Paris

COLIN JONES

Paris

Biography of a City

ALLEN LANE
an imprint of
PENGUIN BOOKS

ALLEN LANE

Published by the Penguin Group
Penguin Books Ltd, 80 Strand, London WC2R ORL, England
Penguin Group (USA) Inc., 375 Hudson Street, New York, New York 10014, USA
Penguin Books Australia Ltd, 250 Camberwell Road, Camberwell, Victoria 3124, Australia
Penguin Books Canada Ltd, 10 Alcorn Avenue, Toronto, Ontario, Canada M4V 3B2
Penguin Books India (P) Ltd, 11 Community Centre, Panchsheel Park, New Delhi – 110 017, India
Penguin Group (NZ), cnr Airborne and Rosedale Roads, Albany, Auckland 1310, New Zealand
Penguin Books (South Africa) (Pty) Ltd, 24 Sturdee Avenue, Rosebank 2196, South Africa

Penguin Books Ltd, Registered Offices: 80 Strand, London WC2R ORL, England

www.penguin.com

First published 2004
1

Set in 9.75/13pt Adobe Sabon
Typeset by Rowland Phototypesetting Ltd, Bury St Edmunds, Suffolk
Printed in England by Clays Ltd, St Ives plc

ISBN 0-713-99321-9

For Jo

Contents

CONTENTS

[Eugene de Rastignac] looked down [from the Père-Lachaise cemetery] on this humming hive in a way which seemed to draw a foretaste of its honey, and spoke these grandiloquent words: 'It's between you and me now!' ('*À nous deux maintenant*')   Balzac, *Le Père Goriot*

Haussmann, faced with a city plan of Paris, takes up Rastignac's cry of '*À nous deux maintenant!*'
                                   Benjamin, *The Arcades Project*

One can never say, like Rastignac, '*Paris, à nous deux maintenant*', but always '*Paris, à nous deux millions!*'
                                   Latour and Hermant, *Paris ville invisible*

From the heights of Père-Lachaise, Rastignac declared to the city, '*À nous deux maintenant!*' I say to Paris, '*adorable!*'
                                   Barthes, *Fragment d'un discours amoureux*

Introduction
An Impossible History of Paris?

'*One never sees Paris for the first time; one always sees it again . . .*'   Edmondo De Amicis (1878)

Writing the Impossible History of Paris

In 1975 the avant-garde writer Georges Perec undertook to record what took place in a single Parisian square in a period of less than twenty-four hours, spread over three consecutive October days. In his *Tentative d'épuisement d'un lieu parisien* (1975),[1] – 'Notes Towards an Exhaustive Account of a Parisian Site' – Perec explained that he chose the Place Saint-Sulpice in the Sixth arrondissement for his experiment. The site was moderately well equipped with the adornments of a modern city: a town-hall, a tax office, a police station, three cafés (one of which was also a tobacconist), a cinema, a famous and historic church, a publisher, a funeral parlour, a travel agent, a bus stop, a tailor, a hotel, a fountain, a newspaper kiosk, a shop selling religious objects, a parking lot, a beautician – 'and lots of other things'. His aim, however, was to leave all these out of his range of vision and to describe the rest – 'what happens when nothing happens except the passing of time, people, cars and clouds.'

The chronicle runs to nearly sixty pages. It is written in a terse, lapidary, informational style.

> Three children being taken to school. Another apple-green
> *deux-chevaux* car.
> The pigeons fly round the square again.
> A 96 bus passes, stops at the bus-stop (Saint-Sulpice section);

Geneviève Serreau gets off and takes the Rue des Canettes. I call out to her, knocking on the café window, and she comes to say hello.
A 70 bus passes.
The church bell stops.
A young girl eats half a cake.
A man with a pipe and a black bag.
A 70 bus passes.
A 63 bus passes.
It is 2.05 p.m.

The experiment 'concludes':

> Four children. A dog. A little ray of sunshine. The 96 bus. It is 2 o'clock.[2]

Perec's efforts to chronicle a Parisian site 'exhaustively' – covering the equivalent of less than a day in the life of the empty spaces of a single Parisian square – yielded a small book.

Let us now examine, through Perec's prism, the task confronting historians who undertake to write the history of the whole city of Paris, rather than a fleeting moment in the life of a single urban square within it. History is normally defined as a discipline which records what happened in the past (and not only the passage of 'time, people, cars and clouds'). And in the history of Paris a lot has indeed happened. Thus in writing its history we historians try to achieve rather more than Perec's aim of chronicling, in a single location, 'what happens when nothing happens'. Yet we find ourselves facing the following daunting 'facts' about our subject (which I set out in a Perecquian manner):[3]

number of squares: 670
number of streets and boulevards: 5,975
length of public highways: 5,959 kilometres
number of municipal buildings: 318
number of fountains: 536
number of public monuments: 40,000
number of shops: 62,546
number of buses: 4,364
number of bus routes: 275

number of bus-stops (*banlieue* excluded): 1,754
number of taxis: 14,900
number of traffic lights: 10,800
number of cafés: 2,050
number of hairdressers: 2,845
number of beauty parlours: 67
number of funeral parlours: 157
number of pigeons: 60,000
number of dogs: 200,000
number of public conveniences: 498
kilometrage of visitable underground tunnels: 300
number of individuals resident in the city of Paris: 2.1 million
number of private households: 1.1 million
length of history: more than 2,000 years (excluding the prehistoric era)
possible number of individuals who have ever lived in Paris or just
passed through, each with their own histories: . . . countless

It is tempting to conclude from such somewhat hallucinatory statistics – of squares, streets, houses, buses, pigeons, dogs, people and so
on – that writing the history of Paris is an impossible quest, certainly
in the Perec manner. But this is not the only moral to be drawn
from the *Tentative d'épuisement*. Certainly, one can never write an
exhaustive history of a city as ancient, diverse and complex as Paris –
but then one knew that anyway. No history of anything will ever
include more than it leaves out. An infinite number of histories of
Paris is possible – and an almost infinite number has indeed already
been produced. As Piganiol de la Force, author of an early visitors'
guide, noted in 1765, 'one would be very wrong if, seeing the vast
number of books devoted to the history of Paris . . . one imagined that
there was nothing more to be said.'[4] (My effort to identify the number
of books in the French national library with *histoire* and *Paris* as
keywords left the poor computer giving up exhausted.) But none of
this infinite series can ever hope to tell the whole story – indeed the
point of Perec's heroic micro-chronicling is to underscore the sublime
impossibility of 'exhaustively' managing that task even when
restricting the story to a single spot in the course of a single day.
The history of Paris may thus be too impossibly rich and diverse to

be encompassed in a single narrative. Yet encompass it is what I will try to do in this book. In this Introduction I give a sense less of what I have included or excluded, than the criteria on the basis of which I have made choices. In so doing I have drawn inspiration from Georges Perec in seeking to write an 'impossible' history of Paris.

Memory and Myth

'Paris has been described so much', noted the Baron de Pöllnitz in 1732, 'and one has heard it talked about so much, that most people know what the city looks like without ever having seen it.'[5] 'One never sees Paris for the first time,' concurred the Italian writer and Parisian tourist Edmondo De Amicis in the late nineteenth century, 'one always sees it again . . .'[6] As these remarks suggest, engagement with Paris in the past has tended to come freighted with expectation. For De Amicis, this sprang from his wide reading of French literature, much of it set, as Balzac put it, in 'the city of a thousand novels'.[7] This meant that De Amicis could not, for example, visit Notre-Dame cathedral or the city sewers without thinking of Victor Hugo, nor the Luxembourg gardens or the Latin Quarter without having a sense of *déjà vu* from Murger's *Vie de Bohème*; nor the Père Lachaise cemetery without reflecting on Balzac's *Comédie humaine*, nor the *quais* and bridges without calling to mind Baudelaire's poetry.

The idea that cultural expectation can get in the way of experiencing Paris 'for the first time' is far from a late nineteenth-century perception. 'A man can die without ever having seen Paris,' confirmed Konstantin Pausovsky. 'And yet he will have been there, he will have seen it in his dreams and in his imagination.'[8] Medieval travellers had expectations too as they approached the city for the 'first' time: many anticipated Jerusalem or Babylon (and some, Sodom and Gomorrah combined). Twentieth- and twenty-first-century visitors have if anything had even more cultural baggage loaded on them by an infinite array of influences including Impressionist painters, surrealist poets, existentialist philosophers, crime fiction writers, classic film-makers, urban photographers, tourist postcards – and other histories of Paris.

The notion, highlighted by De Amicis, that experience of the city is refracted by cultural expectation doubtless applies to other major cities and historic sites. If for Paris it seems to have always been the case, and perhaps more so than for other locations, this is partly because the city has long enjoyed a mythical status. Historians have accustomed us to the idea that Paris was mythologized as the city of modernity in the nineteenth century. The city that Napoleon III and Baron Haussmann thoroughly redesigned in the 1850s and 1860s supplied for several generations the template of modernity which other cities strove to achieve – and which we still inhabit when physically present in the city.[9] But Parisian history was mythologized long before Haussmann was even born. For example, one narrative, developed from the eighth century, had it that Paris was the result of a Trojan diaspora following the fall of the city to the Greeks. From the High Middle Ages onwards at very least, Paris has always been mythically modern. The medieval topos of the city as 'wisdom's special workshop', the post-Renaissance conception of Paris as a new Rome, and the Enlightenment and Revolutionary notion of Paris as the leading edge of civilization comprise three examples which predate the nineteenth-century myth of Haussmannized 'modern' Paris. Part of the myth of Paris is that it has engendered so many myths about itself.

If Paris has always been modern, it has always been historic too. Perec's chronicle of 'the passing of time, people, cars and clouds' excludes what most individuals familiar with Paris will know about the Place Saint-Sulpice probably in advance of physically encountering it, namely that towering over the square is one of the city's most interesting and historic churches. The church is a striking example, in fact, of what an influential group of historians under the leadership of Pierre Nora has in recent years designated as 'a site of memory' – a *lieu de mémoire*.[10] By this term, Nora indicates an institution or location (not necessarily a building) on which the historical consciousness of the French people has focused and which over time has received incremental incrustations of collective memory. It is noticeable that a great many of the *lieux de mémoire* to which Nora and his colleagues have devoted their erudition are Parisian buildings, events or institutions: the Panthéon, the funeral of Victor Hugo, the 1931 Colonial Exposition, the Mur des Fédérés, the Louvre, Parisian statues, the Académie française, the Collège de France, the Palais-Bourbon, Notre-Dame cathedral, the Sacré-Coeur, the Eiffel tower, and so on. It is tempting to conclude that Paris is itself one gigantic 'site of memory', not simply for Parisians, moreover, nor even just for French people. The case is all the more compelling when one widens the perspective to consider the city's incomparable museums and galleries which have acted since the nineteenth century as a major repository of western artistic culture.

If cultural memory, then, lies stored and encoded in the city's built environment, it is pertinent to remember that that environment is inhabited. After all, it would seem rather churlish to exclude Parisians from their own history. The notion that a city is both a site and a community is as old as the Greeks. It follows from this dual recognition that the city's history lies in the interaction between individuals and time, and between ecology and community. In this we can remain true to Perec's project, taking a physical site, and including as our quarry the individuals ('people') as well as the objects, both natural ('clouds') and manufactured ('cars') whose passage makes up a history. Perec's little study is helpful too in another way: it shows how the micro-events which take place in the square run in counterpoint to the square's influence on what happens within it. The passage of the 96 bus, for example, is part of the history of the square, but the location is also an event in the history of the 96 bus. Similarly, the individuals who appear as free agents following their own personal agendas as they pass through the square are, seen from another angle, products of the square as a site of neighbourhood sociability or traffic flow. The history of Paris is a narrative of a place which came to be called Paris, and those who lived in it, or merely, like passengers on Perec's 96 bus, just passed through.

Perec's experiment also reminds us that the individuals whose presence in the square he records do not seem to compose a homogeneous community. Rather, they form a random collection of individuals with – as far as we can judge on the fleeting evidence we are allowed to glean – very different lives, aims, intentions and destinies. For Perec, there is no average Saint-Sulpiçois. It is a good point. It calls us, in writing a history of Paris, not to presuppose the existence of an average Parisian, nor to construct a narrative which – just as bad – imagines that a Parisian community thinks, acts or reacts in unison. That would be very far from the truth.

No Typical Parisians

Power and social status have never been simply distributed among a city's inhabitants. A dominant elite group may lay claim to embody the community in some way or to have special urban entitlements – in Lutetia, this would be through Roman citizenship, in nineteenth-century Paris through a bourgeois lifestyle and possession. Yet it would be an incurious historian who wrote without taking into account the indigenous population and slaves of the Roman era, or without the proletarians, for example, in the period of bourgeois dominance. Indeed, these groups, who formed a large part of the population of the city, contributed powerfully to its history. By the same token, the 'average Parisian' has thus always been both lord and serf, bourgeois and worker, capitalist and proletarian, man and woman.

The 'average Parisian' is a myth in another way too. He or she was almost certainly born outside the city, or was the child of outsiders. The true native born-and-bred Parisian – *le vrai titi parisien* – is a minority phenomenon in Parisian history. Until the late nineteenth century, in Paris as in most major cities, deaths exceeded live births, meaning that population growth was staked on the city's attractiveness for immigrants. At any one time, something between a half and three-quarters of 'Parisians' were thus non-Parisian. Although for more than a century the birth–death ratio has altered, other factors – Paris's cultural attractions, its importance in education and career development, its role as employer – now contrive to produce the same effect of what we might call 'average outsiderdom'.

What is true of the generality is also true of the exceptional individual. Major historical figures who have had an influence on Paris's history, have as often as not been non-Parisians by birth. Julius Caesar was a Roman. The city's patron saint, Geneviève, was most likely of Germanic stock (as of course was Clovis). Philip Augustus was born in Gonesse, Francis I in Cognac, Henry IV in Pau, Louis XIV in Saint-Germain-en-Laye, and Louis XV and XVI in Versailles. Robespierre and Danton were both provincials. Napoleon came from a Mediterranean island which had been Genoan until 1768 (a year before he was born). Baron Haussmann was born in Paris but brought up in Alsace and spoke with a German accent. Eiffel was a Burgundian and Toulouse-Lautrec an Albigeois. Georges Clemenceau was from the Vendée and François Mitterand from the Charente. Victor Hugo hailed from Besançon, while Georges Simenon, the creator of Inspector Maigret, was a Belgian. Édith Piaf at least was Parisian by birth. So is Jacques Chirac, for what it is worth. They are a small minority.

If outsiders have always played a crucial part in Parisian history, Parisians have themselves often remarked on how their fellow citizens act like outsiders in their own history. In his novel *Zazie dans le métro* (1959: subsequently made into a film by Louis Malle), for example, Raymond Queneau tells the story of a little girl's adventures on a weekend trip to Paris as a cross between *Alice in Wonderland* and Dante's *Inferno* (with some nods towards James Joyce's *Ulysses*). Like Alice, Zazie finds it difficult to get her bearings. She is not helped by the fact that the Parisians she meets have no clear sense of the most obvious features of the cityscape that they inhabit. They can just about recognize the Eiffel tower, but are forever mistaking the dome of the Panthéon for the Invalides, or the Sacré-Coeur, or the Gare de Lyon, or even maybe the barracks out at Reuilly, and they mix up the Sainte-Chapelle with the commercial lawcourts.[11] The savant Queneau, a close observer of Parisian ways, here highlights a feature of Parisian history which any historian of the city will recognize. Most Parisians in the past – but then this is probably a fairly universal trait among city-dwellers – had a shaky sense of the shape of their city and the trajectory of its past. It is as though they simply forgot or never learnt the meaning of the sites of memory in their midst. Parisians in the past were less Cartesian than Pierre Nora and his school would have us believe.

Perhaps this quasi-amnesiac tendency derives from the outsider status of 'average' Parisians. It may also link to the often intense parochialism of many city-dwellers. Until relatively recently, some Left- and Right-Bank-dwellers prided themselves on never having crossed the Seine. Nineteenth- and twentieth-century observers noted the tendency of inhabitants of Belleville – and even denizens of the Faubourg Saint-Antoine – to talk of 'going to Paris', a not overly complex manoeuvre which involved crossing the Place de la Bastille and walking in a general westerly direction. The villagey feel of many Parisian neighbourhoods has also contributed to the triumph of a

INTRODUCTION

parish pump mentality, which is no doubt much to the fore in Perec's Place Saint-Sulpice. The tendency of many immigrants to hold on to the identity of their homelands also may count in all this. Scratch a Parisian, one invariably finds a proud Auvergnat, Breton or Tunisian.

Parisians' sense of Paris time has often been as squiffy as their sense of Paris place, if we are to believe chroniclers, antiquarians and historians of the city. Until well into the eighteenth century, for example, it was generally believed that the Roman Baths in the Latin Quarter and the Châtelet prison on the Île de la Cité were constructed by Julius Caesar. These estimates err by about 200 and 900 years respectively. When Parisian builders used stone from the Philip Augustus wall to build new ramparts in the fourteenth century, they claimed that the walls had been built to resist Saracens (who had never in fact been even close to the city). This phenomenon is modern as well as ancient. In his book *Paris insolite* (1952), Jean-Paul Clébert expressed his astonishment at the fact that 'after the enormous quantity of books – good books – devoted to Paris ancient and modern, the inhabitant of Paris is ignorant about his city, disdains it, or else limits his (always identical) thoughts and comments to the poetry of the *quais* of the Seine.'[12] Parisian history, then, may certainly be about memory. But it is also, as Zazie might remind us, about forgetting.

Power, Resistance and Affection

The first account we have of the city of Paris based on first-hand experience is that of the Emperor Julian, who resided in the township of Lutetia (the Roman name for Paris) in 358 AD and then in 360–61 AD. His account starts out '*Cara Lutetia . . .*' ('Beloved (or 'Sweet') Lutetia . . .'), and it goes on to praise the site's pleasant features (including its climate and its excellent wines).[13] Rome and London have attracted paeans of praise over the centuries, but also acres of disappointment and disillusionment. New York only seemed to amount to very much in the twentieth century. One may, if one chooses, see Naples and die, but one does not even have to see Paris with one's eyes, for, as De Amicis has already explained, one has already seen it in one's imagination – and probably started to love it.

Affection seems more integral to Paris's historical identity than is the case for any other, even world-historic city. Julian's is only the first of a very long list of quotations in which those who have got to know the city express their warm feelings for it. Even where judgements are mixed (and all cities have tended to suffer at the hands of the Arcadian tendency), the balance swings towards affection rather than distaste. Most followed Holy Roman Emperor Charles V who on his visit in 1540 declared 'Paris is a world' – and thought that this world could contain good as well as evil.[14] Rabelais thought it 'a bad city to die in' but a good one to live in. Montaigne 'love[d] it tenderly warts and all'; Voltaire thought it 'half gold, half filth', and Goethe, 'the world's head'. Balzac recognized that many thought the city 'a monstrous marvel, an astonishing assemblage of movements, machines and ideas', while George Sand commented admiringly on its unmatchable 'air, appearance and sounds'. Victor Hugo saluted it as 'the focal point of civilization', and the English visitor Matthew Arnold thought 'the free, gay and pleasant life' of Paris the homeland of *l'homme moyen sensuel*.[15]

For his part, the poet Charles Baudelaire regretted that the city could not be fixed in aspic. 'Old Paris is no more. The form of a city changes more swiftly, alas! than the human heart'.[16] With these words, he coined the motto for Parisian nostalgia, but he hardly invented the phenomenon itself. The history of Parisian nostalgia is as long as the history of Paris itself. Present in the writing of Emperor Julian, it is also evident in one of the earliest detailed descriptions of the city we have from the Middle Ages – Guillebert de Metz's 'Description of the City of Paris', dating from the early fifteenth century. Paris had 'been in its flower' in his youth it seems (ah! when else?).[17] On such nostalgic longings for *le Vieux Paris* a whole literary tourist industry would be built in the twentieth century. Read Hemingway, Kerouac, Stein, Miller . . .

Such have been the outpourings of affection from such a wide range of individuals across the ages for the city, that it is important not to lose sight of the fact that Paris is also a site on which the powerful have sought to set an indelible mark. Julian was, after all, a military commander and went on to be Roman Emperor, and the city's development in the late Antique period owed most to the city's strategic position in relation to the barbarian frontier. The Franks too sought to make Paris an expression of their power – and they have been followed by just about every regime since (with the exception of the Vichy regime). Almost no powerful ruler or head of state of note has *not* wanted to impose on the city the force of his authority, particularly through spectacular monumental building.

As a consequence of the embrace of power, the face of the city bears the vestigial traces of now obsolete power systems: the cathedral of Notre-Dame and other ecclesiastical buildings in the Middle Ages, as well as during the Counter-Reformation; the Louvre, palace of sundry monarchs; the royal squares of Henri IV, Louis XIII and Louis XIV; the Place de la Concorde, the École militaire and the Panthéon of Louis XV; Napoleon I's imperial additions; Louis-Philippe's arcades and passages; Napoleon III and Haussmann's boulevards and railway stations; the Eiffel tower and the Sacré-Coeur of the early Third Republic; and, more recently, the *Grands Projets* of Georges Pompidou, François Mitterrand and Jacques Chirac in the Fifth Republic. The list is endless.

Although many Parisian monuments and urban developments are overlaid or juxtaposed against each other, collectively they constitute a surprisingly coherent and intelligible image of the city. The opening up of Paris with boulevards – even before Haussmann's monumental achievement in the 1850s and 1860s – gave the city the potential for developing transport systems which facilitate collective mobility but leave time and space for individual dawdling. Unlike many of its European peers, Paris has escaped major recent wartime destruction and the complications which that brings. Paris grew by radiating outwards from its heart – a fact almost palpably evident to even the most casual visitor. Roman Lutetia was more or less restricted to a single central arrondissement. The medieval city fell largely within the central arrondissements of the modern city (Ie. to VIe.). The Renaissance and early modern city extended to include arrondissements VIIIe. to XIe. The industrialized city from the 1860s drew in all twenty arrondissements. For most of the twentieth century, Paris was getting to grips with its suburbs (*banlieue*).

Yet if Paris has been a pre-eminent site on which power has imprinted itself, it is a city of barricades as well as boulevards and monuments, of resistance to, as well as manifestations of, authority.

Official descriptions have normally claimed that Parisians are full of gaiety, light-heartedness and docility. The trope of satisfied obedience goes back to the Middle Ages, and was being repeated by authoritative sources (including the Parisian writer Louis-Sébastien Mercier) a matter of months before the storming of the Bastille in 1789. In fact the record suggests an altogether more obstreperous aspect to Parisian society in the past. It was presumably not sheer *joie de vivre* which triggered the murders and massacres of the Hundred Years War, the Wars of Religion, the Fronde, the Terror of 1792–4, the revolutionary *journées* of 1830, 1848, 1851 and 1871. Barricades – admittedly in their latter-day appearances as much a symbolic as a military form of resistance – were last erected in anger and in quantity as recently as the May Events of 1968. Their venerable history goes back half a millennium. Collective violence is every bit as Parisian as affection and nostalgia.

Resistance to power and authority within the city can take – and has taken – many forms. Parisians have at times leapt to the barricades, but at other times they have preferred to deploy the 'weapons of the weak'[18] – petty criminality, a refusal to buy into the city's own sites of memory (to the extent, as Queneau suggested, of forgetting what they were!), a well-practised *je-m'en-foutisme*, a shrug of the shoulders, or a raising of the eyebrows. Many authors, particularly since the times of Louis-Sébastien Mercier and Charles Baudelaire, have highlighted the perceived tension between the individual who walked the streets of a city which had been transformed by power and authority, yet who retained an inner sense of alienation and distance from the signs of power inscribed in the city. Baudelaire's fruitful depiction of the *flâneur* – the alert urban stroller – was built around this notion.[19] The German critical theorist Walter Benjamin, whose writings are an inviting reservoir of erudition for any historian of Paris, devoted his life to the idea. Furthermore, urban sociologists such as Henri Lefebvre, Situationist radicals and post-structuralist writers like Michel de Certeau have placed at the centre of their analyses the ability of individuals to resist a city's intended, imposed meanings and to invent their own.[20] The tensions between the imposition of authority and the multifarious expressions of engaged resistance – between power and love, and between community and individualism – figure as insistently recurrent traits of Parisian history. And one does not need a training in Continental Grand Theory to recognize the fact. Indeed, one has only to follow one of Georges Perec's crazy peregrinations (for example: travel from the church of Saint-Eustache in the Halles to the church of Saint-Paul in the Marais by only following streets with names beginning with P); or observe Simenon's Inspector Maigret solving one of his seedier cases; or meditate on the meanings of the Métro with anthropologist Marc Augé ('to take the métro is in some sense to celebrate ancestor worship'), or else read Richard Cobb's wildly imagined rambles around mid-twentieth century Paris to get the hang of the habit.[21]

Time and Space: A User's Guide

In the early 1990s, archaeologists working at Bercy in the XIIe. arrondissement came across prehistoric canoes dating back to between 4,000 and 5,000 BC. Newspapers proudly proclaimed that more than two or three additional millennia had been added to Parisian history. However, in what sense was prehistoric Bercy part of Paris? Paris did not even exist at the time. Bercy was only brought into the city by the annexations of 1859–60, and it is true to say that it has always been a disinherited part of the XIIe. arrondissement, which Parisians have tended if anything to disown. Only in the 1990s in fact has the area been part of the formal urbanization which bids to bring the neighbourhood within the Parisian community.

The Bercy conundrum (Paris/Not Paris) forces us to admit an approach which – in line with most historians of Paris – I have adopted in this book. That is, I have used the term Paris extremely loosely, and with mild but detectable anachronism (and without the tedious convention of quotation marks). Roman Lutetia, for example, covered eight hectares, and was almost entirely containable in the present-day Fifth arrondissement. Yet in writing its history I have tended to regard as Parisian almost anything which falls within the limits of the 10,500 hectares of which contemporary Paris (since the Second World War) is composed and which since the 1960s has been hemmed in by the *boulevard périphérique*.

I shall shuttle somewhat uncomfortably therefore between glossing Paris geographically, historically and anachronistically. This strategy avoids the overly purist option of only speaking of Paris as it was formally delimited at one particular time in the past – as if, for example, we could only bring Montmartre into the history of Paris after its nineteenth-century incorporation. It does have the advantage of highlighting how Paris expanded over time. But it is a fiction, even if a benign and probably unavoidable one. In much the same spirit I have used the convenient shorthand of the arrondissement system, only introduced in 1860, to place locations mentioned in the text for any period. It is of course ridiculously anachronistic to put the medieval cathedral of Notre-Dame, for example, in the Fourth arrondissement in the Middle Ages. But it does facilitate the reader's task of interpreting the city's history through its geography – and vice versa.

I have chosen to tell the story of Paris in chronological order. The chapters progress the chronological narrative of the city of Paris from earliest beginnings to . . . tomorrow. But I have also sought to complicate matters, and to shift dimensions, by including in each chapter a number of feature boxes which jump out of the chronological framework. These are intended to operate like close-ups, fast-forward anticipations or rewind-retrospections. They allow the history of a person, an institution or a monument to escape the chronological window of the chapters, and to be pursued over time – over the *longue durée*, as French historians would say.[22] The Eiffel tower, for example, was built within the period covered by Chapter 9. But it hasn't since disappeared from Paris's story, as readers will most likely have remarked. Its story illuminates the city's history in the twentieth and twenty-first centuries as well as the late nineteenth. Then again, the feature on Montfaucon (Chapter 3) highlights the place of this medieval gibbet in Parisian imagination across the ages – leading up to its metamorphosis by Haussmann and Napoleon III into the 'neo-Swiss' Buttes-Chaumont park (of which the Surrealists made poetic appropriation in the early twentieth century). So again, the feature on the Vél' d'Hiver (Chapter 11), the velodrome on which world cycling records were set – but which was also used as a depot for Jews rounded up in 1943 prior to deportation – will allow me to consider the place of Jews in Paris from Merovingian times through to the Fifth Republic. By examining proto-*haute-couturière* Rose Bertin (Chapter 6), we can glimpse the emergence of consumerism in eighteenth-century Paris –

but also consider the blossoming of the city as a fashion capital in the nineteenth and twentieth centuries.

The feature boxes will focus on an array of phenomena ranging from the great to the humble and from the memorable to the forgettable: the range extends from the Eiffel tower or the Louvre down to a coffee-house (the Procope), a restaurant (the Grand Véfour) or a public urinal (the *vespasienne*). In some ways these phenomena may be thought of as 'sites of memory', but with one major caveat: I will focus as much on forgetting – and sometimes choosing to forget – as actively as on remembering or commemorating. The Roman arena, for example – the *Arènes de Lutèce* (Chapter 1) – is one of the great non-monuments of Paris, now more a playground than a historic or even much-visited place, which Parisians have chosen not to make a fuss about, presumably because it is simply not grand enough, or does not fit into received and sanctified versions of their history. The Philip Augustus Wall (Chapter 2) might be remembered – and was in fact highly important in structuring Parisian topography and memory from the High Middle Ages – but it is virtually invisible on the ground. The *Cour des Miracles* (Chapter 5) – lairs of organized begging in the seventeenth century – probably did not even exist as distinct physical spaces, even though Louis XIV's police authorities are well known for having cracked down on them.

By rising above the course of the narrative and focusing on such phenomena, which may well go against the chronological grain, I want to provide a means of complicating the narrative of the work as a whole. There is no thought that in this or in any other way I can possibly hope to write as 'exhaustive' a history of Paris as Georges Perec managed (or maybe successfully failed to do) in regard to the Place Saint-Sulpice. I shall inevitably exclude more than I can include. Yet my wish is that, like indeed the Place Saint-Sulpice, the resultant book, for all its omissions, will contain enough of interest to manage a *Michelin Guide* recommendation: *vaut le détour*.

I

Paris-Lutetia
From Earliest Times to *c*. 1000

'*Cara Lutetia*' – 'my beloved Lutetia' – wrote the Roman Emperor Julian of his stays in the city in AD 358 and then during the winter of 360–61,

> is capital of the Parisii people. It is a small island lying in the river; a wall entirely surrounds it, and wooden bridges lead to it on both sides. The river seldom rises and falls, but is usually the same depth in the winter as in the summer season, and it provides water which is very clear to the eye and very pleasant for one who wishes to drink. For since the inhabitants live on an island they have to draw their water chiefly from the river. The winter too is rather mild there, perhaps from the warmth of the ocean which is not more than 900 *stades* distant, and it may be that a slight breeze from the water is wafted thus far . . . A good kind of vine grows thereabouts and some individuals have even managed to make fig-trees grow by covering them in winter . . . to protect them from the cold wind.[1]

This is the first description of any length that we have of the city which would become known as Paris. It is written with what was to become a familiar emotion in writings about Paris: affection. Its author was a man of power.

At this stage in its history, Paris was Lutetia. Julius Caesar, who conquered most of the current area of France in the first century BC, bringing it under Roman control, was the first to use the name 'Lutetia' (others said 'Lucotecia') to designate 'the city of the Parisii tribe'.[2] Chroniclers of the city from the Middle Ages to our own time have spilt much ink on determining where the term originates. Fancifully, some have linked it to the Greek term *leucos*, 'white' – 'because of the

Bois.

Bois.

Marais.

Grand Pont.

Petit Pont.

Temple d'Isis
ou de Ceres.

Prez.

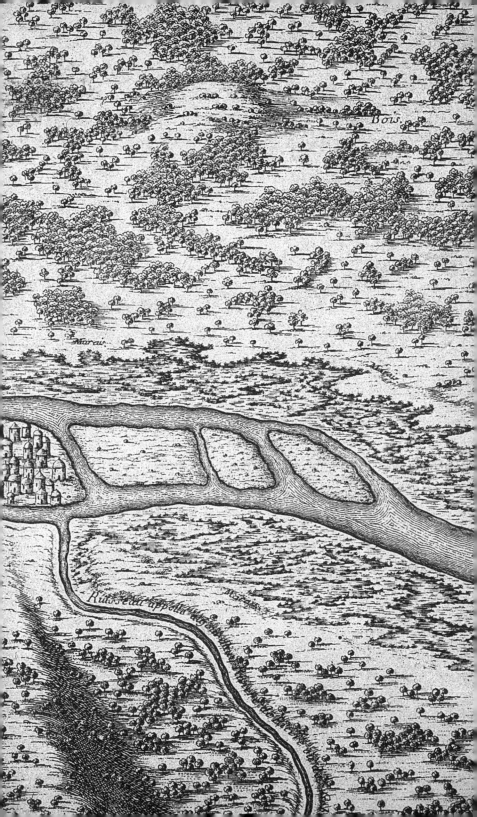

Bois.

Marais

Ruisseau appellé

Marais

whiteness of the faces of the inhabitants or because the houses were built of white plaster', as the seventeenth-century antiquarian Antoine de Mont-Royal pedantically explained, or else, as Rabelais more mischievously thought, as homage to 'the white thighs of the women of that city'.[3] Others have traced it to Leucothea, goddess of sailors and waterways, mentioned in Homer, and who was allegedly worshipped on the site. Less sublimely, scholars also link it to *luco-* or *lugo-*, the Celtic word for marshland, and to *lutum*, Latin for mud. It is probably best to stick with the mud.

The muddy etymology of Lutetia highlights a striking feature of Paris which marked its topography in early times. Despite Julian's Arcadian description, the river Seine played a very significant role in the character of the location. The river's maximum width today is around two hundred metres; then, it may have been up to half a kilometre in places. Perishing wintry conditions – for the climate was less mild than Julian described it – frequently produced an ice-bound river which put bridges at risk of destruction and threatened starvation through the breakdown of food supply. The river was less deep too, and a broader bank of marshy and muddy land stretched on either bank. On the Left Bank a tributary called the Bièvre flowed into the Seine, probably near to the present-day Austerlitz railway station (Ve.). In the distant past, a band of low-lying land on the Right Bank had taken the river waters in a northern arc up to the foothills of high ground at Ménilmontant, Belleville, Montmartre and Chaillot. This had dried out around 30,000 BC and been replaced by the existing course of the Seine. But the area between the river and these confines was left enduringly floodable. At the best of times, this marshy area on the Right Bank served as a city defence. At worst, heavy rains could turn the defunct river course into a raging torrent: the chronicler Gregory of Tours recalled a shipwreck occurring during the AD 582 floods near to the church of Saint-Laurent (Xe.). The old river-course was similarly revived as recently as during the great floods of 1910, when music-lovers could paddle to the Opéra.

Land, water and mud thus had a more dramatic relationship with the city's history than in recent times. If there is some truth in the adage of the geographers that 'Paris is a gift of the Seine', the river could give the city trouble as well as opportunities. It had to be controlled and mastered. This was evident, for example, as regards the Île de la Cité. This was the major island on the Seine which Caesar identified as the principal residence of the local tribal group here. Around it Parisian topography and history was to revolve. The island was some six metres below its present level, and consequently also prone to floods. It was in fact only the most important of a little archipelago at this point in the river, and covered only seven or eight hectares, as against seventeen today. Three islets lay on its western side, just beyond the present day Pont Neuf: the channels separating them were filled in so as to form the tip of the island in the Middle Ages. To the east there were four islets. One of these would be added to the Île de la Cité, two would be remanipulated to form the Île Saint-Louis in the seventeenth century, while the Île Louviers to the east would be conjoined to the Right Bank, establishing the Boulevard Morland (IVe.), as late as 1843. These topographical complexities must have made navigation difficult, and necessitated the use of shallow-draft vessels.

The general features of the Paris basin – the sprawling natural feature in which Paris was set – had been established in the last ice age, when rhinoceroses ambled across the site of the Place de l'Hôtel-de-Ville, and woolly mammoths grazed close to the *Grands Magasins* and up in Belleville. A particular feature of this wider region was the close accumulation of a significant number of slow-moving and there-fore usually navigable waterways (Marne, Essonne, Loing, Yonne, Aube). These were tributaries of the Seine, which itself flowed into the sea far away to the west beyond present-day Rouen. This river network allowed communication from the English Channel in the west towards Alsace, Germany and Switzerland, and through to much of northern, eastern and central France.

The earliest human presence in the broader Paris region dates back 700,000 years, but the most impressive set of ancient human artefacts located in the area – those excavated in 1991–2 at Bercy (XIIe.), a couple of kilometres upstream from the Île de la Cité – testify elo-quently to the role of water in the history of the site. Fortuitously, but not unrevealingly, the artefacts discovered had been preserved over the millennia by Parisian mud. The Bercy excavations demonstrated not only evidence of continuous occupation back to around 5,000 BC in the late Stone Age, but also the centrality of the river in the lives of that early society and those that succeeded it. Holding pride of place amongst the finds are several dugout canoes, over five metres long, and dating back to around 4,500 BC. They mark out these early societies as hunter-gatherer in orientation, living from the fauna of land (deer, boar, aurochs, bear) and water (fish, beaver, water-fowl, water-turtle). Even when these early inhabitants settled down to more sedentary lifestyles, they retained their predatory ways. They preferred herding to farming, and mixed the production of grain with the tending of cattle and pigs and a continuing quest for wild game. Even when Julius Caesar came into the area, many groupings here were still practising a kind of slash-and-burn cultivation, as they moved from clearing to clearing within what was still very dense forest.

From the Bronze Age onwards (c. 1800–c. 750 BC), Paris was the hub of a complex network of trackways, as well as the focus of a major river system. The greater breadth of the Seine in these early times made it a more formidable barrier, so that the presence of the flotilla of islands around the Île de la Cité gave the site real logistic value for long-distance trade and exchange, allowing the river to be crossed more easily than at any comparable location down to the sea. One must not give in to geographical determinism, for it was true that land-based traders from the Channel, from Flanders and from Belgium could if they wished skirt Paris to the north and cross the Marne further upstream to reach west Germany and Italy. The presence of a north–south trackway on the line of the present-day Rue Saint-Jacques (Ve.–XIVe.) on the Left Bank and the Rue Saint-Martin on the Right (IIIe.–IVe.), witnessed to Paris's strategic position in these networks of long-haul trade, especially as regards the south and south-west. Particularly significant was the flourishing exchange conveying British (particularly Cornish) tin, an essential ingredient in the production of bronze, to the copper deposits and the Bronze Age societies located to the south and east. The pivotal situation of the site plus the play of patterns of exchange around it thus encouraged the regular passage of individuals from a variety of backgrounds. This produced a cultural and ethnic mélange at the site which was to prove another long-term feature of Parisian history. Pre-Roman Paris was already a melting-pot.

At some time in the Iron Age, which followed on from the Bronze

Age, a large group of new peoples seems to have settled in the area, washed up here by wide-ranging and amorphous population movements taking place in central and eastern Europe. These were ancestors of the Celts, or Gauls, whom Julius Caesar would defeat and subdue. A branch of one such tribal group – the Quarisii, or Parisii – voyaged as far afield as Yorkshire before settling down, but most of the group came to be located in the region around Paris and towards the Seine's junction with the Marne. The iron weaponry of the Celts suggests that they were warlike peoples, and their dwellings were often grouped round defensible fortresses (*oppida*), which took advantage of the defensive potential of rivers and other natural features. The *oppidum* at Saint-Maur-des-Fossés (Val-de-Marne), for example, nestles perfectly within a bend of the river Marne. The Île de la Cité was, as far as we can tell, the *oppidum* of the Parisii described by Caesar.[4]

Caesar's interest in the region was more than topographical. The Roman Republic was by this period in the midst of a phase of expansion, which brought the whole of present-day France under its authority. The southern, Mediterranean fringe of France – Gallia Narbonensis, as it was called – which linked the Italian peninsula to the Iberian peninsula – had been brought under Roman authority in 121 BC. Caesar's Gallic Wars of 58–51 BC were fought both in order to protect Roman influence within this southern province and also to extend Roman *imperium* against the Celtic Gauls and their turbulent Germanic neighbours. What Caesar dubbed 'Hairy Gaul' (*Gallia Comata*) extended from Belgium, the Netherlands and western Germany through to the Atlantic Ocean. He contrasted it with the allegedly smoother, civilized and more Romanized Gallia Narbonensis.

The Roman military thrust in the 50s BC had in fact been aimed less at the Parisii than at other, more powerful tribes such as the Arverni, who were based in the Massif Central, and the Parisii's neighbours, the Carnutes (based round Orléans) and the Senones (centred on Sens). Initially, the Parisii tried to box clever, by staying out of the conflict. They were sufficiently accommodating towards the Romans that in 53 BC Caesar convoked an assembly of all the tribes of Gaul in Lutetia. The following year, however, the Parisii switched sides. Caesar sent against them a force led by his faithful lieutenant Labenius. With some little craftiness (involving the use of discarded river-craft to convey his forces across the Seine by night), the Roman general forced the Parisii under their commander, Camulogenus, into the field probably in either the region of Grenelle (XVe.) or Auteuil (XVIe.) to the west of the Île de la Cité, and cut them to ribbons. Parisii who escaped the slaughter fled south and joined the composite resistance army led by the Arvernian Vercingetorix. Caesar records that some 8,000 Parisii were involved in the battle of Alesia in 52, in which the Gaulish commander Vercingetorix was forced to yield and his forces given another mauling.

Lutetia did recover from this Roman pounding (as well as from the damaging fire of the Île de la Cité initiated by Camulogenus). In the aftermath of the wars, 'Hairy Gaul' was divided into three provinces, with Lyon (Lugdunum) as their capital. Lutetia, which was located within the northern province of Gallia Belgica, was set back by the advent of Roman *imperium*. For some decades before the conquest, the Parisii had been producing an impressive-looking golden coinage which suggested commercial vitality and prosperity in the region, grounded in the carrying trades. The Roman conquest brought a sharp diminution of the metal value of local coins, indicating a marked economic downturn.

The archaeological record suggests that a true city on the Roman model emerged only very slowly. Lutetia probably had the classic gridiron street plan favoured by the Romans imposed on it straight away, with the role of the *cardo* – the central north–south thorough-fare – being given to the highway already existing on the line of the Rue Saint-Jacques. The built infill within this framework, however, took longer to achieve. Although there may have been a port facility by the present-day Place de l'Hôtel-de-Ville (IVe.), there were few dwellings on the Right Bank. The main building on the Île de la Cité was the basilica in which Emperor Julian lodged, constructed only in the fourth century. The Left Bank (indeed, in modern terms, the Fifth arrondissement) contained nearly all of Roman Lutetia. The area of settlement extended from present-day Rue Mouffetard in the east to the Rue de Vaugirard (VIe.) in the west, and from the level of the Boulevard Saint-Germain where the marshy riverbank ended to a little beyond the top of the Montagne Sainte-Geneviève. Here a porticoed building (near the site of the present-day Panthéon) combined the

The *Arènes de Lutèce*

functions of forum with basilica and temple. There were two theatres, one of them the vast amphitheatre of the Arènes (which would be rediscovered only in the late nineteenth century). Of three public baths, most notable was the complex whose remains are still viewable from the Boulevard Saint-Michel. On the edge of the city three burial grounds, one on the road to the south-west on the upper reaches of the present-day Rue de Vaugirard, another out on the Rue Saint-Jacques towards Notre-Dame-des-Champs (VIe.), and the third, more tardily, by the Gobelins crossroads to the south-east (XIIIe.) An impressive aqueduct originating in the Rungis area to the south of the city and linking with the Bièvre river was erected to supply water for these multiple needs. The system of water-supply provided by Napoleon III in the Second Empire (1852–70) wisely followed the same route. Water – whose quality was highlighted by Julian – was ducted into private dwellings which had the hypocaust central heating systems characteristic of Mediterranean cities.

1.1: The *Arènes de Lutèce*

The Roman arena, or amphitheatre, of Lutetia, situated just off the Rue Monge in the Fifth arrondissement is a 'site of memory' which Parisians have contrived to forget – twice. When the city archaeologist Théodore Vacquer identified the site in 1869–70, he brought to Parisians' attention a monument which had been lost for more than a millennium. Built around AD 200, it was one of the largest examples in France of a Roman amphitheatre, and had been able to contain up to 15,000 spectators – almost twice the probable population of the city itself. This superb regional monument faced west so that spectators enjoyed a pleasant afternoon vista over the valley of the river Bièvre as they settled down to shows which included animal fights, gladiators and aquatic sports. The *arènes* fell into decay with the demise of Roman power. By the fourth century, Christians were performing burials in the centre of the arena. The stone of the building lent itself to pillaging for funerary monuments and other uses. A twelfth-century English visitor to Paris spoke of 'a great circus full of immense ruins', but those ruins were probably reduced even more by the building of the wall of Philip Augustus (1190–1215). A medieval place name – the *clos des arènes* – gave the site of the amphitheatre away, but even this name was virtually forgotten. A mound some twenty metres high gradually formed over the vestiges.

There was much astonishment when in 1869 a construction team came across the surviving ruins during the creation of one of Baron Haussmann's penetrating streets through the heart of unhealthy and run-down working-class housing. The complete rebuilding of much of the city under the Second Empire had revealed important archaeological finds: Vacquer, one of the unsung heroes of Parisian conservation, located the remains of a forum near to the Rue Soufflot, several theatres and the street system. Yet Haussmann and his acolytes were building Paris of the future as the site of modernity and had little time for its past. Although a public debate on the restoration began, one of Haussmann's last acts as Prefect of the Seine was to order the bulldozing of the site, and its conversion into an omnibus depot – a very Haussmannian victory.

In 1883–5 further building work along the Rue Monge revealed, under a former nunnery, the second half of the original arena. The public debate was more strident this time, and it met with triumph when Victor Hugo wrote an open letter in support of this monument. 'It is not possible', he fulminated, splendidly, 'that Paris, the city of the future, should renounce the living proof that it was a city of the past. The arena is an ancient mark of a great city. It is a unique monument. The municipal council which destroys it would in some manner destroy itself. Conserve it at any price.'

And conserved it duly was. Work continued on the site, in confident expectation of a fruitful and imperishable outcome.

This important victory for a nascent conservation movement in Paris turned out not to be as earth-shattering as had been hoped. Although the arena site was very big, virtually nothing remained of its seats and prominent buildings. Expecting companion monuments to the arenas at Nîmes and Arles, archaeologists discovered something which was in essence a pile of rocks and rubble, little more than two metres high. 'In order to preserve the arena,' noted one city official waspishly, 'it would first be necessary to show that the arena exists. Experience seems to demonstrate the opposite . . . As a monument, there is nothing there any more.' This was not the splendid monument of Paris history that Parisian authorities had imagined. The publicity movement for the *arènes* fizzled out. Restoration work was extremely slow. In 1917–18 the archaeologist Capitan finally finished off the site as a public park, the Square Capitan as it became in fact. The 'restoration' of the building was in a great many respects a new creation – Roman Disneyworld, Third Republic-style.

Today, the *arènes* slumber pretty well forgotten – for a second time in their history – in a city whose *Romanitas* does not extend to boosting its Roman status as a third-rank Gaulish city. Tourists are few, save when special seating is erected for summer concerts. Most of the time, the *arènes* are inhabited by parents and babies, and by local lads indulging in scratch games of soccer, invariably played out to the excited squeals of children from the nearby kindergarten. The *arènes de Lutèce* has been transformed into a site of local sociability and *mémoire de quartier*. In a city whose official 'sites of memory' sometimes border on the overblown, maybe this is no bad thing.

Despite the not unimpressive (if slow-coming) trappings of *Romanitas*, Lutetia was never more than a second-rung city throughout the period of Roman rule – until Julian fleetingly associated it with imperial rule. The Romans allowed the existing tribal network to subsist throughout Gaul, and the Parisii had no primacy of any sort over the sixty-odd tribal groupings – now renamed *civitates* ('city-states') – which made up 'Hairy Gaul'. Lutetia was merely the capital city of one *civitas* within the more extensive province of Gallia Belgica. It had little strategic importance. It was quite a distance, for example, from the *limes*, the fortified frontier which was erected to prevent incursions by Germanic tribal groupings across the Rhine and Danube and which guaranteed the *pax romana* throughout north-western Europe. Even when, in the fourth century, the tripartite division of Gaul was replaced by a system of smaller units, Lutetia failed to win administrative promotion: nearby Sens was made capital of the Fourth Lyonnais Division.

Lutetia was no more important socially, economically or culturally than it was administratively. With possibly up to 8,000 inhabitants, it contrasted with Narbonne and Nîmes (in Gallia Narbonensis) as well as with Lyon, Autun, Reims and Trier, each of which had between 20,000 and 30,000 inhabitants (while Rome itself had three-quarters of a million). Lutetia's 50-odd hectares of site made a poor contrast with Reims's 600 hectares, Trier's 285 and Autun's 200 – or even with the pre-Roman Gaulish *oppidum* of Alesia (97 hectares). The fate of the coinage of the Parisii plus the fact that the Romanization of the built environment had taken time to get under way suggest that the city's economic fortunes were slow to recover from the trauma of conquest. Lutetia was one of relatively few Roman cities in northern Gaul in which building could be done in locally quarried stone: the deposits of limestone (for stone) and gypsum (for plaster) within a five-kilometre radius of the Île de la Cité was to provide the raw materials of construction until modern times (the last limestone stone quarry closed in 1939) and over the centuries created vast, cavernous underground complexes. Most public buildings were only erected in the second and even third century AD. Stone, plaster and tile gradually supplanted wattle-and-daub and thatch – which never disappeared altogether. Though the building trades, pottery and metalwork all did respectably in the city's golden age, and led to the formation of manufacturing suburbs, Lutetia was not really a centre of production, and it specialized instead in the carrying trades. Here too the Parisian economy suffered from the imperial decision to build the main road linking provincial capital Lyon to England by way of Sens, Senlis and Beauvais, missing Paris out altogether.

The 'Boatmen's Pillar', an extraordinary archaeological find made in the environs of Notre-Dame cathedral in 1711, and dating from the beginning of the second century AD, suggests that, despite such problems, economic recovery was on its way. The stone pillar, some five metres high (viewable in Paris's Cluny Museum (Ve.) which also contains the vestiges of the Roman bath-house) represents the Roman gods (Mars, Venus, Mercury, Fortuna, Castor and Pollux, and Vulcan) happily consorting with Gaulish deities. It is inscribed (in pretty poor Latin): 'Under the reign of Tiberius Caesar Augustus, the boatmen (*nautes*) erected this monument to Jupiter, most great and most good, at their collective expense.' The pillar highlights the syncretic nature of Gallo-Roman religion, but also the social status and economic power of the boatmen whose organization, which predated the arrival of the Romans, seems to have powered the economic surge of the early second century AD.

Local produce was carried far afield. Beyond the three necropolises on the city margins, large farms on the Roman model were to be found, worked by slave labour, giving Lutetia a garden city look. There was a big farm at Chaillot, for example, and another at Montmartre, which also contained temples dedicated to Mars and to Mercury. One had to go outside the bounds of the present-day *boulevard périphérique* encircling the city to find more densely inhabited locations (Clichy, Gentilly, Bobigny, Ivry, Saint-Denis). The rural character of greater Lutetia increased over the course of the third and fourth centuries, as Roman power wavered, declined and was finally extinguished. From late in the second century, plundering barbarian incursions from beyond the *limes* were starting to spread insecurity across Gaul. As early as 162 and 174 raiding highlighted the danger, but it was really from the late third century that the problem became acute throughout the province. The attacks of the Germanic Alamans and Franks in 275 caused damage to sixty Gaulish cities, Lutetia included. This led, a little after 300, to the fortification both of the Île de la Cité and of an indeterminate area around the forum, using stone from more undefendable buildings. The growing practice of individuals burying hoards of coins and other valuables demonstrated the psychological impact of the barbarian threat.

1.2: A Parisian Child

This is the oldest Parisian face we have (p. 16). It is nearly two thousand years old. It is an accidental death-mask, of almost photographic clarity and intensity, discovered in 1878 during excavations on the Rue Pierre-Nicole (Ve.). The archaeologist Eugène Toulouzé had been working on the Roman necropolis in this area for some time, and located a roughly executed sarcophagus from the first or second century. With great care he prised open the cover to reveal the corpse of a young child, probably between twelve and fifteen months old, alongside which was a beautifully wrought glass milk-bottle. The head of the child, the archaeologist noted,

> was partly covered by a layer of fairly thick cement. After carefully removing it, how great was our surprise to see that the cement had formed a kind of death-mask over the head, thus conserving intact for us, after eighteen centuries, the face of the child. Perhaps as the coffin was being sealed, the cement had become stuck to the lid, and had become detached, fixing itself on the child's head and receiving its imprint.

The child received special treatment in death at least. He was one of only three persons buried in a sarcophagus in this extensive burial ground – most burials were either direct into the earth or else the bodies were placed in wooden coffins. Yet a child's death was a banal occurrence not only in Roman Lutetia, but for most of Parisian history. Perhaps it was no surprise that the largest cemetery in Paris from the Middle Ages onwards was dedicated to the Holy Innocents slaughtered by Herod. When it was closed down in 1786, it contained the mortal remains of two million Parisians, a vast proportion of them children. Statistical evidence suggests that until the late eighteenth and early nineteenth centuries, one Parisian child in three or four died before their first birthday.

This slaughter of the innocents was exacerbated by a range of

social practices. From the late Middle Ages onwards, Parisian bourgeois, shopkeepers and artisans were in the habit of sending their children to be wet-nursed in the countryside, where they were likelier to die than if they had been kept at home. In addition, Paris became a dumping ground for foundlings from outside as well as within the city. Foundling hospitals were created from the sixteenth century onwards, notably the Enfants Trouvés, founded by Saint Vincent de Paul in 1640. Unfortunately, such well-meant institutions stimulated dumping. By the time of the French Revolution, some 8,000 babies were being transported to be abandoned in Paris each year, and during their travels and in the first three months of their care, 90 per cent died. The death rate was highest among babies who – like the Parisian waif excavated by Toulouzé – were fed artificially. Things only improved in the nineteenth century.

Child poverty was as great a problem as child mortality. The child beggar was a frequent target of concern from the sixteenth century onwards. There were horror stories in abundance about child abuse. A mother was executed in 1445 for having poked her girl baby's eyes out so that she would become a more reliable prop for street begging. Stories about leg-breakings and other disablements were common in the picaresque literature of vagabondage. Children had a knack of triggering such rumours and urban legends. On several occasions from the sixteenth century onwards – in 1529, 1663, 1675, 1720, 1741 and 1750 – a panic seized Parisians that children were being kidnapped. In 1750 it was said that they were being killed off so that their blood could be used to bathe the leprous wounds of the debauched Louis XV.

From the late eighteenth century the child beggar seems to metamorphose into the street urchin – the *gamin de Paris* – object of both anxiety and charitable concern to the Parisian elites. It had been a gang of children who mutilated and castrated the corpse of the Admiral Coligny in the Saint Bartholomew Day's Massacre of 1572. The most serious assault on Bourbon power before the French Revolution was named after a child's catapult – the Fronde (1648–53). In the early nineteenth century a Paris police official claimed that their descendants were little better: 'everyone knows this Parisian race of street children who in gatherings shout out seditious words, and in riots are the first to pick up a cobblestone from the barricades and almost always are the first to start shooting.' Alexis de Tocqueville agreed: 'it is usually the urchins of Paris who begin insurrections and generally they go about it gleefully, like schoolboys on vacation.' Parisian children were thus perpetrators as well as victims of violence. Yet Victor Hugo's sympathetic and sentimental portrayal of Gavroche in his great novel *Les Misérables* (1862) helped raise awareness of the conditions which had produced such behaviour. Gavroche dies on the barricades – but not before he has touched the heartstrings of Hugo's readers.

Despite these worrying signs, the invasions seem to have affected Paris relatively lightly by comparison with other northern cities, and problems were not seen as serious enough to prevent individuals building residences outside the fortified areas. Though slightly contracted, the urban tissue which had developed under the *pax romana* stayed essentially intact, albeit probably invaded by weeds and nettles. Furthermore, Lutetia also came to develop a measure of latter-day strategic importance. While the *limes* had been watertight, it was possible for Roman military forces to police the frontier based in cities close to Germany such as Trier. Once the frontier had begun to falter, there was much to be said for a rearguard location such as Lutetia, which was too far distant to be a first target for invading raiders. The excellent system of roads and rivers emanating from the city facilitated the swift movement of troops to any hotspot. It also provided efficient lines of military food supply through to the Cambrésis, the Beauce and Poitou. Wine production (noted by Emperor Julian) established itself in the region, probably even before the decision of Emperor Probus (276–82) to lift the age-old ban on vine cultivation outside Italy. A Lutetian military camp was established in an area on the Left Bank out to the south-east on the road to Italy. A fleet was also stationed in the city to ferry troops along the river system to points where disorder threatened. The city's development into a garrison city offered excellent opportunities to the boatmen of the Parisii: the *nautes* doubtless continued to prosper.

These must have been the overwhelming strategic reasons for the Roman general Julian's choice of the city as his winter headquarters when he was sent to Gaul to combat Germanic raiding in the late 350s. He established a basilica on the Île de la Cité, whose importance seems to have been growing at this time: the city's port was also located on the island. In 360, in an act which was to prove of some significance in Lutetia's later history, Julian was acclaimed Roman emperor by his troops. The latter were mutinous at the threat of being transferred to fight on Rome's eastern, Illyrian frontier – torn from their families, as they put it, in 'a state of nakedness and want'.[5] The legionaries raised a reluctant Julian on a footsoldier's shield in acclaim – a ritual as much Germanic as Roman – and, in the absence of a suitable diadem, coiffed him with a standard-bearer's insignia. The new emperor died three years later, but one of his successors, Valentinian I, also quartered here in 365–6 during campaigns against the barbarians, giving extra sheen to the imperial aura of Lutetia.

Or should one now say Paris? The practice of *civitates* giving their premier city their tribal name was fairly common, and by the early fourth century, 'the city of the Parisii' was also being called 'Paris'. By the end of that century the shift in nomenclature was complete. Under its Roman veneer, Lutetia had never lost its Gaulish, late Iron Age feel. As was their practice elsewhere in Gaul, the Romans had allowed the Parisii to subsist in largely their old political form, and the local aristocracy probably had few new recruits from outside. The *nautes* almost certainly predated the Romans too. Paris-Lutetia was always an outpost in what was still very much a wild and savage land. Emperor Julian's own family hailed from a remote Danubian people which he characterized as 'boorish, awkward, without charm and abiding immovably in its decisions'. Yet he frankly admitted a temperamental likeness to the Celtic peoples of the Paris region, describing his role amongst the Parisii and their ilk as 'like some huntsman who associates with and is entangled among wild beasts'.[6] Although the Romans gave themselves credit for civilizing this relatively insignificant (if, as Julian argued, charming) city of quasi-barbarians, Lutetia was unable to cast off its pre-Roman inheritance. Indeed this became more prominent as the fourth century wore on.

Emperors Julian and Valentinian in the late 350s and early 360s enjoyed a measure of success in pushing back German tribes – notably the Alamans and the Franks – across the *limes*. The shift of the military command from Paris to Trier late in the fourth century suggested a greater sense of security in the region of the *limes*. However, the shades of the *pax romana* flattered only to deceive, as, in the fifth century, Roman power collapsed completely. The development of a dual empire based in Rome and Constantinople failed to rally imperial forces in the west. In 410 Rome was sacked by the Visigoths, and the division between the eastern and western empires was definitively enshrined. Even before that, in 406, the Roman defensive frontier in the north-east had punctured like a balloon, as hordes of Germanic invaders swarmed across the *limes*, effectively ending the Roman provincial system throughout Gaul. The Burgundes settled in eastern France, the Alamans in Alsace, the Sueves and Vandals in Spain while the Visigoths crossed from Italy into south-western France, establishing a kingdom in the Toulouse area which Roman imperial authorities were forced to recognize in 416. In swathes of northern and north-eastern France, it was the Franks who were the dominant force.

Prominent among a loose confederacy of tribes answering to the name of Franks were the Salian Franks who were said to trace their genealogy back to the numinous Merowech (*Mérovée*), son, it was said, of a pagan sea-monster. They became locked in ever more deadly embrace with the last nominal Roman imperial representatives in the area, the commanders Aetius (425–54), Aegidius (454–64) and Syagrius (464–86). In 463–4 the Franks besieged Paris (when they killed Aegidius); they did the same in the late 480s, following the death of Syagrius, who was based in Soissons. The killing of Syagrius plus the death of the last western emperor in 476 may be said to mark the end of the Roman empire in the west.

Losing its sense of itself as Roman Lutetia, Paris was gaining a new identity, in which religion played a key role. Christianity had arrived, and was durably etching itself on the face of the city. Subsequent church tradition had it that the first Christian community in the city had been founded by Saint Denis, who was widely believed to be the Denis the Areopagite mentioned in the New Testament as a follower of Saint Paul. This tradition was based on a confusion of Denises. The Parisian Saint Denis was probably a Christian missionary expedited to the region towards the end of the third century. He worked clandestinely, since Christianity's intolerant monotheism was perceived as threatening to the Roman cult: emperors Decimus (249–51) and Valerian (253–60), for example, had launched bouts of severe persecution. Denis was executed, possibly in 272. His death was the occasion for the miracle on which his canonization was to be based: decapitated on the slopes of Montmartre or *Mons Mercurii*, he was alleged to have picked up his head and walked with it to the place of his burial, over which the abbey of Saint-Denis was subsequently built. The fortunes of Christianity improved drastically when, by the Edict of Milan of 313, Emperor Constantine made Christianity the religion of the state. Although sporadic persecution of Christian communities did not cease – Lutetia's champion Emperor Julian, for example, was a militant anti-Christian – by the early fifth century Christianity was secure. Henceforward it was pagans and heretics who were on the receiving end of persecution.

A young Christian woman – who would be almost at once canonized as Saint Geneviève – symbolized the city's resistance to the marauding barbarian bands in the fifth century. Her hagiographers recalled how, in 451, when the city was threatened by the advent of Attila and the Huns, and when the city fathers counselled mass flight, Geneviève organized resistance. Her reputation as bastion of Christianity in the face of heathen barbarism was duly gilded by the fact that Attila's forces withdrew from the vicinity of Paris and went on to be crushed in battle by Aetius near Troyes and Châlons. Subsequently, Geneviève would be found negotiating with the armies of the Franks under Childeric in 463–4, and then again in the 470s, bringing grain from Troyes to relieve the city from famine caused by Frankish siege. The death of Syagrius following defeat in battle by Childeric's son, Clovis, made continued outright resistance inadvisable, especially as Clovis was beginning to amass a mighty Frankish empire covering much of the territory of erstwhile 'Hairy Gaul'.

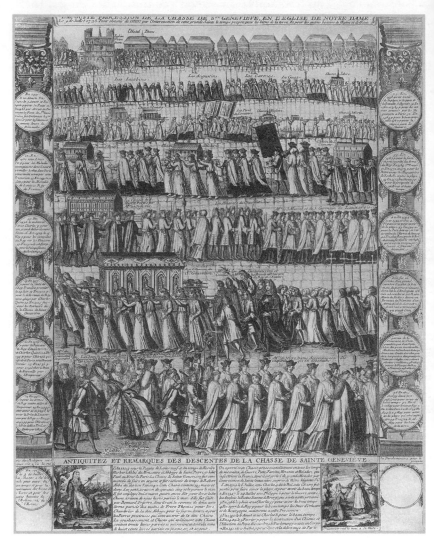

Saint Geneviève procession, 1725

1.3: Saint Geneviève

On the Pont de la Tournelle joining the Left Bank to the Île Saint-Louis stands a towering statue of Saint Geneviève, the patron saint of Paris (422–502), by the veteran public sculptor, Paul Landowski (1875–1961). Set in place in 1928, the statue is located on the eastern limit of the fortified city in the late Middle Ages and faces east. It thereby recalls the principal perceived source of danger in the earliest days of Paris. It was from the east that Attila and the Huns approached Paris in 451, when Geneviève famously rallied Parisian resistance. The Frankish military chieftains with whom she negotiated in the 570s and 580s also came from the east.

Yet by erecting the statue of the patron saint in this position – against the express wish of the sculptor, who had fought at the Somme and who wanted it, in a spirit of peace, to face Notre-Dame to its west – republican politicians were also recalling more recent threats to Paris from the east, starting with the Franco-Prussian War of 1870–71, when Paris was besieged. In 1914 there had been a wave of intercession prior to the Battle of the Marne, a conflict which did indeed save Paris from German invasion. Though her remains were paraded around the city in May 1940 as the 'phoney war' with Germany finally turned serious, she was clearly less successful that time, Paris having to endure four years of Nazi occupation.

The placing of Landowski's statue does not reveal a consistent Germanophobia in the treatment of Saint Geneviève. (Indeed, ironically enough, her name was Germanic in origin and her parents may even have been naturalized Franks.) For most of the millennium or so in which her powers of protection were invoked, she was a capable all-rounder in manifold cases of disaster and catastrophe. This aid could be personal – her inter-cession was judged especially useful for paralysis and fevers. The humanist Erasmus felt she had helped him recover from a life-threatening quartan fever when he was a Parisian student in

1497. She also responded to collective appeals, a development which originated in accounts of the Viking siege of the city in 885, when her remains had been promenaded on the city ramparts as a means of saving the city. (Barbarians like the Franks, the Vikings had approached the city this time from the west.)

From the Middle Ages onwards, each 3 January the reliquary containing her remains was solemnly taken out of the church of Sainte-Geneviève, where Clovis (whom she had helped convert to Christianity) had placed them in 512. They were taken on a procession around the Montagne Sainte-Geneviève down to Notre-Dame cathedral and back again. Until Louis XIV moved the court to Versailles in the late seventeenth century, the kings of France if in residence in Paris would follow the procession. The reliquary was also promenaded at times of disaster – on no fewer than forty-four occasions in the strife-torn sixteenth century. The occasions for processions included times of plague, rain and flood, 'for the prosperity of the arms of the king', against the Huguenots, during the king's illnesses and, especially, in times of dearth and famine. Geneviève had allegedly brought up provisions along the river from her country estates in the region of Troyes when famine threatened the Parisians, and her fame owed more to this skill at provisioning than to Germanophobia.

The police official Nicolas de La Mare, writing in 1738, noted that the cult of Saint Geneviève was 'almost as old as the monarchy'. He was almost proved a prophet. The saint's intercession seemed to be less called for in the secularizing age of Enlightenment: her remains were promenaded on only two occasions over the eighteenth century. They were rudely displaced in the iconoclastic dechristianization campaigns of the French Revolutionary Terror, following the execution of Louis XVI. Her precious gold-encrusted reliquary was taken to the mint to be melted down – 'in much tranquillity and without any miracles', noted the *Moniteur* newspaper.

Geneviève made a spirited comeback in the nineteenth century as a national icon (as well as, curiously, becoming the patron saint of policemen and air-hostesses). Although her remains had been dispersed in the 1790s, a replacement reliquary was constructed, containing a stone from the original sarcophagus. This was now placed in the nearby church of Saint-Étienne-du-Mont, where they remain, the object of fitful devotion – famine and Germanophobia having become, one hopes, things of the Parisian past.

Geneviève may well have been instrumental in the christianization of the new dynasty of Merovingians (that is, descendants of Mérovée or Merowech). The pagan Childebert had been in awe of her personal holiness, and it was possibly under her influence that Clovis and some 3,000 Frankish troops were converted to Christianity in around 498. Clovis ruled the Franks from 481/2 until 511. He and his wife Clotilda inaugurated a cult of Geneviève's memory, establishing the Basilica of the Holy Apostles (where the royal couple would be interred) on the site of what would, from the ninth century, become the church of Sainte-Geneviève on the Montagne Sainte-Geneviève. Clovis's adoption of Christianity allowed him to pose as defender of the faith against fellow barbarians the Visigoths, who had been won over to the Arian heresy, and whom he defeated in the battle of Vouillé in 507. He could also thereby claim cultural capital as the successor of Roman imperial power. In 508 in a ceremony at Tours he received from the eastern Emperor Anastasius I in Constantinople the official title of consul. Lutetia's claims through Julian and Valentinian to be an imperial city as well as, thanks to Geneviève, an iconically Christian community, gave the city the cachet which Clovis sought in his wish to be seen as invested with the legitimacy of Rome. 'Having put on a tunic of purple and a military mantle', Gregory of Tours recounted, in a garbled account, 'he placed a diadem on his head. From that day onwards, he was known as consul or Augustus. Then he left for Paris where he fixed his capital.'[7]

Despite surface appearances, it was not surprising that the Franks should adopt the mantle of *Romanitas* and the aura of Christianity. For they had accepted many of the values of the late Roman empire. Long before Clovis, Frankish populations had been seeping across the *limes*, which was far more porous than it claimed to be. The creeping Germanization of recruitment into the Roman army from the second century onwards was also pertinent here, especially once Paris became a garrison town. The big Gallo-Roman graveyard to the south-east of the city contained the headstone of a Roman (*sic*) legionary called Ursanius, from the Germanic Menapii tribe, usually located on the mouth of the Rhine. He was doubtless far from untypical. The Franks had served on a number of occasions as the Romans' *foederati* – or treaty-based allies – to police the frontier so as to keep other barbarian groups out. Clovis's father, Childeric, for example, had fought along-side Aetius against Attila in 451 and at his death he insisted on being buried with the insignia of a Roman general as well as with Frankish throwing axes (*francisca*). Paris was probably as ethnically and cul-turally mixed as in earlier times, and that mixing included Germanic elements. The Roman legionaries who had raised Julian on a shield in imperial acclamation in 360 were performing, as we have suggested, a Germanic ritual little known in Rome. Even Geneviève – Christian icon in the defence of *Romanitas* – probably had Germanic blood in her veins.

The Merovingian Franks, barbarian poachers, had thus turned imperial (and Christian) gamekeepers. They were reputed for being among the most romanized of so-called barbarians. 'The Franks are not nomads as indeed some barbarians are,' recorded the sixth-century Greek chronicler, Agathius of Mirina:

> their system of government, administration and laws are modelled more or less on the Roman pattern, apart from which they uphold similar standards with regard to contracts, marriage and religious observance. They are in fact all Christians and adhere to the strictest orthodoxy. They also have magistrates in their cities and priests and celebrate the feasts in the same way we do, and for a barbarian people strike me as extremely well-bred and civilized, and as practically the same as ourselves except for their uncouth style of dress and peculiar language. It seems that they are fairly civilized and cultivated for a barbarian people.[8]

Integration was made all the easier by the fact that the Franks were not numerous. They supplied the leading cadres of Clovis's new state, but the archaeological record shows that they did not markedly alter the material culture of the majority of the population in and around Paris (their presence was denser to the east). Significantly, too, no German place-names subsist in the Paris region – only Latin and (especially) Gaulish ones.

The Franks thus probably merged fairly painlessly through inter-marriage and political alliance with existing Gallo-Roman elites. Their conversion to Christianity was a way of signalling their imperial status (for Christianity had been the imperial cult since 313), but it was also a sop to the indigenous peoples, christianized from the late third century. In addition, the Franks accepted intact the established diocesan framework and ecclesiastical hierarchy, tried to maintain the Roman tax system, and accepted pre-existing legal codes. Latin, the tongue of Romans and churchmen, became the recognized language of the Merovingian state, and was used in all official documents, including the code of Frankish customary law. The Franks also worked hand in hand with the church hierarchy. 'You should defer to your bishops and always have recourse to their advice,' Remi, the bishop of Reims, had written to Clovis at the inception of his power. 'If you are on good terms with them, your province will be better able to stand firm.'[9] Out of prudence, Clovis and his successors largely followed this advice.

Clovis's choice of Paris as capital played very clearly to this Merovingian strategy of accommodating existing power structures and also appropriating the symbolic repertoire of *Romanitas* and Christianity. It was impossible to imagine oneself as the heir to Rome without having a city modelled on it. Paris was an obvious candidate as capital in that it had witnessed the effective coronation of Emperor Julian, but the choice also suggests that the city had not lost all traces of its Roman grandeur to the progress of weeds and nettles. Clovis and his heirs – who wore their hair long, perhaps as a magical symbol – combined the aura of the Christian God's elect, the Roman cult of imperial deity, and the Merovingian tradition of godly status as a result of their descent from Merowech. The long-haired kings minted coins showing Romulus and Remus, founders of Rome; sent diplomatic representatives to Constantinople; and maintained in their architecture the Corinthian column. Chilperic (r. 561–84) composed poetry in Latin hexameters, and was said to have staged Roman games in Paris in 577, possibly in the old amphitheatre.

The dynasty's posture as protectors of both *Romanitas* and Christianity was played out in the context of the complex, chaotic and bloody game of Merovingian power-politics described in Gregory of Tours's *History of the Franks*. On one hand, the Frankish kingdom grew from the early sixth century as a result of military conquest: first the Visigoths in Aquitaine, then the Ostrogothic kingdom of Provence were brought under Merovingian control, then the Burgundians in the east of France, and there was also expansion in Germany and Italy. On the other hand, dynastic lands were very frequently subdivided on the death of a king. On Clovis's death in 511, for example, all his four sons co-inherited: Childebert became 'king of Paris' while his brothers ruled kingdoms based in Orléans, Reims and Soissons. Death and an absence of heirs served to counter excessive fragmentation of power, as did those props of Merovingian (as indeed of late imperial) political culture, namely, cold-blooded murder and assassination. But from the time of Clovis until the middle of the eighth century, only one year in four saw a single Merovingian ruler on the throne. Paris's special symbolic role was still recognized in that it was not split up among the rulers, but retained a status as capital of all Frankish dominions and a place in which joint issues could be thrashed out if need be. Yet the city had become little more than a useful bargaining chip in Merovingian dynastic power-politics, all the more so in that the Merovingian kings were not only multiple but also, from the late sixth century, increasingly itinerant around their domains. A Merovingian king very rarely resided in his capital.

Perhaps because of its symbolic status as capital, Paris developed as the location for successive church councils. One such assembly had been held in the city in 360, to fulminate against the Arian heresy, but councils now met regularly here – in 552, 561, 573, 577 and 614, for example. The city also developed a role in providing burial sites for the dynasty. Both Clovis and Clotilda were buried in the shrine they had created for Saint Geneviève in Paris. In 543, moreover, Clovis's son Childebert (r. 511–58) brought back from Saragossa relics of Saint Vincent, and he deposited these in a shrine on the Left Bank which would thereafter come to be known as Saint-Germain-des-Prés. He was buried here in 558, as were all his successors until 629. A royal necropolis also emerged at the abbey at Saint-Denis – the site of the eponymous saint's grave, over which Saint Geneviève had erected a shrine in the 450s. A number of high Merovingian dignitaries chose it as their burial site, and the decision of Dagobert I (r. 629–38), one of the few sole rulers of Merovingian lands, to be buried there marked the beginnings of what would later become a royal funeral tradition which lasted until the French Revolution.

Encouraged by the monarchy, and also by an aristocracy which in the sixth century became heavily committed to building religious establishments, the church was prospering. A new religious topography for the city now emerged. A healing miracle on a leper performed by Saint Martin of Tours on his passage to the north of the city in 385 led to the erection of the church of Saint-Martin-des-Champs on the Right Bank (IIIe.), well to the north of most habitation. Saint Marcel, for his part, was responsible for developing the city in the south-east: his alleged miraculous battle against a dragon on the fringes of the cemetery in which he himself would be buried (c. 435) created a new Christian necropolis around the present-day Gobelins crossroads (XIIIe.), an area formerly used as a military graveyard. The Merovingians sponsored the beginning of work on a massive new cathedral, dedicated to Saint Étienne, on the Île de la Cité, close to the site where Notre-Dame would be built in the twelfth century. By the eighth century, the island also contained around half a dozen other churches, while the Left Bank was also well-provided for with around a dozen Merovingian foundations. These tended to be erected close to the major roads: the churches of Saint-Séverin and Notre-Dame-des-Champs were adjacent to the Rue Saint-Jacques, for example, those of Saint-Julien-le-Pauvre, Saint-Médard and Saint-Marcel to the highway for Italy.

A further new development was the emergence of significant habitation on the Right Bank of the Seine. This was normally around small hillocks (*monceaux*) which, as a result of the levelling attentions of Baron Haussmann in the nineteenth century, are now scarcely if at all detectable.[10] From around this period, churches were built on these topographical features. This was the case at Saint-Germain-l'Auxerrois (Ie.), and at Saint-Merri and Saint-Gervais (IVe.), and in around half a dozen other sites, including Saint-Jacques-de-la-Boucherie (IVe.), close to what was by now a functioning river port. Beyond the soggiest of the Right Bank marshes, there was Saint-Laurent (Xe.) as well as Saint-Martin-des-Champs. Further north, the pagan temples at Montmartre had been replaced by a church on the site of Saint Denis's martyrdom: the *Mons Mercurii* ('Mercury's Mount') became *Mons Martyrum* ('Martyrs' Mount'). Overall, this was an extraordinary array of churches for a city probably no more populous than its Roman predecessor.

The ecclesiastical institutions of Paris bulked ever larger as its political and economic role dwindled. Although the presence here of Syrian and Jewish merchants in the sixth century testified to the continuance of patterns of long-haul trade and exchange, a far more localized economy of gift, tribute and pillage had started to dominate within Frankish domains and beyond. Towns were no longer the engine of trade and exchange as under the Roman empire: an urban civilization was being replaced by one grounded in the countryside. The political force of the Franks was also in decline. Their now often multiple rulers neglected their more southerly conquests, and focused their power between the Loire and the Rhine. Within this area, two poles of activity emerged: Austrasia (eastern France and western Germany, from the Meuse to the Rhine) and Neustria (central and western France from the Meuse to the Loire, and including Paris).

The kings of Neustria were increasingly peripatetic, and although their treasury was still located in Paris, they usually preferred to lodge in the royal palace at Clichy rather than in the city. With the exception of a stopover made by Chilperic II in 717, no king was recorded as visiting Paris in the first half of the eighth century. In addition, the Merovingian dynasty was being sapped from within by the emergence of a new power-source in their household, the so-called 'Mayors of the Palace'. The chronicler Einhard later noted how wealth and power increasingly passed into the hands of these officials, who were in charge of the dynastic accounts as well as assuring the interim when minors succeeded to the throne. These individuals 'exerted ultimate authority. The king had nothing remaining him beyond the enjoyment of his title and the satisfaction of sitting on his throne with his long hair and trailing beard, there to give the impression of rule.'[11]

In 679 the Mayor of the Palace in Austrasia, Pépin II of Herstal of the Arnulfing (later 'Carolingian') house, ended Merovingian rule in the Austrasian half of Frankish domains. In 687 he forced the Neustrians to accept him and his heirs as their Mayor of the Palace. He and his successors built up their power-base in Austrasia, with the result that Paris became ever more distant from the location of real authority. The Merovingian kings, who still enjoyed a certain kind of divine status, seemed little more than dynastic window-dressing. Finally the Austrasian Pépin III the Short decided that they were more trouble than they were worth, and in 751 deposed them.

Pépin was crowned by the pope as king of the Franks in Saint-Denis in 754, and he was buried there on his death in 768. Yet Paris seemed to be on the point of being written out of dynastic politics. After dallying with the idea of basing his government in Paris, Pépin's heir, Charles the Great – Charlemagne – chose to establish his palace at Aix-la-Chapelle, closer to the heart of the huge empire which he had built up and which ran from beyond the Pyrenees to the Baltic and from the Atlantic coast through much of Italy and into the Hungarian plains. Like the Merovingians, the Carolingians sought a sacred basis to their power – yet did not associate Paris with it. They followed the inspiration of one of their ancestors, Charles Martel, who had defeated Arab armies at Poitiers in 732, and became armed crusaders for the faith – notably in Germany. Partly at least in recognition for these spiritual services, on Christmas Day 800 the pope crowned Charlemagne Holy Roman Emperor. Yet Paris was not allowed to share in this new-found glory. The Carolingian state apparatus was based in Aix-la-Chapelle, and the emperor drew most of his officials from Austrasian rather than Neustrian families. Although church councils were held in Paris in 825, 829, 846, 849 and 853, the renaissance engendered by the Carolingian dynasty passed Paris by. The cultural and religious activities involved – the copying and illumination of Latin manuscripts, improvements in musical notation, codification of laws, and workmanship in the fine arts – were at their liveliest in Aix-la-Chapelle and also in monasteries at Corbie, Laon, Metz and Reims, but not, with the honourable exception of Saint-Germain-des-Prés, in Paris.

Paris seemed far distant from the heartlands of Carolingian power. This marginal position was confirmed by the city's relative impotence in the face of a new wave of barbarian attacks – this time by Scandinavian Norsemen, or Vikings. These pagan seafarers had been looting and raiding southern England and the French Atlantic coast from the late eighth century, but from the 840s they made a habit of sailing up the Seine to lay siege to Paris, even from the 850s wintering within France so that they could extend their attacks.

By this time the sprawling Carolingian empire had undergone the kind of political fragmentation which had characterized the Merovingian period. By the Treaty of Verdun in 843, Frankish lands were split between the sons of Emperor Louis the Pious. The imperial title was given to Lothair, who ruled over a long strip of territory running from the North Sea to the Adriatic ('Lotharingia'). This separated the Germanic kingdom of the East Franks (under Louis the German) and West Francia, ruled until the 870s by Charles the Bald (r. 838–77). In the event, however, the latter showed precious little interest in Paris, circulating his court around his domains, and preferring to reside in his palace at Compiègne. His strategy – or maybe lack of strategy – towards the Vikings was to pay them off, an arrangement which developed into a recurrent system of protection money. In the 860s Charles urged the barring of rivers against the Viking raids, and from 870 all cities in West Francia were ordered to repair their city defences. By that time Paris had been pillaged in 845, 856–7, 861, 865–6 and 869, and nearly all the churches of the Left Bank had been despoiled and set on fire. Most inhabitants of the open city swarmed onto the Île de la Cité so as to take advantage of the protection which the river seemed to afford them. The city walls constructed against the Franks and their ilk at the end of the fourth century were half a millennium old and hardly capable of offering military resistance. But from the early 880s new fortifications were built on the Île de la Cité under the orders of Odo (Eudes), the count of Paris (r. 882–98).

In 885–6 the Parisian worm turned. The chronicler Abbo was an eyewitness to the Viking siege of the city which occurred over that winter. The Viking hordes advanced in 'seven hundred tall ships and a multitude of smaller vessels', so densely arrayed that the assembled 'sails, oak, elm and alder' made the river waters invisible for two leagues downstream.[12] The Parisians refused to pay the protection money demanded by the Vikings from their provisional camp on the remains of the despoiled church of Saint-Germain-l'Auxerrois to the west of the city. They trusted instead in the new barrage bridge (the Grand Pont) that was constructed close to the present-day Place du Châtelet (Ie.) on the Right Bank, to block vessels travelling further downstream. Much of the ensuing battle focused on that bridge and on the Petit Pont linked to the Left Bank. The collapse of the Petit Pont allowed some of the Vikings to proceed upstream to continue looting, while others remained to maintain the siege. At a key stage in the operations, Odo brought up reinforcements to the city's aid: Parisian morale was lifted one evening by seeing 'the helmets and shields [of his troops] sparkling in the rays of the sun' up on Montmartre.[13] When West Francian King Charles the Fat (r. 884–7) arrived, he negotiated the retreat of the Vikings. The Vikings returned in 887 and 889, but on both occasions the reinforced defences of the Île de la Cité prevented their pillaging the city or proceeding upstream. And Odo administered them a sound military drubbing.

Abbo – in whose chronicle we suspect more than a little poetic licence and religious over-enthusiasm – highlighted the organizing zeal of Bishop Gozlin of Paris in the city's defence in 885–6, and the protective charms wrought by parading on the city walls the relics of Saint Geneviève, which had been gathered on the Île de la Cité for protection. He also stressed Odo's role in the city's defence against the heathen Vikings, perhaps even rather knowingly comparing it to Geneviève's role as symbol of Christian resistance to the pagan barbarians.

The fact that Parisians looked to their count rather than to their king or the Holy Roman Emperor was a telling sign of political changes taking place in western Europe at this time. All the Carolingian domains were experiencing a fragmentation of power. The dynasty had kept the centrifugal tendencies of their empire in check by delegating political authority, on the understanding that the posts returned within the emperor's gift on the death of the incumbent. By the late ninth century this was no longer happening, so that underlings were becoming both hereditary and, consequently, independent. As it was they who now regulated justice, collected taxes, levied troops and provided military protection, they also commanded the respect of local populations. Some territorially based magnates began to call themselves dukes (and even kings, like Louis, self-proclaimed king of Provence from 910) and to build up a court and a cohort of loyal followers, extending patronage to their followings while emperors looked helplessly on.

Within the Paris region the dominant such sub-dynasty was the Robertians – or Capetians as they subsequently became. Robert the Strong, marquis of Neustria and father of Odo, hero of the 885 siege, had slipped the bonds of dependence on West Francian royal power in the early ninth century, building up an impressive power bloc within northern France. Following the siege of Paris, the prestige of Robert's son Odo, who had taken the title of count of Paris, was considerable. In 892, following the death of Charles the Fat, Abbo recorded, 'to the applause of the people of the Franks (*populus Francorum*), who were very favourable to him, [Odo] obtained the title of king and royal authority; his hand received the sceptre and his head the crown.'[14] The new ruler proved assiduous and energetic, and he handed the countship of Paris over to his brother, Robert, to give himself free rein. Yet on his deathbed in 898, Odo urged fellow magnates to accept as his successor as king of West Francia the Carolingian candidate, Charles the Simple. Such was the degree of fragmentation of power, he perceived that it was more in his family's interests to be counts of Paris than kings of West Francia.

Yet Paris itself – which Abbo had dubbed 'queen above all other cities'[15] – was in poor shape by the tenth century. As a result of extensive Viking depredations, Abbo related, 'the wine-grower and the farmer both suffer, like vines and the earth, the cruel domination of death'.[16] Persistent raiding had destroyed a great many of the urban structures of the Left Bank in particular, and much of the area was turned over thereafter to agricultural purposes. The more lightly urbanized Right Bank seemed to have been spared the worst pillaging, possibly because a defensive wall had been erected to enclose the *monceaux* around Saint-Jacques-de-la-Boucherie, Saint-Merri and Saint-Gervais. Although the city's history so far had been largely conducted on the Left Bank, the post-Viking development of the city, as we shall see in Chapter 2, would favour the Right Bank over the Left. The fortified Île de la Cité was the heart of a capital which still lived in a mood of threat and danger. But it presided over a site which contained a dwindling and seemingly impoverished population.

For most of the tenth century, Paris was significant less for itself than that it was the nominal capital of the Robertian/Capetian line with claims to royalty. Odo's brother Robert held the crown in 922–3, though he died before he could make anything of it. His son Hugh the Great was responsible for bringing back the Carolingian candidate Louis d'Outre-Mer from England to serve as king when the post fell vacant in 936. When the Carolingians ruled, the Robertians strengthened their power-base. In 943 Louis appointed Hugh 'duke of France', and the latter exercised his power throughout the Île-de-France, and also in much of the area between the Seine and Loire rivers including the counties of Anjou, Maine, Orléans and Tours. Yet so fragmented was it becoming that Robertian authority began to be riddled with minor countships and castellanies. The dynasty also had to cope with the growing powers assumed by the bishops of Paris and other ecclesiastical dignitaries, who built up vast landed estates around the city. In this kind of game, Paris itself was largely a political irrelevance. The counts maintained control by juggling alliances rather than by associating their strength with any single location. They circulated round their domains, while the Carolingian rulers used Laon as their capital.

Paris briefly re-entered the spotlight in 978, when emperor Otto II led a short punitive sortie against it. Although he looked down contemptuously on the city from the heights of Montmartre, imperial politics called him back east before he could attempt a full siege – thus seeming only to confirm Paris's symbolic role, highlighted in the associations with Geneviève in 451 and Odo in 885, as a city specially protected by God. When in 987 the princelings of West Francia elected as their king the Robertian Hugh Capet, great-grandson of Robert the Strong, it was not in the expectation that he would wield much authority, nor that this would signify a change in the fortunes of Paris.

Only time would tell what Robertian/Capetian power augured for a place which, frankly, thus far in its history, had not amounted to very much. Paris owed little to Lutetia and its Merovingian-Carolingian successor. Its extraordinary destiny from the twelfth century onwards would, moreover, make these humble beginnings seem meagre, unworthy and forgettable. From the twelfth century a myth of origins developed which attributed Paris's foundation to the survivors from the sack of Troy. A Trojan origin seemed preferable to a Roman one, given Lutetia's third-rank provincial status. The most massive surviving structure from the early period – the bath complex now off the Boulevard Saint-Michel – was thought to be the palace of Julius Caesar or Emperor Julian and fell into absolute disrepair and neglect. To a remarkable degree, Parisians remained ignorant of the early phases of their own history. The forum, the arena and the cemeteries were pillaged for stone for subsequent building, or else so covered in detritus that they survived – but only for nineteenth- and twentieth-century archaeologists. For most of the second millennium, when it came to the early history of their city, Parisians preferred myth over memory.

2

'Queen of Cities'

c. 1000–*c.* 1300

[Paris] is situated at the heart of a delightful valley, in the midst of a crown of slopes enriched by both Ceres and Bacchus. The Seine, this proud river which comes from the east, flows vigorously through it and encircles with its two arms the island which is the head, the heart, the very marrow of the whole city. Two faubourgs (or suburbs), the least of which would cause other cities envy, stretch out to right and left. Each communicates with the island by stone bridges: the Grand Pont is turned to the north, towards the English sea, while the Petit Pont looks towards the river Loire. The first faubourg, large, rich and full of business, is an effervescent theatre of activity; numerous boats, full of merchandise and wealth, surround it. The Petit Pont belongs to the dialecticians, who walk about discussing grave matters.[1]

This idealized description in 1175 by the minor writer Guy de Bazoches of 'the queen of cities', as Abbo had called it,[2] highlighted important features of the city's transformation. Under the early Capetians, Paris had remade itself as a city of three parts, given cohesion by impressive stone bridges. The city had exploded outwards from the Île de la Cité – the 'heart' of the city, in which the foremost symbols of state power (the royal palace) and church authority (the cathedral) were located. The Right Bank had followed a commercial vocation, developing into a major business and trading centre. The Left Bank, heavily damaged by Viking assaults, developed a new role, associated with teaching and learning.

The scale of these changes had turned a modest city of third-rank status into an urban centre to which, for the first time in its history, superlatives could be attached. This period marked the greatest

37

quantum leap in the history of Paris, before and since. Not much more than a dot on the map even in 1100, by the end of the twelfth century it was the largest city in Christendom and a pre-eminent cultural and intellectual centre. Its economy was booming too – indeed with Champagne, Flanders and Tuscany the Île-de-France was probably the wealthiest and most productive region in Europe. The city was also becoming – in a meaningful and significant sense – a state capital, and indeed its emergence into prominence owed much to the influence and growing power of the Capetian dynasty established in such unpropitious circumstances in 987. The growth of the city mirrored the dynasty's successes, as the Capetian kings built up the initially tiny domains under their direct control into possessions which covered the majority of the feudal kingdom of 'France' (as 'West Francia' was now called) and which ranked among the most powerful states in Europe.

Paris would turn out to be a considerable feather in the Capetians' hat. Yet the dynasty took some time to warm to it. Partly this was because there was little to warm to. Viking pillaging had removed much of the city's movable wealth, and caused untold damage to property outside the Cité stronghold. The houses and public buildings which were extant in 1100 were in most respects identical to those of the Carolingians – and even the later Merovingians. Stone from the urban buildings of Antiquity had been pillaged over the centuries to provide the raw materials for fortifying the Cité, and the eminent sites of Lutetia were now passing out of Parisian memory. The amphitheatre had become a graveyard, while the old forum on the Montagne Sainte-Geneviève was widely believed by the thirteenth century to be the remains of Saracen buildings or a haunted chateau. Many of the Left Bank churches were still in ruins after the turn of the millennium. The erection of defensive earthworks on the Right Bank around the hillocks and churches of Saint-Merri and Saint-Gervais (IVe.) provided the basis for further development, but this too was slow to come. The city's population in 1100 may have been as little as 3,000. Yet by 1300 it was around 200,000.

Initially, Paris had thus seemed little for the new dynasty to be proud of. Certainly, the early incumbents showed meagre affection for the city. Hugh Capet was crowned king at Noyon, and chose Orléans as the place where he associated his son Robert II 'the Pious'

(r. 996–1031) with his rule. Robert rebuilt the Cité palace and also donated funds towards the reconstruction of Parisian churches. His successor Henri I (r. 1031–60) helped to reconstitute the fortunes of the cathedral chapter and the abbey of Sainte-Geneviève. Yet none of the early Capetians appears to have visited Paris much, and all chose to reside in Orléans. The fact that dynastic domain lands were scattered throughout the Île-de-France also encouraged the ruler to rotate around a number of locations, including Laon, Senlis, Melun and Étampes as well as Paris and Orléans.

A further consideration was the pattern of power within the city. The Capetians had terminated the post of count of Paris as being a potential threat to their authority. But the Saint-Gervais *monceau* was a feudal fief held by the comtes de Meulan: as late as 1111 the comte profited from the absence of the king to enter the Île de la Cité on a pillaging raid, destroying the bridges and raiding the royal treasury. The bishop of Paris was also a very powerful local figure: his lands probably covered as much territory within the city as the king's, and his seigneurial jurisdiction was wider. Like other religious institutions (notably the cathedral chapter), the episcopacy also enjoyed rights and property in a large number of villages in the Île-de-France and beyond. The Capetians endeavoured to keep the bishops under their control, but they were not always successful. In 1094 there was quite a scandal when Philip I (r. 1060–1108) appointed as bishop the twenty-eight-year-old brother of his adulterous consort. The king was excommunicated for this and other offences, and he remained so up to 1104.

Relations between church and dynasty within Paris were all the more sensitive in that the Capetians were receptive to the growing role which ecclesiastical establishments had in repopulating the city, and developing its prosperity. This was particularly true of the Left Bank. The abbey of Saint-Germain-des-Prés in particular built up in its environs an extensive dependent population of serfs who catered to the various agrarian and service requirements of the monks. It attracted new settlers on to its properties too, allowing them to establish a farmstead or a shop, in return for an annual rental payment, the *cens*. By the end of the thirteenth century the abbey had given the little bourg its autonomy. The nearby parish church of Saint-Sulpice (VIe.)

was built in 1211 to help accommodate the spiritual needs of a growing population, and at the same time two further parish churches (Saint-André-des-Arts and Saint-Côme)[3] were added. Besides cultivating grain, many of the abbey's peasants devoted their land-holding to wine-growing. The same tribute to Ceres and Bacchus – in Guy de Bazoches's terms – was also evident in lands owned by the canons of Sainte-Geneviève, which met Saint-Germain-des-Prés territory at around the level of the present-day Boulevard Saint-Michel. Vines flowed down the slopes of the hill to the very edge of the Seine: the Rue Galande (Ve.) memorializes the 'clos Garlande', one of the biggest concentrations of vines.

The pattern of population development and economic growth was not dissimilar on the Right Bank. The creation of the parish church of Saint-Nicolas-des-Champs (IIIe.) close to the abbey-church of Saint-Martin-des-Champs highlighted the latter's success in attracting new population. To the south of the abbey was a sparser and more disreputable development of wanderers, minstrels and prostitutes in the ironically named 'Beau-Bourg', which abutted on the church of Saint-Merri and the chapter of Sainte-Opportune. Slightly to their south-west was the Bourg Thibourg (or Tibourg), which was named after an eminent merchant: the Rue de la Tissanderie (or Tixanderie: 'Weaver Street') became the core of an important area of textiles manufacture.[4] Further to the west was a developing bourg around the church of Saint-Germain-l'Auxerrois, now recovered from being a Viking stronghold in the 880s (though it still retained a street structure based on that encampment).[5] To the north-east were the extensive domains of the headquarters of the international crusading order, the Templars, based on a towering castle structure on the site of the present-day Square du Temple (IIIe.). On the river the 'Bourg de Grève' developed around the port which had developed on the site of the Place de l'Hôtel-de-Ville (IVe.: formerly Place de Grève). It extended towards the *monceau* Saint-Gervais, especially once, from the mid-twelfth century, the counts of Meulan were ousted from their fief here. Further afield, there was the abbey-church of Saint-Denis; the monastery-cum-leperhouse of Saint-Lazare out on the Saint-Denis road, founded in the 1120s and the focus for the small community of La Villette; and the convent of Saint-Pierre, established at Montmartre in 1134. These religious institutions fostered settlement and also served the city's wider economic interests. Saint-Germain-des-Prés, for example, held a fair which lasted a fortnight. In 1120 the Lendit fair was placed in the hands of the abbey of Saint-Denis, while in 1137, a new fair was confirmed for the Saint-Lazare leperhouse. These strengthened Paris's market functions and helped integrate the city more closely within the region.

The wealth which religious establishments derived from their extensive agrarian and commercial activities was spent in supporting a wide range of handicraft, especially at the upper end. The church was a major patron for architects, sculptors, stained-glass experts, jewellers, goldsmiths, manuscript illuminators and the like. In many of these arts Paris achieved international primacy. It was under the aegis of the church too that the city developed a reputation as a centre of learning. Although there had long been a cathedral school of some repute, and a solid tradition of learning at Saint-Germain-des-Prés and Sainte-Geneviève, Paris was no more than the equal of other ecclesiastical centres in northern France, such as Laon, Orléans and Reims. The cathedral and chapter viewed the granting of licences to teach theology and canon law as a money-making enterprise, and, in reaction to this, a number of clerics relocated to the Left Bank, within the jurisdiction of Sainte-Geneviève. The area around the Petit Pont – located then as now close to Notre-Dame cathedral at the foot of the Rue Saint-Jacques – became a special place for students to come and listen to teachers engaging in intellectual jousting in open-air settings which gave the site the atmosphere of 'a sort of amphitheatre'.[6] The name of the Rue du Fouarre (Ve.: 'Straw Street') evokes the bales on which clerics would sit to enjoy the heady intellectual atmosphere. The arrival here of the charismatic Peter Abelard further burnished the Left Bank's reputation. Abelard's brilliance eclipsed his master, Guillaume de Champeaux, who in ignominy and shame left the Petit Pont community in 1108, establishing the abbey of Saint-Victor out to the east of the Montagne Sainte-Geneviève in what was formerly a wild and deserted site. Saint-Victor won the support of the dynasty and developed into a powerful centre of learning in its own right. In 1147 monks from Saint-Victor were entrusted with the reform of the community of Sainte-Geneviève, which had become spiritually decadent. In its new form, it too developed into a further beacon of learning.

By the mid-twelfth century, Paris was proving a magnet for younger clerics wishing to engage in intellectual work. Guy de Bazoches's image of these teachers and pupils walking about 'discussing grave matters' in the shadow of the Petit Pont was reflected in the memoirs of the English cleric John of Salisbury, a student here in the 1140s, who likened the Left Bank to Jacob's Ladder, with angels ascending and descending. 'And there I saw,' he added, 'such a quantity of food [a nice student touch!]; so happy a people; such respect for the clergy; the splendour and dignity of the whole church; the diverse tasks of the students of philosophy.'[7] The student body was highly diverse, socially and ethnically. Their needs in what – in recognition of the *lingua franca* in use – was only much later called the 'Latin Quarter' were met by the development of a service sector ranging from parchment-makers, binders, illuminators, copyists and the like through to taverns, inns, bath-houses, food shops and roasteries.[8]

The air of intellectual, religious, commercial and agrarian vitality developed by the church served the interests of the Capetian dynasty very nicely. Significantly, this cohort of monarchs – Louis VI (r. 1108–37), Louis VII (r. 1137–80), Philip II Augustus (r. 1180–1223) and Louis IX (1223–70: 'Saint Louis') – used the city as their primary official residence, and all looked on the church as an ideological buttress of royal power. Churchmen were in particular responsible for developing the idea of the dynasty as specially favoured by God – like the Merovingians and Carolingians before them, with whom the Capetians stressed their links. Even during the reign of Hugh Capet, Robert the Pious had become renowned for the miraculous power to cure scrofula, the 'King's Evil'. The practice of the 'royal touch' was taken up by his successors, and became a quasi-official ceremony, which highlighted the miracle-working powers of the Capetian line. Almost the first thing which Capetian kings did when they were crowned was to undertake their first bout of practising the royal touch.

The Benedictine monk Suger, abbot of nearby Saint-Denis, played a key role in amplifying this strain of royal propaganda, cunningly linking his own abbey with the crown's aspirations. The growing prestige of the monarchy would owe much to a Paris–Saint-Denis axis. While kings of France had been crowned at Reims from the ninth century, they had been buried at Saint-Denis since the times of

Dagobert in 639. The abbey-church developed into a royal necropolis. Louis VI added to the monastery's prestige by lodging his own and his father's crown there, where it joined other sacred royal regalia including the crown of Charlemagne. The sense of the dynasty's religious mission was further served by its prominent place in the crusades to recapture the Holy Places from the Seljuk Turks. No other nation in western Europe was as prominent in the crusades as the French. The First Crusade was launched by the pope at a church council in Clermont in 1095; the last, in 1270, was led by the king of France (Saint Louis). In the period between, more than half the French nobility and three French kings went on crusade. So numerous were they in the crusading forces that the Turkish term for crusaders was 'Frenchmen' (*Franci*).

2.1: Saint-Denis

It would be tempting to say that the histories of Paris and Saint-Denis were twinned by fate – were not the difference of size between the two so grossly disproportionate. Saint-Denis today has around 100,000 inhabitants, as against Paris's two million or more. A difference of this magnitude has been a constant feature of their histories. Even so, Saint-Denis has played a pivotal role in regard to Paris's history in two utterly contrasting ways.

In the Middle Ages Saint-Denis served as the dynastic patron of the Capetians, whose capital was Paris. The medieval linkage derives from the fact that Saint-Denis is the reputed site of the death of Saint Denis, in legend the first bishop of Paris. In the late fifth century Saint Geneviève, patron saint of Paris, added to the sacredness of the site, which was already a place of pilgrimage, by building a church here. This subsequently became the basis of an abbey, which Napoleon made into a basilica and which in 1966 became a cathedral. In the twelfth century Abbot Suger reinforced the Paris–Saint-Denis connection. He confirmed the abbey as the necropolis (since the seventh century) of the dynasty; established it as the home of the sacred regalia of the monarchy; developed the gothic style which became a symbol of the dynasty's prestige; served as minister and regent to Louis VI and VII in one of the most formative periods in the history of the French state; and presided over the school of historians of the abbey who rewrote the history of France from its allegedly Trojan origins to the present, in ways which glorified their own site as well as the dynasty. The bond between the two was so close that *chansons de geste* called the French ruler 'king of Saint-Denis'. The abbey's wealth grew not only from this royal generosity but also as a result of the numerous privileges the monarchy accorded the abbey, including the right to hold the Lendit fair on the plain to the south of the city.

In the thirteenth century the necropolis underwent a massive refurbishment so that it could be a more visitable and impressive shrine to the greatness of the kings of France. Pilgrims and travellers to Paris visited Saint-Denis in droves, highlighting its role as propaganda organ for the monarchy. The tombs became more ornate. In the early sixteenth century, for example, Louis XII and Francis I underlined their claims to be considered Renaissance monarchs by each building imposing and highly decorated Italianate mausoleums. A century or more later, the Bourbons preferred a much more austere style, signalling changing conceptions of death.

Saint-Denis, sacred site of the dynasty, could never rival Paris in any way save the symbolic. The Capetians' capital benefited from having Saint-Denis at arm's length. In royal *entrées* to Paris the city fathers always waited on the monarch at the Saint-Denis gate, and his mortal remains often left by the same route on their way to the royal necropolis. Though Saint-Denis was sacked by the English in 1436, Joan of Arc dedicated her armour here and Henry IV subsequently renounced Protestantism in the abbey-church. When Holy Roman Emperor Charles V came to Paris in 1540, he was taken out to Saint-Denis, where in addition to the tombs of dozens of rulers, he was also allowed to inspect a bizarre array of relics including Solomon's golden cup, Virgil's mirror, Joan of Arc's sword, Charlemagne's chess set, Roland's

Alexandre Lenoir defends the royal tombs against destruction during the
French Revolution

ivory horn and the largest unicorn horn in the world. A great deal of this was despoiled in the sacking of the abbey by iconoclastic dechristianizers during the French Revolution in 1793–4. By that time, Saint-Denis's sacral primacy within France had largely faded anyway.

Though restored by Eugène Emmanuel Viollet-le-Duc in the nineteenth century in ways which captured something of its original gothic grandeur, the basilica was not the focus of the second phase in the history of relations between Saint-Denis and Paris. Indeed, by the late nineteenth and twentieth centuries the building seemed a compelling anachronism, set in aspic in a fast-developing context. As Parisian heavy industry relocated beyond the twenty arrondissements, Saint-Denis became the most genuinely proletarian commune in the suburbs (or *banlieue*). The canal system added to the railway network to allow the speedy provision of raw materials for heavy industry there, and the diffusion of finished goods.

In the inter-war period in particular, the city played up to the role of champion of left-wing causes in the 'red belt' (*ceinture rouge*) formed by Socialist and (especially) Communist municipalities. This played into Parisian bourgeois fantasies of an irreducible oppositionist suburb, always needing careful control. Although the left-wing orientation holds good, the deindustrialization of the area from the 1960s onwards has moderated its militancy, and dissipated the myth of 'Saint-Denis-la-Rouge'. The placing of a national sports stadium there – the Stade de France – and an extensive programme of urban renewal form part of a move to give it a very different national identity.

When Louis VI left for the Second Crusade in 1147, significantly, he made Abbot Suger regent in his absence (which lasted until 1149). Suger established himself in Paris close to the Rue Saint-Martin (IIIe.–IVe.), which he judged 'a more convenient location'[9] for running the kingdom. The Paris–Saint-Denis axis was also apparent in another domain in which the church glided the reputation of the Capetian dynasty, namely the architectural style which subsequently became known as gothic. It was Abbot Suger who had assembled the key components of the style (pointed arch, ribbed vault) in rebuilding the abbey of Saint-Denis from the 1130s. The construction of the cathedral of Notre-Dame on the Île de la Cité from the 1160s, covering the site formerly occupied by the Saint-Étienne cathedral (about which we know next to nothing), gave the style its cachet. The gothic – *opus francigenum* ('French-style work') – was soon adopted elsewhere in northern France, and in the following century it became enormously influential throughout northern Europe. Besides increasing the international prestige of the Capetians, the gothic changed the face of Paris, as it was subsequently adopted by local churches, such as Saint-Julien-le-Pauvre (Ve.), Saint-Martin-des-Champs (IIIe.) and, most brilliantly, the Sainte-Chapelle on the Île de la Cité, which was erected from 1247 by Saint Louis as a shrine for a relic of the Crown of Thorns. The gothic also entered the vocabulary of civil buildings, such as the present-day Conciergerie on the Cité, part of the royal palace of justice which was extensively rebuilt by Louis VI and Louis VII.

The Paris–Saint-Denis axis was further glorified by the dynasty's military successes, at home and abroad. A particular target was the English Angevin dynasty, which in the late eleventh and twelfth centuries had established an area of domination down the western side of France from Calais to the Pyrenees. In the wake of the indignities Louis VI suffered in Paris at the hands of the comte de Meulan in 1111, he then lost the royal standard (and his horse) in a humiliating military defeat by Henry I of England at Brémoule in 1119. But in 1124, faced with invasion from the east by the German emperor, he rode out to Saint-Denis to adopt the institution's oriflamme – a banner based on the imperial insignia of Charlemagne – before moving east at the head of his troops to beat back the German forces. Henceforth, the taking of the oriflamme from Saint-Denis became a quasi-liturgical ceremony initiating the monarch's military campaigns.

The military efforts of Louis VI, Louis VII and Philip Augustus to establish the Capetian dynasty as a major power in medieval Europe involved not only defeating foreign enemies but also bringing under their control the crown's feudal vassals (including the kings of England). At the start of Louis VI's reign, it was impossible to venture

around the Île-de-France without risk of highway robbery or worse. With a mixture of brutality and guile, Louis VI established security and royal authority within the Capetian power-base in the Île-de-France against truculent brigands, barons and castellans. He and his successors then went on vastly to extend royal territory throughout France. One of the crowning moments of this process was the battle of Bouvines in 1214, in which Philip Augustus – with oriflamme aflying – crushed the coalition forces of the king of England, the Holy Roman Emperor and various rebel barons. The Angevin empire in France shrivelled away, and Capetian power proportionately increased. The chronicler William the Breton recorded the triumphant entry into Paris which the king and his forces made following Bouvines: the people and the students feted the event 'with very great feasting, chants and songs'. The most illustrious of the hundred or more prisoners the French had taken on the field of battle were imprisoned within Paris. It seemed difficult to ascertain 'whether the king loved his people more or was more loved by them'.[10]

By associating Parisians with Capetian triumph, the dynasty seemed to be bonding irresistibly with its elective capital. Philip Augustus was present in Paris on some seventy-five occasions over nearly half a century, in the company of a royal household which grew to about five hundred persons. State ceremonial, moreover, was increasingly played out within the city. Notre-Dame became the dynasty's parish church, where kings took mass. In 1215 the king married here and in 1219 received the pope. Philip Augustus resided not only at the old royal palace on the Cité, but also the fortresses which he developed at the Louvre and at Vincennes, as well as at the abbey of Saint-Germain-des-Prés and the Temple. Despite this itinerant quality – which would remain a feature of the monarchy throughout the medieval and early modern period – the idea was gaining ground that royal authority was fixed and stabilized in the kingdom's capital. Indeed, the phrase *caput regni* ('head of the kingdom', 'capital') became current from precisely this period.[11] By the early fourteenth century, the idea that 'the city of Paris is, as Rome was, the common fatherland'[12] was gaining currency.

The deliberate use of comparisons between Rome and Paris – which Philip Augustus exemplified in his adoption of the imperial name – was intended to bolster the dynasty's claims to unfettered sovereignty.

Philip required his capital to be as strikingly associated with his own power as Rome had been for Augustus. This Roman and imperial theme was increasingly evident in dynastic propaganda. It interwove with an older theme, which pictured Paris as having been founded by descendants of survivors from the fall of Troy. One version of this myth of origins had it that the founder of the city had been King Priam's son Paris. Others provided a different trajectory which fitted in with the idea that the Franks as a people had originally been descendants of a Trojan diaspora.

Philip Augustus and his successors thus strove to make the capital a place worthy of such distinguished origins. The city came to house the state's embryonic administrative structures as well as the royal household. The royal seal had been lodged permanently in Paris since the time of Louis VI, and it was used to certify state documents in the physical absence of the king. In 1194 the king had actually lost the royal archives on the field of battle of Fréteval, and it was decided that in future duplicates of all state documents should be housed permanently in the royal palace on the Île de la Cité. The royal treasury was also located in Paris, for the most part in the Temple – the Templars were acknowledged financial experts. The royal chancery and the Parlement of Paris – which from the second half of the thirteenth century was the kingdom's high court of law – shared the palatial premises on the Île de la Cité too. Justice was now dispensed in the king's name from Paris and was no longer merely a personal attribute of the ruler.

Perhaps the most striking and influential way in which Philip Augustus helped to change the physiognomy of Paris in line with its vocation as a royal capital was his decision to build a fortified wall around its perimeter. The wall of Philip Augustus was constructed on the Right Bank between 1190 and 1209 and on the Left between 1200 and 1215. Whereas the merchant class contributed to the building of the Right Bank wall, the extension on the south of the river was done entirely at the crown's expense – and somewhat on the cheap. Rabelais's later contention that 'a cow's fart'[13] would bring the whole thing tumbling down was an exaggeration, but one which highlighted the limited long-term military effectiveness of the perimeter wall on the Left Bank. Yet in the short term, the wall's military purpose is more than evident. Over five kilometres in length, three metres wide at the base, between six and eight metres high, the wall was studded with some seventy-one towers, mostly at an interval of between sixty and eighty metres. Neat engineering conducted water from the Seine and from rivulets to the north and east to supply a moat round the Right Bank wall; the Left Bank had to make do with dry defences. The wall had twelve heavily defendable gates, marking the main entry points into the city. Following an incident when the king was – the chroniclers relate[14] – mightily offended by the stench of Parisian mud and effluent passing his window, he ordered that the main pathways leading to each of the gates be paved. On the wall's western edge, overlooking the Seine, and facing out towards the direction of Anglo-Norman power, the fortress of the Louvre was constructed, its central tower some thirty metres high. The Louvre made the existing fortifications on the Île de la Cité obsolete. No matter, they were maintained, and indeed Philip and his successors strengthened the fortifications of the palace[15] and of the fortresses overlooking the Grand Pont linking the Right Bank to the Île de la Cité (the Grand Châtelet) and over the Petit Pont (the Petit Châtelet).

2.2: The Philip Augustus Wall

Though generally recognized at the time as almost a wonder of the world, very little remains in place of the city walls which Philip Augustus erected between 1190 and 1213. The small outcrop of wall on the Rue Clovis (Ve.) on the Montagne Sainte-Geneviève has long been a (very) minor tourist spot, but the most impressive remains have only recently been exposed.

The wall was never put militarily to the test, and was in time encompassed – indeed virtually lost sight of – within the growing city. The Left Bank wall remained functional for many centuries, but on the Right Bank the creation of the Wall of Charles V in the late fourteenth century made the Philip Augustus Wall obsolete and redundant north of the Seine. The gates were gradually demolished, and fragments of the wall were often incorporated into subsequent buildings, thus entering a kind of memory deep-freeze from which only disparate pieces have been released. The hundred metres or so of wall on the Rue des Jardins-Saint-Paul (IVe.) in the Marais were uncovered by demolition and 'conservation' work in what was a poor and overcrowded area in 1946, while the restoration and public viewing of the base of one of the ramparts under the Tower of John the Fearless on the Rue Étienne-Marcel (IIe.) dates from restoration work done in the 1990s.

Despite its rather meagre functionality, the Philip Augustus Wall has played an extremely important role in the history of the city in a number of ways. It highlighted to the king's fellow European monarchs his determination to make his capital a key piece in his general system of power. To some extent he built the monarchy into the wall – not merely by commanding its construction and contributing to its cost, but also by placing his royal palace, the Louvre, at one of the western limits of the wall. As France's main military threat – the English – would approach the city from the western side, this was a way of underlying a dynastic commitment to the protection of Parisians.

Furthermore, building the wall was a way of inhibiting external expansion and stimulating the consolidation of undeveloped land within the walls. *Intra muros* agricultural and wasteland – such as the area of the Champeaux ('little fields') around the Halles on the Right Bank, and a good deal of marginal land on the Left Bank – provided potential food supply in time of siege, but was also a site for urban infill. It is likely that all present-day streets within the wall on the Right Bank had been laid out by the end of the thirteenth century (with the numerically small exception of nineteenth-century Haussmannian additions). The gridiron pattern of streets around the Halles, for example, dates from this period. To the south of the market halls, the Rues des Étuves, de la Four-de-la-Couture-l'Évêque, des Prouvaires, and de la Tonnellerie (all Ie.) are spaced equidistantly at 65 metres, while a similar gridiron pattern is detectable to the east of the Halles too, involving Rues Mondétour (Ie.), Quincampoix and Aubry-le-Boucher (both IVe.). These streets were probably sold off in parcels of roughly the same size, parcels which still make up a good proportion of housing and business in the neighbourhood. The impact of this phenomenon was all the more significant in that the structure of urban parishes was also set at this time so as to accommodate the changes in *intra muros* space. It would remain unchanged until the seventeenth century.

There were no ditch-works or ramparts outside the walls, but in fact the perimeter fixed the course of a number of streets both within and without the wall. This is most apparent on the Left Bank, where the track of the wall can be followed along the line of the ditches (*fossés*) dug outside the wall in the fourteenth century. It can be followed almost without interruption from east to west: in the Ve. arrondissement the Rue des Fossés Saint Bernard leads from the Seine through to the Rue des Fossés Saint-Victor (now du Cardinal-Lemoine), then swings west through the Rue des Fossés Saint-Jacques into the VIe. arrondissement (where it has been renamed Rue Monsieur-le-Prince). This then leads into the Rue des Fossés de Nesle (now Rue Mazarine). It rejoined the Seine at the Tour de Nesle, an imposing feudal structure opposite the Louvre and, like it, a military defence against attack from the west.

This kind of street continuity is not so evident on the Right Bank, but there are fragments of such influence. The trace of the streets to the north of the present-day Rue Jean-Jacques Rousseau (Ie.), for example, runs in a curve parallel to the line described by the wall. The same is true in the case of Rues du Grenier Saint-Lazare (IIe.) and Michel-le-Comte (IIIe.). Despite its virtual invisibility, then, the Philip Augustus wall has been a major shaping influence on Parisian topography – and memory.

This was power architecture. It made Paris the most heavily – and the most conspicuously – defended military stronghold in western Europe. Yet its meanings were not confined to international power politics. The choice of Paris as royal capital meant that the cronies and clients of the monarch became eager to establish themselves in the city. In emulation of their master, they built impressive local residences. As late as the middle of the twelfth century, princes and barons who visited Paris literally camped out on the Pré-aux-Clercs, the wasteland running eastwards from the Saint-Germain-des-Prés abbey, famous as a place for student skittles and ice-skating, open-air preaching, lovers' assignments and surreptitious duelling.[16] Now, high courtiers built permanent residences, particularly in the Saint-Germain-l'Auxerrois area close to the Louvre. Alphonse de Poitiers, Saint Louis's brother, for example, set a trend by building a private hotel on the Rue d'Osteriche (now Rue de l'Oratoire, Ie.). This subsequently passed to the counts of Périgord and Alençon. Religious houses and personages – following Suger's example – also saw the advantage of a Parisian pied-à-terre. Episcopal residences tended to be on the Left Bank.

There is evidence that Philip Augustus actively encouraged development, notably on the Left Bank, offering compensation from the royal purse for damage caused by the erection of the wall. Yet the priority which the king gave to the building of the wall on the Right Bank highlighted the preference which he accorded the commercial north over the university and wine-growing south of the city. Philip followed the lead given by his predecessors in sponsoring the Right Bank's trading vocation. Before his death in 1137, Louis VI had created a public market on the open spaces to the north of Saint-Germain-l'Auxerrois, in partnership with the bishop, who had property interests here. In this market location – soon called Les Halles – Philip Augustus had two large warehouses built, one for grain merchants, the other for a variety of other food sellers. The success of the Halles did not mean that all commercial activity ended in the rest of the city. The commercial and provisioning links with the region were too intense to allow a monopoly to emerge. There were still significant market-places, for example, at the Saint-Germain-des-Prés bourg (VIe.), as well as at the Palu market at the heart of the Île de la Cité, and at the Apport Paris and the Place Baudoyer to the rear of the Grève port (IVe.).[17] The city's livestock market was held out on the Rue Saint-Honoré (Ie.). Yet none of these other markets enjoyed the extensive privileges accorded the Halles. In 1181 the king transferred the Fair of Saint-Lazare to the site, providing compensation to the Saint-Lazare monastery, including the right to hold a new fair on the day of Saint

Laurent (10 August). The crown would also make the same purchase and transfer of the Saint-Germain-des-Prés fair in 1285. Philip Augustus also had a wall built to protect the Halles from the adjacent Cemetery of the Innocents, a notorious repair of ne'er-do-wells.[18] During the thirteenth century a range of other market halls was constructed (for drapers, mercers, cobblers and flayers), which added to the volume and diversity of commercial activity present here.

The Philip Augustus Wall and the location of its gates not only outlined the city's physical shape. It also helped to structure internal mobility, communication and sociability in ways designed to serve the dynasty's interests. The wall appears to have been deliberately planned so that it could keep out major religious institutions – and to weaken them more by splitting their territories into *intra* and *extra muros* sections. This was the case with the Temple and the abbey of Saint-Martin-des-Champs on the Right Bank and Saint-Germain-des-Prés on the Left. These institutions were forced to fortify their *extra muros* possessions. The Templars built a high, crenellated wall with no fewer than seventeen towers, including 'Caesar's Tower' (*la Tour de César*) which housed the royal treasury.

These exclusions from the city were combined by a sustained royal assault on religious authority within city walls. In 987 all city markets had been under the authority of ecclesiastical bodies. Kings had chiselled away at this situation. Louis VI's arrangement with the bishop over the Halles was a landmark arrangement: the bishop renounced most of his seigneurial rights and property claims in the area, in return for a cut of the profits from the new market. The *Forma Pacis* treaty which Philip Augustus signed with the bishop in 1222 enduringly adjudicated the relationship with and respective rights of episcopacy, cathedral chapter and crown in a way which was regarded as satisfactory all round. The church retained fewer rights, but they were worth more by virtue of royal ratification. And the crown's authority henceforward had no obvious rival. 'Maintain [cities] in favour and in love,' Saint Louis's advice to his son would be. 'Because of [their] strength and wealth ... your subjects and foreigners, especially peers and barons, will fear doing anything against your interests.'[19] Throughout France, the monarch was using towns to counterbalance the authority of his great feudal vassals. Part of this process was the effort to transform Paris from contested ecclesiastical space into uncontested urban, royal space.

The crown's adjudication of seigneurial and property rights on a partnership basis was all the more sensible in that the economy of western Europe was booming, and offered landowners considerable profits. Buoyant commercial development was based on greater agrarian production in and around Paris and the growth of the manu-facturing sector. One did not need to travel far from Philip Augustus's wall to find all the elements of a fast-developing economy. Thick woodland was nearby – there was still a band of it between Paris and Montmartre, for example, while at Vincennes in the east and Boulogne to the west were coming to be recognized as specialized wooded sites. But land-reclamation, stimulated by mushrooming urban demand, also allowed new settlements to form and existing villages to expand outside city walls – as well as within the circumfer-ence of the twentieth-century *boulevard périphérique*. Particularly notable in this regard was the advent of market-gardening in the so-called 'Marais' area.

The Marais at this time did not include the neighbourhood known since the seventeenth century by that name and based on the IIIe. and IVe. arrondissements. The medieval Marais formed a sprawling northern arc around the edge of the Right Bank wall, extending from the river close to the Bastille in the east to Chaillot in the west.[20] In 1153–4 the king authorized the canons of Sainte-Opportune to reclaim extensive terrain to the west, which was mostly waste or pasture. They turned it into cultivable land (*coutures, courtilles*), using the ancient course of the Seine river as an irrigation channel. Little bridges spanning that channel-cum-gutter – commemorated in the Rue des Pont-aux-Choux ('Cabbage Bridge Street': IIIe.) – allowed farmers to bring into the city most of the vegetables which the in-habitants ate. The development brought untold wealth to Sainte-Opportune, and stimulated others to try the same thing. The bishop, for example, began to convert his extensive holdings in the Ville-l'Évêque to the west of the city along the same lines.[21] There were soon numerous *coutures* in the north-east area enclosed by the walls, developed by groups such as the Templars, the abbey of Saint-Martin-des-Champs, the church of Saint-Gervais and the convent of Sainte-Catherine, to the north of the Place Baudoyer (IIIe.–IVe).[22] The bourgs around these developments could be quite considerable: in the early thirteenth century the Villeneuve-du-Temple contained some 600 inhabitants, while at the same time Saint-Germain-des-Prés – clinging 'like a barnacle to its rock'[23] – contained some 121 tax-paying households (perhaps 700–800 individuals) – and numbers probably doubled over the course of the century. All around the north of Paris – at Ville-l'Évêque (VIIIe.), La Grange-Batelière (IXe.) and Courtille (XIe.), for example, but also a little further out at Chaillot (XVIe.), Clignancourt (XVIIIe.), La Villette (XIXe.) and 'Poitronville' (soon to be Belleville: XIXe.–XXe.) – what had been a few isolated farmhouses were developing into substantial villages.

Vines and cereals still came up to Paris's gates, especially in the south, and reflected the pattern of agriculture throughout the Île-de-France. A more diversified economy developed to the south-east of the city. In 1148 the abbey of Saint-Victor diverted the waters of the Bièvre, a tributary of the Seine, towards its own property.[24] Also close to the Bièvre was the settlement around the abbey of Saint-Marcel, on the site of a Gallo-Roman necropolis at the present-day Gobelins crossroads, where something of a bourg emerged around the parish churches of Saint-Martin, Saint-Hilaire and Saint-Hippolyte.[25] The banks of the Bièvre attracted wine-growers, butchers, tanners and dyers. The wool mill on the river at Rue de Croulebarbe (XIIIe.) remained in place until the nineteenth century. Limestone quarrying was much in evidence in this area too, right around the arc formed by the present-day XIIIe., XIVe. and XVe. arrondissements. A great deal of the limestone from which medieval Paris was built came from these areas.

The volume and character of urban demand also promoted long-term currents of trade. On the Right Bank, in an almost military-style operation which ended up at the nearby Halles, the Montmartre gate received daily consignments of fresh fish from the Norman coast. The other gate in the city wall close to the Halles allowed communication with the plain of the Lendit outside the bourg of Saint-Denis. The annual Lendit fair, specializing in spices, wines, cloth and horses, grew into a massive operation, which even began to skim off some of the trade which had ensured the wealth and fame of the fairs of the cities of Champagne.

Communications within the city were notoriously poor as a consequence of narrow, winding streets, nonexistent levels of street cleansing, and an over-dependence on a small number of bridges. The street system was incoherent and cluttered. The Rue Saint-Honoré to the west, for example, petered out before meeting the Rue Saint-Antoine coming in from the east. Similarly the Rue Saint-Jacques brought traffic to the Petit Pont from the south – but one then had to push one's way through the Île de la Cité before negotiating the perennially over-crowded Grand Pont linking to the Rue Saint-Denis. Where it was not at a standstill, traffic could be dangerous: in 1131 Louis VI's son and heir was killed when he was unhorsed by a runaway pig – an odd first in the colourful history of Parisian traffic accidents. The river was a more reliable means of communication, particularly for long-distance trade and for bulky cargoes. The poor quality of Parisian bridges made it difficult to ship goods straight through the city, but generally the water route was less hindered by deficient infrastructure. The Grève port was built up, but there were numerous additional landing-places and safe havens. The Seine brought the city, as one writer enthused, 'the riches of all parts of the world, . . . wines of Greece, of Grenada, of La Rochelle, of Gascony, of Burgundy . . . and quantities of wheat, rye, peas, beans, hay, charcoal and wood'.[26] From upstream came a host of Norman produce too – apples, cider, fresh and salt fish, salt, hay, wood – and some commodities from along the Atlantic seaboard, while from downstream there were wines from Burgundy, cereals from the Beauce and the Brie and most of the foodstuffs which made their way into Parisians' diets. There were links to places further afield such as Genoa, Florence and the Mediterranean in the south, and to the north much more powerful currents of exchange with Flanders, Germany and the Baltic states.

The economic grouping most instrumental in this commercial vitality were the water merchants – a kind of Capetian equivalent to the Roman *nautes*.[27] We only gain some sense of their importance from the period in which the monarchs began to recognize and support their activities. The first mention of them dates from 1121. In 1170 Louis VII confirmed the privileges of the 'bourgeois of Paris who are water merchants', which included the monopoly of all imports brought into Paris along the river. This right involved a good deal of policing, and the water merchant cartel – or *hanse*, as it was called – was given wide latitude for enforcement. The king made the area round the Place de Grève where the main ports were located immune from any sort of building, and encouraged investment in port facilities. The corporate power of the water merchants received a considerable accolade in 1190, when Philip Augustus left on crusade. He appointed his mother and the bishop of Paris as co-regents but gave supervision of royal administration to 'six upstanding and worthy' Parisians, all of whom were leading lights among the water merchants. The six were instructed to audit accounts which royal officials not merely in Paris but from throughout the realm presented to them thrice yearly. There was no clearer example of the crown's use of its towns as a lever against feudal power.

After Philip Augustus's return from crusade, he continued to treat the group well; in 1220, for example, he gave them authority and policing over weights and measures in the city. Standard measures were kept in a raised building near to the Grand Pont, known as the 'Parloir-aux-Bourgeois' where the merchants met and transacted business. Faulty or defective measuring equipment was ceremonially burned on the square outside this building. As their privileges were made more extensive and as their wealth grew, the water merchants came to be seen as a surrogate municipal council. Early in the thirteenth century they were using a seal, which showed a simple depiction of a ship. The provost of Paris (*prévôt de Paris*), a position held by a merchant and sold to the highest bidder, was based at the Châtelet fortress, and enjoyed very wide-ranging judicial, policing, administrative and military functions. Yet the water merchants began increasingly to contest his authority. Between 1260 and 1265 Saint Louis reorganized local government. The Paris provost was made a state functionary: Étienne Boileau was the first to hold this charge, from 1261 to 1270. He shared local power with the water merchants whose officers were now transformed into aldermen (*échevins*). These chose from among their number a merchants' provost, or *prévôt des marchands*. For more than a century the monarchy had been recognizing powers of local government to bourgeois in townships throughout France. The refusal to do the same in Paris highlighted the crown's wish not to relax its grip or to inhibit the income it derived from this source – in the 1290s, it has been estimated, the city provided some 14 per cent of the crown's revenues. Yet the water merchants were in essence a city council and the *prévôt des marchands*, the city mayor. Their seal became the seal of Paris.

The recognition of the water merchants as a constituted body with legally enforcible rights was accompanied by the extension of moral and legal responsibility to other groups of traders and artisans. The crown favoured this practice, as it derived income from the bodies in the form of taxes of various sorts. It also valued the self-policing functions which they performed. And it regarded the legal basis of their existence as a form of authority superior to feudal vassalage. By the end of the twelfth century there were more than a hundred incorporated trades, forming a kaleidoscopic array of groupings. Some were tiny, notably in sectors in which there was a considerable task of quality control – there were only six goldleaf-beaters, for example. Economic boom conditions could also stimulate an extreme division of labour: thus there were separate bodies for hatters making headgear in felt, cotton, flowers (including some of the relatively few women within the system) and with peacock-feathers. At the other extreme from these microgroups, there were indeterminate hundreds of weavers, bakers and cobblers. There was a definite hierarchy within the trades – the religious image-makers, for example, snootily claimed that their produce was aimed exclusively at 'the holy church, princes, barons and other wealthy men and nobles'.[28] Yet this did not always reflect levels of skills: one of the most powerful of trades was the butchers who were incorporated early on, in 1134. These men were exceptional too in being allowed to employ workers outside their own shops – the rule was that tradesmen and artisans worked only from their own premises.

A particularly important group were the money-changers. These were Italians for the most part, though from 1141 they were generically known as Lombards. They were obliged to pursue their activities out in the open on the Grand Pont linking the Cité to the Right Bank, and henceforth known as the Pont des Changeurs ('Exchange Bridge'). Most lived on the Rue des Lombards on the Right Bank (Ie.–IVe.).

The other incorporated trades also imprinted themselves on the urban topography in the same way, with street-names providing a guide to industrial and shopkeeping specialism. The guide was not always infallible: although there were numerous weavers (*tisserands*) working in the Bourg Tibourg, not a single one resided in the Rue de la Tissanderie to its south when the 1296 taxrolls were drawn up. Fiscal documentation revealed, however, numerous furriers (*pelletiers*) on the Rue de la Pelleterie, cobblers (*savetiers*) on the Rue de la Saveterie on the Île de la Cité and the helmet-makers (*heaumiers*) on the Rue de la Heaumerie just to the north of the Grand Pont.

Not all groups of workers – even those with a good deal of collective awareness and activity – achieved full legal status. This was true, for example, of the washerwomen (*lavandières*) to be found on the Rue des Lavandières close to the banks of the Seine. The more disreputable trades were also known for residential concentrations. The Rue des Jongleurs off the Rue Saint-Martin, close to the present-day Pompidou Centre (IVe.), did indeed house jugglers, while it was more than apparent who were the denizens of the Rue de la Grande Truanderie ('Great Rascal Street': Ie.) and the Rue Coupe-Gueule ('Cut-Throat Way': Ve.). Prostitutes – who had their request to finance a window in Notre-Dame cathedral, on the same basis as other trades, rejected by the bishop – were to be found in locations such as the Rue Pute-y-Muse ('Whore-Hides-Here': IVe.) and Impasse Putigneaux ('Scabby Whore': IVe.). In 1270 Saint Louis sought to confine licensed prostitution to a small number of streets throughout the city.[29] (Interestingly, most locations were on the Cité and the Right Bank: students had to cross the Seine in order to sin.)

The trades enjoyed a local monopoly of production and sale in their specialism, plus a range of privileges. The stone-cutters solemnly claimed that some of theirs derived from Charles Martel in the eighth century. Each trade also ensured training through a familiar routine of apprenticeship. The number of apprentices was normally fixed, as was the number of journeymen and supplementary workers (*valets*) permitted in each workshop. The aim thereby was to keep prices steady and ensure the peaceable transmission of businesses across the generations. Competitive pressures were moderated through a very active life of piety, sociability and charitable mutual aid, which was channelled through the confraternities associated with each trade. The butchers' confraternity, for example, was associated with the church of Saint-Jacques-de-la-Boucherie on the Right Bank, close to many of their businesses, and where much of their social life was conducted.

The multifarious trades of the economically vibrant capital city were thus incorporated in a way which, while maximizing the state's income and interests, also buttressed the position and served the perceived interests of petty producers, artisans and shopkeepers. It was another example of the way the crown used partnership arrangements as a way of strengthening its authority within the city. The same phenomenon was also found in regard to another of the great interest groups within medieval Paris, namely the university.

Initially, the Capetians must have wondered whether the university was more trouble than it was worth. The endless turbulence and town–gown conflicts which dotted the twelfth century made the rumbustious cosmopolitan student body one of the biggest problems of local policing. At one stage Philip Augustus even seems to have considered dissolving the teaching groups entirely and banning them from the city. Even many churchmen found this rather worldly Left Bank sociability not to their taste. 'Flee this Babylonian milieu', Saint Bernard of Clairvaux urged keen young clerics, 'and save souls ... You will discover far more in the midst of the forests than in books.' Peter of Celles described the city as a place in which 'the nets of vice and the traps of evil and the arrows of hell lose innocent hearts'.[30] Jacques de Vitry reported that many masters shared their premises with brothels, and he provided a thumbnail sketch of the prevalent vices of all the nations whose students ended up here: the Normans, for example, were 'vain and boastful' and the Bretons 'fickle and inconstant', while the English were 'drunkards', the Dutch 'soft as butter and indolent', the Romans 'seditious, violent and foul-mouthed', and the Germans 'wild and obscene'.[31]

By the late twelfth century, however, while some churchmen retained their doubts about this unruly assemblage, the monarchy was swinging towards a more positive line. It may have been that the stream of Parisian graduates into the crown's embryonic administrative structures gave the crown good reason to appreciate certain of the skills being inculcated on the Montagne Sainte-Geneviève. The international fame which Parisian scholarship was gaining also must have appealed to a dynasty very sensitive to its own propaganda. Flattering for the capital city's image of itself was the idea which became current of a *translatio studii* – a 'transfer of scholarship' – whereby the centre of the world's learning had passed from ancient Egypt through Athens and Rome to Paris. Though they were a threat to public order, students and their masters also represented an important sector of urban demand. The Left Bank would have been denuded without them and the service industries they nurtured – from accommodation and catering to manuscript copying and illumination. Many French students were from relatively poor backgrounds, but the Parisian cachet also brought into the city the scions of wealthy foreign families, who had a lot to spend.

It still, however, took a public order matter to start the monarchy on the road towards dynastic approbation. A town–gown flare-up in a Left Bank tavern in 1200 which left five students dead led to students threatening to quit the city unless their grievance was properly addressed. Philip Augustus placed all students under episcopal writ, rather than the lay justice dispensed by the Châtelet court. By extending the principle of benefit of clergy to them, this act constituted students and their clerical teachers as a corporative entity, placing them more directly under the papacy than the state. By so doing, it removed them from the direct influence of the bishop of Paris, whose wings Philip was busily clipping. Pontifical letters a few years later referred to them as forming a 'society' (*societas*); the term *universitas* was soon in use.[32] The process by which the body strengthened its corporative identity and extended its privileges over these early years of the thirteenth century is murky. While the statutes given in 1215 by the papal legate Robert of Courson (himself a Parisian master), confirmed existing rights and added some new privileges, there remained some fragility about the university's position. In 1229 an incident occurred in which, after a student rampage in the Bourg Saint-Marcel, a student was killed. Neither the bishop nor Blanche of Castille, Saint Louis's mother and queen regent, gave redress, whereupon the students as a body threatened to quit the city altogether. Indeed they carried out their threat, only returning in 1231 at the behest of the pope.

The papal bull *Parens Scientarum* ('Parent of the Sciences') of 1231 ending this episode confirmed the 1215 statutes and recognized the university as 'the mother of the sciences, . . . ornament of the church, shield of the faith, spiritual sword of the christian militia'.[33] The university's claims to autonomy from the bishop and his chancellor were upheld, as were its members' claim to benefit of clergy, and the right to strike. The university's syllabus, model of teaching and system of examinations were also approved. Though in theory the bishop's chancellor retained the right to issue teaching licences, in practice this power lay in the hands of the masters. Following a master's degree in the arts faculty, students could progress to higher instruction in theology, medicine and canon law (the teaching of Roman law, based on imperial precedent rather than ecclesiastical conventions, was forbidden in 1219). These faculty structures would be solidified in the 1260s, but they were already implicit in 1219, when the right of each faculty to have its own leader, or proctor, was recognized. In 1221 an official seal was granted. From the same period, the student body was organized in four 'nations'. None of these corresponded very closely to national frontiers: the French nation included students from the Île-de-France, the Midi, Italy and Greece; 'the Normans' covered Normandy and Brittany; 'the Picards' extended to Flanders and much of northern France; while 'the English' were the most multifarious of all, including alongside students from the British Isles, others from the Low Countries, Scandinavia, central Germany, Hungary and the Slavic lands. Each nation was represented by a proctor, the four of whom elected the university's rector. The nations provided a framework for student spiritual and secular sociability and mutual aid – and a sure-fire recipe for rivalries. Students stayed as rowdy as ever: in one dispute in around 1280, for example, the English tore down houses in which the Picards were lodging, killing several and forcing the others to flee the city.

The corporative structure of the university thus took scholars out of the control of the bishop, and placed them under the patronage of the papacy and the crown. For more than two centuries, the support of popes and kings rarely faltered. The biggest crisis the university had to face was in the 1250s, over the role of the mendicant orders. The thirteenth century had witnessed the foundation of large numbers of religious institutions which collectively enriched the spiritual texture as well as the architectural brilliance of the city (for they were richly endowed): the Augustinians were here from 1250, ending up on the Quai des Grands-Augustins (Ve.), the Chartreux in 1257 and the Carmelites in 1259. The mendicant orders came too: the Franciscans in 1207, the Dominicans in 1217. Both groups stimulated much university ire by developing a popular programme of teaching, by granting lodging and tuition to poorer students and by acting as strike-breakers during the university commotion of 1229–31. The battle with the mendicants had a doctrinal element too, the friars' opponents painting them as subscribers to heretical millenarian beliefs. Efforts by the university in the early 1250s to restrict the holding of teaching chairs to one per monastery led to a major conflict. Pope and monarchy both upheld the rights of the religious orders, and their opponents were forced to recant and to accept the teaching of the two Dominicans (and future saints), Bonaventura and Thomas Aquinas.

The reputation for superiority which the religious orders were gaining within the university was partly countered by the emergence of the collegiate system – a further sign of the university's institutional maturity, and a development of considerable importance for the future. The creation of a rash of new colleges aimed at non-mendicants from the middle of the thirteenth century onwards was part of a concerted effort to improve on what the mendicants could offer. Most of the institutions were glorified lodging-houses, but a new template was provided by the college instituted in 1257 by the royal chaplain, Robert de Sorbon, with heavy financial backing from Saint Louis. The Sorbonne offered tuition as well as lodging. This ensured that the intellectual development of the students was more closely monitored than before. Inmates also enjoyed access to probably the best library in Paris. New collegiate creations now rained down thick and fast, the legacies of bishops, other secular clergy as well as laymen and women, permitting the considerable enlargement of the student body. There were probably around 3,000 students in Paris by 1300. Often the colleges were specifically designed for students from a given locality. The Collège d'Harcourt (1268) was reserved for forty Norman scholars; the Collège des Cholets, founded by the bishop of Beauvais (1292) was for students from the dioceses of Beauvais and Amiens.

The establishment of the Collège de Skara for Swedish students dates from the 1290s, while around the turn of the century there were many important creations including the Collège du Cardinal Lemoine (1302: for 120 students from northern France), the richly endowed Collège de Navarre (1304) and the Collège de Bayeux (1309).

2.3: Robert de Sorbon

There is often a mismatch between the reputation of an institution and that of its founder. This seems particularly apposite in the case of Robert de Sorbon's Sorbonne. The institution is perhaps the most famous and most historic university in the world, yet its founder was a humble, somewhat intellectually limited and subsequently little-regarded thirteenth-century cleric, Robert de Sorbon.

Born in eastern France in 1201, Sorbon pursued his studies in Paris in conditions of personal poverty, before becoming canon of the cathedral chapter of Cambrai. A reputation for piety attracted the attention of Louis IX (Saint Louis), who appointed him his chaplain and subsequently his confessor. He profited from his position to establish a community of clerics dedicated to providing free lessons for poor students in theology – such as he himself had been. In 1250, while Saint Louis was away on crusade, the king's mother Queen Regent Blanche of Castille donated to Sorbon 'a house which had belonged to Jean of Orléans and the adjacent stables situated on the Rue Coupe-Gueule, in front of the Palais des Thermes'. On this material basis was founded the college of the Sorbonne, for sixteen poor scholars, in 1253. Saint Louis made further donations and appointed Sorbon as director (*proviseur*) of the new institution, a role he retained until his death in 1274. The Sorbonne's orientation around the advanced degree of theology marked it out as different – the numerous colleges founded prior to this had been for students following the lower, arts degree – though like the other colleges, it bore a legal and cultural resemblance to the trade guilds and other medieval corporations.

Sorbon had a particular interest in questions of morality and cases of conscience and this interest was reflected in the Sorbonne's developing specialisms. It was consulted on such issues by successive popes and rulers across Europe from the Middle Ages onwards. The eminence of the theologians of the Sorbonne was such that it came to represent the theology faculty of the university, and indeed on doctrinal issues it represented the university as a whole. In time its international eminence was reduced by the proliferation of universities across France and Europe in the later Middle Ages, by its overly close association with the losing Burgundian cause in the Hundred Years War, and by the advent of the world of print. Its institutional autonomy was reduced too and it was brought much more closely under the aegis of the monarchy.

Until the seventeenth century the Sorbonne comprised a random scattering of houses and buildings around the Rue Coupe-Gueule (now Rue de la Sorbonne, Ve.). In 1625 Richelieu, Louis XIII's great Cardinal minister and himself director of the Sorbonne, began a programme of consolidation and construction. The courtyard and the chapel of the present institution were started in 1635 and completed in the 1640s.

A key player in the Counter-Reformation, the Sorbonne was less prominent in the more secular eighteenth century. The *philosophes* of the Enlightenment jeered at its useless assemblage of knowledge, thus preparing the way for the abolition of the institution (along with all universities) in the Terror in 1792–4. Reopened by Napoleon in 1806, it adapted well to the post-revolutionary educational scene, becoming the administrative head of the Paris university. Extensive building works between 1885 and 1901 resulted in the imposing existing structures.

For most of the first half of the twentieth century, more than one French student in two was attached to the Paris university. The system was under strain from rapid increases in student numbers in the 1950s and 1960s. The situation was dramatized by the May Events of 1968, when the Sorbonne became one of the principal theatres of student protest. The post-1968 move to break up the University of Paris into smaller more manageable units, and the shift of much research work into research institutes, has reduced the Sorbonne's institutional role. The 75,000 students who attend the University of Paris I (Panthéon Sorbonne), III (Sorbonne Nouvelle) and IV (Paris-Sorbonne) represent only around one-third of university students in the Paris region, and less than 5 per cent of university students throughout France.

Robert de Sorbon had a kindly but rather loftily unworldly view of what students should be like. 'The scholar walking on the banks of the Seine in the evening ought not to indulge in sports,' he maintained, more than a tad optimistically, 'but rather think about his lesson and repeat it to himself.' His intentions have been massively transgressed by successive generations of Sorbonne students. They enjoyed a reputation for licentiousness and riotous behaviour throughout the Middle Ages and Renaissance. Rabelaisian would be a word for it, and indeed François Rabelais was a close observer of student mores and his writings received two formal condemnations by the Sorbonne. By the early nineteenth century, students had become part of the revolutionary tradition of barricades and street rioting – a role which they latterly and briefly resumed in 1968.

The emergence of the university highlighted the intellectual dynamism and energy which students and masters had begun to generate in what Pope Gregory IX referred to as 'wisdom's special workshop'. Yet this movement of intellectual emancipation which burnished the university's international fame was also one of intellectual regulation. It accorded both with the monarchy's policing concerns, and with the papacy's emphasis on doctrinal rigour and spiritual orthodoxy. The colleges were agencies of discipline as well as of student support – as the battle against the mendicants had suggested. The colleges stood *in loco parentis* and concerned themselves with students' morality too. Also significant in this respect were efforts to use Parisian scholars as agents for the wider enforcement of religious orthodoxy. In 1205 the crusader King Baldwin of Flanders requested the pope to send out to him in Constantinople doctors from Paris to preach the true faith. In

1217 Pope Honorius III requested Paris doctors to be sent out to help to christianize Languedoc. As a consequence of this they would act as spiritual storm-troops repressing the Albigensian heresy in this region. Furthermore, the university stood and watched as the infrastructure of Jewish learning was attacked and destroyed over the course of the thirteenth century.

In 1323 the monk Ferrulo was glossing the etymology of Paris ('Parisius') to derive from the word paradise ('paradisus'). Yet paradise was not evenly shared and indeed had a darker side even at this brilliant era in the city's history. Those darker elements and those inequities would come to the fore as the fourteenth century progressed. The extraordinarily dynamic performance of the city of Paris since the twelfth century had derived from an apparent synergy of forces: a booming agriculture in the environs (a *sine qua non* in effect); a resourceful and enterprising merchant class, led by the Parisian *nautes*; a burgeoning skills base within the trades; the cultural hegemony of the university; and the support of one of the most powerful states in western Europe. From the early fourteenth century, all these factors were compromised to some degree. The city suffered accordingly – and terribly.

3

The City Adrift

c. 1300–*c.* 1480

Paris was, noted an anonymous eulogy written at the beginning of the fourteenth century, 'the mother and mistress of all cities'.[1] The superlative status which the city had acquired over the previous two centuries now extended across a wide range of domains. Paris was by far the largest city in christendom: the 61,098 hearths recorded in the 1328 census suggests that its total population was probably in excess of 200,000 or even 250,000 individuals. This, moreover, was at a time when no other city in France reached the level of 50,000 and when European rivals (Florence, Genoa, Venice) only barely attained six figures. No other region in Europe save possibly Flanders was as densely populated as the Île-de-France. The wealth concentrated within the city walls was commensurate with its immense size, and highlighted not only a wide array of crafts but also the largest and wealthiest concentration of consumers in the west. Intellectually too, Paris still towered over any of its rivals, its university's fame so widespread that any European with claims to academic intelligence who had not studied there felt guilty about the fact. All this was made possible, moreover, by the very close and beneficial relationship which the city enjoyed with the Capetian dynasty. Politically, Paris was the capital of a state which had emerged from humble beginnings in 987 to become one of the most dynamic powers in western Europe. The city contained a collection of buildings and monuments – from the walled periphery through to the royal palace on the Île de la Cité – which underlined the international prestige of the French dynasty.

There was nothing about the reigns of Philip III (r. 1270–85) and in particular Philip IV the Fair (r. 1285–1314) in which one could detect a weakening of royal power, or a reduction in that dynastic commitment to the capital city which had been a crucial ingredient in Paris's prosperity. The periodic convocation from 1302 onwards of a national representative body, the Estates General, composed of delegates from the clergy, nobility and the towns, and usually meeting in Paris, seemed to fortify rather than weaken the crown. Yet within a matter of years, political stability in France in general and in Paris in particular was at an end. Symptomatically, the mutually supportive relationship between the monarchy and its capital would be placed under severe strain. With the exception of a few oases of calm, the years down to the end of the fifteenth century would rank among the darkest days in the city's history. This was truly, as the poet Eustache Deschamps, writing at the turn of the fifteenth century, characterized it:

> Age of iron, time out of joint, sky of bronze,
> Fruitless land, sterile and barren,
> Wretched people, full of pain.[2]

The Capetian dynasty had been very lucky in the marriage bed: an unbroken line of eleven generations had ensured uncontested male heirs from the time of Hugh Capet to the reign of Philip the Fair. Then Capetian luck ran out. Philip had three sons – Louis X (r. 1314–16), Philip V (r. 1316–22) and Charles IV (r. 1322–8) – each of whom ruled briefly without producing an heir. The throne in 1328 passed to Philip IV's nephew, Philip de Valois, but the rightfulness of the claims of Philip VI (r. 1328–50), as he became, was contested – and durably so. King Edward III of England was the son of Philip the Fair's daughter and though he did his Valois cousin homage in 1329, he soon afterwards registered a claim to the throne. By 1337 England and France were at war. The succession issue would remain at the heart of a series of military challenges which, retrospectively, have been called the Hundred Years War (1337–1453). War was, however, both symptom and cause of an even more wide-ranging malaise which characterized most of the period.

Paris's troubles over the fourteenth and fifteenth centuries sprang not simply from the fact that kingship was contested, more that its kings were physically or mentally absent from the city for most of the period. Despite modernizing the Cité palace, Philip VI elected to reside at the hunting lodge turned fortress-cum-summer-palace out at

Vincennes. John II (r. 1350–64) lived for a couple of years on the Île de la Cité. His successor Charles V (r. 1364–80) preferred the more defensible Louvre, and built a palace complex in the east, off the Rue Saint-Antoine (IVe.), at Saint-Paul (or Saint-Pol), complete with extensive orchards, gardens and a soon-legendary menagerie. Charles VI (r. 1380–1422) spent much of the time in Paris, but from 1392 was subject to lengthy bouts of insanity. As aristocratic factions jockeyed for power, he ceased to be a political actor. From 1422, kings simply did not reside in Paris at all, except when passing through, preferring palaces in the Loire valley. From 1420 to 1435, moreover, as we shall see, the kingdom was divided, with the northern half being governed out of Paris by the viceroy of the kings of England, and with the southern part under the Valois pretender, Charles VII (r. 1422–61).

The changed fortunes of the city in the course of the fourteenth and early fifteenth centuries could be told as a story of walls, gates and bridges as well as of dynasties. No stone had been hurled in anger against the city wall constructed by Philip Augustus between 1190 and 1215, and indeed it had played a vanguard role in peacetime urban development. By the mid-fourteenth century, in contrast, a new wall had to be built to provide more adequate protection from outside aggression. The defensive qualities of that wall would be much tested over the next century. The municipal authorities had begun to build the wall immediately following the disastrous French defeat by the English in the battle of Poitiers of 1356. Not finally completed under royal direction till the early fifteenth century, most of 'Charles V's Wall' had been put in place by the 1390s. Nearly five kilometres long, it enclosed some 439 hectares as against the 272 hectares of the Philip Augustus Wall. All the new space was located on the Right Bank, on which four Parisians out of five now lived.

The new defences testified to a sharpened perception of the need for better protection against more sophisticated siegecraft. The striking feature of the new Right Bank ramparts in particular was their depth. A series of deep and wide ditches and towering banks ensured that the defensive system was, at its most complete, up to one hundred metres wide. The marshes of the eastern areas were drained so as to provide a moat, and a supplementary system of locks was put in place to keep that moat supplied (though the Left Bank wall made do with only dry defences). New, stronger gates were built throughout, and on the eastern side a massive new fortress was constructed from 1370, which matched the towering Louvre on the west side. The Bastille, as it was soon called, would have a vivid part to play in Parisian history.

Charles V's Wall also testified to the scale – and the topography – of the last phase of medieval urban expansion. A good deal of agricultural land was included. This made good siegecraft sense. But also now enclosed were many of the zones outside Philip Augustus's wall where there had been economic and social expansion in the interim. These were all on the Right Bank. Growth areas outside the old walls on the Left Bank such as Saint-Germain-des-Prés, Saint-Victor and Saint-Marcel were not incorporated within the Charles V wall, which left them more fragile in the face of disaster. Right Bank inclusions embraced land along the Rue Saint-Antoine, for example; the *coutures* (garden lands) of the Temple, of Sainte-Catherine and of Saint-Martin-des-Champs (IIIe.); outgrowths from the Halles (notably beyond the old Saint-Denis and Montmartre gates: IIe.); and property along the Rue Saint-Honoré, including the Louvre (Ie.) This boosted further development. The Temple zone, for instance, which had seen *intra muros* development under Philip Augustus, now expanded to cover the neatly spaced gridiron of nearly a dozen streets leading off the Rues du Temple and Vieille-du-Temple, north of the Rues de Braque and des Poulies (IIIe.). In the late fourteenth century the turreted hôtel of the nobleman Olivier de Clisson gave some architectural variety and social tone to the area.[3]

A more longlasting consequence of the greater military orientation of the city was the emergence of neighbourhoods or 'quarters' (*quartiers*) as a framework of social and administrative life, including urban defence. The construction of Charles V's Wall increased the number of *quartiers* to sixteen, in each of which a *quartinier* was assisted for city watch and gate duty by *cinquantiniers* and *dizeniers*. This framework overlaid – though it did not always correspond geographically with – the quarters used from around 1420 for policing and for tax assessment and collection. A new basis of intra-urban neighbourhood sociability was being laid.

One irony of Charles V's Wall was that by 1450 it contained only around half as many individuals as the Philip Augustus Wall – half its length – had enclosed prior to the 1350s. Paris's population fell by more than 50 per cent between the 1320s and early 1420s, when the city may have contained as few as 80,000 to 100,000 inhabitants. Although recovery followed, total population in 1500 was still only around 150,000. A further ironical feature of the wall was that the increased number of gates did not have an effect on boosting circulation or exchange. Indeed, because of the insecurity in which the city so frequently found itself, many of the gates were bricked up completely or kept closed to traffic for lengthy periods, making points of ingress and egress fewer than had been the case with the Philip Augustus Wall. The city had turned in on itself.

Walls and gates thus had much to say about how unexpansive and inward-looking Paris was becoming. So had bridges. The city's bridges had never really achieved the level of efficiency which a great economic centre required. Their condition now got worse. The bridges seemed to obstruct rather than facilitate exchange: goods from upstream were unloaded at the Saint-Germain port near to the Louvre and then moved across town by land to the Grève ports for despatch downstream – and vice versa. In 1296 a new Grand Pont had been built: the Pont aux Changeurs (or Pont-au-Change) linked the Cité with the Right Bank close to Charles the Bald's old barrage bridge.[4] Floods in 1393 carried off the Petit Pont which would be endlessly repaired over the next century. In 1407–8 both it and the Pont Saint-Michel – built in 1378 at the end of the Rue de la Harpe (Ve.) – were washed away. The same fate befell the wooden passageway, the 'Planches Mibrai', an extension of the Rue Saint-Martin over the Seine. In 1413 the 'Planches' were reconfigured as the Pont Notre-Dame. Unfortunately, this was done on the cheap, for the structure was on the point of collapse for most of the century and was washed away completely in 1499.

These sombre circumstances need to be put in the context of the slowing down of the European economy from the early fourteenth century onwards. Harvest failures between 1314 and 1316 produced in Paris, a local chronicler recorded, 'great dearness of corn . . . [T]he common people were sorely burdened and oppressed.'[5] Outright famine elsewhere in France suggested that the population was growing faster than the economy's capacity to feed it – although price hikes in

Paris were also probably caused by merchant speculation and hoarding. Crisis levels of mortality were observable in 1323, 1328, 1334 and 1340–41. The climate may have been deteriorating at this time: certainly natural catastrophes appeared to rain down more frequently than hitherto, adding to man-made problems. Floods were not new to Parisian life: one in 1196 had Philip Augustus fleeing the Cité in fright and taking refuge on the Montagne Sainte-Geneviève, and there were further inundations in 1281 and 1296–7. Yet in the fourteenth century the Seine would overflow or burst its banks on no fewer than twenty-seven occasions. The winter of the century was 1407, when icebergs floated down the Seine, and ink froze on the quill.[6] The floods of 1432 brought the economic life of the city to a standstill for six weeks. From the 1420s wolves scavenged in the city at night, jumping up to gnaw at the limbs of executed felons on the city's gibbets out at Montfaucon, and in 1439 killing more than a dozen people in the market gardens to the north of the ramparts.[7]

3.1: Montfaucon

Strollers enjoying the Swiss kitsch pleasures of the Buttes-Chaumont park (XIXe.) pass unawares over one of the grimmest, most notorious low spots of *le Vieux Paris*, namely, the gibbet of Montfaucon. Established by Saint Louis (r. 1223–70) as a sign of royal justice over the city, the gibbet was institutionalized under Charles IV (r. 1322–8), when the wooden scaffold was converted into an elaborate stone structure with some sixteen columns, each ten metres high. From it literally scores of decaying criminals' bodies could be hanging at any time. The gibbet was a place of execution in its own right, but also the place of exhibition of the remains of individuals tortured and executed in one of the many execution sites in Paris, such as the Place de Grève. Bodies could be left there for two or three years or more, at the end of which time – crows and (in bad times) wolves having done their worst – they were a gruesome sight, and their noisome stench wafted towards the Faubourg du Temple. When

The medieval gibbet at Montfaucon

they were cut down, their remains were cast into a pit at the centre of the gibbet structure.

This impressive monument was on a raised mound in still fairly open country, and situated on the main road out to Meaux. It was unmissable from miles around. Its fame rested not simply on its visibility, but also on the high status of several who had ended their days swinging from it. Royal ministers and favourites, Parisian *prévots* and, latterly, the mutilated remains of the Huguenot leader Coligny all famously found their way there. King Charles IX, visiting the site in the aftermath of the Saint Bartholomew's massacre to view Coligny's remains rotting on the scaffold, is alleged to have muttered to his gagging courtiers that 'the body of a dead enemy never smells bad'.

Yet the heyday of Montfaucon was over by the sixteenth century. Executions ceased in 1627, and a smaller gibbet was erected nearby, for ceremonial and display purposes more than as a place of execution. City maps in the early eighteenth century showed only the stumps of the once-famous stone pillars at Montfaucon. Yet other forms of life – all of the darker sort – were already relaying the spot's sinister connotations. It had become one of Paris's principal sewage dumps. It now acquired a new role as knackers' yard for clapped-out horses. Some years as many as 15,000 nags were despatched here. Their remains nurtured a panoply of petty trades (powdered sewage – known as *poudrette* – for gardeners, skins for tanners, horse-hair for brush-makers, maggot-producing gut for fishermen and so on). It also fed a plump army of rats, who could strip a corpse to its skeleton within twenty-four hours. Bull-fights and other animal combats were staged at the nearby Place du Combat (now Place du Colonel-Fabien), adding to the dark and unsavoury aura of the place. In addition the quarrying for gypsum, or plaster of Paris, in the environs had left an extraordinary scarred and somewhat lunar landscape, underpinned by a honeycomb of underground caves and passages in which robbers and beggars were said to have their lairs.

It really was therefore a historic metamorphosis that Napoleon III and Baron Haussmann designated for the area in choosing it as the most significant of the very few green spaces they opened up in the east of the city. Haussmann used the scarred landscape to picturesque effect, and added to it by importing truckloads of stone so as to provide a sedately mountainous appearance to the new park. Completed in three years and opened to coincide with the 1867 Exposition, the Buttes-Chaumont did not, however, take its new fate lying down: it became a Communard refuge in 1871, until government shelling from the heights of Montmartre flushed out the rebels. It would take the poetic inspiration of the Surrealists in the 1920s to strip away much of the long-ingrained grimness of the site. By saluting the park as 'a legendary paradise', 'an apartment of dreams', Louis Aragon helped to launch a very different trajectory of Parisian memory.

This sequence of atrocious winters was made more appalling still by epidemic disease. The advent of bubonic plague in 1348, following a gap of more than half a millennium, could not have happened at a worse time. The Black Death of 1348–52 probably reduced France's population by between 30 and 40 per cent. Paris lost perhaps 50,000 individuals. Although initially the city recovered rather well, population growth was halted by further major epidemics throughout the 1360s, and then in 1374 and 1400. There would be no fewer than thirty-six years of plague in the city between 1348 and 1480, more than one year in four. If this was not bad enough, other epidemic diseases also reaped a rich harvest: the *tac* (mumps) in 1414, for example, scarlet fever in 1418, the *dando* in 1427 and smallpox in 1433 and 1438.

Poverty and nutritional deficiencies were a poor defence against epidemic disease and it was invariably the poor who suffered most. Furthermore, the city's charitable infrastructure proved unable to expand in order to face up to these worsening social problems. The medieval economic boom had triggered an outburst of charitable giving, promoted by the church. Under Saint Louis the ancient Hôtel-

Dieu adjacent to Notre-Dame cathedral on the Île de la Cité, run by the cathedral chapter and staffed by a dedicated community of Augustinian nuns, was expanded so it could hold up to 600 paupers a day. Hospitality and care were also offered in a range of smaller foundations such as the Hôpital Sainte-Catherine on the Rue Saint-Denis (IIe.) and the hostel attached to the church of Saint-Julien-le-Pauvre (Ve.). Other establishments were more specific in their function: the Hôpital de la Trinité had been founded in 1202 by two bourgeois to provide shelter for the needy, for example; another bourgeois, Étienne Haudri, had created an institution for impoverished widows (subsequently known as the Haudriettes); while it was a king, Saint Louis, who was responsible for the establishment of the Quinze-Vingts to provide care for three hundred blind persons.[8] There were leperhouses too, for this scourge of medieval society. These establishments were usually located far enough outside city walls for urban inhabitants to feel safe, yet near enough for them to be able to tap the charity of citizens. Paris's main institution, the Hôpital Saint-Lazare, was out towards Montmartre, while on the Left Bank there was a small establishment near Saint-Germain-des-Prés – on the site currently occupied, in fact, by the *Bon Marché* department store.

The establishment of foundations and charitable giving continued after 1300 of course, but their impact and effectiveness were small, given the wide range of need which troubled times produced. New establishments were too limited in scope, while some inherited institutions were probably over-provided for: the Quinze-Vingts rarely had three hundred blind persons, for example, while the decline of leprosy was reducing the number of inmates in leperhouses who actually suffered from the disease. In addition, the crown, which had boosted the city's fortunes prior to 1300, now seemed to be adding to Parisians' social problems, notably through engagement in warfare. In the thirteenth century the monarchy had developed an aggressive foreign policy and a majestic style of living. These were fundable – notably through royal domain revenue – when economic times were good, but not during periods of downturn. Taxes had thus to be levied. By the early fourteenth century these were passing from being an exceptional burden to becoming regular impositions. Paris was particularly affected by this shift: the dynasty treated the city as a milch-cow. The crown also meddled in Parisian affairs so as to keep its finances in credit. Indeed a currency revaluation in 1306 sparked off a revolt in the city. Rioters from the lower orders marched on the property of the respected merchant Étienne Barbette, who had ordered his tenants to pay him in revalued coinage. Appalled by this attack on popular living standards, rioters sacked and fired his property, and then proceeded to the Temple, where Philip the Fair was dining, to justify their actions and seek royal support. The king temporized, then crushed the revolt with coldly deterrent violence, leaving the bodies of twenty-eight rioters hanging from the city's gibbets.

The Barbette episode was a grim harbinger of worse social tensions to come. An early fourteenth-century chronicler had characterized Parisians as 'agreeable in their charming affability, their urbanity and the gentleness of their spirit'[9] – but such a description beggared belief in the light of what ensued after the start of the Hundred Years War. The state's need for heavy annual taxes in order to finance the war effort was highly unpopular – especially once the French started to lose battles. Following English victory in the battle of Crécy in 1346, English outriders raced towards Paris causing fires and destruction at Saint-Cloud and Rueil, and Parisians hastily renovated their urban defences. The state of emergency in 1356, following defeat in the battle of Poitiers, was even more severe. King John II was captured by the English and held to ransom. English troops encircled Paris, causing severe damage especially to the north of the city round Mantes and Meulan, 'piteously burning and devastasting our fatherland', as the chronicler Jean de Venette put it.[10] Houses which had been built next to Paris's walls were knocked down to make the fortifications more robust, and there was talk of burning down the bourg of Saint-Germain-des-Prés altogether, to ensure that it did not become an enemy stronghold. Refugees from the outlying villages poured into the city, making food supply even more of a problem.

As this example showed, it was not at all the demographic damage done in battle in time of war that was at fault. The main problem was the undisciplined bands of soldiers and marauders who undermined law and order, imposed 'ransoms' on local people, livestock and commodities, and caused wanton damage to rural capital by living off the land. The soldiers also disrupted trading routes and provoked population migration, severing people from their means of subsistence and causing prices of prime necessities to spiral upwards. Nor were these marauders always foreigners. Until the mid-1360s damage was done by English troops alongside disbanded soldiers from the French army profiting from the lawless conditions, and by feudal forces led by the king's vassals. Noteworthy here was John II's son-in-law, Charles 'the Bad', king of Navarre and count of Évreux, who was fishing in troubled waters for his own advantage. By late 1358 around sixty chateaux in the Paris region were occupied by Anglo-Navarrois forces, and the flames caused by the troops' incendiarism were visible from within Paris.

The captivity of King John from 1356 to 1360 caused a good deal of jockeying for power by powerful aristocrats, which the dauphin – the king's son and heir Charles (who himself would rule as Charles V) – did his best to contain. These struggles were made more complex and intractable, however, by the emergence of France's communes as a political force. Paris was the most audacious of all in this respect. At the meeting of the Estates General convoked in 1355 to obtain national approval for new taxes, the Paris delegation pushed itself into the lime-light, putting forward a financial reform programme which involved the rooting out of corrupt officials. The reformers looked back to the nostalgia-tinged reign of Saint Louis when taxes had been irregular and affordable, the currency sound and royal officials paragons of probity. (Or so legend had it . . .) The Parisian cause was laid out by a well-connected merchant and former échevin, who in 1354 had acceded to the post of Prévôt des Marchands, namely, Étienne Marcel. Between 1356 and 1358 this enigmatic figure would preside over an episode which severely damaged the dynasty's relationship with its capital city.

Marcel exploited the extreme embarrassment in which the monarchy found itself following defeat at Poitiers to extract a string of concessions from the dauphin's government. His influence – imposed through his popularity in the city and through the following he attracted from other communes in northern France – ensured that the state adopted the anti-corruption programme which he was promoting. He also prevented an unpopular devaluation of the currency, notably through commandeering a strike of Parisian workshops. And he seemed to be close to getting the dauphin to agree to regular meetings of the Estates General, which it was felt would limit the king's powers. In the event Marcel's influence was annulled by a number of fatal errors of judgement on his part. First, he led a demonstration against the crown's conduct of the war in February 1358, which involved the invasion of the Cité palace, and the assassination, in the dauphin's full view, of the marshals of Champagne and Normandy. At a stroke this murder put Marcel beyond the pale for most noblemen, thus reducing his political options. He compounded his error by publicly humiliating the blood-spattered dauphin over the corpses of the dead marshals. The dauphin, no fan of Marcel anyway, was forced to wear the red-and-blue hood which Marcel had made his emblem, while Marcel donned the royal headgear. The dauphin subsequently adopted the Prévôt des Marchands' reform programme and accepted him into government. But this alliance was grudgingly made and proved ephemeral. Charles now toured northern cities, drumming up antipathy towards Paris and its over-mighty leader.

Marcel's actions were winning mixed reviews among Parisians too. He had provoked criticism as well as praise by sending out troops to join in the brutal anti-seigneurial peasant revolt known as the Jacquerie taking place in the countryside to the north of Paris. The rift with the dauphin looked as though it would lead to open war, and in this context the failure of other towns to come in behind Paris was worrying for Marcel. The latter looked to Charles the Bad for support, though many Parisians were even more suspicious of the heterogeneous Navarrois army than of the dauphin's forces. To rally support, the Prévôt des Marchands led a Parisian force out to dislodge English troops in Saint-Cloud, but the burghers were butchered in their tracks. Marcel now sought to buttress the city's defence by allowing Charles the Bad into Paris with an army which included many English soldiers. The move triggered an anti-Marcel uprising on 31 July 1358 in which the Prévôt des Marchands was assassinated.

Dauphin Charles, now declared regent, played an artful role of benign forgiveness towards Parisians. Executions were kept to a minimum. There were protestations of mutual love and respect between capital city and its king. The seal of the municipality was changed so that over the ship hovered a dynastic fleur-de-lys. Some time later, the device '*Fluctuat nec mergitur*' ('it floats, nor does it sink') was added

Entry of Charles V into Paris

– an apposite gesture for this stormy period. Paris was being brought into line. The newly obedient city went out of its way to make a large contribution to the ransom for King John, and then towards the building of new ramparts, which were clearly needed. In the early 1360s, Charles – who on John's death in 1364 succeeded as Charles V – even determined to reside in the city, though in the lush new complex out at Saint-Pol, rather than in the Cité palace, which had too many bad memories for him. To Saint-Pol's rear towered the forbidding profile of the new Bastille fortress. Significantly, this was fortified in such a way that it offered protection against both external besiegers and internal assailants. A landing stage was built at Saint-Pol to allow the king to flee by water, if required, either downstream to the fortress of Vincennes or upstream to the Louvre. Charles was not of a mind to be dictated to by the Parisian populace ever again. Despite its somewhat benign conclusions, the Étienne Marcel episode had severely frayed the relationship between king and capital.

In the late fourteenth century the theatres of conflict with England shifted away from the Paris basin, and the withdrawal of soldiers and marauders from most of the area in which Paris did its provisioning, produced something of an economic recovery. Though the reduction in population levels had caused seigneurial income to fall by half, many sectors of the Parisian economy enjoyed a welcome spurt of activity and hopes for more. There were encouraging signs of cultural vitality too. Court officials in particular developed a taste for the culture of Antiquity, while Christine de Pisan reformulated the rules of courtly love. A mildly erotic vein was the speciality of Eustache Deschamps, later bemoaner of hard times, but at this time enthusiast for the city and its multiple pleasures, with an expert eye for *un bon cul de Paris*.[11] There were the beginnings of spiritual renewal too in the so-called *devotio moderna* movement which stressed individualized piety.

Despite this respite, things were to get much worse. Parisians had learnt a new repertoire of antipathies in the Étienne Marcel episode, and the advent as king of the eleven-year-old Charles VI in 1380, following the death of Charles V, laid the foundations for a long and drawn-out period of turbulence which lasted well into the next century. Despite the continuation of foreign conflict, there was a widespread demand – reflected in the 1380 meeting of the Estates

General – for the complete abolition of royal taxes, which would mean the king having to live solely off the product of royal domain lands. When in March 1382 royal financial officials started to collect new indirect taxes in Paris, a popular insurrection broke out, with trade organizations to the fore. The rebels seized lead mallets (*maillets*) from the Hôtel de Ville destined for urban defence, and launched attacks on tax officials and money-lenders (including many Jews and Lombards). The 'Maillotin' threat was worsened by the fact that other cities (notably Rouen) were also staging tax revolts at the same time.

The defeat of the tax rebels allowed the regency government – shared between Charles VI's uncles, the dukes of Anjou, Burgundy and Bourbon – an opportunity to take further the curbing of Parisian political independence. Virtual martial law was declared in the city, with up to one hundred notables being executed over the next weeks for their part in the Maillotin disturbances. In January 1383 the posts of *échevin* were abolished, while the Prévôté des Marchands was merged into the royal post, the Prévôté de Paris. In addition, the government ended the legal independence of the trade guilds which had been the vital force of the Maillotin movement.

This imperious move against the spirit and practices of Parisian self-rule was not long-lasting, for political circumstances increasingly militated against firm government on any issue. In 1388 Charles VI had ended the edgy conflicts between his uncles, but then in 1392 the young monarch showed the first signs of the insanity which would dog him until his death in 1422, and keep him out of the power struggle. There was consequently a growing relaxation of the 1383 municipal regulations – in 1389, for example, the merchant Jean Jouvenel was accorded the courtesy title of 'Guardian of the Prévôté des Marchands', and he used this lever to defend trading interests.

High politics now began to polarize between a Burgundian faction and the followers of the king's younger brother, Louis of Orléans. (After 1410, this latter group would be called the Armagnacs.) The king was little more than a pawn in the middle, while Paris became the stage on which factions fought for supremacy, with Parisians swinging first one way, then the other. The local unpopularity of Orléans and Charles VI's queen, Isabeau of Bavaria, was such that from 1405 the new duke of Burgundy, John the Fearless (*Jean*

'*Sans-Peur*'), had little difficulty in setting himself up in power in the city. In 1407 he had his main political rival, Louis of Orléans, mown down by hired killers as he was leaving the home of Queen Isabeau in the Rue Barbette (IIIe.) off the Rue Vieille-du-Temple in the Marais. The killers smote the prince such a blow 'with a halberd, so as to make his brains fly out over the paving stones'.[12] Politics had now reached a state in which sitting on the fence was no longer an option.

For nearly three decades, national power politics would oscillate wildly around a Paris which was itself chronically divided. The city found it ever more difficult to represent national as opposed to factional interests. Parisians themselves were on the receiving end of violence meted out by all factions: in the space of less than half a century, military bandits would be at Paris's gates on three occasions (1406, 1432, 1437), warring factions on four (1410, 1423, 1429, 1435–6) and the English twice (1437, 1441). Within the walls there would be sickening bouts of mass bloodletting, at the hands of Burgundians and Armagnacs – as the rump of Louis of Orléans's supporters were now called, following Louis's replacement as faction-leader by Bernard, count of Armagnac, father-in-law of Orléans's young heir. The anonymous Parisian Bourgeois, whose chronicle between 1406 and 1449 provides an invaluable insight into the city's experience in these years, noted fifteen years in which there was pillaging in the city or its environs – but also eight years of epidemics, eight of long hard winters, four of flooding, one of drought, four in which maybugs caused crop damage, seven of monetary revaluations, four of exceptionally high taxes, plus some twenty years of high prices. 'The great', he commented on the age through which he was living, 'hate each other; the middling sort are borne down by taxes; and the poor are unable to earn a living.'[13] Fifteenth-century chroniclers recorded an extraordinary number and variety of community processions in the city: more than fifty in 1412 alone, most of them in the months of June and July. Yet these moments of collective togetherness were the ceremonial fig-leaf which covered a harshly divided and contentious society.

3.2: The Parvis of Notre-Dame

There is no obvious answer to the question of where the centre of Paris lies. The original site of Paris was on the Île de la Cité and the Left Bank. Yet in the nineteenth century, such was the drift of the most dynamic parts of Paris away from the east that many would have placed the centre on the *grands boulevards*, close to the Opéra. Another candidate would be the Châtelet, which conjoins the north–south and east–west pathways of the *grande croisée* about which Haussmann and his followers made so much fuss. The Châtelet-Les-Halles Métro and RER station – which each day sees many millions of passengers passing through it – endorses such a claim. For several centuries, however, it would appear that all road distances from Paris have been measured from the square facing the west front of Notre-Dame cathedral – the Place du Parvis-Notre-Dame.

The word *parvis* is derived from 'paradisus', though the present square is far from as idyllic as its name would suggest. Despite some latter-day urban landscaping, its drab, wind-swept spaces are dull in every respect save as viewing point for the cathedral. Though some six times larger than the site prior to Baron Haussmann's quasi-vandalizing 'improvement' of the Île de la Cité in the 1850s and 1860s, the much smaller, historic *parvis* has had an important place in the life of the city since late Antique times.

The Parvis existed in the odour of sanctity. The cathedral of Saint-Étienne, built in the early sixth century and pre-dating Notre-Dame, was in close proximity to the basilica of Notre-Dame, which was converted into the present-day cathedral in the twelfth century. Also clustering round Notre-Dame was a host of minor churches eventually liquidated by the combined fervour of Enlightenment reformers and French revolutionaries: the baptistry of Saint-Jean-le-Rond (destroyed in 1748), the churches of Notre-Dame-de-la-Pitié and Saint-Christophe (1747), the priory of Saint-Denis-de-la-Châtre and the church of Saint Landry (1790 91). The cathedral was the ceremonial heart of the city too, around which community processions often revolved.

Mingling with the odours of sanctity on the Parvis were other, more worldly emanations. Around the corner at the heart of the island was the Rue de Glatigny, a famous centre of prostitution, authorized to exist by Saint Louis. The carnal/spiritual juxtaposition must have pleased Rabelais, whose giant Gargantua took refuge on the towers of Notre-Dame, urinating on the Parisian masses below and killing, it was recorded, some 260,418 individuals (not including women and children). Notre-Dame itself was not above more carnal concerns: Thomas Platter, a Swiss medical student in the late sixteenth century, noted how the cathedral was 'in all times a place of rendezvous favourable to debauchery'. From 1748, moreover, products of debauchery could be dumped outside the new foundling hospital built on the Parvis. Outside the cathedral's west front too were stocks in which the bishop had the right to place individuals who had infringed his seigneurial rights. The west door was also the conventional spot where arch-criminals made honourable amends and sought God's mercy before undertaking an itinerary across the city at the end of which they might be burnt alive or broken on the wheel on the Place de Grève outside the Hôtel de Ville.

Adjoining the cathedral on its river side was the main hospital of Paris, the Hôtel-Dieu, whose close location highlights the bishop's traditional role as fount of hospitality and father of the poor. The hospital may date from the seventh century, and it grew markedly in the Middle Ages, adding rooms and extensions in an unplanned and rather chaotic way. By the seventeenth century the hospital had colonized two bridges and a tract of land on the Left Bank backing onto the Rue des Rats (now Rue de l'Hôtel-Colbert: Ve.). The hospital continued its role as a refuge for Parisians – around one-third of city-dwellers died within its walls in the seventeenth century. Yet by this time it was acquiring its terrible reputation as a disease trap which would last until the nineteenth century. By the time of the

Revolution of 1789 a quarter of individuals admitted were dying here, often of diseases contracted within its walls. The habit of piling inmates three or more to a bed was hardly conducive to good health. Only the shifting of the hospital into a new purpose-built home – across the other side of the Parvis, where it has remained – did much to dissipate that reputation. (And even so, the Hôtel-Dieu remains a cold and cheerless place.)

A seething cauldron of piety, poverty, disease, delinquency and crime, the Parvis was also a renowned centre of trickery. 'In front of the Hôtel-Dieu', noted the antiquarian François Colletet in 1664, '[is] a big statue that is believed to represent Esculapius, god of physicians according to the Ancients.' Parisians had the malicious habit of asking provincials up in the city for the first time to go to the Parvis and ask for the shop of 'Monsieur Le Gris'. Humiliated to find no such tradesman existed, they were then frogmarched back to the square to have their noses rubbed hard up against the three-metre-high statue, which stood close to the cathedral door.

The enigmatic statue had other identities assigned it besides those of Esculapius and Monsieur Le Gris: these included the god Mercury, a previous bishop of Paris and a Merovingian magnate, and it has also been argued that it was a representation of Christ, relocated here from the old Saint-Étienne cathedral. The statue acted as a boundary marker too and the custom of measuring road distances from it had been adopted by the monarchy's highways services since time immemorial. The statue-cum-marker was removed in 1748 as part of the adaptation of the square to house the new foundling hospital. But the spot on which it stood – some 30 metres from the west door – remains the centre of Paris and, in a sense, of France.

John the Fearless fled Paris following the outrage caused by his admission of responsibility for the murder of Louis of Orléans, but the following year he was back, with a bevy of canon lawyers in tow, arguing that the assassination had been justifiable tyrannicide. He sought to establish a Burgundian power-base to put himself beyond reversals. As a visible emblem of his power, he built a towering citadel-residence at the Hôtel d'Artois, to whose precincts the bloody footsteps of Orléans's murderers had led. Nearly 27 metres high, and situated on the old Philip Augustus Wall on the Right Bank, it competed for prominence with the Louvre donjon and with the Tour de Nesle on the Left Bank owned by the pro-Armagnac duc de Berry.[14] At its very highest level was a bedchamber designed to allow John to sleep free from fear of assassination. The tower was crenellated and fortified, and walkways from the tower opening up on the rampart walls meant that the duke's troops could move swiftly within the interior of the city. In fact, it could not have resisted siege attack: it was designed more to evoke impregnability than to embody it.

The tower was the centrepiece of an ambitious bid to make Paris a Burgundian stronghold. John the Fearless sought to fashion the city's most influential traditional groupings into a power-base for the Burgundian cause. The university, which had formerly stayed aloof from political factionalism, was increasingly drawn in on the duke's side and acted as Burgundian apologist. John restored to the trades many of the powers they had lost in 1383, reinvigorated the water merchants' guild and in 1412 even restored the Prévôté des Marchands. These economic interest groups were predisposed to rally to the Burgundian cause anyway by the fact that the extensive territories of the dukes contained not just Burgundy (one of the city's main provisioning sources in wine), but also the Netherlands: Flemish cities provided Parisian merchants with their major mercantile and manufacturing links, while Bruges had become the main financial centre of northern Europe. John brought vats of wine up from Beaune to distribute as political gifts to his supporters. An additional feature of his political project was his use as his particular henchmen of the wealthy guild of butchers, who formed a kind of aristocracy of guild labour. The two thousand armed men commandeered by the butchers formed the duke's personal bodyguard. They also constituted the core of the forces who joined with English troops in 1412 to inflict signal defeats on Armagnac besiegers at Saint-Denis and Saint-Cloud.

Yet John the Fearless found it increasingly difficult to keep Paris within the bounds of order and legality. A series of insurrections in

April and May 1413 headed by the butcher-flayer Claude Caboche
led to an invasion of the Saint-Pol residence of Charles VI's young
dauphin Louis, and then crazed hunts through the streets and in the
prisons of Paris for presumed supporters of the Armagnacs. It would
take further episodes of terroristic violence led by Caboche and his
butcher-led forces and involving the murder of hundreds of individuals
before the warring barons and Parisian notables were provoked to
overthrow the Cabochiens. The latter brought the duke down in their
fall. John the Fearless had lost credit in Paris for failing miserably to
curb Cabochien violence, and in August 1413 he fled the city, leaving
it in the hands of Armagnac supporters.

In the five years in which they controlled Paris, the Armagnacs
would prove even less adept than the Burgundians at mastering a
difficult situation, and Parisians would even welcome back John the
Fearless with open arms in 1418. The situation for the Armagnacs
was, admittedly, worsened by the disastrous defeat of French forces
at the hands of English longbowmen in the battle of Agincourt in
October 1415 and by the death of Dauphin Louis. In Paris an Armagnac terror now followed the Burgundian one, and was blithely
accepted by Bernard of Armagnac himself ('crueller than Nero', in the
Paris Bourgeois's opinion).[15] This threw much Parisian sympathy
back to the Burgundian cause. In the night of 28–29 May 1418
anti Armagnacs opened the city gate at Saint-Germain to Burgundian
forces, who, to cries of 'Peace! Peace!', swept through the city, forcing
their enemies to flee. Following a fortnight of fear and confusion, the
Burgundian forces committed a massacre of prisoners, including the
count of Armagnac himself, and sundry bishops, barons and high
functionaries. John the Fearless found himself allied again with the
most violent and bloodthirsty elements of Parisian society, led now
by the executioner Capeluche, 'the vast majority' of whose victims, it
was recorded, 'were folk of poor estate'.[16] The duke did his best to
bring the murder gangs under the control of more bourgeois elements,
but in November 1419 he was assassinated in an ambush set up by
Armagnacs, now in the entourage of the young new dauphin Charles
(r. as Charles VII, 1422–61).[17]

The decision of the new duke, Philip III 'the Good' of Burgundy, to ally with the English as a means of seeking revenge was supported by many Parisians. Not since the time of Clovis, opined the Paris Bourgeois,

> has France been so desolated and divided ... and the Dauphin has no other intention than to put the whole of his father's country to fire and sword, while the English are causing as much evil as Saracens would. It would be better to be captured by the English than by the Dauphin and his so-called Armagnac followers.[18]

And so it came to pass. In a ceremony held at Notre-Dame cathedral on 21 May 1420, Charles VI signed the Treaty of Troyes which made King Henry V of England the regent of France and heir apparent to the French crown. He married Charles VI's daughter as a pledge of political union. The Prévôt des Marchands and the university ratified the treaty, and the two kings along with Duke Philip the Good made a much applauded entry into Paris on 1 December 1420. English garrisons were established at the Louvre, at Vincennes and at the Bastille. English forces at the latter were commanded by Sir John Falstaff (with whom Shakespeare would later take some liberties). Though Henry V died in August 1422, the death of Charles VI a few months later brought to the French throne Henry VI of England – a mere baby, born the previous year. The Valois dauphin remained pretender.

The capital city on which the Capetians had built a mighty European reputation had thus turned into an English fief. Control of the city was in the hands of Henry VI's regent (and uncle), the duke of Bedford, who settled down in the Hôtel des Tournelles, which Charles V had constructed in the Marais to the north of the Hôtel Saint-Pol. Neither the English king nor his Burgundian ally appeared to show much interest in the city. Duke Philip managed only short visits totalling a mere six months over the whole period, rejected the offer of the regency in 1429, and stayed focused on building up his Burgundian-Flemish state as a major European power. In 1431 Henry VI was crowned king of France at Notre-Dame cathedral. But he spent less than a month in the city.

The Parisians seemed not to miss the pretender. 'Charles VII' fell back on the insignificant city of Bourges, and bided his time. There were only around one hundred Englishmen in the city for most of the occupation, so 'English' Paris was administered by Parisians. When in 1424 Bedford won a significant victory over the forces of the 'king of Bourges' at Verneuil, he and his wife were acclaimed in Paris by celebrations unparalleled, the Paris Bourgeois noted, since Roman times. In Notre-Dame cathedral, the duke was 'received like a God', to the sound of hymns, bells, trumpets and organ.[19] Indeed even when Charles VII's cause was being spectacularly rallied by the dynamism of Joan of Arc, Parisians remained unimpressed. In 1429 the 'Maid of Orléans' led an assault on the city gates at the Faubourg Saint-Honoré which was stoutly resisted. It was not an English but a French archer who fired an arrow which wounded her. Many Parisians regarded *la Pucelle* – the Maid – as a witch, and were frightened that Charles VII would launch a bloodbath if he penetrated the city.

Parisians had been keen to welcome the Anglo-Burgundian 'solution' to civil war. They had expected the urban economy, crippled by Burgundian-Armagnac mauling, to recover, and were dismayed that no light was appearing at the end of the tunnel. Civil war was continuing. Prices had increased up to sixfold between 1410 and 1420, and they showed little sign of dropping. Anglo-Burgundian domination worsened a very grave situation. Provisioning difficulties and the prevalence of pillagers and marauders in the environs meant that almost everything for sale in Paris sold with one or more ransoms incorporated into the price. By the early 1420s half the population had fled, causing a massive disruption of all economic indicators. The depopulation of the city caused the property market to collapse, with rents falling by anything up to 90 per cent: tax-rolls revealed hordes of tenants marked down as 'left because of poverty'. Many traders dependent on a large and prosperous local market went to the wall as a result of the savage contraction of demand. Taxes stayed high, not least because the Anglo-Burgundians had to maintain large standing garrisons in order to be able to face up to the sporadic raids launched by the 'king of Bourges' throughout the city's main provisioning region (the area to the south-east and east). Parisians were convinced that they were being bled dry by the English – even though the English treasury was in fact subsidizing the Anglo-Burgundian state.

A rising sense of grievance was exacerbated by the fact that the duke of Burgundy played little role in the new state, which consequently seemed more Anglo than Anglo-Burgundian. The English showed no sensitivity to the niceties of constitutional protocol and acted more as conquerors than allies. Henry VI's coronation at Notre-Dame in 1431 seemed rather shabby, especially considering that Charles had been crowned two years earlier in Reims following venerable rituals, including anointment with holy chrism. Moreover, the English child king's retinue made a series of gaffes following his coronation. The principal banquet was an unseemly scrum rather than an orderly ritual, with 'cobblers, mustard-makers, scullery lads, bar staff and builders' mates' claiming precedence to food over the most prestigious corporate groupings of the city. The usual gestures of liberality were simply not observed. The food was also judged both meagre and *réchauffé* – an appalling culinary error, highlighting an enduring tradition of French disdain for English cooking. Henry's advisers had not grasped that being king of France involved being the liberal-handed patron of Paris.[20]

The English crown had failed to elicit popular affection in Paris. This meant that, once Bedford died in 1435 and Charles VII's cause was regaining ground, Parisians were not averse to passing back under the authority of the kings of France. With Charles VII promising an amnesty, members of the pro-French party in the city started an insurrection, forcing the English to fall back on the Bastille. The rebels then opened the Saint-Jacques gate to royal troops. The defeated English were permitted to embark for their homeland. Although it would still take more than a decade for the endless cycle of wars to grind to a halt, at least by 1436 Paris was French again, and the basis of a renewed relationship between capital and king had been laid.

In 1437 Charles VII rode into the city, 'he and his men all armed' against surprise misfortune.[21] He proved merciful and forgiving towards Parisians. An amnesty was introduced, and pillaging and ransoming forbidden. But the wounds were slow to heal, and there was no hiding the dynasty's enduring suspicion and resentment of things Parisian. The English occupation had confirmed the severance of the special relationship between city and king caused by the Étienne Marcel and Maillotin episodes. Charles VII and his successors – Louis XI (r. 1461–83), Charles VIII (r. 1483–98) and Louis XII (r. 1498–

1515) – rarely stayed any length of time in the city, preferring the lavish palaces which they had built in the Loire valley. Louis XI seems even to have considered moving the capital to Tours. A royal ordinance in 1450 confirmed Paris's complicated electoral system for local government, but this was now brazenly manipulated by the crown. Charles VII imposed his own man, the parlementary magistrate Henri de Livres, as Prévôt des Marchands in 1460. He was prolonged in office by Louis XI to 1465, who then reimposed him on a restive municipality in 1466 and again between 1476 and 1484.

Parisians had a chance to demonstrate their fidelity, as political struggles with Burgundy continued. In the so-called War of the League of the Public Weal in 1465, for example, the cards were stacked against Charles VII's successor, Louis XI – with Bretons and Burgundians plundering and pillaging on the edge of the city, in Clignancourt, Montrouge, Gentilly and Ivry. But Paris came good. The city defiantly refused to open its gates to besieging barons (who included the future Charles the Bold of Burgundy). 'The bourgeoisie and all the inhabitants of the city of Paris had great honour [through this],' a chronicler recorded, 'in that they defended very well both for the honour of the king and for their own honour and maintained themselves in good union and obedience with the monarch.'[22] They showed similar loyalty in the 1470s, doing their bit towards the collapse of the Burgundian cause.

After decades of strife and division, the cleric Thomas Basin had noted in the 1440s that 'Paris began to breathe again and to return to better circumstances.'[23] Significant changes were occurring within the urban economy. The water merchants had constituted the cream of Parisian society under Philip Augustus and Louis IX, and held their corner against all but the very wealthiest and most powerful of noblemen. In the early fourteenth century, in emulation of noble chivalric forms, for example, they held public jousting competitions against urban rivals in which they replayed the Trojan wars – a nice allusion to local patriotism.[24] These highly self-conscious patricians who thought themselves as good as any noble were hit hard by economic contingency, particularly by the dynasty's long-term failure to enforce law and order within the Paris region. They lost many of their boats to pillaging or ransoming, and were unable to enforce their privileges over interloping Rouen merchants. Many merchants seem simply to have migrated to seek out safer and more secure locations.

If the carrying trades were damaged by the breakdown of law and order in the Paris region, the most dynamic sector of medieval manufacturing, the cloth trade, also fell into a vertiginous decline. In 1300 some 360 weavers had paid taxes; by 1421 only two managed even to make it onto the tax rolls.[25] Nor was the reduction in numbers caused by industrial concentration: on the contrary, the rule that all artisans had to practise within their own workshops meant that the kind of industrial concentration taking place in areas of the Low Countries and northern Italy was not replicated here. Paris's financial system seemed increasingly rickety too when compared with these commercial rivals: indeed the Lombards who had been in the forefront of financial services in the past in Paris were increasingly scapegoated. Philip Augustus (in 1291) and Philip VI (in 1347) expelled them, and though they were soon back in business, the crown proved unable to protect them from the kind of plebeian xenophobia which also targeted the Jews: both groups, for example, would be the object of Maillotin wrath. By 1450 there were precious few Lombards left in the city. Many financiers chose to locate closer to the royal court on the Loire, while those left on the Pont-au-Change were jostled by doll-makers and hatters.

The collapse of Parisian cloth-making owed something to technical backwardness too. By the fourteenth century the best-selling cloths were carded to produce a smoother finish – but Parisian masters resisted this technical improvement. Significantly, only the drapers out at Saint-Marcel showed themselves willing to innovate in this respect (they learnt much from Italian dyers too). A kind of de-industrialization was taking place in the eastern reaches of the city, around the old weaving centre of the Bourg Tibourg. Cloth-makers were driven out by competition from the Saint-Marcel industries and by an influx of fashionable money: many high nobles also started to build residences in this area, so as to be close to the royal Saint-Pol and Tournelles palaces.

Paris's cloth-finishing and dyeing industries did rather better than cloth-making, as did silk manufacture. These fitted in with the traditional orientation of Parisian manufacturing around luxury and semi-luxury produce. But the picture even here was one of decline, linked to the relocation of the royal court and the political elite away from Paris. The king's absence from the city in various Loire residences instigated a massive emigration of the political elite, who now had less pressing reasons for maintaining a Parisian residence. The kind of power building represented by John the Fearless's tower-residence was a thing of the past: no duke of Burgundy after him resided in Paris. The bishops of Sens built a residence on the Right Bank in 1475, and the Cluniacs erected an impressive dwelling over the old Roman baths on the Left Bank in 1485.[26] But these were the exceptions. Three-quarters of the bishops who had a Parisian pied-à-terre in 1400 had abandoned it by 1500. 'Neither the king nor any seigneur comes to Paris any more than they would to Jerusalem', grumbled the Paris Bourgeois, presciently, as early as 1438.[27] The Parisian manufacturing sector had got too used to the easy days of producing for the wealthy indigenous elite to change its ways and go out seeking outside markets. The Halles, symptomatically, were in poor shape too, and their international status was in vertiginous decline.

These political and economic dislocations caused a darkening of the social atmosphere over the fourteenth and fifteenth centuries. An unpleasant scapegoating reflex, endorsed by the crown, had been emerging even by 1300. In 1307, for example, Philip the Fair had launched a brutal attack on the Templar Order which had served as the crown's treasurers and whose wealth he coveted. Following a trial of massive bad faith, the Templar leaders were burnt at the stake as heretics in 1314 on the western tip of the Île de la Cité. The Lombards were another group whose financial expertise was held against them. So were the Jews: expelled by Philip the Fair in 1306, then recalled, they would be definitively expelled from Paris and the kingdom in 1394. They were victims of popular as well as royal wrath. In 1320 accusations had swept through France that Jews were poisoning wells, and the charge was repeated in 1321 (though then aimed principally against lepers, another scapegoat group) and in 1348–9 following the Black Death. At the end of the century witchcraft became the focus of increased concern too: in 1398 the Sorbonne condemned some twenty-eight forms of magic and witchcraft, and the first witch-hunts began – notably in the south-west – shortly afterwards. Joan of Arc

Riotous soldiers pillage a house in Paris

would be swept along into these panics at her trial in 1431. This more repressive and intolerant strain in Parisian life was evident in regard to migrant workers, vagrants and beggars – as well as prostitutes, who were subject to increasing bouts of repression for constituting a threat to public order. Attacks became more systematic in the wake of the Hundred Years War. In 1473 the Paris Parlement ordered local policing officials to make a concerted attack on 'bandits and vagabonds'.

The top as well as the bottom of Parisian society was also in flux in the period. In 1467 Louis XI convened a muster outside the Saint-Antoine gate of all Parisian males of arms-bearing age. The chronicler Jean de Roye recorded the scene, remarking

> the standards and the pennants of the court of the Parlement, of the Chamber of Accounts, of the Royal Treasury, of the officials from the tax administration, the Mint, the Châtelet and the Hôtel de Ville, under which there were as many and indeed even more warriors than under all the banners of the trades.[28]

This observation highlighted an underlying truth about late fifteenth-century Paris. Because of the oscillations of the previous century, the city was changing from a major economic and political centre into an administrative stronghold, a change that impacted powerfully on the city's topography and social hierarchy. The trend had been set by the monarchy, which had already by 1500 begun to sell off in lots its sprawling residence of Saint-Pol: the last lions in its much-loved menagerie, visited by plebs and royalty alike, died in 1487 (leaving a street-name in commemoration).[29] Many departing bishops allowed their Parisian residences to become university colleges, while the residences of other prelates and of the high nobility passed into the hands of the wealthy elite within the financial and legal administration. By the late fifteenth century the Hôtel d'Armagnac (former home of the comtes d'Armagnac and the duc de Berry), the Hôtel du Porc-Épic (once owned by Louis of Orléans) and the Hôtel de Clisson were all owned by the state's financial officials.[30]

Given the vicissitudes of the economy, it was perhaps not altogether surprising that merchants should look for more solid areas of invest-

ment than trade and manufacturing. The reunification of the kingdom after the expulsion of the English in 1453 meant that the state required a much enlarged administrative, legal and financial machinery. Though there was a growing move to decentralize some state business – thus by 1500, there were six parlements in France, five chambers of account and six courts of aides – this was outweighed by a counter-vailing growth in the volume of state business. After the violent oscillations of factional politics, royal service was ideologically attrac-tive to much of the monied elite, who also regarded entrance into the tertiary sector as a social promotion as well as an economic investment. Even if there were problems about the prompt payment of salaries in royal service, the latter was probably still a more steady and reliable income source than trade or manufacturing offered. The reorganized municipality required staffing too: the Prévôté des Marchands alone employed some 250 persons (including two inspectors each for strings of onions and for walnut-bundles . . .).[31] In 1438, of the 281 wealthiest individuals whose social background we can identify, 103 were from the world of office, law and finance. The proportion was probably even higher by the end of the century. There was also a growing tendency – already visible in the fourteenth century, when even Étienne Marcel, for example, had held a little rural retreat in Ferrières in the Brie – for this elite to match the lifestyle of the old nobility by buying rural property for leisure and to mark their social promotion.

The growth of the state and the reordering of the social elite also affected the University of Paris. Charles V called the university 'his eldest daughter', and in the early fifteenth century University Chan-cellor Jean Gerson saluted the institution as 'mother of study, mistress of science, tutor of truth, . . . the fine clear sun of . . . all Christendom'.[32] The medical faculty's report on the Black Death won international renown and legitimacy, while throughout the fourteenth century the theologians, now concentrated at the Sorbonne, were ceaselessly con-sulted by both the monarchy and the papacy, its historic patrons, on all major doctrinal issues. As a result of Philip the Fair's power-politics, the papacy relocated to Avignon in 1309, where it remained until 1378, with France providing a preponderance of popes, who loyally looked to the Sorbonne for doctrinal guidance. Schism occurred in

1378, with counter-popes henceforth based in Avignon and Rome. France's support for Avignon alienated most other countries which traditionally sent students to the University of Paris.

The University of Paris had lost its aura of universality. Although it was to play a key role in ending the schism in the Council of Constance between 1414 and 1417, by then its international prestige was dwindling, and decline continued throughout the century. The flow of English students slowed to a trickle under the impact of war, and the 'English nation' by the end of the fifteenth century was made up almost entirely of Germans. Study was simply not safe in a city oscillating between Burgundians and Armagnacs, and the university's drawing power seemed to be increasingly restricted to northern France and Burgundian lands. Town–gown conflicts were exacerbated by these tensions. The reckless career of the poet François Villon – a master of arts in 1452, who killed a man in a brawl (but managed to escape punishment for it) and engaged in other scrapes – suggests the existence of a world of student delinquency which put a strain on town–gown relations. One conflict between students and townspeople in the middle of the century ended with the latter yelling, 'Kill them! Kill them! There are too many of them!'[33]

3.3: François Villon

François de Montcorbier, known as Villon, France's most accomplished late medieval poet, spent all the parts of his life about which we know anything in the student milieu of Paris. He was perhaps less Parisian than he claimed, for his family was from the Bourbonnais to the south. Such a claim to Parisian identity was, however, not uncommon. The city's population had fallen to less than 100,000 in the 1420s, following Armagnac and Burgundian faction-fighting, but by the 1440s and 1450s was bouncing back. Villon was far from alone in being a 'new' Parisian.

The life of this would-be Parisian was to be lived in the shadow of the wave of social and political discipline being imposed on the city in the aftermath of the political crises of the earlier decades. In its quest for order the monarchy drove out beggars, marginals and delinquents, and also reduced the university's institutional autonomy. For its part the university was also seeking to clean up its reputation: in 1444, for example, the Sorbonne condemned the 'feast of fools' at carnival time, in which students had always been to the fore. The behaviour of Villon was probably no worse than many of his student predecessors. But he fell spectacularly foul of the campaign for urban and university order.

From a humble background, Villon studied in Paris in the 1440s before receiving his mastership of arts in 1452 – a year before the end of the Hundred Years War. Parisian student life was still pretty rumbustious at this time. A famous night-time prank in 1455 saw students – with Villon most likely among them – moving a huge and ancient boundary stone on the Right Bank known familiarly as the *Pet au Diable* ('Devil's Fart') over onto the Montagne Sainte-Geneviève, producing a major legal rumpus. As a kind of perpetual student, Villon was involved in a series of scrapes with the law. In 1455 he killed a fellow cleric in a brawl, and fled the city. Friends arranged a pardon in his absence, but as soon as he was back he became involved in an organized theft from the Collège de Navarre, and fled the city again to avoid detection. He seems to have spent the next years on the road as a traveller, but by 1461 was back in prison for an uncertain offence at Meung-sur-Loire in the Orléanais, where he may have undergone judicial torture. Pardoned by King Louis XI, Villon returned to Paris only to be recognized as an accomplice in the Collège de Navarre affair – for which he received a stiff fine. By now, Villon had sufficient a reputation as a delinquent that when he was arrested for being on the fringes of a tavern brawl in 1461, he was sentenced to death. He seemed exactly the kind of individual upon whom both state and university were trying to crack down. If yet again Villon managed to secure a pardon, it was at the expense of ten years' banishment from the city. He left in 1463, and was lost to history for ever.

In the following century Rabelais told of Villon's life after 1463, claiming he had settled down in the provinces, but this seems to have been invention. Certainly Villon was only post-humously a celebrity. His poetry was published by a Parisian bookseller in 1489, and King Francis I ordered the poet Clément Marot to draw up a full collected works in 1533. But his poetry fitted poorly into the developing classical canon – there were no further editions of his work between the early sixteenth century and 1742. Thereafter it has tended to be most attractive to those who sympathize with his life as a reveller, a rebel and an embryonic bohemian – late nineteenth-century aesthetes like Huysmans, modernists like Ezra Pound, para-Surrealists like Pierre MacOrlan.

The content of Villon's poetry certainly focuses on a life lived on the margins, replete with boozing, womanizing, thievery and legal scrapes but also with hunger, cold and want. But his verse is also complex, compressed and difficult, full of stylistic and scholastic parodies, and shot through with untraceable references and with playful and enigmatic ambiguity. For all its animation and dynamism, the poetry also dwells upon death: one poem is an imaginary valediction penned on the way to the gibbet of Montfaucon; another – his most famous, the *Testament* – is an imaginary will, in which he makes as though to leave legacies both sincere (his heart to his faithless mistress) and comic (his cobwebbed window-frames to the poor, his hairclippings to his barber, etc.). His poems also evince a sad warmth towards the past: the line *'mais où sont les neiges d'antan?'* ('where are the snows of yesteryear?') has become one of the most heavily used citations in the literature of nostalgia. It alone marks him out as a true Parisian.

The university's decline was also partly a consequence of the emergence of new centres of learning throughout western Europe. In 1200 Paris had been one of only three universities (with Bologna and Oxford) in the whole of Europe; by 1500 there were more than a dozen in the French zone alone, and some of these had claims to undermine Parisian supremacy – notably Montpellier for medicine and Orléans for civil law (which was not even taught in Paris). The Paris masters were furious with the establishment by England of universities at Caen in 1424 and at Bordeaux in 1441, which was targeted very precisely against Paris's intellectual supremacy.

With a multiplicity of rival establishments reducing the international drawing-power of the Montagne Saint-Geneviève, the university also found it impossible to rise above the factionalism which bedevilled French politics in the period as a whole. The rector had forbidden the wearing of party badges during the Étienne Marcel episode, as though to highlight the need for the university to rise above partisan politics. Wooed by the dukes of Burgundy, however, and allying themselves with a pro-Burgundian municipality, the doctors soon capitulated. University masters justified John the Fearless's cold-blooded murder of Louis of Orléans as a tyrannicidal defence of the public good. The university was a meek and unprotesting – indeed spasmodically sycophantic – supporter of the Anglo-Burgundian regime after 1420. They willingly provided prosecutors for Joan of Arc's trial, which sent the Maid of Orléans to the pyre.

Having chosen to back the wrong horse in the Armagnac–Burgundian struggle, the university was in no position to cut a dash once Charles VII was the uncontested ruler. In the kind of state which was emerging from the Hundred Years War, the university seemed only one of a welter of corporate bodies making claims for special treatment – and finding that the state was less generous than of yore. From the early fourteenth century onwards, scholars found their privileges being progressively whittled away. When they protested, the ruler gave them short change: 'You are not worth me bothering about,' was the disdainful expostulation on one occasion of Louis XI (who had been annoyed at the university's failure even to attend his formal entry into Paris in 1461).[34] Two of the most important and innovatory acts of the resurgent state were the declaration in 1439 that the king could tax at will (and the new *taille* tax was introduced without consultation with the Estates General); and the formation of a standing army in 1440. In both respects the university found its liberties overridden. Its claims as an institution situated under the aegis of the papacy were diminishing; it was becoming an institution of state. This was made increasingly apparent over the course of the century. In 1437 the state ended any thought which the university had that it was exempt from normal state taxes; in 1470 Louis XI imposed a loyalty oath on all students from Burgundian lands (triggering a mass exodus); and in 1475 students were sent off to battle notwithstanding the former understanding that as clerics they were exempt from military service. In 1445 their judicial independence had been ended too, as they were brought directly under the authority of the parlements for the first time. A severe reform of the university's statutes in 1452 cut back on perceived abuses, though it proved incapable of reversing the dwindling intellectual dynamism of the institution. In 1498–9 the university would lose its venerable right to strike, and scholars' claims for benefit of clergy would also be further restricted. Perpetual students like Villon were increasingly equated with vagrants, who received short shrift from the police.

While the university slumbered in its scholastic and pedagogic certitudes, cut adrift from papal support, less internationally respected and more tightly incorporated within the legal structures of the French state, a new type of institution was bidding to contest the university's primacy as a centre of learning and research, namely, the printing press. It was two scholars at the Sorbonne who in 1470 attracted print workers from Germany, where from mid-century Johann Gutenberg and his emulators had begun to experiment successfully with movable type. The demand was there: readership of books increased by a factor of ten. The new print technology would not be bound within university structures, and its revolutionary impact on communications would soon be apparent. It would leave indelible marks – for better and for worse – on the history of sixteenth-century Paris.

4

Paris Reborn, Paris Reformed
c. 1480–1594

On 15 March 1528 King Francis I (r. 1515–47) solemnly proclaimed to the Paris city council: 'Henceforth it is our intention to live and reside for the most part in the good city of Paris and its environs more than in any other part of the kingdom. Recognising our chateau of the Louvre to be our most fitting and convenient lodging, we hereby order the said chateau to be repaired and put in order.'[1]

In the event, things were not to be quite as straightforward. It would be nearly two decades until, in 1546, one year before his death and the accession of his son Henry II (r. 1547–59), Francis actually set to work on rebuilding the Louvre. When he resided in Paris, it tended to be in the old Tournelles palace by the Saint-Antoine gate, and he spent more time outside the city, at residences in Fontainebleau, Saint-Germain-en-Laye and at the country house of Madrid in the Bois de Boulogne. Yet in the long run this declaration did as it promised: it restored the kind of close relationship between the monarch and his capital which had characterized Paris's salad days in the Middle Ages. This meant the end of the century-long orientation of the Valois dynasty around the river Loire: Louis XI (r. 1461–83) had even debated moving the capital to Tours, while Charles VIII (r. 1483–98) and Louis XII (r. 1498–1515) had been infrequent visitors to Paris. After a quarrel with the city council in 1496 over taxes to pay for the Italian Wars to which he had committed the crown from 1494, Charles had sworn he would never set foot in the city again. Earlier in his life, Francis too preferred to luxuriate at Chambord and his other Loire valley residences.

4.1: The Louvre

In the early 1980s Fifth Republic President François Mitterrand launched plans for a *Grand Louvre*, involving the erection in the main courtyard of the chateau of I. M. Pei's glass and steel pyramid which would act as a point of public entry into the enlarged museum. There was considerable public outcry against an alleged desecration of a historic heritage site. Yet if the Louvre has come to seem a changeless and unchangeable symbol of western civilization, in fact one of the most striking traits of its history has been its role as a kind of soft wax on which men of power have sought to impress their influence and personality. The Louvre has always signified the display of power – but its form has been more protean than is usually imagined.

From the late Middle Ages onwards, this protean trait was acknowledged in one of the claimed derivations of the Louvre: the name, it was said, was a corruption of *l'oeuvre* – the work, or the building site – and signified that the palace was always in process of transformation and indeed would never be finished. Other place-name hypotheses (some of them equally fanciful) include derivations from the Celtic *levrez*, 'leperhouse', suggesting the (uncorroborated) existence of a leper hospital; the Latin *rubrum* (red: corrupted into *lubrum*), evoking the colour of the tiles allegedly fashioned from the adjacent tileries (*tuileries*); the Latin *luparia*, 'site of wolves'; the Frankish *lure*, 'to be on watch'; and the Anglo-Saxon *leouar*, 'castle'.

Perhaps the last two meanings are most plausible in terms of the first shape which Philip Augustus imprinted on the building: a massive feudal tower which was part of the city's new defences. The tower's height allowed advance warning of the approach of troops from the west. It also looked frightening, even from afar. Moreover, the defensive qualities of the chateau were amplified rather than diluted in the building of the new wall of Charles V in the mid-fourteenth century. Only archaeological excavations in the late twentieth century have revealed the massive scale of the medieval bastion. The remains of the Charles V bastions are now visitable in the shopping mall beneath the Louvre.

In the Hundred Years War no king resided here and the building became an arms dump and prison. Even so, the old Louvre had an almost legendary reputation. The seventeenth-century antiquarian Henri Sauval thought that there was 'no other tower so talked about in the history of the world'. There was much astonishment then that Francis I, as part of his campaign to install himself properly in the city from the late 1520s, demolished it and replaced it with a more Renaissance-style *palazzo*. The Renaissance palace was a very public affirmation of royal glory, in which major state ceremonials took place. This official dimension and the unfinished state of the building – 'if it were ever finished,' noted the secretary of the Venetian ambassador in the late 1570s, 'one could rightly say that it was one of the world's most beautiful edifices' – led Catherine de' Medici to build a more homely, if still pretty grand, palace to the west, the Tuileries. She – and subsequently Henry IV – built a gallery joining the two palaces along the riverside. From this time onwards a division of labour was established whereby the Tuileries served as the home of the reigning monarch, while the Louvre was the official expression of state power. Over the centuries only very few rulers could bear – or else were allowed by their rebellious subjects – to live in it for very long.

The Louvre's emblematic status as the site of official and ceremonial grandeur was amplified by Henry IV and Louis XIII but most especially by Louis XIV. With Colbert's enthusiastic direction, the palace frontage designed in the 1540s by architect Pierre Lescot and sculptor Jean Goujon was made one side of a closed courtyard, the *cour carrée*. Colbert pulled off quite a coup in persuading the celebrated Italian maestro of the baroque Gianlorenzo Bernini to come to Paris to work on a design for the east front of the palace. Bernini soon retired hurt from the vicious court infighting against him, and his enemies, led by Claude Perrault, brought forward more classical plans for the colonnade.

Perrault's superb colonnade was figuratively as well as materially a façade. Louis XIV's decision to shift his court to Versailles starved the Louvre of funds even for properly completing the Perrault plans. Henry IV had allowed artists and luxury artisans to reside in part of the palace, and under Colbert royal academies were also housed here. But the palace was now so neglected that hordes of marginals invaded the vacant space as well, setting up huts and shacks even inside the *cour carrée*.

In 1806 Napoleon drove out the artisans and other royal hangers-on from the palace premises, and sought to restore to the whole site a more official look. Yet it was Napoleon III who, as part of his programme of urban modernization, did most to turn the Louvre into what is currently visible. In particular he built the courtyard to the west of the *cour carrée* – the *Cour du Carrousel* – and opened out the area between the Louvre and the Tuileries as an enormous public piazza. This involved destroying infamously insalubrious tenement blocks which had divided the two palaces since their creation. The destruction of the Tuileries palace by Communard fires in 1871 had the unexpected additional effect of opening the western frontage onto the Tuileries gardens and down to the Champs-Élysées. It was thus the Third Republic – by deciding not to rebuild the Tuileries – which set in place one of the greatest of political vistas.

If the Louvre had presented an image of raw military power under Philip Augustus, and a stately centre of ceremonial from the Renaissance to the Second Empire, it was also increasingly developing a reputation as a cultural focus for what it contained as well as what it was. Paris Salon art shows were established here in 1737, but it was really the First Republic which, by establishing the Musée de la République here in 1793, sealed its future. The Louvre has been one of the great public art galleries ever since. What has hung on its walls has been as influential in the development of western art as the city of Paris itself.

François Mitterrand's decision in the early 1980s to make the idea of a *Grand Louvre* one of the defining *grands projets* of his presidency was grounded in an artful awareness of the traditions embodied in the Louvre's history. The thorough renovation of the galleries sought to make a more worthy and viewer-friendly context for the art on display. The expulsion from the northern side of the buildings of the Finance Ministry offices similarly opened up considerably more space for display. The novelty of Pei's pyramidal design lay partly in its reflective exterior surfaces, which mirror and intensify the image of the surrounding historic buildings. In addition, however, the commission was calculated to establish Mitterrand firmly in the illustrious lineage of heads of state back to Philip Augustus who have accumulated political capital by imprinting their tastes and their political vision on what is one of France's foremost 'sites of memory'.

The 1528 declaration was in some degree a thank-you note from king to Paris. Despite Charles VIII's pique, the city had made – and would continue to make – important contributions to the financing of Valois war-making in the Italian Wars, a loose series of conflicts lasting from 1494 to 1559 which, though predominantly conducted in the Italian peninsula, pitted France against the Habsburgs, who controlled Germany and Spain. After two centuries which had profoundly shaken the crown–capital relationship that had been so mutually beneficial in the Middle Ages, that relationship seemed to be back on track – though as we shall see there were to be more than a few bumps along the way.

In this repeat honeymoon period the crown now regularly consulted the city fathers on matters of national importance. From 1522 it devised a system of state borrowing, the *rentes sur l'Hôtel-de-Ville de Paris*,[2] which used the city's financial credit in order to tap national wealth. In 1525 Paris would stand politically firm while Francis was in captivity in Italy and Spain following disastrous defeat in the battle of Pavia. The city was subsequently generous as regards the ransom which the Habsburg Holy Roman Emperor Charles V (also king of Spain) demanded for Francis's sons, exchanged for their father in 1526. The 1528 declaration thus confirmed a contractual arrangement between the dynasty and its capital city which was already being developed.

There were to be two symbols of the renewed pact between crown and city: a new royal palace and a new city hall (or Hôtel de Ville). The massive old feudal donjon tower of the Louvre was knocked down. Reconstruction work was eventually begun under the eye of principal architect Pierre Lescot, who built the south-western corner of what became the Louvre's *cour carrée*. The main gate to the old Louvre had been on the river, but it was now shifted to the eastern front, opening the palace directly onto the city. The environs of the Louvre became something of a palace complex. Francis purchased the nearby Hôtel de Neuville for his mother Louise of Savoy, and in the 1560s Henry II's widow Catherine de' Medici took over this residence and the surrounding site (including an old tile-kiln or *tuilerie*). She had the architect Philibert de l'Orme build her a new palace – the Tuileries – which became renowned for its magnificent gardens, complete with maze and grotto. In the 1570s she decamped to a splendid new residence, the Hôtel de Soissons, near to the Halles (of which all that remains is the astrological tower now attached to the Bourse de Commerce) (Ie.).

The classical features in the development of these royal palaces – Lescot had Jean Clouet provide superb sculptures for the Louvre frontage, for example – were also evident in the new Hôtel de Ville to which Francis committed the crown in 1529. Since the time of Étienne Marcel the municipality had been lodged in the so-called *Maison des Piliers* on the Place de Grève – now known as the Place de l'Hôtel-de-Ville (IVe.) – and the new building was erected just across the square from it, on the site of the present-day building. (The latter is an 'improved' replica, constructed after the original was burnt to the ground by the Communards in 1871.) Work on the site started in 1532 and lasted several decades. It followed plans drawn up by the Italian architect Boccador, and featured Corinthian columns and niched statues, these Italianate features contrasting pleasingly with the high French-style pitched roofs.

The showy brilliance of the Louvre and the Hôtel de Ville conformed to Francis's wider notions of Renaissance monarchy. Like fellow rulers across Europe, the Valois kings of France were increasingly seeking to burnish their reputations through display, in ceremony, buildings and court activity. Like other rulers, they sought to ground their cultural

activities in a rediscovered Antiquity. Humanism – the loose intellectual movement which sought out the most authentic texts from the
ancient world as a means of offering a pathway towards knowledge –
had spread widely within Europe, and particularly Italy, from the
fourteenth century onwards. Initially, however, it had experienced a
false start in France. In the late fourteenth and early fifteenth centuries,
the Collège de Navarre and the royal chancery had been the foci of a
new interest in the culture of the Ancients, which spilled into a concern
to develop a more individualized conception of piety – the so-called
devotio moderna. But the growing turbulence of the Hundred Years
War from the 1410s put paid to such developments. It was really
only from the end of the fifteenth century that Parisian intellectuals
reconnected to wider European intellectual currents. From 1494 military campaigning in the Italian peninsula brought the dynasty and the
political elite directly into contact with both Renaissance culture and
the Antiquity on which it was based.

A crucial stimulant in the development of humanism in France as
in Europe more widely was print. Printed books published in Germany
were available in Paris from the 1460s, and it was the advantage the
new technology offered in providing access to more, and more stable,
texts derived from Antiquity which led to two scholars from the
Sorbonne inviting German workers to Paris in 1470 to set up the first
printshop in the country. By the 1480s Paris was seventh in Europe in
terms of book production; by 1500 it was second only to Venice; and
during the sixteenth century it became the most prolific printing centre
in Europe, producing some 25,000 titles, as against Venice's 15,000.
Even in the early sixteenth century Paris possessed 102 presses, mostly
on the Left Bank, especially around the Rue Saint-Jacques. At one
time there were 160 printshops to be found in 80 houses along the
street. Initially, religion was at the heart of production, ranging from
exemplars of *devotio moderna* such as Thomas à Kempis's *Imitatio
Christi* and handbooks on the arts of dying through to weighty theological tomes. Yet print culture soon embraced far more than that:
staples in the 1490s were aimed at all purses and included the classics
of Antiquity, Arthurian romances, Villon's poetry, conduct books,
descriptions of royal ceremonials and even battlefield reports from
Charles VIII's Italian Wars. By the 1530s printed maps of the city

were appearing, and these became an important vector of Parisian propaganda about itself.

The humanist respect for Antiquity harmonized with the crown's wish to rethink the city in a new spirit of cooperation. Francis I, influenced by humanism and highly Italophilic (he imported both Leonardo da Vinci and the celebrated goldsmith Benvenuto Cellini to work for him), was also receptive to the ideas about urban renewal which he had seen being implemented within Italian Renaissance cities. The result was a quest to re-create Paris as a new Rome – indeed as better than Rome. The inspiration was reflected in a renewed interest in the history of the city, stressing its origins in mythic Troy (more ancient, and thus, it was now said, more prestigious than Rome). Some writers claimed an antediluvian origin for Paris, with the city allegedly tracing its origins back to Japhet, Noah's son, born before the Flood. Gilles Corrozet, writing in 1532, was only marginally less fanciful: the city was founded nearly a millennium after the Flood – though this still made it 70 years older than Troy and 498 years older than the so-called Eternal City of Rome.[3] These ingenious genealogies were exercises in political legitimation more than in grounded historical research.

An early cultural marker of the Valois dynasty's commitment to new ideas about urban space was the bridge erected to replace the Pont Notre-Dame, which had collapsed from storm damage in 1499. The new structure was built in stone between 1504 and 1512 according to plans drawn up by the Italian Fra Giocondo. Like the other Parisian bridges, it had houses on it, but what was new was that the sixty-eight houses were built according to the same model, containing a shop and arcade as well as living space. They formed a symmetrical and systematic series topped off at both ends with a monumental arch (another classical touch). The impact of the bridge on visual space was intensified by efforts to open up vistas towards it in a fashion which the Via Giulia in Rome had recently initiated. The Rue de la Juiverie – the present-day Rue de la Cité (IVe.) – on the Île de la Cité was widened and straightened, and in 1530 the 'false gate' of the old Philip Augustus Wall on the Rue Saint-Martin was demolished. These changes for 'the good, profit, utility and decoration of the city' made it possible to have an uninterrupted sight line from the Saint-Séverin church on the Left Bank through to the Saint-Martin gate in the Charles V Wall. The change was infectious, for in 1533 the city condemned all the Philip Augustus gates on the Right Bank, 'in order that the streets should be lighter, straighter and better aligned'.[4]

The opening out of the city was intended to allow the better display of royal power. From the fourteenth century in particular, it had become customary for monarchs to make formal ceremonial entries into the city. The most important of these *entrées* followed the coronation, when the whole city paid honour to the king, who in return confirmed urban privileges. But *entrées* also occurred for other signal royal events. They came to be played out with an international audience in mind, and publications described the order of march, the participants, the monuments traversed and so on. From the late fifteenth century, contemporaries referred to the *entrées* as 'triumphs'. This term highlighted a growing sense of majesty and *Romanitas* about the occasions, which were accentuated by the building of triumphal arches for the king to pass under. From 1531 the ceremonial route was redrawn so that the cortège passed over the Pont Notre-Dame, whose ceremonial arches were especially brilliant. The upper windows of the houses along the bridge were leased out to city councillors, affording them and their guests a grandstand seat for the procession.

The Roman motif influenced the content of the ceremonies. It had been the custom to stage little passion plays along the route, but these were outlawed by the Paris Parlement in 1549 as 'the mummeries of past times'.[5] They were replaced by more mythological and allegorical tableaux and dramas. These highlighted significant events in the life of the city – even though the allegorical content of the *entrées* was so abstruse that it defeated even the best educated of Parisians. One could just about calculate what was going on, for example, with the appearance of five horses bearing the words *Paix, Amour, Raison, Joye, Seureté* ('Peace, Love, Reason, Joy, Security') – the five initial letters added up to the word 'Paris'. But in the Louis XI *entrée* no one could quite work out the coded meaning of having three women naked to the waist at one point on the line of procession. One clearly baffled observer noted that they had 'fine breasts, standing out, separate, pink and firm (and it was extremely pleasing)'.[6] Perhaps this was allegory enough.

Urban improvement in the early sixteenth century extended beyond walls, gates and bridges. The quais on both the Left and the Right Banks were aligned, slightly raised (so as to reduce the risk of flooding) and, from the late 1520s onwards, paved. Water supply was a particular concern: there were seventeen public fountains in 1500 and these were embellished and added to: the most striking addition was the Fountain of the Innocents, which was erected close to the cemetery of the Innocents. It was on the route of the royal *entrée* of Henry II in 1549 and was adorned with statuesque nymphs carved by Jean Goujon. More mundane but also important in urbanization plans were efforts to produce more aligned housing frontages and to remove obstacles on public thoroughfares. Municipal edicts of 1554 and 1560 forbade overhanging eaves on houses in an effort to improve the amount of daylight reaching the street. There were also much-repeated orders for householders to put candles in their windows at night so as to make the streets more walkable and less dangerous. In 1506 a so-called 'mud tax' (*taxe aux boues*) was established to pay for a (still pretty rudimentary) street cleansing and waste disposal service.

The crown played a major role in these improvements and in the development of urban housing stock and new areas of habitation. This was achieved notably through the familiar process of *lotissement* – that is, the parcelling of land into small lots situated so as to face onto newly designed streets. Royal edicts in 1516 and especially 1543 put on the property market the remainder of the old Hôtel Saint-Pol, whose division had begun late in the fifteenth century, and other royal domain land within the capital. The death of Henry II in a freak jousting accident in 1559 led his widow, in the 1560s, to try to dispose of the Tournelles palace too – especially now the renovated Louvre was in place. If sales were poor (much of the area became a horse market), this was mainly because supply in the eastern zones had already been saturated by earlier *lotissement* – and because the area was incredibly smelly, as a consequence of the propinquity of the city gutter. The decision of the convent of Sainte-Catherine in the 1540s to raise money by selling its extensive *coutures*, turned market-gardens into prime real estate for precisely the kind of wealthy individuals attracted to Paris by the relocation of the royal court. The transformation of the *coutures de Sainte-Catherine* was remarkably rapid: Gilles

Corrozet noted in 1550 that 'the *couture* has been given over to building', and in 1561 was recording that 'there are now fine streets here and sumptuous dwellings'.[7] The area forms the heart of the present-day Marais, and it was precisely in this period that some of the often Italian-influenced architectural gems which still stud the neighbourhood were constructed: the Hôtel de Ligneris (the Hôtel de Sévigné, which now houses the Musée Carnavalet), for example, the Hôtel de Lamoignon, home to the Bibliothèque historique de la ville de Paris, and the Hôtel Donon, where the Musée Cognacq-Jay is located. The *lotissement* of the sprawling Barbette estate off the Rue Vieille-du-Temple in 1561 also attracted wealthy buyers of building plots.[8]

The monarchy's renovation of the Louvre meant that its neighbourhood and the area towards the Halles also began to attract wealthy hôtel-builders in the Marais mould. Francis I's disposal of the old Hôtel de Flandre and John the Fearless's Hôtel d'Artois (now known as the Hôtel de Bourgogne) provided new space for development.[9] In the 1550s, Henry II oversaw the redevelopment of the Halles, simplifying and improving the street system in a way which attracted housing clients into the area. The local parish church was the sumptuous Saint-Eustache, 'cathedral of the Halles', which was completely remodelled from 1532 onwards on a lavish scale.

Much of the new development was outside the city walls in the faubourgs (suburbs). In 1471 Louis XI's establishment in the Faubourg Saint-Antoine out beyond the Bastille of a 'liberty' under the protection of the female abbey of Saint-Antoine-des-Champs had allowed woodworkers and furniture-makers to establish businesses which were exempt from the city's corporate restrictions yet benefited from the closeness of the city's wood port and depot. Other faubourgs also boomed. To the west, the presence of the Louvre and the Tuileries stimulated growth along the Rue Saint-Honoré: the establishment of the parish church of Saint-Roch confirmed the neighbourhood's vitality.[10] Housing which developed outside the Saint-Denis gate on an old rubbish tip – a *Mons superbus* reached by the Rue Mont-Orgueil (IIe.) – expanded sufficiently for the area to become known as Villeneuve-des-Gravois, and to receive a parish church in 1563, Notre-Dame-de-Bonne-Nouvelle (IIe.).[11]

On the Left Bank the crown's influence was less strong. There was development close to the river in the west around the Tour de Nesle and the Rue Saint-André-des-Arts (VIe.), and on the eastern side the property of the Bernardins college from the Quai de la Tournelle up to the Rue Saint-Victor (Ve.) was sold off in lots. This whole area had long since spilled over its ramparts, leaving little room for *intra muros* development. Most growth consisted of a thickening of the existing faubourgs. The opening up of a ferry (*bac*), which allowed stone from Vaugirard to be transported across for the building of the Louvre and Tuileries, led to development of the hinterland around the new Rue du Bac (VIIe.). The reopening of the Porte de Buci (VIe.) in 1539 after a century of closure, and the establishment of a new gate in the west, the Porte de Nesle, eased communication with the city, encouraging wealthy nobles and state officials to lodge here or else to establish summer retreats. The lively Saint-Germain fair held in spring each year, and popular with princes and paupers alike, further boosted the vitality of the area, especially after 1511 when permanent shops were built. There was a good deal of *lotissement* from the Faubourg Saint-Jacques eastwards too, notably around the Rue Mouffetard. By the early sixteenth century a region called the Villeneuve Saint-René was forming beyond Rue Mouffetard, down to the Faubourg Saint-Victor and the present-day Jardin des Plantes (Ve.).

The location of the king and his court in Paris also provided a fillip to sectors of the city economy which supplied a growing demand for luxury commodities. Since the Middle Ages the crown had passed sumptuary legislation seeking to restrict private expenditure on luxury items for social and economic reasons. Sumptuary legislation was still recycled – in 1517, 1547, 1549 and 1567, for example – yet Parisians still found it easy to live it up. Paris was no longer a cloth-producing centre of note: the city's drapers imported cloths from Bourges, the Beauvaisis and Normandy and dyed and finished them. The clothing trades did particularly well, as the old custom of individuals having a single robe was being replaced by a move in elite circles towards more variety, with cut, cloth, colour – fashion, in fact – becoming paramount. Dyers, seamstresses, embroiderers and tailors now came into their own as never before, as did a dynamic second-hand clothes trade. There were a dozen shops selling feathers for hats – quite as many as those selling pen-quills.[12] The quality of the waters of the Bièvre for dyeing was already renowned, and the dyeing trade out at the Faubourg Saint-Marcel increasingly diversified into tapestry-making, in which the numerous Gobelin dynasty made a name for themselves. Francis I created a tapestry works at Fontainebleau, and Henry II opened another at the Trinité hospital on the Rue Saint-Denis (IIe.).

4.2: The River Bièvre

The history of Paris has been so closely bound up with the history of the river Seine that it is easy to forget the role played by other waterways: the network of rivers within the Paris basin putting Paris in touch with a broad hinterland, for example, and the Canals d'Ourcq, Saint-Denis and Saint-Martin around which much of the city's industrial prosperity in the nineteenth century was based. Not the least important river in the city's history has been the Bièvre, named (unlikely though this may seem) after the beavers (Celtic: *befar*) which lived here even before the Romans arrived. It has also been the most discreet of rivers – indeed, by the late twentieth century it had become invisible, paved over or diverted into storm drains.

The source of the Bièvre lies in the Versailles area, and the river wends its way into Paris from the south, crossing the present-day *boulevard périphérique* close to the Stade Charléty (XIIIe.), then moving north around the Butte-aux-Cailles, across the Boulevard Blanqui, and then following the edge of the Rue de Croulebarbe (named after a mill present on the site in the thirteenth century). Indeed the poplar trees in the Parc René-Le-Gall in that street are nourished by the now subterranean waters of the Bièvre. Crossing the Rue Mouffetard (Ve.) at the so-called Pont-aux-Tripes, the river originally reached the Seine around the Gare d'Austerlitz. However, in 1148 the monks of the abbey of Saint-Victor put in place a diversion which took water away from the river and ran it through their gardens, incidentally powering mills there too. This diversion changed the course of the river in such a way that it now reached the Seine more or

Tanneries on the river Bièvre, 19th century

less across from Notre-Dame – along what is now the Rue de Bièvre (Ve.). The erection of Charles V's Wall led to a further diversion of the waters too.

The uses of the river for industrial purposes was noted by others besides the monks of Saint-Victor. From the fifteenth century Bièvre waters were used by dyers, tanners and starch-makers from the Bourg (soon Faubourg) Saint-Marcel. The butchers who were located there also used the waters as a dump for their waste products. There resulted an unhealthy stench for which the river became famous (though river pollution did not prevent beer-makers also installing themselves in the neighbour-hood). Rabelais provided an inventive explanation for this unhealthy aspect of the river, according to which it had been formed by the collective urination of some six thousand dogs. In much the same spirit the seventeenth-century poet Claude Le Petit queried whether the stream more resembled mud or water, soot or ink. His conclusion was that it was in essence a chamber pot for pigs.

Nevertheless, the purity of the waters was what had attracted Flemish dyers and many of their ilk to the locality in the fifteenth century. This vocation for the river was confirmed in 1666 when Louis XIV's finance minister, Jean-Baptiste Colbert, purchased the dyeing works in the locality from the heirs of dyer Jean Gobelin and his peers, and instituted the Royal Manufactory of the Gobelins. The Gobelins specialized – as in fact it still does – in tapestries, combined with carpet-weaving and furniture-making. The Bièvre was thus a major and enduring source of employment on the Left Bank over many centuries. In 1860 the river supplied water and power for over one hundred factories or workshops within city limits, including 24 tanneries, 21 leather dressers, 9 specialists in leather-goods, 8 laundries, 4 dyers and 3 breweries. By the time that Marville photographed the site, the river looked like an industrial yard.

Despite the industrial uses of the river in its lower reaches, the river had retained something of a reputation as a rural backwater in the shadow of the city. Out beyond the present-day Boulevard

Auguste Blanqui (XIVe.), the river ran through a series of streams which iced over in winter – providing skating opportunities for Parisians, but also an ice industry provisioning the city (a function memorialized in the name of the Glacière area). Upstream too washerwomen had always scrubbed Parisian laundry clean and hung it out to dry. Here Jean-Jacques Rousseau botanized in the late eighteenth century. The wine-harvest (*sic*) was just over, he recalled, and 'the peasants were leaving the fields until the winter tasks. Still green and smiling, albeit leafless in part and almost deserted, the countryside presented throughout the image of solitude.' The Romantic writer Senancour similarly warmed to the memory of 'the most wooded, the nicest and the most tolerable sites of a region which is not beautiful but which is fairly agreeable and fairly varied'. Later in the nineteenth century, the aesthete J. K. Huysmans eulogized 'this strange river, this outlet of all kinds of filth, this cesspool the colour of slate and lead' as a last refuge of the countryside within the reach of Parisians.

Yet it was not just the countryside which was disappearing as a result of Parisian growth. So was the Bièvre. Work to canalize it and reduce pollution levels within it started from the 1840s. Although they were halted temporarily, by 1910 the whole of the river had been placed under stone and concrete. Factories could still draw on its waters. But the river had gone.

The monarchy's quest to impress through ostentatious display played neatly into the hands of the high-quality end of the city's luxury trades. Paris had long been famous for the quality of its goldsmiths: the introduction of hallmarks in 1506 led to Paris masters adopting as their own the dynastic fleur-de-lys – a satisfying emblem of the re-emerging crown–city contract. One estimate in the late sixteenth century put the numbers of goldsmiths at around 300, and there had probably been even more than this earlier in the century.[13] Artisans working with precious stones, ivory, glass and fancy metals were also much in demand, as were the products of the new trade of clock-making. A booming leisure industry was also developing, as was attested by the existence of over two hundred tennis courts (*jeux de paume*).

Economic boom conditions reaffirmed Paris's status as the largest city in Europe, a fact which the monarchy's relocation here helped to promote. Population was reaching pre-Black Death levels by late in the fifteenth century, but surged to unparalleled heights around 1560, when the city probably contained as many as 300,000 individuals. Around one French person in fifty was now a Parisian.

The Valois dynasty welcomed and stimulated urban development and economic growth. Yet successive rulers found it depressingly difficult to bring these teeming developments within the framework of a classic Renaissance city and also to cope with the social problems which ensued from urban dynamism. In 1548 Henry II expressed concern about the rate and direction of growth by forbidding new building in the faubourgs. Although the edict was reversed almost at once, it highlighted the anxieties which faubourg expansion caused. The faubourgs required protection and defence, which did not come cheap. There were a number of military scares throughout the first half of the sixteenth century following defeats at the hands of the English (in 1512 and 1523) and the Holy Roman Emperor. In 1536 Emperor Charles V reached Saint-Quentin and Péronne; in 1544, Château-Thierry; and in 1552, Metz. There was a growing sense of the inadequacy of the city defences. This focused on the Right Bank ramparts in that although the distended growth on the Left Bank had made the southern defences highly vulnerable, it was generally assumed attacks would come from the direction of the northern and eastern frontiers. Right Bank Paris was much bigger too. Desultory efforts to reinforce the ramparts in 1512, 1523 and the mid-1520s were given more urgency by invasion threats from the 1530s. From the early 1560s a new trench was dug which included the Left Bank faubourgs, while tentative steps were taken to extend the Right Bank wall so as to cover the Tuileries palace.

Besides security concerns which subverted the dynasty's Renaissance notions of a more open city, the 1548 edict on faubourg building highlighted other anxieties too. Trade regulations within the faubourgs were less restrictive and this inhibited the prosperity of *intra muros* artisans, and risked producing labour shortages. The excess population could be an added strain on urban provisioning, yet the faubouriens paid disproportionately low taxes. In addition the areas were a notorious haunt of the lawless, the delinquent and the diseased. The internal policing of the city was in a lamentable state too. In 1518 a gang of delinquents had burnt down the royal scaffold at the Halles – and murdered the executioner to boot. In 1534 another gang actually stole the royal dais from the Louvre palace.

Despite the appearance of a luxury-driven boom in the city, the economic processes in train produced victims as well as beneficiaries. For much of the century, real wages were falling for most of the Paris trades, partly as a result of increasing population and a growing supply of workers. The latter also found it difficult to integrate demobilized and deserted soldiers from the royal armies, who were a serious social menace. The conditions were in place for crime to prosper. Only in the late 1550s and early 1560s were systematic efforts made to reorganize and to professionalize the police forces of the capital so as to fit them for a widening range of duties.

The Renaissance project of opening up the city thus involved more attention being devoted to policing issues than the dynasty probably had wished. Beggars, vagrants and other undesirables were increasingly represented as a kind of polluted and polluting yeast embodying infectious disease, unlicensed vice and crime. In 1496 Charles VIII had decreed that all *pipeurs, ruffians et coquins* could be expedited to the galleys, and drives to expel similar undesirables became more intense from the 1520s. Toughness against beggars and vagrants extended to prostitutes. The ancient brothels of the Glatigny neighbourhood on the Île de la Cité were closed down in 1518. In 1561 the crown would outlaw brothels throughout France. In Paris the brothel trade had been diminished by the habit of devout Catholics of waiting outside the premises and raining down pious imprecations on any person entering or leaving.

For some time the city had been edging into charitable territory formerly dominated by the church. In 1505 municipal appointees were put in charge of the Hôtel-Dieu, whose management by the cathedral chapter had proved increasingly inept. New municipal regulations regarding public assistance were introduced from the 1530s, making poor relief an arm of city governance. Orphans and foundlings were a special object of concern: the Hôtel-Dieu's special service from 1535 was called the Enfants Rouges; from 1541 the hospital of the Saint-Esprit also started to admit them; and in 1545, the so-called Enfants Bleus service was established at the Trinité hospital out on the Saint-Denis road. In 1544 the Grand Bureau des Pauvres was established: a poor tax was to be collected, and charity was to be devoted solely to the deserving poor, with the able-bodied unemployed being set to work on public schemes. The aim was to put the 'undeserving' poor beyond all excuses, thus justifying harsher punishment.

This concern for the repression of socially marginal groups linked to measures of control against contagious diseases. Bubonic plague was still a recurrent nightmare. Concerted efforts were now made to control the disease, though it is unclear whether these did much to lessen its demographic impact. The use of neighbourhoods outside the city for quarantining victims of the disease had been tried out in 1496–7 and 1506 for the 'new disease' of syphilis, and the experiment was extended to plague victims from 1519. Locations outside Saint-Germain-des-Prés were used for this purpose. From 1531–3 the city council coordinated a wide raft of measures, in consultation with the crown and with Paris's medical faculty. There was a repressive aspect to plague policies that aimed to reduce human contacts regarded as dangerous – and thus linked to more general policing measures. Thus bath-houses, brothels and theatres were forced to close, while beggars and vagrants were expelled from the city (possibly taking the disease elsewhere – though that was elsewhere's problem).

These efforts to repress crime and vice, to control disease and to assist 'worthy' poverty were no more than a partial success, highlighting the fragility of the dynasty's achievement over the first half of the century in making Paris a Renaissance showcase of its power and prestige. The quest to reshape urban space and reconfigure the city in ways which evoked the grandeur of Antiquity had not produced durable results. The dynasty had devoted more time and money on its Italian Wars than on urban embellishment. Symptomatically, Francis I was to die in Rambouillet rather than Paris. Henry II did achieve the feat of dying in his capital city, yet it was out at the old Tournelles palace rather than in the refurbished Louvre.

For most of the sixteenth century, defective weapons of social control struggled to keep up with runaway population growth. Utopian ideals of urban renewal thus fell foul of unanticipated social and demographic developments. The crown seemed to be running ahead of popular taste too: for all the Italianate Renaissance influences in evidence on buildings sponsored by the crown, most of the churches built over the period preferred a flamboyant form of the gothic – still seen to brilliant effect at Saint-Germain-l'Auxerrois (Ie.), Saint-Eustache (IIIe.) and Saint-Étienne-du-Mont (Ve.)[14] Yet there was little change to Paris's overall urban landscape, which retained most of its medieval features. Indeed the city was essentially a medieval tapestry, studded with a number of Renaissance jewels.

If Paris thus continued to impress, it was less by its architectural distinction or cultural rebirth than by its sheer size: at 300,000 in the 1560s, it still towered over all French cities as well as its major European rivals. The legacy of the past thus overwhelmed the shock of the new – which was minimal. Paris was still a city, as Henry II put it, of 'mire, muck and filth'.[15] One of the reasons the dynasty moved to the more open, western side of the city had been the almighty stench in the Hôtels de Saint-Pol and des Tournelles caused by the open drain, the *Grand Égout*, which ran on the trace of the present-day Rue de Turenne (IVe.), and which caused fish which swam its way to die instantly.[16] The Spanish nobleman Gaspar de Vega passed through Paris in 1556 specifically to see the Louvre. The palace amounted to 'very little for such a great city', he wrote to King Philip II of Spain. 'I noticed no notable edifice at all, and the town presents nothing of interest save its size.'[17]

It was, however, the size and social dynamism of Paris which was to be put to the test in a different way from the 1560s onwards, as Renaissance ambitions for urban planning and cultural renewal gave way to a dynastic fight for survival. The premature death of Henry II in 1559 led to a generation of political uncertainty. Henry's fifteen-year-old son Francis II (r. 1559–60) lasted little more than a year, while his brother Charles IX (r. 1560–74) fell terminally ill shortly after his achievement of majority. Their reigns were marked by the forceful presence, as queen mother and sometime regent, of Catherine de' Medici, whose influence continued under her third son Henry III (r. 1574–89). Henry III was to die childless, and according to royal

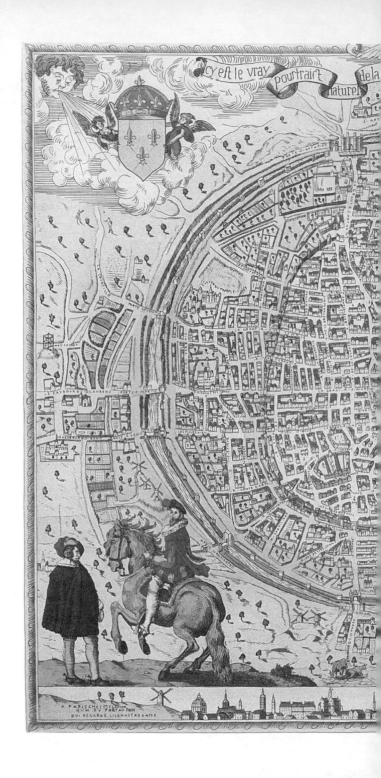

Icy est le vray pourtrait de la naturel

1576 plan of Paris

laws of succession, the throne should have passed uncontested to the collateral Bourbon branch, in the person of Henry, king of Navarre. Henry was, however, a Protestant – and thereby hung a tale. Following the Reformation sparked off by Martin Luther in Germany in 1517, religious disputes between Protestants and Catholics throughout France became increasingly venomous. Religious schism and dynastic struggles after 1560 mixed a cocktail which was well-nigh lethal for French stability – and Parisian prestige and prosperity.

The Protestant Reformation soon made an impact across France, and in Paris in particular. Luther's critique of the church became more extreme as his conflict with ecclesiastical authority became more bitter. Yet the spirit of much of what Luther had to say – if not the actual letter – chimed with pre-existing trends within French intellectual circles. The Lutheran quest for highly individualized forms of piety was an extreme version of the *devotio moderna* popular in humanist circles. Similarly, the close attention which humanist scholars paid to Greek and Hebrew as well as Latin texts had already been directed towards religious texts as well as the canonical works of Antiquity. The movement of ideas deriving from these developments linked with a continuing demand for reform of the church, which appeared in desperate need of revitalization. The national Estates General of 1484, for example, had berated the French church for decadence, and urged its reform.

The call for thoroughgoing and spiritually driven church reform was not unheeded within the French ecclesiastical establishment. Étienne Poncher, bishop of Paris from 1503 to 1519, for example, was vigorous in attacking delinquent and unworldly clerics and in reforming monasteries, literally breaking down monastic gates on occasion to do so. He also did his utmost to prevent the Sorbonne from condemning outright the Christian humanism of Erasmus and Lefèvre d'Étaples, whom some held were sailing close to the Lutheran wind. Lefèvre d'Étaples's pupil Guillaume Briçonnet, who had been abbot of Saint-Germain-des-Prés, was made bishop of Meaux in 1516 and tried to introduce reforms. Though the Sorbonne was intellectually etiolated at this time, some university colleges had welcomed new concepts of piety and become seedbeds for the Protestant message. Notable here were the Collège de Navarre and the Collège de Montaigu. The austere

life of piety created in the latter by the Flemish divine Jan Standonck
put the fear of both God and the college master into the young
Erasmus. The college, noted a Dutch visitor later in the century, seemed
'more like a prison for torture than an educational establishment'.[18]
At the Collège du Cardinal-Lemoine, German students were among
the first and most enthusiastic followers of Luther, whose writings
were now all the more widely diffused for being in print form. Johann
Gutenberg had laid the egg which Martin Luther was in the process
of hatching.

It was, significantly, the so-called Placards Affair of 1534, in which
printed posters (*placards*) attacking the Catholic belief in the mass
were posted around Paris, which led to a polarization of the religious
struggle. The conflict was already extremely bitter. The Sorbonne had
gone on the offensive in 1521, condemning both Luther and some of
the Christian humanist work of Lefèvre d'Étaples. Two years later
ensued the first burning of a Lutheran at the stake in Paris (alongside
mounds of books by Luther). There would be a string of others over
the 1520s. The desecration of a wayside statue of the Virgin Mary on
the Rue du Roi de Sicile in the Marais (IVe.) in 1528 led to a massive
Catholic outcry, and mass processions of repentance led by Francis I
himself, 'bareheaded with a torch in hand'.[19]

Despite these acrimonious and sometimes bloody exchanges, however, Catholics were far from having everything their own way in the
1520s and 1530s. Francis I's cultural outlook predisposed him towards
a degree of tolerance towards Christian humanism. In 1517 he had
created the Collège du Roi – now the Collège de France – outside the
framework of the university system, later endowing the new institution
with chairs in Greek and Latin as well as Hebrew studies and oriental
languages. The king's sister Marguerite of Angoulême, an accomplished poet in her own right and a major patron of the humanist
cause, was linked to the Meaux humanists under Briçonnet. She
protected a pupil of Lefèvre d'Étaples, Louis de Berquin, who had
translated Luther into French, from the Sorbonne's clutches (at least
for a time – he was executed in 1529). Marguerite married Henri
d'Albret, king of Navarre, in 1527, but continued to reside in Paris.
In 1533 she appointed her confessor Gérard Roussel, one of the Meaux
grouping, to preach a Lenten sermon which was widely regarded as

Protestant in its message. In the same year Nicolas Cop, the rector of the university, and a young lawyer from Noyon called Jean Calvin co-authored a university address in much the same spirit: they had to scamper across the rooftops to escape a mass round-up of Parisian Protestants. The two men fled eventually to Geneva, which was to become the spiritual home of French Protestantism.

The Placards Affair swung the political balance towards a Catholic cause newly energized by the iconoclasm of 1528. The king was said to be furious that one threatening poster had been unceremoniously plonked on the door leading to his own bedchamber. Widespread arrests of Protestant suspects ensued. Francis, who now declared he would send his own children to the stake if they strayed towards heresy, led a mass procession of repentance in January 1535. It climaxed (after a copious dinner) in the execution of six men who were alleged to have played a part in the affair. The anti-'Lutheran' net spread increasingly wide. Antoine Augereau, who in the past had published works by Marguerite d'Angoulême-Navarre, was burnt at the stake in November 1534. The first printer to be executed was followed in January 1535 by the first woman to receive the same punishment: schoolteacher Marie La Catelle had read the Gospel to her pupils in French and eaten meat on a Friday. From 1544 the Sorbonne drew up an 'Index' of prohibited books. Robert Estienne, who had been appointed royal printer in 1538, fled as a religious refugee to Geneva in 1551. If Francis I had grown increasingly impatient with dissident opinions before his death in 1547, his successor Henry II was even more aggressively intolerant. The *chambre ardente* ('burning chamber') which he established in the Louvre in 1547 conducted five hundred trials over a three-year period, and sent thirty-eight individuals to the pyre.

The 'Lutherans', moreover, were turning Calvinist. The now Genevan-based jurist Jean Calvin published his famous *Institutions of the Christian Religion* in 1536, offering both a refinement of Lutheran doctrine and a new form of church organization based on cellular communities of believers. By the mid-1550s there were four secret Calvinist churches in Paris, based in the Latin Quarter, which sought, in the words of one adherent, to work within structures 'as much as possible like the example of the early church at the time of the apostles'.[20] Proselytization by 'Huguenots' – as the Calvinists were called from around 1560 (for reasons which remain mysterious)[21] – was proving highly effective, notably among university students and individuals who worked within the print industry and the royal administration (including the Paris Parlement). Public Huguenot preaching was banned by the authorities. Yet it went on in secret tavern rendezvous and out at the Pré-aux-Clercs on the Left Bank, in the less guarded faubourgs, notably around Saint-Médard on the Rue Mouffetard, and in country houses of Calvinist supporters out at Popincourt. The work of conversion attracted an increasingly popular following. In 1559 a national synod meeting in Paris brought together representatives from some seventy-two churches, and the national network hereby established could by 1561 boast more than 1,200 communities, and a total population of at least a million individuals.

The bold resistance of the Huguenot community was buttressed by the emergence in the 1550s of new converts from within the social and political elite. A raid on a Huguenot gathering on the Rue Saint-Jacques in 1558 revealed a score of nobles among the participants. Supporters in high places included the queen of Navarre Jeanne d'Albret (Marguerite d'Angoulême's daughter), her husband Antoine de Bourbon, a leading representative of the collateral branch of the Valois line, and his brother the prince de Condé, plus the doughty Gaspard de Coligny, war veteran and Grand Admiral of France. Coligny and Condé, together with the Catholic Chancellor Michel de l'Hôpital, were the leading figures on the regency council of Charles IX's mother Catherine de' Medici and preached counsels of toleration. However, the Colloquy of Poissy at the end of 1561 between representatives of both sides failed to find the basis of agreement. Matters were aggravated by a series of incidents including Protestant and Catholic atrocities and burnings in the parish of Saint-Médard from late 1561 and an outrage in March 1562, in which the troops of the Catholic paladin, the duc de Guise, attacked a Protestant assembly at Wassy in Champagne, leading to dozens of deaths. Against this background, crown legislation allowing concessions to the Huguenots was like a red rag to the Catholic bull.

Symptomatically, it was the 'massacre of Wassy' rather than the Saint-Médard 'atrocities' which proved the trigger for religious war.

For whereas in the first decades of Reformation, Paris had been at the heart of the humanist, then Lutheran, then Calvinist projects, the capital city was gradually becoming less pivotal in the evolution of religious conflict. Some eight religious wars would unfurl between 1562 and 1598, dotted with truces and peaces and vain attempts to heal the confessional divide. The theatre for those wars was the country as a whole. Within this generous arena the conflicts would pit faith against faith and political dynasty against political dynasty. While the Bourbon house, now centred on the petty Pyrenean kingdom of Navarre, became the champion of the Huguenot cause, the powerful Guise family, which had extensive possessions in northern and eastern France, headed the hard-line Catholic cause, with the Montmorencies (including Coligny) oscillating between the two. Above it all, and desperately trying to keep some kind of confessional balance and to prevent the monarch becoming a prisoner of faction, was Catherine de' Medici. Yet her failure to come down on one side or the other only dismayed both sides and encouraged them to think in terms of self-determination.

The regent's assumption of the title of 'Mother of the City of Paris' in 1563 was to prove about as futile a political gesture as one could imagine in such circumstances. Indeed the resolution of the wars became all the more problematic as Paris became identified body-and-soul with the Catholic side. A single crucial event effectively wiped out the Huguenot cause in a city which had hitherto been pivotal to its success. That event was the massacre of Saint Bartholomew's Day in 1572, which left a deep scar on the city of Paris and on the religious and political history of France. In the previous decade the Huguenots had come to represent a powerful military and political force within France. A great many cities particularly in the south and south-west declared for the Huguenot cause, and powerful dynasts – notably Condé and Coligny – provided them with protection and with their main force. There seemed no military solution available to the crown, for it proved difficult to find the resources to keep an army in the field, let alone guarantee its fidelity. Catherine found it impossible to work out a solution which matched the shifting factional balance with the strength of local feeling at grassroots level. In the battle of Saint-Denis in 1567 Parisian bourgeois militias had successfully resisted the

Huguenot attempt to seize Paris, but only at great human cost, which embittered Parisian Catholics. In an effort to circumvent another such assault, the queen regent sought to calm down factional strife by arranging the marriage of King Charles IX's sister Marguerite de Valois with Jeanne d'Albret's son Henry of Navarre, a leading Huguenot. They were to be wed in Notre-Dame cathedral in August 1572.

The political situation swiftly turned ugly. Historians still debate the participants' degree of responsibility for the events which followed. It would seem that at an early stage the ultra-Catholic leaders resolved to murder an indeterminate number of their opponents, most prominent among whom was Admiral Coligny, who appeared to have won a dominant voice on the regency council. Whether the plotters were merely profiting from the presence of large numbers of Huguenot noblemen in the city for the first time for the wedding festivities, or else genuinely afraid that these were about to commit a *coup d'état*, is moot. An assassination attempt on Coligny on 22 August failed, but only spurred on the Catholic plotters, with some tacit support from the young Charles IX – and a great deal from his mother. On Saint Bartholomew's Day, 24 August 1572, the dawn tolling of the bell of the church of Saint-Germain-l'Auxerrois, adjacent to the Louvre, was the signal for Catholic vigilantes to set about a systematic butchery of Huguenots within the city. Henry of Navarre and the young prince de Condé were spared, but only as bargaining tools and on the understanding that they would convert to Catholicism forthwith. Coligny was defenestrated, and his body defiled: 'his head was removed and his shameful parts cut off by [hundreds of] small children.'[22]

'The killing of all the Huguenots continued all day Sunday and on the next day which was a Monday,' noted a Catholic chronicler in chillingly matter-of-fact style.[23] The violence appeared to have been legitimized by the king: 'Kill them all, the king commands it,' Guise had ordered.[24] At one stage, matters looked to be getting out of hand as plebeian Catholics, profiting from the general lawlessness, started attacking and sacking the homes of wealthy Catholics as well as Huguenots. Lawlessness was such that Geitzkofler, a terrified German witness, noted, 'whoever had an enemy could have him cut to pieces by calling him a Huguenot.'[25] The Seine ran red with the blood of corpses dumped in the river. It was, one charmless ditty put it, a way of 'taking the news to Rouen [a Protestant stronghold] without a boat'.[26] Semi-curfew conditions lasted for several weeks, but by the evening of 27 August, between 1,500 and 2,000 Huguenots had been massacred – contemporary accounts set the level even higher – in conditions of the most ghastly cruelty.

Saint Bartholomew's Day was a massive setback to the Protestant cause, for it had wiped out their political cadres at a stroke. When combined with the killing of between 8,000 and 10,000 Huguenots in provincial cities sparked off by the Parisian massacre, it constituted the single greatest atrocity in the confessional wars of Reformation Europe – a bloody accolade in the context of conflicts which were far from anemic. Parisian Catholics, accustomed to superlatives, seemed actually to glory in the event: 'full of wellbeing', Geitzkofler noted, 'the population cried Vive le Roy! as if the massacre had been praise-worthy.'[27] It also effectively ended the Huguenot cause within Paris. The city passed from being the city of religious confrontation between two communities into the fanatical cheerleader for the Catholic cause in general and the Guise clan in particular.

After 1572 much of the military action of the Wars of Religion passed into the south and west of France, as dreary truce followed sporadic fighting, and with a new king, Henry III (r. 1574–89), who found it too expensive to keep an army in the field in a way which would command respect from both sides. The Estates General which Henry convoked in 1576 proved a platform for the expression of views soon to be known as politique – that is, in favour of a return to political stability and some form of religious toleration. But the politiques as yet lacked the battalions available to the Catholic and Huguenot causes. There was talk of Huguenots establishing a new state in the southern half of the kingdom on the lines of the Dutch 'United Provinces'. Catholic opposition to the plan was uncon-ditionally hostile. From 1584, moreover, the Huguenot commitment to the integrity of the French state was strengthened by the fact that the death of Henry III's younger brother the duc d'Anjou made Henry of Navarre, as a Bourbon (his mother, Jeanne d'Albret had married Antoine de Bourbon), the rightful heir to the throne. It was widely assumed that Henry III – despite much worthy effort – would fail to produce an heir. For a time the shape, functional viability and sexual preferences of the king's penis had become a hot topic of secret diplomatic exchanges, but by 1584 most European statesmen had written off the organ as terminally defective.

The political stakes were consequently much higher after 1584 – and those stakes included Paris, for the capital's assent to any political arrangement involving a Protestant seemed both essential and extremely unlikely. Paris, a magistrate from the Parlement told one of the Guise clan, the duc de Mayenne, 'is the first flower in your hat. If you lose it, our party will at a stroke lose its credibility with all other cities.'[28] Faced with the possibility of the Navarre succession, the Catholic cause set down a marker, when the most eminent members of the Guise clan – notably Henry, duc de Guise 'le Balafré',[29] and Mayenne, his younger brother – signed a secret treaty at Joinville with representatives of the king of Spain committing them all to 'the conservation in perpetuity of the Catholic religion'. This *Sainte Ligue* – the 'Holy League' – providing international endorsement for the unity and catholicity of the French state was a daunting blow for Henry of Navarre – but also, in some measure for Henry III.

4.3: Henry III

'Oh, ungrateful city! I have loved you more than my own wife!' This regretful expostulation by Henry III was perhaps less of a compliment to the city of Paris than it appears, for Henry married against his will, soon abandoned his partner and lived apart from her all his life. Furthermore, he rubbed in his disenchantment by continuing to nurture a long list of lovers, both male (the *mignons*, or 'darlings'), and female. Yet however we judge his remark, it remains true that Henry III was one of the great unrequited lovers of the city of Paris. Brought up in the Louvre, to whose embellishment he gave affectionate attention, Henry studied his capital's history carefully and appreciated its intellectual and cultural atmosphere. He was also a devoted *flâneur* – a leisurely stroller in Parisian streets – who relished the bustle and sociability of the busiest neighbourhoods, revelled in the fun to be had at events such as the riotous Saint-Germain fairs each spring, and even initiated a Parisian craze with his love of bilboquet, the cup-and-ball child's game. It was he who began work on the Pont-Neuf, the great bridge linking Left and Right Banks with the Cité – but typically his successor Henry IV took all the credit for its completion.

Henry took the role of Renaissance monarch seriously. He enriched the cultural life of the city with music, court masques and festivals and a (soon-aborted) academy, the *académie du palais*. But it was his courtiers and cronies who most profited from his predilections. His emphasis on Renaissance-style court entertainments cut him off from the people of Paris, as did his attachment to matters of etiquette which prefigured court protocol under Louis XIV. His sense of exclusion accounts for the absence during his reign of royal *entrées*, a favoured form of festive urban inclusivism. His love of fine clothes, jewellery, earrings, facial cosmetics and other expensive fashionable Italian imports Parisians found difficult to stomach. Parisian xenophobia was amplified by the fact that the king relied heavily on Italian financiers.

The Parisians reproached Henry for his lack of orthodox piety. Yet this Renaissance princeling was also a committed Counter-Reformation ruler. He probably played a key personal role in the Saint Bartholomew's Day Massacre, and was a devout Catholic who introduced new forms of piety into the city, notably the confraternity of penitents copied from Saint Charles Borromeo of Milan. He urged the French church to adopt the Counter-Reformation edicts of the Council of Trent. On occasions he lurched hectically from hedonism into bouts of austere piety – though he found that this trait annoyed Parisians even more. After 1583 this arch-*flâneur* could no longer walk the streets of Paris without protection. In 1588 he fled the rebellious city to save his life, as the English gentleman Robert Dallington later noted, 'in his doublet and hose and one boote off for haste'.

Henry faced an unenviably difficult task as ruler of a polity saturated with religious violence that crippled the machinery of government, and which was already suffering acute economic problems. He was temperamentally ill-suited for the delicate game of balance which politics had become by the 1580s. 'What I love', he proclaimed, 'I love extremely' – and Paris had too many of its own extremes to take to those of Henry III. A wave of League pamphleteering ruined his reputation long before his death in 1589, which took place outside his beloved Paris. Although the loyalist Parlement of Paris hanged the lawyer Le Breton for sleazy attacks on the king's reputation, crowds of Parisians came to kiss the feet of the swinging corpse. By 1589 Parisian preachers were calling for the assassination of the 'tyrant'; public prayers were said beseeching his death; and when that death came, it was greeted with great pleasure within his beloved capital.

Henry's lifestyle and above all his free-wheeling sexuality was what irked Parisians most, and their shock has been echoed down the ages by some rather strait-laced historians. Sodomy was seen not only as a form of social deviance but also as outright heresy, and the fact that Henry was widely accounted to be *un bougre* gave carte blanche to his opponents to damn him in any way they could – as transvestite, dissembler, devil worshipper, black magician, murderer, and much more besides. Rarely can a ruler so committed to his capital have drawn such sweeping condemnation.

Despite his own genuine affection for Paris, Henry III was increasingly unpopular within the city. His bisexual escapades disenchanted pious Parisians. A growing swell of discontent focused on the lavishness of a royal court which seemed to be parasitic on the body politic. Taxes were high, state rentiers were not being paid regularly, while the overuse of venality of office had caused the public-service ethic to be lost in a welter of corruption and sleaze. Nor could royal justice be counted on: it was expensive, tardy and partial. The crown's resort to Italian financiers also nourished a latent Parisian xenophobia.

Since the eradication of the Huguenot cause from the city in the 1572 massacre, most Parisians were supportive of the 'Ultra' Catholic position represented by the Guise faction, and found Henry's more accommodating attitude towards his Huguenot subjects increasingly intolerable. Even though the king was forced to ally with the Guises in 1585, to accept the League, and to allow Guise supporters in provincial cities wide-ranging rights of self-organization, this only encouraged the Ultra opposition.

More than a touch of religious fanaticism was rooting itself in the city. Prodigious wonders and portents of disaster were widely reported and collectively viewed – strange lights, flying dragons, figures seen fighting in the clouds, and so on. It was confidently asserted that the city contained some 30,000 witches, organized under a king.[30] On the day after the Saint Bartholomew's Day Massacre, a dead hawthorn tree in the cemetery of the Innocents had suddenly blossomed. This was taken as a sign of divine approbation for the previous day's activities, and the tree became a popular pilgrimage site. A kind of processional frenzy increasingly gripped the city. In the early 1580s there were 'white processions' of peasants seeking 'to pacify [God's] ire and to preserve the poor people from the contagion of the plague'[31] – as pestilence, dearth and famine added to political calamities. The days were too short for all the processions Parisians seemed to want: parish priests were woken up in the middle of the night to lead nightshirt processions through the streets (though these were stopped after a while because of some unwanted pregnancies). The processions were often the work of religious confraternities. This ancient form of spiritual sociality had been revitalized in the movement of Counter-Reformation, and proved an important organizing framework for religious activism. Henry III had himself actually contributed to the movement by popularizing in the city confraternities of penitents, who did good works from behind slit-eyed hoods. A millenarian strain increasingly evident in Ultra propaganda glorified Paris as the new Jerusalem. Ideas of the Renaissance city as the new Rome seemed very far away.

In this context there was therefore something poignantly elegiac about the eulogy for the city which the writer Michel de Montaigne penned in the aftermath of the Saint Bartholomew's Day Massacre.

Humane and tolerant, Montaigne's words are overlaid with a familiar nostalgia for better times:

> However much I rebel against France, I look warmly on Paris. It has had my heart since I was a child . . . The more I have seen other fine cities, the more Paris's beauty gains in my affections. I love it for itself, and for itself alone. I love it tenderly warts and all. I am only French through this great city . . . the glory of France and one of the noblest ornaments of the world. May God drive out of it all divisions![32]

This was indeed a pious wish for a city which increasingly took pride in being 'the goal and fortress of all christendom'[33] – Catholic christendom, that is. From the mid- to late 1580s onwards the Catholic cause was passing into the hands of a clandestine organizing committee known as the '*Seize*' ('the Sixteen': indicating the widespread basis of their support in the city's sixteen neighbourhoods). These men, in the main of Parisian stock and from solid bourgeois backgrounds, consolidated the League position and spread its influence among the lower orders. They issued black propaganda about Huguenot atrocities and intentions, causing the printing presses to work over-time: 'the braziers of rebellion', opined Pierre de l'Estoile, a *politique*, originated in 'discourses, replies, memoranda and apologias'.[34] The League also worked hand-in-glove with parish priests who preached hellfire sermons increasingly targeting the king as well as Henry of Navarre. The impassioned stamina of these League preachers im-pressed the Venetian ambassador: they spoke, he noted in wonder-ment, 'for three or four hours at a time, without even spitting: a truly amazing feat'.[35]

In May 1588, stung by the way in which the popular Guises were openly flaunting their disobedience, Henry III attempted a *coup de force* against the capital, sending royal Swiss troops into all the neigh-bourhoods. He only succeeded in triggering a popular insurrection: chains were put up across the streets and barricades were built – a significant first in Parisian history – so as to inhibit troop mobility and to prevent lawless elements in the population taking any initiatives. The Swiss soldiers were massacred in droves. Cowering in the Louvre, Henry realized the game was up and fled the city (for ever, as it would prove), leaving the League cause triumphant. Paris was in a condition of wilful kinglessness, and would remain thus until the moment in 1594 when Henry of Navarre – from 1589, King Henry IV (r. 1589–1610) – entered the city.

The apparently unconditional nature of Parisians' rejection of both Henry III and Henry IV was seen in growing support for the idea of electing a Guise monarch. Such thoughts were dealt a mighty blow by Henry III in December 1588. The king had manoeuvred with some adroitness since fleeing Paris, attracting support from within the Parlement of Paris and building up anti-League feeling throughout France. In December 1588 during the Estates General that he had convoked, he cunningly drew Henry Balafré and his brother the Cardinal de Guise into his palace at Blois and had them assassinated. 'So dies the king of Paris,' Henry III is alleged to have said, with his rival's body motionless at his feet. 'I have killed [the duke],' he informed his mother. 'I want to be king, not a prisoner nor a slave . . . Now I begin to be king again.'[36]

The deaths were greeted with anti-monarchical horror in Paris: 'from the smallest to the greatest, everyone burst out crying.'[37] The League proclaimed Henry of Navarre's uncle, the Ultra-Catholic Cardinal Charles de Bourbon, as the rightful successor. This move, whose constitutional legality was debatable, threw Henry III temporarily at least into the Protestant camp. He joined Henry of Navarre in marching on Paris in the summer of 1589. It seemed clear that for political authority to be re-established in France as a whole, the capital's wild independence would have to be curbed.

Paris was both potential victim and principal prize in what was to prove the end-game of the Wars of Religion. Any chance of the *politiques* developing a groundswell of support was, however, at least temporarily halted. For on 2 August 1589 Henry III was assassinated. His murderer, the monk Jacques Clément, was enthusiastically hailed in Paris as a miracle-worker sent by God. Significantly, however, the dying monarch had recognized Henry of Navarre as his successor – a long-term *politique* master-stroke which Huguenot propaganda did everything to exploit.

It would take Henry IV nearly a decade to stabilize the political system and establish religious peace. These were years which he spent very largely on campaign around the country, and military success was a crucial part of this story. Henry regarded the winning over of Paris as essential for the claiming of his inherited right to the throne. But Paris was not easily wooed. Parisians were hardly well-disposed to the Huguenot 'Pretender', especially as the latter had just been besieging them alongside their *bête noire* Henry III. The Navarrois decided to try force over seduction. He gathered new troops in Normandy and returned to besiege Paris again. He defeated Mayenne at the battle of Arcques, took Saint-Denis, captured all the adjacent villages and overran the feeble outer faubourg defences, causing a great deal of wanton destruction. He actually looked down on the hostile city from the tower of the abbey-church of Saint-Germain-des-Prés; but his artillery could not shift the Philip Augustus Wall here, which led him to accept that military assault was unviable. He settled down to a prolonged siege of a city inhabited by 'a mutinous populace, lacking form, order or reason'.[38]

The siege of 1590 brought out tensions within the city. Parisians had reacted to the loss of its Guise leaders by establishing the 'Council of the Forty' (*Conseil des Quarante*), a kind of war cabinet of local notables including three bishops and seven high nobles, who appointed Guise's younger brother the duc de Mayenne as military commander. The parish clergy, fanatical supporters of the League, organized massive street processions to maintain morale – which did, however, begin to crack. With the Seine coincidentally running low because of drought, the lack of food supplies was soon driving the inhabitants to eat every animal that moved within the walls, down to horses, cats, dogs and rats. 'I myself saw,' stressed an Italian witness to the siege, individuals biting into living dogs because they could not afford to buy wood to cook them. 'And several fed themselves with cats, that they ate at home,' reported another witness.[39] As many as 30,000 individuals may have died in these famine conditions, and taken together with those who fled (and whom initially Henry had let leave), the city's population shrank from 300,000 to 200,000. War-weary voices, at first only muffled, began to be heard calling for 'bread and peace'.

The siege was lifted when the duke of Parma brought Spanish troops within the vicinity of Paris, causing Henry IV to retreat. The Leaguers were still in command, and presided over an ever more terroristic programme of spiritual renewal. They sniffed out *politique* plotting wherever they perceived opposition to their own position. In one incident in November 1591 they even purged the Paris Parlement of magistrates whom they adjudged to have sold out to the enemy. The execution of the parlementaires, which shocked bourgeois opinion, caused Mayenne to react strongly. Yet by punishing League extremists, he only heightened growing tensions within the city. The death of the individual whom the League championed as royal pretender – the doddery 'Charles X', Cardinal Charles de Bourbon – added to League woes, since there was no obvious candidate left, and the growing interest of the king of Spain in the issue raised fears that Paris was becoming a Spanish puppet. Always a makeshift coalition anyway, the League turned highly fissiparous. Under surface loyalty to the Ultra position, moreover, a peace movement was taking shape.

By March 1592 cracks within the League had widened sufficiently for Mayenne to begin negotiating with Henry IV. The issue of Henry's abjuration of Protestantism was soon aired. In July 1593 the Navarrois converted to Catholicism, formally abjuring at Saint-Denis – a site he had chosen because of its hallowed associations with the monarchy. It is difficult to plumb the depths of any person's religious convictions, particularly when they were under the kind of conflicting pressures which surrounded Henry after more than three decades of confessional strife. Yet his famous comment that Paris was 'worth a mass' was probably less glib than it sounded.

On 22 March 1594 Henry entered Paris. He was cautious about the manoeuvre, suspecting there would be military opposition, but there was none to speak of. Indeed Parisians now seemed more than resigned to see him: happy in fact. He manifested his good intentions by conspicuously playing the role of a Catholic ruler. He went straight to Notre-Dame to hear mass; he washed the feet of the poor on Maundy Thursday; he touched for the 'King's Evil'; and he ostentatiously attended Easter communion. By deliberately using the most historic – and Catholic – rituals and ceremonies of the monarchy, he aimed to make whole again the rent body of the state.

The new king flaunted a sense of forgiveness, so as to win Parisian support. His first Parisian royal declaration set an example of deliberate royal amnesia. It was not the first time during the Wars of Religion that such formulas of forgetting had been deployed. But it was the case which counted. 'His Majesty,' it was declared, 'wishing to unite all his subjects, notably the bourgeois and inhabitants of his good city of Paris, and to allow them to live in amity and harmony, wishes and intends that everything which has occurred since the troubles began should be forgotten.'[40]

Henry's capture of the French capital had made his wrapping up of the Wars of Religion only a matter of time. By 1598 the Edict of Nantes re-established a regime of formal toleration of religious diversity which was to prove long-lasting. There was no one left to fight. But Henry appreciated that the thought of his new dynasty losing the capital was too dreadful to contemplate. He realized that he had made Parisians suffer in the past. And he now wanted to make it up to them. His reign was to witness a Parisian rebirth more significant than the Renaissance. And the reforms he and his successors were to introduce proved more long-lasting – especially in the light of the appalling events of Saint Batholomew's Day and the official cult of amnesia proclaimed by the new king – than even the Reformation. Paris's future would lie as a new Rome, not a new Jerusalem.

5

Grand Siècle, Great Eclipse
1594–1715

The city which Henry IV 'of Navarre' (r. 1589–1610) won to his cause in the Wars of Religion was in pretty bad shape. Under the Navarrois and his son and successor Louis XIII (r. 1610–43), it bounced back energetically, going on to enjoy a dynamic period of growth. There was a marked surge in population, especially before 1650: demographic recovery after the 1589–90 siege was swift, and by 1600 the city was seemingly up to its 1560 level of 300,000; by 1680 it had reached half a million. The city's surface area grew even faster, at least doubling over the period as a whole. Much of the new building was of high quality, and indeed still gives the neighbourhoods of central Paris much of their charm. The close correlation between Parisian prosperity and the dynasty's commitment to its capital city seemed to be holding good once again. With 'Sun King' Louis XIV (r. 1643–1715) – initially at least – ensconced in the capital, science, ideas, literature and the fine arts all enjoyed an especially fertile period. The so-called *grand siècle* was also characterized by a formidable build-up of the state – the number of royal officials doubled between 1560 and 1640, for example – and by the consolidation and expansion of French territories.

Jean-Baptiste Colbert, Louis XIV's principal minister from the 1660s until his death in 1683, drew on the legacy of his master's royal predecessors in explicitly setting out to renew the dynasty's engagement with Renaissance ideals of the city. By the third quarter of the seventeenth century, indeed, the pieces seemed to be coming together to make of Paris a new Rome, a new eternal city – 'not buried in its own ruins' like the Italian metropolis, as a travel writer had put it in 1643, but, instead, 'numerous in its citizens, superb in its buildings and magnificent in its churches and religious houses'.[1] With its mixture of political strength, cultural allure and international recognition as a great power, Paris was, opined Louis XIV's great military engineer Vauban, 'the true heart of the kingdom, the common mother of all Frenchmen and the condensation of France itself'. The legist Julien Brodeau would in 1669 similarly salute Paris as 'the France of France', 'the capital of the kingdom, the centre of the state, . . . the source of law, the common fatherland of all Frenchmen, the pole of all the world's nations'.[2]

In the event *Louis le Grand* ('Louis the Great') – and Parisians were the first (in 1672) to accord Louis XIV that sobriquet – flattered only to deceive. Initially attracted by Colbert's notion that the glorification of France's capital city would add to his own and his dynasty's lustre, the king subsequently chose to abandon Paris for a new site made specifically to his measure, the palace of Versailles. Despite the cultural éclat of the city in the period, from the 1680s the city witnessed relative eclipse in the face of the new court-based city of Versailles, the solar temple where the Sun King spent all of his time. If for one high state servant in 1697, Paris was still 'the foremost city of the world', Versailles was, he asserted, of its type 'the first, the greatest and the most magnificent in all the world'.[3] By then another kind of eclipse was also on the horizon, moreover: after more than half a millennium of being the largest city in Europe, Paris was being approached and would soon be overtaken in size by London.

If this late twist in the story of Paris at the end of the seventeenth century seemed like a political renunciation on the part of the Bourbon dynasty, it had not started out like that. Indeed Henry IV showed an almost unconditional commitment to his capital city. Paris's importance in terms of the régime's legitimacy and strength had been underlined in the last stages of the wars. Henry appointed himself the city's governor and made it the lynchpin of his efforts at national recuperation. In phrasing which echoed the epochal remarks of Francis I in 1528, he stated his intention of 'spending his time and residing in this city . . . and rendering [it] beautiful and full of all the decoration and utility possible'.[4] (As with Francis, incidentally, this promise was marked more in the breach than in the observance, for Henry spent a good deal of his time in rural retreats in the Île-de-France.) The

ambitious new king strove to shape the city so that it could match the grandeur to which he aspired for the nation and for his dynasty. In the year of his death a pamphlet would note that 'from the moment [Henry IV] became master of Paris, we have seen nothing but builders at work'.[5] His considerable efforts at construction and reconstruction were to be taken still further by his son Louis XIII. Both Louis XIII and his successor Louis XIV came to the throne as infants; their regents – Marie de' Medici in the case of Louis XIII (1610–17) and Anne of Austria in that of Louis XIV (1643–51) – also played an important role in ensuring this continuity. Major players in this respect too were the crown's cardinal ministers, Richelieu, whose ascendancy lasted from 1624 to 1642, and Mazarin, in post from 1642 to 1661.

Henry IV took Francis I's cue in seeking to make the Louvre the splendid centre-piece of his power. The new king began the palace's refurbishment almost as soon as he had entered Paris in 1594, and went on to build a long, quarter-mile gallery to connect up with the Tuileries palace erected by Catherine de' Medici. The gallery was turned into a series of workshops for luxury artists and artisans – but it also made a good escape route in the event of political crisis. Its beauty was observable from the new Pont Neuf – the bridge, begun by Henry III in 1578, linking Left Bank to Right via the tip of the Île de la Cité. Work had ceased in 1588 as religious strife in Paris reached fever-pitch, but Henry got the builders straight back to work after conquering the city. By 1603 the king was nimbly prancing across the almost-finished bridge (though others who sought to follow his example fell off and ended up in the Seine). In 1606 it opened to acclaim.

5.1: The Pont Neuf

The Pont Neuf was the Eiffel tower of the Ancien Régime. Endlessly reproduced in engravings, paintings, sketches and urban landscapes, it was one of the first Parisian monuments to be captured on a panoramic photograph – and photography further extended its fame. Its shape and situation were well known enough to brook no uncertainty. Like the Eiffel tower, it evoked Paris. Indeed, it *was* Paris.

In 1991 film-maker Leos Carax produced a stir when for his film *Les Amants du Pont-Neuf* ('The Lovers of the Pont Neuf'), he recreated the bridge in all historical exactness in a chalk pit near Aix-en-Provence. Yet much of the fuss missed the point. Because of the passage of years, the material components of the original Pont Neuf have been wholly renewed more than once. Not a stone on the twenty-first century structure remains in place from the 'New Bridge' created by Henry III and Henry IV (though several of its decorations adorn Parisian museums). All the *mascarons* – its decorative, open-mouthed gargoyle heads – were renewed in the 1850s. Even the bronze statue of Henry IV is ersatz: the 1614 original was melted down for cannon in 1792 for the revolutionary armies, and the current replacement was erected only in 1818. Yet in a way this concern for exact veri-similitude – both in its conservationists and its film-makers – attests to the affection which Parisians, at least until relatively recently, have accorded the structure, or at least the shape of the structure.

When it was opened in 1606 the Pont Neuf represented – as would the Eiffel tower in 1889 – something special. The longest of Parisian bridges at 278 metres and the widest at 28 metres, it was the first to be built without overhanging houses on it. This made it both a royal and a Parisian bridge: for it was financed by the king not out of selling bridge-houses but by means of city-dwellers' regular taxes. The absence of houses made crossing the Pont Neuf an alfresco adventure for Parisians (especially as what Laurence Sterne called the 'unpremeditable puffs' of wind on the bridge often threatened the removal of hats and wigs). The existence of pavements on each side – a Parisian first too – and the presence of shops in the *demi-lunes* (the semi-circular space above each bastion) helped make it seem like a promenade as well as a piazza. The Samaritaine – the first functioning Parisian water-pump drawing water from the river, decorated with a sculpture of the Good Samaritan – was established in 1608. It helped the bridge to become famous for being crowded – and crowded for being famous. A German visitor in the early seventeenth century recorded the Parisian proverb according to which there was 'not a moment of the day on which one did not see [on the bridge] a carriage, a white horse, a priest and a prostitute'. Taken as a whole, moreover, the bridge represented a decent political allegory: a new means of communication joining together in harmonious concourse Parisians who for two generations prior to 1594 had been segregated from each other by political and religious strife.

The Pont Neuf solidified its position in the imagination of successive generations by being at once a place of power and authority, and of contestation and merry-making. It provided a grandstand view over aquatic ceremonials, fireworks displays and festivals being played out for the king's benefit in the adjacent Louvre palace, while Henry IV and his bronze steed – the *cheval de bronze* – became the focus of demotic royalism. The ceremonial pathway leading from the Louvre to the Palais de Justice or Notre-Dame cathedral always passed over the bridge. On occasion Parisians revelled in subverting the official character of this royal bridge. It was here that the cadaver of Marie de' Medici's hated counsellor Concini was desecrated (and probably spit-roasted) by rebels; here, that Frondeur ribaldry was at its height in 1648–52; here, that royal ministers were burnt in effigy in the run-up to the 1789 Revolution; and here, that the tumbrils bearing aristocrats to guillotine sites on the Right Bank passed during the Terror.

More mundanely and in less troubled times, the Pont Neuf offered passers-by a daily dose of the carnivalesque. Street trades proliferated on the bridge, each with its own distinctive cries to attract attention. (The *cris de Paris* formed a literary and artistic form of lasting popularity.) Pedlars jostled against a motley crew of *bouquinistes* (second-hand booksellers), pamphlet-sellers, pickpockets, acrobats, dog-barbers, street entertainers, flower-sellers, umbrella-hire merchants and recruiting sergeants. In addition the bridge was famously 'the rendezvous of charlatans'. One Italian visitor in the 1690s noted that 'some [quacks] replace lost teeth, others make glass eyes, while others heal incurable ills ... Another will assure you that he rejuvenates the aged, while others will drive wrinkles away from your forehead or eyes, or else make you a wooden leg.' Toothpullers were a particular speciality of the bridge, back to before the Fronde. From the 1710s to the 1750s the folkloric *Grand Thomas* set up his stall daily next to the *cheval de bronze*, and pulled out the teeth of two generations of Parisians to stupefied admiration.

In his *Tableau de Paris* in 1788, Louis-Sébastien Mercier declared the Pont Neuf to be 'to the city what the heart is to the body: the centre of movement and of circulation'. Yet by then its fame was on the slide. In the 1770s public stalls were banned and though a more sedate assemblage of shops was allowed back, even these were removed in the 1850s. The Samaritaine was demolished in 1813. Haussmann and the motor-car completed the ruin. The only *cri de Paris* henceforth to be heard on the bridge would be the terminal croaking of a run-over pedestrian (to paraphrase one of Raymond Queneau's poems). The decision of performance artist Christo in 1985 to 'wrap' the bridge as if it were a parcel marked an attempt to bring the Pont Neuf back to the attention of Parisians – but it was a desperate last throw. While we can today be made aware of the bridge's once legendary status in Parisian life we can perhaps only read about it rather than genuinely feel it.

Henry's antiquophile predecessor Francis I had made a new bridge the leading edge of a commitment to reshaping the city in ways which were in line with Renaissance urban ideals. Yet unlike Francis, Henry really did achieve a great deal, making considerable inroads into this still highly medieval city. At the heart of his thinking was the notion of the *place royale* ('royal square'). Each square – modelled on the piazzas which had been appearing in Rome and in north Italian cities – was a development opportunity, with the king providing the design and street layout, but with private capital injected into the costings. Henry was personally responsible for the conception and execution of no fewer than three such *places*. The most ambitious scheme was the one least far advanced when Henry was assassinated in 1610 and it died with him. This was the Place de France, located on the north-eastern fringe of the city (IIIe.), which Henry scheduled as the government office and ambassadorial neighbourhood. Only a few street names – which were destined to evoke France's multiple provinces – survived. The development was centred on the district in the Third arrondissement around the Rue de Bretagne, with Rues de Normandie, de Poitou, de Saintonge being obvious survivors.[6]

Henry made a stronger impact on city planning with his two other royal squares, the Place Royale in the Marais and the Place Dauphine on the Île de la Cité. The idea behind the Place Royale – which was renamed Place des Vosges in the Revolution (IVe.) – lay in Henry's plan to use the shell of the old Tournelles palace in the Marais as a site in which to develop a silk industry which could, he hoped, combat that of the Italians and boost the domestic economy. Yet the scheme swiftly raced beyond the notion of providing a workers' village, and the *place* was transformed into an elegant urban square, dominated by the aristocracy and without much space for plebeian elements. Committed to residence in Paris himself, Henry wanted to draw to the capital the high nobility, whom he preferred to have under his purview rather than out in the provinces stirring up dynastic or religious turbulence. It was, he adjudged, 'more necessary than ever to increase the size of Paris so as to accommodate the seigneurs, gentlemen and other officials of our entourage'.[7] The project was a co-funded enterprise. Henry invested his own money, notably in the Pavillon du Roi on the south side of the square, but the remaining three sides were subdivided into plots into which he and principal minister Sully shoehorned the political elite, insisting that the other residences should follow the Place's distinctive white stone and red brick design. The top names in the old Sword aristocracy and the newer Robe nobility of state administrative service were soon queuing up to purchase. The royal inauguration of this impressive project – a tournament-like *carrousel* held in 1612 in the central square at the heart of the Place – took place under Henry's successor Louis XIII. Richelieu placed a statue of the latter in the centre of the square in 1639.

By this time the development had sparked new phases of expansion around it. Just to the west of the Place, for example, the old city gutter (*égout*) was paved over, making the Rue Neuve-Saint-Louis –

subsequently renamed Rue Turenne after one of its most famous residents – a highly fashionable street. It ran through the *coutures* of Saint-Gervais and the Temple and these areas were subsequently developed too, further amplifying the neighbourhood's expansion. Henry was insistent, moreover, that architects follow building regulations – some of them dating back centuries – which kept a straighter building line on the street. This helps to explain why the extant remains of housing in this area of the Marais chime so harmoniously with the architecture of the present-day Place des Vosges. Here as elsewhere, moreover, timber-framed buildings were banned, and greater care taken to make building heights more uniform.

The early seventeenth century also witnessed the creation of a new island, the Île Saint-Louis, which became an offshore extension to the ever-more exclusive Marais. From 1614 a group of private businessmen headed by Christophe Marie devised the idea of putting together into a single development two semi-abandoned islands in the lee of the Île de la Cité, namely, the Île Notre-Dame, which was owned by the cathedral chapter, and the smaller Île des Vaches ('Cow Island'). With royal help, they circumvented the cathedral chapter's opposition to the use of the land and the building of what became a network of new bridges. The Pont Marie (1614–35) linked the island to the Right Bank (the Marais side), the Pont de la Tournelle (1620) continued the line of the Pont Marie to join up with the Left Bank, while a smaller wooden walkway linked the new island to the eastern tip of the Île de la Cité. The Marie syndicate touted building plots with a façade on the river, offering wonderful views for those with money enough to enjoy them, while rather humbler dwellings were planned for the heart of the new island, where a new church, Saint-Louis-en-l'Île, was constructed from 1622. The island's existence and fast-growing prosperity also helped revitalize the neglected area on the Left Bank behind the Quai de la Tournelle, and further east, out towards the botanical gardens created in 1633. From 1640 the Jardin du Roi – the present-day Jardin des Plantes – was open to the public and became a favoured Parisian leisure spot.

A similar combination of urban utility, social engineering and decoration was served by Henry's development of the Place Dauphine (Ie.). The third of the king's royal square concepts, it was located on the western tip of the Île de la Cité, just to the rear of the Pont Neuf. Laid out in 1608, the Place was targeted not at the aristocrats who haunted the Place Royale but at financiers and merchants, who stood to benefit from its closeness to the city's main trading zones. Though fewer of the original buildings have survived than is the case with the Place Royale, it is still possible to get an idea of the elegantly enclosed and exclusive character of the triangular plot. The *quais* around the bridge and on the Île were repaved to add tone, and the finishing touch was an equestrian statue of Henry IV which was placed in the middle of the Pont Neuf, close to the apex of the Place Dauphine. Commissioned from an Italian sculptor in 1604, the *cheval de bronze* was shipwrecked in the Mediterranean in transit from Italy, and was only inaugurated by Henry's widow in 1614.

No ruler prior to Henry IV had put his effigy on display in his capital city in this way. The gesture accorded with Renaissance notions of sovereignty developed in the city states of north Italy, but it was also remarkable in that it highlighted the confidence which the ruler had in Parisians' support for the Bourbon dynasty – earlier rulers had feared defacement of an effigy of themselves in a public place. Henry also made the Pont Neuf and the Place Dauphine the springboard for a broader urban development on the Left Bank, now more tightly conjoined with the Louvre neighbourhood. A wide new street – the Rue Dauphine (VIe.) – was laid out continuing the line of the Pont Neuf on the Left Bank. Although Henry's plan that the new street should be lined with houses of uniform design came to nothing, the street did stimulate development: it was crosscut by a number of new streets, all of which were laid out for housing development.[8]

The creation of the Rue Dauphine also played a role in the closer integration of the Faubourg Saint-Germain into the city. The English visitor Robert Dallington thought the Faubourg as large as Cambridge – it seems in fact to have exceeded 20,000.[9] Beginning as a downmarket Marais with a still rural feel, the neighbourhood would emerge as the ultimate in fashionable living by the end of the reign of Louis XIV. Two royal palaces also played a key role in Saint-Germain's success. One was the sprawling residence built after 1607 by *la Reine Margot* (Henry IV's first wife, his partner in an arranged marriage preceding Saint Batholomew's Day in 1572, but whom he had long since discarded). It was located on land purchased from the university on the old Pré-aux-Clercs (which was fast being gobbled up by development), where it faced onto the Louvre. On her death in 1615 the queen left the property to Louis XIII, who permitted the demolition of the house and use of its grounds for residential development. The street plan which was laid out to the south of the Rue de l'Université (VIIe.) – notably Rue de Bourbon (now Rue de Lille) and Rue Verneuil parallel with the Rue de l'Université – supplied a grid for the building of smart private residences (or *hôtels particuliers*).

If the Reine Margot development pulled the Faubourg Saint-Germain further towards the Seine, the building of a palace for Henry IV's widow Marie de' Medici stimulated development towards the Montagne Sainte-Geneviève. This was the so-called Luxembourg palace (Marie did not reside there long enough to impress her identity on a site still named after an earlier owner). The palace, which was constructed from 1612 to the 1620s, deliberately mimicked the Pitti palace in her native Florence, and the Luxembourg's spacious gardens which were to become a favourite promenade of Parisians were a version of the Boboli gardens (VIe.). John Evelyn in 1644 thought it 'perfectly beautiful and magnificent'.[10]

The expansion of the Faubourg Saint-Germain – in the long term at the expense of the Marais – highlighted a gradual but clear-cut drift of the city's centre of gravity to the west, notwithstanding developments over in the Marais and the Île Saint-Louis. This was even more evident on the Right Bank. The Louvre's new-found role as royal residence had stimulated aristocratic building in its environs, including on and beyond the old walls of Charles V. In particular the Faubourg Saint-Honoré (out along the street of the same name) saw several spurts of new building. Plans to extend Charles V's city walls to the west and north-west to enclose the newly developing neighbourhoods had stalled during the Religious Wars. Henry IV's building of the gallery connecting the Louvre along the river-front to Catherine de' Medici's Tuileries palace signalled renewed intentions in this neighbourhood. Marie de' Medici put in place a superb promenade, the Cours-la-Reine, out to Chaillot (where Catherine de' Medici had built a palace) and towards the Bois de Boulogne. Expansion also benefited from Cardinal Richelieu's decision to build himself a new residence, a stone's throw to the north of the Louvre palace. The Palais-Cardinal – or Palais-Royal, as it became more durably known from 1643 – was an extensive structure with colonnaded gardens. Almost adjacent to the site to the north, Richelieu's successor Mazarin constructed a palace too: the Palais-Mazarin occupied the present-day Site Richelieu of the Bibliothèque Nationale.

Both cardinal ministers recognized the need to provide military defence for these fast-developing areas where they had chosen to locate their residences. There were two aspects to this strategy: first, cracking down hard on housing extensions in the suburbs – edicts in 1627, 1634, 1638 and 1644 echoed various sixteenth-century precedents, attacking such developments; and second, by extending the defensible area of the city. In the 1630s new bastions were constructed along a line already mapped out from the late sixteenth century and running westward, then south-west, from the Porte Saint-Denis (IIe.), and providing an addition of some 84 hectares. This was equivalent to around a third of the fortified area on the Right Bank, and swelled the total city's area to 567 hectares. The Fossés Jaunes ('Yellow Ditches') ramparts as they were called (from the colour of the earth turned over in their creation) reached the Seine on the line of the gardens of the Tuileries laid out in the 1660s (a remnant of it still forms the western limit of the Tuileries gardens, and faces onto the present-day Place de la Concorde: Ie.). The zone now covered by defences encompassed, besides the Tuileries, much of the Faubourg Saint-Honoré as well as the Faubourg Montmartre to the north. The framework for development in the new neighbourhood was provided by a north–south Rue de Richelieu which intersected with an east–west street parallel with the Rue Saint-Honoré, the Rue des Petits-Champs. The latter area had been less bucolic than its name made it sound, for also located here was the towering city rubbish-tip known as the Basse-Voirie. This was levelled in the 1630s, allowing the creation of the Rue Sainte-Anne (Ie.–IIe.). The following decades saw the progressive development of this whole area, a process in which Richelieu invested. The district attracted many of the financial elites of the state – Louis's principal minister Colbert, for example, was another devoted resident.

The golden age of the private hôtel was now in full swing, both in the Richelieu district and in other fashionable neighbourhoods such as the Marais, the Île Saint-Louis and the Faubourg Saint-Germain. Dwellings – whether for old court and aristocratic families or for denizens drawn from the financial, legal and administrative cadres of the Bourbon state – were larger and airier than their sixteenth-century forebears. Foreign visitors often called them 'palaces' rather than 'residences', and were impressed by the vibrant cultural life which many housed. Elegantly appointed from the exterior, they invariably boasted munificently decorated and luxurious interiors. The Hôtel Lambert de Thorigny on the eastern tip of the Île Saint-Louis is a brilliant example of the genre. Constructed by Le Vau, and subsequently decorated by Eustache Le Sueur and Charles Le Brun, its first owner was a ruthlessly successful state financier, one of those 'runts of fortune' evoked by the Parisian historian Henri Sauval, 'that brigandage and extortion had laden with wealth'.[11] The aristocratic style of life which the new hôtels encouraged extended to the new financial elites as well as old noble families.

5.2: Madame de Sévigné

'It is an excellent affair,' the celebrated letter-writer Marie de Rabutin-Chantal, Madame de Sévigné (1627–96), wrote excitedly to her daughter in 1677 about the residence she was planning to buy for them both to live in. 'We shall have a beautiful courtyard, a lovely garden and a fine neighbourhood.' The residence in question, in which Madame de Sévigné was to spend the last two decades of her life, was the Hôtel Carnavalet. Set in the fashionable Marais neighbourhood (IIIe.–IVe.) on the present-day Rue Sévigné, it today houses the Musée de l'Histoire de Paris. Paris's major history museum is well sited: the Hôtel Carnavalet was one of the jewels of the Marais in a highly distinguished period in the city's cultural life. There was little of that life, moreover, that Madame de Sévigné was not plugged into, and did not comment upon in her copious and highly readable correspondence.

Henry IV's construction of the Place Royale (now Place des Vosges) in the Marais had stimulated an efflorescence of fine

building. The poet Scarron sang the praises of each house in the
Place:

> Their sumptuous interiors, and superb panelling,
> Their rich ornaments, their priceless paintings,
> Their rare cabinets, their daises and balusters . . .

Such comments were also applicable to a great many of the
hôtels particuliers being built in the wake of the opening of
the Place Royale, and which continue to give the Marais its
characteristic beauty. The king had intended the Place Royale
to act as a cultural cement, unifying the fractious social elite –
and Madame de Sévigné, who was born in a residence on the
square, was particularly well placed to benefit from this. The
daughter of a misalliance between a financier and the daughter
of an ancient noble house, she had access to the royal court but
was also an active citizen in her neighbourhood. Although she
travelled widely throughout France, she was a denizen of the
Marais through and through – indeed all her adult life in Paris
was spent in the neighbourhood. Her status and gender ruled
her out of certain cultural activities: she could not possibly slum
it by attending a theatre, while the bold intellectual libertinage
of Mersenne (sometime host to Descartes and Gassendi), Saint-
Amant, Cyrano de Bergerac and others was beyond her. Yet if
she did not attend a city theatre, she read plays and saw them
performed at court: she was 'mad on' Corneille, a friend of
Racine (and the story that she had declared that the craze for his
plays would pass as swiftly as the craze for coffee is probably
apocryphal) and appreciated Molière's comedies for their underlying moralism. La Fontaine dedicated one of his fables to her
daughter. She regarded Pascal as providing rules for her to
live by. She was also friendly with Scarron (as well as his wife
who, when widowed, would become Madame de Maintenon,
Louis XIV's morganatic wife), the poets Boileau and Voiture,
the lexicographer Ménage, the Jansenist Arnauld family, the
composer Lully – all the great names, indeed, of the *grand siècle*.
  Madame de Sévigné's Marais was a centre of cultural effer-

vescence. Many of the artists (Vignon, La Hyre, etc.) and architects (Mansart, Mansart-Hardouin, Libéral Bruant, Le Vau, etc.)
responsible for the new building and decoration had chosen to
live here. The theatre was booming here too: the troupe of
players at the Hôtel de Bourgogne – the nucleus of the Comédie-
Française that formed later in the century – started off at the
Impasse Berthaud (across the road from the present-day Centre
Pompidou). Salons were held in which cultural issues were discussed and intellectual debates held. On the Rue Pavée (in a
residence which is today the Bibliothèque historique de la ville
de Paris), Lamoignon hosted a salon attended by the writers
Racine, Boileau and La Rochefoucauld and the physician Guy
Patin.

No shrinking violet – the great memoir-writer Saint-Simon
recalled her as being 'so lovable and such excellent company' –
Madame de Sévigné was very much part of this scene. She was
particularly warm in support of bluestockings, who also gave
the Marais its character. The salon of Madame de Rambouillet
earlier in the century was followed by that of Mademoiselle
de Scudéry on the Rue Vieille-du-Temple, while on Rue des
Tournelles there were the gatherings of the fabled courtesan
Ninon de Lenclos (who incidentally seduced both Madame de
Sévigné's husband and, twenty years later, her son). Madame de
Sévigné was also a supporter of Madame de Lafayette, whose
Princesse de Clèves (1678) is one of the earliest novels in the
French language.

We read Madame de Sévigné today not only for the wit and
liveliness of her style (despite its bowdlerization by her prissy
descendants) and the insights she provides on this moment of
the cultural supremacy of the Marais (soon to be overtaken by
the Faubourg Saint-Germain). In addition her letters provide
incomparable, villagey gossip about the neighbourhood she
knew so well. Who was marrying whom, who had unfortunate
financial affairs, how the seasons were passing, the fortunes of
her pets, duels on the Place Royale (she knew at least by sight
the real-life d'Artagnan, whose musketeer regiment was housed

close by) – all was grist to her mill. A particular obsession was health, both her own and that of her beloved daughter (to whom she gave some of the first contraceptive advice on record). Some sixty medical men are mentioned in the correspondence and they range from the grave physicians of the Faculty so wickedly satirized by Molière through to out-and-out quacks. Every medical fad is there too, from Vichy waters through to coffee and chocolate, to quinine and to every imaginable sort of purge (for Madame de Sévigné was an ardent believer in the bowels being open). In such manifold ways she brings the old Marais to life.

The mixture of state and private finance which had led to the development of Henry IV's *places royales* and the major urban housing developments during the first half of the century also characterized another major feature of this period: a boom in ecclesiastical building. Henry IV had ended the Religious Wars with the Edict of Nantes of 1598 which accorded Huguenots rights of toleration within France, and he himself set an example by choosing his counsellors from both sides of the confessional divide. Protestant worship was permitted in a number of French cities, but, following long-established practice, not in Paris. Although Paris's 20,000 to 30,000 Huguenots – many of whom grouped together around the Rue de l'Université in the Pré-aux-Clercs area – were offered legal protection, they worshipped at their temple at nearby Charenton, a short boat-trip away.

Nevertheless, despite the Protestant presence, Calvin's hopes of making Paris a bastion of Protestant Reformation had been comprehensively baulked. Indeed, in the course of the seventeenth century the city became a belated storm-centre of Counter-Reformation, following the doctrinal line established at the international church's Council of Trent (1545–63). This was sealed by the decision in 1622 to elevate the bishopric of Paris into an archbishopric. That Paris had become a uniconfessional city, in terms of public worship at least, was underlined by the profusion of religious constructions. There had been only one Catholic church built in the whole of France throughout the decades of the Religious Wars. The situation now changed drastically:

perhaps as many as one hundred churches were built or given major overhauls over the course of the seventeenth century in Paris alone. Some initiatives – as for example Notre-Dame-des-Victoires (1629–1740: IIe.) and Saint-Jacques-du-Haut-Pas (1630–85: Ve.) – were linked to the creation of new parishes to cope with population expansion. Work was also restarted on churches whose construction had become bogged down by the troubles – Saint-Merri, Saint-Gervais, Saint-Germain-des-Prés, Saint-Sulpice, Saint-Eustache and Saint-Étienne-du-Mont, for example. Particularly striking in architectural terms were the churches of Saint-Roch on the Rue Saint-Honoré (Ie.) and the Jesuit church of Saint-Louis-et-Saint-Paul (now Saint-Paul: 1627–41) on the Rue Saint-Antoine (IVe.). Both were completed with the elegant 'Jesuit-style' façade involving three orders of classical columns. The scale of building in these as in many other churches was so substantial that there were problems of completion – the rebuilding of Saint-Sulpice, started in 1646, was not finished until the eve of the French Revolution, in 1788.

The regular clergy made a massive contribution to the spate of clerical building. New religious houses had been pretty scarce throughout the sixteenth century, but there were no fewer than sixty new establishments between 1600 and 1660 and a further thirty by 1700. (There would only be another ten between 1700 and 1750.) A clear majority were on the Left Bank. Much of the faubourg area here after the Religious Wars was 'ruined and utterly desolate', as one visitor put it,[17] but in peace conditions it represented cheap land physically close to the city's heart and was consequently latched on to by ecclesiastical builders. Two-thirds of new constructions were for women. The institutions had a range of spiritual missions, including the mystico-contemplative, such as the Carmelites introduced by Barbe Acarie in 1603 in Notre-Dame-des-Champs on the Rue Saint-Jacques (Ve.). At the other extreme, communities dedicated to the active life (notably in charity and education) and living 'in the world' rather than behind monastic walls comprised one of the most striking examples of Tridentine piety (the liturgical and doctrinal reforms and the revival of the monastic movement agreed at the Council of Trent). Among the most famous of the female orders were the Daughters of Charity

Carrousel in the Place Royale, 1615

founded in 1633 by Saints Vincent de Paul and Louise de Marillac and whose mother-house was located on the Rue du Faubourg Saint-Denis (Xe.).

Some of the new convents and monasteries were built with sobriety. The abbey of Port-Royal, for example, the spiritual home to Jansenism, the movement of Augustinian piety which developed from the 1630s, was appropriately austere. Yet a stone's throw from this site out on the southernmost fringe of the city was the gloriously exuberant Val-de-Grâce convent. The latter's chapel was constructed from 1624 onwards on a site purchased by Queen Anne of Austria, and it was associated with her prayers for a son. (These were answered in 1638 with the birth of Louis XIV when she was nearly forty.) The chapel was crowned with a dome, and this feature was, in fact, a mark of the more Italianate, baroque forms of piety promoted in particular by Cardinal Mazarin (a Roman by birth). Other domes in evidence included the Sorbonne chapel erected by Richelieu (1642), the church of Saint-Louis-et-Saint-Paul in the Marais (1641), the Invalides (1670), the hospital of La Salpêtrière (1670) and the Collège des Quatre-Nations (1688).[13] The Paris skyline was indelibly transformed into a mélange of the Italianate and the gothic.

The ostentatious profusion of religious building sought to 'Catholicize' Parisian space in a way which could only make remaining Huguenots uncomfortable – as the government, which was closely associated with these developments, was well aware. The implementation in France of the edicts of the Council of Trent which had thoroughly reformed the Catholic church had been slowed by the Religious Wars, but after the turn of the century they began to swell a revival of Catholic piety from which the divinely ordained monarchy stood to gain. The post-Tridentine church and its lay elites seemed to have renounced open violence against Huguenots. The confraternities which had acted as a spiritual avant-garde for League factionalism in the Religious Wars now turned to charitable, educational and more sedately devotional purposes. Richelieu frankly told the Estates General in 1614 that conversion now came not by violence but through 'us setting a good example, and through teaching and prayers, which are the only weapons we wish to do battle with'.[14] This was a pertinent point to make, in the light of the assassination of Henry IV only four years previously at the hands of a *dévot*, a fanatical relic of the Religious Wars, Jean-François Ravaillac. Richelieu's comment would also, however, prove an exaggeration, in that the Revocation of the Edict of Nantes in 1685, ending tolerance towards Huguenots throughout France, would be accompanied by overt violence and naked aggression (though the worst of this would be in the provinces rather than in the capital). Yet the general point – that the Catholic church aimed to reform itself and to make more of an appeal to the laity – held good. Catholics offered a sensorial and intellectual bombardment to their opponents and to the laity in general. Churches and monasteries constituted a visual agent of proselytization, inside as well as out. The interiors of churches were lavishly decorated with paintings, sculptures and stained glasswork. Organ music and sacred choral music flourished as never before. The kind of vivid processional and ceremonial culture evidenced in the 1580s was still rife, though now shorn of eschatological elements: the notion of Paris as the new Jerusalem seemed to have had its moment. The post-Tridentine church also sought to combat Protestantism on the ground of doctrine, which implied a thorough reform of clerical training. A cluster of new seminaries emerged, the most famous of which were those of the Oratorians on the Rue Saint-Honoré (1611), Saint Vincent de Paul's Lazarists on the Rue Saint-Denis (1625) and the Saint-Sulpicians (1642). This was consequently a golden age of the Catholic sermon.

Religious publishing also received a great deal of attention, ranging from the most cerebral of theological treatises through to works of elementary proselytization and popularization. The Bourbon dynasty gave the church its head – indeed Louis XIII and Anne of Austria were in many ways classically devout post-Tridentine rulers. Yet the scope for religious and intellectual discussion was severely limited in comparison with the freedoms claimed under the Catholic League. Rulers did not want churchmen to become a focus of political opposition. Henry IV completed the domestication of the university begun by his Valois predecessors. The institution was in poor shape – its numbers, notably, had dwindled sharply as a result of the Religious Wars. Richelieu made doubly sure of its theological docility by becoming provisor of the Sorbonne (to whose architectural refurbishment he also contributed). The cardinal minister also much increased censorship, while his establishment of France's first newspaper, Théophraste Renaudot's *Gazette de France* (1631), was less about diffusion of information than news management and manipulation of opinion. Richelieu also used royal arrest warrants (*lettres de cachet*) against political and intellectual opponents, making the Bastille fortress the sombre and notorious site for the repression of dissent which it was to remain until 14 July 1789.

The cardinal ministers continued the efforts of their predecessors to make Paris's city council the crown's poodle. Since 1415 the council's *Petit Bureau* which transacted routine business comprised the Prévôt des Marchands, four elected aldermen (*échevins*) and three salaried officials, while for the *Grand Bureau*, at which major issues were discussed, twenty-four urban notables were added. The crown began to muzzle the municipality in the aftermath of the Hundred Years War. Subsequently Francis I and Henry II ensured that no municipal election was valid save with the crown's approval, and both interfered constantly in electoral processes. By the late sixteenth century, apart from the senior posts, which were electable, other positions were filled through the play of influence, cooptation, venality and corruption. During the Religious Wars the city council had lost so much authority that its wishes could be openly flouted by ad hoc *dévot* groupings. In the long term the council also found itself losing out to the extension of the powers of the Châtelet. The Prévôt de Paris was invariably now a titled aristocrat, so his lieutenants tended to be agents of crown authority. In the military domain the post of governor of the city (before as well as after Henry IV) was usually given to members of the royal family or other grandees, who showed little concern for the feelings of the municipality.

A Prévôt des Marchands could only now expect to be effective if he was carrying out the wishes of the king. This was certainly the case, for example, with François Miron, who held the post from 1604 to 1606. Son of a Châtelet lieutenant, Miron served in the Parlement and then as Châtelet lieutenant himself from 1596, before he was projected into office by the personal backing of Henry IV. The king, it was said, in a comment which well illustrates the lack of a public-service ethic in Parisian municipal affairs, 'knew him to be faithful in his service, not greedy and because of this [he knew that he] would steal less than the others'.[15] Miron and his successor François Sanguin, Prévôt des Marchands from 1606 to 1612, became the effective instruments of Henry's wish to rejuvenate Paris. They reorganized its finances following the bruising caused by the Religious Wars, and sought both to repair and to embellish the city in the Renaissance spirit championed by their ruler.

The city council was changing socially as well as politically. Partly this reflected a long-evident transformation of the urban elite away from commerce and manufacturing.[16] A number of measures confirmed and exacerbated the trend. The creation of a Commercial Tribunal in the city in 1563 had reduced the commercial dimension of the authority of a city council which had after all begun as a hanse of water-merchants. A regulation in 1615 stated that at least two of the four *échevins* were to be merchants, but this was widely flouted. The prohibition of 1554 on members of 'the mechanical arts' being elected removed some of the council's function of representing those in trade outside the elite. Successive rulers winked at the tendency for elected councillors to be members of the Robe nobility with ties of loyalty to the crown rather than independent merchants. Such individuals often enjoyed noble status, a phenomenon which was extended by a royal decision in 1577 to accord nobility to the Prévôt des Marchands and *échevins* whose fathers had also served on the council. More than half of city councillors in place in 1614 were members of the Paris Parlement and the other sovereign courts (who had purchased their posts). The same processes were in train lower down the urban hierarchy too: in 1633 the practice of venality – the sale of offices in the state administration – was officially extended to the *quartiniers* responsible for the different neighbourhoods.

The crown's domestication of the city council, the transformation of the Parisian cityscape, and the recharged intellectual and spiritual atmosphere might have given the impression that social and religious elites were politically docile. Nothing could have been further from the truth. Because religion still counted, it proved difficult to control. Though most Catholics had renounced the violence of the League, there were many Catholic militants – or *dévots*, as they were called – who urged more energetic action against Protestantism than Henry IV had

offered. They influenced Louis XIII and the queen regent Marie de'
Medici in the 1620s in particular to take steps in order to reduce the
military autonomy of Huguenot communities in the south and west
of France. The *dévots* also were highly critical of the foreign policy
which Bourbon monarchs introduced, on the grounds that the French
state, by making strategic alliances with Protestant princes against
France's long-term enemy the Habsburgs, was putting its own interests
– *raison d'état* – before considerations of the international church's
spiritual harmony.

The *dévot* critique was all the more politically threatening, moreover, in that it developed in a period in which the Bourbons' state-
building plans placed a great strain on French society. Initially the
French stayed out of the Thirty Years War (1618–48), offering covert
support only to the Habsburg Holy Roman Emperor's German opponents. In 1635, however, France entered the war, and conflict would
continue with Austria until 1648 and with Spain (also Habsburg) until
1659. A sharp increase in army size meant that the costs of warfare
spiralled frighteningly fast. The government reacted by massive tax-
hikes, colossal borrowing and an ingenious range of financial stratagems aimed at squeezing more money out of the population – or
making the state pay less than full value for the goods and services it
required. All this occurred at a time when harvests were poor and
bubonic plague a recurrent visitor. Every single year from 1620 to
the 1650s, one or more of a gamut of forms of protest – rural
risings, urban riots, noble plots – occurred somewhere in France. The
troubles climaxed in the Fronde (1648–53), a novel cocktail of civil
war, peasant insurrection, urban rebellion, noble conspiracy and
constitutional turbulence.

Paris had more than its fair share of involvement in these troubles.
A conspiracy in 1617, led by the young Louis XIII against his own
mother and her principal adviser Concino Concini, resulted in the
latter being murdered on the king's orders and buried secretly in
the church of Saint-Germain-l'Auxerrois. Parisian mobs, resentful of
Concini's tax policies, proceeded to dig up the corpse, cart it to the
Pont Neuf and chop it up and burn it in scenes which were alleged to
have included cannibalism. The city stayed mercifully calm in the
following years, but there was some alarm in 1636. Spanish troops

from the Netherlands defeated the French at the battle of Corbie, then sent raiding parties down the Oise river valley to threaten Paris. A panic exodus from the north and north-east of the country led to hordes seeking refuge in Paris, while concomitantly hosts of Parisians headed south in fright, blocking the roads with carts and carriages. Cardinal Richelieu and Louis XIII kept their heads when all around them were losing theirs, and their show of steadfastness impressed the Parisians, who volunteered to fight in number, obliging the Spanish to withdraw.

By the 1640s Richelieu's successor Mazarin was placing Parisian loyalism under severe strain by a range of policies which seemed to be targeted very precisely at Parisian pockets. With the state's financial needs reaching stratospheric levels, Mazarin determined that Parisians were better equipped than most French subjects to contribute to the war effort. The *Toisé* Edict of 1644 and the Tariff Edict of 1646 were brazen money-making schemes designed to squeeze cash out of the numerous Parisians who had developed housing beyond the city ramparts. The Redemption Edict of 1647 was much the same: it used the otherwise almost completely ignored seigneurial rights of the king as a fiscal lever, kindly permitting those living in property within royal domains to buy themselves out of future obligations. In January 1648 this was followed by a raft of further financial measures, targeted particularly at the wealthy magistrates of the Paris Parlement.

It was noticeable that resistance from within Paris to these fiscal manoeuvres tended to be headed not by the municipality but by the Parlement. The erosion of the independence of the city council had left political space which the Parlement was only too keen to occupy. Despite the fact that all magistrates were venal rather than elected officers, and that the institution was essentially a high court of law rather than a parliament, the Parlement proved able to carve out for itself a significant representative role. From the fifteenth century it played up its capacity as defender of the interests of city-dwellers as a whole – over food supply and high prices, for example. Its duty of registering all royal legislation made it a constitutional watchdog which had the right to delay or even block royal legislation if this was viewed as out of keeping with tradition. The institution's role was amplified by the fact that from 1614, the Estates General, the national representative body which had met some five times over the sixteenth century, was put on ice. The Parlement, located in the ancient royal palace on the Île de la Cité made redundant as a royal residence by the building of the Louvre, played up its claim to constitute an integral part of sovereignty.

Provoked by this raft of draconian fiscal legislation aimed at themselves and at fellow Parisians, the Parlement reacted vigorously. It was thus venal state officials in the Parlement – rather than elected city councillors – who headed an organized movement in March 1648 to demand a dismantling of the military and financial apparatus of the state and a cessation of the dynasty's orientation around military expansion. The response of the Regency Council under Anne of Austria and Cardinal Mazarin was to arrest those magistrates they adjudged ringleaders – a step which almost led to them having a revolution on their hands. The Fronde – named after the catapult which Parisian children used to pelt their betters – was under way.

Law and order in Paris seemed on the point of breaking down as street barricades were constructed – not for the last time. In negotiations from which the city council was totally excluded the regent made as if to agree to the rebel programme. Yet she and the king slipped out of Paris in January 1649 and used the prince de Condé, a Prince of the Blood and the greatest general of his generation, to launch a siege of the city to force it back into obedience. The situation recalled Henry IV's 1589–90 siege of Paris. Cardinal de Retz, then coadjutor to his uncle the archbishop of Paris, and whose memoirs constitute a breviary of aristocratic revolt, recalled seeing weapons from the Hundred Years War and cockades from the League being paraded through the streets.[17] The religious divide, however, was no longer at issue – royalists and rebels were Catholics almost to a man, and the Huguenots kept their heads down.

The siege was ended by a conciliatory treaty between the regent and the rebels. However, the situation – especially with war against Spain still continuing – was going to get much worse before it got better. The next few years were to see endless and often unpredictable turns in events. What had started as a Parisian tax dispute became a national conflict. Complicating matters was the self-interested intervention of the grandees of the realm, all seeking to feather their individual nests, but also hoping to use the weakness of the monarchy during a period of regency to reduce the moves towards monarchical centralization which Richelieu had started to push through. Also stirring the pot were some well-connected and quite remarkable aristocratic women, such as the duchess de Nemours, as keen as their male partners to act out an epic role like the heroes of romances or dramas by Corneille. Sometimes the Frondeurs adopted the strategy of the grandees of the Wars of Religion in using their clientage in the provinces to build up private armies. At other times they sought political alliance with the Paris Parlement. And on occasion some of the Frondeurs – including Retz, Condé and Louis XIV's uncle the duc d'Orléans – used hired hacks to write inflammatory pamphlets (the so-called *mazarinades*) to stir up the Parisian populace. Many Frondeurs were willing to be bought out of rebellion at the right price – but in the tough circumstances of the late 1640s and the early 1650s the state simply did not have enough power even to give away.

There is no easy way for historians to comprehend the complexity of the issues in play – and the same was true for many contemporaries. In 1652, for example, many peasants from the villages around Paris welcomed Condé and his army under the impression that he was serving the king, when in fact by then he had become the principal Frondeur rebel. In the changeable and spasmodically shambolic course of events, everyone seemed to suffer for at least part of the time. Mazarin was obliged to go into exile on no fewer than three separate occasions. He and Anne of Austria were continually and publicly humiliated in violently partisan and often obscene *mazarinades*. And on one occasion the young Louis XIV was obliged to endure the indignity of hordes of Parisians trooping past his bed at night to ensure he had not fled the city.

Despite its frivolous name, the Fronde revolt was desperately serious, and especially so, in fact, for the inhabitants of Paris and its rural environs who suffered most of all. There were two periods of siege – 1649 and 1652 – in each of which the price of bread rocketed causing enormous hardship – and swelling the ranks of the Frondeurs. The death-rate doubled between 1651 and 1653. Things were even worse in the surrounding region, since they also had to endure indisciplined marauding and pillaging by troops from both royal and Frondeur armies, causing famine and steepling death-rates in the city. 'We are being killed like chickens,'[18] wrote the Jansenist nun Angélique Arnauld, and she went on to recount a whole slew of massacres and atrocities taking place just outside the gates of the city. 'Two-thirds of the villagers around Paris have died from illness, want and suffering,' noted one of the Paris magistrates.[19] It would take many districts in the Paris region more than a generation to recover from the economic and demographic damage.

The structures of Parisian municipal government were much embarrassed by the turn of events. With royal officials either in flight or failing to function at all, the municipality failed to seize the opportunity to act as Paris's protector. Nor was the Parlement any better, duped as it was by the unreliability of aristocratic Frondeurs such as Condé, Retz and the interminably vacillating duc d'Orléans. The fiasco of urban government was cruelly exposed in the spring of 1652. With Parisian authorities refusing to open city gates to either Frondeur or royal troops, Condé and his Frondeur army were driven up against the city walls outside the Saint-Antoine gate, where they risked being cut to pieces by the royal army under Turenne. In the event the soldiers were saved by some nifty cannonfire from city walls personally supervised by the Frondeuse duchesse de Montpensier, Orléans's daughter. The duchess, who was a possible marriage partner for Louis XIV, even playfully (one hopes) trained cannon on the party of the young king who was watching events from the hillock at Charonne (XIe.). Although the king survived, she had thus 'killed her husband', as Mazarin put it.[20] (She never married.) The relieving cannonfire allowed the city to open its gates to Condé's forces.

Yet Parisians soon had cause to rue the step. A couple of days later, on 4 July, Condé's forces committed the 'Massacre of the Hôtel de Ville', killing more than a score of city notables and going on to take over urban government themselves in conjunction with the more radical members of the Parlement. The seizure of power – with its echoes of the League's purge of the Parlement in the 1590s – had, however, been at the cost of alienating almost all support within Paris itself. As in the 1590s, a peace movement was soon emerging.

The Frondeur rebels had anyway fallen out among themselves, and lacked either an army or the requisite administrative machinery and financial means to continue the wars. Condé fled to the Spanish, and it was with joy, but more than a little apprehension, that the city opened its doors to young Louis XIV for an official *entrée* on 21 October 1652. Though the still teenaged king, who installed himself at the Louvre, was willing to accord an amnesty to the city, all Frondeur leaders were punished. Nor did his government, which Mazarin returned from exile to head, shift its war policies: the struggle against Spain continued, and high taxes, currency instability and fiscal expedients would remain political currency throughout the decade. The Parlement tried to raise its head above the parapet on a number of occasions, but the crown overrode objections to its policies, eventually removing the institution's constitutional right to remonstrate against royal edicts.

Yet despite continuing problems, from 1652–3 the government was back in the saddle. The autonomy of city government had been terminally liquidated. Only loyalists were allowed into municipal office, and successive Prévôts des Marchands outrivalled each other in craven sycophancy. On July 4 1653, the first anniversary of the Massacre of the Hôtel-de-Ville, the king laid on a firework display and festivities for Parisians. Its centrepiece was a statue of himself, placed directly outside the city hall, represented 'as a demi-god, with a bolt of lightning in his hand, and with one foot stamping on the flame of discord and the other resting on an upturned ship which bore the coat of arms of the city of Paris'.[21] The statue would remain in place several decades. Unlike Henry IV in 1594, Louis would not indulge in voluntary political amnesia.

There followed a period of uncertainty in which it seemed that the king might grow to love Paris and things Parisian after all, and outlive his earlier resentments. In 1661 Mazarin died and the young king determined not to appoint a successor to him, but to rule as his own principal minister. 'Everyone here is hoping that the king is going to do great things in terms of justice and for the welfare of his people,' noted the arch-Parisian physician, Guy Patin in 1661. 'The king has said,' he noted later, 'that he wants to make of Paris what Augustus made of Rome.'[22]

Romanophilia was a sentiment which Louis XIV shared with Colbert, who served as the king's general ministerial factotum from the

Day of the Barricades, 26 August 1648

death of Mazarin until his own death in 1683. The sentiment was expressed in a variety of media – history, panegyric, painting and the arts generally. Although there had been much enthusiasm for Renaissance ideals as far back as the fifteenth century, there was a good deal of dispute as to how those ideals were to be put into practice. The contribution of Louis XIV and Colbert was to seek to establish and implement these through royal academies which were both paragons of taste and the fount of normative rules. The Académie française established by Richelieu in 1635 was now joined by academies for painting and sculpture (1648), the sciences (1661), inscriptions and belles-lettres (1663) and architecture (1671). Guided by these bodies, Louis and Colbert embarked on a frenetic bout of power-building in which the influence of Antiquity was very much to the fore.

Francis I's wish to fashion Paris as a new Rome had had little practical effect, while Henry IV's efforts in this direction had been geared round a combination of utility and decoration. What distinguished the programme of Louis XIV and Colbert was an emphasis on monumentality. Particular emphasis was placed on public buildings, which would overpower the viewer with an impression of strength and force, and care was taken to implant them in the city in such a way that they transformed the surrounding cityscape. The Academy of Architecture was to play a key role in producing a more homogeneous, French-style version of classicism which would be enduringly influential on most forms of building above the very humble. In 1665 Louis had called in Bernini, the brilliant Italian sculptor and architect, to design a new façade for the Louvre of requisite majesty. Ultimately the king rejected the Bernini model for a more classical – and classically French – design by Charles Perrault and Louis Le Vau, but this was no less splendid in conception. The interiors of both the Louvre and the Tuileries were thoroughly overhauled and at one stage 3,000 masons and 600 joiners were hard at work on the dual site. The garden designer André Le Nôtre was set to work on redesigning the Tuileries garden. Across the river the Tour de Nesle on the edge of the old Charles V Wall was demolished, and the site and its environs were given over to the erection of the Collège des Quatre-Nations, for which Mazarin had provided an endowment.[23] Le Vau was architect of this building, which at present houses the Institut de France. Topped with a dome, its integration into the cityscape made the westward vista from the Pont Neuf an impressive statement of dynastic power.

The monumentalism favoured by Colbert and Louis XIV worked to best effect when seen as part of vistas uncluttered by the muddled over-building which traditionally characterized the city. Bridges were now in favour – such as the Pont Neuf, which did not carry tenement building and which increased city-dwellers' awareness of the river. This was the case too with the Pont Royal which replaced the old Rue du Bac ferry. Constructed in wood in the 1630s by the entrepreneur Le Barbier, it was rebuilt in stone at the king's expense in the 1680s. The region down to the Pont Neuf, flanked by the Louvre and Tuileries on one side and by the Collège des Quatre-Nations on the other, became a kind of public amphitheatre where fireworks, river jousts and ceremonial water processions were held.

Other examples of such urban power-building were the weighty triumphal arches built in the north of the city: one at the end of the Rue Saint-Denis, commemorating victories in the war of Dutch Devolution (1667–8), and the other on the Rue Saint-Martin, celebrating the annexation of Franche-Comté into France in 1678. Public fountains were redecorated in a more impressively monumental style too. The Samaritaine pump which had been erected on the Pont Neuf in 1608 was a famous Parisian monument and a similar one was built on the Pont Notre-Dame in 1676. Another landmark building was the Observatoire, the scientific observatory which Louis had built in 1676 to the south of the Luxembourg garden, and which was designed by Perrault. The astronomer Giovanni Cassini would have preferred a location on higher ground outside the city where the building could be more functional – thus showing he did not understand the new visual grammar of absolutist power practised by the king and his ministers.

The Observatoire and the new triumphal arches were located outside the formal line of the city walls. But the walls were no more. In 1670 Louis ordered the demolition of all the ramparts and their replacement by raised and tree-lined 'boulevards' (a Louis-Quatorzian coinage from the Dutch *bolwerc*, or rampart). Although in 1674 he established a city building limit a few kilometres outside the area of construction, this was just a series of boundary-stones, which had nothing military about them. To make Paris an open city in this way marked a newfound confidence in France's military might. The dense network of putatively impregnable fortresses and earthworks – the so-called 'iron belt' (*'ceinture de fer'*) – being constructed by military engineer Sébastien Le Prestre de Vauban around French frontiers put effective protection at a distance. In addition, one lesson of the Wars of Religion and the Fronde was that city walls allowed cities to hold out against rather than for the king. It was hoped that the removal of the walls would strengthen Parisians' affection for the dynasty, in that their security was utterly dependent upon it.

The 'boulevardization' of the ramparts – the course of which the *grands boulevards* of the nineteenth century followed fairly exactly – was accomplished speedily on the Right Bank. The novelty value of removing urban ramparts, yet being certain that the city was adequately defended, made quite a splash internationally, and the Paris example would subsequently be much copied across Europe. Although the gates from the old Philip Augustus Wall were demolished between 1673 and 1683, the boulevardization process was only completed on the Left Bank quite late in the eighteenth century. It was envisaged that the space around the ramparts – which had been about one hundred metres thick – should be used for open walkways, offering advantageous vistas on the city and on the surrounding countryside. Louis XIV's monumentalist reforms of Paris were thus presented under a favourable aspect for the leisured stroller.

This combination of viewing space and urban monuments was evident in other developments which the king promoted. To the west of the city the Cours-la-Reine (VIIIe.) on the Chaillot road to the south-west of the Tuileries opened up a similar urban vista, and in 1670 Le Nôtre created a *Grand Cours* through the centre of the Tuileries garden on the line of the present-day Champs-Élysées. On the Left Bank an even more impressive use of space was seen in 1670 in the creation of the veterans' hospital of the Invalides (VIIe.). The church's dome seemed almost literally to tug the city further to the west. It allowed linkages to be made with the developing network of streets on the edge of the Faubourg Saint-Germain, around the Rues de l'Université, Saint-Dominique and de Grenelle, where elegant housing was being constructed. The Invalides' service institutions brought new life and habitation to the area to the west too, amid the village of Grenelle and former rabbit warrens. At the same time a splendid boulevard-style avenue (the Avenue de Breteuil) was constructed leading due south from the site. To the north a prohibition was placed on any type of building down to the river, leaving the vista pristine.

Louis and his publicists made much of the Invalides as a grace-and-favour institution established out of the king's personal generosity towards valiant ex-soldiers. More mundanely, it was also part of an extensive police operation aimed to clean up Paris and provide optimum security in the wall-less city. Disruptions caused by the Thirty Years War in the north and east of France had caused an exodus of refugees into cities such as Paris, while the troubles of the Fronde also exacerbated the problem of rootless poverty. In these circumstances, demobilized soldiers and deserters were an invariable cause of public disorder and petty crime – as indeed they had been since the Hundred Years War if not before.

The enclosure of veterans within the Invalides was at least partly intended as a means of preventing such men from extracting their livelihoods from the civilian population. Much the same logic also applied to the project for building what was called a General Hospital (*Hôpital Général*). This had been a concept favoured by post-Tridentine *dévot* activists such as the influential (but clandestine) Company of the Holy Sacrament. Enclosure of beggars, vagrants and petty criminals alongside the deserving poor in multi-purpose poorhouses would allow the genuinely needy to be succoured at low cost while the deviant and delinquent could be moralized into better ways by an unremitting diet of spiritual pedagogy. The notion also appealed to political economists who held that the massed ranks of paupers could be set to work in artisanal trades which would serve the country's balance of payments. A further argument for confinement was the fact that the poor still tended to be equated with contagious diseases which risked the health of the social elites. In 1606–11 Henry IV had built the Hôpital Saint-Louis (Xe.) for plague victims roughly midway between the north of the city and the village of Belleville. The hospital was in pretty much permanent use between 1618 and 1636, when bubonic plague seemed quasi-endemic in the city. Thereafter, as the scourge hit less frequently, the institution was either devoted to skin diseases or else kept closed. Even though it was shut for four years out of five between 1650 and 1700, the threat of bubonic plague was perceived as being as real as ever. The Hôpital Général (as indeed the Invalides, for syphilis and skin disease were endemic amongst the troops) was thus viewed as having the additional advantage of housing many of those who would be likely to spread disease.

The establishment of the Hôpital Général in 1656 was a messy and higgledy-piggledy affair, with a much more repressive aspect than originally planned, which alienated many humanely minded *dévots*, such as Vincent de Paul. In their finished forms the different houses of the institution either warehoused paupers who did not have a home to go to (notably foundlings, orphans, and the aged, infirm, disabled and insane) or else imprisoned various kinds of delinquents (especially prostitutes and individuals adjudged moral deviants). The largest houses were those established for girls and women at La Salpêtrière, whose chapel, topped with a cupola, was designed by Libéral Bruant, and Bicêtre, for men and boys. La Salpêtrière's name comes from being built alongside old gunpowder stores in a distant part of the disinherited Faubourg Saint-Victor – indeed such was the bad reputation of the poorhouse that it blocked further urban expansion in this area for several generations. Bicêtre was erected on the site of an abandoned chateau several kilometres south of the city; the new institution was characterized by an Italian visitor in the 1660s as housing 'an assemblage of rogues who are there in order to rot in filth and to squabble ceaselessly among themselves'.[24] By 1663 there were around 5,000 paupers confined within the Hôpital Général as a whole, two-thirds of whom were in either Bicêtre or La Salpêtrière. By 1700, numbers had doubled.

With the exception of leperhouses, medieval hospitals had tended to be in the heart of the city, where the sight of suffering humanity was thought likely to provoke the charitable giving on which the institutions depended. Thus the ancient Hôtel-Dieu, for example, was next to Notre-Dame cathedral. For the generation of the *grand siècle*, when it came to poverty and disease it was a case of out of sight, out of mind. The Invalides, plus the hospitals of Saint-Louis, La Salpêtrière and Bicêtre, along with a foundling hospital in the Faubourg Saint-

Antoine, were all outside the line of the city walls. There were some smaller institutions on the Left Bank within the city, but no such institutions at all *intra muros* on the Right Bank. The strategy of aiming to keep poverty at a distance also applied to disease. *Cordon sanitaire* techniques were the key here, and they were successfully deployed in 1666–8 to keep the plague from coming downstream from Normandy into Paris. Without knowing it, the city had said goodbye to plague after a sombre acquaintance of more than three centuries.

The government's social policy of containment was the counterpart to the strategy of removing the old city walls and producing an 'open' city. Opening the city meant shutting away those who seemed of most threat to urban order. New policies of policing within the city also conformed to this pattern. Paris appears to have been a very dangerous place in the early seventeenth century. No fewer than 372 persons were murdered in the city in the single year of 1643. On one day in 1644, 6 June, there were fourteen murders. The crown had cracked down hard on the practice of duelling from the 1620s, but there were still numerous such mortal assignations. Organized crime was rife, and gangs of beggars and petty criminals were alleged to reside in impenetrable inner-city zones called 'courts of miracles' (*cours des miracles*). The existence of many 'liberties' where the Châtelet's powers were circumscribed, as well as the existence of a number of seigneuries enjoying judicial powers (especially those belonging to the bishop, the cathedral chapter and some monastic houses), seemed to encourage rather than deter lawlessness.

5.3: The *Cour des Miracles*

Seventeenth-century Parisians were gripped by a moral panic. Beggars and delinquents had grouped together into quasi-military organizations, and were living off the credulity and good intentions of honest Parisians. Wayward individuals were living in parts of the city where the law of the land simply did not run. The late seventeenth-century historian of Paris Henri Sauval claimed to have visited the most famous of these urban 'liberties', the *Cour des Miracles* which was located adjacent to the Filles-Dieu convent and is currently bounded by the Rues Réaumur, Damiette and des Forges (IIe.). It was, he noted, 'a square of a very considerable size, and a great cul-de-sac which was stinking, muddy, irregular and unpaved'. It was 'like in another world [and] situated in one of the most poorly built and dirtiest of neighbourhoods'. The *Cour* was the headquarters of professional thievery, highway robbery, prostitution and begging. The 'miracles' which were performed there were the actorly gestures by which beggars made themselves up to seem blind, disabled, crippled and covered with sores and wounds. Back home after a day of unlawful begging, Sauval stated, 'they take off their paint, clean themselves up and become healthy and jolly in an instant – without any miracles'.

This extraordinary *Cour des Miracles* had features which resembled those of a guild or corporation – the beggars had their own laws, for example, their own rituals and rites of passage, their own training procedures and code of honour. But the *Cour* also travestied the royal court (also a *cour*) which the Bourbons were currently building. The denizens of the *Cour des Miracles* had their own king, the so-called Grand Coesre, plus, Sauval noted, 'laws, estates general, and a language all their own'. Whereas the kings of France accentuated their divine right, in the *Cour des Miracles* 'everyone lived in great licentiousness; no one had faith or law, and baptism, marriage and the sacraments were unknown'. Some, moreover, were gypsies.

The *Cour des Miracles* story had little factual foundation, however, and functioned as a comforting myth for the propertied classes. Nothing in police and judicial records or on contemporary city maps confirms this level of organizational sophistication in the world of begging, prostitution and crime. But the idea of such a counter-culture fortified Parisians in the belief that they should be much more sparing in their charities towards the poor, for fear of subsidizing vice and crime. The idea also gave justification to the efforts of Louis XIV to implement stricter social discipline on a Paris whose turbulence had been confirmed in the Fronde. The establishment in 1656–7 of the Paris Hôpital Général – the sorry assemblage of poorhouses and prisons in which the needy and delinquent paupers were to be confined – drew its inspiration from the idea of eradicating street begging and closing down such havens of vice. Similarly, one of the first claims of Nicolas de La Reynie, Louis XIV's new police official, the Lieutenant-Général de Police, established in 1667, was that he had led a physical assault on the *Cour des Miracles*, purged it of its denizens, and brought the area back within the realm of law and order. Straight new street developments later in the century cut swathes through the site of the old *Cour des Miracles*. Its last vestiges disappeared with the expropriation and development of the Filles-Dieu site in the Revolution and Haussmann's redesigns of the Second Empire (notably along the Rue Réaumur).

The idea of an urban counter-culture of poverty and beggary was one which appealed to the Romantic side of Victor Hugo, who in his 1831 novel *Notre-Dame de Paris* drew heavily on Sauval and writers like him in his depiction of the gypsy Esmeralda, Quasimodo and the rest. Hugo and others who followed his lead were partly at least reflecting contemporary fears about the level of self-organization of the industrial urban working classes in Paris. This is not, of course, to say that there were not appalling levels of poverty in Paris in Victor Hugo's time as under Louis XIV, nor some forms of organized crime. Yet like the mid-seventeenth century, the early nineteenth century was a period of large-scale urban immigration, in which existing structures of social control were placed under heavy pressure. The *Cour des Miracles* story was a myth which played into wider bourgeois anxieties about public order rather than a straight ethnographic account of an established social reality. Unhappily the myth re-emerges at other times of social concern – it has been much used and abused, for example, in descriptions of immigrant communities in late twentieth-century Paris. The *Cour des Miracles* was a genuine group of streets. More importantly, it was also a figment of the indignant bourgeois imagination. Its sombre ideological significance cannot be exaggerated.

In 1665 matters were brought to a head when Paris's senior policing official – the *lieutenant criminel* of the Châtelet, Jacques Tardieu – was murdered in his home along with his wife. It proved well-nigh impossible to find a replacement. A high-level government committee sat in 1666 to review policing in the capital. The city watch was reformed and expanded. More crucially, in 1667 a new royal officer with very wide-ranging powers was established to oversee all policing throughout the city, namely the Lieutenant-Général de Police. The first incumbent, La Reynie, lasted thirty years in the post, until 1697, and his successor, the marquis d'Argenson, nearly two decades. Their half-century of tenure of what became effectively a minister-level position, established it as absolutely key to Parisian life. The remit they were given by the 1667 edict was 'to purge the city of everything that can cause disorder, and to procure abundance'.[25] Characteristically drawing inspiration from the Roman Empire, Colbert maintained that it was essential 'to prevent the city of Paris from getting so big that it should share the destiny of the most powerful cities of Antiquity which found within themselves the source of their own ruin, for it is very difficult to ensure that order and good administration [*police*] should be distributed appropriately in all parts of such a large body'.[26]

The ending of non-royal seigneurial rights within the city in 1674 meant that police powers were deployed evenly across urban space. A few 'liberties' were maintained, such as the Temple precincts in the Marais, in which the absence of police harassment allowed authors to escape censorship. But these were few, and were invariably penetrated by police spies. Round-ups of street beggars and petty criminals led to mass transfers to the Hôpital Général. The *cours des miracles* were (allegedly) demolished. There were much tougher policies towards prostitution and sexual deviancy too, especially from the 1680s, as the ruler became more prudish and *dévot* in his old age.

Although the powers of the Lieutenant-Général were powerfully repressive, there was also a creative and even benign aspect to his work. Concern was shown for poor relief and assistance, notably in times of dearth and epidemic disease. The Lieutenant-Général introduced a much more efficient system of street cleansing and multiplied street-paving and street-widening programmes. The arrival of the carriage as a means of transportation within the city was relatively recent. Foot, horse and mule were what Parisians had previously used. Carriages had been virtually unknown as recently as the reign of Henry IV, who on one occasion had even excused himself from seeing his principal minister because 'my wife is using the carriage'.[27] (By grim irony, Henry would be assassinated in his carriage, which had got caught up in a traffic jam.) By the mid-seventeenth century there were said to be 300 carriages, and a profitable carriage hire business had developed. There were more than ten thousand of them by the start of the following century. There was a quality leap in the provision of street lighting too as a result of police action, a fact on which foreign travellers to the city often commented. After 1700 a new fire-fighting system was introduced, boasting state-of-the-art Dutch fire-pumps.

The king and his police chief also worked in tandem in regard to the world of work. Ever since Henry IV's infatuation with the idea of boosting the Parisian silk industry, Bourbon rulers had shown a concern – subsequently labelled 'mercantilist' – to stimulate the production of luxury goods, so as to reduce dependence on imports. Colbert was particularly active in this respect, and Paris was one of his most worked-on trial sites. An impressively large state manufactory was established out in the Faubourg Saint-Marcel at the Gobelins (XIIIe.), under the artistic direction of the king's First Painter Charles Le Brun, to specialize in goods needed at the royal court: tapestry, sculptures, fancy ironwork, cabinetwork and the like. The Savonnerie house of the Hôpital Général at Chaillot (XVIe.) was organized for carpet-production, and a mirror-works was created at Reuilly (XIIe.), beyond the Faubourg Saint-Antoine.

It was La Reynie's job to deal with labour discipline, not only in state manufactories but across the face of Paris. Considerable efforts were made to repress the clandestine workers' associations known as *compagnonnages*. Royal legislation in the sixteenth century had sought to ensure that all artisans and shopkeepers formed part of a legally founded corporation or guild. Colbert renewed this legislation in 1673 and looked to La Reynie to enforce it in Paris. Though even the king himself had doubts about enforcing the legislation, the number of legally constituted guilds in Paris doubled within two decades. The notion of restricting labour to guilds which were under police surveillance was ideologically consistent with the strategy of confining of the poor. The containment policies also found an echo in the system of neighbourhoods (*quartiers*) into which Paris was reorganized in 1680, then again in 1702. The new system sought to replace the old one of local bourgeois solidarities with a more heavily administered, top-down structure under the tutelage of the Châtelet. Each neighbourhood was patrolled by commissioners of the Lieutenance-Générale.

Several decades of a kind of royal dressage were thus expended in seeking to make Parisians live up to the notions of *Romanitas* which inspired the monumental building projects of Louis and Colbert. By the early 1670s, however, it was becoming evident to both men that they were fighting a losing battle. Colbert realized that he had proved unable to remove Louis's distaste for Parisians forged in the dark days of the Fronde. When resident at the Louvre the king pined for Fontainebleau, Saint-Germain-en-Laye and other royal residences in the environs of Paris. The most prominent of all of these in Louis's affections was becoming Versailles, which for his father had been little more than a hunting lodge. 'Oh! How tragic,' Colbert had once apostrophized the king, 'that the greatest and most virtuous king . . . should be judged by Versailles!'[28] Yet such was to prove to be the case.

The 1660s and 1670s were decades in which Louis was building up a high estimation of his own role in European affairs. Yet he found Parisians irredeemably critical and unappreciative of his efforts, and unwilling to play their part in the magnification of the king's international *gloire*. On acceding to sole rule in 1661, for example, Louis had ousted Nicolas Fouquet as his finance minister and put him on trial for corruption. Yet the longer the trial lasted, the more Parisians warmed to Fouquet's cause against Colbert, his cold and ruthlessly businesslike successor. Parisian opinion was scandalized by the heavy sentence handed down against the former finance minister. If Louis was disdainful of the Parisian populace, he was contemptuous of the city council, and highly suspicious of the Parlement. Even once he had got rid of arch-conspirator Retz as archbishop of Paris, he still found the lower clergy Frondeur in its sympathies. Many ecclesiastics were attracted to the austere ideas of the Jansenists, and Louis never got it out of his head that these had formed Retz's militia during the Fronde. His tough line towards the Jansenist convent at Port-Royal in the

1680s attracted him much criticism from within the church, the Parlement and among the people of Paris (as his police agents were now able to tell him in detail). Even his Revocation of the Edict of Nantes in 1685, which the king had expected would win him plaudits from this hyper-Catholic city, failed to ignite unanimous praise. Violent aspects of the outlawing of Protestantism – the destruction of the Huguenot temple at Charenton, the attempted dragooning of consciences – caused concern even in some *dévot* circles.

Religious enthusiasm was starting to inhibit the rumbustious and Rabelaisian street culture of which Parisians had always been proud. The playwright Molière satirized pious bigotry in his *Tartuffe* (1664), but he was swimming against the stream, especially when Louis, from the 1680s, took a turn towards ostentatious piety. In addition the association of the Pont Neuf with Frondeur seditiousness alienated the king and his cronies. Rulers in the past had been keen visitors to the annual Foire Saint-Germain. The fairground extravaganza continued to attract the crowds – one German visitor recorded having seen there a bearded lady, a man without any hands who wrote with his feet, a lionness, a camel, a two-headed dolphin, an aquarium, a five-footed cow, puppet-shows, strongmen lifting cannons, tightrope walkers and much, much else besides[29] – but the king was no longer part of the crowd. His own preference was for a court-based culture – masques, plays, ballets (at which he excelled as a performer), concerts and the like. Pioneered by Henry III, such courtly entertainments were now firmly established as the cultural repertoire of monarchs. They had little room for the Parisian people.

The death of Louis's mother Anne of Austria in the Louvre in 1666 saw the king sloping off to Versailles as 'the spot where I can most be by myself',[30] and this sense of specialness became increasingly pronounced. Louis did not return to the Louvre for nearly two years, and thereafter spent only two months of the year there. He left the Louvre – as it would turn out for ever – on the rainy night of 10 February 1670, returning to the city on no more than twenty-four occasions over the next forty-four years until his death, but never again spending the night there. The shift of his government to Versailles, on which he began devoting ever more colossal sums of money, was gradual, and only in 1683 did the court move for good and all to

Versailles. Everything was makeshift for quite a while: his foreign minister had to sleep in the menagerie in 1672. Even after 1683 the problems were clear enough: ministers were obliged to reside at Versailles, but their offices and archives remained three hours' journey away in Paris.

By 1683, in addition, Colbert – with whom Louis had forged the idea of Parisian *Romanitas* – was dead. The sense of making something special out of Paris died with him. Louis had in fact left Paris in his mind long before he established his court at Versailles. Over the course of his reign he was to spend a good deal of money on new building in Paris: the sum amounted to about 20 million livres, around half of which was spent on the Louvre and Tuileries, with the Gobelins and the Invalides also representing very substantial sums. Yet this was dwarfed – in the proportion of about one to ten – by the amount expended on Versailles. Symptomatically, despite the high price of Perrault's east frontage to the Louvre, the building did not even receive a roof until well into the eighteenth century. There was a real danger of Paris being eclipsed by this new court city. Louis still asked his courtiers, 'What are people saying in Paris?', yet there was wide concern in the city itself that Paris was becoming, as La Bruyère put it, 'the ape of the court'.[31] For the last decades of his reign, Paris suffered a royal eclipse.

Paris had been remodelled to the measure of a Roman-style ruler, but the city now had to make do for the most part with only his image. Court gazettes, tame newspapers and royal medallions proclaimed the king's glory. His image was also made available to Parisians in sculptures, notably in the Place des Victoires and the Place Vendôme. These two latter-day attempts to link up with the tradition of the *place royale* mapped out by Henry IV were located in the new western areas of the Right Bank. The Place des Victoires (Ie.), just to the east of the Rue de Richelieu, was laid out by François Mansart around a statue of Louis XIV commissioned by the practised courtier the duc de La Feuillade. The king visited the statue in 1687, when the site was just being cleared for construction. A similar statue of himself was the centrepiece of the Place Vendôme to the west (Ie.). The houses were built to the same style, as in Henry IV's Place Royale, but they breathed an urbane elegance and sophistication which made Henry IV's favoured square seem quaintly bucolic and archaic. Like the Place des Victoires, the new square's inhabitants were the heads of the wealthiest financial houses on which the king depended to fight his wars.

Despite the centrality of his representation to the whole concept, Louis did not even bother to attend the ceremonial inauguration of the Place Vendôme in 1699, sending along the duc d'Orléans in his place. Indeed both squares were important less for the glorification of the royal image than for the subsequently much-imitated use of classical forms in domestic architecture for non-aristocratic clients. Louis's few final visits to Paris after 1700 all had to do with the Invalides hospital. Yet if he showed commendable concern for military welfare, he seemed insouciant as regards the well-being of civilians. The generous, palatial spaciousness of the royal *places* struck a contrast with popular living conditions. In 1698 the English visitor Martin Lister commented: 'Here the palaces and convents have eat up the People's dwellings and crouded them excessively together and possessed themselves of the far the greatest part of the ground.'[32]

Almost continual warfare from the late 1680s placed an enormous strain on the country, leading to higher taxes and a round of financial stratagems. In 1693–4 and then again in 1709–10, France also suffered among the very worst mortality crises of the early modern period. The problem was essentially climatic: appalling harvests across Europe caused by bad weather meant there was just not enough food to go round. In 1693–4 more than one-tenth of France's total population died, and one eyewitness recalled that in Paris, 'there were 1,400 to 1,500 deaths daily, some in the Paris Hôtel-Dieu, others on piles of mud in the middle of the street.'[33] The crisis of 1709–10 was less pronounced, but still drastic. The harshness of the winter became legendary, and in the subsequent thaw much of Paris suffered flooding. The severity of the conditions caused the city's population to drop, possibly by as much as a fifth, from around half a million to about 400,000.

There was only a limited amount that the royal government could do against this kind of scourge, but this did not prevent it from receiving a great deal of blame for inaction in the face of suffering. Resentment crystallized into rioting in Paris in 1709, after public works schemes aimed to provide subsistence for the needy were overrun by numbers. The house of Lieutenant-Général de Police d'Argenson (who worked hard to mitigate the effects of the crisis) had to have an armed guard to prevent popular attacks, and there was some shooting which left a number of Parisians dead.

'Shooting: the only way to make Parisians shut up,' the nineteenth-century writer Gustave Flaubert was to note sardonically.[34] This kind of comment only really becomes intelligible in Parisian history from the time of Louis XIV. Kings had often found themselves fighting Parisians in the past – but this was principally so as to control the city and to make it a central piece in their political strategies. Overt violence was still very much the exception, but now that the monarchy had relocated its ritual centre to nearby Versailles, government sought to keep Parisians in line by measures of containment, confinement, restriction, policing – and, in the last resort, by overt violence. By removing city ramparts, the monarchy had attempted to make Parisians more dependent on the dynasty. Yet this is not what transpired. With the monarchy keeping itself at a distance, and apparently turning lukewarm towards the idea of constructing a new Rome, it seemed that it was more up to Parisians now to make their own history.

6

The Kingless Capital of Enlightenment
1715–89

Paris had lost its status as royal residence in 1683. The death of Louis XIV in 1715 saw the infant Louis XV (r. 1715–74) transferred to the Tuileries and his uncle the duc d'Orléans installed at the Palais-Royal as regent. Yet the child-king was so dazzled by the charismatic image of his great-grandfather, that he was scarcely in his teens before, in 1722, he relocated his court back to Versailles. Here it stayed. Louis's grandson and successor, Louis XVI (r. 1774–92), had no thought of moving back to Paris. Although in 1789 he would return to reside in the city, it would be under duress, at the end of the pikes and bayonets of his rebellious subjects. But that is a story which will have to wait for later.[1] What concerns us in the present chapter is how a city whose historic identity had been constructed around its status as royal capital, and which had tended to enjoy its best times when the monarch was in residence within it, coped with a condition of physical kinglessness.

Neither Louis XV nor Louis XVI felt at home in Paris: each had a low embarrassment threshold in public venues and their crowd appearances lacked the artful nonchalance of a Henry IV or Louis XIV. It was Parisians who, in 1744, following an episode in which Louis fell dangerously sick in Metz, had dubbed their monarch 'Louis the Well-Beloved'. Yet the affection was neither deep nor durable. Louis XV's visits to Paris were already becoming rarer and more perfunctory when a riot in 1749 over alleged child-kidnapping by royal officials soured relations for good. After the so-called 'Vanishing Children' episode, even Louis himself commented lugubriously that he had become 'Louis the Well-Hated' in the eyes of his Parisian subjects.[2] He ordered that a road should be specially built so that he could skirt

round his capital when travelling between Saint-Denis and Versailles. Henceforth he never overnighted in Paris, made no royal *entrées*, shunned taking mass at Notre-Dame or the Sainte-Chapelle, and scarcely graced the Louvre with his presence. Louis XVI did nothing to reverse the trend: indeed, in a horrible street panic close to the Tuileries palace during the evening of festivities in May 1770 marking

Crowd panic during royal marriage celebrations, 1770

his marriage (while still dauphin) to Marie-Antoinette of Austria, more than a hundred Parisians were crushed to death – a misfortune which soured relations from the start.

The crown's estrangement from Paris was linked to anxieties regarding the continued growth of the capital city. Following the lead of

Louis XIV and Colbert, the government feared that the city might replicate the experience of the vast megapolises of ancient times and 'die of its own size', as police theorist de La Mare put it.[3] There was a danger of the city becoming rotten with disuse through flight to the suburbs, with the city centre becoming silted up and resistant to circulation and effective policing. In 1724, scarcely installed at Versailles, Louis XV had shown his concern in this regard by formally endorsing his predecessor's ruling of 1674 which prohibited the building of new streets in the faubourgs.

The city's development over the century did not, however, seem to suffer from relative royal eclipse, nor from governmental inhibitions on urban growth. Indeed the eighteenth century would prove one of the most prestigious and dynamic in the history of this now seemingly kingless city. Its population grew from around half a million in the last years of Louis XIV to 650,000 or more in 1789. Its trade and manufacturing sectors boomed; its role as a centre of consumption reached new heights; and its intellectual prowess soared. Paris became unofficial capital of the European Enlightenment, the movement of ideas stressing the rational improvement of humanity. The city's cultural institutions flourished in ways which the rest of Europe envied and tried to mimic. 'Paris is the world,' wrote Marivaux in 1734, 'the rest of the earth is nothing but its suburbs.'[4] Whereas in the previous century La Bruyère had sneered at the way in which the city aped the Versailles court,[5] this relationship was now reversed. By the 1780s the dramatist and urban analyst Louis-Sébastien Mercier would describe Versailles's relationship to Paris as being 'like a satellite round a whirlwind'.[6] Tourists from home and abroad were sure to make a trip out to see the royal court in action, but it was Paris, not Versailles, which, as Mercier avowed, 'rivets the gaze of the entire world'. Paris was, Charles de Peyssonel agreed in 1782, 'the Epitome of the Universe, a vast and shapeless city, full of marvels, virtues, vices and follies'.[7]

Earlier guidebooks to Paris had stressed its antiquities and the archaeological record that it embodied. In Germain Brice's *Nouvelle Description de la ville de Paris*, much reprinted over the course of the century,[8] however, the emphasis shifted to the here and now, and stressed the utilitarian over the historic, supplying shop addresses rather than interminable lists of monuments. Paris was great because of what it was, not what it had been. There was a growing concern to calibrate the full extent of the city's vibrant social and cultural life, and to represent it in a way less hidebound by tradition. Brice's guide led the way by including a map of the city, and there were indeed to be over a hundred maps of the city published over the century – far more than ever before. They invariably marked the 1702 administrative division of Paris into twenty *quartiers* rather than the age-old tripartite division of Île de la Cité and Right and Left Banks. Maps, guidebooks and almanacs were increasingly made available in pocketbook size, moreover, for the inquisitive pedestrian.

The face of Paris seemed palpably to be changing in ways which attenuated the traditional visual vocabulary of royal authority. The ostentatious display of royal military power was less important than hitherto, especially given Louis XIV's removal of the ramparts. The creation of a string of seemingly impregnable fortresses on France's national perimeter had produced a *pax borbonica* from which Parisians benefited: there would be no military incursions against the capital between the Fronde and 1792 (though there were a couple of invasion scares). Charles V's Bastille fortress became a prison, as did the heavily turreted Châtelet. Both establishments were only demolished after the collapse of the Ancien Régime – the Bastille in the weeks after 14 July 1789, and the Châtelet between 1802 and 1810. Yet both were already seen as anachronistic, and there were numerous projects for their erasure from the Parisian cityscape. They were out of place in an open city. Furthermore, with some exceptions,[9] ecclesiastical building projects – one of the means by which the divine-right basis of Bourbon power had been affirmed at the zenith of the Counter-Reformation – were less evident in a century which in any case was becoming increasingly secularist and materialist. Ceremonial religious processions now became the prompt for more secular pastimes: in 1786 the English visitor Mrs Cradock was astonished to witness 'religion and amusement mixed up together', as a solemn religious procession outside the church of Saint-Sulpice and involving hundreds of priests transformed itself into a street show including 'a camel with a monkey on its back, and a clown dancing, singing and making lewd jokes to the public', accompanied by other street entertainers.[10]

The scale of dynastic commitment to the city may have been in flux, but Louis XV and Louis XVI emphatically did not seek to disengage from the city. After all, Parisians supplied roughly one-sixth of the total state tax revenue. Paris might be physically kingless, but it was still primed to bear the signs of dynastic authority and dynastic strength – and to accept the demands of the royal taxman. Ceremonial welcomes to foreign ambassadors and heads of state were still played out in the city streets as well as the *salles de parade* of Versailles. Praise of the king on these occasions was, however, invariably vicarious. In the absence of the king, the Paris-loving princes of the royal blood, such as successive ducs d'Orléans and Louis XV's cousin the prince de Conti, personally associated themselves with such celebrations. Ominously too, the Parlement of Paris had regained its power to remonstrate against royal edicts and started to accentuate its disputed role as defender and representative of the Parisian people – and indeed of the French nation. The magistrates became involved in frequent political clashes with Louis XV. These were most notable in the late 1720s and early 1730s and then in the 1750s – over financial issues and also concerning the Jansenist movement within the French church. Both king and Parlement curried favour with Parisian opinion and vied with each other to seem more patriotic and more caring towards Parisians.

There was indeed a noticeable change in the style of urban represen-tation favoured by the crown. Rulers put behind them the tradition of highlighting the king as military warrior who commanded obedience or as the awesome lieutenant of God on earth. Instead royal propa-ganda stressed that the king should be seen as a kindly – if somewhat remote – father figure, eager to ensure his subjects' welfare and who looked to elicit from them love, respect and gratitude rather than fear or awe. Kings might thus personally disassociate themselves from Paris; but they had not renounced the monarchy's enduring wish to try to shape it in their dynasty's image.

This new development was evident in Louis XV's establishment in 1752 of a military college, the École militaire. This registered the crown's association of the city with another object of royal affection, his military nobility. A grand philanthropic gesture, like the creation of the Invalides and the La Salpêtrière hospital, the École was located, as they had been, on the less built-up Left Bank (on a site incidentally well outside the 1674/1724 city limits set by the crown). Its construction was masterminded by the financier Pâris-Duverney and Louis XV's mistress the Marquise de Pompadour, and it was designed to provide career training for impoverished country gentry. The École had a somewhat chequered history until the Revolution: it had been designed with royal beneficence in view, but was never properly funded, and took years to complete. But its establishment was important in pulling Paris further to the south-west and stimulating infill through to the Faubourg Saint-Germain. The tiny fishing hamlet of Gros Caillou (VIIe.), hemmed between the École militaire and the Hôtel des Invalides, now prospered by servicing these institutions.

Wide, tree-lined avenues were created in the vicinity of the École militaire and the Invalides on the model of the lay-out being gradually extended to the city's perimeter boulevards. This development was complemented by the creation outside the École, on what had been vegetable allotments, of a parade and exercise ground, the Champ de Mars. The terrain was lengthened by filling in a rivulet of the Seine: the former Île des Cygnes was incorporated in such a way as to extend the Champ de Mars down to the Seine (at a spot later to sport the Eiffel Tower). Tens of thousands of individuals could and did gather here for military tattoos, horseracing and other public spectacles.

The Champ de Mars highlighted the monarchy's continued desire to contribute towards the remodelling of the city. It also showed the king's developing concern with dynastic self-promotion and generosity through public spectacle. The latter policy was also evident in a range of minor projects and initiatives. The Tuileries gardens, for example, were opened to the public (a gesture which Louis XVI obliged royal princes to replicate in the case of the Palais-Royal and the Luxembourg gardens). Plans were made to extend the squares in front of the churches of Saint-Sulpice (VIe.) and Saint-Germain-l'Auxerrois (now Place du Louvre, Ie.) in order to allow them to form similar locations for assembling crowds. Such public squares, notably the *places royales*, became the site of orchestrated public rejoicing for the announcement of peace treaties, major battles, dynastic events and so on. The quais alongside the Seine were redesigned too so that they could accommodate large numbers who wished to watch river entertainments on public holidays. There were magnificent river-jousting competitions (*joutes*) held on the Seine in 1739, for example, to celebrate the marriage of the eldest daughter of the king to a Spanish prince (though very characteristically none of the royal family bothered to turn up in person).

Dynastic grandeur was increasingly expressed in the neo-classical style. A re-emergent taste in government circles for Antiquity owed much to the visit which the Marquis de Marigny, Madame de Pompadour's younger brother, made to Italy in the early 1750s. On his return the born-again antiquophiliac Marigny became Director of Royal Buildings, a post which gave him control over royal artistic and architectural commissioning for two decades. The Hôtel des Monnaies (the royal mint), constructed by architect Jacques-Denis Antoine under Marigny's instruction in the 1770s on a highly visible location on the Seine frontage,[11] was one example of his passion. It could have passed muster as a mildly updated Greek temple. The same was also true of both Jacques Gondouin's College of Surgery on what is now the Rue de l'École de Médecine (VIe.), which Louis helped to sponsor, and the church of the Madeleine (VIIIe.), started by Constant d'Ivry in 1764. The crown also had a hand in the extensive developments around the new Théâtre-Français (now the Odéon: VIe.), another pseudo-Greek temple. Louis XV purchased the site from the prince de Condé in 1773, but work had not got far when the king died. Louis XVI handed over responsibility for the construction to his brother, the comte de Provence, who was given the nearby Luxembourg palace as his residence. The site was divided into a radial set of streets focusing on the theatre, which was constructed so as to open up a large square in front of it. The Roman style was more in favour for the grain-market (*Halle aux Blés*) (Ie.) constructed in the 1760s on the lines of a colosseum on the site of Catherine de' Medici's Hôtel de Soissons.[12]

The greatest product of the Antique revival and a particularly fine example of the crown's spectacular monumentalism was the church of Sainte-Geneviève (Ve.). When he had recovered from near-fatal illness at Metz in 1744, Louis XV made a vow to reconstruct the very dilapidated abbey-church of Sainte-Geneviève, resting-place of the remains of Paris's patron saint, as well as of Clovis and other Merovingian dynasts. The design of the new church was the work of Jacques-

Germain Soufflot, one of Marigny's companions on his Italian cultural tour. The first stone was laid in 1764, and the church completed in 1773. It was to become the Panthéon, resting-place for the remains of great men (and, extremely latterly, a tiny smattering of great women). Significantly, despite its royal pedigree, the remains of kings and queens would never pass under the dome of this imposing pile: the Revolution made sure of that. In order to give the church room to breathe, the Rue Soufflot (Ve.) was opened up, running towards the Luxembourg gardens. Although the new street only reached as far as the Rue Saint-Jacques, the operation involved considerable expense and vast administrative operations.

The complexities of major urban development within existing urban tissue influenced the location of another major royal initiative, the Place Louis XV, a project which similarly combined royal paternalism, spectacular monumentalism and Greco-Roman taste. The idea for a new royal square followed a vow of the city government to honour Louis XV for his success in the War of Austrian Succession (1740–48). Two competitions were held, in which architects and engineers were invited to suggest a location and design for the square. Well in excess of a hundred applicants entered into the spirit of the project, proposing a wide and imaginative series of sites (the Île de la Cité, for example, the Place de l'Hôtel-de-Ville, and even, ironically enough, the Bastille). Almost any of these sites would have opened up the heart of the city, and stimulated mobility and connection. Yet such projects would have been politically, financially and administratively difficult to drive through, and in the end the king preferred an easier option: he donated to the city fathers land he owned at the end of the Tuileries garden, on the western fringe of Paris. The new Place Louis XV (later the Place de la Concorde, Ie.) offered less scope for urban renovation than seventeenth-century *places royales* such as the Place des Vosges and the Place Vendôme. The square opened the possibility of a link to the Champs-Élysées, which were being laid out as an urban promenade, with tree-lined boulevards extending out to the new bridge at Neuilly. Yet this was not followed through – the square was seen as being on the outer limit of the city, and a moat separated it from the Champs-Élysées. 'Surrounded by gardens and bosquets,' noted one writer, 'it merely suggests an embellished esplanade in the midst of an

agreeable countryside.'[13] With Edmé Bouchardon's masterly equestrian statue of the king (destroyed in the Revolution) adorning the
centre of the square, this was dynastic power-building of a sort which
accentuated the popular contemplation of royal authority over
improved urban utility or circulation. Only with the building of the
Pont Louis XVI (now Pont de la Concorde) in the late 1780s, which
joined together the Faubourg Saint-Honoré on the Right Bank and
the Faubourg Saint-Germain on the Left, did the Place start to show
potential as a catalyst for urban development.

The Faubourgs Saint-Honoré and Saint-Germain in fact supplied
the most fashionable addresses in eighteenth-century Paris, overtaking
the once-chic Marais, now increasingly viewed as fuddy-duddy and
passé. The prosperity of the two neighbourhoods showed that the very
wealthiest and most powerful individuals in the kingdom, despite
passing time at the royal court in Versailles, were also committed to
the kind of lifestyle that could be found only in Paris. Entrée to the
royal court might be a vital affirmation of aristocratic status, but many
found that court life got very boring very soon. Louis XV and XVI
were unable to prevent the Gadarene rush of aristocratic courtiers
who formed the audience for the king's absolutist ceremonials at
Versailles from drifting towards Paris. Old 'Sword' nobles (those
whose rank derived from their military functions) on the run from the
inanities of the court built the same kinds of private residences as
wealthy 'Robe' nobles (whose status derived from legal and administrative service) and financiers. Intermarriage and shared interests in
cultural activity solidified this tendency – as did residential propinquity. The fashionable Parisian faubourgs offered a framework for
the heterogeneous elements within the social elite to pursue a relatively
homogeneous lifestyle.

The fact that much of the apparatus of central government was still
located in the city was also important in this mixing together of the
monied elite. It was not until the 1760s that the war, navy and foreign
affairs ministries were transferred to Versailles. Even then, the offices
of the Contrôle Général (the finance ministry) and subaltern branches
of all the ministries were still located in Paris. Moreover, the city
remained the centre of the state's judicial and financial systems. The
Robe nobility, who dominated the Parlement, were among the most

solidly based elements within the elite, and like the high officials within the state's financial machinery showed a strong preference for Paris over Versailles. The General Farm, which was responsible for gathering indirect taxes, had its offices on the present-day Rue Jean-Jacques Rousseau (Ie.), close to the church of Saint-Eustache on one side and the exclusivist Place Vendôme on the other. Whereas the Faubourg Saint-Germain was more the haunt of the older nobility, nine-tenths of Farmers-General in 1789 were resident in the vicinity of the Rue Saint-Honoré and its extension, the Rue du Faubourg Saint-Honoré. The area developed the aura of the city's financial district (the stock exchange was nearby) as well as a cultural powerhouse, for the financial elite also prided themselves on being among the city's cultural pace-setters.

Only the Faubourgs Saint-Germain and Saint-Honoré, noted a memorandum in 1733, 'were appropriate for building big houses which would be the residence of persons of distinction'. These areas were consequently, it continued, 'so increased and so full of superb new dwellings that several would justly merit the name of palaces'.[14] Both neighbourhoods enjoyed good air, had space to allow the creation of extensive gardens, and boasted a relative absence of the lower social orders. On the Left Bank the development of the Faubourg Saint-Germain was most marked along the set of long streets running parallel to the Seine: the Rues de Bourbon (now Rue de Lille), de Verneuil and de l'Université, and further south, the Rues Saint-Dominique and de Grenelle (VIe.–VIIe.) – all of which retain much of this impressive eighteenth-century building stock. Later in the century the fashionable area of the Faubourg would spread towards Saint-Sulpice and the Odéon.

The installation of the king in the Tuileries and the duc d'Orléans at the Palais-Royal in 1715 had attracted to the Saint-Honoré neighbourhood a sizeable chunk of the political elite. The tenure of the state financial ministry by the Scottish speculator John Law sparked a speculative boom based on massive over-production of paper money. Although Law's notorious 'System' collapsed in ignominy in 1721, by then it had already kick-started major building projects in these neighbourhoods. The process was well served by the canalization and then the complete paving over of the Great Sewer (*le Grand Égout*)

(1739–67),[15] which ran to the north and parallel to the Grand Boulevards. The removal of this source of stench and infection made its environs altogether more desirable. Massive residences now started to be built on the southern side of the Rue du Faubourg Saint-Honoré, with their gardens opening out onto the Champs-Élysées. The Hôtel d'Évreux, for example, constructed between 1718 and 1722, became in the 1740s the Parisian residence of the king's mistress, the Marquise de Pompadour, an avid shopper on the Rue Saint-Honoré, where the finest silks, furniture, porcelain and fashionable clothing were to be found. (Later renamed the Élysée palace, the Hôtel d'Évreux has since 1871 served as the official residence of Presidents of the Republic.) The Chaussée d'Antin neighbourhood (IXe.) to the north-west of the Rue de Richelieu was another fashionable area in the vicinity. What under the regency had been meadowlands, dairies and market gardens was changed seemingly overnight into a residential district containing spacious and elegant homes for wealthy financiers and their like.

The Chaussée d'Antin area's growth stalled somewhat in the late 1720s, but it re-emerged strongly from the 1760s and 1770s, a period which witnessed the beginnings of a major speculative building boom in Paris, much of it in the radius of the wealthy western neighbourhoods. The 1724 building limitation became increasingly redundant, particularly because those who sponsored urban developments in the city and its faubourgs were in a powerful position to extract royal favours. It was Louis XVI's brother, the comte de Provence, as we have seen, who fronted development operations around the Odéon.[16] Provence's younger brother, the comte d'Artois, similarly built up the Roule neighbourhood out beyond the tax wall along the Faubourg Saint-Honoré on what had been royal nursery gardens established by Louis XIII (VIIIe.)[17] The ruined minister the duc de Choiseul, who chose to raise money by developing the gardens of his residence on the Rue de Richelieu, supplied another high-profile example of this tendency: a home was built here for the Opéra-Comique theatre company and fashionable new properties were constructed alongside (IIe.).[18] Similarly, Louis XVI's finance minister Jacques Necker and Farmer-General Jean-Joseph de la Borde were involved in speculative building in the fashionable Chaussée d'Antin neighbourhood. To the east of the Chaussée d'Antin, the Faubourg Poissonnière (IXe.) saw a similar exercise in high-grade speculative building around the same time, notably on the former domains of the Filles-Dieu and of the Saint-Lazare monastery.

Ecclesiastical property in fact played a not inconsiderable part in this late-century building boom. Many religious houses – such as the Filles-Dieu and Saint-Lazare, in fact – had extensive gardens and grounds, dating back to the Counter-Reformation age of faith and even beyond. Yet as the eighteenth century wore on they suffered from financial mismanagement and misfortune, a decline in charitable giving and a fall in religious vocations. Property deals offered a way out of their problems, and a new financial instrument emerged, namely leasehold, which allowed them to circumvent mortmain (the legal prohibition on the sale of church land). On the Right Bank the Feuillants used ninety-nine-year leases on their properties along the Rue Saint-Honoré in order to achieve solvency. In the Marais the properties of the Order of Malta in former Templar domains permitted major building developments (IIIe.–XIe.), while the Aligre market place and its environs were carved out of the properties of the abbey of Saint-Antoine-des-Champs (XIIe.). On the Left Bank the abbey of Saint-Germain-des-Prés developed the Rue Jacob while the Carmes did the same along the Rue de Vaugirard down to the Rue du Regard (VIe.).

A stroll around the Musée Cognacq-Jay in the Marais (IIIe.) will give the twenty-first century visitor a sense of the lusciously if sometimes cloyingly beautiful interiors to be found within the cream of these new fashionable residences: the museum exhibits the kind of features which made of the reigns of Louis XV and Louis XVI a golden age of the French decorative arts. The stern classical values espoused by Colbert and Louis XIV had, from the regency onwards, given way to the rococo. The latter term, coined only later in the century, denoted a multiform movement of elegant asymmetrical and luxuriant ornamentation, often presented in a hedonistic and mildly erotic style, which dreamily highlighted the activities of nymphs, pagan goddesses and shepherdesses. The rococo suited the materialist ostentation of the monied elite, and indeed in turn influenced royalty – across Europe as well as in France. Support for the rococo from Madame de Pompadour – whose purchasing and commissioning, aided by her brother,

Marigny, was on an extraordinary scale – installed the rococo in princely pleasure houses in the Paris region (such as the Marquise's own favourite, the country house at Bellevue) as well as in the choicest of Parisian private residences. Although the emergence of the neo-classical style in architecture stimulated a move away from a rococo style and thematics from the 1750s and 1760s, the infiltration of Greco-Roman motifs and a more elevated and moralistic decorative style did not affect the aesthetic quality nor the expense of the workmanship on view.

In theory at least, the criteria for intellectual work and artistic taste were set by the royal academies put in place in the seventeenth century.[19] Yet the eighteenth century saw the blossoming of new bodies which came to rival the intellectual and artistic authority of the crown's cultural apparatus. The pleasure domes of the wealthy elite in particular provided the venue for the expansion of cultural institutions independent of the state. Aristocratic hôtels often housed art collections, natural history cabinets, coin and medal collections and libraries to which any well-bred tourist or literate intellectual could gain access. Certain residences hosted salons, worldly gatherings of individuals drawn from the social, literary and artistic elites and meeting regularly to engage in conversation on the affairs of the day and in other cultural pursuits (music, poetry, play-readings, etc.). Most salons were male in composition, even though they were usually ruled over by a woman, who umpired proceedings in the lush sur-roundings of some of the choicest private hôtels of the city's most fashionable neighbourhoods: the Rue Saint-Honoré (Madame du Ten-cin, Madame du Deffand, Madame Geoffrin), the Rue des Moulins near to the Place Vendôme (the Baron d'Holbach), the Chaussée d'Antin (Madame Necker), and the Rue Saint-Dominique (Julie de Lespinasse).

Pride of place in the meetings of the salons was taken by the writers and journalists who proclaimed themselves as philosophers of reason and enlightenment. The *philosophes* – men like Voltaire, Montesquieu, Diderot, d'Alembert, Grimm – set the intellectual pace, adjudicated public taste and campaigned for more rational social institutions. Foreigners remarked on the cultural prestige which such men of letters achieved, and saw as something quintessentially Parisian the custom of 'not only admitting but courting the Literati to adventure into the beau monde . . .'. '[Y]ou will behold [them],' continued an intemperate English visitor, '*habillè au dernier gout* [*sic*], blended with uniforms and shoulder-knots, giving zests to *petits soupès* . . . or adapting Ovid's art of love to the genius of modern toilets.'[20] Although salon habitués were drawn from a broader social range than the royal academies, such was the fame of the *philosophes* that visiting heads of state eagerly lined up to attend the gatherings so as to imbibe the heady rationalist talk and agreeable politeness on offer.

Not only did the denizens of the salons often express views which ran counter to those of the cultural apparatus of the absolute monarchy, they also increasingly claimed to embody the rational views of public opinion in general. The idea that canons of taste should be regulated not on high by the crown and its cultural minions nor even by the Parlement but rather from below, from within polite society, was simultaneously being developed in another cultural venue, the Paris art Salon.[21] From the late 1730s the holding of a major annual (later biennial) exhibition of new paintings in the Salon, within the Louvre, provided a highly prestigious venue for artists. The popularity of these art shows – there were 30,000 visitors in 1781, for example – provided a clue to a subtle transformation taking place. What increasingly gave the Salon its prestige was less crown endorsement than public acclaim. 'It is only in the mouths of those firm and equitable men who compose the Public,' claimed the art critic La Font de Saint-Yenne in 1747, '. . . that we can find the language of truth.'[22]

Public opinion was king in this emergent range of cultural institutions, which seemed beyond the control of the monarchy. Cultural and intellectual pursuits were attracting a wider audience from within the urban bourgeoisie. The latter, guided by the *philosophes*, was becoming increasingly self-confident in its own judgements. They dominated the Masonic lodges, for example, which had started up in Paris in the 1720s. Although some of these were socially exclusivist, in most of them individuals ranging from nobles down to artisans and shopkeepers happily rubbed shoulders with businessmen, state officials and professionals, as they performed arcane secret rituals and engaged in clandestine acts of philanthropy. Around one hundred lodges existed in Paris by the end of the Ancien Régime, containing perhaps as much as 5 per cent of the adult male population and a very high proportion of the commercial and professional bourgeoisie.

Just as there was more than earnest and clandestine do-gooding taking place in Masonic lodges, there was more than coffee being consumed within Paris's coffee-houses. These too formed a forum of discussion and debate especially popular with the middling sort. Around 400 in number under the regency, coffee-houses were probably three or four times as numerous by late in the century. A standard feature in the coffee-houses were newspapers. The press was indeed a vital component in the emergent bourgeois public sphere. The number of books published over the century rose threefold, with theological subjects plummeting in favour of a lighter menu of history, travel and belles-lettres. Even more significant was the rise of the periodical press, particularly in the second half of the century. Government censorship restricted the way in which public affairs and politics were reported, but it was evident that there was a fast-growing demand for news and views of all sorts. From 1777 Paris had its first daily newspaper, the *Journal de Paris*. By the 1780s this was turning out 10,000 copies a day, many of which were eagerly devoured within the city's coffee-house culture.

6.1: The Café Procope

The supreme merit of Paris, Ralph Waldo Emerson opined, was that it was 'a city of cafés and conversation' – and the two were inseparable. The city owes much, then, to Francesco Procopio dei Coltelli. François Procope, as he became, was a Sicilian who is generally accredited with establishing the first coffee-house in Paris. If the coffee bean had been making the odd appearance in France since the 1640s, it was Procope who was said, after promoting the new beverage at the Foire Saint-Germain in 1672, to have set up his own shop on the Rue des Fossés-Saint-Germain (now Rue de l'Ancienne-Comédie: VIe.) in 1686. Procope's business sense was sound: by placing his up-market premises adjacent to a bowling green and a tennis court he could be assured a steady flow of thirsty customers. The transformation of the bowls amenity into the home of the Comédie-Française assured another set of idlers (the audiences, that is). Picked up by fashionable society, coffee became a fad on which everyone had an opinion.

Like many fads, coffee could have faded. Medical interest in the therapeutic value of the new substance was intense, and this helped promote its use. Yet if coffee endured and established itself as an item of absolute necessity in the life of most Parisians, this was substantially because it was associated with a new form of sociability which made its consumption a pleasurable and collective activity – the mixture of coffee and conversation. The Dutch and the English had coffee-houses slightly before the French, but when the Dutchman Nemeitz visited Paris in the 1720s he was struck by how numerous the institutions had become. Some streets had between ten and a dozen coffee-houses – indeed there were probably around 400 in existence at this time. Some of them, he noted, 'are held in great esteem and often visited by princes and other great figures'. They were not such havens of smokers as the Dutch coffee-houses (this would change), and not so given to receiving newspapers (this would too). They were different from workers' bars, and the general atmosphere was boisterous but in a bourgeois rather than ple-beian way. What really marked them out in Nemeitz's eyes was the fact that people loved listening to conversations on the affairs of the days. The coffee-house had become a forum for the bourgeois public voice.

The eighteenth century was the heroic age of the Café Procope. All the principal *philosophes* were regulars: Diderot and d'Alembert (the two hit on the idea of the *Encyclopédie* here one day), Voltaire, Rousseau, Marmontel, Beaumarchais, Mer-cier and so on. The Revolution brought a new wave: Danton, Marat, Hébert, Camille Desmoulins and numerous journalists and members of the sans-culotte intelligentsia. The red bonnet was first displayed here. Though the Procope had its Romantic phase – with Musset, George Sand, Gautier, Balzac, Hugo and, later, Verlaine – it fell on hard times later in the nineteenth century. It became a vegetarian restaurant (a real curio in Paris prior to the late twentieth century), and was run by the Assistance publique. International tourism saved it (sort of): the café was restored, albeit as a restaurant which now plays mostly to the credit-card tourist crowd.

The Procope's fame had been slipping even before the Revolution. The great cafés of the late eighteenth and early nineteenth centuries were those situated in or around the Palais-Royal. The first thing that the soldiers of the allied armies did on entering Paris in 1814 was to rush to the Palais-Royal's cafés where they could soak up the atmosphere – and check out the prostitutes. By the mid-nineteenth century the brand leaders – the Café Riche, the Café Anglais and Tortoni – were out on the fashionable western boulevards. By this time a distinctive café decor had established itself too, initially at the top end of the trade, but soon spreading more widely: mirrors, chandeliers, marble-top tables, ornate stucco work and gilding. *Cafés-concerts* showed a diversification of the leisure activities to be found in such places. Also, from the 1860s, starting on the boulevards, the habit of spreading café tables out onto the pavement began, opening out Parisian street life as a kind of absorbing theatre. Paris has never been the same since. One American visitor's jaw dropped in 1869 to discover 'persons of all classes sitting [in pavement cafés] smoking, drinking, chatting, reading the journals. Here is a true democracy – the only social equality to be seen in christendom.' (He may have exaggerated.)

Karl Marx first met Friedrich Engels at the Café de la Régence in the Palais-Royal. There was nothing exceptional about this, for the café's early history had been associated with bourgeois and bohemians: Marx and Engels were both. However, the proletarian class whose cause both men espoused also, as the nineteenth century wore on, became attracted to the café as well as the bar and wineshop. Indeed there was not always much to distinguish between such institutions – alcohol had long been a café staple. By the 1880s the city contained some 40,000 cafés. (This fell by 1914 to around 30,000; there are currently around 2,000.) Working-class sociability demanded tobacco. Many

Café Procope

bourgeois establishments had resisted them hitherto, but soon gave way. These were places of conviviality, but also of consolation, 'cathedrals of the poor', according to the writer Leroy-Beaulieu. Edmond de Goncourt visited working-class Belleville a week after the bloody destruction of the Commune in 1871 and found 'people drinking with faces of ugly silence'. It could have been worse. For it was confidently said that 30,000 Parisians would have hanged themselves if cafés were closed on Sunday nights as in England.

During the Second World War the café had a moment which would long live in Parisian nostalgia. Shortages of fuel and basic foodstuffs drove individuals into cafés for a little warmth as well as the coffee, alcohol and company which were café staples. The intellectual cafés of Saint-Germain-des-Prés spawned the existential movement of the *après guerre*. Sartre developed his philosophy by using the actions of a café waiter as a kind of existentialist parable.

By the turn of the twenty-first century the café was undoubtedly under pressure. Fast-food outfits and the like had seduced away a massive segment of potential café crowds, and changing mores led to many cafés closing early, especially out in the suburbs, sometimes triggering a downwards spiral in attendance. Fortunately the café was putting up good resistance. The welcome now given to women, in institutions which had been bastions of varying forms of masculinity, increased the potential clientele. In addition, café proprietors responded to the tendency towards segmentation of markets by developing niche cafés: musical cafés, literary cafés, philosophical cafés, gay cafés, teetotal cafés, and – not least – cybercafés. Symptomatically, museums began to be invaded by cafés. Café entrepreneurs gave the institution a style make-over – witness the chain established by the Coste brothers including the Café des Hauteurs in the Musée d'Orsay and the Café Marly overlooking the Louvre Pyramide, or else the Café Beaubourg next to the Centre Pompidou, designed by the architect Christian de Portzamparc.

The consumption of coffee – on which Parisians spent some three million livres a year (more than on cheese, incidentally)[23] – transcended social distinctions. The exotic commodity was the *raison d'être* of the coffee-houses which were the new bastions of intellectual and political vulgarization. Yet one of Louis XV's little pleasures was to make coffee for his guests at private dinner-parties hosted by Madame de Pompadour – another example of the crown now following fashion rather than setting it. At the other end of the social spectrum, moreover, *café au lait* was fast becoming a standard breakfast item for the Parisian labouring classes. This kind of cross-class sharing of taste was evident in other cultural and leisure venues. Certain of the elite's cultural institutions, for example, became more socially expansive over the century. There had been only around 4,000 places in all Paris theatres in 1700, for example; by 1789 there were 13,000. The Opéra-Comique and the developing boulevard theatres played to popular as well as elite taste. Furthermore, while coffee-houses, theatres and public gardens saw an invasion by the lower orders, conversely, some haunts of the labouring classes were increasingly frequented by their social betters. Nobles, for example, may well have been proportionally over-represented in Parisian bars and drinking haunts, while the city's numerous tennis courts pitted princes against master-glaziers.[24] The ancient fairs of Saint-Germain and Saint-Laurent went into decline after the 1760s, but other venues picked up their habitually cross-class custom – notably the north-western boulevards, which offered a smorgasbord of puppet theatre, acrobat performances, automata demonstrations, waxworks museums and freak-shows. Paris, noted one visitor, striving for an appropriate simile, was a collection of 'swarms of sprites and shadows flitting about amongst the spaces of chaos'.[25]

Although public executions and animal fights (both invariably rated a good day out) also drew a wide range of enthusiasts, perhaps the best emblem of this emergent collective urban culture – as well as a satisfying symbol of the age of enlightenment – was the fireworks display, which became the invariable accompaniment to popular, municipal and royal festivities. The spaces newly opened up in the city by royal projects and speculative developments – the Place Louis XV, the Champ de Mars, the *quais* and so on – allowed the promiscuous mixing of the orders. The Parisian predilection which Mrs Cradock had noted for turning public events into entertainment and revelry,[26] attested a secular materialism which contemporaries interpreted as a sign of waning religious faith.

Since there proved a market for such class-blind rubbing of shoulders, there were soon entrepreneurs and projectors eager to stimulate further public demand. New leisure industries were soon appearing, which catered for the burgeoning tourist trade. In 1764 the Italian pyrotechnist Torré created a 'Summer Vauxhall' on the Rue de Bondy (now Rue René-Boulanger, Xe.), while his compatriot Ruggieri established a 'Winter Vauxhall' on the premises of the Saint-Germain fair. (The use of the term 'vauxhall' highlighted a more than linguistic debt to London, prime consumer market of eighteenth-century Europe.) A particularly striking location of this sort was the *Colisée*, a huge amphitheatre built in the 1770s to the north of the Champs-Élysées (VIIIe.), and modelled on the Roman coliseum. Capable of holding up to 40,000 individuals, the *Colisée* offered a wide range of entertainments and shopping experiences for everyone from 'the lowly through to men of title'.[27] Even more impressive in this respect was the Palais-Royal. In the early 1780s the duc d'Orléans turned his ancestral Parisian residence into a semi-public space, a kind of neo-classical shopping mall brimful of businesses and thronged with strollers and passers-by (and no shortage of prostitutes). The Italian dramatist Goldoni noted that there were more than enough shops in the Palais-Royal arcades to 'supply everything one needs for appearance', as well as a host of 'coffee-houses, public baths, restaurants and caterers, hôtels, social gatherings, spectacles, paintings, books, concerts'.[28] 'With money in one's pocket,' remarked the Marquis de Bombelles in 1786, 'in a single day and without leaving its precincts one can buy as prodigiously much in the way of luxury goods as one would manage in a year in any other locality.'[29]

As the Palais-Royal seemed to indicate, the new cultural milieux evident in eighteenth-century Paris and the accompanying social life eroded social deference. Visitors had often in the past remarked upon the light, irreverent gaiety of Parisians; this now seemed to be developing into a freer and more egalitarian outlook on life, often exhibited in the street or in locations such as the Palais Royal. 'Apart from the very highest nobility, everyone is equal in Paris,' noted one commentator with no little (but still revealing) exaggeration. 'A cobbler won't give way to a marquis in the street. That's what is fine about Paris.'[30] For customary deference to operate, however, the cobbler and the marquis would have to recognize each other's social station. This was becoming increasingly difficult – because of the emergence of fashion.

Fashion was the subject of much moralizing lamentation as cynosure of all the vices. Yet sumptuary sermons did not inhibit its growing popularity across all the classes. Traditionally, what you were was what you wore – but this time-honoured equation was becoming less cogent. The swift-changing playfulness of fashion parodied norms of dress and acted as a solvent on the display of rank through costume. It came to be a truism that it was now impossible to tell a duchess from a dairymaid. Madame de Pompadour and, latterly, Louis XVI's queen Marie-Antoinette played by dressing up as dairymaids, while dairymaids for their part were adopting forms of dress – silk stockings, light colourful dresses, jewels and trinkets – which had formerly been the exclusive preserve of the elite. Each year the mercers of the Rue Saint-Honoré on which Madame de Pompadour and the fashion elite did their shopping dressed a doll in clothes adjudged to represent the season's new fashion. A regiment of the dolls was then expedited to the provinces and to far-flung foreign locations. The fashion doll informed royal mistress and shop-girl alike across Europe just what they had to live up to for the year.

Fashion caused a similar problem of visual indeterminacy as regards men too. At the highest level the plain English riding-coat became a desired item for much of the social elite: even Louis XVI wore one – to the extent that, when mingling with his cronies, strangers could not always pick him out. 'The most senior personages of the state walk the streets dressed like the least elevated of citizens,' noted Charles de Peyssonel in the 1780s. 'You think you are talking to an attorney's clerk, and it turns out to be a Prince of the Blood.'[31] In a related development, wealthy clergymen preferred to dress as aristocratic fops, sporting a sword and a cane.

The revolution in dress evident in the streets, boulevards and parks of the capital formed part of an even more extensive development evident in virtually all aspects of material life. Analysis of the post-

The Palais Royal in the late 18th century

mortem inventories of the lower orders demonstrate that the lush interiors of the monied elite found an echo in more materialistic and fashion-conscious lifestyles further down the social ladder. There were more clothes to be found – and in different cuts, colours and cloths – in popular wardrobes. And people had wardrobes, in fact – a century before, most had merely managed a linen chest. Other new kinds of furnishing became widespread: chairs, side-tables, chests-of-drawers, lamps, engravings and wall tapestries, mirrors and screens, for example. More people ate off china and manipulated jugs, vases, knives, forks and spoons. Nearly half of all homes had a coffee-pot. These changes extended to body furnishings too: the watch became a standard feature – even 'the tiniest of street urchins' boasted one, complained one provincial student.[32] So did female jewellery, wigs, snuffboxes (and, consequently, handkerchieves: between 1700 and 1789, Daniel Roche has remarked, Paris learnt how to blow its nose).[33] Razors, wigs and toothbrushes changed the way people looked, and offered means of adapting appearances to the vagaries of fashion.

The proto-consumer revolution brought a hedonistic buoyancy not only to the city but also, increasingly, to its surrounding countryside. Outside the exterior boulevards, villages and hamlets which a century before had been isolated and abandoned now found themselves swept up in the vortex of a booming material culture. The fact that commodities consumed outside the customs barrier were exempt from state taxes encouraged the emergence of a leisure industry just beyond the reach of the taxman. Here a network of drinking establishments called *guinguettes* emerged. These were especially lively on Sundays, 'Holy' (that is, unworked) Mondays and feast days, when Parisians would come out to enjoy themselves and get drunk cheaply. As a result, levels of street violence (and, it was said, extra-marital conceptions) were notably high here. At a slight remove, villages and hamlets such as Roule (VIIIe.), La Chapelle (XVIIIe.), Fontarabie (near to Charonne: XIIe.), Bercy (XIIIe.) and Vaugirard (XVe.) were caught up in the same movement of collective leisure.

A further feature of these changes was the predilection of the monied elite for building country houses, retreats, summerhouses and follies. Here they could indulge the polite taste for gardening, botany and nature in all its forms. *Maisons galantes*, that is, pleasure hideaways for mistresses, were another local speciality. The renewed appreciation of the close countryside had started during the regency: Orléans had built the chateau of La Muette for his daughter the duchesse de Berry, for example, while his wife built a country house at Bagnolet. Out in the Bois de Boulogne the maréchal d'Estrées built the Bagatelle residence in 1720; in the 1770s it would be completely redesigned and refitted by the comte d'Artois, Louis XVI's brother. Subsequently, most of these *résidences secondaires* – in places such as Passy, Auteuil, Nanterre, Saint-Cloud, Asnières, Sèvres, Ivry, Vincennes, St Maur, Villejuif – were destroyed by nineteenth- and twentieth-century over-building. With the notable exception of the Bagatelle, there are few extant signs of this very marked development, save only the fact that existing street plans sometimes overlie what once were estate roads.[34]

In order to reach their *guinguettes* or *résidences secondaires* beyond the line of the old ramparts, Parisians might still pass through agricultural land. Rye and barley were grown at Grenelle (XVe.) and in the Faubourg Poissonnière (IXe.). Viticulture was still widespread to the south, out to Passy (XVIe.), Vanves and Vaugirard (XVe.), while in the east Belleville and Charonne (XIe.–XXe.) were still wine villages, and in the north more than a quarter of Montmartre (XVIIIe.) was given over to the grape (and the latter locality also boasted more than a dozen windmills). In general, however, plough-land and vineyards in the vicinity of Paris were in marked retreat; the immediate country-side was being urbanized. Besides being devoted to parkland and summerhouses, growing amounts of farmland supplied the more diversified agrarian goods characteristic of a consumer economy. Market-gardens were now displaced outwards from the vicinity of the boulevards, stimulating formerly sleepy villages into commercial life. A division of gardening labour developed, often based on the horse manure trucked out from the city each day. There was asparagus at Argenteuil, La Villette and Montmartre, for example. Mushrooms came from Vaugirard, peas from Clamart, cherries from Montlhéry, gooseberries from Charonne, haricot beans from Arpajon and flowers from out beyond the Faubourg Saint-Marcel. Late in the century the agronomist Parmentier would experiment with potato cultivation at Grenelle.

Industry also developed alongside the long-established quarries found around the city's perimeter. Madder dye was grown at La Villette (XIXe.), while the nearby hamlet of Goutte d'Or (XVIIIe.) specialized in saltpetre extraction. Chemical works were being introduced on the island of Javel (XVe.) to the west of the city: *eau de Javel* – that is, bleach – would be devised here in 1789. Porcelain was another Parisian speciality with suburban outreach. In 1756 Louis XV transferred the Vincennes porcelain works to Sèvres in the south, where it was almost literally under the eye of its patron, Madame de Pompadour, in her overlooking chateau at Bellevue. Clignancourt, Sceaux, Meudon, Saint-Cloud and Poissy all developed important porcelain works too, many of them sponsored by members of the royal family.

Compared with other places in Europe at this time, however, the spread of industry into suburban and rural areas was still relatively limited. The orientation of Parisian manufacturing had always been – and continued to be – around luxury and semi-luxury goods. (Destroy the Paris luxury trades, the baronne d'Oberkirch reckoned, and French international supremacy would collapse overnight.)[35] And these luxury trades were almost exclusively concentrated within the old city. At mid-century the city contained perhaps a little over 50,000 artisans and industrial workers; by 1789 the figure was closer to 100,000. On the surface, production was organized in innumerable guilds and corporations. Yet these were on the defensive. The crown aimed to destroy them (and almost did so in 1775) for obstructing the free market, and winked at all manner of infractions of corporative regulation. In addition there were more than a dozen guild-free 'liberties' such as the Temple and the Faubourg Saint-Antoine (which enjoyed protection from the adjacent abbey of Saint-Antoine) and where the guilds dared not meddle.

Much Parisian industry was focused round finishing raw materials drawn from the provinces or else objects manufactured there. Past masters at this were the merchant mercers, who numbered over 2,000 members and who constituted the largest of the powerful 'Six Corps' which formed the prestigious apex of Paris's corporative pyramid.[36] Specializing in commodities including everything from silks, fashionable clothing and fine furniture through to jewellery, paintings and tapestries, mirrors, clocks, porcelain, lacquer, fashion accessories (buttons, lace, braid, etc.), umbrellas and toys, they straddled both the different productive specialities of which luxury goods were made and also the worlds of production and consumption. These versatile specialists in 'prettification' (as a commercial dictionary phrased it)[37] catered to the fashion season and to the individual needs of their often wealthy clientele by customizing their products. A fashionable mirror retailed on the Rue Saint-Honoré might have come up from the Saint-Gobain glassworks before having rococo fittings attached; a clock might combine elaborate machinery, bronze and gilt fittings and porcelain statuettes or plaques; a chest-of-drawers might have had Chinese panels of the fashionable varnish of the Martin company added; and a fashionable dress would similarly be an elaborate confection of the cloth, lace, button and braid wares of an army of specialists. What started as expensive customization for the elite would then be vulgarized in cheaper materials for sale in markets targeted at foreign tourists, the middling sort or even the aspirant labouring classes. European taste followed Paris's lead.

6.2: Rose Bertin

'Fashion is to France what the gold mines of Peru are to Spain.' Louis XIV's minister Jean-Baptiste Colbert thus highlighted, in 1665, the economic benefits that being an acknowledged leader in the field of fashion brought France – and Paris in particular. The court of the Sun King set styles which the rest of Europe sought to emulate. Even though the court was based in Versailles, the Paris clothes trades supplied the goods. A new development in the late eighteenth century was a productive synergy between a style-setter and a dress-maker. The style-setter was Louis XVI's queen Marie-Antoinette, and the dress-maker Marie-Jeanne (aka Rose) Bertin, whom contemporaries jealously acknowledged as the monarchy's 'minister of fashion'.

Born in Picardy in 1741, and from a humble background, Rose Bertin trained in Abbeville before moving to Paris. Here her talents were recognized by a host of court ladies, including the duchesse de Chartres (wife of the future Philippe-Égalité, duc d'Orléans) and the princesse de Conti. Through their patronage, Rose opened a shop on the Rue Saint-Honoré in 1770 with the exotic-sounding title 'le Grand Mogol'. In the early 1770s she was presented to Marie-Antoinette. A friendship blossomed between them.

In the mid- and late 1770s Rose Bertin was Marie-Antoinette's principal clothes stylist. The two women launched a fashion style each season, which all well-born ladies hastened to emulate. 'The crowds rushed round to one Madame Bertin,' one memoir-writer later recorded. 'It was a real revolution in the ways our ladies dressed.' Rose attracted hatred by refusing to let any female courtier wear a season's style before Marie-Antoinette had launched it. She talked of her twice-weekly sessions with the queen as her 'work' (*travail*), the word used for the king's sessions with his ministers. Such self-inflation was hardly popular – the baronne d'Oberkirch called her 'puffed up with self-importance, treating princesses as her equal', and Rose sparked a sensational court case by spitting in the eye of a rival. But as long as she retained the queen's favour she was unassailable.

Rose was a *marchande de modes* – a word best translated as either 'milliner' or 'fashion merchant'. The bodice and train of a dress were the work of a tailor, a seamstress (*couturière*) provided the petticoats, while the *marchande de modes* supplied the decorative features which gave the dress (and accompanying headgear) its distinctiveness. As Mercier noted, Paris's 7,000 tailors and seamstresses were the building-workers, but the score or so of *marchandes de modes* the architects and decorators.

One of Rose Bertin's distinctive fashion accessories was the *pouf*, pieces of gauze and other materials (flowers, feathers, fruit and knick-knacks of every sort) which were threaded into the hair or wig. From 1775 *poufs* and other Bertin creations provided a kind of allegorical running commentary on public life. In 1775 there was the *pouf à l'inoculation* (an indecipherable confection including a serpent, a rising sun, flowers and an olive branch, created to celebrate Louis XVI's smallpox inoculation) and the *pouf à la révolte* (commemorating a peasant bread riot);

the following year the colour puce was given Bertin endorsement. There followed a style of enormous head-feathers, up to two or three feet high; Henry IV hats (evoking Louis XVI's patriotic efforts to emulate his illustrious predecessor); the *coiffure aux insurgents* (displaying support for France's allies in the American colonies); the *coiffure au Dauphin* in 1781 (celebrating the birth of a royal son and heir); the Montgolfier style of 1783 evoking the first balloon ascent; and many others. Many of these styles were depicted in portraits of the queen by the court artist Madame Élisabeth Vigée-Lebrun, adding to Bertin's renown.

In the 1780s Rose had less unmediated access to the queen, as Marie-Antoinette adopted less extravagant (but still highly costly) styles, and as rival *modistes* found royal favour. Yet she carried on serving the queen, even after the latter was imprisoned in the Terror. Though Rose emigrated in 1792, she was sub-sequently able to prove to the Revolutionary government that she had been chasing her aristocratic creditors across Europe in the interests of the thirty-odd women – 'true sans-culottes', she claimed – whom she had working under her. She had made 'an exchange of the gold of France's enemies in return for the bullets fired by the Republic's armies'. Resettled in Paris in the late 1790s on the Rue de Richelieu, she died in 1813 – not, in the end, a rich woman. Her wealthy clients – the queen not least – had been bad payers.

Rose Bertin was a disaster for the crown. Her expensive fripperies became the target for much anti-monarchical satire and critique, and nourished the myth that the state's financial problems were mainly due to courtly extravagance. The fashion styles of the French Revolution would be anti-Bertin creations stressing simplicity and virtue and with worthy titles such as *négligé à la patriote* and *déshabillé à la démocrate*. In the long run, however, her importance for Paris was tremendous. She confirmed the fashion leadership of Paris, and provided the first example of a denizen of the clothes trades acting as arbiter of national and indeed international fashion. With Marie-Antoinette's help she constructed a fashion cycle which set the

tempo of work and invention in the Paris clothes trades. In addition her use of media was pioneering: besides using an emergent fashion press, she also dressed actresses and other figures in the public eye (such as the hermaphrodite the Chevalier d'Éon). The Parisian clothes trades developed an international repute which they were never to lose: 'through its fashions,' one contemporary noted, 'Paris is mistress of the world.' Henceforward the international jet-set would want to be dressed according to Paris fashion because they had read and seen that it was Paris fashion. Worth, Poiret, Chanel, Schiaparelli, Dior, Saint-Laurent and Galliano are Rose Bertin's heirs. So are the hundreds of thousands of men and women who since her times have composed the labour force of one of Paris's most enduring industries, which uniquely combines glamour and sweatshops.

Consumerism was reworking the framework of production within the city but also contributing to the subtle transformation of its social character in ways which transcended centuries of tradition. Parisian neighbourhoods had always in the past tended to contain a mixture of social types and vocations. This was endorsed by the ancient tradition of 'vertical' social differentiation, whereby the higher up the storeys of a house one went, the poorer the residents became. This still persisted, but it was being undermined by 'horizontal' differentiation. There were lots of servants, but few workshops and artisans, for example, to be found in the cliquey Faubourgs Saint-Germain and Saint-Honoré. With its overpopulated tenements and winding, narrow streets clogged up with waste and detritus, the historic heart of the city – the Île de la Cité and the area around the Hôtel de Ville – was viewed as an eyesore: the neighbourhood, noted architect Pierre Patte, 'constitutes old Lutetia and has not changed since the days of gothic barbarism'.[38] Elites were gingerly extricating themselves from this historic slum. The Halles and the Hôtel de Ville neighbourhoods in particular were noble-free zones. Few nobles were to be found either in industrial neighbourhoods like the Faubourg Saint-Antoine, whose booming specialization in furniture production was now augmented by the production of mirrors, porcelain and wallpapers, or the more

disinherited Faubourg Saint-Marcel, with its tanneries and dye-works.
'There is more money in a single house in the Faubourg Saint-Honoré,' remarked an informed observer in the 1780s, 'than in all the Faubourg Saint-Marcel put together.'[39] In the impoverished southern reaches of the city were to be found La Salpêtrière and Bicêtre – the two principal houses of the Paris Hôpital Général – two massive, and massively depressing, poorhouses encompassing more than 10,000 individuals. It was from this disinherited southern side that the young Jean-Jacques Rousseau, his brain full of big-city fantasies, as he later recalled, entered Paris for the first time in 1731.

> I had imagined a city as beautiful as it was great, and of the most imposing appearance. Entering through the Faubourg Saint-Marcel, I saw only little stinking streets, wretched black houses, an air of dirtiness, of poverty, of beggars, of carts, of seamstresses, of tisane-sellers and hat pedlars . . . Something of this first impression has always stayed with me and given me a secret distaste for the dwellings of the capital.[40]

6.3: Rue Mouffetard

The Café des Amateurs was the cesspool of the Rue Mouffetard . . . The squat toilets of the old apartment houses, one by the side of the stairs on each floor with the two cleated cement shoe-shaped elevation on each side of the aperture so a *locataire* would not slip, emptied into cesspools which were emptied by pumping into horse-drawn wagons at night. In summer time, with all windows open, we would hear the pumping and the odor was very strong . . .

Ernest Hemingway's memoir of his times spent as a novice writer in the 1920s on *la Mouffe*' – the Rue Mouffetard (Ve.) – is a reminder of how slow the progress of material comfort and conveniences was for working-class areas within Paris. This did not affect his warm view of the street itself, which he adjudged a 'wonderful narrow crowded market street'. The market element still predominates – as a glance at any twenty-first century guide-book will confirm – so that it is easy to lose sight of the street's distinctive past.

The early history of the street was not without a certain dignity. What became Rue Mouffetard had been one of the most ancient major streets in Roman Lutetia, leading out from the Petit Pont by the Île de la Cité through the present-day Rues Galande, Lagrange, the Place Maubert, and Rues de la Montagne Sainte-Geneviève and Descartes towards Lyon and Italy. From Merovingian times the church of Saint-Médard – around a kilometre south of the Seine and located at the point at which the street intersected with the course of the Bièvre river – had acted as a pole for population expansion, and a little further south a necropolis emerged. Much of this was razed by Viking raiders in the ninth century, but once times got better, the fortunes of the 'Bourg Saint-Médard', along with the 'Bourg Saint-Marcel' a little further south, improved. From the twelfth century some major ecclesiastical institutions and high-placed individuals set root in the area.

Nevertheless, the foul smells evoked by Hemingway have had a long association with the site – and indeed the smell of tanneries disappeared only a matter of decades ago. Etymologists inform us that the name Mouffetard derives from *Mons Cetardus*, the Latin name for a mound on the present-day Place d'Italie. No matter, just about all the early Parisian antiquarians assumed that the term came in fact from the French word *mofette*, signifying putrid stench. From the late Middle Ages tanneries, starch-makers, dyers and butchers on the nearby river Bièvre had turned the Mouffetard area smelly. But these trades boosted industrial employment, which gave a plebeian character to the Rue Mouffetard and its growing network of side-streets.

'If one ventures into the area,' noted Louis-Sébastien Mercier at the end of the eighteenth century, 'it is out of curiosity; nothing summons us there, for there is not a single monument to be seen there.' Incorporated within the city in 1724, the neighbourhood bore the marks of marginality. 'No neighbourhood in Paris is more horrible nor so unknown,' commented Balzac, reinforcing the point, some decades later. The denizens of the Latin Quarter might make spasmodic visits: in the sixteenth century the Pomme au Pin tavern on the present-day Place de la Contrescarpe had been the haunt of Rabelais, Ronsard and others. Yet by the eighteenth century the area also had an acknowledged reputation for violence and savagery. 'The population bears no relationship whatever to the Parisians, civilised inhabitants of the banks of the Seine,' Mercier recorded. In 1561 the so-called '*vacarme de Saint-Médard*' ('the Saint-Médard racket') had been an early atrocity in the Religious Wars triggered by the decision of the church's bellringers to ring all their bells continuously so as to prevent assembled Protestants outside from hearing their preacher; blood flowed copiously as a result. In the 1720s and 1730s the church's cemetery had become the theatre for the hysterical fits and spasms of the Jansenist convulsionaries. After 1800 popular dancehalls in the area became known for instigating street fights and demotic violence. Furthermore, men from the Mouffe' were always to be found in the ranks of rebels in the Revolutionary *journées* of the 1790s, and again, later, on city barricades in 1830, 1834, 1848 and 1871. 'Mouffetard country [*le pays Mouffetard*],' noted Georges Duhamel in 1920, 'has its own customs and laws which have neither meaning nor jurisdiction over the other side of the Rue Monge.'

Baron Haussmann and his disciples did their best to tame this proudly independent area through aggressive urbanization. The plan for a Haussmannian boulevard to bisect the street came to nothing, but the building of the Rues Monge and Claude-Bernard reduced the size of the Mouffetard neighbourhood, and also brought a more bourgeois population into the area. The development of the lower reaches of the street – which now became the Avenue des Gobelins – had a similar effect. Despite part of it being earmarked as an *îlot insalubre* ripe for redevelopment after the Great War, the Mouffe' retained its popular character and villagey feel. The cheapness of the neighbourhood attracted impoverished writers such as Hemingway and also George Orwell, whose *Down and Out in Paris and London* (1933) presents a lightly disguised Rue Mouffetard. The political radicalism of the past was on the wane. The Mouffe' had a final radical fling in the late 1950s and 1960s, when anarchists and 'Soixante-Huitards' installed themselves here, initiating a number of local projects, including a street-theatre based in a disused bus. But the radical glory days were over, and gentrification and consumerism were well on the way.

The local market was becoming the neighbourhood's most obvious point of reference. At the turn of the twentieth century the writer Georges Duhamel, in *La Confession de minuit* (1920), compared it to an oriental souk, 'bordered with modest-looking shops which are stuffed with succulent merchandise. Meat, cheese, vegetables and fruit are on display onto the street. We see prodigious triperies, patisseries . . . walls of carrots, hillocks of potatoes, continents of cabbages . . .' This is a recognizable description for the twenty-first-century *flâneur*, who can set it alongside the more recent effloresence of sushi bars, fast-food outlets, internet cafés and the other impedimenta of post-industrial consumerism.

By the 1760s when Rousseau recorded these first impressions, a gulf opening up between rich and poor within the city was becoming apparent – but so too was a discourse critical of the city precisely as a generator of social inequality and human alienation. Rousseau was a key actor in this developing drama. His famous 'Two Discourses' – on the sciences and the arts (1750), and on the origins of inequality (1755) – had criticized the assumption that social advancement and urban culture inevitably brought happiness in its train. In his best-selling novels, like *La Nouvelle Héloïse* (1760) and *Émile* he warmed to the theme: a city like Paris was less the beacon of civilization than 'the abyss of the human species', which bred dissatisfaction and unhappiness.[41] Rousseau was not the first to attack the artificiality of urban life, but he did crystallize existing critiques in a striking way. Indeed, by a quirk to become familiar, the denizens of the 'abyss' were among the most captivated readers of his work. From Rousseau's angle of vision the ostentatious and hedonistic materialism of much of the city seemed a heedless aggravation for the poor. 'This paradise on earth,' one commentator noted, 'is becoming a place of torture all the more cruel for the wretched in that the abundance, pleasure, joy and festivals of which they are witnesses and in which they have no part, retrace more tellingly the frightful image of their miseries.'[42] The last decades of the Ancien Régime were thus to be characterized not solely by enthusiasts for cosmopolitan and civilizing Parisian values but also a developing anxiety about the social problems of the city.

Enlightenment Paris certainly had its dark side. The great mortality crises of the past may have ended – the last outbreak of bubonic plague in Paris was in 1652, the last great famine in 1709–10 – but latent poverty and deprivation still prevailed. The consumerist city consumed the bodies of the poor. Despite its egalitarian pretensions, roughly one-third of the population was regarded as poor by the standards of the time, but this proportion could rise sharply: there were dearths in 1725–6, 1739–41, 1765–75 and 1788–9, and major labour dislocation caused by post-war demobilizations after 1715, 1748, 1763 and 1783. Most children born in the city were farmed out to rural wetnurses; perinatal death rates of one in three or four were common. The city received a horde of abandoned children: a sizeable sector of the transport system was given over to conveying such waifs from across the face of northern France: there were 3,150 of them in 1740, and double that number a generation later. Children who managed to survive until they were three months old were then prone to a wide range of diseases, notably smallpox, which, following the demise of bubonic plague in the previous century, was the biggest epidemic killer. Syphilis was an additional threat. Babies were often born with the ravages of the disease on their bodies – for both prostitution and venereal diseases were rampant. There were perhaps as many as 20,000 prostitutes in the city, though the numbers involved in casual and commercial sex were vastly greater. The rate of illegitimacy rose over the century from one in eleven to nearly one in four.

Given high mortality, especially among the very young, and a failure to achieve population growth by natural increase, the city needed to recruit an endless stream of immigrants from the surrounding areas. More than three-quarters of Parisians had been born outside the city, and by the 1780s around 3,500 new recruits entered the city annually. They crowded into the poorer faubourgs, where they found existing networks of their fellow countrymen. From this, geographical labour specializations developed: the Limousins were often building-workers, for example, the Savoyards water-carriers, the Lyonnais stone-cutters. All such outsiders were viewed as semi-savages by Parisians, though as one provincial pluckily noted in 1787, 'all Parisians are not wits any more than all provincials are imbeciles.'[43] (Parisians, however, were less sure about this.)

Up to the seventeenth century, plague and other epidemic diseases were usually conceived of as penetrating the city from the outside; now the stress was on the city as a source of its own pathology. It was less the crowds of immigrants who were responsible for the prevalence of disease than the conditions of the city itself. Paris, wrote medical topographer Menuret de Chambaud, is 'an atmospheric cesspit in which we all swim'.[44] Other physicians claimed that the area adjacent to the Halles, the old Cemetery of the Innocents, Paris's main grave-yard, caused serial epidemics. Such medico-social problems seemed all the more severe in that the institutions of poor relief were experiencing financial and logistical difficulties over the course of the century, which made them incapable of meeting increasing demand for their services. Charity was not keeping pace with inflation, while the finances of many hospitals had been severely damaged by the John Law fiasco. The Hôtel-Dieu, the main hospital of Paris, was in a scandalous state: the sick were stacked up between four and six to a bed, and one entrant in four died within the institution, often of a disease contracted after entering it. Care for the poor was becoming deadly. Entering Paris, said the Italian writer Vittorio Alfieri, was like being 'sucked into a fetid sewer'.[45]

Growing awareness of social inequality and urban pathology stimu-lated a vigorous movement of urban reform and development, particu-larly from mid-century onwards. A medical lobby urging greater urban hygiene was increasingly vocal, demanding that air should circulate, streets should be paved, aligned and cleared of obstructions, water supplies should be improved and that war should be declared against pollution. These hygiene campaigns meshed conveniently with the wish of statesmen and political economists to make the city's inhabi-tants more productive. There was an aesthetic component in the reform movement too. The *philosophe* Voltaire was a mouthpiece of this movement for 'urban embellishment' (the ideas of urbanization and planning were not yet current). In his *Les Embellissements de Paris* (1749) he combined humanitarian, hygienic and utilitarian considerations with a concern for urban beauty. Kings, financiers and municipal authorities were roundly attacked for failing to remodel their city in such a way as to make it 'as convenient and as magnificent as possible'.

> We rightly blush to see public markets in narrow streets displaying dirtiness, spreading infection and causing public disorders . . . We need to open public markets, water fountains which work, regularly laid-out crossroads, new theatres. We must widen the narrow and unhealthy streets, and openly reveal hidden monuments and make them visible.[46]

Voltaire's call for monuments to be cut away from the surrounding urban tissue derived from a wish that their 'magnificence' could be better appreciated, a wish which echoed Renaissance urbanist notions as well as Louis-Quatorzian classicism. But Voltaire also recommended the move because it would bring beneficent fresh air into a stagnant urban site in ways which physicians were advocating.

A particular concern for the street was one of the characteristic aspects of the reform movement. In the time of Louis XIV the Furetière dictionary had defined 'street' in utterly minimalist, functional terms as 'a space between houses which serves to let the public through'.[47] Now there was a growing sense that the street had to be a key focus for remodelling the city on hygienic and aesthetic, as well as utilitarian, grounds. Visitors and tourists continued to be scandalized by the practices of throwing urine and faeces out of windows onto the heads of passers-by, but police regulations on nuisances, obstructions and lighting were tightened up. Collected weekly in 1700, street waste was now removed on a daily basis. In the 1750s and 1760s the major city dumps were relocated well outside the city limits. Latterly, measures were taken to improve water supply. There was a move to pave streets (though the provision of pavements for pedestrians was still in its infancy). A further feature of the campaign was to remove housing from bridges. A fire on the Petit Pont in 1718 had left a gap of four houses on the bridge. On the eve of the Revolution of 1789 a pamphleteer claimed, on the basis of careful scrutiny of death registers, that the adventitious ventilation had resulted in the reduction of the neighbourhood's death rate – and saved 20,000 lives over half a century! No new bridge would have housing allowed on it in future, and in the 1780s a start was made on demolishing houses on existing bridges. From the 1760s attention was devoted to improving the quality of the *quais* and river banks too, and this encompassed the removal of tenements backing onto the river.

A particular target of the hygiene reformers was the presence within the city of a plethora of sick or deceased bodies. A fire at the Hôtel-Dieu in 1772 led to a series of enquiries aimed at relocating the pathogenic institution in a more hygienic environment away from the city centre – but nothing was done, and death rates continued to be scandalously high. Significantly, in their efforts to improve hospital care, reformers tended to bypass the Hôtel-Dieu: nearly a dozen small hospitals with up to around 100 beds each were established from 1778 to 1788. There seemed a better chance of such more rationally designed institutions serving as 'healing machines'[48] rather than as generators of sickness. Greater success crowned efforts to remove dead bodies to the perimeters of the city. Since the 1760s there had been moves to try to stop the practice of burying the dead within churches, which were increasingly viewed as disease traps. Architect and urban theorist Patte quite cheerfully called for a cull of virtually all gothic churches (including, for example, Saint-Germain-l'Auxerrois) on hygienic as well as aesthetic grounds. These survived, but the antique Cemetery of the Innocents did not. Following a wide-ranging public hygiene campaign, burials ceased there in 1780 and, from 1786, existing bones were shifted to the site of the Tombe-Issoire (XIVe.) to the south of the city, where catacombs were created.[49] The evacuated site was turned into a vegetable market annex to the adjacent Halles.

Particular care – on grounds which characteristically mixed the utilitarian and the aesthetic – was now given to issues of street width and housing height. New streets set out in the building frenzy after the 1760s were increasingly subject to regulations which insisted on width. Added width not only made streets easier to keep clean, but also opened up the kind of pleasing prospect on houses which Voltaire had recommended. Developing practice was codified in building regulations of 1783–4. In theory at least, house height was henceforth regulated in direct relationship to street width: wooden buildings should be no higher than 48 feet, with street width at between 24 and 29 feet, whereas on streets with stone façades height was limited to 60 feet and street width set at between 30 and 45 feet. These building regulations – subsequently refined and increasingly applied – were to make a massive and enduring impact on the Parisian cityscape.

Although the development of the cityscape over the course of the century displayed the combined activities of private entrepreneurs, church authorities, the Paris Parlement and the central government, it was the central government which was increasingly in the driving seat. Kings blew hot and cold about their capital city, as we have suggested,[50] yet they still wanted the royal imprint on Paris to be evident, marked, and in line with the welfarist agenda which the crown had adopted early in the century. The crown expected the municipal government to play a significant role in urban regulation; but it did not brook any expression of independence from it. The city finances were placed directly under the eagle eye of the state Controller-General. Still without a mayor, Paris had a Prévôt des Marchands who was elected by the city authorities every two years – but was always a royal nominee. He and his fellow councillors were increasingly criticized for being so many political eunuchs whose embonpoint showed evident signs of having enjoyed too many municipal dinners.[51] In fact even the dinners were under attack, since from the 1760s the monarchy launched a campaign to reduce the ceremonial trappings of power which city councillors enjoyed: municipal budgets were purged of expenditure on banquets after municipal elections, carriage hire, purchase of ceremonial robes, and even uniforms for their ceremonial guards. From 1768 the age-old midsummer bonfires which lit up the Place de l'Hôtel-de-Ville on St John's Eve were suppressed. The framework of Parisian ceremonial life, it seemed, should be royal, not municipal.

The Lieutenance-Générale de Police, established in 1667, was the leading edge of the monarchy's onslaught against the municipality's ceremonial prestige and political authority.[52] A crown nominee, the Lieutenant-Général was responsible for the city's *police* – a term which was interpreted increasingly broadly, and given a secularist twist. Policing was no longer, police official Guillaute proclaimed, 'about turning society into a monastery' by a web of interdictions. The matter in hand was to administer the city coolly, rationally and in ways which encouraged the civilizing aspects of urban life by means of 'keeping an eye on an infinite pile of the tiny little details without which citizens would be neither secure nor at their ease'.[53] Public order was a major consideration: the streets of Paris were now generally viewed as being safe to walk in (except for the traffic): the police had crushed the last big criminal gangs in the 1750s, and attentive provisioning ensured that disturbances over the price of bread were few. As well as control of public order, the Paris police had responsibility in food supply, shops and markets, the printing and book trades, surveillance of strangers, road maintenance, philanthropic activity and much else besides. Under Police Lieutenant-Général Lenoir between 1776 and 1785, the department devoted a fifth of its budget and a quarter of its personnel to issues such as street clearance, lighting, emergency services, charity and public works. Urban initiatives now tended to originate from the Lieutenant-Général's office rather than from the city fathers: in the last two decades of the Ancien Régime, for example, the police were pivotal in regulating the wetnursing industry, building a hospital for syphilitic babies and establishing a charity pawnshop for the poor.

Yet the monarchy failed to derive as much ideological credit from such operations as it might. First, as we have seen, neither Louis XV nor Louis XVI showed any real interest in personally engaging themselves in the dynamic cosmopolitan culture which was emerging in their capital, each preferring the closeted ceremonials of Versailles. Second, some of the work of urban 'improvement' was very manifestly at the expense of part of the citizenry: the removal of houses from bridges and slum clearance around the Cemetery of the Innocents may have been hygienically desirable, for example, but it also threw tenants out onto the street with no compunction. Third, the crown attracted a good deal of unpopularity through the royal agents who had most to do with the city on the royal behalf. Despite his philanthropic role, the Lieutenant-Général de Police was seen as nefariously and despotically powerful. He presided over a large criminal police force, an army of informers and spies, and a host of censors – and was widely held to run the city's vice trade. Lenoir himself complained of his

Parisian reputation for omnipotence, evident in the 'belief that nothing happened in Paris [that] was unknown to the Lieutenant of Police'.[54] Such a belief might deter; but it could also anger and enrage.

The idea that monarchical institutions were not simply irrelevant but were in fact actively toxic to the welfare of Parisians became increasingly current in the last decades of what the Revolutionaries of 1789 would dub the Ancien Régime. The blossoming of the public sphere and of a more open and egalitarian culture in the city provided an alternative – and increasingly oppositional – template to Bourbon values. Despite the monarchy's welfarist agenda, kings and their courtiers often gave the impression of fostering a culture of political cronyism, which devalued public responsibility in favour of the pursuit of personal profit and private pleasure. Court nobles, many of whom had come from the most ancient of families, were drawn into financial deals with business interests which were negotiated in Paris and then sealed at Versailles with royal endorsement and accompanying privileges. This caused growing concern in the public sphere. As if to signal that worms can indeed turn, even the Prévôt des Marchands in 1787 commented that 'minds are indeed inclined to censure indiscriminately everything which appears to present the slightest idea of privilege, which is always accompanied by profits to the public's prejudice'.[55]

'About this time,' Thomas Blaikie, a Scot who was making his way in Paris in the 1780s as a gardening consultant to royalty, later noted, 'people began to speak very disrespectfully of the Court.'[56] Gossip, conversation and attacks on privilege were amplified by the press, both licit and illicit, while criticisms of what was increasingly referred to as 'ministerial despotism' were now also gravely articulated by the Paris Parlement, which increasingly posed as the true defender of the interests of all Parisians. The magistrates encouraged Parisians to believe that only the worst would come out of Versailles. They accused Louis XVI's unpopular finance minister Calonne of being little more than a crook, manipulating the stock market in the interests of his family and allies, and engineering a stock-exchange crash in 1785–7. The minister was also involved in a cut-throat political battle over the city's water supply which saw two cartels of businessmen and statesmen (including the Lieutenant-Général de Police and several royal ministers) jockeying for a contract which was widely viewed as a means of naked self-enrichment at the expense of the people of Paris. 'What is *not* up for sale in this extraordinary city?' enquired a stupefied Mercier, when faced with 'a company to sell us the water of the Seine'.[57]

The air of moral turpitude and corrupt dealing which hovered over the political system spread increasingly towards the royal family. In the 1770s anti-Austrian court factions had launched pornographic pamphlets alleging that the king was impotent and the queen an unbridled sexual pervert. By the 1780s these accusations of moral corruption and debility were circulating widely within Paris and the provinces. In 1786 Parisian crowds openly applauded the Parlement's legal humiliation of Marie-Antoinette in what became known as the 'Diamond Necklace Affair', which seemed to prove the queen's sexual licentiousness.[58] State surveillance over the grain trade – which was instrumental in removing the spectre of famine from the lives of Parisians for the first time in the city's history – was viewed with suspicion whenever bread prices rose. Despite the paternalistic language which they affected, both Louis XV and Louis XVI were accused of involvement in a *pacte de famine* which involved speculating on grain prices in a way which caused widespread hunger and misery while they enriched themselves and their courtiers and financiers. By the same token, the crown's engagement in Parisian 'embellishment' and the post-1760 building frenzy were construed as actions that were sectional, selfish and likely to be against the public interest.

Louis XV had attracted a good deal of unpopularity in Paris by his 1724 ruling (in whose transgression, as we have seen,[59] he had played a leading part) that Paris should not expand beyond defined limits. Louis XVI, for his part, now created an even greater wave of hostility in building a new customs barrier – the so-called 'Wall of the Farmers-General' (1784–7). The barrier was some twenty-four kilometres long, placed well outside the built-up areas, and encompassed a good deal of terrain formerly free of taxes. It was presented as a rational step which would protect against smuggling and fraud, which were harming Parisian businesses. In a way it also showed the king's positive commitment to a city which hitherto the monarchy had neglected, for the wall was situated in such a way as to allow further growth and development. To Parisians, however, the wall seemed anachronistic in an age increasingly won over to notions of free exchange. They felt hemmed in, and did not like it. A collection of interest groups consequently assailed the royal council, which claimed in bewilderment that the establishment of this new customs barrier could only be construed as in the interest of Paris's 'happiness and pleasure'.[60] 'The wall walling Paris in makes Parisians wail,' went the ditty, however.[61] Parisians did not relish the idea of paying more for their drink in the *guinguettes* of the formerly tax-exempt periphery. Medical men fantasized about such a wall engendering more disease (one physician even providing exact calculations of how many cubic feet of air would now be denied Parisians). Urban legends were soon spreading like wildfire about smugglers bringing wine and eau-de-vie illicitly within city limits through underground pipes and by mini-balloons. Resentment was all the more acute in that the wall seemed to show the crown totally in cahoots with the Farmers-General – number-one hate figures of eighteenth-century France. To add insult to injury, the wall was constructed with enormously expensive designs, the architect Claude-Nicolas Ledoux supplying a set of tollgates which combined the neo-classical with the visionary-utopian.[62] When he realized what was being done in his name, Louis XVI sacked Ledoux and scaled down the building projects. But by then the damage to the crown's reputation had been done.

'A riot which might degenerate into sedition,' noted Mercier in 1788, in one of the great failed prophesies of world history, 'has become morally impossible [in Paris] . . . Everything seems in place which can repress forever the likelihood of a serious uprising.'[63] Effective policing had indeed reduced the occurrence of dangerous rioting over previous decades. Paris in the age of Enlightenment had been tranquillity personified in comparison with the sixteenth and seventeenth centuries. Yet an articulate public sphere had emerged which was critical of government for seeming to shut itself off from the city's social, economic and cultural dynamism. Cocooned in Versailles, the monarchy was increasingly imagined as being immoral, corrupt, self-seeking and – as the Farmers-General Wall imbroglio indicated – seriously out of touch. These changes had brought the possibility of serious conflict back on the Parisian agenda. The targets for popular fury on 14 July 1789 included not only the Bastille – state prison, arms depository and the timeworn (and anachronistic) symbol of naked military might – but also the major tollgates of the infamous Farmers-General Wall. These assaults signalled that Parisians had got too used to inhabiting an open city, and that they no longer believed in the paternalist goodness of a dynasty whose disassociation from its capital city over the previous century was now costing it dear.

7

Revolution and Empire
1789–1815

The short period from 1789 to 1815 did not change the face of Paris radically or in new ways. Indeed the material environment of the city was probably changed less than in the decades leading up to 1789, which had witnessed a feverish explosion of urban building. Yet events which took place within the city over the quarter-century period inaugurated by the Revolution of 1789 had a dramatic impact on French and indeed world history. Paris was both the motor of Revolution and Revolution's most conspicuous setting. Paris and Revolution became, in some contexts, synonymous. The role which the city played affirmed and endorsed the set of images which Paris had developed over the course of the previous century. Enlightenment Paris had been – as Louis-Sébastien Mercier, journalist, dramatist and observer of Parisian mores, put it – 'the capital of light', 'the centre of the republic of letters', the 'New Athens'.[1] There would be many who would see the events of 1789 in particular through that lens. Although there were discordant voices such as that of Edmund Burke in Britain, in general the intelligentsia of two continents (Wordsworth, Coleridge, Priestley, Kant, Goethe and Schiller in Europe, Washington, Jefferson and Madison in the new United States of America) hailed the Revolutionary process in the most glowing terms. 'How much the greatest event it is that has happened and how much the best!' exclaimed Charles James Fox. Yet the city's experience in the early and mid-1790s in particular would also cast Paris (and indeed the Revolution) in a new, sinister light, as the home of popular violence, bloody revolt and political Terror. Fount of civilized and enlightened values, Paris now also became a Pandora's box of political horrors.

The people of Paris were to thrust themselves memorably and

Retour de la Famille

Paris le 25 Juin 1791.

durably into the course of radical change in the political crisis of 1789, but in ways which were not easily anticipated in the light of events leading up to it. After all, politics took place at Versailles, around the king's councils, not in Paris. The crisis began with the realization of Controller-General Calonne that the state was facing bankruptcy. The political crisis of 1787–8 that ensued – which historians call the 'Pre-Revolution' – derived more from the financial problems of the Bourbon monarchy than from any particular developments within France's capital city. The crown had spent too much on wars over the course of the eighteenth century, yet had not developed methods of finance which would draw sufficiently on the country's immense and burgeoning wealth. Calonne urged the king to set up a hand-picked national representative body called the Assembly of Notables to endorse a radical package of tax reforms. The Assembly had met at Versailles in February 1787 and refused to play ball, forcing the resignation of Calonne and his replacement by the Archbishop of Toulouse, Loménie de Brienne. When the latter tried to force through a similar reform package, he found himself facing the combined opposition of the thirteen parlements of France, led by the august magistrates of the Parlement of Paris. The parlements had the duty of endorsing all royal legislation. They used this power to argue that they would be infringing their duty to the state if they allowed radical tax legislation to go through against the constitutional spirit of the country.

The stand-off between the government and the parlements made the developing political crisis of 1787–8 more than a question of Versailles-based machinations. Yet activity within the city of Paris tended still to be rather limited in scope. There were noisy demonstrations on the Pont Neuf in late 1787 and early 1788 in support of the Parlement. In August 1788 Brienne's effigy was ceremonially burned on the bridge, as the crown reluctantly sacrificed the principal minister and agreed to the convocation in 1789 of the Estates General, France's national representative body, which had last met in 1614.

If one observer noted that the Pont Neuf demonstrations amounted to little more than 'attempted sedition by schoolboys',[2] this was partly because the riots were led by law students and trainee attorneys rather than workers from the faubourgs. The conditions were by then emerging, however, for a social widening of the conflict. The French economy had taken a downturn from the 1770s, and consecutive harvest failures in 1787 and 1788 sent the price of bread rocketing. Popular hunger fuelled a growing number of market disturbances and riots throughout the country. Paris too was badly affected by the nationwide economic crisis. Around a quarter of the region's harvest was lost in the terrible hailstorm of 13 July 1788. In the frost and snow throughout the winter of 1788–9 the rivers which supplied the city froze over, and roads were passable only with difficulty. Poor families found themselves spending 80 or 90 per cent of their income on bread. The consequent slump in demand for manufactured goods affected Parisian industry, which was already suffering the impact of competition from cheap English goods caused by an Anglo-French trade treaty in 1786. In April 1789 there was a major riot in the Faubourg Saint-Antoine, of a sort which contemporaries claimed had not occurred since the times of the Fronde. It was directed at the wallpaper manufacturer Réveillon who was rumoured to have demanded the forcible reduction of workers' wages as a way out of the crisis. The riot was repressed by the Gardes-Françaises regiments, who were normally garrisoned in Paris, with a ferocity which aggravated rather than appeased popular anger.

Anger was taking a more political form by this time too. In 1788 royal censorship had collapsed – the crown could no longer ignore the clamour of dissent bubbling up to greet the new Estates General. This triggered an explosion of political pamphleteering, much of it making political claims which had formerly been well out of bounds. The expressed desire of the Paris Parlement that the Estates General should meet within the forms of the 1614 meeting intensified debate, for it implied that the Parlement wanted to join with the nobility and the clergy in a single repressive bloc and manage rather than respond to wider popular concerns. By this single gesture the Parlement of Paris, hero of the pre-Revolutionary crisis, converted itself almost overnight into a political villain in the eyes of most Parisians. This meant that when the long and laborious procedure of elections to the Estates General got under way in early 1789, Parisians and provincials were suspicious of the political machinations of what were now called 'the privileged orders', that is, the clergy (the First Estate) and the nobility (the Second). Electoral assemblies of the Third Estate (non-clerical commoners) as well as of the clergy and nobility were accompanied by the compiling of books of grievances (*cahiers de doléances*) which expressed hopes for reform. The *cahiers* of the Paris Third Estate were a not untypical hodge-podge of demands, ranging from the radical – the Estates General should meet in Paris rather than at Versailles; Paris should have proper self-government; the Farmers-General customs wall should be knocked down, as indeed should the Bastille – to the mundane – sources of urban pollution should be checked; there should be better hospitals, etc. Wide-ranging reform seemed to be on the agenda.

The multi-tiered electoral system introduced for the city of Paris took place within sixty electoral districts, and was so complicated that it was not completed until the end of May 1789. The Third Estate delegates from Paris joined their peers at Versailles, only to find the Estates General in a state of political deadlock, with the Third Estate deputies refusing to start business until the crown had made clear that voting should be done in a way which prevented the privileged orders from dominating.

The summer crisis of 1789 impelled the people of Paris from the sidelines to the heart of Revolutionary politics. Under popular pressure, Louis XVI seemed to give way to the Third Estate on the voting principle, but instantly called up troops around Versailles and Paris as though planning a coup to sweep away political arrangements he was already regretting. He also sacked the popular minister Necker, replacing him with known reactionaries. Fears were expressed that a 'Saint Bartholomew's massacre of patriots' was on the cards. Forced into a defensive stance by apparent royal bad faith, the Parisian populace reacted energetically. The electoral assembly which had made the final selection of Third Estate deputies – numbering some 407 Parisian bourgeois – had been meeting informally to follow political events, and they now stepped in, taking over the reins of local government at the Hôtel de Ville. Flesselles, the Prévôt des Marchands, had no choice but to fall into line. The Commune – as the grouping was now called – formed a bourgeois militia, strengthened by many Gardes-Françaises, who by now were mutinous against royal authority. The militia, which was later given the official title of National

Guard, prepared to defend Paris against royal troops and also tried to keep order among an over-excited populace. The liberal aristocrat Lafayette, a veteran of the American War of Independence, was called on to command the Guard. The latter was unable to stop the destruction of the tollgates on the Farmers-General Wall, which were blamed for popular hunger. But it joined in a hunt for weapons and gunpowder which led to the seizure first of the Invalides and then, on 14 July, of the Bastille. Learning of the loss of the Bastille and its garrison, Louis agreed to pull the army back from Paris, to reinstate Necker and to accept the existence of a National Assembly (into which the Estates General had transformed itself). On 17 July the king journeyed from Versailles to his capital, to receive a rhapsodic ovation from Parisians. That day, the national tricolore was created, from placing the ceremonial white of the Bourbon dynasty between the heraldic red and blue of the city of Paris. The decision was also taken to demolish the Bastille, symbol of a political tyranny which it was hoped had now passed.

Many contemporaries regarded the king's action on 17 July in accepting the Parisian revolution of 14 July as a satisfying symbol of rediscovered political unity between ruler and nation. Alas! Unity was to be only an evanescent, if insistent, dream for the next decade. Opposition to the revolutionary process had not vanished: hardly had the Bastille fallen than royal princes and high-ranking aristocrats were fleeing the country in order to rustle up support across Europe against the National Assembly. These political exiles – the *émigrés* – were to prove an enduring thorn in the Revolution's flesh. The events of mid-July had also highlighted another important feature of the next decades – the threat of violence constituted by the Parisian population. The latter had not only captured the Bastille; they also murdered the governor of the Bastille, the Prévôt des Marchands, the Intendant of the Île de France and sundry other hate-figures, parading their heads around Paris on the ends of pikes like trophies.

The National Assembly sat down to work on the constitution. In the next couple of years they would pass an extremely wide-ranging set of reforms, grounded in the principles of freedom and equality before the law outlined in the Declaration of the Rights of Man and the Citizen introduced on 26 August 1789. But the crisis would not go away. Against a backcloth of continuing high bread prices, and stirred up by rumours that the king and queen were allowing the court at Versailles to become the storm-centre of armed counter-revolution, the Parisian people organized a march out to Versailles. In the *journées* of 5–6 October 1789 they forced the king to accept the return of the court to Paris, where he and his family were rehoused in the Tuileries palace (rather uncomfortably, it seems). After a century of absence the king was physically back among Parisians again. The deputies of the National Assembly, who had accompanied Louis back to his capital, also established themselves within the city.

The *journées* of 5–6 October 1789 confirmed the double reality of counter-revolution and Parisian popular violence – and double-underlined the importance of the city itself in political events henceforth. The king felt a prisoner in the Tuileries, and to all intents and purposes he was. The National Assembly also felt itself under the scrutiny of the Parisian people, who packed the public galleries and provided a lively and often critical running commentary on events. Paris had written itself into the script of the Revolution in a way which would prove difficult to erase.

If Paris-based violence – both popular and counter-revolutionary – hovered uncertainly on the margins of menace for the most part until 1792, Paris also thrust itself into the Revolutionary limelight in another way, namely as the privileged forum for political ideas. In a sense the early Revolutionary years were a culmination of the bourgeois public life which had developed in what Revolutionaries were now calling the 'Ancien Régime' ('former régime'). With the guarantees now offered by the constitution, opinion had never been freer. Visitors to the city concurred that Parisians were eager to discuss politics in a new and quite animated way. They also highlighted the role of informal public oratory in sites such as the duc d'Orléans's Palais-Royal and in the numerous political cafés with which Paris was now populated.

7.1: Philippe-Égalité, duc d'Orléans

Louis-Philippe-Joseph, duc d'Orléans (1747–94), was the black sheep of the royal family. The Orléans were the cadet branch of the reigning Bourbons. The duke was the wealthiest man in France except Louis XVI, and he owed his royal cousin massive debts. This did not prevent him from cultivating Paris as counterpart to the ruler's possession of Versailles, from being elected to the first republican assembly in France's history, from renouncing his ducal title for the name 'Equality' (*Égalité*), and from voting for the death penalty in the king's trial. The latter, wayward gesture of unfamilial republicanism – which shocked even many of his intimates – failed to prevent him from losing his own head to the guillotine shortly afterwards.

Philippe's execution in Paris was particularly striking in that the Orléans house had long cultivated links with the city. The shift of the affections of Louis XIV and his successors from their capital to Versailles had left a royal niche which successive dukes of Orléans strove to fill. In 1715 Philippe-Égalité's great-grandfather had shifted the royal court back to Paris when he became regent (though Louis XV soon removed it to Versailles once more). Successive dukes acted as royal representatives for ceremonial events in Paris which the king could not be bothered to attend. Philippe's father had cultivated allies in the Paris Parlement, and during a political struggle in the 1770s he even had Parisians hanging placards outside his residence urging him to seize the crown.

Philippe's political ambitions were difficult to fathom. A hard-won reputation as a slightly disgusting hedonist made him unpopular at the court of Louis XVI and Marie-Antoinette. His pronounced taste for self-publicity (he took a balloon flight, for example) and for things English (horse-racing, gambling and male fashions like the frock-coat) also irritated the king. If he had political ambitions, however, he put them on hold as long as he depended on Louis to grant him permission to develop the

Orléans family's Parisian residence, the Palais-Royal. Built by Cardinal Richelieu from the 1620s, the erstwhile Palais-Cardinal had housed the young Louis XIV during the period of the Fronde (thus leading to a change of title to Palais-Royal), before passing permanently into the hands of the Orléans dynasty. Philippe was financially hard up – amazingly so, considering his stupendous wealth – and he saw the opportunity for realizing commercial potential by developing his residence as a kind of mall, full of luxury shops and cafés which would attract fashionable Paris to linger and dawdle under his aegis. He sought and obtained the king's permission for this development in the early 1780s (though not without Louis mocking his cousin's newfound career as a 'shopkeeper'). A new theatre was built as well, and there was a 'circus' too – a kind of exhibition hall within the bounds of the gardens – and a waxworks museum, run by Curtius, protector of Madame Tussaud.

By the late 1780s the Palais-Royal seemed to be the launching-pad for Philippe's quietly nurtured political ambitions. The enormous popularity of the location placed him very much in the Parisian eye, a feature he accentuated by crossing swords with the king in 1787–8 and earning himself a martyrish period of exile. By 1789 he had a team of hack writers working for him, pushing his political cause. By then the Palais-Royal had turned into the engine-room of political radicalism, and was full of illicit pamphlet-shops and printing-houses pouring out radical propaganda. All Parisians, reported one newspaper, hurried there 'to find out the news and to keep abreast of what was going on elsewhere'. It was also where political cabals met to sharpen their programmes for the upcoming Estates-General.

The storming of the Bastille on 14 July 1789, which saw Parisians force Louis XVI to accept a liberal constitution, had its origins in the Palais-Royal. It was there, legend has it, that the journalist Camille Desmoulins stood on a café table to denounce the royal court's military manoeuvrings and to launch a call to arms. Thereafter the Palais-Royal confirmed its place as the urban forum of public debate and the formulator of Parisian opinion. As Victor Hugo later put it, it was 'the core of the comet Revolution'. The Russian writer Nikolai Karamzin, who was here in 1790, called it 'the heart, the soul, the brain, the very synopsis of Paris'. It was also a home of more furtive pleasures. In 1791 the English poet William Wordsworth 'coasted round and round the line/Of Tavern, Brothel, Gaming-House, and Shop'. High-class shopping, eating and drinking, gambling and more or less open prostitution were – with sheer *flânerie* – essential parts of the Palais-Royal's attraction. The worlds of consumption and revolutionary politics often harmonized: the main political groupings foregathered in cafés on the premises.

Although much of this activity reflected an enormous amount of credit on Philip, he found it difficult to cash in. He showed the requisite signs of patriotism, even going off to fight in the army in 1792 along with his son, the duc de Chartres. But by the time the French people discovered they wanted to get rid of Louis XVI, they had made up their mind that they did not want to replace him with his Orléanist cousin. Orléans was thus reduced to increasingly extreme political actions to prove his republican credentials, including consigning his cousin to the guillotine. Yet within a year he had been arrested himself and executed. The tumbril conveying him to the scaffold stopped momentarily outside his former home – a sadistic touch – but he remained impassive and stoical in a death which was more impressive than his life.

Under Napoleon and then even more after his fall, the Palais-Royal remained a legendary site of pleasure rather than a site of popular politics. 'There is no spot in Europe quite like it,' noted an awe-struck visitor in 1813. In 1815 the returned Orléanists moved back in and straight away sought to ingratiate themselves with the Parisian people. Philippe-Égalité's son did accede to the throne on the overthrow of the Bourbons in the 1830 Revolution – though he lasted only until 1848 when he too was removed. By then the Palais-Royal was an altogether more sedate place.

The prohibition of both gambling and prostitution in the 1830s had ended its giddy reign as the home of Parisian hedonism.

The bulk of opinion and news was carried in newspapers. Probably more people learnt of how the Bastille had fallen through reading about it in newspapers than in any other way. The press had been lively and committed prior to 1789; it was the Revolution which made it into a genuine mass medium. This was nowhere truer than in Paris, where 90 per cent of men and 80 per cent of women had at least the rudiments of literacy. In 1788 there had been 200 booksellers and 36 printing works in the capital. By the late 1790s the figures were 500 and 218 respectively. The capital had had only one daily newspaper in the Ancien Régime – the sedate *Journal de Paris*, founded in 1777. By 1790 there were twenty-three dailies and an indeterminate number of periodicals appearing less frequently. In that year alone more than three hundred new titles appeared. Theatre – another target for close state control and censorship under the Ancien Régime – also benefited enormously from the new conditions, and showed a growing propensity for politicization. The city had housed around a dozen theatres in 1789; in the Revolutionary decades there were thirty-seven (the majority of which were on the Right Bank, especially on the Boulevard du Temple (IIIe.), which was becoming Parisian theatreland). Salons also boomed, and often took on a more political hue than hitherto.

Political clubs – more or less illicit prior to 1789 – also emerged, often meeting in church premises made vacant by ecclesiastical reform. The most famous of the clubs, which met in the old monastery of the community of Saint Jacques on the Rue Saint-Honoré, was the Society of Friends of the Constitution, or Jacobins. Starting as a political lobby preparing the following day's business in the Assembly, the Jacobins contained a higher proportion of deputies than other clubs, but also opened their sessions to the public. They achieved notoriety too by sponsoring affiliated provincial clubs – over a thousand in time. By 1793 the city contained forty-nine clubs (two of which were for women), around a quarter of which were Jacobin affiliates.

The national organization of clubs, which affirmed Paris's strategic role in the political process, was copied by clubs of differing hues,

Des Citoyens chantants l'hyme des Marseillois,... ils en sont au refrain...

aux armes Citoyens!..........

Citizens singing the *Marseillaise*

such as the Feuillants, a moderate breakaway from the Jacobins in 1791. Other clubs sponsored newspapers and pamphlets to spread their ideas nationally. The utopian group the Cercle social, for example, published a radical news-sheet called the *Bouche de Fer*, while the popular Cordeliers club had the crude and demotic mouthings of Jacques Hébert's *Père Duchesne* newspaper (in which radical ideas jostled alongside multitudinous *bougres* and *foutres*). The Cordeliers club along with the neighbourhood clubs formed at local level, often had a more plebeian membership than the Jacobins, admission fees to which were high – and more radical policies too. Many such clubs were unable to get their message out to the provinces, and they focused on ways of influencing policy-making within the National Assembly such as collective petitioning on issues. Delegations from the clubs made a custom of presenting their petitions flamboyantly to the Assembly in sessions full of dramatic interest. The radical groups also sought to coordinate their action through Paris's system of municipal government.

Although it was all to end in tears, a properly municipal form of government had indeed been introduced in 1789, rewarding Parisians for their pivotal role in events and also bringing the city into line with other towns and villages across the land. Paris was one of three districts within the Department of Paris. The ad hoc Commune established at the time of the taking of the Bastille was the core of a municipal commission which oversaw government until the decree of 21 May 1790. The worthy astronomer Bailly, Third Estate delegate from Paris, was acclaimed as mayor at the time of the king's visit to Paris on 17 July 1789. He was assisted by the almost wholly bourgeois representatives of the city's sixty electoral districts for the Estates General. In May 1790 the sixty districts were compressed into forty-eight electoral sections, though other essentials remained the same. Local government was in bourgeois hands. It was to take the overthrow of King Louis XVI and the establishment of a republic to bring a more populist feel to city politics.

In truth, despite the popular enthusiasm of 1789, the king had found it extremely difficult to accommodate himself with a Revolution which set aside his erstwhile 'absolute' powers and obliged him to operate within a political system that placed more power in the hands of an elected, one-chamber legislative assembly than in his own. Although he had presided in person over the Fête de la Fédération, a massive ceremony of celebration organized on the Champ de Mars on 14 July 1790, with delegates from every department in France presenting their arms to king and nation, he had severe qualms about the processes in play. The king was repelled by the threat of violence which seemed to be hovering within Paris, and out of loyalty felt supportive towards his family and aristocratic servants who were now in external emigration or internal exile. He was also extremely unhappy about the religious reforms being introduced by the National Assembly. In November 1789 the Assembly had nationalized all church property, as a means of achieving state solvency. This was followed by the Civil Constitution of the Clergy of July 1790. This attempt to provide a kind of liberal housecleaning for an ancient and touchy organization – monastic vows were ended; the number of dioceses and parishes reduced; election to clerical office introduced, etc. – was certain to cause feathers to fly. Primed by the pope, Louis sympathized with clergy critical of the Civil Constitution, who refused to take the oath of loyalty demanded of all clerics. In France as a whole some 55 per cent of clerics swore the oath (though some subsequently retracted). In Paris, where the number of parishes was reduced from 52 to 33, the figure of 'jurors' among the parish clergy was 66 per cent, though when all other forms of clergy are taken into account the figure was only around 40 per cent.

Louis's unwillingness to take mass from the hand of any but a non-juring priest roused suspicions that he was not supporting the Revolution. Even prior to 1789, as we have seen, there had been a good deal of distrust as regards the king's commitment to the welfare of his people. Suspicions were now amplified by Louis's effort to flee his Parisian 'prison' in June 1791. The 'Flight to Varennes' finished in fiasco. The king was captured and brought back into the city of Paris as though in a kind of royal anti-*entrée*, moving through serried ranks of ominously silent Parisians. Louis escaped deposition only by the skin of his teeth – and mainly because he was willing to humble himself by feigning unqualified support for the Revolutionary cause. Moderates in the Assembly also preferred to have him under their control rather than to allow the increasingly radical popular movement to institute a republic, which risked alienating the rest of France, and indeed the whole of Europe.

As we have seen, Paris had got used to its odd status as a kingless city in the course of the eighteenth century. In addition there was a good deal of secularization of attitudes during the Enlightenment across the social spectrum. Yet little in 1789 would indicate that within four years Parisians would have led a successful movement to overthrow the king and institute a republic, nor that the city would have become the theatre of a campaign of vicious 'dechristianizing' anti-clericalism. In 1789 republicanism was a political option taken seriously by no one (or no one serious). Furthermore, the triumphant *journées* of the early years of the Revolution were celebrated in church services across the land – and Paris was little different in this respect.

The conduct of king, court and non-juring clerics made anti-monarchism and anti-clericalism politically respectable, and indeed patriotically desirable. What above all produced this change was warfare. In April 1792 France went to war with the Holy Roman Empire (the rest of Europe would follow in early 1793). The Girondins, a group of deputies from the Gironde department (round Bordeaux) and their allies, had launched a campaign for war as a means of forcing Revolutionary doubters, king included, off the fence. Yet the strategy rebounded badly. War polarized political attitudes, especially as the war initially went very badly. Indifference towards the Revolution by non-juring clerics or by the king and his supporters was now glossed to signify treason. Punitive legislation aimed at *émigrés* and non-jurors only made the king vacillate even more – in ways which increasingly seemed treasonable too.

With the National Assembly hopelessly divided on the way out of the political impasse vis-à-vis the king, it took the organized activists of the popular movement to break the deadlock. In the war crisis of the summer of 1792, popular militants started to attend sectional meetings and join the National Guard – both forms of engagement formerly restricted to propertied citizens. They also volunteered in droves for the front. By late July many of the sections were not only openly voting for a republic, but also covertly organizing a new *journée* to overthrow the king. They moved to take the place of the existing municipality, and formed themselves into an Insurrectionary Commune ('*Commune insurectionnelle*'). On 10 August, in a dramatic day of violence, they forced the National Assembly to accept the king's abdication. The Assembly agreed to convoke a National Convention to write a new, republican constitution for France.

While elections were organized, Paris was effectively run by the Insurrectionary Commune. It prepared the city for defence, should German troops break through France's eastern defences, as seemed quite possible. It ordered the melting down of church bells for cannon. It introduced a wide range of surveillance measures, and sought to control opinion by closing down counter-revolutionary printshops and censoring the press. And it recruited passive citizens into the National Guard and encouraged volunteering for the army. When on 20 September 1792 French troops repelled the invaders at the cannonade of Valmy, some 200 kilometres from the capital, there were more than a few Parisians among them. On the same day, the new National Convention met and immediately declared a republic, 'one and indivisible'.

Despite their fundamental role in establishing the republic and their heroic part in national defence, Parisian popular militants were to receive only mixed reviews on their achievement. For what they did was also accompanied by acts of savagery which repelled not only most of European opinion, but also a great many sincere republicans even within France. The *journée* of 10 August was accompanied by horrible atrocities committed on the king's Swiss Guard – whom, some said in mitigation, had opened fire first. There seemed no excuse at all – save only an unsubstantiated fear of a counter-revolutionary 'prison plot' – to explain the September Massacres of 2–5 September. With the more or less open encouragement of the surveillance committee of the Commune, gangs of militants toured the Paris prisons massacring those confined there: common-law prisoners such as prostitutes, thieves and vagrants as well as non-juring priests and individuals imprisoned for political reasons. A number of atrocities were also committed, including the murder of Marie-Antoinette's intimate friend, the princesse de Lamballe, whose severed and desecrated head was unsteadily waved on the end of a pike outside the queen's cell in the Temple prison. Over 1,300 individuals perished. The stones ran red in the city's prisons (the Conciergerie, the Abbaye, the Force, etc.), poorhouses (Bicêtre, La Salpêtrière) and former religious buildings turned into makeshift detention centres (the Carmes, the Bernardins, Saint-Firmin). Many of these places were at the heart of Paris; Parisians heard the screams and walked past.

'It was the best of times; it was the worst of times.' The opening words of Charles Dickens's great French Revolution novel, *The Tale of Two Cities* (1859), were never more apt than at this moment of Parisian history which so dramatically mingled the great and the ghoulish, the heroic and the ignoble. Once in place, the Convention acted swiftly to dismantle the Insurrectionary Commune, and set up new municipal elections. These took months to end, giving the new Convention a breather from municipal pressure. A moderate, the physician Chambon de Montaux, was elected mayor. Yet the ignominious reputation which the Commune had brought on the Parisian Revolution was not easy to expunge. Activists from Brest and Marseille had been prominent among the rebels on 10 August, and a majority of 'Parisians' were provincials by birthplace. No matter: the September Massacres were laid squarely at the door of the Parisian popular movement. Many Revolutionary well-wishers turned counter-revolutionary overnight. 'The Revolution of the Declaration of the Rights of Man is one thing,' commented the Italian writer Alfieri. 'Revolutionary Paris in the hands of this plebeian mob (*plébaille*) is altogether different.'[3] In his *Nouveau Paris*, published in 1799, Louis-Sébastien Mercier would seek to differentiate between 'two distinct peoples' living alongside each other in the city, which in his eyes had both made and spoiled the Revolution: on one hand there was 'the people of 14 July and 10 August', 'hurling itself selflessly towards freedom, ready to undertake anything, invincible and generous', who had truly made the Revolution; and on the other there were the 'subtle, greedy and cruel' people, seeking only 'power and wealth', who had spoiled it.[4]

Mercier, elected to the Convention in 1792, sat among the Girondin grouping. Many of the latter had formerly warmed to the historic role of Paris as bastion against political tyranny and provincial intellectual backwardness – but they now viewed Paris as public enemy number one. The intellectual Condorcet had earlier contended that 'France needs to be strong in order to resist its enemies, and to be strong, it needs a common centre'. Louvet had sung the same tune as recently as July 1792: 'Paris is the palladium of our freedom. The city will be forever guilty in the eyes of tyrants for having started the Revolution.'[5] Now both men shared the fear of another fellow Girondin, that 'Paris will become the tomb of freedom across the universe.'[6] This anxiety was increasingly widely held out in the provinces.

The Girondins believed that Parisian activists managed to influence the Revolution only through the support which they received from the radical wing of the National Assembly. Their enemies in the new Convention were thus figures with a popular following in Paris (and many of whom had been members of the Insurrectionary Commune). Such pro-Parisian radicals went by the title of Montagnards. They included figures like the Arras lawyer Maximilien Robespierre, nick-named 'the Incorruptible' for his altruistic and principled stands on moral issues; the volcanic orator Danton, linked with the Cordeliers club; and the campaigning journalist, ex-physician Marat. All three men were subject to fierce Girondin attacks in the Convention, especi-ally for their putative part in the September Massacres. All three were, however, becoming increasingly aware that without a radical programme of reform which attracted the support of the labouring classes, the nascent republic risked being still-born. They tended to excuse the violence of their plebeian allies as natural justice or else as generous excesses of the will for freedom. The republic would have to be forceful and not shrink from violence – or it would fail.

The split within the republican political elite was dramatically high-lighted in the trial of Louis XVI, which turned into a Girondin–Montagnard squabble in which the fate of the king was sometimes overlooked in the heat of the exchanges. Louis was indeed executed on 21 January 1793, but this solved nothing. Political divisions tended to revolve around the Parisian activist – or sans-culotte as he was often now called. To be *sans culottes* was to be 'without knee-breeches', a style of dress which was supposed to characterize trouser-wearing workmen as against effete breeches-wearing aristocrats. There was no little exaggeration in this contrast. Most of the individuals who counted themselves as sans-culottes in 1792–4 were master artisans, small shopkeepers and petty clerks, and the pre-Revolutionary ward-robes of such individuals had invariably included breeches. Political correctness Terror-style thus involved dressing up (or rather, down) – wearing trousers, plebeian waistcoat and clogs (leather was reserved for soldiers' boots), sporting a tricolore cockade pinned to a red 'phrygian' bonnet (based on the headgear awarded freed slaves in Antiquity), and carrying a pike, as sign of readiness to spring patrioti- cally into action. True sans-culottes also intoned various Revolution- ary anthems, including the 'Marseillaise', popularized by the Marseille militants who had contributed to the overthrow of Louis XVI.

Although Robespierre and other Montagnards nurtured a rather idealized picture of good-hearted sans-culottes, which stressed their obedience to the will of the people as expressed through the National Convention, in fact members of the Paris popular movement were a pretty boisterous and independent crowd. They might hate the Parisophobic Girondins, but they were quite capable of differing in their views from the Montagnards too. Nurtured on ideas of a moral economy as regards food supply, they were more willing than the Montagnards to countenance measures of economic egalitarianism such as price fixing, taxes on the rich and the death penalty for hoarders. Encouraged by ambitious radicals like the cleric Jacques Roux and the journalist Hébert, they also saw themselves, in their sectional assemblies, as embodying popular sovereignty – a doctrine which went down well with none of the Conventionnels. 'We do not here defend the interests of the city of Paris,' Commune officials had instructed a sullen Convention in the autumn of 1793, 'but those of the whole of France. Paris has made the Revolution, Paris has given the rest of France freedom, Paris will maintain it.'[7]

The period from the spring of 1793 till early 1794 saw a complex multilateral political conflict unravelling in Paris. The Montagnards were willing to allow popular pressure to be put on the Convention to expel the Girondin deputies, and the latter's provocations were hardly tactful: 'Paris will be annihilated,' one Girondin exclaimed in the Assembly, if the sans-culottes took action against them, 'and men will search the banks of the Seine for signs of the city.'[8] Nevertheless, by the *journées* of 31 May–2 June 1793 the Girondins were expelled as a result of sans-culotte pressure, and many of them would go to the guillotine in October. On the other hand the Montagnards proved less reluctant to embrace the radical economic programme being urged by

Roux and his supporters, the so-called *enragés* ('wild ones'). It needed further sans-culotte demonstrations (notably on 4–5 September), plus the worsening international and military situation, to make such policies palatable to the Convention. The latter now moved to accept a radical social programme: a maximum price on foodstuffs (the Maximum); relief programmes for the poor; the prohibition on discounting the Revolutionary paper currency (called the *assignat*); approval of the pillaging of conquered territories abroad; the death penalty for hoarders and other economic miscreants; and so on. In order to deliver this programme, the Convention also implemented a vigorously centralizing policy of state Terror. Executive power in what was now referred to as the Revolutionary Government was placed in the hands of a committee of the Convention, the Committee of Public Safety (from July headed by Robespierre). This enjoyed extensive powers regarding war operations as well as for the implementation of Terror within France. A Revolutionary Tribunal dealt with counter-revolutionary crimes. A Law of Suspects threatened with death all manner of political dissidents. Sweeping powers were placed in the hands of the police and of local surveillance committees. Sans-culotte vigilante forces known as *armées révolutionnaires* were directed to go out into the countryside and enforce the Maximum and indeed all Revolutionary legislation. The guillotine – unveiled in 1792 as a more humanitarian means of meting out capital punishment than the horrible tortures of the Ancien Régime – now stood as a sinister emblem of repression. Around it an elaborate public theatre of punishment developed.

This arsenal of Terroristic legislation which combined the carrot with the stick was also designed to keep in line the remainder of the country. The increasing crescendo of Parisian violence, and in particular the expulsion of the Girondins, had caused widespread opposition throughout France, so the departments needed to be bullied, cajoled and seduced back into conformity. Although the Montagnards had come to accept much of the programme of the Parisian popular movement, they were hostile to the latter's vaunted autonomy and its claim to represent the people of France. At the same time as passing *enragé* programmes, therefore, they also had Roux and a number of his allies either imprisoned or intimidated into silence.

Roux's successors as sans-culotte agitators, notably Hébert and Chaumette, both ensconsed within the Commune, sought to open a new
front, by swinging towards policies of radical dechristianization. They
diffused their policies through political allies from the Convention
who were enforcing the Terror in the departments. But Paris was the
special centre for their activities. The city had already lost a good deal
of the Catholic veneer which had characterized it since the days of
the Counter-Reformation. Some 6,000 ecclesiastics had thronged the
streets of pre-Revolutionary Paris – by 1793, they were numbered in
hundreds. Religious processions in the open air had been banned.
Most church bells had been melted down for cannon. Before 1789
there had been numerous religious edifices in Paris – fifty-odd parish
churches, over one hundred and thirty monastic buildings, more than
sixty university colleges and a dozen seminaries. All of these had been
made 'national lands' (*biens nationaux*), and a great many were now
either closed, sold off or put to alternative use. (Notre-Dame-des-
Victoires (Ie.–IIe.), for example, served as a stock exchange.) Since
mid-1792 there had been a plethora of iconoclastic attacks on signs
of royalty, nobility and feudalism in the city: all royal statues on the
city's *places royales*, for example, were unceremoniously destroyed.
Royal tombs out at the Saint-Denis basilica were systematically desecrated. The mortal remains of more than a millennium of French
monarchs were tossed into a common grave and covered with quick-
lime. The remains of Louis XVI and Marie-Antoinette shared the same
fate. Street crosses and religious way-stations were destroyed. Now
this movement extended to a systematic assault on religious imagery.
The figures on the west front of Notre-Dame cathedral – thought
(wrongly) to represent the kings of France – were removed, though
not before they had been symbolically beheaded. Saints' names were
removed from Parisian topography, especially once, from October
1793, a new, secular calendar was introduced, which replaced the
names of saints with natural products and agrarian implements.
(Chaumette had himself got into the spirit of the new epoch by
changing his Christian names Pierre-Gaspard to the very classical
'Anaxogoras'.) The Palais-Royal became the Palais-National, for
example; the Place Royale, the Place des Vosges; the Place Louis XV,
the Place de la Révolution; the Rue Bourbon, the Rue de Lille; the Rue

Saint-Denis, the Rue Franciade; the Rue Saint-Honoré, the Rue de la Convention; the Rue Saint-Sulpice, the Rue du 31-Mai (1793); and so, wearingly, on.

Chaumette and his supporters in the new and reformed Commune sought to stage dechristianization activities in the capital to give themselves more political clout. On 7 November 1793 Gobel, the archbishop of Paris elected under the provisions of the Civil Constitution of the Clergy, publicly abjured his faith and donned the red bonnet; a dozen of his parish clergy would follow his lead, and some would even marry, again in ceremonies high in anti-clerical content. On 10 November a 'Festival of Reason' was staged, with a procession and a secular service held at the new 'Temple of Reason' (a.k.a. Notre-Dame cathedral). On 23 November the Commune ordered the closure of all churches within Paris. Hébert also wanted to knock down all the city's steeples.

The total dechristianization of Paris was, however, resisted by Robespierre and many of his Montagnard allies. They feared that Chaumette was going too far towards atheism, and risked triggering a clerical backlash even among individuals thus far devoted to the Revolutionary cause. Robespierre also suspected Chaumette's political motives, and feared the attempts of the Commune to reimpose its influence in ways which implied that it, rather than the Convention, represented the people of France. With Danton, Robespierre reaffirmed the principle of freedom of worship, attacking atheism as an aristocratic rather than a popular creed, and this was followed by the Law of 14 Frimaire Year II in the Revolutionary Calendar (4 December 1793). The law affirmed the Committee of Public Safety's wide-ranging powers, tightened up bureaucratic controls, set limits to the degree of political coordination Paris's forty-eight sections were permitted and also recalled many of the dechristianizing deputies in the provinces. By March 1794 the Committee of Public Safety was ready to arraign Hébert before the Revolutionary Tribunal on trumped-up charges. Chaumette and sundry followers would follow shortly (as would the more moderate Danton). Robespierre also devised a humanist Revolutionary cult in order to replace the Commune's atheistic efforts: on 8 June the Convention staged an elaborate Festival of the Supreme Being, parading through the streets of Paris under Robespierre's mastership of ceremonies. With a faceless Robespierre nominee Fleuriot-Lescot brought in as mayor from May 1794, the Commune was a shadow of its former self. It proved hostile to the workers' side in labour disputes occurring throughout the spring of 1794. On 23 July – 5 Thermidor Year II – it even implemented the Maximum for wages as well as prices for the first time. The measure drastically reduced Parisian workers' wages.

Four days after this labour legislation – on 9 Thermidor Year II (27 July 1794) – Robespierre was overthrown by his fellow Conventionnels. Much of the assembly had become fearful for their lives in a Terror which seemed to be spinning out of control the more that 'Year II' advanced. The Law of 22 Prairial (10 June) had facilitated convictions in the Revolutionary Tribunal, so that the streets of Paris witnessed the ever-more frequent passage of tumbrils on the way to the guillotine. It was rumoured that it had been decided to shift the place of execution out to the east of the city in the present-day Place de la Nation (XIe.–XIIe.) because the soil under the guillotine on the Place de Grève was becoming so sodden with blood that there was a risk of contamination of urban water supplies. Some 2,600 individuals perished in this way at the hands of the Revolutionary Tribunal. Many moderate deputies had accepted the need for Terror in the war emergency of 1793. Yet by June 1794 the war situation was immeasurably better. Finally frightened into action by Robespierre's wild talk of even more political proscriptions, a group of Conventionnels conspired to overthrow him along with his seemingly untouchable clique of followers. In a turbulent *journée* Robespierre was arrested, but escaped his captors. From the Hôtel de Ville, the Commune's headquarters, he called on the sectional militants to save him from the Convention's coup. The sans-culottes simply refused to come out in numbers and defend a man who by this time – as the Maximum ruling of 5 Thermidor showed – seemed more their persecutor than their friend.

Robespierre would be conveyed to the scaffold on 10 Thermidor with angry Parisians shouting 'Fuck the Maximum!' as he passed. Over the next couple of days the crowds would also witness the execution of some eighty-seven members of the Revolutionary Commune. Dozens more were imprisoned. There seemed little move within the city to speak up for individuals who had claimed to represent the people of France, and who were indeed the legal representatives of the Parisian population. This demonstrated that the alliance between the Revolutionary government and the popular movement which Robespierre had helped to create in the previous year had now disappeared. Robespierre had so neutered the Parisian popular movement that it had neither force nor will to support him when he needed it.

The fall of Robespierre also meant the end of the short period of municipal self-government which Paris had enjoyed since 1789. Even before the time of Étienne Marcel in the fourteenth century, there had been a sense that Paris was too important to the state to be allowed self-government of a type which other cities enjoyed. The experience of the Paris Commune between 1789 and 1794 now seemed to prove the monarchy right on this detail at least. While this process had begun before 9 Thermidor, the post-Thermidorian Convention was more than happy to take it further. It sought to ensure that a reprise of the Terror in Paris was unimaginable, and that the Parisian populace was no longer a political actor. The forty-eight sections which had been the crucible of popular militancy were scrapped and replaced by twelve arrondissements, which the ex-Terrorists of Year II were frightened out of attending. The Department of Paris, now renamed the Department of the Seine, was given increased powers. Yet in fact in the short term most of the responsibilities of local government, including policing, were handled by the committees of the Convention. The closure of the Jacobin clubs was followed by harassment of sectional militants. Somewhat pathetic attempts by the remnants of the popular movement to impose themselves on events only gave the government licence to clamp down even more. The abortive *journées* of Germinal and Prairial Year III (April–May 1795) protesting the high price of bread and the rightward drift of national policy were followed by the demilitarization of the faubourgs, the imprisonment of popular activists and the arraignment of left-wing deputies attracted to the popular cause. The Convention planned a new constitution which was less radical, and more liberal and decentralized, than anything imagined under the Terror. When Parisians sought to protest – in the *journée* of 13 Vendémiaire Year IV (7 October 1795) – their demonstrations were crushed by a few artfully aimed bouts of

Arrest of Robespierre

cannonfire ordered by the young army officer Napoleon Bonaparte.

Bonaparte's 'whiff of grapeshot' established the scale of priorities to be observed by the Directory, which was instituted by the new constitution. Issues Parisian were eclipsed by matters military. It was on the battlefields of Europe, not on the streets of the capital, that the continuing drama of Revolutionary politics would henceforth be played out. Furthermore the Thermidorian and Directorial periods were characterized by theatrical and symbolic attempts to reclaim the streets and institutions of Paris from those who had dominated in Year II. In 1795–7 old Jacobins and sans-culottes were subjected to pitiless harassment by the so-called *jeunesse dorée* ('gilded youth'), sons of middle-class families with a sprinkling of ex-Girondins, released prisoners and crypto-royalists. Anyone sporting a red bonnet or the unofficial sans-culotte uniform of Year II was attacked and ragged. Renditions of the 'Marseillaise' – whether in cafés, streets or theatres – were drowned out by counter-revolutionary anthems. The remains of Revolutionary heroes which had been interred at the Panthéon were dragged out and desecrated. Even though there was still much generalized suspicion of Catholicism, the dechristianizing gestures of Year II were resisted. Street-names, for example, were 'de-dechristianized' or else reclaimed their historic identities. The old Rue des Cordeliers (named after the religious order, not the club) had become the Rue Marat in 1793; it now was transformed into Rue de l'École-de-Santé (now Rue de l'École-de-Médecine, Ve.). Even the Rue du Roi-de-Sicile (IVe.) – Rue des Droits-de-l'Homme from 1792 – got its name back, though the Place Louis XV – Place de la Révolution – was renamed (durably) Place de la Concorde. *Concorde* – 'harmony' – was, however, in short supply.

The popular movement appeared to have shot its bolt. In 1796 the Left mounted a conspiracy against the new regime, in the form of a clandestine organization around the radical and communistic writer 'Gracchus' Babeuf. Yet the 'Babouvists' looked to the army rather than the faubourgs for support. Even so they were easily crushed. The complex electoral regime instituted by the Directory allowed the provinces more of a say in national politics, but though this did counterbalance Parisian influence it brought its own problems – an endless oscillation between Right and Left, producing a political instability made dangerous by shifting fortunes in war. The brilliant military victories which Bonaparte carried off in the Italian campaigns of 1796–7 signalled that the war of national defence in Year II had metamorphosed into a conflict for territorial aggrandizement in Europe. War seemed to palliate the political wounds of the 1790s, but only as long as it was crowned with success. Matters were different when the war effort faltered, as it did in 1798–9. Bonaparte's attempt to strike at British power in the East in the Egyptian campaign of 1798 ended in fiasco, while the Austrians dealt out defeats to French troops across Europe. A political crisis flared up in Paris, with vestiges of the old Jacobin Club and popular movement from Year II calling for measures of national security on the lines of those instituted under the Terror.

Most of the political class shrank in horror from a shift in approach which would bring Parisian sans-culottes back to the heart of governmental strategy. They preferred to look for a strong general who would deliver them victory on the battlefield but who also had the prestige to rewrite the constitution giving more power to the executive, so as to end the now almost paroxysmal oscillations of political opinion within the country at large. They found the general in the formidable shape of Bonaparte. Returned to France from Egypt, the latter hastened to Paris where he paraded himself around different political lobbies, hobnobbing with intellectuals and artists – but making sure not to make the most minimal gesture of fraternity towards the people of the faubourgs. The Brumaire coup which he orchestrated in November 1799 was premised on manufacturing a political scare that would force the legislature to declare an emergency and relocate government to Saint-Cloud – some 10 kilometres to the west of the capital, and several hours of clog-shod walk from the eastern Faubourg Saint-Marcel. Parisian popular militants were forced into the position of observers rather than participants in the change of constitution which led to the installation of the Consulate, dominated by First Consul Bonaparte. This was the first time since 1789 that national domestic politics had not been made within the confines of the city of Paris.

In 1802 Bonaparte would make himself Consul for life, and Emperor in 1804. He also confirmed the state's control over the city of Paris put in place by the Thermidorians and Directorials. A law of 11 October 1795 had confirmed the replacement of the forty-eight sections by twelve arrondissements. In addition a governmental 'commissary' appointed to keep the department of the Seine under surveillance was given special responsibilities as regards the capital. On all security issues he worked closely with the ministry of police which the Directory established in 1796. These arrangements were maintained and supplemented by Napoleon. The twelve arrondissements were all municipalities in their own right and each had a mayor – but these were not elected officials but governmental nominees. The mayors were under the close control of the newly instituted Prefect of the Seine (the institutional heir of the Directory's departmental commissary), who was, as Napoleon admitted, 'a sort of minister'.[9] If the Prefect of the Seine had far more powers than the old Prévôt des Marchands, he had even less independence. Security matters were now given over to a Police Prefect, who replicated many of the attributes of the old Lieutenance-Générale de Police. He had an extensive staff, and appointed police commissioners in each of Paris's twelve municipalities. The other influence on Parisian matters would be the Minister of the Interior – most issues relating to urbanism passed across his desk. Paris was thus placed in the firm grip of an institutional triad – Prefect of the Seine, Police Prefect, and Minister of the Interior – each of whom reported directly to their new master.

Napoleon himself was well aware of the importance of the city of Paris for his new regime, but he harboured intense distrust of its inhabitants. 'By nature,' he held, 'Parisians are ungrateful *frondeurs*.'[10] His comment on the events of 10 August 1792 was revealing: 'If I were king, it wouldn't have happened like that.'[11] Louis XVI had shown no gumption; Parisians despised weakness. They needed force to keep them in line, as Napoleon had illustrated in the 13 Vendémiaire *journée*. Louis XVI had felt a pathetic prisoner when residing in the Tuileries; Napoleon set himself up in the palace with no such neuroses (though, truth to tell, he tended to treat the Tuileries as a hotel, as he was away on campaign around three-quarters of the time between 1805 and 1814). When faced with the decision as to where he should be crowned as emperor, he considered both Rome and Lyon – the classical symbols with which he associated his imperial regime would have worked in both – before settling on Paris. Yet he recoiled with horror from the thought of locating the ceremony on the Champ de Mars, site of the Fête de la Fédération of 1790: 'It is important that the people of Paris should not believe itself to constitute the Nation,' he insisted. 'One must not subject oneself to popular hubbub (*brouhahas*).'[12] His selection of Notre-Dame cathedral proved most apposite: it was a suitable venue for the pope, who attended the ceremony (though Napoleon chose to crown himself), and with whom Napoleon had in 1801 concluded the Concordat, restoring religious peace after the anti-clerical escapades of the 1790s.

Parisians liked the fact that Napoleon had chosen Paris for his coronation. Yet this sprang from no particular liking for the new regime but rather because the ceremony brought in the tourists and was good for business. Only eighty Parisians had voted against the establishment of the Consulate, as against over 60,000 who voted for. Yet this was par for the course in the kind of plebiscitary democracy Napoleon was creating (eighty-one voted against the shift to the Empire, so clearly overt opposition was only expanding slowly). Parisians generally had little spontaneous affection for Napoleon. They warmed to his cause a little when he nearly fell victim to a bomb attempt on his life – the affair of the *machine infernale* of the Rue Saint-Nicaise just outside the Tuileries in December 1800. But many disliked his repressive response – over a hundred alleged Jacobins were deported. Though Napoleon had negotiated a European peace at Amiens in 1801, this soon broke down and Parisians had to accept the perpetuation of a war regime.

The tight rein on which Napoleon kept the city was strongly resented by a great many Parisians. The destruction of city-level self-government was only part of a more general campaign to curtail Parisians' political engagement. This had begun even before Thermidor, as we have suggested, and Napoleon took it further. Popular engagement in Revolutionary politics in the early and mid-1790s had usually been a minority phenomenon in aggregate terms, but it was still considerable and marked a step up from anything experienced before 1789. Participation at major elections was limited: around one-fifth of the male, propertied electorate – in total about 15,000 individuals – voted in the election of Bailly as mayor in 1789, for

Arrival of Napoleon at Notre-Dame cathedral

example. This level was sometimes approached but rarely surpassed thereafter. Maybe around the same number were regularly involved in factional politics in Year II. Yet far larger numbers were involved in the Revolutionary *journées* which constituted Parisians' most marked and most genuinely collective civic input into the Revolutionary process. Parisians also showed their ardour by military commitment: at the height of the war emergency of 1793 over 100,000 men were in the National Guard, and the Parisian *armée révolutionnaire* spreading Terror to the countryside numbered around 7,000 men. Over the 1790s as a whole between 6 and 9 per cent of male Parisians served in the army. Most adults in the city were literate, and they proved assiduous readers of political newspapers and periodicals. The *Père Duchesne* of Commune stalwart Hébert was published in national print-runs of up to 200,000; readership was several times higher than this number. Parisians were among the keenest participants in political clubs and associations, and involvement in the capital reached deeper than elsewhere into new political constituencies – notably the labouring classes and domestic servants, but also women.

The Revolution gave a stronger impetus towards political engagement by women than any other mass political phenomenon in history hitherto. Women were often to the forefront of revolutionary crowds on the great Revolutionary *journées*. They participated in political life, attending sessions of successive national assemblies and the Paris Commune, many of them following the Commune's injunction during the Terror to knit socks for frontline troops while listening to debates. They capitalized massively on freedom of speech and publishing: four times as many women were in print in the 1790s as in the decade before 1789. Playwright Olympe de Gouges's *The Rights of Women* (1791) was a sonorous public demand for equal rights. Women benefited too from new legislation on divorce to free themselves of abusive husbands. They joined some political clubs in their own right and also set up women's clubs. The most famous of these, the Society of Revolutionary Republican Citizenesses, included in its ranks Pauline Léon and Claire Lacombe who were strategists for the *enragés*. Yet just as the Revolutionary government before Thermidor had sought to muzzle political radicalism, it also set about eradicating women's claims to equal political rights. De Gouges went to the scaffold.

Chaumette's Commune, then the Revolutionary government formally outlawed female clubs. The highly sexist language used in these debates highlighted the extent to which Revolutionary males had been influenced by the strong code of virility promoted by Revolutionary warfare. Women, the Convention was informed, were prone to 'an over-excitation which is deadly in public affairs'.[13] From March 1795 the National Assembly forbade women from attending political meetings or even gathering in groups in the streets to discuss public affairs. Napoleon scaled back on social legislation which had benefited women such as the laws on divorce. The Napoleonic Civil Code introduced in 1804 more or less reduced women to the status of minors under the authority of their husbands or fathers. Medical writings which purported to demonstrate that women were biologically equipped for little more than love and motherhood set the seal on a long-lasting domestication of women. The Napoleonic regime was bad news for the rights of women within the city.

The removal of women from political life, the banning of political clubs, judicial repression, the vigilante harassment of left-wing activists, the dismantling of the electoral system and the muzzling of the structures of municipal self-government all combined to produce a massive deactivation of participatory politics from the late 1790s onwards. Napoleon liked crowds to proclaim loyalty and to spectate the ceremonies of consular, then imperial power. He expected obedience not reasoned political involvement. The rights of political assembly were much curtailed, and the number of newspapers drastically cut. The number of printers was reduced from over 200 in the late 1790s to 132 by 1804 and 80 by 1811. Political militancy might have been something of a minority luxury even at the height of the 1790s; from 1799 it became taboo.

Political demoralization was heightened by the severe social strains in Paris attendant on the deregulation of the national economy after the Terror. Revolution and war had brought dislocation to a city already suffering the impact of the economic downturn of the last years of the Ancien Régime. The luxury trades were hit hard by emigration and by the pruning of the high ecclesiastical elite: workers from the carriage-trade, from luxury furniture and from hairdressing were among the keenest (and hungriest) of sans-culottes. The sudden shrinkage of consumer demand was one factor – military enlistment was another – in the overall stagnation and probable decline of the city's population. In 1789 it numbered 650,000 or more, but there were certainly fewer in 1795. A census of 1801 put the figure at only 547,576. This registered the approximate order of magnitude of population loss, although it underplays the mobile population which the city attracted.

The 1790s were not, however, a total economic disaster for all Parisians. The establishment of the new Revolutionary institutions in the city attracted a new major source of consumption. Politicians needed somewhere to eat in the evenings, a demand in which lay one of the origins of the emergence of the restaurant in this period. The Révolution's positively gargantuan appetite for print also meant that anyone with connection to the print trades was likely to prosper (as long as they could keep their political noses clean): rag collectors, papermakers, printers, publishers, binders, booksellers, ink-manufacturers, hawkers, pedlars – and authors. Journalism achieved sufficient critical mass to develop into a profession. The size of the bureaucracy probably increased by a factor of ten – a phenomenon which led to the social acceptance of the new word *bureaucratie* (or *burocratie*). The centralization of higher education and research – a Directorial and Napoleonic legacy which would prove an enduring feature of French life – also benefited the city. The Parisian location of Bourbon creations such as the old Jardin du Roi (now mutated into the Museum of Natural History and the Jardin des Plantes), the Ponts et Chaussées (1747) and the École des Mines (1778) was confirmed, while the Institut (1795) was an umbrella organization for the old national academies. Major new creations included the École Normale (1794), the Conservatoire des Arts et Métiers (1794) and the École Polytechnique (1795). The revived medical faculty, the École de Santé (1794), also dominated provincial rivals such as Montpellier and Strasbourg. Henceforth the bulk of state-funded research and the overwhelming majority of students were to be found in the capital.

7.2: The Grand Véfour

Just as coffee antedated the coffee-house or café, the *restaurant* came before the restaurant. Originally, it seems (as Rebecca Spang has demonstrated), the restaurant was a place in which one went in order to 'se restaurer' – to restore oneself – through the consumption of a medicinal bouillon called a *restaurant*. In the decades preceding the Revolution of 1789, owners of premises offering this refined service were shrewd businessmen: they were playing on the contemporaneous cult of sensibility; exploiting current anxieties about the damaging effects of modern urban living on the nervous system; and positing a link between health and food consumption which has been an effective leitmotiv in food advertising ever since. In the 1770s the first such establishments often styled themselves *maisons de santé* ('houses of health', 'infirmaries'). Despite the restaurant's subsequent association with digestive overload, these early establishments used marketing devices to pose as places where one really did not eat much at all. It was *nouvelle cuisine – avant la lettre*. In a restaurant one could be seen picking solitarily at bouillons, light dairy produce and sweets and fresh fruits. There were around fifty restaurants in the city by 1789.

So strong is the sense of Paris as the acme of gastronomy and good eating that it is easy to be unaware that this reputation has been acquired so relatively recently in the city's long history. Medieval and Renaissance Paris had their hospitality sector, of course, such as inns, taverns, and various types of eating and drinking establishments. But the restaurant as we know it was a product of the late eighteenth-century history of the city. The Grand Véfour restaurant – still to be found and eaten at in the Palais-Royal – was one of relatively few such institutions to continue offering *restaurant* bouillons well into the nineteenth century. By that time the new establishment had been changed radically, notably by developments during the Revolution. Chefs of aristocratic houses were forced to find new forms of work when their employers went into political emigration in the 1790s: many opened restaurants. The institution also benefited from the long-term presence in Paris after 1789 of provincial deputies in the National Assembly, needing to find appropriate dining facilities. In addition the sector was powerfully influenced by the emergence, notably from the period of the Directory, of the science of gastronomy. From this conjunction of factors a set of practices and conventions emerged which have stayed durably in place: flexible mealtimes, printed menus (instead of eating what was served up, *table d'hôte* style), individualized meals, and fine furnishings which combined privacy (small tables, separate rooms, theatrical protocol played out by waiters) with publicity (mirrors, common dining space). The restaurant meal was now presented in a social setting which mixed business with pleasure and utility with festivity. Unlike in most cafés, moreover, women could feel comfortable here.

The Grand Véfour came relatively late to the table. Its founder Jean Véfour purchased one of the Palais-Royal's eminent political cafés the Café de Chartres, repair of royalist factions and post-Thermidorian *jeunesse dorée*. Worried about the possible desertion of the Palais-Royal by the social elite during the changed political atmosphere of the Empire, in 1814 he decided to diversify by adding a restaurant. His gamble paid off, and the Grand Véfour, as the restaurant renamed itself in 1820, became popular for its elegant 'fork luncheons', attended by all the celebrities of the age. Its fame flared particularly brightly in the Second Empire, when it absorbed the adjacent Véry restaurant, in which Balzac's Lucien de Rubempré chose to dine on arriving from Angoulême, to initiate himself into 'the pleasures of Paris' – the Ostend oysters, fish, partridge, macaroni and fruit, washed down with Bordeaux, were 'the ne plus ultra of his wishes'. Wanting to evoke the extremities of Parisian poverty, Baudelaire has a poor beggar-girl fishing through the garbage outside the Véfour.

The Véfour remains a highspot of Parisian haute cuisine. But even by the close of the nineteenth century it was a deliberately old-style version of it, looking out as it does over a semi-deserted Palais-Royal and decorated with the beautiful painted walls and ceilings which self-consciously recall the Ancien Régime (even though they were largely 'refreshed' in the Second Empire). By the end of the 1800s the restaurant as an institution had diversified enormously. Working-class restaurants – among which the Bouillons Chartier stood (and indeed stand) out – showed the triumph of the institution across the social board. 'Rustic' restaurants were also appearing which served regional food to curious Parisians and nostalgic provincials. The bistrot now offered a more informal version of bourgeois dining too. In addition the loss of Alsace and Lorraine to Germany in 1870 brought to Paris a refugee population of eastern French businessmen, who established the brasserie style of restaurant (Bofinger, Lipp, Brasserie Flo, etc.) which is often taken to typify the genre.

Changes in dining styles in the late twentieth century have certainly left their mark on the Parisian restaurant sector. Renovated with new styles and fads – *nouvelle cuisine, cuisine minceur*, fusion foods – it still holds on to its international reputation for fine dining, not least because of the excellent supply system for fresh raw materials. Perhaps the most truly adventurous dining to be had in early twenty-first century Paris is in the restaurants associated with Paris's immigrant populations – North African just about everywhere, the Indo-Chinese in the XIIIe. arrondissement's China Town, West Indian, Indian and African out in Belleville and the XXe. Like the Alsatian brasserie, they too may well influence what diners come to expect of a Parisian restaurant.

The economic centralization of the Terror gave Paris an advantage over its provincial rivals, many of which were suffering from the collapse of the colonial trades. The emergence of a huge standing army – over a million strong in 1793–4 – also stimulated war industries (armaments, uniforms, boots). Many of these were located in Paris, partly, it must be said, to placate the sans-culottes. Areas of manufacturing hit by the loss of the luxury trades were now enlisted into military production: 'let locksmiths cease to make locks,' the Committee of Public Safety had declared. 'The locks of liberty are bayonets and muskets.'[14] As it now renounced as unworthy the 'ridiculous fashions, numerous baubles, brilliant rags and nice furniture' for which the city had been famous, Paris could become 'the arsenal of France'.[15] In Year II there were some 7,000 workers in armament production; under the Ancien Régime there had been none.

The deregulation of the economy after the Terror produced a great deal of hardship, which was worsened by appalling winters in 1794 and 1795. It made the winter of 'nonante cinq' one of the coldest, hungriest and most lethal in the eighteenth century. Yet the shift away from state control over production also helped boost the consumer industries (porcelain, glass, jewellery, watch-making, etc.) which by the late 1790s and early 1800s were staging a strong comeback. A new cotton industry was breaking all records for growth. The continued presence of a skilled workforce, the availability of capital, the readiness of factory-style buildings (in the form of disused ecclesiastic constructions) played into the hands of canny manufacturers. In 1798 Minister of the Interior François de Neufchâteau organized an industrial exposition on the Champ de Mars to try to show the rest of Europe that Paris was back in business. There were over a hundred exhibits, including Gobelins tapestries, fashionable clothes and wallpapers among the consumer goods, plus a steam engine, examples of industrial metalwork and chemical techniques to signal Paris's inventive and productive side.

By the late 1790s and early 1800s the Paris property market was also picking up. The building boom of the 1770s and 1780s had fizzled out shortly after 1789. The political emigration of a numerically small group of wealthy nobles – maybe a couple of hundred families in total – removed from the city one of the most lucrative sources of building and decoration. Construction almost dried up in the mid-1790s. Yet the potential for recovery was still there, in that property had become an excellent hedge against the inflation and monetary depreciations which plagued the 1790s and ruined numerous ancient families who had invested in government bonds and annuities. Moreover, the state's decision to sell off much of the nationalized property of the church (and, latterly, the expropriated property of *émigrés* too) revitalized the Parisian property market. One thousand edifices changed hands as a result. In northern Paris around a quarter of all property had the status of *bien national* and passed onto the market over the course of the 1790s. Though the post-Terror deregulation of the economy brought hardship to poorer Parisians, the business climate of those years was favourable to the amassing of huge fortunes by property speculators, army suppliers and financiers. According to Charles de Constant, a visitor to the city at the turn of the century, while the east of the city looked terribly impoverished and run down, and while emigration had turned the formerly aristocratic Faubourg Saint-Germain into a ghost town, in the western and north-western parts of the city it was quite a different story. Along the Rue du Faubourg Saint-Honoré, in the Roule district and around the Chaussée d'Antin (Ie., IIe., IXe.), lovely new private residences were to be found, invariably tastefully fronted by Greek columns, and not infrequently decorated with statuary which had once adorned now disused churches. Their owners were 'all those whom the Revolution has made prominent, made stand out and made rich: army suppliers, generals who have made war in Italy, artists and actors'.[16]

The property boom in the western neighbourhoods highlighted the process of re-establishment of the Parisian elite along lines of wealth rather than birth. The Society of Orders had seemed anachronistic in Paris at least by 1789; by 1799 it was totally defunct. The emigration of many high nobles and the ruination of others, notably in the legal elite, by the abolition of venal office and the collapse of the state paper currency, left room for newcomers. Property was a privileged marker of status in the new class-oriented elite. Many *arrivistes* into the Parisian elite signalled their position by the purchase of a second home in the Paris environs, where there were plenty of bargains to be snapped up. Around a third of *biens nationaux* sold in the area around Versailles until 1795 went to Parisians; the latter represented one buyer in six on the market around Chartres.

The recovery of the private property market in the late 1790s, linked to the growing prestige of western neighbourhoods and the consolidation of an urban elite based on levels of wealth, was to continue along the same lines once Napoleon was in power. The consequences of the church losing control of its extensive range of edifices and properties were also still being worked through. Demolition was not uncommon: the keep of the Temple (IIIe.), in which Louis XVI had been imprisoned, was destroyed in 1808 (Napoleon worried about it becoming a place of royalist pilgrimage), the abbeys of Saint-Victor (Ve.) and the Carmes (VIe.) in 1811 and 1813. Yet purchase had often not been followed up with development in the early and mid-1790s because of shortages of money and poor business conditions. More propitious conditions from the late 1790s saw some substantial projects under way. This was particularly evident on the Left Bank. The nationalization of the massive estates of the abbey of Saint-Germain-des-Prés (VIe.) provided a developer's bonanza, with important new streets being opened up: from 1800 the Rue de l'Abbaye to the north of the abbey cut across the heart of the estate, while on a north–south axis the Rue Bonaparte opened up the neighbourhood towards the Seine. A number of old buildings were lost in the process, but some became the core of construction projects: the abbey stable block, for example, was converted into the hauntingly beautiful Place Furstemberg. The Rue d'Assas (VIe.), constructed between 1798 and 1806, was another good example of this phenomenon. Leading from the Rue de Vaugirard up to the Observatory, it crossed property formerly owned by a number of monastic houses. In the same neighbourhood the demolition of the seminary of Saint-Sulpice allowed the Place Saint-Sulpice to be opened up in front of the church. Similarly the Rue d'Ulm (Ve.), due south of the Panthéon, was created after 1807 over the former lands of the Visitandines, the Ursulines and the Feuillantines.

The recovery of the private property market in the late 1790s and early 1800s contrasted with the sluggish state of public building. For most of the 1790s the national and local authorities were more preoccupied by politics than construction. In 1794 the Convention established an advisory group to advise it on potential urban development. The Commission des Artistes had eleven members, seven of whom were architects while the others had served in the city's highway department (*voirie*), and they produced a number of projects for urban 'embellishment' (as they still called it, following the inspiration of Enlightenment urbanism). Later claims that the work of the Commission was a precursor to Haussmann are wide of the mark: although they did urge the creation of several streets and boulevards which cut into existing urban tissue, there was no overall sense of a unified urban plan. Besides, though a few of the Commission's plans were followed up – the demolition of the Grand Châtelet prison after 1802, for example – this was more accidental than by design. There was simply not enough money to implement anything much in the 1790s, and even the limited projects of the Commission largely fell on stony ground.

New theatres were the most notable additions to the pool of public buildings. Other Revolutionary monuments of note often tended to take the form of changes of use: thus Soufflot's church of Sainte-Geneviève became the Panthéon for Great Men, the Louvre's use as a museum was amplified, and the Val-de-Grâce monastery became a military hospital. There were statues too: the Place de la Révolution, for example, contained one representing the Republic and the Place des Victoires an obelisk to fallen warriors. A column imitating Trajan's column in Rome and decorated with military scenes from Napoleon's career was erected in the Place Vendôme from 1806 to 1810. Temporary structures for Revolutionary festivals were numerous, like the public amphitheatre built on the Champ de Mars for the Fête de la Fédération in 1790. Overall the 1790s witnessed more monumental destruction (the Bastille, sundry disused churches, royal statues, etc.) than construction.

One of Napoleon's big ideas for Paris was to revitalize its monumental record. 'Paris is short of monuments,' he noted. His conclusion: 'It must be given them.'[17] The wish to reshape Paris through an ambitious public building programme sprang from a desire to make Paris into an apposite venue for his acts of political ceremony and imperial theatre. 'Men are only great through the monuments they leave behind them,' he stated – and he was clearly thinking of himself. Yet there was also a more pragmatic edge to his ideas. He once observed that he 'would rather face 20,000 soldiers on the field of battle than 2,000 workers on the streets of Lyon' (he could as well have said Paris).

The economic system which he established throughout his European conquests was designed to cushion potential sans-culottes from radical action by filling their stomachs and providing them with employment. *Bellum napoleonicum* would thus have the same effect of shielding Parisians from the harsh facts of warfare as the *pax borbonica* of the eighteenth century. The provision of public works was one recommended way of keeping Parisians happy – and loyal to a regime to which they had not naturally warmed. Monuments could play their part in fixing popular memory in ways helpful to the regime: 'my aim,' Napoleon noted in 1805, 'is to push the arts towards subjects which will perpetuate the memory of what has happened these last fifteen years.'[18]

Napoleon believed that 'the four most important things for the city of Paris are: water from the river Ourcq, new markets in the Halles, abattoirs and wine warehouses.'[19] This is a curious list of superlatives for someone as obsessed as Napoleon with imperial grandeur. His plans to extend the city towards the west – out to Saint-Cloud, he stated grandiloquently on one occasion – necessitated a more sizeable economic infrastructure. In addition his concern that Paris should be adequately provided with clean water and basic foodstuffs was grounded in his desire to ensure that the people be given no excuse to be mutinous. Though he did not include it in his list, the key in this respect was the cheap and proficient supply of grain to his capital: after all, as he well knew, the provision of bread (and circuses) had an impeccable Roman-imperial pedigree. The price of bread had acted as a barometer of popular discontent throughout the eighteenth century, and he sought to stabilize it. He revolutionized grain storage in the city, modernizing and reroofing the Halle aux Blés which had burnt in a fire in 1802, and supplementing it with an ensemble of reserve stores in the east of the city. 'I want the Halles,' he stated, 'to be the people's Louvre.'[20] In the same area, he constructed wine-warehouses in the shape of the Halle aux Vins, built out on the Quai Saint-Bernard (IVe.). Distribution and retailing of bread, wine and other prime necessities was ensured by the construction of a good number of covered markets dotted around the city, most of them located in former religious buildings (and some of them only completed after 1815). On the Left Bank, for example, the Marché Saint-Germain

(VIe.: the only one of Napoleon's markets still standing) was built over the premises of the dilapidated site of the old Foire. Near by, the Marché des Carmes was erected over the old Carmes monastery, site of some of the most horrible of the September Massacres. Market-building was sometimes accompanied by improvement in approach roads or the construction of new streets: the Marché Saint-Martin built in the grounds of the ancient abbey of Saint-Martin (IIIe.: now the site of the Museum of Arts and Métiers) entailed the construction of the Rues Vaucanson, Montgolfier, Borda, Conté and others.

While food was brought closer to Parisians, food preparation was put at a distance: new abattoir regulations introduced in 1810 stipulated that five new abattoirs be placed on the outer margins of the city. Hygienic considerations were uppermost too in the continuation of moves to locate places of interment away from sites of human inhabitation, a process started by the decision to close the Cemetery of the Innocents in the 1780s. By the time Napoleon came to power, only a few locations within Paris permitted burials. Frochot, the first Prefect of the Seine, continued the relocation of burial remains out towards Tombe d'Issoire (XIVe.). He was also responsible for making these ossuaries into catacombs on the Roman model. Soon tourists were lining up for a view of the 'tastefully' arranged remains. Frochot also created three major municipal cemeteries in places at that time well outside the city. The most celebrated of these was the Père-Lachaise cemetery (XXe.), out beyond the Faubourg Saint-Antoine, which was opened in 1804.

7.3: The Catacombs

Paris's catacombs were created in the late eighteenth and early nineteenth centuries out of bones and other remains moved from the Cemetery of the Innocents in central Paris out to the Tombe d'Issoire neighbourhood in the XIVe. arrondissement. Although the catacombs are only one 800th of the total area of underground passages which lie beneath the twenty arrondissements of modern Paris, they cover an area more than extensive and impressive enough for the chilly visitor.

The catacombs were given their present form – corridors of neatly arranged skulls and tibias – in 1809 when Napoleon's Prefect of the Seine Frochot and the Inspector-General of Quarries Hériart de Thury undertook to arrange the huge volume of remains in a pattern designed to impress visitors. Rome had its catacombs, so the idea was that the now-imperial city of Paris should have them too – and that preferably they should be better. The remains of some two million Parisians are estimated to have been located in the Cemetery of the Innocents over nearly a millennium of Paris's past, but this number was consistently replenished until well into the nineteenth century by the continuing relocation to that site of the contents of the city's churches and charnel-houses.

The catacombs are perhaps less impressive when viewed in the perspective of imperial construction and display than as part of a massive change in the cultural meanings of death within the city, which took place over the late eighteenth and early nineteenth centuries. The Romans had placed their burial grounds on the margins of Lutetia, so that one could not enter the city without passing funeral monuments. Subsequently death had installed itself at the heart of Paris, in the cemeteries of the city's churches, and often within those churches. When in the twelfth century the city expanded to the north-west so as to open a major urban marketplace – the Halles – a cemetery (the Innocents) was placed next to it.

The juxtaposition of the dead and the living at the heart of the city seemed to pose few problems to late medieval and Renaissance Parisians – indeed, it activated numerous forms of piety and devotion. It was only in the more secularizing eighteenth century that public hygiene was raised as a reason to remove the remains of the dead from the heart of human habitation. A marker in this respect was the testamentary request of Lieutenant-Général de Police La Reynie in 1709 not to be buried in his parish church of Saint-Eustache (adjacent to the Innocents) so as not to contribute to the infection of the air in the neighbourhood. Late in the century a medical lobby picked up the relocation of cemeteries as an important plank in its policies of sanitary improvement. When their arguments were adopted by the Parlement of Paris, the time was ripe for change.

The placing of death at a distance was accompanied by a parallel decision to establish new cemeteries outside the perimeter of the city – a policy that was applied to every commune in France in 1803. From this ensued the creation of the Montparnasse, Montmartre and, especially, the Père-Lachaise cemeteries. Revamped under Haussmann, the latter became a sign of the urban modernity which Paris represented more generally: the Emperor of Brazil, the city fathers of San Francisco and Glasgow municipal council were among those who wanted to build a Père-Lachaise in their own back gardens.

Death might have been more out of sight for nineteenth-century Parisians than it had for any of their ancestors. Yet it was not out of mind. Indeed, the turn of the nineteenth century saw the emergence of a veritable cult of death and remembrance. The visit to the cemetery on All Souls' Day, the creation of family tombs, the landscape gardening of cemeteries to make a more 'natural' site – plus of course the opening of the catacombs to public viewing – were accompanied by an array of more personalized devotions. The cemetery had gone from the heart of the city, but its literary and visual representation had not. The hill on which Père-Lachaise was set, for example, became a well-known spot for viewing the city. It is here that Balzac's hero Rastignac stands, to contemplate his future career, defiantly determining to conquer rather than submit meekly to the city which has brought him so much pain.

The modern medium of photography was another means which was used to maintain the cult of the dead in the city in the absence of the dead themselves – and not only with portraits of the defunct. The early Parisian photographer Nadar, for example, was famous not only for his aerial panoramas of the city, but also as being the first person to photograph Paris's underground world. In his 1867 essay 'Le Dessus et le dessous de Paris' ('The Above and Below of Paris') he highlighted the 'confused equality of death' to be found in the catacombs, 'where all comes to vanish, even the memory of the father in the son', and where the remains of the marquise (Pompadour, for example) lay alongside those of the milkmaid, and those 'who had loved, had been loved' jostled alongside individuals 'without name, forgotten, lost'. Nadar's efforts to conjure up this spectre involved some conjury on his own part. Because he had to use long exposure times to capture an image, he decided that the human figure he needed to give a sense of scale to his photograph would be replaced by a tailor's dummy, clad in workman's clothes. The representational familiarity of death under (rather than within) the city was thus based on a convenient illusion.

The regulation of the food trades sprang from hygienic considerations as well as from anxieties about social disorder. Health issues were all the more important in regard to water supply. It was not that the population was growing so fast as to necessitate new supplies – in fact population was relatively stable, not surpassing 1789 levels until around 1815. It was rather that, as we have seen from his list of priorities for Paris, Napoleon regarded plentiful water as a key component of public health. He insisted that the city's fifty-six public water fountains should run day and night, and ordered the construction of an additional fifteen. An Egyptian-style fountain was placed on the site of the horrible old Châtelet prison (IIIe.). To ensure that the city had sufficient water for such purposes, he supervised the building of the Canal de l'Ourcq from 1802 onwards. This involved canalizing the river Ourcq for eleven kilometres, then constructing nearly one hundred additional kilometres of canal to bring the waters to the La Villette basin to the north-east of the city (XIXe.). The basin, opened in 1808, also connected up with the Canal Saint-Denis, which joined the Seine close to Saint-Denis to the north, and the Canal Saint-Martin, which ran down to the Seine south of the Place de la Bastille (IVe.).

This remarkable engineering feat was a triumph for communications, making Paris a location which technically at least was extremely easy to provision. A concern for better communications

The catacombs photographed by Nadar, *c.* 1890

was demonstrated within the city too. When Napoleon came to power, Paris had twelve bridges; when he was overthrown it had fifteen. None had houses on them – this ruling of Louis XVI had now become standard. The iron-frame Pont des Arts footbridge linking the Louvre to the Institut was a heavy symbolic statement: knowledge conjoined to power. There was a symbolic element too to the building of the Pont d'Iéna, which linked the end of the Champ de Mars to Chaillot, where Napoleon was planning to build an imperial palace for his son. More utilitarian in intention was the Pont d'Austerlitz joining the Jardin des Plantes area to the Faubourg Saint-Antoine.

Communication was also at the heart of Napoleon's most impressive achievement in urban building: the cruciform development around the Place de la Concorde and the Pont de la Concorde (the latter of which had been completed, using stone from the Bastille prison, in the early 1790s). The area remains the part of Paris most marked by the Napoleonic imprint. This development was the outcome of Napoleon's perception that, to grow and prosper, Paris needed to develop towards the west, building out from the prosperous Saint-Honoré area and the Faubourg Saint-Germain. On the north–south axis the Madeleine church (VIIIe.) to the north of the Place had been started in 1764 under Louis XV, though work on it had ceased under the Revolution. Work resumed in 1806, when Napoleon dedicated it as a temple of glory to his armies. A similar Greek temple façade was now placed over the river frontage of the old Palais-Bourbon facing it across the river (VIIe.). The neo-classical idiom was also employed on other Right Bank buildings to the east of the Madeleine: the temple-like stock exchange (*Bourse*), on the site of a disaffected convent(1807–13), and the Trajan Column placed in the Place Vendôme.

The neo-classical style was even more apparent on the east–west axis through the Place de la Concorde. Napoleon's development here built on, extended and ornamented what was already a well-established symbolic axis of power. Work to level off the fairly steep hill to the west of the Place had begun under Louis XV, and Napoleon's idea was to extend beyond the present-day Rond-Point des Champs-Élysées out to the site of the Place Charles-de-Gaulle (VIIIe.). To

crown the vista effectively, a massive monumental structure was necessary, and from 1806 work began on the first *arc de triomphe* to be
built in Paris since the 1670s, and what proved to be the largest such
structure ever built. The Arc de Triomphe de l'Étoile would only be
completed under the July Monarchy. Its situation at the centre of a
star ('*étoile*') of streets also facilitated the subsequent development of
the area. It was matched with the much smaller Arc de Triomphe du
Carrousel, placed along the Louvre–Étoile axis outside the Tuileries
on the present-day Place du Carrousel (Ie.).

Colbert and the 1794 Commission des Artistes were among the
many who had urged the extension of the line of the Champs-Élysées
eastwards towards the site of the Bastille. The increased volume of
traffic along the prosperous Rue Saint-Honoré had necessitated some
attempts at urban reform, and the nationalization of a number of
religious buildings along a line extending eastwards from the Rue
Saint-Honoré made possible the creation of a new, twenty-metre-wide
highway, the Rue de Rivoli. Only the riding school of the Tuileries
palace – the Salle du Manège which had housed the National Assembly
from 1789 to 1793 – required demolition. The section of the street
from Concorde down to the level of the Louvre was opened in 1802.
A set of side-streets were also constructed, notably the Rue Castiglione
which linked up to the Place Vendôme, and which was extended to
the north by the Rue de la Paix (Ie.). Lots for shops and businesses as
well as residential developments were created, though the rather
meagre returns from speculative building meant that the area was not
really complete until the 1830s.

The slow progress of commercial development on the Rue de Rivoli
highlighted Napoleon's failure to coordinate his monumentalism with
the needs of business and the exigencies of the private property market.
Yet if the emperor failed to shape his city in the grandiose way he had
hoped, this derived mainly from a shortage of both time and money.
He would be overthrown in 1814, and his brief return in 1815 was
marked only by a desperate concern for survival. The heavy costs of
war meant that he failed to supply the resources required for a
thorough reshaping of the city. Neither was there sufficient time,
money and imagination on hand to develop a distinctive imperial

style: his buildings drew their inspiration from the neo-classical idiom established before the Revolution. Building heights were maintained within the regulatory limits fixed in 1783–4. Fittingly for a statesman longer on talk than performance, the street-names with which he supplied the city – usually commemorating his military victories (Castiglione, Pyramides, Rivoli, Ulm, Iéna, Austerlitz, Montebello and so on) – are one of his most enduring legacies. Many of his projects were not even completed in his reign – this was true of the grandest (the Bourse, 1827; the Arc de Triomphe, 1836; the Madeleine, 1845) and the most mundane (Rue de Rivoli, sundry markets, etc.). All bear the marks of successor regimes. He wanted to place a 180-foot-high obelisk on the site of the *cheval de bronze* at the tip of the Île de la Cité, but had to content himself with the paste-board model which stood here in 1810–11. He constructed the Arc de Triomphe de l'Étoile out of wooden scaffolding and canvas so that it could impress Parisians out to welcome his new empress, Marie-Louise of Austria, into the city in 1810. Despite the grandeur of his ambitions, Napoleon's efforts were redolent of the stage-set. Some of that ersatz grandeur was, moreover, the product of plunder rather than construction, such as the war trophies which he paraded around Paris in 1798 after his Italian campaigns before placing them in the Louvre. Some of the most striking of these – the horses from St Mark's cathedral in Venice, for example – were restored to their owner states in 1815.

The areas of construction in which his impact was genuinely useful and long-lived – the Canal de l'Ourcq, markets, granaries, fountains, abattoirs and so on – related to the provisioning of the city in order to keep its citizens contented with his regime. It was ironic, there-fore, that by 1810–12 his unpopularity was growing, as he failed to prevent Paris from feeling the brunt of an economic crisis caused partly by poor harvests but partly by his economic grand strategy. The elaborate machinery established to supply cheap bread did not work: the subsistence crisis of 1810–12 replicated that of 1787–9 in all essentials. The Continental System by which he sought to break British economic power by prohibiting its exports to enter Europe rebounded against him; even his client states mutinied against the policy, while British imports caused widespread unemployment in Paris as well as across the Empire. The old Farmers-General Wall, which he had converted back into a tax barrier for the collection of municipal tolls (the *octroi*) intended to sustain city finances, was now held against him.

Parisians also found it difficult to forgive Napoleon for exposing them to foreign occupation. Vauban's *ceinture de fer* had kept foreign armies out of France with some success since the seventeenth century, but Napoleon's growing military weakness meant that Parisians in 1814 had to face up to the prospect of defending themselves without even a fortified city wall to hide behind. With Napoleon's armies powerless to prevent them, the allied armies began a siege of the city on 30 March 1814. After one not unheroic bout of fighting, the Parisians surrendered. 'Louis XVIII' – Louis XVI's brother, the ex-comte de Provence – entered the city on 3 May, ready to restore the Bourbon monarchy.

There would be more tears before bedtime for Napoleon. He was packed off to the tiny Mediterranean island of Elba, but his dramatic return to France in 1815 had the Bourbons fleeing with great alacrity. Napoleon found it easy to re-establish himself in the Tuileries – but this owed less to his popularity in the city than to the unpopularity of the Bourbons, who had failed to protect Paris from a severe economic crisis caused by the occupation of the city, and whose excessive piety seemed out of kilter with Parisian opinion. Had he played his cards differently, Napoleon might have elicited a stronger response from the city. But like his Prefect in 1814, he steadfastly refused the idea of giving rifles to the workers of the Faubourg Saint-Antoine. To the end, the spectre of armed and dangerous sans-culottes dominated his vision of Paris. Parisians heard the news of the battle of Waterloo and Napoleon's exile to Saint Helena with a great deal of indifference.

When the allied troops had entered Paris for the first time in 1814, many of them wore a white cockade to signify their peaceful intentions towards Parisians. Thinking that they would show the invaders their appreciation for this gesture, many Parisians wore the white cockade in return. However, Bourbon sympathizers among the troops imagined that by wearing these cockades, the Parisians were showing their undying support for the Bourbon cause (white being the monarchy's ceremonial colour). This misunderstanding led the allies to imagine that Paris was massively pro-Bourbon and pro-Restoration. The years

Russian soldiers in the Champs-Élysées, 1814

after 1815 would show how wrong this was. Indeed the regimes which followed Napoleon produced a nostalgia for his rule which his rule had done relatively little to justify.

8

Between Napoleons
1815–51

With hindsight the period between 1815 and 1851 takes on the character of a Napoleonic interregnum. The three regimes which followed the overthrow of the First Empire – the Restoration monarchy (1814–30), the July Monarchy (1830–48) and the Second Republic (1848–52) – all started with a good deal of optimism about their durability. Nor was there anything inevitable about the re-emergence of Bonapartism. Napoleon died in exile at Saint Helena in 1821 to much Parisian indifference, and although the Napoleonic legend developed thereafter, not many hopes were pinned on the Bonapartist pretender, Napoleon's nephew, prince Louis-Napoleon Bonaparte. The latter's unprepossessing personal appearance and his advanced (some said crackpot) ideas made him widely discounted as a serious politician. The pathetic fiasco which ensued from his two efforts, in 1836 and 1840, to lead a Bonapartist rising in France also harmed his reputation. In the event the prince, who in 1848, to Parisian astonishment, was elected President of the Second Republic, in 1851 organized a *coup d'état* to strengthen his powers, and in 1852 imposed his appointment as emperor.

As we shall see,[1] the Second Empire of Napoleon III (1852–70) would return to the inspiration of Napoleon I, seeking to make Paris an emblem of the dynasty's power. The regimes which held power between the two Napoleons, in contrast, maintained altogether less grandiose and more nuanced policies towards their capital city. The Bourbon dynasty re-established after Napoleon's 'Hundred Days' had seen out the allied occupation with some staunchness. The English novelist Sir Walter Scott recorded Parisians in 1815 mocking the restored Louis XVIII (r. 1814–24) as 'the English Prefect' and 'Louis

the Inevitable'.[2] Yet despite a poor start the king won a fair degree of popularity, ruling within a moderately liberal Constitutional Charter and presiding over the social and economic recovery of the city.

The international settlement of 1815 forced France back to its 1792 frontiers. The king also had to allow many of the plundered artworks with which Napoleon I had bedecked Paris – such as the bronze horses from San Marco in Venice – to return to their homes. Paris was no longer the imperial capital which Napoleon had sought to make it. The question facing Louis XVIII was: how could it be made into a royal one again? His decision to reject returning the court to Versailles, centre of Bourbon power, was a brave conciliatory gesture. He established a court life in the Tuileries (where he slept in Napoleon's bed). Although his zealous enthusiasm for matters of protocol and etiquette made it rather stiff and dull, the court did begin to break down the barriers which had separated the elites of Paris from the world of courtiers under the Ancien Régime. The phrase le Tout-Paris began to be used from the 1820s to denote the mixed social, political and cultural elites of the city.

Louis also followed a moderate policy in regard to making Paris pay for its Revolutionary sins, not least towards his own elder brother and sister-in-law. One of the first things he did on returning to Paris was to seek out the bones of Louis XVI and Marie-Antoinette where they lay in a common cemetery-pit on the Rue d'Anjou (VIIIe.). The writer and statesman Chateaubriand had been smiled at by the queen when he had visited Versailles on the eve of the 1789 Revolution. Chillingly his memoirs would recount how the memory of that smile, framed by the famous Habsburg jaw, would allow him to recognize the queen's skull in this lugubrious identification exercise.[3] The remains of Louis XVI and his queen were removed to Saint-Denis, where efforts were being made to reconstitute the ancient royal necropolis. Although royal bones had been thrown out of the abbey into a common pit, the antiquarian Alexandre Lenoir managed to retain many of the Saint-Denis funerary monuments and display them in a museum in the old Petits-Augustins monastery on the Rue Bonaparte in Paris (VIe.) These were now returned to Saint-Denis too.

Louis XVIII ordered the building of an 'expiatory chapel' (chapelle expiatoire) on the site of the former royal resting-place. It came to

house the remains of victims of the Revolutionary Tribunal. Commemorative monuments were also established at the Conciergerie prison
on the Île de la Cité, where the queen had spent her last hours in 1793,
and in the Jardin de Picpus, for other victims of the Terror.[4] In addition
the king ordered that the Panthéon should become a church again
rather than a secular monument to great men. The royal equestrian
statues, which had been melted down for cannon in the 1790s, were
also restored. Henry IV and the famed *cheval de bronze* reappeared
on the Pont Neuf in 1818, and Louis XIV on the Place des Victoires
in 1822. It took till 1829 to replace Louis XIII in the Place des Vosges
– or rather Place Royale, as it had become again.

Renaming, alongside the diffusion of the heraldic white flag and the
royal coat of arms, was another means by which the restored Bourbons
sought to 'royalize' their capital city. Many of the more outlandish
Revolutionary names had in fact already been changed by Napoleon.
The Place de la Concorde now reverted to the name of Place Louis XV.
The nearby Rue Royale (formerly Rue de la Concorde), Rue Dauphine
(Rue de Thionville from 1792 to 1814), the Quai Conti (ex-Quai de
la Monnaie) also underwent rebaptism. (There would of course be a
reversion to pre-Restoration titles after 1830.)

Louis XVIII did not extend this process of symbolic reoccupation
of Paris as far as some of the Ultra-Royalists wanted. He felt that to
over-emphasize demands for the city's expiation would be unpopular
with most citizens and rebound against the dynasty. However, he
placed a good deal of emphasis on the restored Catholic religion as a
guarantor of the city's good behaviour in the future. Religious rituals
and street ceremonials of public worship in fact helped spark something of a spiritual revival in the city. A number of new churches were
begun, especially on the smarter side of town – Notre-Dame-de-Bonne-
Nouvelle (IIe.) in 1822, for example, Notre-Dame-de-Lorette (IXe.)
the following year and Saint-Denys-du-Saint-Sacrement (IIIe.) in
1826.[5] In 1830 a Daughter of Charity called Catherine Labouré
claimed to have been visited by the Virgin Mary in the chapel of her
mother-house on the Rue du Bac (VIIe.) – and soon scores of miracles
were being claimed throughout the city and further afield.

The religious revival intensely irritated the large sector of the
Parisian population indifferent to Christianity or suspicious of the

DESC

Du Char funèbre qui transportera les cendres des Héros de la gr[...]
sa largeur, sa longueur et sa hauteur prodigieuse.—Détails des [...]
rois, en l'honneur des Victimes, et pendant la descente de leur[...]
de la Bastille, son intérieur et son extérieur;—Liste des noms des

Le char qui transportera les cendres des héros de juillet aux caveaux de la Colonne de la place de la Bastille est d'un aspect imposant; jamais la capitale n'aura vu pareil corbillard, tant par ses riches draperies et décorations que par sa forme gigantesque. Son élévation égale au moins la hauteur d'un deuxième étage d'une grande maison. Du reste, les chiffres suivans donnent une juste appréciation de ses formes et dimensions:

supporte une statue exécutée par M. Dumont. C'est le Génie de la Liberté tenant un flambeau d'une main, des fers brisés dans l'autre, et déployant ses ailes. Où s'arrêtera son vol?

Les fondemens sur lesquels repose la colonne de Juillet présentent l'aspect le plus extraordinaire et le plus monumental; ils sont placés à cheval sur le canal St-Martin qui passe sous la place de la Bastille. Une ogive

sonne peuvent aisé[...]
me tems; l'escalie[...]
attache aux nerv[...]
éclair par le haut[...]
teau; c'est tout en b[...]
la plate forme ento[...]
pés, également en [...]
laissés au centre pa[...]

ON

ine aux caveaux de la place de la Bastille;—Son poids énorme,
es religieuses qui auront lieu à l'église Saint-Germain l'Auxer-
s leur nouvelle sépulture.—Description de la Colonne de la place
es inscrits sur la colonne de Juillet, qui sont morts pour la liberté.

dre en mê-
la Colonne
nontans et
du chapi-
vendoit sur
s d'espace

prend aux nations que la France ne dégénère jamais ;
que nous sommes d'âge en âge les héritiers du patrio-
tisme de nos pères.

Depuis long-temps nous demandions à grands cris
cette Colonne, qui désormais nous si fiers. La patrie a
enfin compris et comblé le vœu de ses enfans : ce monument impérissable s'élève aujourd'hui pour charmer
leurs regards avides, et chacun d'eux

sieux. J. Chéviron. L. Clément. P. Cléry. P. M. Corbel. P. A. Gor-
duapt. A. Cormier. P. Cortilleux. J. Cottin. J. L. Coudère. R. Cou-
dray. L. Cousin. J. F. Couve. L. Crabay. J. L. Crampon. B. J.
Crespelt. J. G. Crouillié. J. Crespel. A. Curier. A. Curier.

T. Dablies. A. Daissy. A. Dalifer. L. G. Damas. L. E. Damal.
M. Danse. F. Darbour. J. J. Dariois. N. F. Daubert. A. Dauphin. P.
Dauteuil. L. M. David. H. David. H. Deblond. L. G. Debovet. J.
Décourty. J. Dodieu. M. Deguette. N. Deheurles. L. J. Debon. J. C.
Delacourt. P. F. Delamotte. L. C. Delattre. A. Delmas. C. Denance.

1840 commemoration of the 1830 Revolution

regime's enthusiasm for the union of 'Throne and Altar'. Political divisions within the capital were accentuated, moreover, when the monarchy moved away from its initial mood of conciliation. The assassination in 1820 of Louis XVIII's nephew the duc de Berry, son of Louis's brother the comte d'Artois, pushed the king towards more Ultra policies. Pro-émigré and pro-clerical positions were even more to the fore under childless Louis's successor Artois, who reigned as Charles X (r. 1824–30) and was the last ruler of France to touch for the 'King's Evil'. A move by the king against press freedom and constitutional legality triggered three days (*journées*) of riots in Paris in 1830 – the so-called *Trois Glorieuses* of 27–29 July – which the regime proved unable to master. Significantly, rioters targeted the symbols of Bourbon rule diffused across the city with which the Bourbons had sought to 'royalize' the capital of Revolution. Thus royal troops were attacked and barricades built to prevent them asserting control over the streets; the Louvre and Tuileries palaces were pillaged; the white flag of the Bourbons was everywhere unceremoniously replaced with the tricolore; and royal coats of arms which businesses supplying the royal family had placed on their shop-fronts were torn down. Aristocratic hôtels were also attacked and crosses removed from the roofs of city churches.

Although rioters seemed intent on expunging royal symbols in the city, the *Trois Glorieuses* produced neither a republic (the thought of which frightened the middle classes) nor a Bonapartist restoration. Political manoeuvring centred on the Hôtel de Ville, where Lafayette, in a deliberate replay of 1789, was appointed commander of a reconstituted National Guard (it had been disbanded for political indocility in 1827). The upshot was the continuation of monarchy, albeit with a new king. The throne of the so-called July Monarchy was offered to, and accepted by, the duc d'Orléans. The Orléans house had cultivated support in Paris since the time of Louis XIV. The new ruler, Louis-Philippe the First (and last), was eldest son of Philippe-Égalité, the Revolutionary duke who had turned his residence the Palais-Royal into a hotbed of radicalism, and voted for the death of Louis XVI. Louis-Philippe himself had served with some distinction in the republican army before fleeing the Terror in 1793, and since 1815 had been reinstalled in the Palais-Royal. The new king now abandoned his ancestral Palais-Royal to establish himself in the Tuileries (which still lacked, it must be said, some elementary comforts – there was no running water until 1848).

In the *Trois Glorieuses* Paris had changed the government of France – and done so with little damage to itself: only 600 rioters and 150 soldiers died in the disturbances. The city which had served Louis-Philippe his crown on a platter received warm royal endorsement. The new king declared Paris to be 'his native city', named his first grandson the comte de Paris, confirmed the continuance of the National Guard, resided in the Tuileries and walked the city streets with an umbrella on his arm. 'What the people need now,' Lafayette had told him during power negotiations in 1830, 'is a popular king, surrounded by republican institutions.'[6] Louis-Philippe consequently introduced a more liberal constitution, and nurtured a popular personal image. He distanced himself from the aura of the Restoration by rejecting anything which smacked of the old union of 'Throne and Altar'. The Rue Charles-X was thus renamed the Rue Lafayette; the old Royal Household was disbanded; the king ostentatiously refused to attend mass in public each Sunday; and public religious processions in Paris were banned. Royal ceremonies became secular, populist occasions. In a commemoration of the *Trois Glorieuses* in 1840, for example, the king inaugurated a column honouring the July combatants in the Place de la Bastille, where it still stands.

Modest in its political claims, the new regime was modest in its attitudes towards public monuments within the capital. The July Monarchy was more of a finisher than an initiator in matters monumental. Most of its major achievements were inherited projects, many of which had ground to a halt at some stage since 1789. All were in the western half of the city. The Madeleine church (1842: VIIIe.), for example, had been begun under Louis XV. A neo-Greek, temple-style building, it incongruously resembled the Bourse (1827). Further completion and embellishment included the Arc de Triomphe de l'Étoile, and a remodelled Place de la Concorde (both 1836). A well-attended spectacle saw the planting that year, on the site of Louis XV's old equestrian statue, of the Luxor column, dating from the thirteenth century BC – making it the oldest object in Paris by more than a millennium. This too was a bequest from the former regime: the obelisk had been promised to Charles X by the Egyptian ruler Mohammad Ali in 1829 as a gauge of diplomatic friendship. There was updating and reorganization too of the Palais-Bourbon (VIIe.), which housed the Chamber of Deputies; the Luxembourg palace (Ve.), home of the Senate; the municipality's Hôtel de Ville (IVe.), which was tripled in size; the Palais de Justice on the Île de la Cité (Ie.); and the Sainte-Geneviève church (Ve.), which was transformed back into a Panthéon for France's great men (1830). A not insignificant part of the city's budget was devoted to establishing churches as well as restoring ecclesiastical buildings which had been sold off as national lands in the Revolution. Saint-Julien-le-Pauvre (Ve.) had been rescued from being a warehouse in 1826, and the flour depot that was the Sainte-Chapelle (Ie.) was rededicated as a place of worship in 1837.

The most imposing of these gestures of continuity with Paris's past was the decision to bring back Napoleon's remains from Saint Helena. The publication in 1823 of Las Cases's memoirs of Napoleon on Saint Helena had helped to stimulate a more positive reassessment of the Empire. In these hard times Napoleon's reputation rose too among Parisian workers, for whom the emperor had always tried to provide work, bread and circuses. Following several years of negotiations with the British, the transfer was agreed in 1840. After a long journey by sea and land, the imperial remains made a long procession through the streets of Paris on the freezing day of 15 December 1840. The hearse, designed by the architect Henri Labrouste (whose work includes the cavernous Bibliothèque Nationale on the Rue de Riche-lieu), was a highly decorated and monumental assemblage ten metres high and four wide. Its progress under the Arc de Triomphe and along the Champs-Élysées towards the Invalides, where the remains would rest henceforth, was watched by hundreds of thousands. 'It feels as though the whole of Paris has slipped into one half of the city,' noted Victor Hugo, 'like liquid in a tilted vase.'[7]

Louis-Philippe's consistently palliative attitude towards the regimes which had preceded the July Monarchy sprang less from strength than weakness. The king had a desperate lack of confidence in his regime's reputation for legitimacy – within Paris, in the country at large, and more generally in Europe. Highlighting the monumental record of preceding regimes seemed a way of associating himself vicariously with their symbolic capital. Yet there was a danger that he would thereby fan the embers of the political movements still attached to those regimes. The English novelist William Makepeace Thackeray, who was present in Paris at the return of Napoleon in 1840, noted the salvoes of '*Vive l'Empereur!*' which accompanied the progress of the procession, alongside marks of disrespect for Louis-Philippe.[8]

Louis-Philippe's star did not rise high in Paris, despite his best efforts. He was the target of half a dozen assassination attempts and the butt of pitiless satirical lampooning. To add to the slings and arrows of Parisian life, his son was killed in a traffic accident. (Fatal traffic accidents were averaging around twenty per annum at this time.) Parisians cynically noted that the king spent less money on Paris than on his out-of-town residences at Fontainebleau, Compiègne, Saint-Cloud and Neuilly, as well as on Versailles. At great expense he converted the latter into a museum of national history – a move that was widely regarded as another somewhat pathetic bid for legitimacy.

What contemporaries took from the transfer of power in 1830 was thus less the importance of the Orléanist candidate than the dynamism and energy of the people of Paris, who by their actions were viewed as reaffirming their capacity for revolutionary agency. One curious and somewhat unlooked for symptom of this demonstration of Parisian vitality was that the city changed sex, passing from female to male. *La ville de Paris* had long been allegorically personified following French gender declension as feminine.[9] In 883, for example, the monkish chronicler Abbo had hailed 'the queen of cities', while at the height of the Wars of Religion in the sixteenth century, Montaigne had announced that he loved Paris 'for herself'. The Romantic poets of the early nineteenth century, who personified the city more than any other literary movement, extended the range of epithets and descriptions. In 1828 Victor Hugo had imagined Paris as a 'giantess sleeping at his feet'. Yet by 1831 he was saluting 'the giant [*sic*] Paris'.[10] It was as though the Revolution of 1830 had revealed that Paris was no lady. The feminized crowd (*la foule*) was now transformed into the masculine 'people' (*le peuple*). Henceforward the Left in particular variously lauded and mythologized the city as a majestic 'hero', 'gladiator', 'soldier', 'sentinel' and 'toreador'. Although the Right insultingly referred to Paris as a monstrous Babylonian whore, it too now tended

1835 attempt to assassinate Louis-Philippe

to view the city as masculine rather than feminine: Paris was 'a tyrant', 'a satrap', 'a parvenu', 'a beggar', 'a murderer' or 'a charlatan', 'a clown' and so on.

Louis-Philippe cut a rather dwarfish and insubstantial figure when compared against his city, embodied in this way as a collective (male) force of nature. The king's efforts to bring the city under his mastery added to his unpopularity. The government's unwillingness to bring the ministers of Charles X to trial caused a good deal of agitation in the capital, where radical groupings were now re-forming in the newfound freedom. A provocative decision by Bourbon supporters to hold a commemorative mass in the church of Saint-Germain-l'Auxerrois on the anniversary of the duc de Berry's assassination led to the church being sacked and burned by the anti-clerical descendants of the sans-culottes. Although the cholera epidemic of 1832 quietened things down somewhat, 1833 and 1834 witnessed a long series of acts of collective militancy. In a horrible incident in 1834 – the so-called 'massacre of the Rue Transnonain' – the forces of order killed rebels and bystanders in cold blood. If popular agitation died down from mid-decade, it had not gone for good, as was to be shown by the revolutionary *journées* of February 1848 which deposed Louis-Philippe.

8.1: Rue Transnonain

One day when he was fifteen years old, standing in front of a grocer's shop on the Rue Transnonain, he had seen soldiers with their bayonets red with blood and with hair sticking to their rifle butts . . .

This graphic description of the aftermath of the massacre of the Rue Transnonain of 12 April 1834 is a literary one. It comes from Flaubert's *Sentimental Education*, completed in 1869. The massacre it evokes occurred during the 'pacification' of Paris, following an uprising instigated by the radical *Société des Droits de l'Homme et du Citoyen* in solidarity with an insurrection by silk-workers in Lyon. A score or more barricades went up on the Right Bank in the region of the Rues Saint-Denis, Saint-Martin and Beaubourg   a far from isolated occurrence in the turbulent period which followed the 1830 Revolution. Economic conditions and the ravages of cholera had disenchanted much of the working population of Paris with the July Monarchy. 'The people were all the more saddened and angered following the promises that had been lavished upon them by the government,' the stonemason Martin Nadaud would later recall. The barricade was an active symbol of resistance and a political demand for change.

As in other such risings, the National Guard under Louis-Philippe's orders along with troops of the line set about bringing calm to the area, moving systematically through it over a period of several days. Responding to alleged sniper fire from number 12 Rue Transnonain, close to one of the highest and most impressive of the barricades, troops under the orders of General Bugeaud (who subsequently denied responsibility) entered the building. When they found doors slammed in their faces, they proceeded to clear the building, shooting, sometimes at point-blank range, all its inhabitants. Twelve individuals, men, women and children, died at their hands.

Although the rising ended almost immediately, this incident caused a tremendous outcry. The government's version of events – that the troops were encountering armed resistance and firing in self-defence – was baldly contradicted by numerous eyewitness accounts published in the press. Several months afterwards the caricaturist Honoré Daumier published a famous lithograph of the scene in which a defenceless man dressed in nightcap and gown lies dead over the corpse of a young child.

It was the mismatch between civilians and soldiers which gave the incident the appearance of an atrocity. The massacre appalled the Left, and even caused shock within the army: Bugeaud was nicknamed 'the butcher of Rue Transnonain', and his men were for some time shunned by other troops. Flaubert's reference to the incident shows that it had become a kind of urban legend. Stendhal too cited it – at a time when the blood was still warm – in his novel *Lucien Leuwen*, which was unfinished when he died in 1834. The massacre disgusts Stendhal's eponymous hero with thoughts of a military career. Victor Hugo's *Les Misérables*, published in 1862 but the fruit of decades of work, also drew on events of this uprising (in which he claimed almost to have been shot by the National Guard as a Saint-Simonian radical). The pathos of the death of the young Gavroche on the barricades in *Les Misérables* draws on the powerful emotion which the Transnonain massacre had stirred.

The Rue Transnonain massacre occurred at the heart of one of the most turbulent areas of *le Vieux Paris*, where the spirit of local community had shaped a powerful tradition of political radicalism. It was also one of the poorest and most disinherited parts of the old city. Haussmann seems to have had both radicalism and poverty in mind when he set about transforming the neighbourhood in the 1850s and 1860s. A number of straight, wide streets and boulevards were driven through crumbling urban tissue. Running north from the Rue Transnonain was the Rue Beaubourg, and the two streets were realigned and widened. At the same time the creation of a new crossroad, the Rue de Turbigo, which ran from the Halles through to the Place de la République, also involved extensive demolition along these streets. Haussmann took the opportunity to merge the Rue Transnonain into the Rue Beaubourg, and thereby to expunge from the Parisian atlas the name of a key site of working-class memory. An old street sign at 79 Rue Beaubourg and a few old houses are all that now remains of the Rue Transnonain.

If the Rue Transnonain massacre lost its emotive charge in Parisian memory, this was partly due to Haussmann's street-name deletion. But probably more important was the fact that the radical tradition in Paris would have far more bloody events to commemorate before long – the repression of the 1871 Commune.

The *Trois Glorieuses* and the popular agitation of the early 1830s reinvigorated Paris's world-wide renown for revolutionary activism in the name of social progress. For good or ill, Paris seemed to be the embodiment of revolution, an irresistible, elemental source of energy. Writing in 1833, Auguste Bazin defined 'riot' as 'the almost recurrent convulsion in an illness that we acquired in breathing the air of freedom. We carry it in our breast; it walks with us; we sleep with it.'[11] Prominent among home-grown radicals who warmed to the myth of Paris-as-Revolution were the numerous students of the Latin Quarter, whose bohemian lifestyles (idealism, attics, hunger, romance, *grisettes*, etc.) were presented eulogistically by Henri Murger in his *Scènes de la vie de bohème* (1851). Every imaginable revolutionary sect in political exile also regarded Paris as their *patrie*. Karl Marx lived here between 1843 and 1845 and met his lifelong collaborator Friedrich Engels in a café in the Palais-Royal.

While the political elite lauded (or else deplored) Paris's role as the bearer of a powerful tradition of political upheaval, for many other contemporaries it was the way of life that one found in Paris that made it truly modern. For Balzac, Paris was 'the head of the world, a brain exploding with genius, the leader of civilisation, the most adorable of fatherlands'.[12] The city had reassumed its reputation as a maelstrom of intellectual and artistic activity. After 1815, partly by dint of the sale of the art commodities of the Napoleonic elite, it became the centre of the European art trade. Despite the loss of many treasures, the Louvre remained the most renowned art gallery in the world, while the Salon provided a brilliant showcase for new work. Paris took over from Vienna as world capital of music at this time too, attracting most of Europe's greatest composers. In a Europe in which French held on to its traditional kudos as the language of cosmopolitan civility and international scholarship, the intellectual life of Paris also enjoyed massive repute. Successive governments provided generous funding for scientific institutions such as the Museum of Natural History, the École Polytechnique, the Collège de France, the Ponts et Chaussées, the Arts et Métiers, and the Paris medical faculty (which was busy inventing modern medical science). The city became an international Mecca for all young scholars, scientists, engineers and physicians with vision and ambition. Paris was a place where everyone seemed to be reading – one visitor spotted a coachman thumbing through Horace in Latin![13] Cheap books, a booming newspaper press and an overworked postal service (Paris had 3.2 per cent of France's population, but received 27 per cent of its letters) seemed to visitors to have produced a genuinely inclusive public.

Part of the thrill of Paris was the sheer urban spectacle it presented to the pedestrian and the passer-by. An 1846 tourist guidebook caught the tone by describing Paris as 'the heart of Europe, the capital of civilisation'.[14] Such guides provided readers with a kaleidoscopic topography of Parisian pleasures: the Champ de Mars for horse races, for example, the *barrière du Combat* for animal fights (including games of darts with rats as targets), the boulevards for the best plays, concerts, cafés, dancehalls, restaurants, gambling dens and high-class brothels, the Tivoli gardens or the *Jardin d'Hiver* for leisured strolling and celebrity-spotting, and so on. Then there were the best addresses and spectator spots for open-air concerts and dances, fairground entertainments, firework displays, military demonstrations, carnival processions, marionette shows and masquerades.

In the 1830s the Polish publicist Frankowski described the city as pulsating with a quite extraordinary creative energy. The city, he noted,

> is rapid, it is ardent, it is seething . . . In the streets, in the passages, in the gardens, on the squares, on the quais, on the bridges, and under the bridges, men, animals, carts and boats walk, run, roll, and slide. The air vibrates. It is torn by brusque notes and long notes, and it is worn out by blasts of bizarre sound that suddenly erupt and suddenly vanish. The street is always babbling, and the paving stones groan or complain, grind or hiss . . .[15]

Frankowski entitled his account of the city *Études physiologiques sur les grandes métropoles*. The *physiognomie* or *physiologie* became a new literary genre in the 1820s and 1830s. Often drawing on the distinguished precedent of Louis-Sébastien Mercier's classic *Tableau de Paris* (1782–8), works of this genre subjected all the diverse and dynamic aspects of Parisian life to the lorgnette of the *flâneur*.

The *flâneur* was the sentient ambler through urban space. He – for the *flâneuse* was a rarity – was a characteristic figure of early nineteenth-century culture. Walking the streets of the city, experiencing the distinctive anonymity of the urban crowd, and drinking in appearances, the *flâneur* was, for Bazin, 'the sole, true sovereign' of all Paris, which he characterized as 'this outside life, this open-air world, this commerce of glances, comments, compliments exchanged in passing, this ambulatory sociability'.[16] The urban crowd was a place for a non-hierarchical, potentially democratic social experience. It gave street-life a scintillating and almost erotic charge in a city 'where every eye was a gay one'.[17] If a kind of lingering hedonism was the mark of the true *flâneur*, the latter also sought to comprehend the new social phenomenon in which he was placed. 'Ah! To wander in Paris!' Balzac mused. 'Adorable and delectable existence. To be a *flâneur* is a form of science, it is gastronomy for the eye.'[18] The *flâneur* did not just revel in the city; he also sought to understand it.

The renewed sense of the city as an exciting, mythic, personified entity was explored in poetic invocation, political propaganda, tourist guides, *flâneur* odysseys and countless *physiologies* and *physiognomies*. Claims to scientific understanding of the city were given added endorsement by the invention of photography. Louis Daguerre, master of visual illusion and impresario of the diorama, achieved the first daguerrotype from his studio looking down on the Boulevard du Temple (IIIe.) in 1838. Within a year the astronomer Arago was explaining the importance of the discovery to the Academy of Sciences. Over the next decades the city of Paris would be the laboratory for the advancement of photographic method. There are probably more early photographs of Paris – its monuments, its streets, and (as long as they would stand still) members of its *petits métiers* (tramps, organ-grinders, umbrella-sellers and so on) – than of any other city. In his book *Lutèce* the German Heinrich Heine noted how photography now provided an inspiration for the urban analyst-cum-*flâneur*: 'A painstaking daguerrotype has to reproduce the humblest fly as well as the proudest steed. My "Lutetian Letters" are a work of daguerrotype history, in which each day depicts itself.'[19] The camera was prized as the urban eye that could not lie.

The quest to seek a punctiliously correct record of the surface experience of urban life, as part of a move to understand what was going on beneath, also chimed with a resurgence of historical and archaeological enquiries at this time. Dulaure's *Histoire de Paris* (1821–9) was a

popular success; the Protestant statesman Guizot founded the École
des Chartes in 1822 for archival training and conservation; and in
1834 the Société française d'archéologie was established. A conservationist lobby was by this time emerging, including the writers
Montalembert, Prosper Mérimée and Victor Hugo. The latter's *Notre-
Dame de Paris* (1831) in particular helped awaken an interest in the
medieval patrimony lying untended at the heart of the city or obscured
by subsequent over-building. A similar trope of unmasking was also
evident in a spate of works of social investigation. A key event here
was the establishment of the *Annales d'hygiène et de médecine légale*
in 1829, which served as mouthpiece for a developing lobby of social
reformers eager to tackle urban problems of disease, poverty, crime
and vice. A more politically radical version of this trend was provided
by the thinkers Marx would later brand as 'utopian socialists' –
Fourier, Saint-Simon, Louis Blanc, Proudhon and Blanqui. The theme
was also fictionalized in the embryonic forms of the detective novel
with which Balzac and Edgar Allan Poe were experimenting: clues
detected by the skilled observer allowed underlying truths to be
brought to the surface. In his novel *Le Père Goriot* Balzac also mythologized the way in which the search for understanding the city merged
with the quest for mastery over it. At the end of the novel his disabused
hero Eugène de Rastignac looks down from Père-Lachaise cemetery
on the city below him, and addresses Paris: '*À nous deux maintenant*'
– 'It's between you and me now!'

8.2: Victor Hugo

The state funeral of Victor Hugo in 1885, remembered the
sociologist Maurice Halbwachs, was 'the first event which penetrated the framework of my childhood impressions (I was eight
years old at the time)'. The writer Jules Romains could not claim
a memory – he was then a foetus of six months, but he knew
that his mother had been present. People remembered where
they were when Victor Hugo was buried.

State funerals in the nineteenth century owed something to
the Ancien Régime traditions of royal burial, and something to

civic rituals developed under the First Republic in the 1790s. They were predicated, first, on the assumption that the deceased was a 'great man' (and those 'men' were almost exclusively of the masculine sex). And second, on the understanding that greatness could come in many forms. Politicians and military men were high in the Third Republic's list of individuals to whom state funerals were accorded, for example: Louis Blanc (1882), Léon Michel Gambetta (1882), Jules Ferry (1893), Félix Faure (1899), alongside sundry generals. But also present were scientists (Claude Bernard in 1878 and Louis Pasteur in 1895), men of letters (Renan in 1892, Zola in 1902) and men of the arts (the composer Gounod in 1893).

There was little doubt that the towering intellectual and literary figure of Victor Hugo would feature on this list. Even before his death his work was enshrined in the French literary canon as the product of genius. Though a royalist in his youth, Hugo's political sympathies had come to rest on the Left. The theatrical polemic over his play *Hernani* in 1830 had broken the stranglehold of classical conventions and opened up the possibility of Romantic forms of theatre which highlighted passion and social movements. A committed anti-Bonapartist, Hugo had to spend most of the period of the Second Empire in exile in the Channel Islands. His return to Paris in 1870 was a great Parisian event: he shook the hands of ten thousand delirious, 'Marseillaise'-singing Parisians in his first few hours back in the city, he reckoned. His eightieth birthday in 1882 had already been an occasion for state honours being showered on him. A Burgundian by birth, Hugo was thus an adoptive Parisian through and through. On this account alone, it was expected that Paris would provide a suitable venue for the ceremonial theatre which would be played out around his burial.

Although he never developed a consistent political philosophy, Hugo's radical commitment to the cause of the Parisian poor had come out in much of his writings, not least in *Les Misérables*. He mythologized the people of Paris. And he also mythologized its buildings: he saw the best architecture as a direct expression of the people. No fan of Haussmannism, he was an early conservationist. His novel *Notre-Dame de Paris* (1831) played an important role in alerting Parisians to the destruction being perpetrated on the gothic remains of their city. He adopted a public stance in a number of *causes célèbres* which opposed planners to conservationists. 'Demolish the building?' he rhetorically enquired on one such occasion. 'No, let's rather demolish the planner.' His writings and his activism helped form the notion of *le Vieux Paris* as something worth saving. By the time of his death, this defender of *le Vieux Paris* had become a piece of *le Vieux Paris* himself.

Hugo had requested that he be conveyed to the Père-Lachaise cemetery in a pauper's hearse, and buried in a pauper's grave. Third Republican politicians wanted more than this. They grasped that the funeral of Hugo could provide an occasion for the regime to draw the nation (but most especially the people of Paris) into affirming republican and democratic values around this iconic figure. To this end, they ordered that the church of Sainte-Geneviève be restored to its erstwhile role as a pantheon for great men – and receive the last remains of Hugo.

'It is not a monument, it's a thermometer,' quipped a journalist describing the fluctuating history of the Panthéon. In 1791 the National Assembly had commandeered the Sainte-Geneviève church as the resting-place of great men, and gone on to place the mortal remains of the *philosophes* Voltaire and Rousseau there. A church as well as a mausoleum from 1806, it was converted back solely into a church by the Restoration government in 1822. The July Monarchy turned it back into a mausoleum in 1831, but Louis Bonaparte made it a church again in 1851. It was the death of Victor Hugo which led the Assembly to reconvert it – definitively, as was to prove – into France's Panthéon.

Although the Right feared that the funeral would turn into a Revolutionary *journée*, the government did everything to ensure that the ceremony became a kind of sermon in republican values. The body lay in state under the Arc de Triomphe. The plan was that the procession should progress down the Champs-Élysées and round the boulevards to the Opéra, where special national hymns commissioned from Saint-Saëns would be sung. This idea was shelved, however, because it was felt that it would give too much time and space to pro-Communard radicals to organize counter-demonstrations. A more direct route was taken. On the day it still took eight hours, such was the pressure of the crowds. The event passed off peacefully, triumphantly. The lack of disorder in crowds variously estimated as between one and two million individuals was what most struck contemporaries. A new, participatory republican ritual had been created. The people of Paris had been their own pacifistic, political spectacle. And not a barricade in sight.

The concept of Paris as either a monstrously or else benignly disposed (male) colossus, the understanding of whose mysteries required a penetrating scientific gaze, highlighted a sense that urban society was changing in important ways. It was perhaps no coincidence that the most evident feature of change was a growing surplus of young, adult, economically active males. Paris, in sum, was being masculinized demographically as well as allegorically.

The steady pace of population growth in the eighteenth century – and the oscillations of the Revolutionary and Napoleonic periods – was replaced by more dramatic trends. The city's population of 550,000 to 600,000 in 1801 had risen to 700,000 in 1817, and was nearly 800,000 in 1831. By mid-century Paris contained in excess of a million individuals. This represented an approximate doubling in fifty years. Strikingly too, the male–female ratio in the city shifted from a historic norm of 100:117 to something like 110:95 in the 1830s – an astonishing gender reversal. The city's demographic structures were clearly in flux. In the eighteenth century births and deaths had been in rough balance, with the birth rate bobbing along a little way under national norms. Although there was now a miniscule rise in the birth rate and a drop in perinatal mortality (largely as a result of smallpox inoculation), some 90 per cent of the city's growth was accounted for by the arrival of waves of adult males – especially in their twenties and thirties and especially in the years 1831–6 and 1841–6. Though there were some contingents of individuals hailing from the south – Limousins in particular continued to man the building trades – most immigrants derived from areas north and north-east of a line stretching from the Mont-Saint-Michel on the edge of Normandy and Brittany through to Geneva on the Swiss frontier. The northerly disposition of migration was also evident among foreign nationals in the city. There was a fair number of Italians, but Germans, English, Dutch and Belgians composed the largest contingents.

Balzac bewailed the fact that Paris contained 'more foreigners and provincials than Parisians', while Bazin confessed his difficulty 'in finding the primitive race [of Parisians, and] in recognising the traits of the indigenous family'.[20] By the 1830s more than half of all residents had been born outside the city walls, to whom could be added provincials and foreigners passing through as itinerant workers, tourists, political refugees and students. What is worth stressing, however, is that this kind of pattern was well rooted in Parisian tradition. Individuals born in Paris had always been a minority in their own city. The sheer volume of immigration in these years – and the challenge which the new arrivals placed on existing infrastructure – seems to have convinced contemporaries that they were witnessing something new and frightening. The labouring classes were also dangerous classes.[21]

The 'push' factor behind migration into Paris included the incapacity of many rural areas to absorb surplus population. But 'pull' factors such as the availability of work were also important. Paris represented about 3 per cent of national population; it made around a quarter of French total production. In 1827 Paris-produced goods represented 13 per cent of the total value of French exports; twenty years later the figure was nearly 25 per cent. The city contained around one-sixth of France's total urban population at the start of the nineteenth century, but one-fifth by 1850. If Paris offered work, it also paid wages which were generally higher than in the rest of France (though ambitious provincials sometimes failed to appreciate that the cost of living was higher too).

Paris was slow to follow the British style of factory-based industrialization, and the workshop remained the dominant framework of production. The traditional luxury, semi-luxury and finishing trades needed skilled labour which was supplied predominantly by native Parisians. New arrivals in contrast were drawn to the booming building trades and to textiles manufacture (though a crisis in the cotton industry between 1827 and 1834 shook out a good deal of labour). In 1848 the city contained some 350,000 workers, around a third of whom worked in the clothes and textiles trade, while one in nine was in building and construction, one in ten in furniture trades, and the same in the metallurgy industry. The jewellery and print trades each supplied one worker in twenty. Despite the predictions of gloom by the critics of the 'dangerous classes', the immigrant population was a net contributor to new levels of wealth.

The industrial geography of the city was changing under the pressure of these forces. The Faubourg Saint-Antoine still specialized in furniture, while other traditional strongholds continued to exist for textiles manufacturers on the Rue de Cléry and the present-day Rue d'Aboukir (IIe.), for the food trades in the Halles (Ie.), and for luxury and semi-luxury trades on the Rues Saint-Denis (Ie., IIe.), Saint-Martin (IIIe., IV.) and Saint-Honoré (Ie., VIIIe.). Improvements in communications were, however, starting to create new agglomerations of casual workers. The river basin created by Napoleon out at La Villette was linked to the Canal Saint-Martin in 1825, and by extension to the Canal Saint-Denis. Heavy goods could henceforward be imported from up and downstream, and factories began to spring up on cheap land outside the old Farmers-General Wall formerly devoted to market gardening. The river Seine – whose steamships plied from the early 1820s onwards – also witnessed vigorous activity. By the 1830s Paris was France's largest port.

Railway stations – probably the monuments constructed under the July Monarchy which were most truly the regime's own work (rather than inherited from its predecessors) – played a part in Paris's industrial realignment too. The establishment of the Gare Saint-Lazare (1837–40), the Gare du Nord (1843) and the Gare de l'Est (1847–50) amplified the industrial vocation of the Right Bank. On the Left Bank too, mainline stations provided new poles for economic expansion: notably around the Gares d'Austerlitz (1838–40) and de Lyon (1847–53) in the south-east and the Gare Montparnasse in the south-west of the city (1848–9). Some six million inhabitants were using

France's rail services by mid-century. The centring of the rail network on Paris, at the expense of lines connecting provincial centres, probably had some effect on increasing immigration into the city. Yet the majority of new Parisians by 1850 had reached their destination on foot, by coach or by boat rather than by railway carriage. The railway age post-dated Paris's population transformation.

The heavy migration into Paris in the early nineteenth century produced problems of integration and accommodation into existing urban space. In the continuing absence of a Parisian mayor, the official most directly concerned with dealing with such problems was the Prefect of the Seine. The latter was a representative of central government who was only fitfully constrained by Paris's elected representatives (whose independence and electoral base were limited). Equipped with the wide range of powers accorded them by Napoleon, the Prefect commanded a budget bigger than many middling European states. Most of this came from the *octroi* (municipal tolls), which were still levied at the old Farmers-General Wall.

The two most striking figures holding the prefectoral position in the period between Napoleons were Gilbert Joseph Gaspard, comte de Chabrol de Volvic (1815–30) and Claude Philibert Barthelot, comte de Rambuteau (1833–48). It would not fall to them as it would their Napoleonic predecessors and successors to work for masters committed to major urban transformation. Both men anyway favoured the small rather than the large scale. Rambuteau in particular reserved his scorn for 'what are called synoptic frameworks [*plans d'ensemble*] which would result in compromising the interests of the city and those who live within it'.[22] Yet if they rejected grand visions of urban transformation, they were able to achieve a great deal while working within a narrower compass. Chabrol spent six times what his Napoleonic predecessors had managed on highway repair and renovation and on street paving, and twice as much on canals and water supply. Much of this was dedicated to the completion of unfinished Napoleonic schemes – the Canal d'Ourcq, many urban markets, fountains and so on. There was incremental improvement too in water supply, drainage schemes, street lighting (gas lights were introduced in 1822) and road paving. In 1822 Paris could boast only 267 metres of pavement; in 1824–5 alone, three kilometres of paving were laid. The two prefects also played an important role as regards improving house-alignments on Parisian streets, and in strictly maintaining building regulations which allowed new construction to integrate harmoniously within the existing built environment.

Rambuteau, who prided himself on planting trees as well as building roads, once described his task as providing Parisians with 'air, water and shade'. 'True politics,' Chabrol once stated, 'consists of making life comfortable and people happy.'[23] An important part of their battery of improving measures was the establishment of new roads and streets. These offered the simultaneous possibility of renovating poorer neighbourhoods, of improving communications and of embellishing the city. Legislation in 1841 made it easier for the prefect to expropriate private property where there was an issue of public utility (and especially public health) at stake. This was crucial in Rambuteau's most significant – and prophetic – achievement in this domain, namely, the creation of the Rue Rambuteau (Ie.–IIIe.). This drove a straight, 13-metre-wide street through a dense and overcrowded urban zone stretching from the church of Saint-Eustache in the Halles to the Rue des Francs-Bourgeois in the Marais, absorbing a host of tiny, labyrinthine medieval streets along the way. Haussmann would learn much from the experience.

The river islands (IVe.) received the attention of Chabrol and Rambuteau too. A medical topography from the Restoration period described the Île de la Cité as 'a bizarre assemblage of badly built buildings, squeezed together, dark and damp'.[24] Rambuteau made a start on remodelling the island with the creation of a new street, the Rue d'Arcole (1834), and the extension of the Rue de Lutèce (1838). The narrow rivulet separating the Île Louviers from the Right Bank upstream was filled in, creating the Boulevard Morland (1843). The prefect worked hard at improving liaison between the Left and Right Banks, for the island seemed to soak up and obstruct traffic rather than facilitate it. To Chabrol's creations – the Pont de Grenelle (1827), Pont de l'Archevêché (1828) and the Pont des Invalides (1829) – he added the Pont Louis-Philippe (1833), the Pont du Carrousel (1833–4), a suspension bridge at Bercy and a number of pedestrian pontoons (*passerelles*).

Between 1815 and 1848 some 150 new streets were opened in the city under Chabrol's and Rambuteau's stewardship. Yet the project of integrating the historic heart of the city into the channels of communication and exchange developing around it was not crowned with success. The city had contained 24,000 houses under Napoleon; in 1848, by dint of the worthy efforts of successive prefects, it had some 31,000. Yet the 30 per cent increase in housing stock compared poorly against a virtual doubling in population over the same period. Furthermore, over-building of expensive residences aimed at the middle classes meant that valuable property lay vacant and unlet, especially in the north-west of the city, while overcrowding in popular neighbourhoods in the east reached scandalous levels. Significantly too, despite the flagrant growth in levels of need, the city budget devoted to poor relief was relatively stable throughout the 1830s and 1840s, and the capacity of hospitals and poor-relief institutions relatively unchanged.

Efforts to improve housing stock and social conditions in the most crowded and impoverished areas of the city were made more complicated by the fact that many middle-class individuals wished to put distance between themselves and the dangerously swelling ranks of the poor. Tourists expressed astonishment at the juxtaposition of social extremes within the city – 'a palace opposite a stable and a cathedral next to a chicken-run', noted an American visitor.[25] This had roots in the kind of 'vertical stratification' which was traditional in the city, whereby both rich and poor coexisted in the same dwelling, but on different levels – the poor at street and roof level, the wealthy on the first and second floors. This pattern, however, was being progressively displaced by more 'horizontal stratification', whereby rich and poor lived in different parts of town. As we have seen, this trend was already very visible in the eighteenth century. In the following century it became even more pronounced. Although there were still some good addresses at the heart of Paris – in the somewhat dowdy Marais, for example – a subtle shift was under way, attracting wealth and prestige to the western parts of the city, while the east and centre became increasingly viewed as impoverished.

Tourist guidebooks noted how the core of the city's dynamism was relocating away towards the *grands boulevards* in the north and north-west, which represented 'one of the points of the earth,' poet

Alfred de Musset held, 'where the pleasure of the world is concentrated'.[26] The monumental projects of both the Restoration and the July Monarchy, as we have seen,[27] hugged the western half of the city. A further symptom of this development was the fate of the duc d'Orléans's Palais-Royal, whose intoxicating mixture of shopping and sociability had led Mercier to dub it 'the capital of Paris'. The excitement which the institution had generated in the late eighteenth century – and, fleetingly, at the height of the Revolution of 1830 – began to pall. The prohibition on public prostitution (1828) and gambling (1836) may have had something to do with that. Social energy now seemed to hover around the arcades, or *passages*. These were institutions less insalubrious, cleaner, better lit and more fashionable than the Palais-Royal and offered an ideal ambience for the leisure pursuits of the *flâneur*. Their proximity to theatres and cafés constituted an important part of their appeal. Popular theatres and dancehalls tended to be located on the Boulevard du Temple (IIIe.) in the east. But from the Rue Saint-Martin westwards to the Boulevard Montmartre (IIe.), there were theatres which offered the melodramas lapped up by the well-heeled and well-to-do. As the Boulevard Montmartre ran into the Boulevard des Italiens, moreover, the most fashionable restaurants and cafés were to be found, notably the Café de Paris, Tortoni (famous for its water-ices), the Maison Dorée and the Café Anglais.

8.3: The Arcades

The *passages* or arcades were early nineteenth-century shopping malls. They represented an enclosed space which mixed social types in the pursuit of retail purchase, sociability and leisure. Their inspiration was the duc d'Orléans's Palais-Royal, opened to the public as a commercial and leisure enterprise in the 1780s. Where the buildings of the Palais-Royal observed classical lines of French public architecture, however, the arcades stood for modern building. They highlighted glass roofs, skeletal iron construction and (from 1817) gas lighting: modernity, in fact.

The arcades answered to a variety of social needs. The lack of pavements, the variability of the Parisian climate and the levels of street filth even in the better-tended parts of Paris made an indoor shopping location desirable. So did the dangers of traffic in a city in which, as Baudelaire whinged, 'death comes at the gallop from every direction at once'. The arcades also met the demand for places in which a society based on class (rather than rank, as under the Ancien Régime) could socialize and engage in emulative spending habits. Although in theory anyone could walk into an arcade, the most successful *passages* employed Swiss flunkeys to eject individuals lacking the necessary bourgeois credentials. Furthermore, from the point of view of retailers, the arcades concentrated shops in ways which opened up the opportunity for impulse buying and emulative purchases. From the point of view of the post-Revolutionary property-developer, moreover, the arcade was a cheaper option than building a street within a block of housing, and offered the possibility of higher rents.

Though the bottom line was always a commercial one, the arcades also functioned as places of elite entertainment: besides cafés and restaurants, they tended to have attractions which combined the trapping of science with sheer entertainment. The Passage des Panoramas (IIe.: 1800), for example, on the Boulevard Montmartre became the core of a labyrinthine leisure complex, which did indeed extend, as its name suggested, to panoramas and dioramas. Other regular participants in arcade life were bookshops, reading-rooms, milliners, pâtisseries, umbrella-shops, toy-makers and tobacconists. 'The shops are brilliant and well-stocked,' noted one guidebook in 1828, 'but somewhat dear.'

The success of an arcade tended to be highly site-specific. There were virtually none on the commercially riskier Left Bank. Under the Restoration, many were located close to existing business and commercial centres. The Passage Véro-Dodat (Ie.: 1826), for example, linked the Palais-Royal area to a major stage-coach terminus on the Rue Jean-Jacques Rousseau. Similarly the Passage du Grand Cerf (IIe.: 1825) was located in the environs of the Rues Saint-Denis and Saint-Martin, and the Galeries Colbert and Vivienne (IIe.:1823, 1828) were established just to the south of the Bourse. Under the July Monarchy, new establishments hovered on and in the vicinity of the *grands boulevards* and Parisian theatreland.

Although the first arcade was opened in the late eighteenth century and there were several Napoleonic additions, it was really the 1820s and 1830s which marked their heyday. By the end of the Second Empire they numbered 150. By then, however, they were palpably in decline. Unsuccessful attempts to open new arcades linking to the Gare Saint-Lazare in the 1840s suggested that their commercial élan was on the wane. The Passage des Princes on the Boulevard des Italiens (IIe.) in 1860 was the last to be constructed.

The decline of the arcades owed much to Haussmann. As the writer Edmond Beaurepaire noted in 1900, 'our wider streets and our more spacious pavements have made easier the sweet *flânerie* which our ancestors could only manage in the *passages*'. The arcades passed the torch of modernity to the *grands magasins*, in comparison with which they seemed tawdry and lilliputian. Most *passages* closed down or else adapted to survival by scaling down their ambitions and their modus operandi. Some now specialized in wholesale business and the second-hand trade. Makers of herniary trusses and corsets and retailers of used false teeth started to make their appearance. Characterized by a general dinginess and dank odours which maddened the Fascist writer Céline, who was brought up in the Passage Choiseul, one of the grimmest, they worked (and work) best in small doses.

If a number of arcades have seen a renewal of life since the 1960s, this reflects their place within a heritage industry well adapted to turning a profit from institutionalized nostalgia. In the 1920s the Surrealists had highlighted the faded magic of the arcades. For Aragon, 'these human aquariums are already dead to their original life yet deserve to be regarded as containing a number of modern myths.' The German philosopher Walter

Passage de l'Opéra, *c.* 1860–70

Benjamin devoted his life to investigating a phenomenon which he saw as constituting a kind of vestigial substratum of high capitalism in which were enshrined popular fantasies and desires. The Surrealists were unable to stop the demolition of their beloved Passage de l'Opéra in 1925, but the literary mystique they extended to the arcades has helped their more recent fight-back.

The growing prestige of the western and north-western side of the city set a premium on building land within striking distance of the hyper-fashionable boulevards – notably an outer ring of land to the west and north of a line running from the Champs-Élysées through to Montmartre. It was here that the young ambitious heroes of Balzac's novels – who usually started life in seamy digs in the Latin Quarter – dreamed of ending up as evidence of their social success. From the 1820s the fashionable types living here could be conveyed to the boulevards by horse-drawn omnibuses, a means of transport still too dear to be available to the working classes. By 1850 there were eleven companies, running over forty lines with around 5,000 carriages.

Housing development in the north and north-west took the form of private–public partnership schemes, which recalled the frenetic property boom in the last decades of the Ancien Régime. The most successful projects presided over by Chabrol and Rambuteau were located in the environs of the Chaussée d'Antin (IXe.), which retained its fashionable aura. The neighbourhood contained the homes of much of France's financial elite – men like Jacques Laffitte, Casimir Périer, Benjamin Delessert and James de Rothschild. Near by, the 'New Athens', an area to the east of the present-day Gare Saint-Lazare, was another case in point. The developers' prospectus lauded the project as 'a homogeneous ensemble of houses and residences inspired by the aesthetic canons of neo-classicism, as shown in their simplicity and in their decoration which exhibits discreet devotion to Antiquity'.[28] The area attracted individuals from artistic as well as political and financial milieux: George Sand and Chopin were early buyers and they were followed into the area by Alexandre Dumas, the actor Talma, and painters Delacroix and Ary Scheffer (whose residence houses the present-day Musée de la Vie romantique). The success of this project encouraged similar development in the Saint-Georges district, serviced by the church of Notre-Dame-de-Lorette. The Square d'Orléans, whose layout was based on the great London squares, served as model to nearby developments along Rues La Bruyère, Trudaine, Malesherbes, Chaptal and Pigalle. The development of the area to the east, around the church of Saint-Vincent-de-Paul (1824: Xe.) and along the Rue Lafayette (IXe.), was further stimulated by the building of the Gare du Nord. Conversely, however, the establishment of the Gare Saint-Lazare actually inhibited the expansion of the Quartier de l'Europe (VIIIe.) to the south of the Place de Clichy, which had been developed on similar speculative lines: railway lines broke up the unity of the area.

As during the First Empire, redundant property expropriated from the church during the Revolution often formed the basis of speculative building. This was the case to the north of the city, notably towards the Rue Saint-Denis on the grounds of the old Saint-Lazare monastery (IXe.–Xe.) and on the former convent of the Filles-Saint-Thomas close to the Bourse (IIe.). Elsewhere there was similar development in the grounds of the old abbey of Saint-Martin-des-Champs (IIIe.), for example, and on property formerly belonging to the hospital sisters of La Roquette (XIe.). Before the Revolution these religious buildings had been integrated into the texture of neighbourhood life, so housing developments there tended to prosper. There could be problems, however, where projects opened up new terrain which was more off the beaten track and which lacked the infrastructure to support fresh injections of population. The company which in the 1820s sought to develop the Quartier François I to the south of the Champs-Élysées and the Avenue Montaigne (VIIIe.) on what had been market-gardens failed to attract custom, and the same was initially true of what had been a leisure complex at the Beaujon gardens (VIIIe.), in which the Rues Chateaubriand, Lord-Byron and Fortunée were now laid out.[29]

The social geography of all such outer areas was massively transformed by the government's decision in 1841 to build a new, militarily defensible wall. The old Farmers-General Wall, two metres high, might keep out smugglers, but was incapable of resisting armed attack – as had been proved in 1814 and 1815. Military men had begun calling for proper fortifications during the Restoration, but it needed a rise in the temperature of European diplomacy in the late 1830s due to tensions in the Middle East to put the issue on the governmental agenda. Even then, all the determination of Louis-Philippe and his powerful minister Adolphe Thiers was required to force legislation through an Assembly fearful of expense and anxious about foreign adventurism. The 'Thiers Wall' caused as much unpopularity among Parisians for Louis-Philippe as the Farmers-General Wall had for Louis XVI. (Parisian horses tended not to like it either: they automatically stopped at the old Farmers-General Wall, as if unable to break the habits of an equine lifetime.) The building of the new wall employed 25,000 workers and was complete by 1846. Some thirty-four kilometers long, it was situated between one and three kilometres outside existing city limits, between the Farmers-General Wall and the borders of the department of the Seine. There were forty-five gates, as well as entry points for railways and canals. Building was prohibited on land 250 metres from the wall, and grassy knolls there became favoured spots for Parisian Sunday picnicking, stimulating the emergence near by of inns, dancehalls and *guinguettes* for the leisure trade. Business was helped by the fact that the inner ring of *la petite banlieue* ('the little suburb'), as it was called, was outside the Farmers-General Wall and thus exempted from the city *octroi*, meaning wine was cheaper than within the city.

A paved road was constructed adjacent to the wall roughly on the site of the present-day *boulevards des maréchaux* – the roads, named after marshals of France, which encircle the city marginally within today's *boulevard périphérique*. This meant that movement around the rim of the new line of defence was easy. It also stimulated development along this new road, around the principal gates, and on many of the streets linking the city gates to the old tollgates. As well as the exemption from the *octroi*, land prices here were much lower than in Paris. This stimulated an influx of both labour and business. Municipal regulation at around this time aimed at eliminating noxious substances from residential city areas was also forcing many businesses – tanneries, chemical works and the like – out into the rim of the 'little suburb', whose population mushroomed from 75,000 in 1831 to 173,000 in 1856. The thickening of population outside the formal city limits but inside the defensive wall prepared the area for its full integration into Paris in 1860.[30]

Parts of the 'little suburb' were strongly working-class and industrial in character. This was perhaps most evident in the sector which ran from Montmartre (XVIIIe.) to the cemetery of Père-Lachaise (XXe.) in the east. This area already contained dense levels of poor housing. Particular centres of working-class settlement included the neighbourhood below Montmartre around the Place des Abbesses and the Rue d'Orsel (XVIIIe.), the Rue de la Goutte d'Or towards the present-day Place de La Chapelle (XVIIIe.), and the increasingly industrialized La Villette area. The disinherited villages of Belleville, famous for its quarries, and Charonne, both now within the Thiers Wall, also witnessed considerable growth.

Victor Hugo had described early nineteenth-century Montparnasse and its environs as 'these strange places that no one knows'.[31] The establishment of the Gare Montparnasse (XVe.), however, saw the area brought within the urban framework for the first time. To the south of the station the Plaisance area down to present-day Rue Raymond Losserand became a centre for railway workers. The adjacent neighbourhoods of Thermopyles and the Nouveau Village d'Orléans saw semi-organized housing developments. To the east of the station the Rue de la Gaieté (XIVe.) became, as its name suggested, a centre for popular theatres, eating-houses and bars. Much of this Left Bank area still retained a rural flavour, however, notably towards the villages of Vanves and Vaugirard in the west (XVe.), and in the area to the south east of Montparnasse (XIVe., XIIIe.). The fields around the Buttes-aux-Cailles (XIVe.) contained some of Paris's last vineyards, while the Glacière area contained ice-houses (and pools for winter skating). Further south, and to the east of the river Bièvre, Petit-Gentilly was customarily bedecked with the city's drying laundry.

Development characterized by a mixture of rural and urban was also evident in the western and eastern extremes of the inner ring of the Thiers Wall. In the east the area from Charonne through to Bercy (XIe.–XIIIe.) was one of the least inhabited parts of the 'little suburb', though Bercy's development as a wine warehousing centre brought it some incomers. At the western extreme the low-lying, floodable land beyond the École militaire at Grenelle (XVe.) had been relatively uninhabited farmland, but it now began to spawn housing developments, both for workers and bourgeois, on either side of the present-day Rue du Commerce (1837). The area's population almost quadrupled between 1841 and 1856. On the opposite bank of the Seine the villages of Auteuil, Passy and Chaillot (XVIe.) were developing into centres of comfortable residential housing. Here, and to the north of Chaillot, particularly towards the Batignolles area (XVIIe.), market-gardens and nurseries became mixed with some minor industry. In 1800 there was only a windmill at Batignolles, and its population was recorded as being nil. In the 1820s, however, the area was a target for development companies offering middle-class housing. An influx of workers into the heavy industry which developed towards the Avenue de Clichy changed the area's complexion. It became an outpost of the heavy industry of the north-east zone, its population growing from 6,000 in 1831 to 30,000 in 1851.

Paris 'between Napoleons' may thus have appeared politically less dramatic than the Revolutionary and Napoleonic regimes which preceded it, as well as the Second Empire after 1851. Yet in fact this belied the extensive reshaping of the city and the major social shifts that were taking place in the first half of the nineteenth century. Population increase caused largely by immigration was, moreover, placing the existing structures under severe strain. Parts of the centre were coming to be perceived as a zone of economic stagnation and social deprivation, but the far bigger problem was the widening divide between a wealthier north-western sector and an eastern half of the city which was more heavily industrial and more impoverished. Paris seemed to have become a two-tiered, two-speed city.

This emergent social geography was starkly evident in the impact of the cholera epidemic of 1832. There was no clinical reason why the disease should not have been evenly spread among the population, yet in fact, as the journalist Jules Janin acerbically noted, cholera turned out as an affliction pre-eminently of the poor, 'who die first and alone, and whose death gives the lie, bloodily and fundamentally, to the doctrines of equality with which we have diverted ourselves for half a century'.[32] Indeed the cholera-specific death rate of the wealthiest rentiers and landowners actually fell in the course of 1832 (largely because they were able to protect themselves by flight and seques-tration), while that of day-labourers doubled. The poor areas, with their narrow, high-sided streets, mired in filth, were consequently more heavily hit than the wealthier north-west of the city. 'Cholera', a placard posted in the Faubourg Saint-Antoine announced, 'is an invention of the bourgeoisie and the government to starve the people.'[33]

In fact, even though cholera was socially selective, the horrid (and horridly swift) lethal outcome of the disease severely distressed the social elite. For there seemed a real threat of a vaguely understood contagion reaching into wealthy as well as poor homes. The water-borne character of the disease was only appreciated much later, and the presence of epidemic disease was normally equated with bad smells. It fed a haunting feeling among the bourgeoisie that the city as a whole had become pathological. In the 1780s Mercier's *Tableau de Paris* had expatiated at length on pathogenic environments within the late eighteenth-century city. But this was before the massive influx of adult labour had placed added strain on the structures of everyday living. One of the most striking experiences recorded by early nineteenth-century tourists to the city, for example, was the range of sensory extremes to which the visitor was exposed. No pure sensation seemed possible in this context. The dazzling brilliance of shop-windows, arcades and the like contrasted with the aerial assault by emptying chamberpots and the acts of 'bestial filth' which Fanny Trollope complained she had to witness in the streets (she was referring to casual urination and defecation).[34] Similarly, the pleasing conver-sational hum of the cafés and salons was set in stark relief by the unsettling din and racket of the streets. The perfume of bourgeois interiors was unable to resist the sheer stink of the city. When the east wind blew, the emetic stench of the rubbish tip out at Montfaucon penetrated into the very heart of the city.

The city's death-rate was higher than that of the rest of the country – or other contemporary big cities such as London. One-third of all births were illegitimate, and around one-tenth of new babies were abandoned to the foundling hospital. Sixty per cent of abandoned children died within the first year of their life in care. One-sixth of all French suicides occurred within the department of the Seine.

Poor-relief expenditure was double that of France as a whole. Immigrants to the city found that, despite Paris's evident attractions, its streets were not paved with gold. Indeed at mid-century, perhaps as much as one Parisian in ten was dependent on charity or poor-relief, and three deaths out of four produced pauper funerals. All demographic data was also socially skewed. It was among adult male immigrants in the eastern parts of the city that death-rates were aberrantly high. Those eastern, and some disinherited central neighbourhoods, provided disproportionately more illegitimate births, more foundlings, and much higher levels of poor relief. They were also centres of vice and crime. There were fashionable brothels up in the wealthy north-west of the city, but the east was the home of working-class prostitution – on a massive scale, given the gender imbalance among adults. Criminal underworlds seemed to thrive here too, particularly in the Faubourgs Saint-Victor and Saint-Marcel in the south-east, where nearly all the indices of deprivation, crime and social pathology (begging, theft, infanticide, insanity, suicide, etc.) were highest.

Careful scrutiny of crime statistics has led many historians to adjudge Paris's reputation for pathological levels of vice and criminality exaggerated.[35] No matter, it was the view of contemporaries which counted: the *classes laborieuses* (working people) were equated with the *classes dangereuses* or 'dangerous classes'. Crime and vice proceeding from the poor were viewed as social diseases which might stop the city of modernity in its tracks, just as the contagion of cholera had threatened to do in 1832. Crucial in bringing this message home to the urban bourgeoisie were the best-selling novelists of the age, who dramatized the 'facts' uncovered by social investigation in ways which made them more palatable. Balzac's summary of the underlying urban plot was brutally succinct: in Paris 'life can be considered as a perpetual conflict between rich and poor'.[36] The sixty-five volumes of his *La Comédie humaine* (first edition 1842) provide a purposefully panoramic vision of Parisian society revolving around this theme, and drawing copiously on the work of social investigators. Similarly, Eugène Sue's *Mystères de Paris* (1842–3) purported to enlist his readers into knowledge of the grim class realities beneath the city's glittering surfaces – and in the process used Parent-Duchâtelet's investigation of Parisian prostitution, Frégier's work on urban workers and Villermé's analyses of public health problems. Again, in Victor Hugo's classic account of the Parisian underclass, *Les Misérables* (1862), the memorable passages on the Parisian sewers had as their inspiration Parent-Duchâtelet's erudite work on the topic.[37]

Parisian public health issues and questions of crime and vice would have made good melodrama even without the novelists. But the way in which novelists narrated social distress gave them immense cultural visibility. For Balzac, the newspaper byline, 'Yesterday at four o'clock a young woman threw herself into the Seine from the Pont des Arts' represented the kind of *fait divers* 'before which drama and fiction pale in comparison'.[38] Yet Balzac's fiction deliberately used such social 'facts' as the raw material for his plots – which allowed him to claim that his novels were quasi-ethnographic documents of scientific validity. Like many of his contemporaries he saw the impoverished inhabitants of the city as forming a race of savages or barbarians, subject to some degenerative condition: 'a horrible people to behold', was his expression, in *La Fille aux yeux d'or* (1834). Their faces – 'wan, yellow, weatherbeaten, . . . contorted, twisted' – were 'masks rather than faces, masks of weakness, masks of force, masks of wretchedness, masks of joy, masks of hypocrisy'.[39] A similar conceit was evident in Alexandre Dumas's *Les Mohicans de Paris* (1854), in which the novelist brought the eye of the anthropologist of North American Indians to the world of Parisian vice and crime. Paris's subterranean caverns and catacombs were an occasional decor of much of this kind of fiction – the underground was a suitably apocalyptic milieu for the dangerous new underclass. More generally, however, such fictions were set in the workers' faubourgs. These were viewed – again the words are Balzac's, in his novel, *Facino cane* (1836) – as so many 'seminaries of revolution, which contain heroes, inventors, practical savants, rascals, rogues, virtues and vices, all compressed together by poverty, stifled by necessity, drowned in drink, worn out by strong liquor'.[40]

The idea that the faubourgs fostered political radicalism and potential anarchy as well as vice and crime became more firmly entrenched as the July Monarchy wore on. The government, wedded to a stringent laissez-faire social philosophy, was patently failing to find adequate remedy for the social problems linked with the capital city. This was certainly the message of French radicals, international political exiles and campaigning journalists, who were becoming increasingly vociferous through the 1840s. Yet even conservative critics of the regime saw the class struggle in the city as becoming more than superficial political squabbling. By January 1848 Alexis de Tocqueville was telling his colleagues in the Chamber of Deputies that 'we are sleeping on a volcano', and he prophesied 'the most redoubtable revolutions'.[41]

In the same year the volcano duly exploded in a new political revolution. A conjunction of political crisis engineered by the regime's opponents and economic hardship triggered by bad harvests and a downturn in the business cycle produced an uprising in February 1848, with barricades springing up again around the city. The king abdicated with almost indecent haste, racing to the Channel ports to take refuge in England. Mérimée correctly concluded that the Orléanists had 'destroyed royalty in France':[42] Louis-Philippe was indeed to prove the last king of the French. Paris's Hôtel de Ville again held the destiny of France in its hands – and this time plumped for a Republic, which immediately introduced humane liberal legislation, bringing in universal male suffrage, abolishing slavery in French colonies, setting the working day at ten hours and establishing national workshops to provide work for the hungry and unemployed.

Yet the seeds of the Second Republic's destruction were sown almost straight away. Just as in 1794, the bourgeoisie had drawn away from the radicals of the popular movement once they felt that popular energies were worsening matters, so now the provisional government turned on the Parisian radicals, closing down the national workshops and driving the descendants of the sans-culottes to the barricades in protest. Radical wild-man Auguste Blanqui had warned that 'a Saint-Bartholomew's Massacre of proletarians' was on the cards.[43] And in the 'June Days' of 1848 the regime brutally crushed the radical street opposition of the Parisian faubourgs. Despite the apparent unanimity of the February Revolution, social division was now placed at the heart of the new Republic. Some 4,000 civilians were killed (there were over a thousand military casualties) and 11,000 taken prisoner. In the subsequent clean-up, over 4,000 of the rebels would be deported to Algeria.

The February Revolution of 1848 had seen Parisian street militancy – as in 1789, 1792–3 and 1830 – dictating to France's government. The June days reversed the trend. In fact the elections in April 1848 had already undermined the capital's claims to represent the nation, by returning a massively conservative majority. In December 1848 the people of France elected Louis-Napoleon Bonaparte as its president, incidentally humiliating Parisian politicians who had made their name in the course of the Revolution. Universal male suffrage had given rural France a voice – and with that voice it elected a man who was untainted by Parisian politics and who was a nephew of a man whom the peasantry credited with the land settlement of the First Empire and restoring Catholicism. Though the political elite tended to write off the new Bonaparte, he had the last laugh. Furthermore the Second Empire which he inaugurated in 1852 would again make Paris the centre of his projects; but it would not be the Paris of Revolutionary modernity, but the city of urban transformation and new styles of living.

9

Haussmannism and the City of Modernity
1851–89

The return to power of a Bonaparte in 1848 instigated a reprise of the imperial themes and the grandiose scale of operations which Napoleon I had sketched out for the capital of his European empire. Even while he was still President of the Republic, Emperor Napoleon III (as Louis Bonaparte made himself in 1852)[1] was planning the revitalization of the nation's capital. Legend had it that he had arrived at the Gare du Nord in 1848 with a rolled map under his arm containing the future new boulevards sketched out in coloured pencils. His seizure of executive power in 1851–2, which roused widespread opposition on the streets of Paris, increased the resources at his disposal and boosted his ambitions. The period up to the overthrow of the Second Empire in 1870 and the establishment of the Third Republic (1870–1940) was to be characterized by a programme of urban renewal perhaps as ambitious and as far-reaching as any in western history. The result was a Paris which by the end of the century had new boundaries, a new configuration and, in some respects, a new identity, as the city of modernity.

The Second Empire innovated not by building alongside and outside the old centre, but rather by locating innovation at the very core of the city almost for the first time, in the heartlands of the radical sans-culotterie which had opposed Louis Bonaparte's rise to power, and indeed had demonstrated against his 1851 *coup d'état*. Perhaps the most striking feature of the transformation was a new and more highly integrated system of straight and broad roadways which tore through the antique fabric of what was already coming to be called *le Vieux Paris* ('Old Paris'). Others included the prioritization of circulation, the harmonization between monuments and means of

344

communication, the provision of green space and the articulation of an infrastructure which could cope with a larger and more densely occupied site. The surface area of the capital rose from less than 3,500 hectares to nearly 8,000 by the 1860s; the population increased from roughly one million at the fall of the Second Republic in 1851 to 1.9 million in 1872, 2.4 million in 1891 and nearly three million by the time of the First World War.

The personal influence of Napoleon III on his proclaimed mission of renovation should not be underestimated. Nevertheless, it is difficult to disentangle his activities from the role also played by Baron Georges-Eugène Haussmann, whom in 1853 Napoleon III designated the Prefect of the Seine, and who remained in power until only a few months before Napoleon's own overthrow. The loss of vital documents, notably in the extensive incendiarism of 1871 following the ignominious end of the Second Empire, makes exact adjudication of their respective parts impossible – as do Napoleon III's tendency to vainglorious self-promotion, and Haussmann's rhetorical propensity for stressing his own role as mere 'instrument' and 'servant' of his 'master'.[2] If contemporaries tended to ascribe more credit to Haussmann, this was partly because they found it difficult to imagine that a man like Napoleon could possibly have a profound influence on a city he appeared to know so little. Before 1848 he had never lived in Paris save as a baby and as a fleeting tourist, and as emperor he would on occasion get lost making the simplest of journeys. Haussmann, the 'Alsatian Attila', in contrast, had spent a happy childhood in the capital before his family had moved to eastern France. It was the name of Haussmann which, moreover, was to endure. The Bonaparte name was execrated throughout the Third Republic, so that it was not 'Napoleonism' but 'Haussmannism' that was recognized as an influence – a continuing influence – on the remodelling of the capital.

What perhaps most marks out what contemporaries were already beginning to call Haussmannization from the processes of urban development which preceded it was the unitary, holistic vision which underpinned it – even if that unitary vision was the work of two men. Few of the elements in this vision were new. After all, the city had been used as a dynastic power-site since the Romans. The straight

urban street had been highly valued during the Renaissance. Boulevards had existed since the time of Louis XIV. There had been moves to extend the city's perimeters by royal edict under Louis XVI. Napoleon I had attended to the city's infrastructure and sought to highlight prestigious monuments within the cityscape. Furthermore, much of the detail of urban renewal which would be associated with the notion of Haussmannism had already been trialled by Prefects Chabrol and Rambuteau. The latter in particular had devised the method of renovating decaying neighbourhoods by creating new streets.

Nonetheless, it was under the Second Empire that these existing features of urban transformation were fused together into a programme of urban renewal covering all the functions which the city performed. Whereas Rambuteau and Chabrol had eschewed the idea of any *plan d'ensemble*, Haussmann and Napoleon III gloried in it. For them the modern city was an organism which needed to be analysed according to a strictly utilitarian examination of urban functions. Napoleon and Haussmann saw themselves as physician-urbanists, whose task was to ensure Paris's nourishment, to regulate and to speed up circulation in its arteries (namely, its streets), to give it more powerful lungs so as to let it breathe (notably, through green spaces), and to ensure that its waste products were hygienically and effectively disposed of. These were all aspects of the new Paris which Napoleon proudly showed off to the world at the international Expositions which he held in the city in 1855 and 1867. The world was duly dazzled.[3]

In the past Paris had often been viewed as a great city whose grandeur could be registered in the vestiges that the past had left on its face. This equation between greatness and the monumental record had already been eroded during the eighteenth century under the pressure of more utilitarian approaches.[4] Although Napoleon III accentuated his regime's links to both Roman and Napoleonic empires, Paris's own history played very little part in his vision for the city. Similarly, although Napoleon referred to his projects as 'embellishments', Haussmann himself admitted he thought essentially in terms of Paris's 'security, circulation and salubrity'.[5] Neither man displayed much nostalgic or aesthetic appreciation of the lived environment of the old city. Haussmann, it is true, employed photographers such as Charles Marville and watercolourists like Davioud to make 'before-and-after' pictures of areas being transformed by his works – but the emphasis was less on nostalgia for a world that was being lost than relief at its being consigned to history.

History was notable only by its absence from the list of core features of the programme of Haussmannization which Napoleon highlighted to the municipal council in 1858. His vision was of

> major arteries opening, populous areas becoming healthier, rents tending to get lower as a result of more and more building, the working class getting richer through work, poverty diminishing through better organization of relief, and Paris responding to its highest calling.[6]

The 'highest calling' which Napoleon III, in this vaguely messianic way, planned for Paris was the metamorphosis of an ailing city into the capital of the world, the shining light of the modern age. Like all such missions, the project of renewal stressed how bad the state of Paris had been prior to its own advent. The political economist Victor Considérant vehemently described Paris in 1848 as 'a great manufactory of putrefaction in which poverty, plague . . . and disease labour in concert and where sunlight barely ever enters. [It is] a foul hole where plants wilt and perish and four out of seven children die within their first year.'[7] 'Paris, in its state following the 1848 Revolution,' the writer Maxime du Camp later agreed,

> was on the point of becoming uninhabitable. Its population [was] suffocating in the tiny, narrow, putrid, and tangled streets in which it had been dumped. As a result of this state of affairs, everything suffered: hygiene, security, speed of communications and public morality.[8]

To some degree these damning verdicts on the condition of mid-century Paris are exaggerations which accentuated the Second Empire's achievement. Paris at mid-century obviously faced many major social problems. Yet, despite the doom-sayers, it was still the largest manufacturing city in the world, was a major financial centre, had a young and dynamic workforce, had put in place a railway infrastructure and was beginning the work of reinventing itself as a modern city. The criticisms of pre-Haussmann Paris did, however,

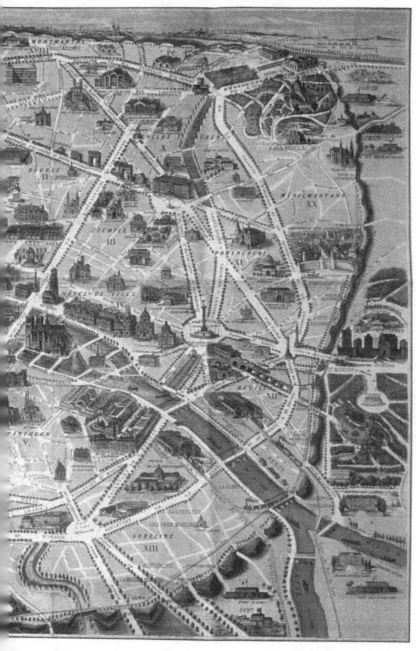

Map of Haussmann's Paris

contain an important nugget of truth: namely, that by mid-century the city was widely perceived as a dangerous, unhealthy and frustratingly difficult place to inhabit. This meant that there was a groundswell of desire from within the urban community for a more liveable city. This does not mean to say that if Haussmann had not existed, the Parisians would have invented him. But it does signify that Haussmannism was already in the air.

Even before Haussmann was appointed Prefect, an imperial Commission for the Embellishment of Paris had already begun to devise plans for the renovation of the city which in many details prefigured Haussmann's programme. Interior Minister Persigny was also developing similar ideas at the same time.[9] These precursors may have had a scintillating vision of the modern city, however, but they lacked the political, financial and administrative clout to bring that vision to life. This is what Napoleon and Haussmann were able to provide – albeit only from 1853 onwards. The plans of renewal which Napoleon tried out when he was still only president of the Republic, for example, had failed to make much impact. Haussmann's predecessor as Prefect of the Seine, Jean-Jacques Berger, regarded Napoleon's plans as over-costed: 'I'm certainly not going to be involved,' he noted privately, 'in the city's financial ruin.'[10] He proved a perennial wet blanket. Napoleon's seizure of Paris by *coup d'état* in December 1851, however, and then his declaration of the Empire in November 1852, swung the balance of power his way. In Haussmann, whom he put in Berger's place in June 1853, he found an energetic and committed political fixer, who was altogether more receptive to his ideas, and who was more than happy to strong-arm the municipal council – whose members he personally appointed anyway – into assenting to his master's wishes.

Haussmann's streets and boulevards displayed the same kind of insouciant authoritarianism which he showed in most of his political dealings. This 'demolition artist',[11] as he jocularly called himself, shunned the older piecemeal methods of improvement through the alignment of existing streets, and deployed the method pioneered by Rambuteau, which consisted of driving new streets through existing neighbourhoods. It was, he opined, 'easier to cut though a pie's inside than to break into the crust'.[12] This urban butchery was facilitated moreover by regulations introduced in 1848 and confirmed in 1852 which strengthened the hand of the Prefect in street-building projects. The 1841 regulations, originally designed to facilitate railway development, and which Rambuteau had used in his urbanization project, permitted the expropriation of properties for purposes of public utility where the property was actually on the track of a new street. The 1852 decree stated that property adjacent to the street and affected by the plans should also be subject to compulsory purchase and made available for development. This allowed chaotically complicated street- and house-plans to be almost surgically replaced by rectilinear roadways. It also permitted the construction of new buildings in replacement of what was torn down. Characteristically, the operations became self-financing, for the usually insanitary old buildings were sold at low cost to urban developers who replaced them with attractive prestige properties which could be sold or else rented out as homes and businesses. This allowed the accumulation of capital, which could be invested in further speculative building, a tendency which was also favoured by the emergence of a modern banking sector in these years.

For those involved in this whirligig of property development, Haussmann appeared to have invented a kind of virtuous circle which conjoined private and public energies in a way which built new homes, provided mass employment (one-fifth of the Parisian workforce was in the construction trades at the height of Haussmann's development), made a signal contribution to public health, beautified the city and supplied the financial bourgeoisie with fat profits to boot. The notion of the 'highest calling' which Napoleon and Haussmann had for a modernized Paris was, moreover, grounded in an optimistic calculus which assumed that urban growth would be self-financing in the long term. Many financial pessimists – such as ex-Prefect Berger – argued that the city simply could not afford the scale of new building which Haussmann wanted. Yet this was steady-state financing. Haussmann built into his calculations the assumption that 'productive expenditure' – in effect, debit financing – would make the city bigger, richer and more attractive. By developing Paris as a world city whose inhabitants had more in their pockets, and which tourists would want to visit in droves, it would be all the easier to siphon off part of this surplus wealth, notably in the form of indirect taxes on consumption (the major item in the city's budget). This developmental logic meant that the government renovated Paris on the cheap, comparatively speaking: the state treasury bore only around 10 per cent of the total costs of the public works undertaken in these two decades. Virtually all the rest of the money came from loans, permission for which Haussmann was able to force through the municipal authorities by a combination of bullying, finagling and optimistic accounting.

Broadly speaking, the reconstruction of Paris by Napoleon III and Haussmann over the 1850s and 1860s proceeded from the inside out. Initially the prime task was to renovate the centre of the old city according to the blueprint which the emperor had devised. The focal point of the early work was the imposition of a major crossroads – the so-called *grande croisée* – at the centre of old Paris, thus bringing the beneficial effects of circulation to its very heart. Napoleon I's Rue de Rivoli (Ie.) was an essential link in a major east–west axial roadway originating at the Arc de Triomphe on the Champs-Élysées and running through to the Place de la Bastille and beyond. The idea was that the street should follow the northern limit of the Louvre and Tuileries. At Napoleon III's accession the street was still only partly in place, from the Place de la Concorde down to the Palais-Royal. The Rue de Rivoli was now extended well past the eastern front of the Louvre down to the Rue de Sévigné (IVe.) in the Marais, where it joined up with the Rue Saint-Antoine leading to the Place de la Bastille. The extension of the Rue de Rivoli, and the related demolition of housing between the Louvre and Tuileries palaces, was at the expense of a score of tiny streets, the names of some of which were venerable in Parisian history (Rue de la Tixanderie, Rue de la Heaumerie, etc.). 'Get these warts off my face,' was Haussmann's expostulation when confronted with such historically sensitive demolition.[13]

The extension of the Rue de Rivoli also involved the remodelling of the Place du Châtelet, the centre of the *croisée*. Two major theatres were erected on an expanded site. The Place du Palais-Royal and the Place de l'Hôtel-de-Ville were given similar treatment – indeed the latter was quadrupled in size. It had always been a historic centre of urban sociability: it was now turned into a mixture of a road junction and an empty space from where one could get a good view of the city hall. In addition, along the Rue de Rivoli between the Châtelet and the Hôtel de Ville, the medieval tower of the church of Saint-Jacques-de-la-Boucherie (IVe.) was modernized (rather anachronistically in fact) at the centre of a little garden square. As a result of extensive flattening of terrain along the Rue de Rivoli, the tower's entrance was henceforth several metres above its historic level.

Haussmann had thus developed a very personal urban recipe in working on the Rue de Rivoli extension: wide streets to promote better circulation and bring more air and light; the levelling of relief; a pivotal role accorded enlarged, open squares; ruthless demolition of anything standing in his way; insensitivity to the claims of history; and (limited) attention to green space. This formula was replicated more generally in the development of the Boulevards Sébastopol, de Strasbourg and Saint-Michel, which were to form the north–south axis intersecting with the Rue de Rivoli at the Place du Châtelet to form the *grande croisée*. Like plans for the lengthening of the Rue de Rivoli, the idea of the creation of the Boulevard Sébastopol had been brought to Paris in Louis Bonaparte's suitcase. He was adamant about the need for it, ignoring critics who argued that Paris had perfectly serviceable north–south arteries, namely the Rues Saint-Denis and Saint-Martin on the Right Bank and the Rue Saint-Jacques on the Left. Only by extending the Boulevard Sebastopol, however, could a direct alignment be run from the Place du Châtelet junction through to a major railway station, the Gare de l'Est. This kind of link was another cardinal point in the Haussmannian strategy. The complete remodelling of the densely occupied Right Bank neighbourhood was also furthered by the creation of three crossroads linking the Rues Saint-Denis and Saint-Martin: the Rue Étienne-Marcel (accidentally uncovering the old tower of John the Fearless, which had been almost solidly encrusted into post-medieval overbuilding), an extension of the Rue Réaumur and the new Rue de Turbigo (named after one of Napoleon III's few successful battles).[14]

The creation of the Boulevard Saint-Michel (Ve.–VIe.) on the Left Bank achieved the southern leg of the *grande croisée* – indeed it was initially called the Boulevard de Sébastopol-Rive-Gauche when it was opened in 1855. The boulevard opened up to public scrutiny the Roman baths, and indeed was very much on the line of a Roman street. It attracted traffic away from the medieval Rue de la Harpe which ran alongside, and which a contemporary had described as characterized by 'mud and misery, shady drinking halls and argumentative eating-houses'.[15] (The street was now lost to Parisian memory, only being rediscovered by Greek restaurateurs in the 1950s.) The impact on the neighbourhood of the new boulevard was amplified by the creation from 1855 onwards of the Boulevard Saint-Germain (Ve.–VIe.–VIIe.), which acted as a kind of Left Bank Rue de Rivoli, facilitating west–east circulation.

While the *croisée* was thus being put in place, Haussmann set about making a further section of central Paris, namely the Île de la Cité, fit for his new image of Paris. Despite Rambuteau's best efforts, mobility and circulation still seemed the antithesis of what the Cité had become. Yet by the 1870s, almost at a stroke, Haussmann had converted the Cité from overcrowded residential zone into administrative centre, its population tumbling from 15,000 to 5,000. Virtually all private dwellings were removed, with the exception of a few hundred metres of old housing left on the north-west of the island. Notre-Dame cathedral and the Palais de Justice (with the Sainte-Chapelle) were left intact, but were now stripped of surrounding housing. The Hôtel-Dieu hospital straddling the Seine towards the Left Bank was demolished, and the institution relocated in a new building the other side of the Parvis de Notre-Dame (which was vastly increased in size) on the site of what had been slum housing. This left the cathedral – at that moment undergoing aggressive restoration by the medievophile Viollet-le-Duc – looking uncannily isolated. At the centre of the island were now located the commercial courts (the Tribunal de Commerce) and the city's police headquarters, the Préfecture de Police. Haussmann had succeeded in making the Île de la Cité a passageway from Left Bank to Right: few in their right minds would henceforth choose to linger there, save on the quais or in the cathedral.

As well as targeting the central zones of the city, Haussmann sketched out developments through to the city limits and, in particular, to the mainline railway stations. He was not alone in regarding the latter as new gateways to the city, which involved a rethinking of urban space. His aim was consequently to establish a framework for circulation which dovetailed with the new Paris street-plan and also with the national road and rail systems. Both were anyway highly (to be frank: overly) Parisocentric in orientation. Each terminus received duly monumental treatment, often using modern materials of glass and iron. The stations were increased in size so as to keep up with expanding passenger numbers, and they were often massively over-decorated too – like the Gare du Nord, rebuilt in the early 1860s by Jean-Jacques Hittorff, one of the regime's many talented architects. In addition they were provided with capacious approach roads to make them stand out. Drawing a straight line along the Boulevards de Strasbourg and Sébastopol towards the Gare de l'Est necessitated the mutilation of the medieval churches of Saint-Leu-Saint-Gilles and of Saint-Laurent, the latter among the most ancient ecclesiastical sites in the city. For Haussmann, straight lines and urban functions prevailed over the claims of history. On the Left Bank the Rue de Rennes gave the Gare Montparnasse a similarly impressive vista from the Boulevard Saint-Germain (though plans to extend the street through to the river Seine came to nothing).[16]

The wish to combine optimal traffic flow with visual perspective on major monuments, evident in the radial street networks around rail-way termini, was a more general feature of Haussmann's work. He was said to have nurtured a secret wish to knock down the church of Saint-Germain-l'Auxerrois so as to allow an uninterrupted vista between the Hôtel de Ville and the east front of the Louvre, but he realized that, as a Protestant, his authorization of the demolition of a church whose bell had in 1572 tolled the opening of the Massacre of Saint Bartholomew's Day would cause a major interdenominational incident. The most visually exuberant project to reach fruition was the appropriately star-shaped Place de l'Étoile (now Place Charles-de-Gaulle) on the outer western reaches, and already the conjunction of some five roads. These were now better aligned and in 1857 seven others were added to them, making the Arc de Triomphe the focus of a dazzling number of perspectives. The Place de la République – or Place du Château-d'Eau, as it then was – located on the cusp of the IIIe., Xe. and XIe. arrondissements, offered a more subdued example of the same phenomenon. The square itself was much enlarged, with the result that the number of popular theatres for which the neighbour-ing Boulevard du Temple was renowned was much reduced, and the square's legendary and raffish plebeian sociability attenuated. It now served as the focal point of a number of new roadways: the Boulevard Voltaire (then Boulevard Prince-Eugène), which linked in the south-east to the Place de la Nation (then still called Place du Trône: XIe., XIIe.); the Avenue de la République (the Avenue des Amandiers until 1879) connecting through to the workers' neighbourhood of Ménil-montant (XIe.); and an array of wide streets leading out towards the northern and eastern barriers.

The decision in 1861 to construct a new opera-house slightly to the north of the Boulevard des Capucines led to the creation of another major new radial *place* in the fashionable IXe. arrondissement. The building was not to be ready until the Third Republic, and the sur-rounding street reorganization spanned the two regimes too. Spoke-like around the new Place de l'Opéra (1862–4) were set new creations which included the Boulevard Haussmann, the Rue Auber (at first called Rue de Rouen), the Rue du Quatre-Septembre (initially called Rue du Dix-Décembre) and the Avenue de l'Opéra.

The desire to have every boulevard vista focusing on a monument became a little overdone and fetishistic. The architect Bailly, for example, was obliged to place the dome of the Tribunal de Commerce on the Île de la Cité askew of the structure so that it could open up a perfect sightline down the Boulevard Sébastopol. The Boulevard Henri-IV (IVe.), leading from the Bastille across the gardens of the old Célestins monastery, opened a wonderful vista on the Panthéon, and allowed a junction to be made with the Boulevard Saint-Germain. Yet this was only at the expense of arriving at the bank of the Seine at such an acute angle that two new bridges, the Ponts de Sully, had to be built obliquely across the river. By the same token, the Italo-Byzantine church of Saint-Augustin (VIIIe.) built by Baltard in the 1860s had to be constricted onto an awkward triangular plot, just so that it could provide a powerful point of view along the new Boulevard Males-herbes. Another example of this obsession with geometric precision was the shifting of the obelisk on the Place du Châtelet a matter of twelve metres in 1858 so that it could be in the exact centre of the remodelled square.

Slowly, a second circle of boulevards – often on the site of the old Farmers-General Wall, and stretching from the Étoile in the west to the Place de la Nation in the east – was coming to be added to the boulevards which Louis XIV had traced out on the old ramparts. This expansion gave room for liaison and infill. The Boulevard Malesherbes between the Madeleine and the Parc Monceau (by way of the Saint-Augustin church) (VIIIe.–XVIIe.) was one of the first Haussmannian creations not simply to carve swathes through established poor housing (in this case the rather sordid Petite Pologne neighbourhood) but also to open up space for new development. Indeed once Haussmann had sold off part of the Parc Monceau to the financier Émile Pereire for housing development, the neighbourhood became one of the swishest in the city, triggering a flight of big money from the Chaussée d'Antin. The latter's star was on the wane, anyway: much eighteenth-century luxury housing here had been demolished to make way for the Boulevard Haussmann and surrounding new streets.

Haussmann was given an even more expansive canvas on which to paint by the decision in 1859–60 to incorporate into Paris the full extent of the terrain up to the Thiers Wall established in the 1840s. This meant the addition of eleven communes in their entirety, plus thirteen portions of other communes (which were thus split in two by the new arrangements).[17] At a stroke Paris's surface area was more than doubled, and its population increased by nearly 50 per cent. The customs barrier was shifted out to the fortifications, though the Farmers-General Wall retained a vestigial significance in providing the rough boundary for the inner and outer ring of the twenty arrondissements into which Paris was – and remains – divided. Critics held that Haussmann had bitten off more than he could chew in making the 1859–60 addition. 'They have sewn rags onto the dress of a queen,' was the view of radical journalist Louis Lazare.[18] Yet the Prefect remained unabashed, certain that bringing in more individuals who used Parisian institutions would increase the city's potential tax-base and boost city income. On the same grounds he even considered extending the city's limits out to the frontier of the Seine department.

Some of the areas annexed in 1859–60 were villages with long traditions of independence, such as Auteuil, Passy and Vaugirard in the west, Montmartre in the north and Charonne in the east. Yet other ex-communes were far less developed, and their integration proved painful. A third of roads in the outer ring were unpaved, and all were of mediocre quality. Water supply was desperately short, drainage

Place de l'Opéra in 1889

poor, and policing almost non existent. A token of Haussmann's intentions was his construction of bridges so as to link these outer areas together: the Alma bridge (VIIe.–VIIIe.) was added in the west, and the Bercy and Pont National bridges (XIIe.–XIIIe.) in the east. A start was made on road-building along the perimeter trackway adjacent to the Thiers fortifications, and in 1851 a 'beltway railway' (the *chemin de fer de ceinture*) was opened at roughly the same distance out from the centre; from 1862 this carried goods as well as passengers. New radial roads were also begun with the aim of tying the periphery more closely to the centre: the Avenue Daumesnil (XIIe.) connected the Gare de Lyon to Vincennes, for example, from where the Rue des Pyrénées (XXe.) linked back northwards to Belleville. In the west the Avenue de l'Impératrice (present-day Avenue Foch: XVIe.) provided a majestic route from the Étoile out to the Bois de Boulogne.

These latter developments highlighted a further feature of the Haussmannian programme, namely the concern for green space. The notion that green space played the role of the lungs for the urban organism was one of the Emperor's hobby-horses, based on his love for and envy of London's parks. In 1852 he donated the Bois de Boulogne to the city, and in 1860 followed up with the gift of the Bois de Vincennes (both amenities had been state property hitherto). The municipal engineer Alphand was instructed to make English-style parks of both. In the Bois de Boulogne, for example, some 95 kilometres of pathways were laid out, endless flowerbeds were provided and two lakes dug. These two *extra muros* parks were at the apex of a complex hierarchy of green spaces. Within the bounds of the city, Napoleon modernized the Luxembourg and Tuileries gardens, developed the Parc Monceau, opened the park of Montsouris (XIIIe.: curiously and unpicturesquely divided by a railway line), and created the Buttes-Chaumont (XIXe.) on the site of the old medieval gibbet of Montfaucon. Over a score of city squares were created too, including the Square du Temple (IIIe.) and the Square de Saint-Jacques-de-la-Boucherie. Then there were boulevards and approach roads – in 1873 these were graced by over 100,000 trees. New churches also provided respite from the Haussmannian style. They tended to be more eclectic than the state's public building: Saint-Augustin on the Boulevard Malesherbes, as we have seen, combined modernist use of iron and steel with a neo-gothic finish. There were similar Romanesque, Gothic and Byzantine tendencies, often mixed up together, evident in the churches of Sainte-Clotilde, which the architect Théodore Ballu completed in 1857, of Saint-Ambroise (1869), in Joseph-August Vaudremer's Saint-Pierre-de-Montrouge (1868) and in the same architect's later church of Auteuil (1877) – as well as in the Russian Orthodox cathedral of Alexandre-Nevski (1861).[19]

Like his uncle Napoleon I, Napoleon III showed a particular concern with public buildings for food supply, and one of his earliest projects was the building of new pavilions in the city's central markets, the Halles. After a false start in design – 'I just want big umbrellas,' Napoleon admonished the architect Louis-Pierre Baltard when the latter showed him his plans[20] – Baltard devised an iron-frame pavilion blueprint for a thoroughly refurbished and modernized Halles. Haussmann also established a wide range of neighbourhood markets across Paris, invariably using the new iron-based architecture which Baltard popularized, such as the Carreau du Temple (IIIe.) in 1863, and the La Villette market (XIXe.) in 1868. From 1867 La Villette contained a massive municipal abattoir.

The provision of green space and concern for food supply formed part of a broader interest in public health. Hygiene was, as we have seen, one factor in the street-building which was central to Napoleon III's vision for the city, but it was Haussmann who took particular responsibility for the other infrastructural features of the programme of works. Most of what he achieved lay underground. Advised by his trusty assistants, the municipal engineers Alphand and Belgrand, that water supply was deficient for an expanding city, he restricted the river waters of the Seine and the Ourcq for public consumption, and for private usage brought in water – at enormous cost and by means of an impressive set of aqueducts – from other rivers in the Île-de-France. By the early 1870s Parisians were using ten times the amount of water which those in the 1850s had consumed, and around two-thirds of all private residences had running water. Around one-fifth at that time also enjoyed gas supply.

Waste disposal was an accompanying concern, its necessity highlighted by the cholera epidemics of 1832, 1848–9, 1853–4 and 1865. A gargantuan underground system of sewers was constructed, which harmoniously networked with the street pattern – 'my own idea', Haussmann was later proudly to proclaim.[21] The network ensured safe, efficient and hygienic waste disposal. Haussmann had doubled the mileage of Parisian streets. Striving to make of the city 'the imperial Rome of our times', he also quintupled the length of its sewers.[22] The Roman parallel clearly struck home: 'almost two thousand years had to pass,' reported a guidebook in 1867 of the sewer tours which were inaugurated in 1855, 'before such a trip was taken in Paris.'[23] The king of Portugal was the first guest of honour to make this tourist descent, which was thought entertaining yet anodine enough to attract women as well as men: 'the presence of lovely women can add charm to a sewer,' one North American visitor noted.[24]

Impressive achievements though these projects were, what was also very apparent was that the areas best served by them were those in which the rich lived. The one-third of homes without running water and the four-fifths without gas supply were disproportionately situated in poorer neighbourhoods, characterized by slum tenements, railway sidings, factories and warehouses rather than plush bourgeois apartments. Of twenty-four urban squares laid out by Napoleon, only two were situated in the eastern workers' suburbs to the east of the Canal Saint-Martin. In addition to the traditional east–west divide between poverty and wealth, a new configuration of need was emerging, which set the renovated central arrondissements against the more disinherited outer ones. In the Xe., XIe., XVIIIe., XIXe. and XXe. in the north-east, 40 per cent of houses in 1865 were adjudged to be in such bad shape that they were untaxable. In 1870 Louis Lazare dubbed these poorest arrondissements 'a veritable Siberia'. 'The capital has been turned into two cities, one rich and one poor,' noted another commentator, 'and with the latter encircling the other.'[25] It was these outer areas where dysentery, typhoid fever, diphtheria, whooping cough, smallpox and tuberculosis were most likely to be prevalent. This was not the avowed intention of Haussmann's sanitary programme, of course – but it made the Prefect's claims to be motivated by a generalized concern for public health seem hollow.

To a considerable degree the process of pushing industry out of the central neighbourhoods did form part of the Haussmannian project. 'There is no need,' the Prefect wrote to his master in 1857,

> for Paris, capital of France, metropolis of the civilized world, favourite destination for leisured travellers, to contain factories and workshops . . . Paris should be a centre of intellectual and artistic activity, the centre of the financial and commercial movements of the country at the same time as the seat of government.[26]

Changes in the city's food supply were an important consideration in this respect. The establishment of a national rail network allowed fruit, vegetables and wine to be despatched speedily to the capital from outlying areas, thus obviating the need for local sources of supply. The vestigial Parisian wine industry simply could not cope with competition from the *vin ordinaire* of the Midi. Pushed out of the centre of the city, industry would thus find its home on agricultural land whose *raison d'être* was now defunct. This would leave the central parts of the city increasingly devoted to the service sectors. In practice the deindustrialization of *le Vieux Paris* of the central neighbourhoods was never complete, especially at the workshop level. The rise in property prices at the centre did, however, squeeze out many of the poor and deterred immigrant labour from establishing itself here. The industrial face of Paris was moving to the outer arrondissements – and so was the working class. Some argued that wealth would in time trickle outwards to the poorer neighbourhoods and allow more harmonious developments. Others were less sanguine. 'The city of luxury,' Lazare warned, will be 'held back by the city of poverty.'[27]

Some 350,000 persons were displaced by Haussmannization. There was a 20 per cent reduction in the population of the classy Ie. and IIe. arrondissements between 1861 and 1901; the bourgeoisie wanted more elbow-room. Yet over the same period the population of the outer arrondissements, from the XIIIe. in the south-west clockwise through to the XVIIe. in the north-east, doubled. The critics of the regime saw this population displacement as a product of a deep-laid punitive logic at work in Haussmann's projects. 'What is called the embellishment of Paris is in essence merely a general system of defensive and offensive arming against riot, a warning shot against revolution,' fulminated the antiquarian topographer Victor Fournel, who reserved his choicest barbs for the Haussmannian boulevard whose design, he sneered, had 'all the subtlety and intelligence of a cannon-ball'.[28]

Evidently no smoking gun exists in the shape of an order of Napoleon III or Haussmann to build boulevards for military and repressive purposes. Nor would it be helpful to underestimate the variety of non-repressive motives which contributed towards the Haussmannization of Paris. Yet there seems little doubt that the wish to undermine Parisian popular militancy by a combination of social improvement and 'strategic embellishment'[29] did weigh on the minds of Haussmann and his collaborators. Popular radicalism was widely viewed as a kind of anti-social contagion like cholera or dysentery. Napoleon feared a replay of the June Days of 1848, or of the popular resistance which Paris had staged against his December coup of 1851, when crowds in the Faubourg du Temple had only been dispersed by repeated cavalry charges. Haussmann's vision of urban modern life was predicated on the eradication of popular resistance. 'He worked simultaneously', noted Fournel, 'against plague and against revolutions.'[30]

'It's the evisceration of old Paris,' Haussmann commented of his work of destruction in the working-class districts, 'of a neighbourhood of riots and barricades.'[31] Boulevards certainly made the deployment of barricades, the stock-in-trade of traditional Parisian radicalism, rather obsolete (they were already more of symbolic than military value, according to Friedrich Engels). The width of the boulevards allowed detachments of cavalry to be used effectively.[32] The levelling of the terrain also made cavalry manoeuvres more practicable, especially on side-roads, where hillocks (*monceaux*)[33] which had been familiar to the Merovingians were now flattened. The placement of boulevards also permitted the rapid deployment of police from the barracks which now studded the city: the garrison in the Rue Lobau (IVe.) behind the Hôtel de Ville, for example, offered the potential for armed support if the municipality was in trouble, while the Rue de Rivoli also allowed the Louvre and the Tuileries to be provided speedy military aid.

The strategic placement of major streets and boulevards was another form of social discipline, since this broke up swarming zones of militancy into discrete and more manageable chunks. The Boulevards Saint-Michel and Saint-Germain, for example, cut exemplary swathes through the Latin Quarter, one of Paris's traditional points of sedition, home to rebellious students from the twelfth to the twentieth centuries. Whether intentionally or not, Duret's statue of Saint Michael crushing a dragon underfoot which adorns Davioud's Fontaine Saint-Michel close to the Seine – 'a massive artistic abortion', in the view of one of Haussmann's critics[34] – recalled the post-Fronde statue of Louis XIV standing triumphantly over the forces of sedition.[35]

The story was much the same in the eastern neighbourhoods extending from the fringes of the Marais through the Faubourg Saint-Antoine up to Belleville, Ménilmontant and Charonne. The radial streets culminating in the Place de la République were strategically astute: the Avenue de la République, the Boulevards Voltaire and de Magenta and the Rue de Turbigo cut through poor and radical working-class areas, while a massive cavalry barracks was constructed on the Place in 1854, making it 'a dangerous spot for any subversive ideas which wandered that way'.[36] The containment strategy was complemented by the decision to pave over part of the Canal Saint-Martin, to form the Boulevard Richard-Lenoir (XIe.). During the June Days of 1848, rioters had taken refuge over on the east side of the canal knowing that government troops had limited access into the Faubourg Saint-Antoine; the paving project made the faubourg easier to control. 'In the past we mastered riots by rifle and cannon,' commented one imperial lackey in 1858. 'Today we use pick and trowel.'[37]

The Haussmannization of the Faubourg Saint-Marcel over in the XIIIe. was a similar combination of urban improvement and community mutilation. The Boulevard du Montparnasse was extended by the Boulevard du Port-Royal; the new Boulevard Arago was laid out; and the latter now met up with a reorganized Rue Mouffetard. Part of the latter was 'boulevardized' and became the Avenues des Gobelins and d'Italie. When this work was completed under the Third Republic, virtually nothing remained of one of the most ancient parts of the Parisian street-plan, on which traces of the independent moated medieval 'Bourg Saint-Marcel' had hitherto been observable.

Haussmannization offered these mutilated neighbourhoods an

impressive array of churches, schools, town halls, hospitals and other features of modern infrastructure – and no shortage of preachy progressive pedagogues: 'If the hammer of the demolishers has annihilated some vestiges of the past that one would have liked to preserve,' noted one writer in 1864, 'it destroys even more haunts of thieves and places of debauchery.'[38] Beneath the rhetoric, the demolition, dislocation and displacement involved in the Haussmanization process did great damage to the sense of community which had developed within many working-class neighbourhoods around the street corner, the square, the wineshop and the public laundry. The circumstances of the fall of the Second Empire and the establishment of the Third Republic would show that the Haussmannian logic had not, however, totally extinguished working-class radicalism. But the urban transformation of the Second Empire had, as it proved, changed its location and its character.

In January 1858, on his way to the opera, Napoleon III narrowly escaped a bomb attempt on his life by the Italian radical Orsini. Rather than becoming more repressive as a result of the incident, the emperor initiated a more liberal phase of his reign. A political opposition began to form which channelled much of its bile against the emperor's choice as Prefect of the Seine. Haussmann's imperious nature had crushed any thought that Parisians might have of influencing the transformation of their city. The liberalization of the Empire made his style seem increasingly anachronistic. The increase in the size of Paris due to the 1859–60 annexations involved considerable financial outlay, especially on infrastructure. Haussmann devised new financial instruments to get himself through, notably the *Caisse des Travaux de Paris*, a kind of privileged savings bank designed to attract loans. He was increasingly under pressure, however, and matters were worsened for him by the increase in the rates of interest at which he had to borrow. An air of cronyism and corruption increasingly hovered over the Prefect's head. There was concern too that his deficit financing might hobble the welfare of generations to come. Opposition politician Jules Ferry regaled the political elite with stories of the baron's '*Comptes fantastiques*'.[39] Ferry and his allies proved able to force him out of office – but just at the moment when the Second Empire was heading for its débâcle.

9.1: Felice Orsini

The fact that since the time of Clovis Paris has been both the capital of France and the frequent residence of its head of state has meant that the city has often been the theatre of acts of violence targeting kings, emperors, presidents and the like. The Orsini outrage on Napoleon III thus had a distinguished lineage – and was one of nearly ten attempts on the life of the Emperor.

Felice Orsini, a member of the Italian radical nationalist group the Carbonari, who regarded Napoleon III as standing in the way of Italian unification, threw three bombs at the emperor as he drew up outside the old Opéra building in the narrow and crowded Rue Le Peletier (IXe.). Napoleon was pretty shaken, but unscathed. The horses pulling his carriage were less lucky; they were blown up. Eight bystanders died and well over a hundred were wounded. Orsini ended up on the scaffold. Unusually for a would-be assassin, however, he seems to have had a positive impact on his target. Napoleon adjusted his foreign policy and in 1858 swung behind the cause of Italian unification. Orsini's act also accelerated Haussmann's plans to shift the opera-house to a new, less teeming and crowded site. When the present-day Opéra-Garnier was constructed, it would have a well-guarded private entrance for the emperor, so as to avoid a repetition of Orsini's action.

The Orsini affair is a reminder that Paris, mythically renowned for its barricades, rebellions, revolutions and days of militant action, has frequently been the site of individual as well as collective political violence. The successful ventures are better known, but they form only the tip of a considerable iceberg of individualized political violence, which continues to the present day, as witnessed by an attempt on the life of Parisian mayor Bertrand Delanoë in 2002.

The ideological dimension to political assassination seems to have become more prominent from the time of the Religious Wars in the sixteenth century, when doctrines of justifiable regicide and 'tyrannicide' were developed. Henry III fled Paris precisely in order to avoid being murdered by Parisians. Henry IV, having survived the Massacre of Saint Bartholomew's Day by the skin of his teeth, was also the target of more than a dozen attempts on his life (mostly outside his capital, in fact) before succumbing to the knife of Jean-François Ravaillac while stuck in a Paris traffic jam in 1610. Yet the line between ideologically motivated action and the work of loners bearing an individual grudge is difficult to draw. Jean-Louis Damiens, for example, who tried to stab Louis XV with a penknife on 6 January 1757, suffered revolting tortures in attempts to get him to confess to accomplices among the Jansenist movement. He disclosed only hints at such links. His main motivation seems to have been the exorcizing of personal demons – a not untypical pattern.

Yet assassination attempts have been most frequent in ideologically charged or politically troubled times. The assassination of Marat in his bath by Charlotte Corday in 1793, and covert attempts to dispose of Robespierre at the height of the Terror, for example, were manifestly ideological, as was the successful attempt by ultra-republican Louis Louvel to kill the duc de Berry, Louis XVIII's heir, in 1820. The same is true of the anarchist outrages around the turn of the twentieth century (whose most effective act was the assassination of President Sadi Carnot in Lyon in 1894). With the exceptions of the assassination of Socialist Jean Jaurès in 1914 and the murder of President Paul Doumer at the hands of a Russian anarchist in 1932, the early twentieth century was relatively free from this form of violence. But it re-emerged strongly from mid-century. There were numerous attempts on the life of de Gaulle during the troubled years of the Fifth Republic when the independence of Algeria was being settled. The final years of the twentieth century saw further outbreaks of such violence, though terrorists now showed less desire to target political leaders. The bomb which killed six and injured sixty-two persons at the Saint-Michel Métro station in 1995 had not been placed there to kill the president on his way to the opera, or anywhere else.

Political assassination aimed at major political figures has occurred outside Paris as well as inside, yet the punishment of malefactors has invariably taken place within the capital, so as to give the event maximum publicity. The execution of Damiens in the Place de Grève in front of the Hôtel de Ville in 1757, for example, was a veritable public spectacular. After walking from the steps of Notre-Dame clad only in a nightshirt and carrying a candle in penitence, Damiens was subjected to an exquisitely calculated series of pain-producing tortures, culminating in his literally being pulled apart by four horses. The scene was watched by tens of thousands. Rooms overlooking the square had been rented out to refined ladies and gentlemen anxious to secure a good view.

Damiens's execution exemplifies a Parisian appetite for public displays of punishment which has been intense, and has extended to non-political figures. The cases of Lacenaire in 1836, of Troppman in 1869, of members of the Bonnot gang and of the *apaches* involved in the Casque d'Or case before the First World War, of the Pappin sisters and of Weidmann in the 1930s are all examples of violent domestic, sometimes serial and usually passion-linked murders which excited disproportionate, media-fuelled public attention. Most of this group were executed in public. Public execution had been the norm under the Ancien Régime, but it received an added boost during the Terror. The guillotine was introduced from 1792 as a humane technology aimed at ending the kind of public death meted out to poor Damiens; but it soon transmuted into a gory and vindictive symbol. From the 1830s the place of execution was shifted from the centre to the margins of Paris. Orsini was executed outside the Roquette prison (XIe.), but in the 1850s the execution site was shifted to outside the Santé prison (XIVe.). From 1939, following scenes of lurid zeal for viewing the death of the mass murderer Eugène Weidmann, the decision was taken to perform all subsequent executions out of public sight. This did not stop ghoulish prison vigils on the days of execution – down to 1977, the last time the guillotine was used. The death penalty was abolished in 1981.

Napoleon was ill advised in 1870 to go to war with Bismarck's Prussia, which was spoiling for a fight. He had always been more popular in the provinces than the capital. Sections of the financial elite, the Catholic church and the rentier bourgeoisie within the capital supported him, but his authoritarian streak – evident in his crushing of worker opposition to his *coup d'état* of 10 December 1851 – had never gone down well in Paris. Even though in 1864 he legalized strikes for the first time since 1791, urban workers were hostile to his blandishments. Like his uncle, Napoleon III sponsored policies of public employment which brought Parisians jobs – but unlike under the First Empire, the cost was the loss of many workers' homes. The 1855 and 1867 Expositions had highlighted a policy of grandeur which played better with tourists than it did with many Parisians, who felt they would have to foot the bill. By the late 1860s, moreover, even the most solid citizens were anxious that Haussmann's magic wand was no longer working: the property boom seemed about to burst, rents were skyrocketing, and a housing crisis was on the horizon. In the elections of 1869 three-quarters of Parisian electors voted for opposition parties (as against 60 per cent nationally). Whereas 83 per cent of French men voted for the regime's liberalization in the plebiscite of May 1870, only 43 per cent bothered to do so in Paris.

Napoleon's continuing base of popularity in the country at large was to count for nothing at all when news of his surrender to the Prussians at the siege of Sedan on September 1871 reached Paris. 'There is the menacing roar of the crowd,' noted Edmond de Goncourt in his diary, 'in which stupefaction has begun to give way to anger. Then there are the great crowds moving along the boulevards, crying "Down with the Empire!" '[40] The Emperor's supporters were powerless to resist the call for a (Third) Republic, which was duly declared from the balcony of the Hôtel de Ville on 4 September.

The Second Empire fell with a whimper rather than a bang. The state of extreme agitation in which Paris found itself was intensified, moreover, by the arrival of the Prussians to invest the city. Some of the circumstances of the Prussian siege – the departure of Gambetta and other politicians by balloon, seeking aid from the provinces, for example, and the thriving pigeon-post – passed into popular memory. So did the bombardment of the southern parts of the city by Prussian guns, which caused a hundred deaths and damaged more than a thousand dwellings and some public buildings including the Luxembourg palace and the Panthéon. Famine conditions led to most mammals from the Vincennes zoo – along with any dog, cat or rat that could be found – being consumed by hungry Parisians. In January 1871 Edmond de Goncourt turned down the offer of elephant steak and camel kidneys from a vendor on the Champs-Élysées, and contented himself with recording his satisfaction at having snared a blackbird which he intended to eat for dinner.[41] In the same month the provisional government of the Third Republic surrendered, ending the resistance of the doomed city. King William II of Prussia had made himself emperor of Germany in the Hall of Mirrors of Louis XIV's Versailles palace. By March, triumphant German troops were marching in procession up the Champs-Élysées – an important symbolic gesture to perform before their return east.

The traumatic conditions in which the regime had ended triggered unforeseen resentments. A battalion of the National Guard up at Montmartre refused to hand over their weapons, triggering an attack on the provisional government headed by Thiers. The latter, highly unpopular because of the terms of the peace treaty which had ceded to Germany the provinces of Alsace and Lorraine, withdrew to Versailles, leaving the city in the hands of an even more provisional, ad hoc government, the Commune. This now staged a memorably brave if in the event short-lived and futile episode in urban radicalism, full of symbolic gestures. The Vendôme column first erected by Napoleon I was demolished, allegedly under the skilful eye of the painter Gustave Courbet. A second siege ensued, this time with the French regular army encircling Paris. In the 'Bloody Week' ('*semaine sanglante*') of 21–28 May, troops entered the city, initiating an orgy of end-game violence. 'Here a dead horse,' Edmond de Goncourt noted of his passage across the Tuileries gardens towards the end of that week, 'there, near the paving stones a half demolished barricade; soldiers' caps swimming in blood.'[42] At the end the rebels fell back towards Montmartre, Belleville and Ménilmontant, highlighting how the outer arrondissements now contained the cream of radical workers whom Haussmannization had displaced from the centre. In this sense the Commune had been 'the revenge of the expelled'.[43]

Rue de Rivoli, 24 May 1871

As the republican troops entered the city a wave of fires lit the skies. At least some of the fires were started accidentally, but a good deal of voluntary incendiarism is also strongly indicated. The targets were various: they included the Tuileries palace in which Napoleon had resided, and the Hôtel de Ville, centre of the municipal government. Both buildings were burnt to the ground, while incendiary violence also targeted other institutions symbolic of the regime such as the Préfecture de Police, the finance and foreign ministries and the city archives. Attempts to fire Notre-Dame cathedral and the Louvre palace just failed. Much blame was attached to women – the *pétroleuses* – alleged to be hurling petrol bombs to right and left in the doomed city (though the allegations were fuelled for the most part by sheer misogynistic panic). The regime which had lived by and for new building found its nemesis in an orgy of incendiary demolition. The fires of the Communards and the Communardes had replaced Haussmann's wrecking ball. They wreaked more damage on Paris than the city had experienced since the age of the Vikings.

Yet the rebels paid dearly for their opposition. The number killed in the events of the *semaine sanglante* bears powerful comparison with the death-toll in the Saint Bartholomew's Day Massacre of 1573 (2,000 dead), the Great Terror of 1793–4 (2,600 victims of the Revolutionary Tribunal) and the 1848 June Days (4,000 dead). No fewer than 20,000 individuals were killed in the course of the week. Many executions took place in the green spaces – the Parc Monceau, for example, and the Luxembourg gardens – on whose modernization Napoleon had so prided himself. Over 35,000 Parisians were arrested and subsequently some 10,000 were tried. Nearly 5,000 of them were deported to New Caledonia. When added to the number of workers who fled the repression, the number of individuals who absented themselves from the city following the Commune approached 100,000. Like those other historic traumas, 'Bloody Week' inscribed itself deeply onto Parisian memory. It thus tarnished at the outset the claims of the Third Republic to represent the whole nation.

Paris entered a period of fratricidal enmity: 'Half of the population would cheerfully strangle the other, which feels much the same,' noted the novelist Gustave Flaubert. 'It is clearly evident in the eyes of passers-by.'[44] The National Assembly voted a law calling for the

creation at Montmartre of a basilica of the Sacré-Coeur as if in expiation for the crimes of the Commune. The decision inflamed rather than cooled divisions – the Left would nurture an abiding hatred for the monument. They revered their own sites of memory, notably the 'Wall of the Fédérés' (*le Mur des Fédérés*) – the spot in the Père-Lachaise cemetery at which more than a thousand Communards who had been shot in the repression were buried.

9.2: The Mur des Fédérés

The Mur des Fédérés is the site of one of the most chilling and sickening acts of political violence in Paris's long (and in this domain) rich experience. It far eclipsed the Rue Transnonain incident of 1834. From March 1870 the Parisian National Guard had been formed into 'federations' and, once the Commune experience began, the term *fédéré* was used interchangeably with 'Communard' or 'supporter of the Commune'. On 28 May 1871, following a frenetic manhunt through the tombstones, 147 Communard rebels were shot in the Père-Lachaise cemetery against the south-east perimeter wall. The remains of nearly a thousand more Communards were brought here from killing spots within the city and dumped into grave-pits. After a period in which the simple enormity of the action was duly registered, the wall (*mur*) of the fédérés became a place of left-wing pilgrimage, as it remains.

To the Left the Mur des Fédérés represented the savagery to which bourgeois government was driven by fear of proletarian revolution, but it was also a heroic site commemorating the irreducible bravery of the working classes. At the end of the Paris Commune, the government stationed in Versailles had sent in the army to dislodge the rebel Paris Commune from power. As they moved out of the centre of the city, the Communards not only left a trail of incendiarism and destruction behind them; they also shot prisoners taken as hostages, including the archbishop of Paris, Monseigneur Darboy. There were atrocities on both sides, but in terms of numbers killed the government troops were far more brutal and ruthless: 20,000 deaths, many of them mass shootings as at the Père-Lachaise (plus even more arrests and imprisonments), as against about a thousand army casualties.

What gave piquancy to the Left's commemoration of the Communards at the Mur des Fédérés, was that it was they, rather than the Versailles troops, who were most severely attacked by writers and intellectuals – surprisingly few of whom had a good word to say for what one writer called 'this orgy of power, wine, women and blood known as the Commune'. Some argued it was provincial immigrants who had caused all the trouble, but others simply adapted the long-enduring myth of Paris as Babylon, from which only the worst could be expected. Part of this hostility derived from the fact that the Communards were responsible for one of the most savage mutilations of Parisian memory in the city's history. Although rebuilding made good in many cases, the fires of the Commune throughout the heart of the city targeted many of the most uncontentious *lieux de mémoire*.

The explosion of journalism which followed the repression of the Commune meant that the existence of the wall and the deaths of the fédérés were well known through photographs and engravings. But such was the demoralization of the Left following 1871 that the wall itself was rather neglected. Flowers were placed by relatives in the early 1870s, but it was not until later in the decade that much political interest was shown in the site. In the early 1880s there was something of a scandal when it was found that young men were using skulls trawled from the shallow graves around the wall to play an improvised version of *boules*. More organized political attendance became the rule in the 1880s, but it was under close surveillance. There was a series of scuffles with the police, and, to make matters worse, between different groupings of the Left which claimed inspiration from the Communards. However, the Left united to oppose plans by the municipality to sell off a plot of land in the cemetery including the Fédérés wall for housing development. By this time, a range of left-wing rituals was evolving around the commemoration: the wearing of a daisy in the buttonhole, the placing of roses at the foot of the wall, the laying of wreaths, the unfurling of red flags, political speeches, post-ceremony rallies, and so on.

Gradually, in the words of the Popular Front Prime Minister Léon Blum in 1936, 'the great day of mourning had become a day of celebration'. This was certainly the case after the election of the Popular Front in May 1936: on the 24th some 600,000 people marched through the streets of Paris and then filed past the Mur des Fédérés. The Communist Party took the lead in the act of commemoration – it could always turn out the largest numbers, especially after the Second World War, when the day of memory was extended to commemoration of French prisoners in Nazi camps. It was the Communists who provided five-sixths of the 60,000 individuals who attended the Mur on the hundredth anniversary of the Commune in 1971. On that occasion the ashes of the last surviving Communard, Adrien Lejeune, who had died of natural causes in the Soviet Union in 1942, were interred by the wall.

By this time, however, the ceremony had lost much of its pulling appeal. The decline of organized labour, the slow demise of the Communist Party, and the emergence of alternative forms of political commemoration probably all played a part in this. So did changes in weekend leisure of the Parisian working class. In some ways the decision of Socialist President François Mitterrand in 1983 to grant the Mur des Fédérés the status of classified historical monument marked the 'nationalization' of a site which had only ever been associated with one side of the political spectrum. One wonders whether this was almost a *coup de grâce* for a monument which no longer seems to excite a significant body of political memories.

The Commune had proved powerless to change the character of national politics. As the June Days of 1848 and the demonstrations against Napoleon in 1851–2 had already indicated, the times when France meekly followed Paris's political lead were over. With the

Second Empire out of the way, the new Third Republic and its voters were ill-disposed to afford Paris any grace. The city was maintained in a state of effective martial law until 1876. There was strict censorship, and a curfew was observed. The government only relocated from Versailles to Paris in 1879. In the post-imperial interregnum Paris had seized a chance to elect a mayor, a post filled first by the scientist Étienne Arago, then from November 1870 to June 1871 the centrist politician Jules Ferry. Following the Commune the city's right to have a mayor was withdrawn – indeed the city would not have one until 1977. Although there was an elected municipal council, it was still dominated by the Prefect, while the mayors of the twenty arrondissements were all appointed by the head of state.

Ironically the politicians of the Third Republic who only months before had hounded Haussmann out of office, embraced rather than rejected the Haussmannian legacy. It was as though Haussmann had so changed the syntax of urban improvement that it was henceforth difficult to speak another language – a point endorsed by the fact that several of the ex-Prefect's key associates continued in positions of responsibility within municipal service. It seemed important, the politician Jules Simon noted, 'that we should finish in freedom what was begun by despotism'.[45] Pressed to rebuild major sectors of the city following the Communard fires, the authorities went beyond a policy of mere replacement, and completed a number of the baron's projects. The construction of the Boulevards Saint-Germain and Henry-IV, for example, and the radial roads around the Place de la République – all pet projects of the Second Empire – were brought to fruition. So was Charles Garnier's Opéra building and the complex street system around it. The creation of the Avenue de l'Opéra involved destroying the Butte des Moulins – originally a medieval *extra muros* rubbish tip – and the whole project was only completed in 1876. The shell of the Opéra itself had served as a food store during the Paris siege. At its inauguration, perhaps as some kind of anti-imperial statement, Garnier was obliged to pay for his own seat in the opening concert.

The theme of continuity was also evident as regards the favoured building styles of Haussmannism. The erection of new, largely middle-class housing was integral to the street construction with which Haussmann's name is indissolubly linked. As part of his wish to optimize urban perspectives, the Prefect dusted off and, in 1859 and 1864, slightly updated the regulations regarding building heights and street widths issued under Louis XVI in 1783–4 (and themselves a continuation of previous best practice). This respect for tradition – so unlike Haussmann's general insouciance towards the historic[46] – gave an uncanny sense that the new Paris melded imperceptibly with many features of the old. The power which the Prefect had over granting permissions to build meant that he was able to force builders to observe some of the key features of the urban aesthetic developed over previous centuries in private as well as public initiatives. A sober and restrained classicism was encouraged throughout. There was the possibility of a shop on the ground floor and a small business on the entresol. Then there followed three (or, now, on major boulevards, four) further floors, plus roof space. Façades, including alignments and balconies, were kept flat and were harmonized, with decorative eclecticism kept to a minimum. The fact that much of the best building continued to be done using dressed limestone – now brought in by train from distant quarries, as supplies in the vicinity of Paris were running low – also added an important feature of continuity. A little more decorative variety crept in from the 1890s.[47] Greco-Roman decorative features, such as caryatids, were increasingly adopted, and Art Nouveau made its appearance. Yet in general more of this classic Haussmannian kind of building was constructed in the decades after 1870 than under the Second Empire. It still marks the urban landscape of Paris more profoundly than building of any other kind.

There was a good deal of standardization as regards the interiors as well as the exteriors of Haussmann-style buildings. Built speculatively rather than for individual clients, and aimed to be lived in by bourgeois tenants rather than proprietors, the Haussmannian apartment block minimized the idiosyncratic and maximized the standard. They were *immeubles de rapport* – buildings designed to turn a profit (*rapporter*). The garret (where the servants were put) and the ground floor might have other uses. But all the other floors tended to be built according to the same plan. The obligation of having a *concierge*, a kind of institutionalized eyes and ears (and nose) to guard against intruders and keep up standards among residents, led to the generalization of one of the most distinctive characters among the dramatis personae of modern Paris. The introduction of the lift from the 1880s meant that the most desirable storey was no longer the first or second – traditionally the level of the *piano nobile* – but could be at a more elevated height. Apartments were increasingly built to a new standard model which highlighted a separate entrance and staircase for servants and tradesmen; an ostentatiously decorative entrance-hall; functional rooms leading off from a spinal corridor; the best living and bedrooms enjoying a view to the front; and the gradual infiltration of the 'conveniences' of running water on all floors, gas lighting, boiler-driven central heating, and decent bathrooms and WCs. The philosopher Victor Cousin once indignantly claimed that in his view it was 'killing architecture to subject it to conveniences and comforts'.[48] But the architects and designers of the Third Republic paid him no heed. Conveniences and comforts were becoming a necessity for the middle-class tenants of Parisian apartment blocks.

Third Republic politicians thus warmly embraced the Second Empire politics of urban grandeur. Paris needed to be shown off to the rest of the world to best advantage. This entailed a good deal of patching up or hiding the damage done by the Communards, which took time. A decision was eventually made to demolish the damaged Tuileries palace, and the foreign ministry's offices at the Palais d'Orsay remained a charred ruin until the late 1890s. The Hôtel de Ville was not fully rebuilt until 1882 (in a much extended form, moreover, which gives it every appearance of a nineteenth-century late-gothic pastiche rather than a painstaking Renaissance restoration). Many Parisians had been dismayed at the extent to which their city had been a glorified building site for two decades under the Second Empire; but the building did not stop once the Second Empire had been toppled. Napoleon III had presided over the creation of more than a score of public gardens and squares; the Third Republic managed thirty-seven by 1911. More than three times as many buildings were erected between 1878 and 1888 as between 1860 and 1869.[49] The popularity of the Haussmann formula not merely in provincial cities but in other countries worldwide was establishing Paris as in some senses the paradigm of modern town-planning.

Symptomatically, Third Republic governments also continued Napoleon III's policy of using international exhibitions to showcase

PARIS: BIOGRAPHY OF A CITY

Paris as a world capital. Napoleon had been captivated by the Great Exhibition of 1851 in Crystal Palace, London, and determined to convert the more restrained tradition of French industrial fairs – which went back to François de Neufchâteau's inspiration in 1798[50] – into something altogether grander. The Expositions held in 1855 and 1867 were massive successes, confirming Paris's reputation as the city of light. Paris's share of France's foreign exports, for example, rose sharply in their wake. The 1855 Exposition, held largely on the Champs-Élysées, attracted some five million visitors, including legions of heads of states and other international dignitaries. The 1867 Exposition was even bigger: it occupied much of the Champ de Mars, and attracted seven million people. Not to be outshone, and ardently wishing to demonstrate the nation's recovery from the humiliations of 1870–71, the Third Republic ensured that the 1878 Exposition was even more extensive. It covered land from the Champ de Mars through to the Trocadéro on the Right Bank of the Seine, and along the Left Bank to the Invalides. The 1889 Exposition – forever memorable for the inauguration of the Eiffel tower – attracted no fewer than 32 million visitors, double that in 1878.

The Expositions celebrated the cult of technology and industrial production, both through the impressive iron architecture in which the exhibits were displayed, and the almost demonic energy of the machines and installations in place, which so impressed contemporaries: 'Four locomotives were guarding the hall of machines,' one visitor later recalled,

> like the sphinxes to be seen at the entrance to Egyptian temples. This hall was a land of iron and fire and water, the ears were deafened, the eyes dazzled . . . All was in motion. One saw wool refined, cloth twisted, yarn clipped, grain threshed, coal extracted, chocolate refined and on and on.[51]

The international character of the exhibitors gave a global feel to the show too: 'Jules Verne dreams of travelling around the world in eighty days,' the official guide to the 1889 Exposition pronounced; 'on the Champ de Mars, you can do it in six hours.'[52]

In some respects, however, the prime exhibit at this international event was something altogether more home-grown, namely Paris itself, now a Haussmannian landscape of power. The city which had been transformed almost beyond recognition proudly put itself on show in a way that none of its rivals could emulate. No other state invested so heavily in this kind of event or used the event so effectively to improve urban infrastructure. The tramway had been inaugurated for the 1855 show, and a *bateaux-mouches* service specially laid on in 1867. In 1878 the first experiments with electric street-lighting were initiated.

On the eve of the 1878 Exposition the Anglo-American man of letters Henry James, visiting Paris, marvelled at the 'amazing plasticity of France': despite the destructive violence of the Commune and its aftermath, 'Paris is today,' he reckoned, 'in outward aspect as radiant [and] as prosperous . . . as if her sky had never known a cloud.'[53] The international Expositions played an important role in the persistence of the notion of an eternal Paris, despite all its troubles, the resiliently radiant city of modernity – the 'focal point of civilization', as Victor Hugo put it, 'the microcosm of general history'.[54] The Italian visitor Edmondo De Amicis in 1878 also marvelled at the new cultural experience of being an individual in Haussmannian Paris, over-whelmed by sensations and almost drowned in the spectacular excess of the modern city:

> [One] thinks with amazement of those solitary, silent little cities from which we started, called Turin, Milan and Florence, where every one stands at the shop door and all seem to live like one great family. Yesterday we were rowing on a small lake, today we are sailing on the ocean.[55]

'Europe has gone off to view the merchandise,' the historian Ernest Renan commented drily on the 1855 Exposition, 'and to compare products and materials.'[56] Renan's asperity in fact highlights the increasing congruence between the Expositions and the experience of shopping. What impressed the crowds was not simply the display of technology and raw productive power, but also the way in which these seemed increasingly attuned to individual consumer needs and personal comforts. Thus the Singer sewing machine, photographs and domestic uses of electricity were among the biggest hits in 1855, as were the refrigerator, the typewriter, the telephone, the lift and an embryonic version of the phonograph in 1878. These were all objects soon on sale in Paris.

To some degree the dazzle produced by the Expositions was the extension of a phenomenon – albeit writ large, and mythic – which had more commonplace expression in emergent forms of retailing, notably through the department store. The *À la Belle Jardinière* and *La Samaritaine* stores were established on the Right Bank by the Pont Neuf in 1867 and 1870 respectively, the *Bon Marché* on the Left Bank on the Rue du Bac, on the site of a former leperhouse and VD hospital in 1883, while the *Galeries Lafayette* would be created on the Chaussée d'Antin in 1895. A much enlarged *Au Printemps* store (founded in 1862) would open on the Boulevard Haussmann in 1905. Based on the principles of high turnover and narrow profit margins, these multi-storey *grands magasins* held enormous and variegated stocks of consumer goods and set fixed prices. Their sales figures were boosted by the emergence of mail order catalogues which diffused the Parisian phenomenon throughout the land. Demand for goods to stock the shelves gave a tremendous fillip to local Parisian industry – always a staple provider in the semi-luxury sector. The craft economy of the older as well as the newer arrondissements was thus sucked into the frenetic sales cycles of the *grands magasins*.

The stores provided a new shopping experience, which put their predecessors, such as the arcades of the Restoration and July Monarchy, into a rather dingy shade. They framed that experience in a setting which combined the most modern technology – notably iron frame construction and plate-glass windows – with a decor worthy of the Arabian nights. Crowd phenomena such as window shopping, browsing, mingling with fellow shoppers and impulse-buying entered the lifestyle of a mass audience. These cathedrals of consumption, by parading the exotic trappings of luxury at a gamut of price levels, attracted all classes off the boulevards, 'from the duchess to the flirt and from the millionaire stockbroker to the beggar'.[57] They played on the consumerist fantasies of their customers – a strategy which novelists were sometimes found endorsing. Émile Zola's descriptions of a department store in his novel *Au Bonheur des Dames* ('The Ladies' Paradise': 1883), for example, were clearly modelled on the *Bon Marché*. They indulged the desires and fantasies of his readership, and produced a feedback effect in that within a couple of years the *Bon Marché* was modelling its displays on those described in the novel.

This intermingling of art and reality, illusion and truth, individual desire and collective fantasy, in everything relating to the spectacular representation of Paris, was increasingly intense as the nineteenth century wore on. 'With this magic title, *Paris*, a play or review or book is always assured of success,' noted the Romantic poet Théophile Gautier in 1856.[58] Eighteenth-century novels might have been set in the capital, but they had evinced little sense of place. By the end of the nineteenth century, in contrast, visitors and tourists frankly admitted that, so prepared had their imaginations been by literary engagement with the city's representations that it was sometimes difficult to experience Paris in the raw. As a result of best-selling novels and celebrated plays, the city seemed known in astonishing detail even by individuals who had never set foot in the place. This meant, as De Amicis noted in 1878, that 'one never sees Paris for the first time; one always sees it again'.[59] The list of topographico-literary associations in particular was endless: the Parisian underworld and the crime novels of Eugène Sue, for example; the aristocratic salons or the print culture of the Left Bank (and so much more!) in the prodigious output of Balzac; and the sewers and Hugo's *Les Misérables*. (How many tourists on the sewer tour were merely vicariously reliving Jean Valjean's odyssey in the latter novel?)

The novels of Zola – and particularly his Rougon-Macquart cycle published between 1871 and 1893 and based on the Second Empire period – offer a particularly striking example of this process of literary mythologization. For Zola's collected work offered a kind of parable of Second Empire Paris as a world in transformation – highlighted in wonderful evocations not only of the department store but also, as a sample, the worlds of the Halles, of high-class prostitution, of banking and finance, and of the absinthe-parlour. The novels also exemplified much of the febrile energy of the emergent Paris, its networks of meaning spun in endless cycles of circulation and exchange. In addition, they illustrated a theme which had been increasingly evident across the century, namely that the writer was a witness of historic significance not only in the metamorphosis of a city but also in understanding the meanings of modernity.

The role of *flâneur*, the sentient ambler around the streets of the post-Revolutionary, modern city, continued to play a significant role in perceptions of Paris. The *flâneur* was the individual immersed in the crowd, but not of it. 'For the perfect *flâneur*, for the passionate spectator,' noted the poet-*flâneur* Charles Baudelaire, 'it is an immense joy to set up home in the heart of the multitude, amid the ebb and flow of movement, in the midst of the fugitive.'[60] The *flâneur*'s anonymity allowed him to witness the pulsating street life of the expanding city, and he diffused his perceptions and sensations in novels, newspaper articles, literary guidebooks and urban physiologies – which in their diverse ways assisted the literary myths of Paris we have noted above.

What started as a literary phenomenon was, moreover, from the 1850s and 1860s finding an echo in the art world, notably in the work of Manet and the Impressionist painters as they groped uncertainly towards what Baudelaire championed as 'the painting of modern life'. This openly rejected the established convention of viewing history, religion and mythology as the substance of painting, and it advocated casting an unblinking eye over the impedimenta of industrial urban life. The poet Gautier postulated that 'a modern kind of beauty different from that of Classical Art could be achieved if we accept civilization as it is with its railways, steamboats, English scientific research, central heating and factory chimneys.'[61]

The group's attachment to the portrayal of the here and now caused it to fall foul of the art establishment, notably the annual Salon which secured artistic reputations and which was widely viewed as legitimizing artistic quality. Their emphasis both on a more exploratory stance as regards the representation of reality (particularly through light and colour) and on an extension of the parameters of acceptable content led to some famous artistic battles. Manet's painting *Olympia*, which was exhibited in 1863 and which showed a nude who owed less to idealized past depictions of the female form than to the world of contemporary prostitution, caused a major furore. The Salon was no kinder to others in Manet's circle, whose work was consistently rejected for display. The group responded by setting up a counter-Salon, the so-called 'Salon des Refusés', to exhibit their work. Eight shows were held between 1874 and 1886. At the first of them the group was given a name when a hostile critic attacked a canvas by Claude Monet as 'impressionist'.

As a group, the Impressionists – including, besides Manet and

Monet, Caillebotte, Cézanne, Degas, Morisot, Pissarro, Renoir and Sisley – focused a good deal of their painting on modern Paris, especially the parts in which the signs of the modern were most apparent. The surprisingly meagre range of painting of Paris which had preceded them had focused on urban monuments – the Pont Neuf, Notre-Dame cathedral, various churches, and so on. The Impressionists in contrast favoured life on the street. Their elective terrain tended to be the boulevards, the quais, the Bois de Boulogne and the better-off neighbourhoods in the north-west of the city. If they depicted a monument at all it was most likely to be a railway station, a café or a Haussmannian *immeuble de rapport* rather than a cathedral – locations in which the bourgeoisie felt comfortable and untroubled by political memory. In his painting *La Place de la Concorde* Degas portrayed a man out casually walking on the famous Parisian square. Yet the man's top hat conveniently hides from the viewer the allegorical statue of Strasbourg, lost to Germany in 1870 and since then perpetually clothed in mourning. The Impressionists' taste for the festive here and now had an element of political escapism about it.

When the Impressionists ventured outside Paris in the search for open-air locations, they invariably eschewed the wilderness or domesticated farming environments and portrayed the watering holes of the capital's bourgeoisie. Favoured spots included sites beyond (or not yet invaded by) industrial development such as Asnières, Argenteuil, Bougival, Chatou and Sèvres; or else seaside locations such as Deauville, which the railways had opened up to Parisian day-trippers and holiday-makers and where they could engage in bathing, boating, al-fresco dining, picnicking and the rest.

The myth of Paris as both the epitome of modernity and the filter through which one perceived the city could thus function in politically conservative ways. An American visitor to the city under the Second Empire had noted how a 'mask of gaiety . . . reconciles many a giddy noddle to the loss of the liberty cap'.[62] The dazzling effect caused by modern Paris was equally evident under the Third Republic. Yet as time went on, many *flâneurs* became more sanguine and reflective, and subordinated their sensations to a more astringent and critical intelligence. They fully accepted that a new spectacular city seemed to be emerging. But in the context of the dark days of 1848, 1851 and

1871 for the radical tradition, they noted how this also produced a sense of displacement and alienation within the inhabitants of the modern city. The work of Haussmann amplified this sensibility, for it showed that Parisians were unable to prevent the destruction of their own milieu. The disquiet and disenchantment that this bred was lyrically chronicled by Baudelaire. He was well aware that Paris was 'rich in poetic and wonderful subjects'.[63] Yet unlike those who preferred to luxuriate in the spectacular and consumerist excesses of Paris, he stepped off the tourist route of boulevards, department stores, public gardens and entertainment venues, and frequented the haunts of tramps, rag-pickers, street entertainers and déclassé intellectuals in the dark dives and grubby streets of the poorer neighbourhoods and in the untidily melancholic spaces of the faubourgs. He was thus aware of the degree to which Haussmann's modernity was a myth, superimposed over repression and destruction. Excited and attracted to the idea of the crowd, he also found the tastes of the new mass society not to his liking. He hungered after an older Paris which seemed tragically gone for ever: 'Old Paris is no more (the form of a city changes more swiftly, alas! than the human heart).'[64]

The more Paris was mythologized as the city of modernity, therefore, the more it nurtured a counter-myth of *le Vieux Paris*, an untidy but somehow authentic site, which had allegedly been much more to the human measure. The imposing Haussmannian environment dwarfed individuals, and made them seem functions of the urban organism, which controlled their every action. The average Parisian, claimed Maxime du Camp, was now a passive, contained and administered cipher, who was willy-nilly 'registered, catalogued, given a number, placed under surveillance, given light, cleaned up, led, cared for, given warnings, arrested, judged, imprisoned and buried'.[65] This dystopian, disenchanted vision highlighted the extent to which the name of Haussmann and the cause of modernity were becoming scapegoats for the processes of intense social and cultural change.

From the top of the Eiffel tower, installed in a paean of modernist praise for the 1889 Exposition, one could glimpse something of the continuing variety at the heart of the Haussmannian city. The vista took in not only the chic boulevards and department stores of the western neighbourhoods but also the factories and workers' dwellings of the outer arrondissements. It embraced a city which was – as the Exposition dramatically underlined – a centre for spectacular consumption, but which also continued to be a major focus of industrial and artisan production. Yet the Haussmannian boulevard was not all-conquering, even at the historic heart of the city on which the Prefect had lavished such attention. Though chopped up into smaller islets, *le Vieux Paris* was very much alive and well, a matter of metres off the Rue de Rivoli or the Boulevard Saint-Michel.

9.3: The Eiffel Tower

The Eiffel tower, which even money-grubbing America, we can be certain, would not want, is the dishonour of Paris. Everyone knows that, everyone says it, and everyone is profoundly upset – and we are only the weak echo of the universal public opinion, which is rightly alarmed. One has only to imagine a vertiginously ridiculous tower dominating Paris like a gigantic black factory chimney, crushing by its barbarous massiveness Notre-Dame, the Sainte-Chapelle, the Saint-Jacques tower, the Louvre, the dome of the Invalides, the Arc de Triomphe, etc.

The public petition from which this passage is taken was signed in 1887 by a starry cast of around fifty intellectuals including writers Alexandre Dumas, Leconte de Lisle and Guy de Maupassant, architect Charles Garnier, composers Gounod and Massenet, playwright Victorien Sardou and numerous architects. These avowed 'passionate lovers of beauty' put themselves forward as representatives of all who loved historic Paris yet despised the thought that it should be desecrated by 'the odious shadow of this hollowed-out column of sheet metal' on which building was just starting.

For a construction which was so comprehensively condemned by a substantial part of the literary and artistic intelligentsia before a single one of the 2.5 million rivets it would require had been hammered in place, the Eiffel tower has worn astonishingly well. Gustave Eiffel, the Burgundian engineer who was responsible for the tower's construction – though it was actually designed by his associates Nouguier and Koechlin – wrote a spirited reply, pleading a new kind of beauty for a construction which, he held, transcended rather than transgressed both artistic canons and historical precedent.

> Is it because of their artistic value that the Pyramids have so powerfully struck men's imaginations? . . . The Tower will be the highest edifice which men have ever built. So why should what is admirable in Egypt become hideous and ridiculous in Paris?

The tower has had its intractable haters: J. M. Huysmans, for example, attacked it as a 'hollowed-out candlestick', a 'solitary suppository, riddled with holes'. Yet Eiffel's contemporaries – and just about all of subsequent posterity – rallied to the tower's cause. It had two million visitors in the year of its construction for the 1889 Exposition, and distinguished guests who trudged up the 1,710 steps to the summit of the thousand-foot structure included the Prince of Wales, eight African kings, Thomas Edison, Sarah Bernhardt and Buffalo Bill. The *Au Printemps grand magasin* secured a marketing scoop (and launched an enduring tourist industry) by acquiring scrap metal left over from the site and converting it into miniature Eiffel tower mementoes. The tower's image saturated French society. By the turn of the twenty-first century, total visitor numbers were approaching 200 million.

Though Pissarro was famously anti, most painters rallied to it almost at once: Seurat as early as 1889, for example, and Douanier Rousseau and Signac in 1890, with Chagall, Delaunay, Utrillo, Dufy, Cocteau and a legion of others following in their train. So did poets. Guillaume Apollinaire, who served at the front in the First World War, composed a resistance poem against the Germans with typography set in such a way as to resemble the tower. Apollinaire's gesture highlighted a fact which was already very apparent, namely that the Eiffel tower was an unmatchable memento of the city of Paris. None of the prestigious *lieux de mémoire* with which Paris was filled could match this level of representativeness. Notre-Dame – which the tower also resembled in being the product of an army of highly skilled but wholly anonymous workers – ran it closest in this respect, although the cathedral's religious function put it beyond the pale for the serried ranks of Parisian anti-clericalists. Eiffel himself talked of his tower as a 'three-hundred metre flagpole', topped by the tricolore. The image of the Eiffel tower – from paintings and poems through to photographs, films and tawdry souvenirs – evoked Paris rather than France as a whole. Indeed, for most people it *meant* Paris.

The tower transcended artistic canons; it also transcended any notion of practical function. Purposes were eventually found for it: a wireless mast was erected in 1908, and one for television followed later, and the top also served as a military observation site. It has also been used as a giant advertising hoarding and as a meteorological station. But each of these mundane ends could have been achieved in other ways. For all intents and purposes the tower is sublimely useless. It is a supreme engineering achievement – but then so is Britain's Forth Bridge, which opened at around the same time and which at least took traffic from one side of an estuary to the other (though at greater human cost: around a hundred men died in its construction, while there was only one serious injury on Eiffel's building site).

A tourist location par excellence, the tower also transcends mundane notions of the touristic. As the tower's shrewdest commentator Roland Barthes noted, there is no inside into which the tourist penetrates: the tower is effectively contentless. In a way there is nothing to see in the tower – except Paris. The site which gives the most comprehensive panorama of the city is also an unavoidable skyline presence throughout Paris. No wonder Guy de Maupassant ate in the tower's restaurant: it was, he claimed, 'the only spot in Paris in which one doesn't see *it*'!

The tower's lack of utility has stimulated a compensatory quest to imbue it with meaning. Eiffel prided himself on having overcome considerable odds to construct what stood as a profound human achievement. The challenge of the tower has stimulated more idiosyncratic challenges. Individuals have sought to fly an aeroplane through its legs (1926, unsuccessful; 1945), to make a parachute descent (1912), to come down by bicycle (1923), to have a foot race to the top (1905), to climb using mountaineering techniques (rather than the lifts) (1954), a motorcycle (1983), a mountain bike (1987), and so on. Several of these attempts have ended tragically – and indeed the tower's death-toll, ranging from adventurers through to the rather different challenge of suicide, is around 350.

Early in the twentieth century the sculptor Raymond Duchamp-Villon called the tower 'a dream of super-human exaltation', and its lack of obvious utility has boosted this fantasy element. The tower has been compared to a firework, a derrick, a lightning conductor, an insect and much, much else. The fantasy has often taken an erotic turn. The tower's manifestly priapic dimension (highlighted by Cendrars, Aragon and the Surrealists) has in fact been mixed rather strangely with a sense, drawn out in a poem by Apollinaire, that it also stands like a shepherdess tending over its Parisian lambs (a comparison which in fact evokes the city's patron saint, Geneviève, who was sometimes represented tending sheep). Moreover, viewed from beneath – especially by poets – the tower's first level resembles a monstrous pelvic floor. This shows that the Eiffel tower transcends gender just as it transcends beauty, utility, history, vision and just about everything else.

Paris thus retained its ability to defy interpretation and to divide opinion. Dispute over the meanings of the city had become a debate over the nature of modernity, a debate in which non-Parisians the world over were free to participate. Disagreement over the nature of the present and the past also entailed a particular view of the future. As the turn of the century approached, it did indeed seem unclear what Paris's future held. From one angle Parisians were apparently entering an unparalleled period of contentment and pleasures. The generation after the First World War, who would attach the term *belle époque* precisely to this period, was clearly of this opinion. Yet conversely there were many who highlighted the tensions and the dark sides within the transformations under way. Some even feared an almost apocalyptic outcome: the future might be about endings not beginnings. The period of the *belle époque* was thus also that of the *fin de siècle*.

10

The Anxious Spectacle
1889–1918

The history of Paris as it approached the beginning of the twentieth century might be told as a tale of two exhibitions – the international Expositions of 1889 and 1900. Both were modelled on the style of 1855, 1867 and 1878; both were centred on the Champ de Mars; both yet again highlighted Paris as 'the City of Light' (and indeed both were illuminated by electric lighting); and both were brilliant successes. The 1889 Exposition attracted 32 million visitors – double the 1878 figure – while the 51 million who visited the 1900 show made it the most frequented international exhibition in the world until Osaka in Japan pipped it in 1970. The 1889 show had been timed to coincide with the centenary of the French Revolution, specially envisioned as the inaugural moment of the modern age, while the theme of the 1900 Exposition was 'Paris, Capital of the Civilized World'. Putative birthplace of democracy, then, and leading edge of modern civilization, Paris put its spectacular self on show in this two-edged period of *fin de siècle* and *belle époque*.

It took panache, certainly, to stage such massive shows, considering the troubled political and social atmosphere which had distinguished the Third Republic since its inception. Both Expositions sought to offer a unified image of a political regime which remained bitterly divided, and which had not entirely shaken off the Commune hang-over. For much of the 1870s the monarchist party had been on the point of regaining power, and the Republic looked fragile. Indeed in 1873 the regime was little more than a hair's breadth away from a royalist restoration. The Bourbon pretender the comte de Chambord, grandson of Charles X, who had lived in France only since 1871, even came to Versailles in order to seek the Assembly's ratification of his candidature. His stubborn refusal to abandon the white flag for the tricolore as national emblem sank his chances. The gesture revealed an Ultra sensibility which would probably not have lasted well anyway.

It was only in 1879 that government, its flirtation with monarchy over, moved back to Paris from Versailles where it had been since the dark days of the Commune. In the same year the first batch of released Communard prisoners was allowed to re-enter city precincts. (The authorities sneaked them into the Gare d'Orléans at 4 a.m., only to find some 40,000 workers arm in arm in comradely welcome.) In 1880 the fourteenth of July was inaugurated as a national holiday, demonstrating the Republic's progressive accommodation with its historic anti-monarchical legacy. In the mid- to late 1880s, however, this moment of relative calm in Parisian politics was overturned by a political shooting star, General Boulanger, a kind of intellectually challenged Napoleon. His call for constitutional revision and a war of revenge against the German empire won a good deal of electoral support among working- as well as middle-class Parisians. By 1891, however, the general had shot his bolt (and indeed himself, on his mistress's tomb),[1] but the 1890s would see the emergence of new sources of political instability. The high level of financial corruption in political circles engendered a series of scandals which alienated a substantial section of public opinion. There were sex scandals too, not least the death of President Félix Faure in mid-sexual congress with his mistress in 1899. Although in 1892 the pope urged French Catholics to support the republican regime, the latter was sometimes aggressively anti-clerical. There was still a good deal of clerical anti-republicanism too; the aristocratic Faubourg Saint-Germain, whose ranks were finely analysed by Marcel Proust, remained one of its hotspots.

The Third Republic's constitution had extended the vote to all adult males, and the regime consequently consecrated the emergence of what Léon Michel Gambetta, one of the heroes of the 1870 Prussian siege, called 'new social strata'. Yet this widening of the social base of French politics seemed only to stimulate new perceptions of entitlement – and new anxieties about where mass politics might lead. On the Left a Socialist movement had begun to emerge from the ashes of the Commune, and by the middle of the 1890s had established a

parliamentary presence. In addition the pacifist wing of the Socialist movement maintained a critique of the colonial expansionism to which the Third Republic had become committed. Working-class political engagement was growing apace. On 1 May 1890 more than 100,000 workers celebrated the first Labour Day in Paris – in contravention of the law. In 1895, the *Confédération générale du travail* (CGT) was formed: it would grow into France's most powerful trade union confederation and was at once involved in agitation for an eight-hour working day. In addition the most militant section of left-wing groups launched a campaign of anarchist violence in the wake of the Boulanger episode. A number of Parisian hotels, restaurants, magistrates' homes and other sites were targeted, and deaths ensued. This kind of wild politics drew routine condemnation – but also surprising levels of support among working-class activists and the artistic and literary avant-garde.

If politics and class divided the regime, so did gender. A growing feminist lobby called for measures to extend social and political rights to women. In 1897 Marguerite Durand established the first feminist daily newspaper, with the provocatively Parisian title *La Fronde*. Durand was a shrewd critic of the highly patriarchal situation in which French women found themselves in the nineteenth century, condemned to be confined either to the kitchen or the bedroom. Although achievements in regard to women's educational entitlement, career opportunities, legal equality, control over property and rights to divorce were solid rather than outstanding, the feminist movement had a cultural impact which transcended its political muscle, particularly in Paris, where much of their activity was centred.

Tensions at the heart of politics over mass politics and women's rights were given a new ethnic and political focus in the mid-1890s by the Dreyfus Affair. The wrongful imprisonment of the Alsatian Jew and army officer Alfred Dreyfus in 1895 for alleged spying for the Germans split the political nation into two antagonistic groupings. The Dreyfusard cause was championed by the League of the Rights of Man, and expressed with clarity in novelist Émile Zola's famous article 'J'accuse' ('I accuse'). The article, which appeared in Radical politician Georges Clemenceau's *L'Aurore* newspaper in 1898, triggered a major outcry including street disturbances in Paris and other cities and it obliged Zola to take temporary refuge in England. 'J'accuse' pilloried the anti-Dreyfusard movement in the army, the Catholic church and the political establishment, as well as the hatefully anti-Semitic elements which had been drawn into the matter. In 1899 Dreyfus received a provisional pardon and this temporarily took some heat out of the dispute. Certain enmities caused by it would, however, be long lasting. Erstwhile Impressionist comrades-in-arms Degas and Pissarro never spoke to each other again because of their disagreements over Dreyfus; the anti-Dreyfusard Degas sacked his (Protestant and Dreyfusard) artist's model in pique too. The Affair would not be brought to a close until 1906, when Dreyfus received a full pardon and was reinstated within the army.

Paris seemed to take a good deal of political turbulence in its stride. During a session of the Chamber of Deputies in 1893, a bomb was thrown at the session chairman. He ducked, and the bomb demolished the wall behind his seat. He then re-emerged from beneath the podium to announce with studied sangfroid, '*La séance continue . . .*', for all the world as if he was a character from an Edmond Rostand play (and indeed the playwright's *Cyrano de Bergerac* would be one of the hits of boulevard theatre on the eve of the 1900 Exposition). Such business-as-usual nonchalance overlay a core of anxiety at the heart of the regime.

The 1889 and 1900 Expositions sought to salve the political wounds of the embattled but resilient Third Republic, and present the best possible picture of a France unified around notions of progress and modernity. Behind these international and universalist claims and the commercial success of the two ventures, however, lay ongoing debates over the future of the regime, the nature of modernity and the character of the city of Paris.

The organizer of the 1889 Exposition was Baron Haussmann's erstwhile collaborator Alphand, and it was saturated in Haussmann-ian values. Its highpoint, the Eiffel tower, was a spectacular hymn to science and progress which the whole Exposition had been designed to epitomize. Iron-frame buildings had been becoming more numerous in Paris since the Second Empire, but this thousand-foot structure surpassed any other modern building. It was all the more impressive when linked with the massive iron-and-glass *Galerie des Machines* at

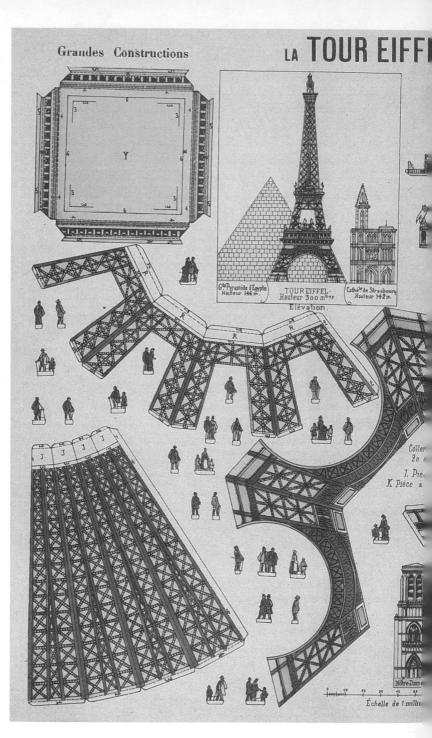

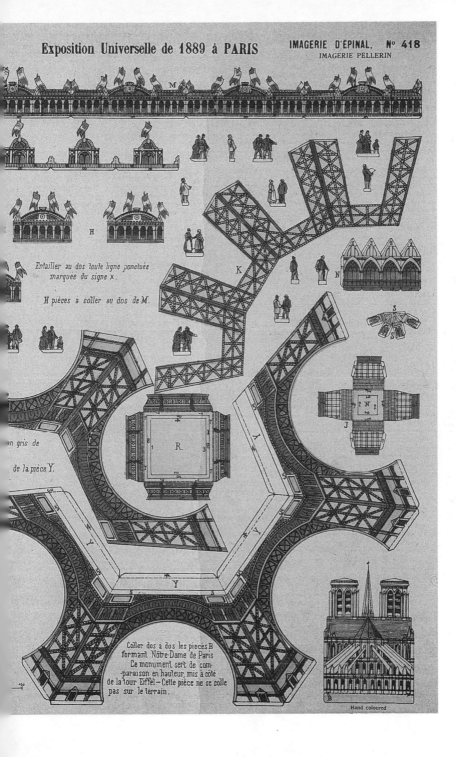

Exposition Universelle de 1889 à PARIS

IMAGERIE D'ÉPINAL,   N° 418
IMAGERIE PELLERIN

M

H

Entailler au dos toute ligne ponctuée
marquée du signe ×.

H pièces à coller au dos de M.

K

N

n gris de

de la pièce Y.

R

J

Y

Y

Y

Coller dos à dos les pièces B
formant Nôtre-Dame de Paris
Ce monument sert de com-
paraison en hauteur, mis à côté
de la Tour Eiffel.—Cette pièce ne se colle
pas sur le terrain.

Hand coloured

its foot, which boasted the largest building span in the world, and in which many of the exhibits were housed. Édouard Lockroy, the chairman of the Exposition Committee, organized an exhibition around the tower's construction which patriotically stressed the conceptual audacity of Eiffel's project, its status as a feat of advanced engineering, and the teamwork required to erect it on schedule. He compared it with Diderot's *Encyclopédie* as a collective work which was based on intellectual rigour, valued manual labour, mobilized energies and served a pedagogic function for society at large. Such objectives chimed harmoniously with the Third Republic's patriotic fervour and its self-assigned 'civilizing mission' in the colonies.

10.1: Alphand

Jean-Charles-Adolphe Alphand (1817–92) was, so the president of the Conseil général of the Department of the Seine proclaimed at Alphand's funeral at Père-Lachaise in 1892, 'the wizard-like organizer of all the great national and Parisian festivities, the magnificent decorator of our Expositions [and] the creator of promenades, squares and avenues'. This was a fitting eulogy for a major (if, since his death, relatively little-known) figure who combined the roles of 'engineer, architect, financier and administrator', and whose 'passionate love of Paris' was warmly saluted by other distinguished speech-givers.

So large a shadow has Baron Haussmann cast over the history of nineteeenth-century Paris that the role of his associates has been neglected. Yet one of Haussmann's most effective administrative gifts was his knack for choosing hard-working and effective agents for the work in hand. The vast sewer network which lay beneath 'Haussmannized' Paris was very much due to the hard graft of Eugène Belgrand, whom Haussmann appointed in 1854 as Director of Paris Water Services. By 1867, when the first tourist visits to the sewers were organized during the Exposition of that year, Belgrand had presided over the five-fold expansion of underground passages, and revolutionized the supply and disposal of the capital's water system. Another

Haussmannian nominee, the architect Gabriel Davioud, attended to the landscaping of the new streets, and in particular was in charge of the design and provision of street furniture (lamp-posts, urinals, park-benches and so on). Jacques Hittorff was Haussmann's favoured architect for redesigning major urban squares, such as the Étoile and the Place Saint-Michel, while the gardener Barillet-Deschamps had the considerable responsibility of the city's nurseries: he replanted Paris. These individuals may have initially followed Haussmann's orders. Yet such was the extent of their responsibilities that they worked independently. Indeed they had to, for although Haussmann left the prefect's position in 1870, they continued in post, Belgrand to 1878, for example, and Alphand to his death in 1892 – one year after that of his master, Haussmann.

Alphand was probably the most important of all the baron's associates: Haussmann called him his 'right-hand man'. His particular role was the development of green space which was one of Napoleon III's most cherished parts of the Haussmannian programme. But he extended his influence across all public works (especially after 1871), and also was master impresario for the international Expositions up to 1889. His gift for management made the latter in particular a massive international success. It was Alphand who selected Eiffel's design for an iron tower three hundred metres high, out of a field of seven hundred.

This great Parisian was, characteristically, a provincial. Born in Grenoble, he (like Belgrand) was trained in the École des Ponts et Chaussées in Paris. He served as a civil engineer down in Bordeaux, where he encountered Haussmann, who was prefect of the Gironde from 1850 to 1853. Haussmann called him to Paris in 1854 to serve as Engineer in Chief of Promenades and Plantations – a post which he retained for thirty-seven years, and to which he added a series of further appointments. The position of Director of Paris Public Works created for him under the Third Republic in 1871 gave him control over highways, promenades, cartography and architecture. After Belgrand's death in 1878 he also took over Water and Sewerage. As if this was not enough, he also played a major planning role in the department of the Seine outside Paris limits.

Alphand's role in consolidating and extending the achievement of Haussmann for more than two decades after Haussmann's dismissal is probably his most considerable achievement. Yet it is run close by his imaginative and creative work on Parisian green space. He rethought and reworked the whole hierarchy of the city's parks, from the Bois de Boulogne and the Bois de Vincennes, through major inner-city parks like the Buttes-Chaumont, the Parc Monceau and the Parc Montsouris down to the dozens of small neighbourhood squares now sprinkled across Paris. While Haussmannism revolved around the straight road and the direct perspective, Alphand's work on green space followed a different artistic course. In the Bois de Boulogne, in fact, he actually eradicated the straight 'Haussmannian' forest roads inherited from Louis XIV and replaced them with curvaceous pathways which highlighted the park's many picturesque features. A great deal of what remains charming if somewhat bizarre about Paris parks – the cascade of Longchamps in the Bois de Boulogne and its grottoes, the iron protectors around the base of thousands of trees, the artificial stalagmites and stalactites out at the Buttes-Chaumont, the Greek temple atop the hill dominating the latter park, the vegetal fencing made out of concrete that he liked to put in the major parks – was originated by him.

Characteristically, just as Belgrand produced a master-work explaining his own achievement as regards water supply, Alphand wrote a book on the *Promenades de Paris*. It was not simply an explanation of all he had done in this regard, but also an erudite account of garden history back to Antiquity, in which he sought to delineate in what ways his own work marked a new stage in urban green space. Yet Alphand's true monument lies elsewhere: one has only to enter a Parisian park and look around.

One may question whether all the visitors to the 1889 Exposition shared this lofty civic vision. Even Lockroy himself was rather disappointed by the ambience of the Eiffel tower show which he claimed (surely with some exaggeration) more resembled the Folies-Bergère rather than the republican classroom. If the vaunting of science and progress had been undercut by the air of frivolity, mass spectacle and sheer entertainment in the 1889 show, this was even more the case eleven years later. The 1900 Exposition eschewed the somewhat fussy and cerebral pedagogic style and the infatuation with useful science which had characterized its predecessor. It chose to emphasize the pleasures of the senses, and to encourage visitors to think of themselves more as consumers than as citizens. The decorative and the feminine now took precedence over Eiffel-style engineering functionality and virility. Even so, there were still a great many scientific displays and competitions. The French made much of their continuing scientific excellence as a source of national strength: the names of Louis Pasteur, Claude Bernard and the Curies were ceaselessly celebrated in the exhibition literature. But the big science and technology prizes were taken home by the Germans. That France's fiercest international opponent triumphed in this way was a cause of concern. Were the French becoming soft? This was a question to which the emergence of feminism gave added pertinence. Significantly, two of the most remarked-upon pavilions on the Champ de Mars proved to be the Pavilion of the Decorative Arts and the Palace of Woman. The Palace of Fashion was the second-most-visited exhibit in the whole show. (Its 1.3 million attendance was surpassed only by the 2.1 million who swarmed to the Swiss village exhibit, with its live cows, *trompe-l'oeil* mountain vistas and yodelling demonstrations.) Moreover, the focal point of the entrance to the Exposition was *la Parisienne* – a five-metre-high effigy of a woman sporting the most up-to-date creations of Paris *haute couture*. What contemporaries called the 'supple and vital'[2] contours of this fashion model contrasted with the taut rigidity of the Eiffel tower, which was already looking quaintly archaic.

It was less that the arts prevailed over the sciences in the 1900 Exposition, or that style triumphed over substance; rather, the show seemed to demonstrate that style – a rather feminized, decorative style at that – *was* the substance which made Paris so distinctive, so radiant, so up-to-date, so modern. The Exposition put the spotlight on the city as the home of the modernist good life, a heady consumerist mix including bright fabrics, *haute couture* (yet also ready-made clothing), patterned wallpapers, bicycles, cameras, light-bulbs, sewing machines and sundry home comforts available through the *grands magasins*. Industry now bent the knee to culture: on the southern flank of the Champs-Élysées, the Palace of Industry from the 1855 Exposition was demolished to make way for two massive exhibition halls – the Grand Palais and the Petit Palais – which housed fine-art displays. Even the technological achievements of the Exposition were dolled up. The iron frame of the *Galerie des Machines* was clad in stone and stucco with elegant grottoes and ornamental fountains. There was a similar rococo and neo-baroque encasement to the iron frames of both the Grand and the Petit Palais and to the newly constructed Pont Alexandre-III, the most gloriously exuberant of all Parisian bridges, linking the Champs-Élysées to the Invalides.

Despite being devoted to the ephemeral and the fashionable, the 1900 Exposition had a more durable impact on the material environment of Paris than its 1889 predecessor.[3] Many of the built features in the 1900 Exposition, so openly oriented around leisure and pleasure, remained in place and made a lasting contribution to Parisian infrastructure. Improvements in mass communication designed to handle the huge crowds expected were a particular and enduring feature of the 1900 Exposition. These far surpassed earlier innovations in this domain – including even the moving walkway introduced at the 1889 Exposition. Vehicular transport had dramatically increased over the 1890s, so special efforts were required to ensure Paris did not become clogged with traffic. The Pont Alexandre-III – named after the Russian Tsar who was one of the many crowned heads to attend and with whom France had recently signed a defensive alliance – was built. The Gare de Lyon was expanded and given its distinctive campanile tower. A new station, the Gare d'Orsay, was opened on the Left Bank of the Seine and linked to the Gare d'Austerlitz to the east. (Closed to traffic on the eve of the Second World War, the building would reopen in 1986 as the Musée d'Orsay, one of the Fifth Republic's *grands projets*.)[4] Yet without doubt the biggest impact on the city's future was provided by the creation of the Parisian metropolitan railway – the Métro, Paris's most successful venture ever in public transport for the dawning mass age.

Utopian dreamers had been juggling with the idea of an underground railway in Paris for more than half a century. Yet while Paris dithered, the rest of the world raced ahead: London had its Underground by the 1860s, New York its Subway from 1872. In Paris, in contrast, an air of intractability hung over the whole idea of *le Métropolitain*. Financially there was the question of how costs might be allocated between state, municipality and private enterprise. Technically there was the problem over whether the system should be powered by electricity (whose energy efficiency seemed problematic) or by steam (but would customers suffocate?). Aesthetically it needed to be determined whether rails should go above ground (if so, what sort of wreckage would be done to Paris's famous skyline?) or below (but would the system be watertight?). It needed the stimulus of the 1900 Exposition to act as a spur to action. Planning at last started in earnest from 1895, and work began in 1898. With some exceptions – mostly along the line of the old Farmers-General Wall, where the aerial option was taken – the Métro was situated underground. Electric traction was used. Metro Line One was inaugurated in July 1900: running from Vincennes to Porte Maillot, it included convenient stops along the Champs-Élysées for fair-goers. The new service proved a brilliant and lasting success. Seventeen million journeys were made on it from July to December 1900, and the following year numbers were up to 55 million. New lines were swiftly opened. By 1914, usage had risen tenfold with nearly 500 million passenger journeys.

The Eiffel tower, the most striking technological achievement of the 1889 Exposition, makes its presence felt throughout the capital, but utility is hardly its strong point. The startling prominence of the tower contrasts with the Métro, the most significant technological achievement of the 1900 Exposition. All that was visible of the Métro were the station entrances whose design, following a requisite level of political infighting, was awarded to Hector Guimard, champion of the *style moderne*, or, as it was known, *art nouveau*. The curvaceous, serpentine and vegetal lines of Guimard's street sculptures (which, following a period of neglect, were finally classified as historical monuments in 1965) seemed almost a mockery of Haussmannian geometrics and the technological modernism of the Eiffel tower. Yet despite being both underground and out of sight, the Métro evoked by Guimard's sculptures had a social and urban utility for Parisians which the Eiffel tower could not match.

The Métro's principal contribution was towards the better integration of the local economy. The 1870s and 1880s had seen a national economic downturn, whose impact on the capital was aggravated by the disruption that Haussmannization – and also the Commune – caused traditional patterns of employment. From the 1890s, however, Paris's economy recovered strongly. The kind of consumerism championed at the 1900 Exposition was a straw in the wind in this respect. The years before the outbreak of the Great War in 1914 saw a transformation in habits of consumption, not merely among the social elite but also among many of the now-enfranchised 'new social strata' across the nation. Bread and wine consumption rose steadily, while that of tea and coffee tripled and that of alcohol rose by two-thirds (though absinthe production rose tenfold). Consumer durables showed a similarly dynamic pattern. Paris's orientation around leisure and pleasure put it in the forefront of this transformation. Around 1900 the *Bon Marché* department-store began to stock kitchenware, cosmetics, photographic equipment and musical instruments – all signs that its clients had more to spend. The store had an art gallery too, where Parisians could if they wished purchase cheap imitations of Impressionist paintings.

By 1900 a new and resilient geography of production was emerging in Paris and its environs. With rents skyrocketing in the central areas subject to Haussmannian improvements, much long-indigenous manufacturing was bankrupted, or else moved out towards or beyond the urban periphery. Government legislation on the location of noxious trades endorsed this shift. So did the tendency to relocate public institutions and key infrastructure such as asylums, hospitals, warehouses, racetracks and sports facilities (plus airports in the fullness of time) away from the central neighbourhoods.

By the start of the new century three main poles of industrial activity had emerged within Paris's twenty arrondissements: the north-east, around the Canal Saint-Denis and La Villette basin (XVIIIe.–XIXe.); the south-west around Javel and Grenelle in the XVe.; and the south-east in the XIIe. and XIIIe. (Picpus, Charonne, Bercy). Even more significant, however, was the strength of industrial development outside the old Thiers fortifications. The number of businesses within Paris fell from 76,000 to 60,000 between 1872 and 1896, while those in the adjacent area – the *banlieue* – rose from 11,000 to 13,000. If most large-scale industry had migrated outwards, it was followed not only by smaller enterprises but also by large numbers of workers. Population was growing faster in the outer than in the inner arrondissements, but it expanded fastest of all in the *banlieue*. The population of this para-urban 'crown' tripled between 1860 and 1914. From 1851 until the eve of the First World War, growth was particularly spectacular in localities with major factories within them: Saint-Denis grew from 15,700 to 71,800, Asnières from 1,200 to 42,600, Boulogne-Billancourt from 7,600 to 57,000 and Ivry from 7,056 to 38,307.

Paris had lost its position as the largest city in the world to London in the eighteenth century, and by 1900 it was being surpassed by New York too, with Berlin, Vienna and Saint Petersburg also catching up fast. The birth-rate, traditionally low in Paris, was becoming lower still as a result of the diffusion of birth-control techniques. (Intra-uterine devices and condoms – vulcanized rubber being one of the star achievements of this phase of industrialization – were becoming as much a part of modern life as telephones, bicycles and decent home plumbing.) What was also noticeable was that the French capital's demographic dynamism was increasingly dependent on its periphery and environs rather than its historic core. This would remain the case during and after the First World War. The *banlieue* represented some 13 per cent of the total Parisian conurbation in 1861; in 1901 it was 26 per cent and rising. The majority of the growth came from new migrants, largely unskilled workers from the northern and central departments. There was also a good admixture of foreigners, including a large Jewish influx from eastern Europe. Foreigners made up around 6 per cent of the region's population in 1890 – a much higher proportion than was the case for any other major capital city.

The word 'suburb', with its Anglo-American connotations of leafy retreats and individual or semi-detached dwellings, does scant justice to the French term *banlieue*.[5] From the middle of the nineteenth century, British, American and other European middle classes relocated their residences away from city centres, which they viewed as dirty, polluted and overcrowded. In France, in contrast, Haussmann had cleaned up much of the centre of Paris in ways which made the middle classes happy to remain there. There was thus no need for suburban retreats. While the outer arrondissements and the *banlieue* were thus being invaded by industrial production, the heart of the city was primed to become a showcase for consumption. Of course the bourgeoisie did not have everything their own way within the bounds of the city. Their presence created tensions over urban entitlement with workers and marginals still located within the city. More than half of Paris's population as a whole was still working-class, and the figure was higher than this in the outer arrondissements. Though the city contained around a quarter of the national wealth, over half of those who died within the city were buried in paupers' graves. Class tensions were even more acute in the *banlieue*, and created a massive fissure within the wider urban community.

The largely unskilled workforce to be found in the *banlieue* was the basis of a major transformation taking place in the region's industrial profile. Traditionally, Parisian manufacturing had been primarily targeted at the consumer market, and textiles had been its leading sector. Textiles still involved 11 per cent of the workforce in 1847; by 1860 it was 3 per cent and still falling. The iron and chemical industries started growing at a great pace, pitching their wares less at Parisian consumers than at the national market. Businesses employing 500 workers or more were three times more numerous in the *banlieue*. The region's river and canal network helped in this remodelling of Parisian industry, but the railways were the most important influence. To the *chemin de fer de ceinture* circle line within the Thiers fortifications – the so-called *petite ceinture* – was added in 1875 an outer or *grande ceinture* linking all the industrial suburbs. This allowed industry to profit all the more from the Parisian focus of national transport systems.

Workers in the large-scale industry concentrated in the peripheral belt were increasingly subjected to the processes of the 'Second Industrial Revolution', namely the creation of a proletariat through deskilling and forcible involvement in mechanized production. This was particularly the case with the economic spurt from 1900 onwards caused by the development of the automobile industry. There were some 600 car-building businesses in the region at the turn of the century, with particularly significant centres at Javel in the XVe. arrondissement as well as at Boulogne-Billancourt in the western *banlieue*. The workforce in both places was increasingly subjected to mechanized production. The automobile industry was only one of a range of new industries emerging in the region at this time, such as aircraft production, machine tools, electrical goods and cinema. Five of France's seven film studios were located in the Paris region.

The workforce remaining in Paris had mixed fortunes. Many traditional craft industries prospered. There would still be far more shoemakers and tailors than car-workers in the region in 1914. Moreover, the skilled workers still numerous within the city constituted an important pool of labour for subcontracting work by the heavy industry of the *banlieue*, especially before automated production methods took hold. Indeed, one attraction of the *banlieue* for many industrialists was precisely its adjacency to an important reservoir of skilled workers. The kind of high-skill, high-quality handicrafts for which Paris had always had an excellent reputation could still thrive. Below the elite level, however, businesses often had to gear themselves for the mass market by subdividing tasks and streamlining production methods. With much of the clothing and furniture trades, this invariably meant increasing the number of workers labouring in sweated conditions in small workshops.

Two other developments complicated labour patterns within the city. The first was the accelerating shift from industry towards the tertiary (services) sector, and in particular towards white-collar occupations. In the wake of the Second Empire, Paris had developed into a major centre for financial services, and the number of clerical employees working for banks, the post office, insurance companies and the railways rose by a factor of three by 1914. The tertiary sector of the Parisian labour market rose from 17 per cent in 1866 to 38 per cent in 1906. The second development – linked to the first in fact – was a spurt in the proportion of women employed in the workforce. Women's jobs were as often as not in sales, office and clerical employment. They composed around 15 per cent within these latter groups in 1870; by 1914 the figure was close to one-third. This was a high figure internationally – and all the more worthy of note in that the culture of the period invariably cast women as essentially decorative objects in the home or the bedroom.

Early in the twentieth century the writer Daniel Halévy looked down from the Montmartre butte close to the Sacré-Coeur basilica on a Paris whose historic spire- and dome-dominated skyline had been ornamented with newer, Haussmannian buildings. But turning his gaze away from this already familiar panorama, he spied to the north, 'another city, apparently as vast as the other, an immense city, with plebeian and sadly leprous roofs, uniformly without spires or palaces and without a history, an unknown city which remains to be discovered.' Where there was any building of distinction, it seemed comically anachronistic – such as the medieval basilica in proletarian Saint-Denis, which seemed 'like one of the mammoths which are sometimes discovered intact in the snow and ice of Siberia'.[6]

Halévy and his contemporaries found it difficult to know what to make of such suburban locations. The *banlieue* seemed to lack identity altogether: 'this intermediary world', novelist and playwright Octave Mirbeau noted in 1888, 'is no longer the city but is not yet the countryside. Nothing ends and nothing starts there.'[7] This sense of intractable otherness between city and *banlieue* was even more evident close to. The uniformly dismal and undistinguished two- to three-storey buildings outside the Thiers fortifications, assembled with an almost total lack of planning or design flair, contrasted with the altogether more *soigné* appearance of post-Haussmannian Paris, where full consideration was given to the impact of individual buildings on the overall skyline and on urban perspective.

The spirit of the building regulations established in 1783–4 and modified by Haussmann in 1859 and 1864 was still very much observed within the city's twenty arrondissements. By the 1880s, however, an aesthetic critical of Haussmann was emerging. There were attacks on 'these new boulevards without turning, without perspectival adventure, implacably straight-lined . . . which recall some future American Babylon'.[8] In 1885 the architect Charles Garnier came out strongly against 'the odious use of the straight line'.[9] The anti-Haussmannian rhetoric was also deployed by a growing conservationist movement, spearheaded by the *Commission du Vieux Paris*, founded in 1897. One of the most-visited exhibits in the 1900 Exposition would in fact be one displaying *le Vieux Paris* in all its picturesque glory.

Some concessions were granted to the burgeoning critique of Haussmannism in changes made to building regulations in 1884 and then in 1902. The 1902 legislation in particular stated a determination to 'favour picturesque tendencies', and 'to allow the most unexpected and picturesque effects'.[10] This championing of the picturesque found no outlet in street design – precious few new major roads were to be built throughout the early twentieth century – but it did influence individual buildings. An annual series of municipal prize competitions for façade design which lasted until 1914 provided a sense of what could be achieved. The Rue Réaumur (IIe.) contains a number of the most powerful designs which used iron, reinforced concrete and plate glass in innovatory ways that broke up the perceived monotony of Haussmannian lines. The 1902 regulations also allowed greater height to buildings. But this was only equivalent to one or (at a push) two additional storeys. The new storeys tended to be above the cornice line, in roofspace which mechanical lifts had now made more desirable. Decorative features at roof level were accompanied by more elaborate and flowing sculpture, by bow-windows and also by façade accessories in brick, plaster, coloured tile and glass which echoed the rococo excesses of the pavilions of the 1900 Exposition. This was evident in neighbourhoods in which there was a good deal of residential building from 1902 onwards aimed at a rich bourgeois clientele. Though still recognizably within the Haussmannian canon, new construction in Auteuil, Passy and Chaillot in the XVIe., for example, behind the redesigned Gare de Lyon in the XIIe., and around the Hôtel Lutétia and the Boulevard Raspail (VIe.–VIIe.), was highly ornate and decoratively picturesque.

Paris at the turn of the century was one of the major financial centres in the world. Capital was mobilized to build Russian railways and colonial infrastructure as well as high-profile bourgeois residences across the city. Yet financial interests were less effective when it came to providing accommodation for the Parisian working classes: the profits were simply not there to be made. Laissez-faire principles at the core of Third Republic ideology inhibited the development of social housing. Indeed the only significant step that the government took in this direction was to encourage private and philanthropic ventures. The unfettered workings of the private housing market were extremely deleterious to the city's workers. There was tremendous variety in the quality as well as the design of residential housing, and in the supply of services. Municipal enquiries suggested that on the eve of the Great War some 43 per cent of Parisians were living in overcrowded and insanitary housing. The municipality was prompted into identifying a number of dense housing blocks within Paris as *îlots insalubres* ('insanitary blocks'), which were picked out for public health measures. In fact nothing was done in these zones until after the war.

10.2: *Îlot insalubre numéro 16*

The notion of the *îlot insalubre* – an urban housing block or set of blocks designated as a public health risk – was a promissory note for urban renovation. The idea was that districts thus designated should be set aside for major sanitary reform, including extensive rebuilding. Although the category originated at the turn of the twentieth century, it was to take a half century or so for systematic action on the *îlots insalubres* to be instigated. For most the promise remained unfulfilled until the 1960s, when a new approach was tried.

Growing concern with public health issues in the poorest and most run-down parts of the city before the First World War had been exacerbated by research which suggested that poor, overcrowded housing caused high levels of tuberculosis. In 1906 a municipal resolution proposed the demolition of six such areas in which TB rates were worryingly high. The war prevented the idea of the eradication of *îlots insalubres* from establishing itself. When the idea resurfaced after 1918, some seventeen such areas, comprising over 4,000 buildings, were so designated. They covered 3 per cent of Parisian terrain, but 6 per cent of Parisians

THE ANXIOUS SPECTACLE

lived in them. An outbreak of bubonic plague, no less, in one of the *îlots*, around the Rue Championnet (XVIIe.), led to instant demolition and rebuilding. But shortage of money prevented anything comparable happening elsewhere.

Also complicating issues was the fact that the municipality recognized that certain *îlots* were situated in buildings of historic value. This was true, for example, of *îlots no. 1*, which covered the Plateau Beaubourg (IIIe.–IVe.: centred on the present-day Centre Pompidou); *no. 3*, covering much of the Left Bank facing towards the Île de la Cité through to the Place Maubert (Ve.); and *no. 16*, an area in the Marais extending from the river Seine up to the Rue Saint-Antoine. The recent immigration into the latter district of large numbers of Jews from eastern Europe had given it a very distinctive character, and it formed part of the *Pletzl*, the area of Jewish sweated labour in the garment trades.

These three areas had different destinies over the course of the twentieth century, which illuminate both the tardiness and the incoherence of Parisian planning policy up to the 1950s and 1960s. The Plateau Beaubourg, first, was extensively demolished in the early 1930s. But the state of the national economy and municipal finances did not allow rebuilding, and the area stayed an untidy open space – until its very emptiness and its central position caught the eye of President Georges Pompidou for the international arts centre he planned to build. The Centre Pompidou was the result. At the other end of the spectrum, *îlot insalubre no. 3* was simply left alone, and indeed remained a centre of pitifully poor housing conditions (though the American writer Elliot Paul managed to make it sound delightfully folkloric in his highly readable account of life along the Rue de la Huchette in the 1920s). By the 1960s, housing here was being bought up by estate agents with bohemian yuppies who appreciated local colour in mind. The area remains a cleaned-up, almost fossilized version of a medieval street (complete with medieval housing, in fact, along the Rue Galande).

The story of the *îlot insalubre no. 16* lies somewhere between these contrasting destinies of erasure (*no. 1*) and fossilization

417

(*no. 3*). Its fortunes were mixed, and, in that, it remains most typical of the other insanitary areas. Despite some Haussmann-ian touches in the late nineteenth century – notably the building of a barracks on the Rue Lobau and the establishment of the Lycée Charlemagne behind the church of Saint-Paul – the area retained its medieval street plan and the bulk of its buildings, which mostly dated from around 1650 to the early nineteenth century. The needs of the Hôtel de Ville for buildings into which it could expand its services meant that from the 1920s right through to the early 1960s, public health pretexts were invariably used to justify demolition, reconstruction and reallo-cation of use. The area lost residential space of considerable historic interest for office blocks, despite bleats of complaints from the *Commission du Vieux Paris*. 'There are cases,' it was noted in 1939, 'in which excessive conservation of old houses is a social crime.' In 1941 a radical programme of demolition was decided.

A Vichy law of 1942, however, established that the pictur-esqueness and historic value of a whole neighbourhood could be adjudged a valid reason for conservation – an important break in state policies which hitherto had tended to be fixated on the clearing of buildings adjacent to historic monuments. However, Vichy did not live up to its promises in this area; in fact it hardened its policy of demolition on health grounds. Furthermore, anti-Semitic policies in occupied Paris meant that it proved easy for developers here to take over property owned or rented by Jews, who had either left or were in no position to resist. Demolition begun in 1942 took down far more property than had originally been planned, including areas which posed no risk whatever to public health.

In 1944 a group of intellectuals and writers active in Paris – including Colette, Valéry, Mauriac, Giraudoux, Cocteau, Galli-mard and the composer Poulenc – wrote a collective letter to Marshal Pétain 'in the defence of and in support of the beauty of Paris'. This checked the full implementation of the demolition plan and, after the war, it was abandoned. But it left the field open to rapacious developers and an expansionist city council, as well as to looters for the antiques trade. Although the most significant historic buildings here, the Hôtel de Sens and the Hôtel d'Aumont, were restored, a great many historic buildings were lost in a barely regulated free-for-all. Much of the historic Rue Geoffroy-l'Asnier went, while part of the Quai des Célestins was demolished between 1959 and 1964 so as to build a Cité des Arts for foreign artists – a good idea but embodied in an architectural disaster. Virtually all new building was architecturally undistinguished, and much just dreary. By this time, however, the idea of the *îlot insalubre* had had its moment. Of the seventeen *îlots insalubres* designated after the First World War, only three had had any development worth speaking of. Paris was henceforth to be developed in ZACs (*zones d'aménagement concerté*) and their like.

In this post-1945 phase of urban renewal, external appearances of buildings were preserved too by the practice of gutting and overhauling the insides of many housing blocks but decorating and even restoring their face onto the street. But in many ways the experience of the area had been a grim one. A great deal of historic value was lost, and the character of the neighbourhood was changed for ever. If one was highly optimistic, one might argue that the experience of the *îlot insalubre no. 16* was a redemptive one. By providing government and public opinion with an object lesson in how *not* to conserve historic areas, it laid the foundations of the much more effective conservation legislation, the 1962 Malraux law, which has done a far better job on the rest of the Marais.

Working-class living conditions were worse in the outer arrondissements to the north and east than elsewhere in the city, but worst of all in the suburbs. In Saint-Denis, some 58 per cent of *banlieusards* lived in insanitary houses, for example, and the figure was 62 per cent in Saint-Ouen and 65 per cent in Aubervilliers. Nine out of ten homes within Paris had piped water; in many *banlieue* locations the figure was between a fifth and a third. One in four Parisian homes had a private WC – the figure was often half that outside the fortifications. Beyond the industrial rim attached to the fortifications line, moreover, a second, outer 'crown' of suburbs was developing, and here things were even worse. At the turn of the twentieth century, Bobigny to the east of the city, for example, had no hospital or health-care facilities, no police station, no running water, no sewer system, no electricity supply, and provision in gas which could only manage some pitifully meagre street lighting.

The *banlieue* was ill-served and ill-regarded in transport and communications too. For the first time in Parisian history, most of the population were working in a different neighbourhood from that in which they resided – and this phenomenon was particularly evident in the *banlieue*. Certain of the suburbs, especially those in the outer 'crown', such as Bobigny, were effectively dormitory towns for people who worked in Paris. Passenger numbers from the *banlieue* into Paris had stood at 3 million in 1869; by 1900 they were up to 40 million; and by 1913 they had soared to 120 million. In the middle of the nineteenth century, *banlieusards* had been at the mercy of omnibus companies which often saw little profitability in running services to poor working-class areas, and railway companies which focused on long-haul destinations. The tramway companies were more responsive: by the 1880s there were services out to Saint-Denis, Gennevilliers, Suresnes and Pantin in the north, and Charenton, Ivry and Clamart in the south. Commuting was made difficult, however, by the fact that no effort was made to take the new Métro out to the *banlieue*. Indeed, despite the fuss surrounding the opening of the Métro in 1900 and its undoubted success, it was not as well integrated into transport provision even within Paris itself as was desirable, making distance commuting all the more of a trial. Métro lines did not connect up with the national rail services. The trains even ran on opposite sides of the track, and Métro tunnels were made deliberately too small to encompass rail rolling stock. In addition the astonishing rise in Métro passenger numbers soon made one thing disappointingly clear: the new service had failed to draw much custom away from the roads. It only seemed to encourage greater mobility among Parisians, adding to transport problems.

Haussmannization had proved a bit of a flop in improving road mobility. Despite the baron's commitment to an aesthetic of speed and mobility, flaws in conception produced a bitter harvest for his successors. Communication between the rail termini was poor, the links to the *banlieue* poorer still, and the straight boulevards delivered traffic speedily to crossroads where they became bogged down in massive traffic jams. The Métro did attract passengers away from the *bateaux-mouches*, with the result that river services went into decline – which in turn led many passengers to desert the river altogether for alternative means of communication. (The *bateaux-mouches* service went into receivership before being resuscitated as a successful tourist service operation in 1937.) According to one estimate there were 23,000 vehicles on the streets of Paris in 1819, 45,000 in 1891 and 430,000 in 1910. Yet if cars were the novelty of the *fin de siècle*, the most characteristic form of transport was the horse-drawn carriage, and the *fin de siècle*'s most characteristic public odour was horse manure. In 1900 the omnibus services alone owned some 16,000 horses, many of them in poor shape, subject to falls in the streets when it had been raining. The end of the era of the horse was, however, in sight: horse-drawn omnibuses and trams were put out of commission in 1913. Steam-driven, then (from 1900) electricity-driven trams were the rule by the outbreak of the war, as were automobile buses, introduced in 1907. Attempts were made to impose some kind of order on this unruly assemblage. Haussmann had imposed driving on the right down the boulevards, and before the Great War his successor as prefect Louis Lépine imposed the principle of priority to the right. In 1910 the first one-way street was introduced. Traffic lights would follow only in 1923.

The golden age of the horse was followed by the golden age of the bicycle. Around a quarter of a million of them were weaving round Parisian streets by the outbreak of war. Hailed as promoter of personal freedom, bicycles were still rather expensive. It may have been only poverty and haemorrhoids which inhibited their use, as one wit put it.[11] But as well as their high price the fact that major working-class fastnesses like Ménilmontant and Belleville were on very hilly terrain also made them as yet more of a bourgeois convenience than a proletarian freedom.

Given the inequities they suffered, including poor access to decent transport, workers in the *banlieue* were increasingly drawn to left-wing political movements, notably socialism, militant unionism and revolutionary syndicalism. The left-wing parties played up to this. Socialist tracts in Bobigny in 1910 evoked workers driven out of Paris by high rents only to be faced with 'absurdly poor transport, rutted streets, insufficient lighting, mounds of garbage, no drinking water and [inadequate] schools'[12] – not in fact very much of an exaggeration. The Paris bourgeoisie for its part was soon expressing its disquiet that its city was being progressively encircled by a *ceinture rouge* – a 'red belt' of disinherited spots that engendered anarchists and criminals. Sensationalist newspapers played to their fears, fabricating any number of moral panics. The so-called *apaches* (violent juvenile criminals) of Belleville, Montmartre and the industrial *banlieue* were a regular cause of fright. 'They do wrong without thinking about it,' noted an appalled *Le Petit Parisien*.[13] In 1911 the Bonnot gang high-lighted a new cause for alarm: they began raiding banks using automatic weapons and a getaway car. Even the city's criminals seemed swept up in Parisian modernity.

The *banlieue* was not the place that visitors and tourists wanted to think about. Travellers' journals in an age in which Paris was a major tourist destination show visitors spending their time at the city's monuments and in its watering holes and fleshpots. If they ventured beyond the city fortifications, it was to Versailles or Fontainebleau rather than out to the industrial suburbs. Tourists – and indeed most well-off Parisians – focused instead on the kind of Paris presented to them by the Impressionist painters. From the 1860s, as we have seen,[14] the latter had offered not only a new philosophy of art, but also a new content, the painting of modern life. That modern life was, however, invariably to be found in places where the Parisian bourgeoisie felt happy and unthreatened – in a world of consumption, in fact, rather than in a milieu characterized by industrial production.

By the 1890s, it is true, new approaches were emerging from the Impressionist camp. Some of the founders of the movement were turning against the City of Light. They found the busy streets with their endless traffic and the spare starkness of much of the urban landscape repellent. In the 1860s Renoir had been more than happy to camouflage Haussmannian properties by conveniently placed tree-foliage, but now he expostulated angrily against Parisian buildings, 'cold and lined up like soldiers at review'. He bewailed the presence of 'all the new-fangled machines', while Degas condemned 'those dirty horseless carriages'.[15] Pissarro coined the expression 'it is worthy of the epoch of the Eiffel tower' to describe ineffably bad taste.[16] Some Post-Impressionists – painters who derived inspiration from the Impressionists, and strove to take forward their experimental approach to the portrayal of light – were of a like mind. Gauguin, for example, preferred the innocent landscapes of Pont-Aven in Brittany or the exotic flora and fauna of Tahiti (where he based himself from 1891). Yet a good number of his peers – painters such as Seurat, Signac, Cross and Toulouse-Lautrec – had a more nuanced attitude towards open-air sites. The veteran Impressionist Pissarro, who linked up with the Post-Impressionists, hated the *grands magasins* and the Eiffel tower, but he warmed to the energy and mobility of the 1890s streets, and undertook a series of superb paintings of boulevard Paris. Seurat's famous 'Bathing Scene at Asnières' was sited at the kind of location which master Impressionists had painted before him. But Seurat now included the smoking chimneys of Saint-Denis in the background. This was hardly, however, an artistic engagement with the problems of the suburbs. Indeed it represented the kind of *banlieue* to which the Parisian bourgeoisie could warm: on the wall rather than in the face.

Besides a taste for the open air the Post-Impressionists also relished more closed and confined locations which the Parisian bourgeoisie might well wish to visit, to explore or to go slumming in: bars, cafés, brasseries, *cafés-concerts*, music-halls, circuses, dancehalls, race-tracks, restaurants – and brothels. In the consumerist world which they portrayed, women often represented or evoked commodified forms of sexual encounter. The types of profession that their women subjects followed – waitresses, milliners, shop-assistants, laundresses, flower-sellers and the like – were well known for supplying the world of prostitution.

The 'painting of modern life' by Impressionists and Post-Impressionists thus often signified a fairly retrograde sexual and class politics. Overall it represented a commodity in which the Parisian bourgeoisie found it easy to recognize itself, or was happy to own. In the early days the Impressionists had had mountains of obloquy

Toulouse-Lautrec, *At the Salon of the Rue des Moulins*

heaped upon them by the artistic establishment – which made it hard for them to sell their canvases at a decent price. In 1880 the state withdrew from the Salon, and more competitive and less mediated forms of artistic judgement evolved. Art dealers in particular played a key role in finding buyers, putting on shows and helping to influence public taste. New market conditions reduced the impact of mandarin artistic judgements in shaping public taste, and this opened the door to a re-evaluation of the Impressionists. Manet's infamous *Olympia* had not even reached its reserve price when it was put up for auction on the artist's death in 1883. Pissarro had been in financial straits before he started his Parisian series in the 1890s: as a result of it he needed never to have worked again. The big Cézanne retrospective organized in 1895 did not win everyone over: the *Journal des Arts* attacked 'the nightmarish vision of these atrocities in oils'.[17] Overall, however, the exhibition was viewed as a triumph, and helped achieve a commercial breakthrough for the movement as a whole. The appearance on the scene of buyers from the USA (Rockefeller, J. P. Morgan, Whitney, etc.) also boosted prices. Canvases which had sold for less than a hundred francs in the 1880s and early 1890s now fetched figures in the thousands. With some difficulty the Impressionists even began to force their way into the Louvre (which Pissarro, in one of his more anarchistic moments, had suggested to Cézanne should be burnt down). Nineteen Impressionist canvases were displayed at the 1889 Exposition; significantly, in 1900 the number was up to fifty-four.

The Impressionists and Post-Impressionists had made Paris not only the site of artistic modernism but also its subject-matter. It meant that artists the world over seeking to explore the cutting edge of their discipline were doubly drawn to the French capital. They longed to frequent its museums, its studios, its masters, its galleries and its dealers – but also its cafés, its music-halls, its *quais*. The number of artists living in the city doubled between 1870 and 1914, at which time (number-crunching French bureaucrats could claim) there were more artists per square metre than in any location in the world. Paris found plenty of new artistic celebrators of its charms – Vuillard, Dufy, Vlaminck, Utrillo, Bonnard, and others. But the city also left its traces on the artistic avant-garde – a term which was becoming current at this time – even when that avant-garde had moved away from

Impressionist-like representation. A mythologized Paris was there, for example, in the impoverished street-entertainers portrayed by Picasso, or in the Métro tickets, newspaper cuttings and advertisements for ladies' underwear of his later, pre-First World War collages. In 1910–11 Picasso and Braque sought to develop Cubism by painting dislocated and deconstructed versions of the Sacré-Coeur. Robert Delaunay did much the same with the Eiffel tower. The styles might change; Paris remained. (And the *banlieue* was effectively invisible.)

The development of the market commodified Parisian art, therefore, and in turn Parisian art helped commodify a certain image of Paris itself, and serve that up for the visual delectation of a much-enlarged mass public. Rampant commercialism (as also witnessed in the 1900 Exposition) thus gave the impression of a city living off itself, and presenting to the outside world a vision of Paris as the site of a particular form of modernity. Literature high, low and bohemian underpinned this message. The battles over Impressionism had been fought out in newsprint – and this fact guaranteed them an increasingly wide audience. Growing literacy was a key factor in making a modern and elegant lifestyle a commodity whose image was presented to a wide audience. Primary schooling was made compulsory in 1882, and the government invested heavily in school building (especially as it was simultaneously seeking to squeeze out private, Catholic schooling). Mass literacy made possible the triumph of popular journalism. By the 1890s *Le Petit Journal*, with its mix of investigative reporting, crime stories, serialized novels, celebrity spotting, and illustrations, had topped a million copies a day, and by 1914 it and the three other largest Parisian titles were printing 4.5 million copies between them daily.

The popular press also played a major part in the growing popularity of organized sport, another form of leisure and entertainment with which the image of Paris was henceforth indissolubly marked. The cycling Tour de France, for example, which started and ended in the capital, was inaugurated in 1903, and derived from an attempt by the sports newspaper *L'Auto* to whip up circulation. Starting a sporting event in Paris was a sure-fire way of giving it maximum publicity, plus some measure of national legitimacy. The annual Paris–Rouen cycle race had begun in 1869, and the Paris–Brest in 1892. Automobile rallies followed suit: Paris–Rouen, Paris–Brest (both 1894) and

Paris–Bordeaux–Paris (1895). The popularity of such events, pumped up through newspaper coverage, also stimulated the emergence of sports stadiums in the capital with a national profile. Horserace tracks – Longchamp, Auteuil, Vincennes – had developed from the last years of the Second Empire. In addition, the Vél' d'Hiv – or the Vélodrome d'Hiver – was built in 1910 to stage major cycling events. In the suburbs the Parc des Princes and the Stade Colombes opened in 1897 and 1907 for team sports. The Olympic Games – the second of the modern era – were staged in the city in 1900 in a variety of these and other arenas.

Publicity for these sporting venues – and for much else – was channelled through newspapers and journals, but also through posters. The description of advertising given by the Moroccan scholar Muhammad As-Saffar on his visit to Paris in 1845–6 makes it sound quaintly hand-made and improvised:

> Merchants write out papers mentioning their goods and their virtues, praising them so that people will want them. The price and the place are also mentioned. Then they affix these papers to walls where people walk by, or on the numerous little kiosks where they relieve themselves, or at the gates to the city . . . and in every place where people gather.[18]

From the 1870s, in contrast, new technical improvements triggered a revolution in publicity in the form of mass-produced, brightly coloured and highly stylized posters. Initial supporters of the new art-form greeted it as a major step forwards for civic education: it constituted, one author opined, 'the town crier who makes himself heard at fifty metres through the eyes'.[19] It did not take long to realize that the poster worked most effectively in a commercial rather than a civic context. The rise of the advertising poster – joyously proclaiming the virtues of department-stores, food and drink, female fashions, sports events, popular entertainments and much besides – both testified to and stimulated the flourishing hedonistic consumer culture oriented around everyday pleasures. A more liberal bill-posting law in 1881 further boosted the sector: advertisements were soon decorating the Parisian streets, from walls and buildings, omnibuses, sandwich boards, public urinals and Morris columns (the latter cigar-shaped columns have remained an enduring part of the Parisian streetscape).

Poster art soon became an art commodity too, with its own stars – Mucha, Toulouse-Lautrec, Chéret, Willette and others. Anarchists diffused information on how to razor posters off walls so that they could bring colour and joy into drab working-class homes.

Other media both reinforced and benefited from the impact of newsprint and publicity. The *belle époque* was a high-water mark of Parisian theatre-going. Performers such as Sarah Bernhardt became household names. Parisian theatre audiences doubled in size between 1870 and 1890 – then doubled again by 1910 and kept growing. At the time of the 1900 Exposition, half a million Parisians were going to the theatre once a week, and half of all Parisians went at least once a month. Telephone technology was just being developed: from 1882 public call-boxes began to be installed around Paris. Significantly, one of its prime uses was the so-called 'theatrophone', through which one could listen in to plays running on the boulevards. In 1895, moreover, the aptly named Lumière brothers had shown moving pictures for the first time. The Sorbonne hosted one of the first public representations of the new art, and there was a growing awareness of the new medium's potential as a form of civic pedagogy. From 1898 Pathé was screening the first newsreels, the *Pathé-Journal*, and in 1899 there was even a documentary on the Dreyfus case. However, in these early years, movies more typically fitted into an existing popular market of dioramas, magic lantern shows, 'disaster' plays with sensational optical effects, and Grand Guignol. One of the earliest uses to which film was put was publicity. The first advertisements on film date from 1895, and were for chocolate, beer, hats and corsets – all very *belle époque* commodities. In 1914 Paris boasted thirty-seven cinemas, many of them along the boulevards.

The boulevards, full of energy and vitality, remained the prime sites for the consumption of the theatrical and spectacular arts which formed such a large part of Paris's image in the wider world. They contained most of the up-market theatres as well as the smartest cinemas. They were also the home of the *café-concert*. These had emerged in the 1840s, and offered a cheap night out for the popular classes in the form of sociable drinking, light music plus some optional turns which ranged from bearded ladies, animal turns and fire-eaters through to the famous *Pétomane* (famous for his virtuoso farting).

The *café-concert* spawned the more spectacular music-hall. The Folies-Bergère was founded in 1886 and the Olympia in 1893. In 1889 the Moulin-Rouge was set up in the Boulevard de Clichy (IXe.). It featured (and may have invented) the can-can dance, establishing an unshakeable cliché of tourist Paris. One writer in the 1890s sardonically described

> the old English ladies and the young misses wrapped up in warm furs even in the midst of summer and who always sit in the front row in order better to ascertain the immorality of the French dancers [and who] cover their faces when it is over and then utter their properly indignant 'Shockings!'[20]

The appearance in the 1890s of the striptease and nude dancing added to the appeal of the city's entertainment industry for a strong current of sex tourism. So did the city's numerous brothels.

Another leisure format which owed something to the *café-concert* and something to the literary café evolved in the 1880s, when the painter Rodolphe Salis established a night club in his gallery on the Boulevard de Rochechouart (IXe.). It attracted a wide range of artists as well as struggling poets and musicians. The Chat Noir management published a literary journal of the same name, and its evening floorshows allowed the performance of its contents, alongside musical turns and light sketches. In 1895 it relocated to the nearby Rue Victor-Massé, but the impresario Aristide Bruant took over the old site and installed his own cabaret the Mirliton, which became the most famous of them all. Mirliton performances comprised a mixed menu of turns, heavy on satire and studied silliness and with a sentimental attachment to *le Vieux Paris* spiced with political attacks on urban developers and corrupt politicians. Such locations allowed the mixing of the literary and artistic avant-gardes. Erik Satie played piano at the Nouvelle-Athènes café which Zola, Renoir, Toulouse-Lautrec, Huysmans and Degas had frequented in the 1870s. The Lapin Agile on the Rue de Saules was re-energized in 1903 when Bruant took it over. Until 1914 it was frequented by a motley crowd including the painter Picasso, poets Guillaume Apollinaire and Max Jacob and novelists Francis Carco and Roland Dorgelès. The bourgeoisie liked to slum it in such arty venues, for which Montmartre acquired a reputation.

Montmartre was also the home for an emerging artistic subculture. The social forces unleashed by Haussmann had made it difficult for up-and-coming painters and sculptors to afford the high-priced new neighbourhoods. The Latin Quarter, it is true, retained its raffish attractions, but on the Right Bank painters sought out haunts off the boulevard track. Montmartre – as, later, Montparnasse (which by the eve of the war was beginning to supplant it) – was made accessible by the new boulevards, but it was less built up with *immeubles de rapport*, so that rents were cheap and space at a premium for artists seeking a studio. Montmartre had been one of the last strongholds of the Commune and its closeness to major railway stations gave it a cosmopolitan as well as a radical feel. These features combined oddly with the villagey ambience of a neighbourhood in which the Sacré-Coeur was only a stone's throw from Paris's last surviving windmills.

10.3: Sacré-Coeur of Montmartre

Parisians often perceive the basilica of the Sacré-Coeur ('Sacred Heart') up on the Montmartre hill as being in rivalry with its approximate coeval, the Eiffel tower. It is not a friendly rivalry. Eiffel's creation on the Left Bank, inaugurated at the 1889 Exposition and commemorating the centenary of the French Revolution, highlights technological progress and republican values. The Sacré-Coeur, in contrast, was the product of a religious vow taken following the *année terrible* of 1870 and is an aggressively clericalist monument.

The cult of the sacred heart had originated in the abbey of Montmartre during the later stages of the Counter-Reformation, and the sacred heart symbol was sported by the peasant counter-revolutionary rebels in the Vendée in the 1790s. For most of the period of the basilica's construction (it was only finally consecrated in 1919), it was viewed as an expiatory and explicitly counter-revolutionary monument, 'a citadel of superstition', in the words of one Third Republic politician. Yet it was the National Assembly of the Republic which, in January 1871, had taken the decision to erect such a monument in reparation for the *année terrible*. There was nothing new about a religious vow of this sort: the Bourbon restoration of 1815, for example, had seen a number of such gestures of atonement. By the time that the conservative majority in the Assembly committed to the idea of situating it in the highly visible location of Montmartre, however, the Commune episode had occurred. Most radical republicans consequently saw support for an expiatory monument as playing into the hands of the clerical Right. The archbishop of Paris had been taken hostage by the Communards and eventually shot by them in the course of the horrific events of the *semaine sanglante*. And Montmartre had been one of the first and also final haunts of the Commune.

If the Sacré-Coeur project had been originally blessed by legislative fiat, the basilica could not count on state funds for its building. Indeed all the 40 million livres required for its construction came from private donations from within the church, which made the basilica an emblem in a wider campaign to instil moral order within French public life. The absence of state support gave the organizing committee greater latitude in its choice of design. They selected probably the most outlandish of the projects submitted. Its architect Paul Labadie had spent time restoring the romanesque church of Saint-Front in Périgueux. He grafted onto a romanesque base a neo-byzantine style which was equally foreign to Paris. Paris had no shortage of domes: Italianate (the Invalides, the Institut de France, etc.) and neo-classical (notably the Panthéon). Yet none of them resembled the dome of the Sacré-Coeur.

Over the centuries most Parisian buildings had been constructed using limestone (*pierre de Paris*) and plaster of Paris quarried from the city's environs (including from caverns under Montmartre). These supplies had been drying up since mid-century and a decision was made to build the Sacré-Coeur out of stone from Château-Landon in the Seine-et-Marne. This stone is whiter than *pierre de Paris* – and indeed gets whiter with ageing. The basilica thus not only has a highly un-Parisian profile; it is also a most un-Parisian colour. Its pallor has proved impossible to imitate or emulate.

This quintessentially un-Parisian monument has, however, become as wholly Parisian as its secular rival – equally inimitable, in fact – the Eiffel tower. What performed this metamorphosis was mass tourism and modern marketing. The communications revolution which had brought millions to the Eiffel tower also enabled the emergence of spiritual tourism. The brilliant success of Lourdes in this period showed that individual pilgrimages on foot were being replaced by collective pilgrimages in railway carriages. The Sacré-Coeur organizers used the media adeptly, producing a monthly *Bulletin du Voeu National* ('Bulletin of the National Vow') to update the faithful on the progress of the building and encourage visits and naming opportunities. Pilgrims were urged to leave an ex-voto (an object symbolizing fulfilment of a vow) in the form of a personalized stone for the basilica building. Licensed vendors on the site also supplied a range of religious souvenir items such as medallions, necklaces and prayer cards.

The compromise with Mammon which the organizers of the basilica made had unforeseen consequences in the environs of the basilica. Prior to its incorporation into Paris in 1859–60, Montmartre was an independent little village. Its unfashionability and cheapness attracted colonies of artists from the 1880s through to the First World War, and around them an important leisure industry emerged. Only 6,000 strong in 1851, Montmartre boasted over 200,000 inhabitants by 1886. The spiritual tourists who came to the Sacré-Coeur could indulge their earthly appetites in the bars, cabarets and cafés of the district. Down the hill from the basilica was the lively red-light district of Pigalle, with its louche dives and criminal milieu. Closer at hand to the basilica was the arty Place du Tertre, which became an important draw for the cultural tourist. In addition the Bateau-Lavoir on the Rue Ravignan, an old piano factory turned artists' colony, would prove the crucible in which Cubism was formed. Picasso painted *Les Demoiselles d'Avignon* here, and Van Dongen, Suzanne Valadon, Braque, Modigliani, Vlaminck and Dufy were among other denizens. Many of these artists – plus Utrillo, another Montmartre resident – would make the still villagey ambience of the district the subject of their canvases. Chicken and sheep probably still outnumbered even artists here (though not for long), and windmills were still in use, but wine-growing, once a local staple, had died out. It would take a special effort of the 'Friends of Old Montmartre' in 1932 to create the existing vineyard on Rue Saint-Victor (XVIIIe.). The theme of *le Vieux Montmartre* – curiously blending the Sacré-Coeur basilica with windmills, vines, artistic mementoes and leisure spots – would join with the notion of *le Vieux Paris* as a major mobilizer of heritage-trail tourism.

The vitality of the Montmartre art scene testified to the strength and diversity of Parisian cultural life at the turn of the century. We have seen how the Expositions of 1889 and 1900 offered a space in which social, cultural and political anxieties could be put to one side in a spectacular display of national unity. The growth of the leisure and entertainment industries in this period did much the same thing, offering the anodyne appearance of harmony to a society riven by divisions. From 1914, however, Parisian society would be put to a different kind of test – mass war rather than mass leisure. The Great War – the First World War, as it was to prove – would destroy the economic foundations of the prosperity on which the myth of the *belle époque* was founded. Many would subsequently erase from their memories the divisions, tensions and anxieties of the *fin-de-siècle* years and give full rein to brazen nostalgia.

Initially the opening of the war against Germany seemed to dissolve anxieties and to put social, political and cultural struggles on hold. The assassination of the eminent Socialist Jean Jaurès in a Parisian café on the eve of the declaration of war removed a leading figure on the Left who might have prevailed against what became an almost Gadarene rush into war. Divisions were set aside and a 'sacred union' (*union sacrée*) was declared for what was confidently predicted would be a short war. As with the Expositions, the Great War would less dissipate tensions than highlight, exacerbate and complicate them.

Paris was closer to the battle-front than any other capital city – and almost at once nearly came a cropper. The Germans broke through Belgium and moved swiftly against the French capital. On 2 September 1914 the government closed the stock exchange and relocated to Bordeaux, taking with it all the gold to be found in the vaults of the Banque de France. Around 35,000 Parisian males of arms-bearing age were detailed for military service and even more than this number of inhabitants now fled. The influx of refugees from the invaded areas to the north of France added to the confusion. The city was placed under the military command of General Gallieni, veteran of sundry African campaigns. He met the expectation of a German siege with great fortitude, as the battle of the Marne (4–10 September) got under way only fifty miles from the capital. Heavy artillery fire on that front was audible in Paris. On 7–8 September General Joffre launched a powerful attack on the weak flank of the menacing German forces. With military vehicles already committed elsewhere, Gallieni requisitioned the Parisian taxi fleet, and made it ferry some 4,000 men to the front for the big push (the drivers asked for the fare, it appears). The French prevailed and the Germans fell back. By Christmas 1914 the war of movement had transformed into a static war, and fighting became bogged down – often literally so – in a long system of trenches running from the Channel to the Swiss border.

The government scuttled back to Paris in December 1914. Life returned to a state which for most of the war remained largely bearable. It did not approach the harshness of the situation which Parisians would endure between 1940 and 1944. But it was no *belle époque*. The government's wish to maintain morale saw it oscillate between a puritanical desire to mobilize the city entirely around the war effort and a more sober realization that, if civilian morale were to be maintained, life had to go on along something like normal lines. The task was not easy, given the sudden removal to the army of over a third of the workforce. Many artisans' shops and small businesses closed down altogether, while the flight of capital and the relocation of non-combatants out of the city caused a slump in demand for many

French soldiers at the time of mobilization, August 1914

manufactured goods. Most museums closed and the Grand Palais became a military hospital. In the early years inflation hit very hard, particularly since, though wages rose, they tended to follow rather than anticipate rises in prices for key commodities. Yet at least there was work, especially as from 1915 the government began to play a more prominent part in the mobilization of industry for the war effort. Paris was indeed extremely well-situated for contributing strategically in support of the western front. Its geographical closeness to the main theatre of conflict was a major asset, in that it allowed the speedy transfer of men and *matériel*. The fact that the road system and the rail network were so heavily centralized on Paris was also a strategic trump card. In addition the orientation of the *banlieue* around heavy industry (plus the fact that rival businesses in the east and north of France were now in enemy hands) meant that Parisian industrialists were in an excellent position to respond to the challenge of total war.

The First World War thus massively reinforced pre-existent trends in the region's industrial geography. The decline of light industry, especially textiles, within the twenty arrondissements was confirmed, while *banlieue*-based, large-scale heavy industry went from strength to strength. The automobile industry converted almost entirely to war production. The Renault workforce out at Boulogne-Billancourt grew from 4,000 to 22,000 workers, and began turning out not only military vehicles but also bombs, cannon and (from 1917) tanks. In 1915 industrialist André Citroën received a government contract to produce a million shells; by the end of the war, his much-extended plant had produced over 24 million. A noticeable aspect of this expansion was the increasing part taken by female labour, accentuating pre-war trends. With so many men in the army, women were now allowed to be bus conductors and Métro officials. The range of jobs they could hold increased as time went on. They ended up playing a crucial role in heavy industry. Around a quarter of Renault's workforce was female, and the proportion was higher in many munitions factories.

Female employment – plus a growing, if still quite limited government commitment to welfare policies, family allowances and so on – allowed Parisian families affected by the loss to the front of their main bread-winners, to get by in the face of rampant inflation. An early government decision to freeze rents was especially important in this respect. Shortages of key commodities caused by the dislocation of the economy were now the main problem. The government's response was to go down the road of food controls and rationing, especially from 1917. Sugar and coal were first to be rationed, and bread followed in 1918. The price of bread was pegged at an affordable level throughout the war in fact, partly by a prohibition of the baking of fancy goods. Parisians had to get through the war without eating croissants. The cafés also had to serve coffee without milk, while restaurants were pressurized into serving meat on only two days each week and into preferring margarine to butter. Mardi Gras was cancelled amid this wave of austerity. The municipality tried to do its bit for the needy in providing free coal and potatoes during the worst winter months. But it was not only individuals with money to spare who engaged in the thriving black market. Any Parisian with a country cousin who could provide additional off-market supplies was instantly befriended. Many families supplemented their food intake by starting petty cultivation – there were around 10,000 garden allotments in the Paris region by 1918. The fact that Parisians' level of health did not deteriorate severely as a result of the privations of war indicates that the variety of circumstances and strategies in play over food supply was modestly effective. Public health authorities took up the challenge of war conditions with great gusto, and led vigorous campaigns of smallpox vaccination. Though there was typhoid in 1914–15 and scarlet fever in 1915, the absence of a smallpox epidemic in these years meant that child mortality figures were relatively respectable. The worst epidemic of the decade was the Spanish influenza of 1918–19, which occurred after the armistice had been signed. Vulnerability to it was not dependent on nutritional status.

Economic difficulties, however, were not without social reactions. Strikes were initially rather rare, while the mantra of the *union sacrée* was still working its magic. But by 1917 civilian morale was affected not only by the worsening shortages and high prices, but also by the fact that war was going badly. On the eastern front France's ally Russia had entered into an era of revolution which removed it from the international conflict. On the western front there were mutinies by French troops against the seemingly senseless mass killing. These were contained by brutal but effective action directed by General

Pétain, who had made a national hero of himself for his role in the battle of Verdun in 1916. Yet the government's commitment to news-management had rebounded against it, producing distrust rather than public confidence. Censorship was frequently over-emphatic – in April 1915, for example, fortune-tellers were formally prohibited from making bad predictions. On the other hand, government propaganda was invariably treated as so much *bourrage de crâne* (brain-washing). These were propitious circumstances for the emergence of political satire: the *Canard enchaîné* – still, almost a century later, France's premier satirical newspaper – was established in 1916.

Morale seemed to weaken as economic circumstances worsened. Women could be as militant as men in labour struggles. Paris seam-stresses went on strike in January 1917 and they were followed by women workers in the munitions factories – the *munitionnettes*. The strike wave then spread to males and to other industries over the late spring. The building trades, the post office, the municipal workforce and the gas industries were all affected. A further bout of strikes occurred in the spring of 1918, involving up to 200,000 workers.

In 1918 other developments were also testing the resolve of Parisians. With the exception of a few raids in 1914–15 and some Zeppelin bombardment in 1916, the city had been spared aerial bomb-ing. In early 1918, however, heavy bombing started, along with the firing of 'Big Bertha', Germany's long-range cannon – a phenomenon which incidentally underlined the technological obsolescence of the Thiers fortifications. On Good Friday 1918 one of the 'Big Bertha' shells struck the church of Saint-Gervais in the Marais (IVe.), causing a roof-fall from which over fifty died. If such bombing was calculated to erode morale, it was probably ineffective, however, for it hardened French attitudes towards the 'Boches' (as the Germans had been insultingly dubbed since 1914). Prime Minister Georges Clemenceau's fiery and tenacious leadership also hardened in this period, which was to prove to be the eve of a general peace.

The total number of directly war-related deaths in the capital was still extremely modest overall: 266 Parisians died during the course of the war from bombing and there were 633 other casualties – nugatory figures when set against the sacrifice occurring at the front. These were small numbers too when set against mortality due to epidemic disease.

The Spanish influenza epidemic of 1918–19 caused 30,000 deaths in the Paris region and 400,000 deaths throughout France.

In the spring of 1918 a German advance, facilitated by the transfer of troops from the eastern front following the Russo-German peace signed at Brest-Litovsk, threatened a reprise of the 1914 invasion scare. There was a predictable getaway rush from the railway stations. But generally morale held, and the military situation was much improved by the arrival of American troops on the western front (as well as in Paris, where they came to love the place and proved very popular). In November 1918 the Germans accepted peace terms dictated by France and its allies. A frenetic bout of celebration which recalled the opening days of the *union sacrée* rocked the city for days. Years of hardship released an extraordinary, carnivalesque joy in the streets of the city.

The *union sacrée* had held – just about. But even before the international peace treaties ending the Great War were being negotiated within Paris, tensions and anxieties which had been put on ice or subordinated to the demands of the conflict in 1914 had started to emerge. Certain features of war-time conditions, moreover, persisted. The fighting might have stopped, but food rationing continued, well into 1919. Then war demobilization flooded the labour market, threatening the position shored up by women workers over the course of the war.

Third Republic politicians seemed unwilling to accept that the basis of France's great power status was eroding – as the events of the next decades would prove. Yet Paris was not what it had been. There was a great deal about the city of modernity which looked decidedly unmodern. The 'City of Light' of the 1900 Exposition did not lack for dark spots in 1918. Although direct war damage had been small, the bulk of Parisian housing stock was in bad shape. No action had been taken against the *îlots insalubres* and a devastating housing crisis was on the horizon. Moreover, a government which had scant resources to devote to housing reform had even less to offer towards the kind of monumental urbanization for which Paris had become world-famous. There would be virtually no Haussmannian boulevards for the next half century, and precious few major monuments. The alacrity with which post-war Parisians latched on to the notion of pre-war Paris as the glamorous cynosure of *la belle époque* was a straw in the wind in this respect. It suggested that Paris was more willing to rest its claims to modernity on the past than on the future. Faded dreams and lost illusions: the motto would encapsulate the history of the capital over the next three to four decades.

I I

Faded Dreams, Lost Illusions
1918–45

In 1935 the German social critic Walter Benjamin, who for much of the inter-war period strove to understand the genealogy of world capitalism through the minutiae of Parisian social, cultural and urban history, wrote a famous essay entitled 'Paris, capital of the nineteenth century'.[1] Perhaps without wishing to acknowledge it, Benjamin was implying something which most Parisians after 1918 might regret, but could scarcely fail to acknowledge – that Paris's greatest moments were in the past.

To a considerable extent, post-war Paris was living off its capital. The future looked bleak and uncertain. A widespread disgust with warfare which lasted until the advent of the Second World War in 1939 was linked to a disillusionment with the kind of liberal democracy offered by the Third Republic. France as a whole had suffered dreadfully from the Great War: material damage caused by the fighting was extremely extensive in the north and east of the country, necessitating special post-war recovery measures, and casualties were proportionately higher than any other warring nation – 1.3 million dead, bringing population size down to 1891 levels, with over three million wounded and disabled. One in ten Parisian conscripts had never returned from the fighting. The war-wounded (*mutilés de guerre*) were given special seats in the Paris Métro and buses, providing a grim reminder of yesterday's horrors. The rapt attention given to Oswald Spengler's gloomily apocalyptic *The Decline of the West* (1918–22), which questioned liberal values, was a useful barometer of the post-war mood. The Bolshevik Revolution in Russia in 1917, which stimulated a powerfully enthusiastic response in the French labour

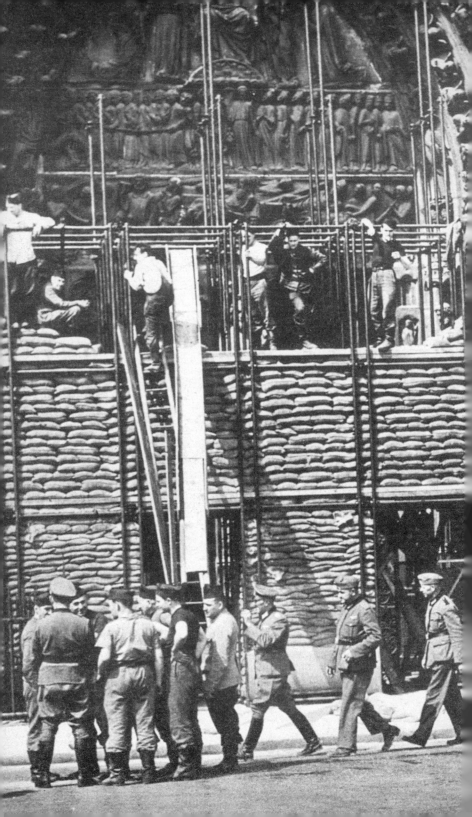

movement, added further piquancy to debates. The years 1919 and 1920 brought waves of social unrest, which seemed to confirm dark bourgeois anxieties about proletarian power. The Right was reinvigorated. The consecration of Montmartre's Sacré-Coeur basilica in 1919 and the canonization of Joan of Arc the following year highlighted the resurgence of the religious Right which had never accommodated to the Third Republic. The dictators Mussolini and Hitler would also find enthusiasts among the French Right. The inter-war years were to be characterized by a polarization of politics.

In the event the regime survived post-war tensions and the general air of anxiety. The 1920s even saw a movement of cautious optimism gaining ground, as Paris's economy cranked back into peacetime life. Although it had lost a sizeable part of its population to wartime mortality, national averages were higher, and the city itself had almost miraculously avoided more than superficial material damage. Paris was still a great international metropolis, as had been duly acknowledged by the fact that the peace treaties which concluded the war were negotiated and signed in Versailles and other royal palaces in the Île-de-France. To some degree, moreover, although Moscow had emerged as the Mecca of international labour, Paris now eclipsed several rivals (Berlin, Vienna, Saint Petersburg) which had threatened its primacy before the Great War.

But Paris's economic recovery in the 1920s flattered only to deceive. The impact of the 1929 Crash in the United States was delayed in France until 1931, but that year initiated an altogether darker chapter in Parisian economic fortunes. The slump of the thirties was the opening event in a wretched period in Paris's history lasting more than two decades, composed of eight years of severe recession (1931–9); six years of war, German occupation and political divisions caused by the collaborationist Vichy regime (1939–45); and a further decade or more of post-war recovery. It was only in the mid-fifties that reconstruction really came to an end, though even then the enjoyment of resurgent economic benefits was hindered by an unstable political situation. The social, political and economic upheavals which Paris witnessed in these middle decades of the twentieth century only strengthened a penchant for looking back wistfully to the 'good old days' of the *belle époque*, plus a tendency to accentuate Paris's international supremacy less in terms of international power politics than of art, culture, ideas and sheer escapist *joie de vivre*.

'1918: Peace', the painter Fernand Léger wrote to a friend.

> The man who for four years has been exasperated, tense and anonymised finally lifts his head, opens his eyes, looks around, stretches, and finds his taste for life: a frenzy of dancing, thinking, yelling out loud, of finally walking erect, shouting, yelling, squandering. An eruption of energy fills the world.[2]

No other city lived the frenetic *années folles* of the 1920s with greater energy, imagination and indulgence than Paris. The city received an influx of foreigners anxious to join the party. 'I feel as if I were biting into a utopian fruit,' the cosmopolitan writer and sometime eroticist, Anaïs Nin, commented of life in the city: 'something velvety and lustrous and rich and vivid.'[3] Pre-eminent among the expatriate community were North Americans, who used the favourable exchange rate and the absence of Prohibition to good advantage, building up a high-living little colony in the city. The early career of US cabaret star Josephine Baker provides a remarkable testimony to the spirit of these *années folles*. So, in a rather different way, did Anglophone writers such as Ernest Hemingway, Scott Fitzgerald, Gertrude Stein, James Joyce, Jean Rhys, Edith Wharton and Henry Miller, who between them spawned some of the masterpieces of literary modernism. Many hung out in the legendary bars of Montparnasse, especially around the boulevard's junction with the Rue Vavin (VIe./XIVe.) – the Rotonde, the Dôme, the Select and (from 1927) the Coupole. These venues also attracted not only part of the Parisian literary avant-garde, but also a highly heterogeneous artistic community. The 'Paris School' of painters and sculptors, for example, had precious few native-born Parisians: its stars were Italian (Modigliani), Spanish (Gris, Miró), Russian (Chagall), Lithuanian (Soutine, Lipchitz), German (Ernst), Dutch (van Dongen), Polish (Kisling), Romanian (Brancusi), North American (Calder), and Japanese (Foujita). These individuals had been drawn to the Montparnasse area by the cheap rents and availability of studio space which had formerly attracted their predecessors to Montmartre – before the latter was spoiled by its fame, was invaded by a criminal milieu dealing in drugs and prostitution, and became the haunt of 'drunk Americans, saxophone-playing negroes and tango-dancing Argentines', as the writer Joseph Kessel snootily put it.[4] Montparnasse, along with the Latin Quarter, also became the centre for a lively jazz scene, animated by touring artistes and black GIs who preferred to delay their return home after the war. The neighbourhood, one denizen recorded, reeked of 'petrol, coffee, alcohol, sweat, perfume, ambition, tobacco, horsepowder, urine, frivolity, gunpowder and sex'[5] – which he was not alone in finding scintillatingly seductive.

11.1: Josephine Baker

The First World War allowed Parisians to have systematic contact with African-Americans for the first time. French prosperity in the eighteenth century had been founded on black slavery in the West Indian sugar plantations, but slaves were a rarity in France – especially compared with eighteenth-century London. The Revolutionaries abolished slavery outright in 1794, though Napoleon reinstated it. Despite the fact that France was a leading abolitionist nation in the nineteenth century, it had little direct contact with blacks. The arrival of US GIs after 1917 was thus an eye-opener for many Parisians – and also for many of their guests. Some 160,000 African-Americans served in France, and many found it a bracing experience. 'There is an air of liberty, equality and fraternity here,' a black private wrote home, with some irony, 'which does not blow in the black man's face in liberty-loving, democratic America.'

In time American visitors would realize that French attitudes to race were not quite as perfect as French republican rhetoric assumed. But many warmed enthusiastically to the hospitality and support they found in France during and after the war. Indeed some black entertainers constructed themselves a considerable French reputation – while remaining little known in their homeland. Parisian infatuation with jazz from the last years of the war onwards provided a fertile terrain for such reputation-building, notably in the arty venues of Montmartre,

Montparnasse and the Latin Quarter. The clarinettist Sidney Bechet, for example, was part of the jazz invasion of the 1920s, and went on to become one of the major figures of the French jazz scene, while remaining little more than a footnote in US musical history. Much the same was true of a friend of Bechet's from the 1920s, Josephine Baker. Partly through her early career in France as an exotic dancer, but partly also due to excellent self-promotion and PR, plus her Resistance credentials in the Second World War, she died in 1975 almost a French national icon.

Josephine Baker had a sad and deprived childhood in St Louis, Missouri, where in 1917 she witnessed race riots which caused dozens of deaths. In 1925, still a teenager, she crossed the Atlantic with a dance troupe, the *Revue Nègre*, booked for the Théâtre des Champs-Élysées. She took the town by storm, receiving literally thousands of proposals of marriage, and numerous other proposals as well. Her reputation was based on her quirky singing and, particularly, her exotic dancing which displayed her semi-naked body in deliberately provocative ways that hovered unsteadily on the cusp of obscenity (most notably, the notorious non-dress composed of up-turned bananas). Her show – and her highly energetic sex-life off-stage – harmonized with ideas of female freedom and independence current in post-war France. It also played quite blatantly on racial stereotypes. One observer, for example, praised the way in which she brought 'a whiff of jungle air and an elemental strength and beauty to the tired showcase of Western Civilization'. But as the New York journalist Janet Flanner noted, black was now beautiful. The verb *bakerfixer* entered the French language, meaning to slick down the hair in the style of Josephine Baker.

The 1930s saw the continuation of the vogue for black dance music – Louis Armstrong toured Paris in 1933 and Duke Ellington the following year. Baker bolstered her popularity by grafting what was to be a durable French persona over the primitivist image she had thus far embodied. Her French was good, and in 1931 she was, famously, singing:

J'ai deux amours –	I have two loves –
Mon pays et Paris	My country and Paris
Paris toujours	Paris forever
C'est mon rêve joli.	That's my pretty dream.

Her soulful cadences brought the song in line with a wave of populist nostalgia-tinged affection for old Paris which performers such as Maurice Chevalier and Lucienne Boyer were already exploiting. Boyer's lyrics might have recalled 'French Montmartre' 'before its annexation by Cossacks and Negroes', but by then Josephine Baker had already made herself an honorary Parisian. Such was her popularity that in 1931 during the Colonial Exposition, the satirical newspaper the *Canard enchaîné* launched a spoof that she was about to be crowned 'Queen of the Colonies'.

Other African-Americans were taken to Parisians' hearts subsequent to the successes of Sidney Bechet and Josephine Baker, including many musicians, film-actors and dancers, but also writers such as James Baldwin, Richard Wright and Chester Himes following the Second World War. The treatment accorded such fêted figures has not always been typical of that accorded individuals from non-French ethnic groupings.

The materialism and hedonism which attracted so many writers and artists to inter-war Paris were highlighted in the 1925 Exposition of the Decorative Arts. The show, which launched Art Deco as a new international style, seemed even keener than the 1900 Exposition to highlight the city's consumerist character rather than any technological or scientific feats. Paris was presented as a dream-machine which generated consumerist fantasies. Sponsorship from the *grands magasins* and *haute couture* houses confirmed the fair's highly commercialized orientation. The Eiffel tower was lit up at night by a dazzling light show advertising Citroën cars. The post-war female styles of short hair and long skirts stressing overall body line and revealing ankles received international consecration (short skirts and exposed knees would soon, excitingly, follow). The great nineteenth-century

Expositions had foregrounded industrial technology and urban infra-structure. Yet in 1925, continuing the trend detectable in 1900, exhibits celebrated the merger of art and consumer culture in the higher echelons of the luxury trades which were aimed especially at the female shopper. The industrial product to receive the most enthusiastic eulogy was the bidet.[6]

In the past Paris's Expositions had showcased the city as the acme of modernity. Yet the fairs of the 1930s placed the city less directly under the modernist focus. The 1931 Colonial Exposition out at Porte Dorée (XIIe.) near Vincennes attracted some eight million visitors. It tried to imprint a becoming dignity on the French civilizing mission (thus belly-dancers were banned), and was considered an organiz-ational success. But the event was a pale shadow of former glories and, significantly, no longer commanded unanimity. Counter-exhibitions were staged by the Communist Party and by the Surrealist movement to highlight the dark side of French colonialism. The 1937 Exposition missed the mark even more blatantly. The left-wing Popular Front government had thrown its full support behind the fair, but the con-struction of the main buildings and exhibition stands was dogged by labour disputes. Previous Exposition inaugurations had been solemn affairs aimed at impressing foreign dignitaries and the world press; the 1937 opening was a fiasco, with visitors picking their way gingerly around what still resembled a building site. The main talking-points of the Exposition also hardly accrued to Parisian grandeur. One was Picasso's monumental painting *Guernica*, housed in the national pavilion, of a Spanish Republic fighting for its life against Francoist aggression. The other was the confrontation across the main concourse of the pavilions of Nazi Germany and the USSR, one crowned by the German eagle, the other by massive statuary figures representing Labour. Instead of the spirit of Paris proclaiming international har-mony, the juxtaposition of these two foreign pavilions, trying to outdo each other in political grandiloquence, was a reminder that by the late 1930s, besides its other problems, the city was overshadowed by threatening international rivalries.

Yet if international Expositions after 1918 no longer performed the role of displaying Parisian grandeur, they did contribute to the emergence of Paris as a world-historic site of memory, adding strikingly, like their predecessors, to the built environment. The 1931 fair saw the construction of what is now the Museum of African and Oceanic Arts out at the Porte Dorée, as well as the modernization of the Vincennes zoo. The 1937 fair required the replacement of the Trocadéro palace, built for the 1878 Exposition, by the Palais de Chaillot across the Seine from the Eiffel tower; this came to house the museums of the Marine and of French Monuments as well as the Musée de l'Homme, devoted to ethnography. Further along the Avenue du Président-Wilson (XVIe.), the new Palais de Tokyo contained the Musée d'Art moderne, while the Grand Palais was also refitted so as to house the Palais de la Découverte, a science museum.

The new wave of museum creations highlighted a fact which was becoming increasingly apparent: the extraordinary array of museums and art galleries that the city had come to contain was a significant feature of Paris's international aura. The history of the city's museums and galleries goes back to the Ancien Régime, and the number of institutions had been much added to in the late nineteenth century. Paris's own history was commemorated, for example, in the Musée Carnavalet (1880) and the Bibliothèque historique de la Ville de Paris (1898). But it was really from the early twentieth century – when Paris continued to hold its rank of the art capital of the world – that this aspect of its cultural reputation came into its own. Besides the Exposition-related creations of the 1930s, major state institutions had also begun to offer their holdings to the tourist gaze, leading to the creation, for example, of the museums of the Police (1909), of Aeronautics (1920), of the Légion d'honneur (1925), of Assistance publique (1934) and of the postal services (1946). Other museums were the fruit of artists' bequests – such as those devoted to the work of Gustave Moreau (1903), Rodin (1919) and Monet (Musée Marmottan: 1934) – or else major philanthropic gestures, such as the museums of Jacquemart-André (1913), Cognacq-Jay (1929), and Nissim Camondo (1937). By mid-century Paris had become the home of an unmatched range of artistic and cultural heritage sites.

Cultural dynamism at the heart of the post-war city was accompanied by demographic torpor. While Paris was increasingly studded by museums, its population seemed in danger of mummification. The population of the twenty arrondissements had grown only slightly since 1900, and in 1921 stood at 2.9 million. This was to be an all-time high. Population level hovered around 2.8 million through to the mid-fifties, decreasing thereafter. Parisians were generally older, more settled and more bourgeois than their predecessors before the Great War. The ageing phenomenon was aggravated by the spread of contraception: the birth-rate, lower in France than in any of its international rivals, was lower still in the capital. If the city was to keep its head above water not only as a composite Sodom and Gomorrah but also as one of the largest cities in the world, alongside London, New York and (soon) Tokyo, its reputation now depended on the demographic vitality of the suburbs. Between 1900 and 1939 the population of the Paris *banlieue* grew by around 50 per cent – as against less than 5 per cent for the twenty arrondissements (and even less for France as a whole). In the aftermath of the Great War, the *banlieue* had contained 1.5 million inhabitants; by the late 1930s there were over two million *banlieusards*, as against 2.8 million Parisians. In some ways this was the big story in Paris's twentieth-century history: the city was on the point of being overtaken, if not dwarfed, by its suburbs.

The fact that both absolutely and relatively Paris's twenty arrondissements were stagnating would have been less worrying had the city been able to harness the dynamism of its suburbs into a coherent vision of its future. In fact it still pained most inhabitants of the core of the city to regard the *banlieue* as being part of the same community. The suburbs accentuated their notoriety as a *ceinture rouge* ('red belt'), full of workers and wild *apaches* whose radical convictions and delinquent excesses contrasted with the growing conservatism of Parisians. Suburban landscapes too were alien, threatening and devoid of meaning for most Parisians. The novelist Raymond Queneau characterized a suburban landscape as 'full of rubbish and old paper, forming a wasteland'. Poet-essayist Blaise Cendrars was even more forthright, depicting Paris's northern suburbs as full of

> gasworks, hospitals, loading yards, old peoples' homes, electricity gener-
> ators, refuges, marshalling yards, cemeteries, schools, missions, the Sal-
> vation Army, sports fields, knackers' yards, flea markets, bread factories,
> storehouses, military depots, monasteries, chapels, American surplus

depots, clandestine propaganda clubs, meeting rooms . . . soup-kitchens, orphanages, cheap food factories, and, like everywhere else, *Au Bon Coin*, a bistro, ten bistros, a hundred bistros . . .[7]

It might have been thought that the removal at this time of the physical boundary separating city from *banlieue* – the Thiers fortifications constructed in the 1840s – would present a golden opportunity for better overall integration. The ramparts were obsolete even in the late nineteenth century, and wartime aerial bombardment underlined the point. Yet the way in which this major change was handled accentuated rather than diminished city/*banlieue* antipathies. Many Parisians saw the *ceinture*, the strip of land – some 34 kilometres long and around half a kilometre wide – as having the potential to ease the city's housing crisis, which had become increasingly severe in the war years. Others hoped for the establishment on this virgin land of green space and leisure facilities of which Paris had comparatively little. The city decided to try to merge both ambitions. Plans focused initially on the bulk of the loop within the fortifications. More ambitious ideas were nurtured for the so-called *zone non aedificandi* – the strip of land hitherto kept free of housing for military purposes beyond the walls. This area had long been occupied by considerable numbers of squatters, the so-called *fortifs'* and *zonards*, who followed a gypsy-like existence, with very little by way of public amenities. These individuals were now elbowed aside.

The work of physical destruction of the old fortifications started in 1919. It developed slowly at first, and was only complete in 1932. Although progress was much slower in the outer ring – the last of the *zonards* were removed only in the 1940s – by this time Paris had come to be encircled by some 40,000 new dwellings. This development marked by far the most ambitious efforts at social housing in Parisian history hitherto. Napoleon III had dabbled in experiments with workers' homes, while the Third Republic had initially made it a priority to involve philanthropic trusts in such schemes. After the turn of the century, however, permissive legislation stimulated the setting up of social housing trusts, under municipal stewardship. In 1914 the Public Office for Cheap Housing (*Office public d'habitations à bon marché*) was created in Paris. Though war then intervened, the defunct fortifications provided the municipality with its big chance once hostilities were at an end. Out by Auteuil and Clichy in the west, some highly desirable bourgeois dwellings were created, but the bulk of new housing took the form of 'cheap housing' (HBMs, or *Habitations à bon marché*). The characteristic, seven-storey sets of buildings, solid rather than spectacular in appearance, were often designed around narrow alleys and courtyards. They form a still largely extant 'red-brick belt' just inside the notorious *ceinture rouge*.[8] There was to be some green-space development, most notably the Cité Universitaire, the student residential campus on the southern edge of the city, which came to contain a hotchpotch of architectural styles, ranging from *faux* gothic through Japanese and Greek temples and Swiss chalets to stark modernism. The space for other such developments was restricted by the municipality's decision to update the circular roadways around the city. Completed in 1939, the so-called *boulevards des maréchaux* (most of the streets being named after marshals of France) were extended from 20 to 40 metres wide. The bulk of traffic they attracted served to distance much of the outer new developments by a wall of noise and metallic mobility – a feature compounded by the advent of the circular *boulevard périphérique* in the 1960s. Building style and boulevards thus reinforced rather than dissolved the poor relationship between Paris and its *banlieue*, and a historic chance for greater integration passed virtually unperceived.

The fortifications project took up much of the energy of the municipal authorities. It represented their best effort at solving an accommodation shortage within Paris which had become the main social problem of these days of lost illusions. The municipal authorities found themselves in a difficult dilemma over housing policy. First, to demolish existing buildings so as to lay down new housing projects would cause a temporary reduction in dwellings, worsening matters in the short term. Second, to allow the laws of supply and demand to determine rent would lead to high rent rises which would trigger mass evictions and aggravate the very housing crisis they were trying to solve. The main method which they, backed by central government, chose for dealing with the housing problem was to continue the policy of rent freezes inaugurated during the Great War. Yet this set up another vicious circle, for rent control meant that private developers had little incentive to invest in building projects (and indeed even to maintain existing housing stock). A sop to landlords was the government's weakening of compulsory expropriation laws (in a way, incidentally, which earlier would have effectively prevented Haussmann from having had any impact on the city). But many landlords simply chose to withdraw their properties from the rental market altogether, worsening the housing crisis. One municipal inquiry revealed that around one-third of Parisian dwellings were overcrowded, but that some 30,000 dwellings were unoccupied and not on the market. Those that were exemplified the effects of overcrowding and low investment. Electricity had spread into most homes by 1939, it is true, yet only half had an inside or unshared toilet, and one-third were still not connected up to the mains sewer. Water-heaters, cookers, irons, refrigerators, vacuum cleaners and televisions were dreamed-of luxuries available only to the bourgeoisie of the western arrondissements.

A further inhibiting factor on major housing development was the emergence of an urban conservation movement. Haussmann had remodelled nineteenth-century Paris within an almost total conservationist vacuum. Yet even though the Haussmannian spirit continued to preside over Parisian development long after his removal from power, by the late nineteenth century an anti-Haussmannian reaction was setting in.[9] No one defended the maintenance of poor-quality and pathogenic working-class housing on principle. But a sense was developing that repair and adaptation was sometimes better (and might even be cheaper) than demolition. Urbanist theory had emerged around the turn of the century. The word *urbanisme* entered the language in 1910 – though it took a quarter of a century for the term to appear in national legislation. Urbanists stressed that the overall material texture of the city was as important as its major public monuments. 'The old monuments left standing,' the Catholic writer Louis Veuillot had complained in 1867 when Haussmannism still held sway, 'don't mean anything any more, because everything around them has changed.'[10] An ancient monument was increasingly seen as deriving its historic meanings within the city and much of its aesthetic charm from this kind of contextualization. The Haussmannian principle of *dégagement* ('separation'), whereby a major monument was denuded of its adjacent buildings, was now increasingly viewed as questionable.

Parisian public authorities were not averse to these developing conservationist arguments, which in some particulars echoed the tradition of municipal building regulations back to 1783. National legislators warmed to the theme too, giving it a chauvinistic spin: it was important to maintain the Parisian tradition against moves to increase building heights which threatened to make the city into New York or Chicago. In 1909 a Commission on Monumental Perspectives was established whose remit was to ensure that no new building in Paris spoiled a favoured urban skyline or obstructed a monumental vista. (National legislation in 1930, then in 1943, would confirm arrangements for giving protection to buildings immediately adjacent to national monuments.) By 1900 the conservationist movement had built up a good head of steam within the wider public too. The *Société des amis des monuments parisiens*, founded in 1885 under the patronage of Victor Hugo and Charles Garnier, had played an important role in blocking some of the wilder schemes for an overground métro in the 1890s. From 1897 the *Commission du Vieux Paris*, conjoining amateur activists with the Prefect of the Seine and other local dignitaries, acted as a voice for the new movement, even though their ability actually to block demolition was limited. Writers, artists and historians both professional and amateur, also became involved in the movement. The latter was also aided by the emergence of neighbourhood history and heritage societies, some of which produced their own learned journals – the *Vieux Montmartre* (1886), for example, the *Montagne Sainte-Geneviève* (1895), the *VIe. Arrondissement* (1898) and *La Cité* (1902). In 1913 national legislation which was a 'first' in European terms provided for a register of protected buildings and also established procedures for listing.

11.2: The *Vespasiennes*

The Roman emperor Vespasian (AD 69–70) was said to have established amphoras in the streets of Rome, and taxed individuals who urinated in them. This seemingly little-known fact was used to provide a euphemistic name for the new street urinals which Count Rambuteau, Prefect of the Seine, began to install around Paris in the 1830s. The *vespasienne* – more vulgarly, the *pissoir*, or *pissotière* – provided a standard and redolent piece of Parisian street furniture until a campaign of urban renovation in the 1960s and 1970s. While Guimard's Métro entrances were saved from the scrap-heap, scarcely one example of a *vespasienne* survives.

The first *vespasiennes* were one-person affairs, resembling sentry-boxes. The people of Paris dubbed them 'Rambuteaus' – a name they also gave to every hole that the street-improvement-mad prefect had dug in the road. Perhaps this is a comment on Parisians' sanitary habits at the time, which caused visitors to wince. *Vespasiennes* developed in time into two-man and ultimately multi-person amenities, each with a light over them, producing a kind of masculine sociability about which their defenders later waxed nostalgic. The poet Barthélemy apostrophized 'boulevard columns [which] prevent the shy / From needing modestly to avert the eye'. (It sounded better in French.) Historian Richard Cobb spoke fondly too of 'these welcoming artistically perforated chapels of fraternity'.

It was of course under the Second Empire that the *vespasienne* really came into its own. Baron Haussmann – and his trusty associate Alphand – sought to equip all the new boulevards, roadways and public parks of the city with an impressive ensemble of street furniture including street lamps, benches, iron railings, street signs, post-boxes, newspaper kiosks, tree-supports, tree-root protectors, publicity columns (the so-called Morris columns), and water fountains (particularly the Wallace fountains installed at the expense of the English philanthropist Sir Richard Wallace from the 1870s). Each piece of street furniture was the object of considerable technical precision in design and placement. There were seven basic models of lamp-post, for example, but no fewer than seventy-eight different types. The multiple variants always had a family resemblance, which helped give the streets of Paris its variously cluttered but familiar and (some said) rather homely air. One Danish visitor in 1891 commended pavement cafés for giving the impression of 'a reserved seat in the street, a sort of comfortable sofa-corner in the great common parlour'.

If in some respects at least, as Walter Benjamin noted, the boulevard resembled the bourgeois home, it was not surprising that the bourgeoisie's critics should resort to vandalism. The Communards of 1871, for example, used Haussmannian street furniture – notably tree-root protectors – as functional trophies in the building of barricades. Another critic of bourgeois culture, the artist Marcel Duchamp, in his Dada and Surrealist phase provided another kind of critique: his famous, scandal-producing art installation 'Fontaine', exhibited in New York in 1917, was a public urinal.

From the earliest days the *vespasienne* had attracted photographers. These curious confections, whose architectural styles ran the range from gothic through classical to the baroque (with occasional pagoda-like accessories), eventually took their place as privileged parts of *le Vieux Paris*. Yet photographers and Impressionist painters seem in fact to have regarded them less as atavistic throwbacks than as icons of Parisian modernity. Symptomatically, from Rambuteau's time onwards they were used for attaching advertising and, from the later nineteenth century, colour posters. These posters could be for almost any modern commodity, though by the 1930s American resident Henry Miller (an enthusiastic devotee of the *vespasienne*) was complaining that they had become the site for public health announcements concerning venereal disease, featuring 'the various stages of syphilis or gonorrhea (from the germ plasm up to the death skull – a leering, grinning figure of death and disease with empty sockets)'. By then, the comic, archaic character of the *pissoir* was being highlighted by Gabriel Chevallier's novel *Clochemerle* (1934), which revolves around the placement of a public urinal.

The decline of the *vespasienne* owed something to the improvement in domestic sanitary equipment. The slow spread of private bathrooms and WCs, particularly in working-class housing, prolonged the relative profusion of *vespasiennes* on the Parisian streets. In 1914 there were 4,000 of them, by 1930, some 1,200. By the eve of the Second World War their number had tumbled by nearly half and from the mid-fifties it bottomed out at around 300 to 350. By then the authorities were focusing on providing more hygienic public conveniences ('*chalets de nécéssité*') which could be used by both sexes. They seem to have disappeared totally from the late 1970s, at which time Mayor Jacques Chirac had introduced hygienic paying *sanisettes* (though the practice of referring to these as 'Chiracs' in his honour never caught on).

The unisex *sanisette* has removed a familiar component of the characteristic stench of Parisian streets on which visitors never failed to comment. It also removed a source of male sociability which was much exploited, as Proust knew all too well, by Paris's homosexual subculture. A questionnaire to *pissoir*-users in the 1960s revealed a high number of individuals who had had their first offer of homosexual sex within a *vespasienne*. Crime – muggings, murders, assaults, prostitution – was also attracted to this site – as were crime writers. The historian Louis Chevalier evoked the way in which

> the tree, the gas street-lamp and the urinal [formed] the Holy Trinity of the outer boulevards, the three props for tragic drama, as indispensable as the outsize bed, the dressing table and, hidden by a Chinese screen, the immodest bidet . . . to that other genre, the *comédie du boulevard*.

The *vespasienne* is gone but not forgotten. For long commemorated in visual culture, fiction and remembrances, it constitutes a significant Parisian site of memory.

The trend towards conservation was helped by the fact that the Haussmannian tradition was now being taken forward by a modernist movement which had failed to secure a popular following. Pivotal in this respect was the 1925 Exposition. The Swiss Charles-Édouard

Jeanneret, known as Le Corbusier, presented a stand, the 'Pavilion of the New Spirit', based on modernist design highlighting a functionalist aesthetic and industrial materials (reinforced concrete, glass, etc.). He also issued the so-called Voisin plan for the future of the city. The plan involved the effective demolition of central Paris. Under his *tabula rasa* approach, only a few approved public monuments would be left *in situ* in the middle of empty green space – there was 'nothing more seductive', according to Le Corbusier, than this kind of Haussmannian *dégagement*.[11] Massive new highways would sweep through the centre from each of the cardinal points, and set the framework for a grid of massive forty-storey skyscrapers – thus evoking a New York few Parisians wanted to be imported into their midst. Le Corbusier and his acolytes would peddle variants of this plan to potential clients for nearly half a century, notably through the CIAM ('Congrès inter-nationaux d'architecture moderne') which they established in the late 1920s and which became the promoter of the modernist aesthetic.

In the course of his life Le Corbusier was to design a small number of buildings in Paris, mostly private dwellings (and mostly, moreover, architectural gems). His seemingly megalomaniacal plans for the rebuilding of Paris, however, gave modernism a bad name and added more grist to the conservationist mill. Buildings in the modernist idiom in the following decades tended to be located on the outer reaches of the city or beyond. Left-wing mayors in some of the suburbs – such as Suresnes, Villejuif and Drancy, for example – started to experiment with high-rise blocks of social housing which were more architec-turally adventurous than the 'red-brick belt' of HBMs. They failed to excite their denizens. (The fact that the Cité de La Muette blocks out at Drancy were to become the major concentration camp for deporting Jews to Nazi death camps in the Second World War hardly added to their perceived charms.) New types of buildings often tended to attract modernist architects too. Factories and showrooms spread the mod-ernist idiom discreetly within the city. So did cinemas – which num-bered 204 by 1922. These combined 'new spirit' inspiration with Art Deco and other, more bizarre elements – as at the 'Grand Rex' on the Boulevard Poissonnière (IXe.), the most glamorous new cinema in Paris (which was a dancehall as well as a cinema), incisively described by historian Richard Cobb as 'a sort of cube in beige cement that looked like a permanent ice cream'.[12] Just within the city limits there was a move to build modernist-influenced churches, usually in reinforced concrete. A related development was the construction in the early 1920s of a Paris mosque off the Rue Monge (Ve.), whose modernist touches were finished off with a 33-metre minaret.

The Parisian public was generally repelled by modernism and increasingly drawn to the aesthetic of the picturesque emerging from the conservationist movement. We have already highlighted the role of painters, especially from the Impressionists onwards, in the mythologization of late nineteenth-century Paris.[13] As time went on, photography also played a significant part in this process. Baron Haussmann had defended himself against conservationist detractors by insisting that 'before and after' photographs should be taken of all areas developed under his administration. The photographer Marville made his name in this way, while Nadar took the first photographic images of Haussmann's sewers and the Parisian catacombs, as well as specializing in aerial panoramas of the city. The growth of a mass market for photographic views – now often placed on the front of postcards, a communications technology which really took off around 1900 – provided a colossal audience for the photographic representation of le Vieux Paris.

The trend was taken further by photographer Eugène Atget, who worked hand in glove with the Commission du Vieux Paris from before the Great War. Although he was to die in 1927 bitter that his great documentary vision of Parisian topography was never published, his copious and well-known images of Paris fuelled the movement in favour of the Parisian picturesque. Yet the latter notion had an ideological double edge. It highlighted the idea that the beauty of Paris derived from its inherited built environment, but also implied that its inhabitants were almost irrelevant to its charms save as folkloric bit-players. 'Poor or dramatic sites,' Georges Cain, curator at the Musée Carnavalet, had written, 'gain by remaining vague and a little mysterious . . . Picturesque silhouettes are extremely striking, but they are dishonoured and devalued by all kinds of things.'[14] By 'all kinds of things', Cain seems to have had in mind the impedimenta of urban distress, most notably the poor themselves. In this sense the quest for the Parisian picturesque was, as Molly Nesbit has put it, 'part of the procedure for not seeing poverty'.[15]

Although Atget was relatively forgotten at the time of his death, his posthumous fame was boosted when his work was championed by a team of young photographers including Man Ray, Brassaï, Berenice Abbott and Walker Evans. Each of these developed individual styles which also often highlighted Parisians and the Paris cityscape. Photojournalism had been pioneered at the time of the 1871 Commune, but it was really in the 1930s that it achieved rounded form mainly, it should be noted, in the work of foreign photographers such as André Kertesz and Germaine Krull. Perhaps influenced by the 'found object' which had pleased the Surrealists, they often focused on mundane but revealing details of everyday life. They influenced the later humanistic work of Robert Doisneau and Henri Cartier-Bresson. Unlike the work of Atget and earlier enthusiasts for the Parisian picturesque, these photographers did not recoil from the poor – indeed tramps and prostitutes were a frequent subject, and they celebrated the everyday actions of *le petit peuple parisien* in time of peace – as well as, all too soon, in time of war. They put the poor back into the timeless picture of Paris.

From the 1920s a notable part of the artistic and literary avant-garde was adapting to the notion of a Paris which was familiar and *déjà vu* rather than a hard-edged modernist vision. The Surrealist movement, which, as we have seen,[16] denounced the Parisian triumphalism of the 1931 Colonial Exposition, was interesting in this respect. The group had grown out of the wartime Dada movement's rejection of western civilization and all its works, and it retained a Dadaist antipathy towards bourgeois values. In the writings of, especially, Louis Aragon (*Le Paysan de Paris*, 1926) and André Breton (notably his *Nadja*, 1928), Haussmann's Paris is largely irrelevant. For them the city was not a site to be read using the aggrandizing emphasis on perspective put in place under the Second Empire. Rather its meanings linked to a kind of collective unconscious which had to be intuited from the odd traces and signs of the past. Aragon's 'Paris peasant' (himself) haunts the relics and vestiges of the still labyrinthine city like a mystical and psychoanalytic *flâneur* seeking commonplace mysteries and epiphanies. Paris for the Surrealists was not the old 'City of Light' but a more dangerous and exciting zone of twilight states, refracted surfaces and looming shadows. Their elective terrain comprised wilfully bizarre locations situated away from the leisure-spots of the bourgeoisie, such as arcade-passages of the early nineteenth century now destined for demolition or else the Buttes-Chaumont park erected over the old medieval gibbet (and preferably experienced at night). The poetic realism of the photographs of Brassaï, who was linked to the Surrealists, similarly highlighted neon-lit boulevards, misty streets, louche bars and the exotic yet mundane brothels as part of Paris's mythic and captivating identity. Such was the force of the mythologized picturesqueness of Paris that a Surrealist vision intended to undercut the mythic view of the city only ended up contributing to the nostalgic myth of the timeless Paris of yesteryear.

Photography, cinema and popular song mythologized Paris by endlessly placing in the same frame love, sex and Paris (and often memory to boot). Although photography increasingly aspired to be treated as high art – the first *Salon indépendant de la photographie* was held in 1927 – it was still massively popular in terms of its audience, and it played a major part in affirming a view of picturesque Paris which combined sometimes gritty realism, seductive charm and wistful nostalgia. (The absence of the medium of colour helped in this.) Much the same applied to cinema. Many of the most popular films of the late 1920s and 1930s were set in a kind of 'populo-nostalgic' Paris, and starred actors associated in the public mind with particular types of working-class Parisian. Maurice Chevalier and Jean Gabin made their names in this way, while the tiny *chanteuse* Édith Piaf was promoted as *le moineau* – the little (Parisian) sparrow. In René Clair's 1933 film *Le 14 juillet*, for example, a female character plaintively, but characteristically, sings:

À Paris, dans chaque faubourg	In every Paris faubourg
Le soleil de chaque journée	The sun, as it rises,
Fait en quelques destinées	For some brings into blossom
Éclore un rêve d'amour.	A dream of love.[17]

In *Le 14 juillet*, as in Clair's *Sous les toits de Paris* (1930), the city's locations and the dreams of its *petit peuple* became an integral part of

French film. Occasionally it did seem possible to set a film in Paris without having a shot of the Eiffel tower, and other locations came to fix themselves in the imagination of the huge film-going public. The dank and atmospheric dockside ambience of the Canal Saint-Martin was one such site, where Marcel Carné's *Hôtel du Nord* (1938) was set. The themes of this type of popular culture – as in Carné's *Le Jour se lève* (1939) – stressed the city as a haunting, unchanging and sometimes spectral site, which offered little to the working classes, who only had their natural spirit to fall back on. The banality of working-class crime in such locations was underpinned by the rise of the detective novel and other crime fiction. Crime novelist Georges Simenon's famous Inspector Maigret – operative in fiction from 1929 – lived on the Boulevard Richard-Lenoir (XIe.), but would not allow his wife near the delinquent dives of the adjacent Canal Saint-Martin.

Extraordinarily, the sense of a never-changing Paris which was being recreated by French film in these years only sparingly used live location shooting. Quite a few of the streets in René Clair's films, as Richard Cobb has remarked, 'look as if they had been put up in Épinay (they had)'.[18] The eponymous Hôtel du Nord was a cardboard creation. For his film *Les Portes de la Nuit* (1945), director Marcel Carné had the whole of the 'aerial' Métro station of Barbès-Rochechouart lovingly recreated in the studio. Only from the 1950s did location shooting become the norm, further expanding the photogenic potential of the city. Jean-Pierre Melville's 1959 gangster movie *Bob le Flambeur* presented a Montmartre *noir* unsuspected by those used to postcard images of the Sacré-Coeur.

If the film studios played a role in developing the notion of the city as timeless, the central parts of the city itself were indeed taking on the character of an unchanging film set. An astonishingly small number of new dwellings were built, particularly in the inner areas, in the 1930s and 1940s. Indeed between 1914 and 1942 some 92 per cent of houses built in the Paris region were located in the *banlieue* rather than within Paris. It was possible to grow up in inter-war Paris without ever passing a building site. The outbreak of bubonic plague in the XVIIe. arrondissement in the early 1920s underlined the seriousness of the public health issues implicit in a decaying cityscape. Yet the public authorities were too short of cash and the private sector too lacking in incentives, for much to get done. Significantly, nearly all the seventeen areas designated as *îlots insalubres* ('unhealthy blocks') as a prelude to redevelopment escaped demolition. Outright demolition was partly discredited by the experience of what often ensued. The original idea had been that tenants displaced by demolition would relocate to less teeming areas, but in fact they simply stayed in the neighbourhood and worsened overcrowding. In practice the urban authorities were again somewhat let off the hook by emerging evidence in the 1930s that there was no close link between overcrowded housing and tuberculosis rates (though the re-emergence of the disease in the Vichy years brought this fear back under the spotlight). Finally, less destructive approaches also were tried: it seemed possible to renovate an *îlot* in line with public health needs by keeping the façade on the street, but creating an airy courtyard in the middle of the block and redeveloping dwellings around this.

While central Paris in the decades following the Great War stagnated, both demographically and in terms of the built environment, the Paris region as a whole boomed – and grew. The city lacked the dwellings to accommodate those who wished to live and work within it: the *banlieue* made up the difference. Yet there were only the meagrest of efforts to plan or to direct the urban growth which followed, leading to a chaotic sprawl. The failure to come to terms with the changing shape of the Parisian agglomeration may be laid at the door of both national and local authorities. The powers of the Paris prefect chosen by government extended to the whole of the department of the Seine. An even wider vision than this was required, however, in that the Parisian sprawl was soon enveloping the neighbouring departments of Seine-et-Oise and Seine-et-Marne, providing an outer ring, or crown (*couronne*), beyond the suburbs abutting the line of the old fortifications. A *Commission d'extension* established in 1910 and comprising engineers, architects such as Louis Bonnier and archivist-urbanists such as Marcel Poëte, endeavoured to deal with urban growth by containment rather than expansion. The enduring unwillingness to countenance the idea, and indeed the likelihood, that the city's growth was set to continue in the future, dogged all efforts to grasp the regional nettle. National legislation in 1919 obliged all France's cities to come up with a development plan, but the plan for Paris was late-coming, slow-moving, timid and generally ineffectual.

In 1925 a *Comité supérieur d'aménagement et d'organisation géné-rale de la région parisienne* was established, reporting to the Ministry of the Interior. In due time it established a working group which produced the 1934 Prost Plan (named after its chairman). Character-istically, Prost accepted as his remit 'organizing Greater Paris rather than extending it',[19] but his plan, which was made law in 1939, was not unimaginative and took a step in the right direction in designating as the Paris region all locations within 35 kilometres from Notre-Dame de Paris – an important mark of acceptance of the logic and extent of suburbanization. The plan urged the protection of green space, a degree of zoning of industrial activity and residential space, and a better transport system, which was to be achieved less through rail improvements than by road construction. (In practice lack of invest-ment in infrastructure meant that there was relatively little construc-tion in the rail and métro sector, while in 1945 France's answer to the German autobahn and the US freeway would be a measly eight kilometres of autoroute linking Paris towards Saint-Cloud.) The hostil-ity of a great many municipalities in the Île-de-France to this degree of direction from on high, plus a level of political deadlock within Paris over the issues, ensured that the Prost Plan – which, despite all these difficulties, remained the prevailing framework for regional development until 1960 – achieved very little.

Political stagnation in Paris made regional development all the more chaotic. The Île-de-France maintained its place as one of the most important industrial zones nationally. This owed something to Paris's historic dominance in a number of sectors, including publishing and *haute couture* (in both of which the city enjoyed a virtual national monopoly), jewellery and the nascent radio-communications industry. Yet the structure of employment within the twenty arrondissements was continuing to evolve. Between 1906 and 1931 industrial employ-ment rose by 32 per cent, but jobs in banking and business rose 52 per cent, in the liberal professions by 60 per cent and in administration and services by 77 per cent. Two-thirds of France's journalists, artists, actors and musicians lived in the city – as did nearly half of the nation's students. As well as all the other branches of leisure in which Paris specialized, virtually all major sports occasions were staged in the city, boosting the tourist trade, and making its sports venues familiar to international audiences. This was helped by the fact that the inter-war period was an exceptional moment in French sporting history: immediately after the Great War the heavyweight boxer Georges Charpentier was world champion, the Olympics were held in the city in 1924, the national soccer team won the World Cup in 1930 and Borotra, Cochet and Lacoste – tennis's 'three musketeers' – enjoyed a run of success through the 1930s.

With Paris itself on the cusp of deindustrialization, the region's industrial heartlands lay out at the periphery, in the ever-expanding *banlieue*. The Great War had confirmed the status of the suburbs as the ideal site for the French car industry and for automobile construction and its associated trades (lorries, army supply, aircraft). Citroën lay just within the Fifteenth arrondissement, but the Renault fortress was out at Boulogne-Billancourt to the west. The chemical and food-refining industries prospered in the *banlieue* too, giving localities such as Aubervilliers a characteristically nauseous smell. The virtual absence of building regulations in the *banlieue* made the construction of industrial plant almost problem-free.

A combination of the relative strength of a regional economy which attracted workers and the high price and scarcity of housing in Paris served to stimulate the building of new housing in the *banlieue* in a context equally devoid of planning regulations. Those who found it most difficult to break into the Parisian housing market tended to be provincials and foreigners. New waves of Poles, Russians and Italians made a big impression on the Parisian melting-pot, while good numbers of Czechs and Slovaks also appeared for the first time. Around one-fifth of population growth in the Paris region between 1921 and 1936 was accounted for by foreigners. The latter made up around 3 per cent of the city's population in 1921 – but nearly 10 per cent by the early 1930s, a level no other major European city could match. Yet though Paris maintained its ethnic heterogeneity, it was beginning to lose many of the young people on whom the economy depended.[20] The *banlieue* acted as the city's demographic safety-net, where disproportionate numbers of younger workers and recent immigrants were forced to establish themselves. Conversely, it was a kind of El Dorado for many Parisian workers who liked the idea of a place in the country with a garden as a hedge against destitution in old age, and the possibility of far more space than they could hope to enjoy in overcrowded Parisian dwellings.

Before the Great War urbanists had enthused over the notion of garden cities on the model being developed in England at the time. Yet garden cities needed planning; and planning was at a premium in post-war Paris. The 'extension' of Paris thus took place in a whirlwind of wild, unregulated initiatives. The most common form these took was the large estate – or *lotissement* – given over to one- or two-storey dwellings. These developments were financed by mutual savings schemes and conducted by property speculation businesses. The *lotissement* they produced turned out to be very problematic. Property companies often sold just the land, meaning that purchasers effectively squatted in temporary housing until they could afford something better. Weak planning controls meant that the companies also were under no pressure to provide the most basic infrastructure.

After a decade of this kind of development producing, in housing terms, what novelist Jules Romains described as 'dustbin scrapings',[21] a growing chorus of support emerged in support of the *mal-lotis*, that is, individuals who had bought property often with the fondest of arcadian dreams only to find themselves stuck on tracts of land without decent streets, rail and road links, or the most basic services. The English writer Aldous Huxley was shocked beyond measure on encountering one such colony of *mal-lotis* at Villejuif:

> We were only seven or eight kilometres from the Paris Opéra, but there were no drains . . . and no water supply. I am not exaggerating when I say that the living conditions in these *lotissements* were considerably worse than the average village of Guatemala or southern Mexico.[22]

By the time that Romains and Huxley were writing in such terms, however, the government was finally acting. The 1928 Sarraut Law put a stop to the kind of uncontrolled development of the past decade, while the Loucher Law in the same year made provision for government support for mortgage schemes in the *lotissements*. Better controls were put on planned developments, and it became mandatory to include in new schemes the provision of roads and pavements (1928), drainage (1929), water supply (1930), and gas and electricity (1931). But the full impact of such changes was limited by the downturn of the economy after 1931 and the impecuniousness of the government. By the mid-1930s money for mortgage schemes under the terms of the Loucher Law was running out.

The poor quality of housing for ever larger numbers of workers in the suburban crown around Paris after the Great War combined with the low quality of life provided there to produce a radicalization of voting patterns, which exacerbated the *banlieue*'s reputation as the *ceinture rouge*. The areas with large numbers of *mal-lotis* invariably voted for the newly formed Communist Party of France (PCF). Tension within the labour movement following the relative failure of agitation in 1918–20 had led to a schism within the Socialist Party (the SFIO). In the latter's Tours Congress in 1921 the fraction who wished to take up membership in the Moscow-run Third International formed themselves into a Communist Party which followed the Soviet line on all major issues. In electoral terms nationally, the SFIO generally outdistanced the PCF, but not in the Paris region, where the PCF was generally (though not always) the dominant partner. The Communists proved especially adept at using local and residential issues – provision of schools, dispensaries, public washrooms, libraries and the like – as well as workplace militancy as mobilizing tools. Success for the Left at the 1924 elections saw the Communists doing well all around the 'red belt': 'Paris encircled by the revolutionary proletariat', crowed a headline in the Communists' newspaper *L'Humanité*. Although the PCF failed to make as great a national impact as it had hoped – its efforts to head a general strike in 1925 were a failure – it set itself up as a major power in the region through its control of municipalities outside the *boulevards des maréchaux*. Communist leaders established local fiefs which in turn acted as a springboard for prominence at the national level: this was true for the Communist leader Maurice Thorez at Ivry, Jacques Doriot at Saint-Denis, Jean-Marie Clamamus at Bobigny and Jacques Duclos in Montreuil. They maintained their own power-base while simultaneously attacking the conservative Paris municipality as 'a haven for fascists'.[23]

PARIS: BIOGRAPHY OF A CITY

The red belt got redder still in the 1930s. The downturn in the
Parisian economy after 1931 led to a jump in unemployment levels.
The PCF attempted to channel working-class militancy not only
against the Right but also against other left-wing parties which barred
its way, and which it accused of being soft on the rise of right-wing
forms of extremism which had already borne grim fruit in Fascist Italy
and (from 1933) Nazi Germany. The Third Republic was by far the
longest-lived of all regimes in France since 1789, but was widely
viewed as having run its course. The aura of corruption and double-
dealing which had hung round it in the *fin de siècle* had not gone away.
Furthermore the critique from the revolutionary Left was matched by
a right-wing movement which similarly prized taking politics out of
the Chamber of Deputies and onto the streets. Die-hard monarchists
combined with dyed-in-the-wool anti-Semites, veterans' associations
and admirers of Mussolini and Hitler to produce a powerful political
bloc. Their cause was given ideological respectability by intellectuals
like the writer Charles Maurras whose movement and newspaper
L'Action française had never got over the outcome of the Dreyfus
Affair.

The streets of Paris were increasingly the venue in which political
extremists from Right and Left fought each other – and protested
against the Third Republic. The demonstrative, theatrical character
of much of this activity was increasingly evident. The transformation
in communications produced by the advent of radio and (soon) television made the simple fact of Parisian protest a national and indeed
international phenomenon. Parisians still read more newspapers
than any other comparable group, but they now listened to the radio
too. From 1898 the Eiffel tower had acted as a radio transmitter, and
by the early 1930s over 40 per cent of homes had a radio set. From
1937 the tower also served for television broadcasting. Although the
tiny TV audience was still restricted to the capital, Parisian radio
stations were very widely received through the country. Audiences
showed particular interest in popular music and national sports. Yet
besides influencing popular leisure, radio also built itself into national
political culture. The municipal elections of 1935 were the first in
which political broadcasts seem to have started to influence voter
choice. Cinema also played an important role here. By 1939 Parisians

were going to the cinema at least once a week, and the newsreels shown with every performance kept them updated on the international news.

That the context for Paris-based political action was changing was highlighted by the extraordinary impact of the Stavisky Affair, a political scandal centred on the eponymous Ukrainian businessman and involving accusations of corruption and police cover-ups. On 6 February 1934 a right-wing protest over the Affair was staged, targeting the National Assembly. The demonstration descended into bitter street fighting on the Pont de la Concorde leading towards the Palais Bourbon in which the Assembly sat. The fighting left sixteen dead and hundreds wounded. The events were almost certainly not part of an attempted right-wing *coup d'état*, as the Left claimed, but a deliberately ostentatious gesture of protest and exasperation. Nonetheless, the day's events highlighted the need for the Left to be politically vigilant and to put an end to internecine squabbling. Prompted by Moscow, the Communists signed an electoral agreement with the SFIO and the Radical Socialist grouping on 14 July 1935 – a day on which the united Left staged a massive street procession in the city. The left-wing parties went into the 1936 elections united and with a common Popular Front programme which in the event carried all before it.

The Popular Front government of Socialist Prime Minister Léon Blum was immediately faced by a nationwide wave of strikes and spontaneous factory occupations by workers determined to see their electoral victory turned immediately into social gains. The occupations, from May 1936 onwards, hit industries and professions across the spectrum. Paris was to the fore, with 150,000 workers on strike at one point in early June. The occupations – which hit not only heavy industry but also shops, the *grands magasins*, banks and insurance companies, hotels and restaurants and so on – marked a touching expression of working-class fraternity in the context of long-deferred hopes for change. The writer Simone Weil remembered her own, and others', 'joy at hearing, instead of the pitiless din of the machines, music, singing, laughter'.[24] Improvised concerts and dances, chatter and gossip, cards and *boules*, passed pell-mell into Parisian folk-memory of this unlikely episode.

Cleaners from a department store on strike, 1936

With essential help from Communist leader Maurice Thorez, Blum negotiated the so-called Matignon agreements with representatives of the unions and with business leaders, which demobilized the whole movement. The package of measures was indeed radical, and included a forty-hour week, paid holidays (which allowed many Parisian workers to break into the holiday and leisure market for the first time), large wage rises, better workplace negotiating mechanisms, and nationalization of key industries (including the railways and war industries). Yet this memorable and historic programme had to be paid for, and this proved problematic. Salary increases in particular triggered an inflationary spiral which then put pressure on interest rates and the balance of trade, and ate away the 1936 wage rises. Blum's attempts at compromise irritated the Communists, causing a marked worsening of the social atmosphere. A fresh round of strikes in the Paris car industry in the spring of 1938 led onto a political crisis in which Blum's government fell. His successors tried unavailingly to boost industrial production, especially as by this time the country was facing a grave international crisis and war was on the horizon. It had taken France until 1924 to restore gross national production to its 1913 levels, but this achievement, and further growth in successive years, had disappeared by 1939, when GNP was back to its 1913 levels.

The Paris which led France into war with Germany in 1939 was in bad economic shape. Morale too was poor. The latent pacifism evident in Parisian culture since the horrors of the Great War had not totally dissipated. Two of the film hits of the late 1930s were *La Règle du jeu* (1937), directed by Jean Renoir (son of the Impressionist painter), a devastating portrayal of the terminal frivolity and egoism of France's ruling elite, and the same director's *La Grande Illusion* (1939), an elegiac paean to universal brotherhood in time of war. After 'the dreadful, naked panic of the summer of 1938',[25] when war seemed on the cards, half a million individuals turned up at Le Bourget airport in October to provide a rhapsodic welcome for Édouard Daladier, who had signed the Munich agreement with Hitler promising peace. As the agreement came to be recognized as worthless, the 1939 German–Soviet Pact put the French Communist Party in an ambivalent position regarding the impending war with Germany. On the Right too there was distaste for going to war with a Nazi power they admired: cocktail chatter had it that Hitler was preferable to another bout of Léon Blum.

After a period of 'phoney war' (*'drôle de guerre'*), the campaign got under way in the summer of 1940, only for the Germans swiftly and comprehensively to out-manoeuvre a French army whose generals were too slow and perhaps too old to react. In early June the fleeing national government abandoned Paris to its fate as an 'open city'. Parisians faced the desperate and terrifying situation of being undefended as German motorized troops swooped towards them. A population exodus erupted, along the lines of the sudden panic emigrations which had occurred during the Great War – but on an even grander scale. The population of the Fourteenth arrondissement, for example, fell from 178,000 to 49,000 in a matter of days. When on 14 June the German troops penetrated the city, they discovered a Paris with only roughly a third of its normal population. The missing were to be found clogging up the roads south, maybe two million individuals joining eight million more from all over northern France, in a caravan of cars, trucks, handcarts, perambulators, livestock, cats and dogs, and hastily assembled possessions. Many who fled came back fairly soon: the city's population stood at around two million in October 1940, and 2.5 million by January 1941. By that time, however, both the city and the nation had been forced to accept a highly humiliating armistice. On 23 June Hitler had flown to the city to indulge in some mild, self-congratulatory sightseeing, as his minions prepared to organize a defeated France into Germany's new European order.

If the campaign of 1940 was a disaster for Paris of epic proportions, the peace with Germany which followed was arguably worse. Very few Parisians had heard Charles de Gaulle on 18 June plead from London on BBC airwaves for his compatriots to continue the struggle. The tank officer and recently appointed Defence Minister had left France as it was becoming apparent that resistance was the last thing on the mind of his government. The latter's peregrinations led it to the spa-town of Vichy where, on 10 July, in the unlikely setting of the municipal casino, the rump of the National Assembly had voted full powers to Field-Marshal Philippe Pétain for the creation of a new constitution. This hero of the Great War, brought into government so as to bolster resistance, now presided over rank capitulation, allowing the German victors to perform brutal surgery on the French body politic. The contested region of Alsace-Lorraine was incorporated into Germany. France was now ruled by an 'independent' government operating out of Vichy under the presidency of Pétain. But the northern half of the country, including Paris, was under permanent German occupation, which was extended to the whole of the country in 1942 when Germany increased the occupied area to cover all of France. As far back as the Merovingians there had been a whole series of projects to relocate the capital of France out of Paris, where Clovis had established it: Pétain was the first to effect the change. A curious consequence of this state of affairs was that the Vichy government maintained an ambassador in Paris, as though the occupied northern zone were a separate country.

The bookseller Adrienne Monnier had noted in her diary on 14 June 1940 people in the street saying, 'What if the Germans are here, there will at least be order.' By the 17th she was recording, 'Gloomy evening. I feel defeat and that it's going to be fascism.'[26] The Vichy state developed home-grown ideological forms derived from Fascism, which were nourished by close collaboration with the Nazi occupiers. The ignominious end of the Third Republic seemed to Pétain and his supporters a righteous condemnation of the liberal and republican values which the former regime had embodied. The Left was in disarray – the Communist Party, already effectively operating underground, would be outlawed when Hitler declared war on the USSR in June 1941, and leader Thorez would slip away from France and spend the war in Moscow. In these circumstances, moreover, Paris's aura as the birthplace of the republican triad of liberty, equality and fraternity was a handicap. The Vichy regime proposed as its slogan the values of work, family and fatherland. This highlighted the regime's endorsement of the allegedly more authentic values of the traditional countryside over those of the modern city. The peasant counted for more in Vichy's scale of values than the proletarian – and certainly the Parisian.

There were a number of often quite divergent strands within the Vichyite camp. Paris contained the leaders of the main political parties and groupings permitted by the regime. The Parti Populaire Français (PPF) of renegade Communist Jacques Doriot, the long-time mayor

of Saint-Denis, supplied the most overtly pro-Fascist political organization, and this was flanked by a group of sinister street-fighters. Deeply
conservative, hierarchical and patriarchal, the regime tried also to
move away from the class politics which had bedevilled inter-war
politics by establishing a more corporatist approach to labour and
industry. At times, formally at least, this recalled the institutions of
the Ancien Régime monarchy, yet it also provided a framework within
which technocratic ideas could be explored. In its short history, before
it was closed down and many of its members went off to join the
Resistance, the École des cadres at Uriage proved a seedbed of the
Fourth and Fifth Republic technocrats. Some liberal and humanist
Catholics such as Emmanuel Mounier, editor of the journal *Esprit*,
were initially attracted by Vichy, though they were soon disenchanted.
Generally the more traditionalist Catholic elites were among the keenest supporters of the regime, and endorsed its stiflingly reactionary
social policies: women were to be kept in the home and to bring up
children. A law of February 1942 made abortion a state crime, and
one female abortionist went to the guillotine in a Parisian prison for
her activities.

Under the new dispensation, only the trappings of Paris's civic
independence remained. Paris's municipal council was dissolved, then
reappointed, but it only met annually at best and in secret. The Prefect
of the Seine department and the police prefect were appointed by the
German occupying forces, to whom each reported. The key figures in
local governance were Germans. Prefectoral responsibilities for Paris
as well as the departments of Seine, Seine-et-Marne and Seine-et-Oise
were assumed by the commandant for 'Greater Paris' (*Gross-Paris*).
(Oddly it took a foreigner to notice a regional interdependence which
Parisians themselves had been reluctant to countenance.) The department's office was placed in the Palais-Bourbon, erstwhile home of the
National Assembly, which had the slogan '*Deutschland siegt an allen
Fronten*' ('Germany is victorious on all fronts') plastered across the
front. The headquarters of the Occupation forces was placed in the
Opéra, and the military authorities inhabited the Hôtel Meurice on
the Rue de Rivoli and the *Abwehr* the Hôtel Lutétia. In the four years
of their Occupation the Germans made no contribution or addition

to the inherited built environment; they merely placed the trappings of their power over what they had found, enjoying their possession of French sites of memory and the swankiest hotels. Vichy achieved little by way of new building either – there was simply no cash for projects. Its embrace of the principle of conservation was based on the assumption that *le Vieux Paris* contained something worth preserving. It also prized traditional craftsmanship, and favoured styles of building recalling medieval-style gabled housing.

The Germanization of Paris was evident in the apparent ubiquity of German army uniforms, the sound of German voices in every nook of the city and in the installation of German signposts throughout it. The hostility which the signposts stimulated was psychological rather than practical in origin, for there was precious little motorized French traffic. The number of cars dropped from 350,000 to a mere 4,500, and of 3,500 buses only 500 survived. Petrol coupons had been introduced in autumn 1940, and shortages of petrol grew progressively worse. Many lorries ran using gas. In these circumstances the Métro provided some compensation – usage was at its all-time high in these years. In the first three months of the Occupation some 22,000 bicycles had been stolen, very much a sign of the times. Production costs of bikes had plummeted since the Great War, and by 1944 there were 2 million of them in the city – almost one per person. The rickshaw-like 'vélo-taxi' became a regular standby. The Occupation thus marked an eery calm in the history of Parisian street-noise, especially in the hours of curfew. Furthermore the start of Allied bombing of factories in the *banlieue* from 1943 generalized the practice of the black-out, plunging the 'City of Light' into uncharacteristic visual impenetrability. The city, noted the photographer Jacques-Henri Lartigue, visiting the city in 1942, 'looks as if it has fainted. You can hardly hear it breathe.'[27]

Wartime and Occupation reintroduced rationing of commodities too, reducing the city of plenty into a site of growing penury and want. Rationing of foodstuffs had begun in the autumn of 1940, but German hegemony made it all the more essential. Under the system of 'exchange' put in place, between half and three-quarters of French agricultural and industrial produce was siphoned off to meet the needs of the Reich. The bureaucratic rationing system seemed designed to

magnify a sense of grievance and to produce long queues and much disappointment. As with petrol, it was often less the fact of rationing than the growing scarcity of key goods that was most galling. Clothing was in especially short supply, leading to all sorts of makeshift solutions. The virtual disappearance of leather led to the widespread use of cardboard and rubber. Fuel shortages made hot water a far from everyday luxury. In all domains there was of course a flourishing black market to supply those who had money. But then most Parisians did not. The decision to plough up the gardens of the Invalides, the Luxembourg and the Tuileries so as to allow the planting of beans, carrots and potatoes played to Vichy's agrarian obsessions; it also showed more than a touch of desperation in food matters. The average daily ration procured each Parisian a mere 850 calories per day. Unsurprisingly the death-rate rose by nearly 50 per cent, from 12 deaths per 1,000 population in 1937 to 17.8 per cent in 1943. Deficiency diseases were rife, especially among the young. Young boys in 1944 were seven centimetres shorter than their predecessors in 1935, and girls eleven centimetres less. The writer Colette's advice to Parisians was succinct but, in these circumstances, understandable: 'Economy and hygiene unite to sum up my message: go to bed.'[28]

If bed could provide warmth and (hopefully) companionship, so could many activities which in less peculiar times would be considered luxury leisure activities. Libraries, for example, saw the number of their denizens double – though newspaper-reading (perhaps insufficiently collective an activity) fell sharply. Authors too used the same stratagems: the fuel shortage drove Jean-Paul Sartre and a group of fellow authors including Simone de Beauvoir to use the cafés of Saint-Germain-des-Prés (notably the Café Flore and the Deux Magots) as their writing-dens. The Occupation marked a golden age of French cinema and theatre too – both were warm as well as convivial. There was escapism aplenty on offer, but also subtle opportunities for political engagement – if only through coughing seizures whenever Pétain's image appeared on the newsreels. Vichy banned pre-war films such as La Règle du jeu and Hôtel du Nord as 'depressing, morbid and immoral'.[29] Yet although many of the famous directors fled and the number of films produced was only a half of pre-war levels, this was still a substantial amount. The margin of freedom which the Germans allowed film-makers facilitated the advent of a new generation of directors (such as Becker, Bresson, Autant-Lara and Clouzot) and a clutch of cinema classics, not least Carné's *Les Enfants du Paradis* (1944–5).

The arts provided a moral crucible for their practitioners. Very few writers or artists gave up their work (most could not do anything else) unless they were forced to do so: Parisian publishing houses were under strict orders, for example, not to accept or distribute anything by Jewish, Communist or American authors. Certain writers and artists were drawn into the welcoming milieu which the Francophile German cultural attachés opened up, for the Germans placed great store by the idea of winning over the French intelligentsia to Nazi ideas. They had some success – authors such as Drieu La Rochelle, Robert Brasillach and Céline not only continued to write, but also placed their pens at the ideological service of the Nazi regime, in journalism as well as fiction. These individuals were drawn into visiting Germany – a fate which also befell popular singers like Maurice Chevalier and Édith Piaf, and artists like van Dongen, Derain and Vlaminck, a fact all had to try to excuse after 1944. Most in the arts world chose to keep their heads down and get on with their work as if cut off from the world. There was a growing amount of clandestine publication, especially from 1942 and 1943. Vercors's *Le Silence de la mer* (1942), published by the underground Éditions de Minuit, was a Resistance classic, while the patriotic poetry of erstwhile Surrealists like Éluard and Aragon was also avidly read. Yet if authors wished to reach a wider audience, they had to negotiate with the Occupation authorities – and square their consciences. Even committed anti-Nazis did so: Sartre, for example, had to delay publication of his multi-volumed novel *Les Chemins de la liberté* (which was published in 1945), but his plays *Les Mouches* (1942) and *Huis Clos* (1943) passed the censor and were performed. His friend Simone de Beauvoir also published her first work, *L'Invitée*, under the Occupation. The Paris stage, similarly, saw first plays by Camus and Montherlant, and the first performances of new work by Anouilh, Cocteau, Guitry and Giraudoux – all important figures in the post-war era.

Authors who had committed to the Nazi cause like Brasillach and Céline cheerfully propagated anti-Semitic ideas, and they were not alone in this. After all, anti-Semitism was a system of belief with a long history in France, as Charles Maurras's newspaper *L'Action française* bore witness. Never before, however, had Jews been recipients of so much undiluted and institutionalized prejudice and violence. This culminated on 16–17 July 1942 when the Parisian police rounded up around 12,000 Jews who were interned in the sports stadium, the Vél' d'Hiv (Vélodrome d'Hiver) in the most appalling conditions – before deportation to Auschwitz.

11.3: The Vél' d'Hiv

The Vélodrome d'Hiver – the covered sports stadium familiarly known as the Vél' d'Hiv – was built in 1910 on the Boulevard de Grenelle out in the Fifteenth arrondissement, and demolished in 1959. There was little fuss about the removal of an amenity which had hosted major boxing matches and staged international cycling events (notably the annual 'Six Jours' between 1913 and 1958). For the building is most famous for being infamous: as the holding place in which Parisian Jews were incarcerated following a major round-up in 1942, before being deported to death camps.

Jews have a long Parisian history: Jewish and Syrian traders are recorded as having lived in the city in Merovingian times, and the subsequent growth, economic prosperity and demographic vitality of the city in the Middle Ages caused the emergence of a strong Jewish community here. Anti-Semitism, however, has a long Parisian history too. Throughout the Middle Ages the Jewish community was subject to bouts of persecution. Kings who took measures against the Jews ranged from the most pious – Saint Louis, for example, who burnt twenty-four cartloads of talmudic manuscripts on the Place de Grève and obliged Jews to wear a distinguishing badge (a little red wheel) – to the most nakedly rapacious – Philip IV, for example, who expelled Jews from France in 1306, though not without first sequestrating their goods.

Subject to a series of expulsions, the Jews returned when

pressure was reduced. In the interim their presence was inscribed on the city in the form of street-names. From 1119 the Rue de la Juiverie on the Île de la Cité contained a synagogue, and there was a Jewish cemetery close by on the Left Bank. The synagogue was converted into a church in 1190, but the Rue de la Juiverie had its name changed – to Rue de la Cité – only in 1834. Similarly on the Right Bank to the east and north of the Hôtel de Ville there were several Rues des Juifs – most notably the present-day Rue Ferdinand-Duval (IVe.), whose new name dates only from 1900. The Jews left their mark in another way too: an incident in 1290 in which a Jew in the parish of Saint-Merri (IVe.) was said to have desecrated the host, led to the execution of the Jew in question but also the establishment of an expiatory chapel and an associated hospital order, who annually commemorated the incident.

Further acts of expulsion in the late Middle Ages down to 1615 – and especially in 1394 – meant that before the Revolution there were very few Jews at all in the city. A list of Jews in Paris in 1715 gives only nineteen names, though this probably expanded to around five hundred by 1789. Most belonged to the petty trades, including peddling, though there were also some money-lenders. The law of 27 September 1791 gave Jews civic rights, thus allowing freedom of movement to individuals who had spent centuries living in ghettoes elsewhere in France. This, and formal government recognition of a Jewish community in 1806, stimulated a growth in the number of Jews in the city. Under the July Monarchy there were 9,000, including wealthy and powerful dynasties such as the Rothschilds.

There was a considerable amount of integration into all levels of Parisian life over the nineteenth century. The situation changed somewhat, however, as a result of the advent of Jewish refugees from Alsace after 1871, and then the arrival of large numbers of Ashkenazi fleeing persecution in eastern Europe. This led to a startling growth in numbers – and also a new geography. By 1939, of France's 300,000 Jews perhaps 160,000 lived in Paris and its environs. The Rue des Rosiers in the Fourth arrondissement became the focus of a strong Yiddish-speaking community, whose synagogue (1913), which Guimard had designed on the Rue Pavée (IVe.), played an important role. Many old aristocratic hôtels were turned into overcrowded dwellings and sweatshops in the so-called 'Pletzl'. The Musée d'art et d'histoire du judaïsme in the former Hôtel de Saint-Aignan on the Rue du Temple (IIIe.) is a particularly good example of this phenomenon, for photographs taken in the 1930s show it as virtually unrecognizable from the recently museumized site.

The virulence of anti-Semitic attacks on the Jews by the far Right during and in the aftermath of the Dreyfus Affair led to a further concentration of Jews in the Marais, as if in self-protection. Charles Maurras, the leader of *L'Action française*, openly attacked the Jews for bringing into France 'fleas, plague, typhus and, in the long run, Revolution'. He was scornful of Parisians for being 'xenophiles' and 'xenomaniacs' – a claim that was put cruelly to the test during the Vichy regime and the Nazi occupation of the city from 1940 to 1944.

The Jewish concentration in the Marais made the application of Vichy laws by the French police all the easier. Even before the Vichy regime had been fully installed, Jews received a special status, and discriminatory laws were made more and more rigorous and all-inclusive, under the surveillance of the *Commissariat général aux affaires juives*. From March 1942 Jews were obliged to wear a yellow star, but even before that many had had their businesses and much of their property confiscated. All were forced to undergo humiliating restrictions: special identity cards; no telephone or bicycle; no right to move homes; no right to enter a café, restaurant or other public place; no right to walk the streets between 8 p.m. and 6 a.m. Their culture was subjected to ruthless jeering in the press, notably in Robert Brasillach's newspaper *Je Suis Partout*. A big exhibition entitled '*Le Juif*' was staged in September 1941, and contained every imaginable kind of race propaganda. The names of streets and buildings were 'dejudaized': the Théâtre Sarah-Bernhardt on the Place du

Châtelet, for example, became the Théâtre de la Cité, while the Rue Henri-Heine became the Rue J.-S.-Bach. The *Institut des Questions juives* provided a pseudo-scientific rationale for regarding Jews as less than human. Moves to deport them, initiated by the Nazi authorities, were implemented, sometimes with an enthusiasm which surprised the Germans, by French police forces. There was little sympathy for Jews resident in France who did not have French citizenship, but even those fully integrated and effectively secularized (including battle-heroes from the Great War) were subjected to the same laws.

The biggest purge in Paris was the Vél' d'Hiv round-up (*rafle*) on 16–17 July 1942. Some 12,884 arrests were made by French police under the orders of Police Prefect René Bousquet: about 3,000 men, 5,000 women and 4,000 children. The Germans were disappointed in that they had laid on trains for the deportation of more than 30,000. The captives had a stay of a week in the most appalling conditions, without proper food or sanitary arrangements. Over one hundred committed suicide and there were more than a score of other deaths. For transfer out of Paris, children were separated from parents in scenes of gut-wrenching sadness. Around 75,000 Jews were deported from France as a whole. Most, including all the Parisian Jews, passed through Drancy near Le Bourget, where a primitive concentration camp had been put together in what had once been a set of modernist housing blocks. Only around 3,000 of the deportees survived.

The Jewish community recovered strongly after the war. Less concentrated on the Marais than hitherto, the community in Paris and its environs exceeds 300,000. The Marais has become a shopper's paradise, and the falafel stalls and kosher butchers emphasize continuity with the past. The tourist also notes the plaques outside primary schools throughout the Fourth arrondissement commemorating the deportation of thousands of Jewish children from the area, many of whom passed by way of the Vél' d'Hiv.

The deportation of the city's Jews contributed towards a growing depletion in Paris's population from 1943 onwards. In addition there was the anti-urban slant of Vichy policy, which meant that conditions were never as bad in the countryside, while Allied bombing caused some inhabitants to flee. Another factor was a push by the authorities to enrol workers in the STO (*Service du Travail obligatoire*), the conscript worker system supplying juvenile labour to Germany's factories. Vichy policies thus had the effect of creating enemies to the regime: Jews and Communists of course, but also workers unwilling to be shipped off to work in Germany. Such individuals fled to hide in the remote mountainous areas (the *maquis*) especially in the south. In time such *maquisards* formed a reservoir of disaffection on which Resistance organizations could draw. And by 1943 the Resistance was growing in strength and ambition.

Occupied Paris simply could not have run without the active collaboration of the French administration. While it is quite possible to draw up a charge-sheet against Parisians who entered enthusiastically into collaboration with the Nazis, it is also true that there was a great deal of more or less covert hostility towards them. For the Germans Paris was 'the sightless city' – no one seemed to wish to return the occupier's glance.[30] The first acts of overt resistance to the Germans had been demonstrations at the Arc de Triomphe led by students in November 1940, but in general Paris was not in the vanguard of Resistance movements in the opening years of the Occupation. Resistance developed faster and with a more radical tinge in the southern zone, where Vichy was as much the enemy as the Germans. The strength of the German presence in Paris and the degree of surveillance that Parisians were under also acted as deterrents.

Initially there were numerous clandestine networks, often with their own political orientation, competing with each other and undermined by informing, betrayal and sheer bad organization. From early 1942 agents from Charles de Gaulle's London-based Free French – notably Jean Moulin, who died under torture in Lyon the following year – began to instil organization and unity within competing Resistance networks. An important coup was the inclusion of the Communist Party, which was particularly active in Resistance work, both in Paris and nationally. The coordination of the Resistance networks from 1943 gave Paris an increasingly pivotal role. Numbers in Paris were still small – probably only 15,000 to 20,000 Resistance fighters in total. But they compensated for small numbers by commitment and ingenuity: one network established its headquarters in the catacombs under the Place Denfert-Rochereau (XIVe.).

Many of the most daring exploits of the Resistance were carried out far from the capital. But Paris was to get its chance to shine in 1944, when the city served as the theatre for the most dramatic of the acts of liberation by which the Germans were eventually driven out of France and defeated. The Allied landings in Normandy in June 1944 reserved only a small, ancillary role to French military forces, and initially the US commander-in-chief, General Eisenhower, sought to bypass Paris in the Allied drive eastwards. In the event, for a variety of reasons and with much perchance, Paris did not have to wait, and Parisians played a major part in their own liberation. On 18 August the Resistance forces in the capital launched an uprising, with memorable hardiness, precious little ammunition and over 600 hastily constructed barricades. On 25 August Free French forces led by General Leclerc came to their relief. Following a bout of fighting in which probably fewer than 2,000 Parisians perished, the Germans surrendered. The same day General de Gaulle arrived in the city to a mighty ovation, and set about organizing the Republic as if the Vichy interlude had never taken place. The symbolic importance of the taking of the city was immense – as was the fact that Frenchmen and women and not only Americans had engineered the success. As the Allied armies proceeded to defeat German forces throughout the country and drive on to Berlin, France had restored a good deal of dignity after four years of national humiliation; and Parisians had played a leading role in that.

Paris was in fact extremely fortunate to be still in relatively good working order. Allied bombing since 1943 had caused more damage in the *banlieue* than in the heart of the city. Von Cholitz, the German commander in the city, had turned a deaf ear to Hitler's orders to raze it and to make it 'nothing but a blackened field of ruin'.[31] From his headquarters in the Hôtel Meurice, Von Cholitz capitulated tranquilly once it became clear that the Germans had no chance of success.

There would be problems aplenty almost as soon as the Germans had surrendered and as Parisians had committed themselves to an ecstatic orgy of removal of German signposts throughout the city. But in all essentials Paris was herself again, and one could at least dream that the era of disappointment and lost illusions had come to an end. On 25 August the photographer Jacques-Henri Lartigue, who had solemnly kept one film for his camera through the years of penury for such a moment, began to take photographs again:

> The end of the German occupation liberates my camera! I look at Paris with new eyes. All of Paris! The miracle is not that she is only scarred nor that she has not been completely demolished, but that she is still *here*.[32]

12

The Remaking of Paris

1945–*c.* 1995

Paris was indeed 'here', as photographer Jacques-Henri Lartigue said, on the day of Paris's liberation from the Germans.[1] Given the horrors of occupation which the city had endured, it seemed almost miraculous that the fabric of the city was still essentially intact, especially when compared with war-razed cityscapes elsewhere in Europe – Berlin, Dresden and Hamburg, for example, or, in France, Cherbourg, Le Havre or Saint-Lô. Around a quarter of French housing stock was lost as a result of fighting. Set in this context, the damage done in Paris in August 1944, added to the destruction wreaked by Allied bombing on factories in the suburbs, was relatively paltry, especially when compared with the scale of damage meted out after the Commune in 1871. Much of the decade which followed the liberation of Paris and Europe would be spent in national reconstruction beyond Paris. This meant that the built environment of the city which had already, as we have seen, been remarkably little changed since the Great War continued largely unchanged. The violent drama of the Liberation and the post-war years was played out against a highly familiar physical backdrop, now a little more run down than formerly, but still in all essentials 'there'.

Paris in 1918 might have been living off its reputation, but the city itself had still been a handsome imperial metropolis. In 1945, in contrast, the wear and tear of decades of neglect were painfully obvious in smoke-blackened stone façades, cracked and untended stucco, and peeling paintwork. Yet once the phase of national reconstruction was over – from around 1954 onwards (and particularly in the period up to the mid-1970s) – the material framework of the city would undergo a remarkably dramatic overhaul, with a scale of rebuilding which rivalled the age of Haussmann. In the interim, however, joy was mingled with an array of less enhancing emotions.

The euphoric Liberation mood did not last long. The aftermath of the war witnessed a continuation of austerity, which was all the more resented in that it had been assumed that the poor state of the economy was largely due to expropriation by Germany. Yet when this ceased, such was the scale of damage to the national economy that shortages of essentials persisted. Rationing of key foodstuffs was reintroduced in 1945 and lasted until 1949. The calorific value of a day's rations had been 850 in 1944, and was still only 1,500 in May 1945. The monthly butter ration in 1944 had been 175 grammes; from 1945 to 1948 it was 100 grammes. 'Nourished by liberation, warmed by the country's return to active battle,' *New Yorker* journalist Janet Flanner had written in late 1944, 'France is still physically living largely on vegetables and mostly without heat.'[2] Six months later the leader of a visiting delegation of Soviet women largely concurred:

> We were told that we would see some beautiful shops in France. But all the shops are either empty or shut. There is nothing to buy. The population as a whole walks on wooden shoes . . . Nobody wears stockings. They wear very short dresses not because it's the fashion but because there's no material.

Yet her admission that 'on the hats one can see whole vegetable gardens and swallows' nests' was a reminder of the ingenuity in keeping up appearances which Parisians had acquired under the Occupation.[3]

The work of economic reconstruction moved ahead only slowly. In 1946 an agency was created under Jean Monnet to institute a national economic plan, *Le Plan*, as it was known. It was to prove vital in the work of reconstruction, as was the availability of US aid, from 1948 channelled through the Marshall Plan. The commissariat of the Plan prioritized heavy industry and the building of infrastructure and also moved France's economy into a more European direction, notably through the creation of the OECD in 1948 and the signing in 1950 of an Iron and Steel union with long-term foe Germany. A sign that the policy was benefiting the recovery of Paris was a striking surge in car-production. After the unearthly quietness of the Nazi years, the streets of Paris were growing reassuringly noisy again.

Post-Liberation street vitality included the kind of militancy which had characterized the 1930s. The fleeting moment of political unanimity in 1944, incarnated in the person of General de Gaulle, had not lasted – a fact which encouraged a weary political cynicism. Once the new Fourth Republic had been established, de Gaulle himself passed, somewhat mysteriously, 'into the shadowland of politics', as British ambassador Duff Cooper put it.[4] The Communist Party, presenting itself as the backbone of the Resistance – and headed by Maurice Thorez, who had returned from his Moscow bolt-hole – stressed the work of political reconstruction in the immediate aftermath of war. The PCF formed part of the post-war governmental coalition until 1947. Subsequently, there proved more than sufficient domestic and international issues to set it at loggerheads with the other parties: the emerging Cold War, the creation of NATO, reports of Stalin's concentration camps, the decolonizing war in Indo-China and, from the early 1950s, the emerging Algerian crisis. The passage of the PCF into opposition meant that Parisians suffered more than most from a series of bitter strikes punctuating the late 1940s and early 1950s. The PCF was strong in the city as well as the suburbs now; the publicity value of street militancy was more powerful in the capital, while the centralized system of transport and power made strikes in these sectors damaging to large numbers of Parisians and *banlieusards*.

The long-term disaffection of the PCF with the workings of the new Fourth Republic was an important aspect of the post-war scene, echoing the Cold War polarization of the world between the victorious allies, the USSR and the USA. The fracture within post-war political culture was, however, even more extreme than this. The euphoria of the Liberation had rapidly been punctured. Within France as a whole there was a powerful call for vengeance against all who had collaborated with the Nazis. This erupted in a spate of vengeance killings and other forms of punitive action, such as the head-shaving and public humiliation of women accused of 'horizontal collaboration'. These incidents – which numbered as many as 20,000 to 30,000 nationally, to add to around 10,000 killings – were less widespread in Paris than in other areas of France. But Paris was soon the theatre for many of the major trials of collaborators and for other purge procedures. An early *cause célèbre*, in January 1945, concerned the writer Robert

Brasillach, accusations against whom centred less on his rabid anti-Semitism than on his traitorous collaborationism. Brasillach was shot, but not before his execution had aroused a call for clemency to which many Resistance intellectuals subscribed. The purges were henceforth less savage, but they were very extensive. Most professional and corporate bodies, for example, organized inquiries into the actions of their members – usually in Paris. Punishment included imprisonment and loss of political rights, a sanction known as 'national degradation'. Leading figures in the Vichy government faced either the death penalty or long prison sentences, although René Bousquet, the police chief who had coordinated the Jewish round-ups of the Vél' d'Hiv, received little more than a rap on the knuckles and resumed his career in public life.[5]

The spectacle of vengeance, contrition and punishment subsequent to the Liberation was, moreover, overlaid by weighty international issues. The final months of conflict in France had witnessed a number of Nazi atrocities, such as the wiping out in its entirety of the little village of Oradour-sur-Glane (Haute-Vienne) in June 1944. Worse was to come. From April 1945 Parisian cinemas were showing horrified audiences pictures of the inmates of Auschwitz and the other death camps taken by Allied troops. In May trains of the deportees started arriving in Paris, where they would be debriefed at the Hôtel Lutétia and other hotels commandeered for the purpose. The crowds who had come to the Gare de l'Est in welcome were horrified to see spectral figures, evident victims of Nazi brutality, stagger unsteadily from the trains. As some returnees, with unbearable pathos, croaked out the *Marseillaise*, the crowds dissolved in tears. In August of the same year the USA unleashed atomic bombs on Nagasaki and Hiroshima, adding a further notch to the scales of twentieth-century horror.

'The Europe of bombed ghost towns,' the novelist, Spanish Civil War veteran and Gaullist Resistance-fighter André Malraux commented, 'is no more ravaged than the idea that Europe has made for itself of man.'[6] The extremities of the ideological conflicts and terrifying technologically driven destruction of the previous years sparked a widespread call for a new start. Only political renewal based on humanistic philosophical premises could resist the moral contamination which had disfigured traditional politics. An approach which stressed humane and committed political *engagement* – commitment – was apparent across the political board. The Communists accentuated their role as partisans of peace, and used their Resistance credentials to develop a strong, broad-Left intellectual and artistic following. These ranged from scientists like the physicist Frédéric Joliot-Curie to artists like Picasso and Léger, writers including ex-Surrealist Aragon and young actors including Gérard Philippe, Yves Montand and Simone Signoret. The 'personalism' preached in the journal *Esprit* by Emmanuel Mounier also stimulated a strong response from young, socially aware Catholics. The most vibrant of the new humanistic currents – and the one which most clearly refurbished Paris's reputation as an internationally important intellectual centre – was the existentialism propounded by Jean-Paul Sartre, Simone de Beauvoir and their numerous acolytes.

Such was the price of fame, that the 'wall-eyed, pipe-sucking, pasty-hued Sartre and his spinsterish moll, de Beauvoir', as American writer Truman Capote unflatteringly described them, were now to be found 'propped up in a corner like an abandoned pair of ventriloquists' dolls' in the basement bar of the Pont-Royal hotel.[7] They had fled the nearby Deux Magots and the Café de Flore on the Boulevard Saint-Germain because the numerous enthusiasts for their writings there made it impossible for them to work in peace. The political journal *Les Temps Modernes*, which the two edited from October 1945, consolidated their fame. The stress the movement placed on the need for moral responsibility in making life choices had its philosophical roots in the phenomenology of Heidegger and Husserl, but few who called themselves existentialists could be expected to gloss these difficult sources, or Sartre's scholarly summation, *Being and Nothingness* (1943). 'I haven't quite got round to any precise conception of what existentialism actually is,' noted the *engagé* painter Jean Dubuffet. 'Nonetheless I feel and declare myself to be warmly existentialist.'[8] Sartre encouraged the movement in artistic and intellectual circles: the novelist and journalist Albert Camus, the ex-convict writer Jean Genet, the philosopher Maurice Merleau-Ponty, as well as artists experimenting in new modes of representation such as Dubuffet, Henri Michaux and Alberto Giacometti were all associated, at least passingly, with the movement.

Existentialism had a precise location on the map. With Montparnasse now seemingly old hat, cafés and bars situated almost literally within the shadow of the ancient abbey of Saint-Germain-des-Prés (VIe.) became the movement's headquarters. The *quartier* also contained the editorial offices of major publishing houses such as Gallimard and Seuil which published members of the movement. It also had an excellent jazz scene, and the existentialists were keen jazzers. Sartre's friend, the brilliant and mercurial Boris Vian, journalist, novelist and poet, was a talented trumpeter who played night-spots in the Saint-Germain area such as the Tabou on the Rue Dauphine and Club Saint-Germain on the Rue Saint-Benoît. Existentialism's fashionable night-club ambience gave what was in essence a philosophical and political movement a media dimension. The press soon noted its capacity for attracting the young, rootless and vaguely politicized – especially once existentialists began dressing in black, and were joined by bright young things (of the night) like chanteuse Juliette Gréco. The publication of de Beauvoir's pioneering feminist classic *The Second Sex* (1949), with its frank discussions of sexuality, was an additional *succès de scandale*.

By 1949, however, the movement's moment of political seriousness and import was passing. Its leaders found it difficult to maintain a meaningful autonomous political stance outside a political culture increasingly polarized by the Cold War, and they fell out with each other: Sartre parted company with Merleau-Ponty, while his relations with Camus also became strained. In addition, media attention had diluted the political core of the movement, turning it almost into a lifestyle option. The revival of international tourism also played a spoiling role: the Deux Magots was soon full of young Americans wanting to place themselves where Sartre normally sat. Where Americans went, estate agents soon followed: before long, Saint-Germain was in the throes of gentrification, as a suave and affluent bohemian crowd moved in.

'Having become a second-class power,' Simone de Beauvoir wrote of the late 1940s, 'France defended itself by glorifying for purposes of export its home-grown products: Fashion and Literature.'[9] A significant number of major *haute couture* designers and houses did indeed establish themselves in this period: Pierre Balmain (1945), Pierre

Cardin (1951), Hubert Givenchy and Guy Laroche (1952) – plus, not least, Christian Dior, whose extravagant 'new look' of 1947 was a major international hit, his creations accounting for three-quarters of French fashion exports in that year. The war had lost the city the rank of the world centre of painting – the art market moved to the more profitable environment of New York. Literature was still in good shape, however, and strove to maintain and augment its international rating. André Gide, now in his late seventies, was awarded the Nobel Prize for Literature in 1947, and the period also marked a moment of international celebrity for authors such as Anouilh, Cocteau and François Mauriac, while Surrealists such as Breton and Éluard were also still producing. The accolade of novelty, however, clung initially to the existentialists, and they and the Surrealists upheld Paris's international status as a centre of the avant-garde. The revival of Parisian theatre owed much to a 'theatre of the absurd' invariably written and directed by foreigners (such as the Romanian Eugène Ionesco, the Irishman Samuel Beckett and the Russian Arthur Adamov), but played out in the scruffily bohemian theatres of the Left Bank. Later in the late 1950s there would be the *nouveau roman* ('new novel'), whose practitioners included Alain Robbe-Grillet, Marguerite Duras and Michel Butor; and also a 'new wave' (*nouvelle vague*) of film directors (and film theorists) including François Truffaut, Jean-Luc Godard, Claude Chabrol, Éric Rohmer and Louis Malle. By the 1970s it would be Structuralist and post-Structuralist 'French theory' (Claude Lévi-Strauss, Roland Barthes, Michel Foucault, Jacques Lacan, Jacques Derrida, Hélène Cixous, Julia Kristeva) which maintained the international renown of the French for intellectual innovation.

Several of the new-wave film-makers highlighted another 'home-grown product' which de Beauvoir failed to mention but which was of considerable export value in the post-war era, namely the image of Paris itself. Post-war photographers such as Robert Doisneau and Henri Cartier-Bresson achieved international repute: Doisneau's famous shot of the kiss outside the Hôtel de Ville played fully into international expectations of the city – love, the street, a recognizable backdrop. Vincente Minelli's *An American in Paris* (1951) and *Gigi* (1958) showed that Hollywood cinema played to the clichés too. Even once the face of Paris had started to change in the 1950s, film's role as promoter of a certain idea of timeless Paris lingered on. Louis Malle's *Zazie dans le métro* (1960), based on Raymond Queneau's popular novel, represented a *vieux Paris* which was just about hanging on, while Jean-Luc Godard's *À bout de souffle*, which appeared in the same year, both highlighted the advent of desirable (and stealable) American limousines, and also provided comforting reassurance about a city which remained true to itself. The consumer hardware had changed, but the timeless backdrop lingered on.

12.1: The Métro in Zazie

For Zazie, Raymond Queneau's eponymous heroine in his 1959 novel, *Zazie dans le métro*, the Métro represents the sum of provincial fantasies about what is special about Paris. Staying with her uncle and his utterly bizarre entourage while her mother tests (with somewhat dismal results) the clichés about Paris as the city of love, Zazie has her heart set on visiting the Métro. But her heart is broken when she discovers it is closed because of labour disputes.

Throughout the novel, pre-teen Zazie tends to express her precocious scepticism about life in the most forthright manner: 'Napoléon mon cul' ('Napoleon my arse') is her characteristic reaction to the idea of the emperor's tomb at the Invalides. But she would evidently never dream of associating her arse with the Métro. The Métro is about fantasy, not body functions. Zazie never enters the Métro – but the tale revolves around the conceit that the Métro is very much inside Zazie: it proves easier to keep Zazie out of the Métro than to take the Métro out of Zazie. The Métro is the absent presence, the mythical grail, around which Queneau weaves a highly sophisticated web of fantasy, albeit in the form of the most mundane and concrete of everyday happenings. Tellingly, Zazie gets her best view of the Métro from the top of the Eiffel tower, that other quintessential feature of Parisian fantasy. Queneau works on the assumption that both phenomena form part of our preconceptions about the meaning of Paris.

Kafka, an early, pre-Great War user, noted: 'the Métro is a frail and hopeful stranger's best chance to think that he has quickly and correctly . . . penetrated the essence of Paris.' In a way this is correct, yet it underestimates the extent to which Métro usage involves a certain apprenticeship. The system requires competence in a number of social rituals: buying a ticket, understanding the meaning of *correspondance*, socially correct behaviour in the presence of buskers and beggars, extremely parsimonious use of eye-contact, and so on. It is at once the most private and individual experience – and yet also one of the most social. This means that care has to be taken in adjudicating between correct public and private behaviours.

The Métro is also replete with a matrix of often arcane meanings which defy even the most assiduous of users. As the anthropologist Marc Augé has noted, so many Métro stops within the old city are named after famed individuals and events in France's history – generals, statesmen, battles, Revolutionary days and so on – that just to take the simplest journey is in some senses akin to celebrating the cult of ancestors. The further out of Paris the traveller ventures, the more the patriotic pedagogy declines, and station names have a geographical rather than a historical denotation (Porte de la Chapelle, Mairie de Clichy, Créteil-Université, etc.).

Within the city, the fact that the Métro was built below existing streets for the most part means that stations are often named after particular streets or crossroads. Walter Benjamin felt that there was 'a peculiar voluptuousness about naming streets' – and this is surely even more the case with Métro stations. Métro topography is full of unlikely couplings. Barbès-Rochechouart, for example, conjoins the names of a nineteenth-century anarchist warrior with a seventeenth-century aristocratic abbess of Montmartre. Sèvres-Babylone commemorates both the street which runs out towards the suburban location of Sèvres and the bishop of Babylon *in partibus infidelium* who founded the nearby monastery of the Missions Étrangères. Richelieu-Drouot miscegenates the Cardinal-

Minister of Louis XIII with a Napoleonic general. Alma-Marceau brings together a Crimean battle and a Revolutionary hero. To complicate matters, there are some singletons who appear to be posing as couples: La Motte-Picquet, for example, Marx-Dormoy and Denfert-Rochereau – three identities in total, not six. To complicate matters further, Métro stations – like streets – often change their name, partly for political reasons, partly as a result of arcane bureaucratic tidying up, partly so as to help tourists. In 1946 Marbeuf-Rond-Point-des-Champs-Élysées was metamorphosed into Franklin-D-Roosevelt, and in 1970 Étoile became Étoile-Charles-de-Gaulle. Then in 1968 Saint-Paul became Saint-Paul-Le-Marais, and in 1989 Palais-Royal, Palais-Royal (Musée du Louvre). There have been nearly fifty such changes since 1945.

Of course relatively few of the daily passengers who have used these stations have much of an etymological clue about these names. But then they have the weirdly redolent poetry of the names – the 'poetical succession of stations', as Richard Cobb put it – to hold on to. Perhaps, in a system in which, as Zazie could testify, fantasy plays such a part, that is sufficient.

The seemingly ahistoric city of the movies was, however, increasingly and ineluctably caught up in the weft of historical change. Besides enduring the tensions of the Cold War, Paris also experienced the issue of decolonization at close hand. Supporters of Algerian independence had been holding demonstrations in the city since the early 1950s, but matters took a graver turn when in 1954 the Algerian *Front de Libération Nationale* (FLN) initiated guerrilla warfare within Algeria. Demonstrations in Paris were now conjoined by FLN bomb attacks and other exploits: by 1958 over sixty policemen had been killed and nearly two hundred wounded. A crisis in Algiers in that year staged by colonists and supported by elements within the colonial army who resisted the idea of negotiation between the French government and the FLN brought matters to a head. Incapable of finding a way out of the crisis, the Fourth Republic summoned Charles de Gaulle back from his self-imposed political exile. De Gaulle profited from the regime's demoralization to institute a Fifth Republic, with a highly 'presidentialist' constitution.

The years after 1958 saw an intensification of FLN guerrilla activity in Paris. National and municipal authorities responded with a tightening of police surveillance and an extension of police powers over Muslims. The French army in Algeria had been fighting a 'dirty war', involving the routine use of torture on suspects. Something of this rubbed off in Paris too. A demonstration on 17 October 1961 of Algerians against the enforcement of a curfew for all Muslims in the capital led to sickeningly vicious police violence, climaxing in the beating and murder of possibly two hundred demonstrators, whose bodies were dumped by night into the Seine. Many Parisians seemed not to want to know about 'the battle of Paris', which had something about it of a Saint Bartholomew's massacre of Muslims.

The Algerian crisis would not go away. Although initially Algerian colonists had welcomed de Gaulle as their saviour, they soon discovered that he had renounced any possibility of keeping Algeria French, and was opening negotiating channels to the FLN. This triggered a violent riposte from the colonists who in early 1961 formed the *Organisation armée secrète* (OAS) dedicated to armed action against decolonization. Linked to high-placed figures in both the political world and the armed forces, the OAS launched campaigns in Paris as well as in Algeria. This involved assassination attempts on de Gaulle himself, but also a number of bomb attacks involving civilian casualties. The view of many Parisians on the crisis was shown on 8 February 1962, when a huge demonstration against OAS violence was organized by the PCF and the other left-wing parties. It descended into running battles with the police. Thousands of demonstrators and passers-by took refuge in the Charonne Métro station (XIe.), where a crowd panic led to nine deaths. Half a million Parisians accompanied the funeral procession of the victims a few days later.

In 1962 the Évian agreements gave Algeria its independence – and this was followed in short order by similar decolonization measures across the French empire. As part of its move to dismantle colonist opposition, the French government passed generous repatriation laws: around a million individuals relocated in France. This included French colonists (some of them from families which had been in Algeria for generations), Italians and other European settlers, plus over 50,000 'Harkis', that is, Algerians who had fought on France's side. Most settled in southern France, though about 100,000 relocated to the Paris region. Évian did not cause OAS outrages to cease at once, while police surveillance measures against North Africans remained in place. Nevertheless, by 1963 the crisis years had passed.

Immigration into Paris consequent on Algerian decolonization was only a chapter in the history of a city which had long had a reputation as a human melting-pot. There had been a sizeable influx, notably of Italians, Germans and Russians, following the end of the Second World War. The repatriation of ex-colonists from across the old French empire in the 1960s – from Tunisia and Morocco and from Indo-China and West Africa as well as from Algeria – added to this. So did a massive, sudden and quite unexpected influx from Portugal: in 1961 some 6,000 Portuguese entered France; in 1963 28,000 did so. Many were women who came to work as domestic helps for Parisian bourgeois families. Again, as earlier in the century, Paris cast many of its newcomers into the *banlieue*. By the end of the century around 13 per cent of the Paris region were foreigners – twice the national average – and one Parisian in six was a foreigner. By that time the ex-colonizer had been joined by the formerly colonized: the push of post-independence poverty and the pull of job opportunities in the metropole triggered major waves of especially North and West African immigration. This added to the capital's religious as well as its ethnic composition: in 1939, the city had four mosques; by 2000 it had over a score, with between 300 and 500 in the *banlieue*. The tendency for the recently arrived to stick together imprinted a new geography on the regional map. Within the city itself, the Jewish concentration in the Marais was confirmed, while Turks (many of them entering via Germany) tended to settle in the Ninth arrondissement, and North Africans (who make up around half of the immigrant community) in the outer eastern arrondissements (especially XVIIIe., XIXe. and XXe.). The large numbers of Vietnamese and Cambodian 'boat people' admitted in the late 1970s grouped in the Thirteenth, and they created there something of a culinary as well as an ethnic (Indo-) 'Chinatown'.

The influx of immigrants made less of an impact on Paris's population than would have been the case before 1945, because the aftermath of the Second World War witnessed a significant shift in French demographic behaviour. In particular a baby boom in the late 1940s and early 1950s shattered the country's long-term record of low birth-rates. Population started to grow again: 41 million in 1946, the national population level stood at 50 million in 1966 and in the late 1990s passed 60 million. Significant urbanization accompanied this growth: whereas agriculture employed 35 per cent of the workforce in 1945, in 1980 the figure was down to 9 per cent, and by 2000 to under 5 per cent. Strong urbanization did not affect the size of the population of the twenty arrondissements of Paris: indeed, the city's population had peaked in the 1920s and until the mid-1950s hovered around 2.8 million, dropping to the current figure of about 2.1 million by the early 1980s. Yet the impact on the Paris region of immigration, urbanization and a resurgent birth-rate was dramatic. The *banlieue* mushroomed in size.

The growth of the Paris region in the aftermath of the Second World War owed nothing to government, which acted to check the expansion of the capital and its environs. Post-war reconstruction had prioritized areas more hard-hit by the war. But it was also predicated on the opinion that Paris had become too big. This view – which chimed with Vichyite opinions – was given ringing endorsement in 1947 by Jean-François Gravier's surprisingly influential book, *Paris et le désert français*, which laid the blame for France's alleged economic underdevelopment at Paris's door. The post-war Minister for Reconstruction Claudius-Petit favoured the decentralization of business and industry away from the capital into more distant departments, and he also approved the idea of a 'green belt' on English lines: if there was to be further growth in the Île-de-France, it should be well away from Paris, and separated from the capital by definable green space. His continuation of Parisian rent control by legislation in 1948 seemed destined to set more solidly in place the vicious circle deterring property investment in the capital – with alarming effects on the housing problem. Recent immigrants to the capital were by now forced into creating shanty towns on waste ground behind the rail termini and on the fringes of the city. The scandal of these so-called *bidonvilles* (a

bidon is a jerry-can) put together from cardboard, corrugated iron
and any other junk to hand, stimulated left-wing parties into calls for
action. Yet the Left simultaneously tended to oppose major urban
developments, which they feared (with real justification in the long
term) could lead to the relocation of Parisian workers in poor housing
in the *banlieue*. The decision of the Left Radical Prime Minister
Pierre Mendès-France in 1955 to forbid any business from building
floor-space in the capital in excess of 500 square metres without
special ministerial permission was very much part of this anti-Parisian
sentiment at the heart of government.

The decentralizing agenda of central government persisted well into the Fifth Republic. Yet a major change of approach to the redevelopment of Paris was in gestation from the early 1950s onwards. Unsuspectedly, the black decades of Parisian urbanism were drawing to a close. In retrospect the end of Claudius-Petit's tenure as Reconstruction Minister in 1953 was a key moment, for his successors initiated a comprehensive policy of construction, supplying public subsidies for major housing programmes. The little building there had been in Paris after the war had generally taken the form of HLMs (*habitations à loyer modéré*: a new, polite way of talking about cheap housing). Now major housing schemes were assembled, and a better environment for property development started to emerge. From 1953 the government also encouraged the Paris municipality to build HLM estates on what remained of the *zone non aedificandi* of the *ceinture*.[10] The drive for new housing over the next few years was helped, moreover, by technological change: the systematic use of prefabricated parts in building reduced the number of work-hours required to build a dwelling unit from 3,600 hours in 1957 to 1,200 hours in 1959.

The wave of new building was surprising in another way too: much of it took place under the guiding star of Le Corbusier.[11] Architects and planners were now enthusiastically drawn to the ideas of this charismatic theorist, who since the 1920s had been the modernist prophet crying in the Parisian wilderness. There had been no real demand for major projects in Paris for decades. Now, however, the idea of *grands ensembles* – high-rise apartment blocks surrounded by green space – as a way of replacing slum housing became intellectually respectable, desirable even. Buildings on these lines were constructed at first out in the suburbs as well as in the *ceinture*, making the old housing estates of one- to two-storey tiled villas seem quaint beyond reason. By the late 1950s and early 1960s, however, *grand ensemble* projects had penetrated into the twenty arrondissements, marking the first time that an architectural trend had been set in the periphery of Paris rather than at the centre.

It was with some wistfulness that the Italian writer Italo Calvino, who visited Paris in the early 1960s, was later to recall this moment in Parisian history at which major new developments were poised to transform the cityscape. As yet, he recorded, the city had 'accumulated the strata of time without the new yet driving out the old'. It presented a picture of

> quaint shops, faded posters, leprous façades, characteristics of a tradition which was thrifty and hostile to novelty and which coexisted with the signs of opulence of a capital whose colonial empire was not yet finally liquidated and in which . . . [one could observe] the dying rays of the *Belle Époque* and of the films of Marcel Carné.[12]

Perhaps the most telling sign that change was irremediably on the way was the fact that central government was beginning to plan for the region's growth, rather than population stabilization and containment. The field was cleared for action by the Fifth Republic's development of a new planning regime for Paris and its region. In 1959–60 the old Prost plan of 1939 was finally consigned to the dustbin. A new planning agency, the *Service d'aménagement de la région parisienne* (SARP), produced the *Plan d'aménagement et d'organisation générale* (PADOG). This was revised on a number of occasions in the 1960s, notably through the energetic action of de Gaulle's nominee Paul Delouvrier, who was responsible for the so-called *Schéma directeur* published in 1968. By then, the formal framework of the Parisian region had been transformed too, by legislation in 1964 which redrew the local map: the department of the Seine was split into four departments (Paris, Seine-Saint-Denis, Val-de-Marne and Hauts-de-Seine); the Seine-et-Marne department remained intact; while the Seine-et-Oise was divided into the departments of Yvelines, Essonne and Val-d'Oise. In 1976 the whole area was designated the region of Île-de-France.

The *Schéma directeur* played a major part in regional policy within the rejigged administrative framework. Unlike its predecessors over the century, it unequivocally accepted that the region would grow. Delouvrier called for the establishment of eight new towns in the Paris region, and a communications network to match. The new towns, it was hoped, would take some of the growing pressure off the city of Paris. They were conceived of less as independent cities than as functional agglomerations, one of whose key roles was to supply Paris with commuting workers. The five new towns developed into major population centres: by the turn of the century, Évry and Melun-Sénart were approaching 100,000 inhabitants each, Cergy-Pontoise and Saint-Quentin had over 150,000, and Marne-la-Vallée nearly 200,000. Each had a slightly different administrative framework and spatial organization. Some, for example, sprang up on open fields formerly reserved for sugar-beet, while others adapted to pre-existing habitation. Yet all were characterized by clusters of high-rise buildings which looked as though they had been drawn from the Le Corbusier back-catalogue. All had a functionally conceived lay-out, with a good deal of surrounding green space and prioritized communications into Paris.

The record of communications improvements in the Paris region in the decades before the 1960s had been little short of pathetic: two autoroutes totalling 29 kilometres between them, overcrowded roads, slow-moving buses (trams had disappeared in 1937) and a Métro which did not reach out far into the *banlieue* and which was poorly coordinated with the national and local rail services. PADOG and then the *Schéma directeur* gave a decisive push to change. From the late 1950s a ringroad autoroute was built on the *zone non aedificandi* outside the old fortifications. It was complete by 1967, by which time an express road had also been constructed on the Right Bank edge of the river Seine to speed cross-city journeys. The latter development was the brainchild of Georges Pompidou, de Gaulle's prime minister from 1962 to 1968, and then president himself from 1969 to 1974 following de Gaulle's retirement. Pompidou was a die-hard modernist in matters urban, an enthusiast for high buildings and motor transport. 'Paris must adapt itself to the automobile,' he declared. 'We must renounce an outmoded aesthetic.'[13]

The 1960s saw a spate of autoroute building out from Paris, allowing great improvements in journey times from the *banlieue* into Paris and linking the capital to Fontainebleau (1960), Mantes and Lille (1967), Lyon and Marseille (1971–4), Metz (1976) and Caen (1977). From 1969 an improving road system was complemented by the *réseau express régional* (RER), a regional high-speed network of trains servicing the *banlieue* and linking to the Métro (Châtelet-Les-Halles, for example) and indeed to main-line stations within Paris (such as the Gares du Nord and de Lyon). By 1976 there were 76 kilometres of RER track; by 1982, 274 kilometres; and by the end of the century the four lines covered nearly 400 kilometres and provided 367 million journeys a year. The quality of rolling stock in the Métro was also much improved over this period.

12.2: The 'Algerian Bridge'

On 17 October 2001 Paris Mayor Bertrand Delanoë inaugurated a municipal memorial on the Quai du Marché-Neuf adjacent to the Pont Saint-Michel in memory of Algerians, possibly numbering in their hundreds, who had died at the hands of the police in one of the sombrest episodes in France's decolonization process. It was an episode whose tragic side was for many decades formally denied by the authorities. It took forty years for the city's acknowledgement of the 'Battle of Paris' of 17 October 1961 to be made public.

In the autumn of 1961 the Muslim community in Paris had determined to protest against the curfew which they had been obliged to observe. The protest came at a highly sensitive time in what were to prove the final stages of the bitter struggle for Algerian independence, which had already, in 1958, triggered the demise of the Fourth Republic. Paris had become the theatre of armed conflict. The rebels wanted to bring the pressure of public opinion against the continuation of French efforts to support the side of the colonizers – and there was no better theatre for their efforts than the streets of Paris. Over the summer there had been numerous bomb blasts and attacks on the police which had already caused several dozens of dead and wounded.

What was planned for 17 October was a peaceful demonstration in which some 25,000 Algerians were to participate. Yet this was considered extreme provocation by the Paris police. They unleashed a torrent of cynical and brutal violence on the demonstrators, clubbing them down in the streets and taking them to holding places – including, with considerable historical irony, the Vél' d'Hiv sports stadium in which Jews had been rounded up in 1942 before deportation to Auschwitz. The

French army had been using torture in North Africa against the rebels. In a wish to extract intelligence from demonstrators concerning the earlier attacks on the police – but also out of unabashed cruelty and vindictiveness – the Paris police now employed the same techniques against demonstrators they had picked up and brought into custody. They went further too. Large numbers of demonstrators were either killed or else beaten up on the streets and their bodies dumped senseless in the river Seine (a practice which was already seemingly in use). The Pont Saint-Michel, just round the corner from the Préfecture de Police on the Île de la Cité, was just one of such venues.

The Algerian community knew what had happened and the appalling scale of the episode. Leading Parisian intellectuals – including many Jewish notables – formally protested, making the comparison with the Nazi period. A Communist newspaper on 7 November ran the headline: 'Sixty bodies of drowned or murdered Algerians discovered within a month in Paris.' Yet much of the rest of the Parisian community were unwilling to believe in such massive police wrongdoing, especially as the police authorities strongly denied all accusations, arguing that virtually all the deaths which had occurred were due to murderous score-settling between Algerian factions. An official cover-up seems to have been organized, in which a leading part was played by the career bureaucrat Maurice Papon, who was prefect of police. In the event even the French Left was unable to make much of an episode whose contours seemed difficult to establish. The subsequent ending of the decolonization process saw a collective wish to forget the bad times, and this meant that such stories passed away and the whole episode became a non-event.

What helped keep the 'Battle of Paris' in the collective memory of some groups on the Left and also within the Algerian community was a photograph taken in the early morning of 18 October 1961 of a graffito alongside the Pont des Arts, downstream from the Pont Saint-Michel. Despite police attempts to hide the slogan, and the swift ensuing clean-up which erased it permanently, the photograph showed a wall-daubing which read '*Ici on noie les algériens*' ('They drown Algerians here'). The slogan was either the work of Algerians or of Far Left supporters of the Algerian cause. The photograph seems to have circulated in samizdat form on the Left, but without triggering a massive popular response.

The possibility of a question-mark against the police story about the 'Battle of Paris' was, however, raised by historiographical reinvestigation from the 1980s of the collaboration of French administrators and politicians in the purges of Jews under the Vichy regime. In 1987 Klaus Barbie, the 'butcher of Lyon' responsible for the death under torture of Resistance leader Jean Moulin, had been extradited from Bolivia and sentenced to life imprisonment for crimes against humanity. Also arrested in the early 1990s was René Bousquet, the police prefect who had ordered the Vél' d'Hiv' round-up in 1942 – though he was murdered before he came to trial. Maurice Papon, who had achieved ministerial rank under the Fifth Republic after his period as police prefect, was also targeted for condemnation. It became clear that as prefect of the Gironde during Vichy, he had signed orders for the deportation of Jews via Drancy en route for the death camps. He was sentenced to ten years in prison in 1998.

Throughout the 1990s Papon had denied any police involvement in the death of Algerians in the 'Battle of Paris', and had referred scornfully to 'the mythical dead' of that day. When the Algerian issue was brought into the Papon trial in 1998, Papon sought to issue a libel writ against Jean-Luc Einaudi, author of a book looking into the episode who had testified in the trial. Einaudi had been prominent in the campaign '*17 octobre contre l'oubli*', which started in the late 1990s to get to the bottom of the incident. The campaign used the graffito photograph as its logo.

A government enquiry in 1999 came to the conclusion that there had been some 48 drownings on the night of 17 October, and that 142 Algerians had died in September and October, 110 of whom had been found in the Seine. It also admitted that the

number of deaths was almost certainly higher. The decision of
the city council to admit that the 'Battle of Paris' had indeed
occurred, and had had such a deadly outcome, brought into
public consciousness an event which had been in the limbo of
oblivion (*l'oubli*) for nearly half a century.

Besides playing a major role in improving regional communications,
the PADOG and the *Schéma directeur* also put the capstone on a
dynamic process of housing construction which changed the face of
Paris. In the two decades from 1954 to 1974 more than 200,000 new
dwellings would be constructed in Paris – plus even more in the
banlieue. In 1958 the government had designated key neighbourhoods in the poorer parts of the city as ZUPs – *zones à urbaniser en
priorité*. In 1969 these were reorganized and extended in the form of
ZACs – *zones d'aménagement concerté*.[14] The ZAC, like the ZUP,
was a designated area, for whose development the government
appointed a part-private company with a wide range of financial,
expropriatory and management responsibilities. In some ways the
ZACs were a belated means of dealing with the old *îlots insalubres*,
which stood like a reproach to urban conscience and whose rehabili-
tation had not been attempted in nearly half a century. But the ZACs
had a wider remit than these districts, also extending to what was
adjudged 'poorly used' urban space.

Suddenly it was like being back in the days of Haussmann. Planners
and architects enjoyed greater freedom and better finance than at any
other time over the twentieth century. As in Haussmann's era the
unlocking of the potential for property development provided opportunities to make quick fortunes – and for corruption and double-
dealing too. Figures in government as well as in business were widely
believed to be up to their ears in illicit enrichment. At least some of
the accusations appear to have been true in this period of easy money
and big profits. Nevertheless, the new business ethos certainly encouraged investors out of their long-term distrust of the Parisian property-
market, and helped to provide the funds for extremely extensive
redevelopment. The latter was focused on the outer arrondissements
(XIIe.–XXe.), where most of the *îlots insalubres* had been located.

There was relatively little new building within the eleven arrondissements which make up the historic heart of Paris – even the few
îlots insalubres within these were subject to restoration rather than
root-and-branch renovation.[15]

Urban developers within the ZACs tended to follow the lead of the
banlieue, and to build in ways which contrasted with Paris's classical
inheritance. Whereas the Haussmannian *immeuble de rapport* had
harmonized with rules of urban construction outlined in the 1783–4
building regulations, the new wave of construction was keener to flout
traditional constraints in the name of modernism. The extra height
provided by the tower block seemed the obvious way to create more
space, as Le Corbusier had underlined. In 1958 building height was
increased to 31 metres in the central arrondissements, and 37 metres
in those of the periphery (compared with 45 metres in the suburbs).
Yet frequent exceptions were made, some of them in the suburbs, such
as the set of office blocks planned for the La Défense development on
the western extension of the line of the Champs-Élysées. The area had
been designated in the 1950s as an overspill zone for the densely
occupied business areas around the Bourse and the Opéra. Within the
twenty arrondissements, the Maison de la Radio – the ORTF building
facing onto the Seine (XVIe.) constructed between 1956 and 1963 –
was allowed to have a central tower of some 75 metres, and the
UNESCO headquarters built behind the École militaire (VIIe.) also
flouted the height regulations. The biggest exception, however, was
made for the Maine-Montparnasse tower on the site of the terminus
station (XVe.), whose construction began in 1959. There are, frankly,
far worse skyscrapers in the world – and indeed in Paris. Yet many
Parisians over the next decade, seeing the tower rising ever higher and
higher to its full size of over 200 metres, felt an appalled sense of
visual transgression. The tower was less a *lieu de mémoire* than a site
of collective apprehension.

By the time that the Montparnasse tower and the surrounding
concourse of shops and offices was fully operational (and a smaller,
uglier, 90-metre-high brother had also been built, at the Jussieu Faculty
of Sciences: Ve.), this kind of building was becoming a standard feature
of the cityscape. The Front de Seine development (XVe.) across the
river from the Maison de la Radio, for example, was composed of

twenty towers up to 120 metres high. The run-down area behind the
Place d'Italie (XIIIe.) received much the same treatment, as did poorer
working-class neighbourhoods out at Belleville (XIXe.) and behind
the Gare de Lyon (XIe.). By the turn of the century these areas would
contain around half of the 160 buildings within Paris classified as
IGHs (*immeubles de grande hauteur*: very tall buildings).

With modern buildings seemed to come a transformation in the
material culture of everyday life. Average national income and consumption rose by over a third between 1949 and 1958 – and carried
on rising. The homes being built in and around Paris were thus
increasingly stuffed full of the contraptions and impedimenta of a
style of life which appeared all the newer and more exciting for coming
so hard on the heels of a period of austerity. In 1939 there had been
500,000 cars in Paris; by 1960 there were one million – and five years
later that had doubled again. Parisians were among the first to benefit
from developments which were national in scope. Only one in fourteen
French homes possessed a refrigerator in 1959; in 1965, one in two
had one. Some 8 per cent of homes had a washing machine in 1954;
by 1970 the figure was 53 per cent (and over 90 per cent in the 1990s).
There had been only 24,000 French television sets in existence in
1950. By 1962 a quarter of homes had a TV, and by 1966 it was a
half. Spending on consumer goods was accompanied by more spending
on leisure too – helped by the statutory provision for three weeks of
paid holiday in 1956 (four weeks from 1963). The life-style changes
were all the more dramatic for being endlessly promoted in aggressive
advertising campaigns in the media and on the walls of the city.

Despite the gusto with which French people – and Parisians in
particular – took to the consumerism of the late 1950s and 1960s,
there was a good deal of questioning about the meaning and the
desirability of such changes. Some of this took the form of a woolly
anti-Americanism, which drew on many sources, including the hoary
anxiety that Paris should not become a second Chicago or New York.
A good deal of sociological evidence began to emerge, moreover, that
the quality of life in high-rise tower blocks was not a bed of roses. The
suburb of Sarcelles, close to Le Bourget airport, was much cited in the
literature. With austerely monotonous modernist buildings slung up
in the 1950s with little concern for communal services or good com-

munications, Sarcelles did not look or feel good. It bred, in the view of the media (who got very excited about the issue), a new social and psychological malaise dubbed 'Sarcellitis', characterized by juvenile delinquency, bored housewives, nervous breakdowns and a rocketing suicide rate. As the modernist architecture of the suburbs infiltrated the heart of Paris, fears grew of a general epidemic of Sarcellitis within the heart of the city. From the late 1940s film-maker Jacques Tati had been providing a light and humorous look at the world of modernist architecture and equally dysfunctional modern gadgets: his *Mon Oncle* (1958) was a satire on the new modernist *banlieue*. Altogether more savage and bleakly dystopic was Jean-Luc Godard's futuristic *Alphaville*, filmed almost entirely in suburban HLMs. *Alphaville* appeared in 1965, a year which also saw publication of the prize-winning novel *Les Choses* ('Things'), by Georges Perec. 'Things' are the commodities of modern living which the hapless young couple who are the novel's protagonists pursue with blandly despairing dedication. Around the same time, Roland Barthes's witty semiological analyses of the minutiae of everyday life were also gaining intellectual currency: new forms of social life – from Citroën cars through to advertisements and wrestling matches – formed myths whose cultural meanings needed to be plumbed with the same ethnographic seriousness as, say, the birthing practices of the Arapaho Indians.

By the mid-1960s doubts were also growing concerning the human costs of the demolition and renovation taking place within Paris. The quality of the housing being replaced by *grands ensembles* in the outer arrondissements was generally poor, so that the developments did not initially stimulate a strong conservationist backlash. But it was apparent that the changes had a notable human cost: whole communities were being destroyed. The area behind the Place d'Italie (XIIIe.), for example, had housed a somewhat sedentary but fairly vibrant working-class community which worked locally in factories such as the huge Say sugar refinery on the Boulevard Vincent Auriol or the Panhard car factory on the Avenue d'Ivry. For the duration of the works in progress, the inhabitants were shifted into accommodation in the *banlieue*. Yet when the development was complete few could afford to come back, for rents were beginning to skyrocket: the effect of rent-control laws was being undercut by runaway inflation. Also, many individuals chose not to return. The Say refinery and the Panhard factory closed down in the 1960s, reducing local employment possibilities. In addition, the rather alienating urban functionalism of the tower-block development had put paid to the cosy street sociability of yore. Here, as in the other *grands ensembles*, wider main streets now allowed the swift passage of car traffic, corner shops were replaced by grouped shopping and business quarters, and raised pedestrian walkways did not respect the old street alignment.

The Place d'Italie developments not only questioned the human aspect of the new architectural gigantism, but also highlighted a decline in both population levels and industrial plant which was more widely evident too. High-rise renovation had increased the total amount of urban space available to Parisians: between 1954 and 1974 some 8 million square metres of floor-space was demolished, to be replaced by 21 million of new space. Yet the area given over to factories and garages fell by 28 per cent. Proportionately more space was now devoted to trade, business and administration: office space increased by 22 per cent. Paris was thus continuing to deindustrialize, and to devote more space to the services sector – a process which would continue for the remainder of the century. Between 1962 and 1982 the number of individuals working in the liberal professions increased by 40 per cent, while the number of workers decreased by 45 per cent. The capital still provided around 10 per cent of national industrial production by the late 1970s, but the figure was falling fast; by the 1990s it was down to around 5 per cent. Industry now took the form of isolated oases and enclaves. The press and the printing trades remained in Paris and expanded relatively to about a quarter of the city's industrial output. The clothing and textiles industries survived and in some cases prospered, especially around the Sentier (IIe.) and also in the Marais and the Eleventh. Furniture was still a speciality of the Faubourg Saint-Antoine. But the Parisian cityscape as a whole had simply lost its industrial character.

The renovations pushed up the number of dwellings within the city: 60,000 units were destroyed, but 270,000 units were built. Housing space grew by 16.8 per cent overall – a substantial increase, then, albeit less than office space. Parisians may have lived in less chronically overcrowded conditions than hitherto, but there were fewer of them. The city's population, hovering around the 2.8 million mark from the 1920s to the late 1950s, began to fall: set at 2.6 million in 1962, it slipped to 2.3 in 1975 and 2.1 in 1982 – at which point it levelled out. Over the decades of renovation, Paris had thus lost more than half a million inhabitants, or one resident in five or six.

Loss of working-class population from the heart of the city was a consequence not only of the modernist renovation of the outer arrondissements but also the new work of urban restoration which began around this time. In 1962 de Gaulle's Culture Minister André Malraux passed an important law which permitted the designation of 'conservation areas' (*secteurs sauvegardés*) – areas of great historical importance or aesthetic value. This pioneering law – no other European country at the time had its like – won its spurs, so to speak, in the Marais, which it turned from one of the unhealthiest and most decaying parts of the old city into a tourist hotspot which was also one of the swishest districts in town.

12.3: The Marais

The Fifth Republic presided over the emergence of a new Paris. More than any of its predecessors, it was actively supportive of the historic patrimony of the city, and nurtured the idea of *le Vieux Paris* as something worth preserving. These two principles of action, however, not infrequently came into conflict. The way in which the authorities sought to negotiate change around them is evident in the restoration of the Marais under the prescriptions of the 1962 Malraux law on conservation areas, or *secteurs sauvegardés*.

The Malraux law provided for the establishment of a private–public company to fulfil the mission of conservation in a given area. Such companies had draconian powers of expropriation, for example, and could get eyesores knocked down, old buildings converted to modern uses and their services upgraded. They could also manage traffic and parking, and work to introduce new economic activities into the designated neighbourhoods. The trick was to do this while retaining some of the historic character not only of the buildings but also of the community.

The Marais was the first area in Paris to be given the Malraux treatment. Even in Balzac's day, Madame de Sévigné's paradisaical seventeenth-century enclave had seen better times. Big money had passed elsewhere in the course of the eighteenth century, and the post-Revolutionary neighbourhood had become dowdy and old-fashioned. Local families – notably rentiers and ageing maverick nobles – were powerful enough to restrict the modernization of the neighbourhood's street plan. The Rues Rambuteau and des Francs-Bourgeois were constructed so as to penetrate the old urban tissue here – but they were emphatically not boulevards. Haussmann preferred to keep his powder dry rather than to enter into conflict with local defenders of the Marais (the fiercely conservationist Victor Hugo had lived on the Place des Vosges from 1832 to 1848), and the same was true of the builders of the Métro, who serviced the neighbourhood only at its margins. Partly as a result the quality of housing in the Marais was falling fast after 1850 – it was difficult to provide modern conveniences in its labyrinthine streets and housing blocks. The establishment of a large East European Jewish community in the late nineteenth century was also marked by a worsening of living conditions.

At the start of the renovation process in the 1960s, the Marais was a highly heterogeneous locality, socially and ethnically. It had a strong artisanal character, and a lively air. Yet it had also become a sink of inner-city deprivation: 60 per cent of homes had no running water and no WC, and the amount of green space was around half the city average. Some housing blocks had 2,000 individuals per square hectare – the Parisian average was around 300. Earlier in the century part of the area towards the river had been designated as an *îlot insalubre* – an insanitary district designated for improvement – but the modernization achieved was generally of poor quality. The success of the Festival of the Marais in 1961 – a cultural festival held in the old hôtels, which attracted large crowds – mobilized the public across the city into believing that the Marais was worth saving.

The aim under the 1962 law was the restoration of this dilapidated area to something like its former glory. This meant the removal of sheds, lean-tos, additions, workshops and the like from the courtyards and inner spaces of the great aristocratic hôtels, with an aim of producing something which approximated the state of the neighbourhood in the mid-eighteenth century. This historical cleansing – *curetage* was the word used – disdained even work of quality which dated from the nineteenth and twentieth centuries, and required a great deal of meticulous care and historical verification, making it slow and expensive.

At its very best the restoration process in the Marais produced many architectural gems. By the 1980s the neighbourhood had been transformed. Its ethnic diversity was retained, but there was a clear shift in its social texture. Despite the best of intentions, many of the workers, artisans and small businesses which had given the district its earlier appeal were leaving in droves. They could not afford the prices, and found the spatial restrictions too confining. With property prices soaring, a new middle-class community benefited from the neighbourhood's beautification.

A particular development was the emergence of a big gay community in the Marais – which had a long history of tolerance of minorities. Gays benefited from the liberalization of the antiquated legislation against homosexuals during the early presidency of Socialist François Mitterrand from the 1980s onwards. Middle-class gays were also in a good economic position to enjoy the new leisure and consumerist orientation of the neighbourhood. Cruising joined *flânerie* as local pastimes.

The Marais remains highly culturally and ethnically diverse, even if the population tends – for the first time since Madame de Sévigné's day – to be rather better-off than before. The beautification of the neighbourhood has placed it directly on the main tourist trails. In this the restoration and establishment of museums here have also played a part. The Musée Carnavalet (for the history of Paris) in Madame de Sévigné's old haunt, the Musée Picasso in the Hôtel Salé, and the Maison européenne de la photographie on the Rue de Fourcy comprise a far from comprehensive sampling.

Indeed, in some ways, mixing respect for *le Vieux Paris* with the exigencies of modernization has produced a kind of museumization of the neighbourhood which has its downside. Old corner shops are now transformed into trendy boutiques. It is obviously nice that a fashionable shoe-shop, for example, chooses to retain outside the old sign of 'Boulangerie' with enamelled figures dating from the late nineteenth century. But the effect it produces is of a kind of fossilization. The enormous disdain which Parisians poured on the establishment of Euro-disney on the outskirts of the Paris region in 1992 may well have masked an anxiety that parts of old Paris were already in the process of becoming historic theme-parks.

The 1962 Malraux law was about enhancement as much as restoration and protection, and the minister underlined this point by reviving an old pre-Haussmannian regulation, long ignored, which required property-owners to clean up the façades of their buildings on a regular basis. The cleansing of historic buildings of their traffic grime – Notre-Dame, for example, was barely recognizable – helped put conservationist issues back on the political map. It turned Paris from dirty grey to a mosaic of light-greys and beige-whites.

Concern about the human costs of renovation – the socio-urban processes in train – and about the role of high buildings was relatively limited while the bulk of development was outside the historic heart of the city. As the Montparnasse tower continued its spectacular ascent, however, '*performing* height', as Roland Barthes could have put it, it became clear that its skyline presence was a reality at the historic heart of the city as well. Conservationist concerns crystallized around plans for the development of the old Halles in the First arrondissement, at the heart of the city. For more than a century there had been talk of the relocation of the city's major marketplace away from the centre, and since the 1930s governments had been buying up property in the neighbourhood with an eye to future development. The Fifth Republic grasped the nettle, ordering the transfer of market functions to new locations at La Villette (XIXe.) and Rungis in the *banlieue*, with effect from 1969. The decision stimulated a debate on the future of the area, which continued even as the work of demolition got under way. (Baltard's Second Empire pavilions, for example, were to be ruthlessly destroyed as late as 1971.) A sense of foreboding that high-rise building was finally reaching the historic central arrondissements was kindled by the digging on the site of Les Halles of a hole of dimensions of which legends were made. *Le grand trou* was so deep because it had been decided to locate beneath the new development the major Métro and RER terminus of Châtelet-Les-Halles. The scale of the hole was such that it raised fears that something gigantesque – of Montparnasse tower dimensions perhaps – was also in the offing, so as to house a world trade centre which was planned for the site. Even though the quality of the pre-existing housing in the Halles neighbourhood was scrappy and undistinguished, concern grew that a long-established working-class community was about to be removed and the area irremediably disfigured by the architecture of rampant modernism.

Many of these anxieties and concerns about the future shape of the city were elaborated in the so-called 'May Events' of 1968. These began as a protest against overcrowding and poor conditions in the university, but developed into an effort by rebellious students to revive the Left's nineteenth-century tradition of Parisian street militancy. For several weeks, riots and barricades became a staple feature of Parisian street life again, and the Latin Quarter a battlefield for cobblestone-hurling students and intimidating riot police. The May Events also provided a forum for fundamental questioning of the values of capitalist society and its emergent consumerism. Student leaders conducted a clever revolt which adeptly used the weapons of the strong on behalf of the weak. Diagnosing consumer capitalism as a 'society of the spectacle',[16] they aimed to put 'imagination in power' (one of their favourite slogans), choosing forms of action which looked good and which were widely reported – even by a media who had supposedly sold out to the political authorities. News coverage by the state-run media, for example, should have allowed the government version of events to predominate. Although the television was 'the government in the sitting room', as the rioters put it, in fact news reportage which showed police brutality in gory detail won their cause much sympathy. The transistor radio – usually tuned to Radio Luxembourg, which was outside government control – was stuck close to everyone's ear. Posters and advertising hoardings promoting modern commodities became the rebels' drawing board, and graffiti were used to inscribe on them mobilizing commands, gnomic reflections on the evils of capitalism, and a wistful commentary on the Events themselves. Participants and commentators contrasted the festive, carnivalesque character of the Events with the nine-to-five monotony of urban working life under the Fifth Republic, encapsulated in the slogan *'Métro, boulot, dodo'* ('Métro-work-bed'). Similarly, the intoxicating sense of community developed by the students and the inhabitants of the city who supported them contrasted starkly with the selfish, Sarcellitis-threatening anomie of consumer capitalism. A common leitmotiv was a hedonistic yearning for nature which contradicted the mechanistic artificiality of contemporary society. As one graffito put it, *'sous les pavés, la plage'* – 'beneath the cobblestones, the beach'. Festive, back-to-nature rebellion was an excellent antidote to creeping Sarcellitis.

In the final analysis, however, these unclassifiable disturbances ultimately confirmed rather than overthrew the commitment of 'middle France' to consumerist materialism. Striking workers who had participated in the breakdown of public order accepted high wage rises to return docilely to work (shepherded by a PCF which had lost the taste for anti-capitalist fight). The 1969 elections, set up as a kind of opinion poll on the May Events, saw the most comprehensive drubbing for the Left in French history. Even though de Gaulle, who had wobbled perilously at one stage in the course of the Events, had retired (hurt) in 1969, his replacement, his sometime henchman and prime minister Georges Pompidou, had been the backbone of government reaction throughout the disturbances and was a modernizer *pur et dur*. Yet even though they were ultimately decisively rejected by the electorate, the ludic (and occasionally ludicrous) May Events constituted a serious questioning of capitalist values. Their most effective influence was as

a semi-subliminal, delayed-action critique of the values of modernization, which was to reverberate durably in the mentalities of Parisians.

Paris in 1969 and the early 1970s was an odd place, with the dust
from May '68 still very much in the air, but with the government of
Georges Pompidou seeming to want only to drive faster along the
road to modernization. Even as public disquiet grew concerning the
looming presence of the Montparnasse tower and the prospect of
something worse at Les Halles, the new president told a *Le Monde*
journalist, with disarming frankness, 'I repeat, there is no modern
architecture without towers,' and he offered the prospect of 'a forest
of towers' at La Défense, whose skyline to the rear of the Champs-
Élysées was also becoming troublingly visible from within Paris.[17]
Pompidou also threw all his weight behind a project to put a major
art gallery and cultural centre in the Plateau Beaubourg in the First
arrondissement – the earliest of the *îlots insalubres* to receive demolition. The Centre Beaubourg, subsequently renamed the Pompidou
Centre, was designed by Richard Rogers and Renzo Piano following
a major international competition. It represented a style quite new to
Paris – though Parisians in the end found it less frightening than many
had feared. After all, they had managed to familiarize themselves, and
even grow to love, other spectacular exceptions to Parisian rules, such
as the Eiffel tower and the Sacré-Coeur.

In the event, by 1977, when the Pompidou Centre was opened, a
remarkable sea-change had occurred in attitudes towards planning
and urbanism. Pompidou's sudden death in 1974 led to a presidential
election which brought to power the liberal conservative Valéry Giscard d'Estaing, a figure who was downright suspicious of Pompidou's
modernizing impulses. The fact that Giscard had only just edged
the vote ahead of the Socialist François Mitterrand highlighted
the national mood for change – the Gaullists had been nowhere in the
contest. More attuned than the Gaullists to the reflective mood of the
nation in the post-'68 period, Giscard also faced the consequences of
a downturn in the economy after several decades of unparalleled
growth. The oil crisis in the West after 1971 hit the French economy
particularly hard – and Paris harder still. Between 1971 and 1973 the

city shed some 42,000 jobs in industry, accelerating the movement of deindustrialization. The *banlieue* was if anything hardest hit by the crisis, with unemployment suddenly emerging as a mass phenomenon. Runaway inflation and a credit squeeze brought to a close a period of surging economic growth and rampant materialism. A steep fall in the birth-rate, and a slackening of immigration into the Paris region were further signs of uncertainty about Paris's future.

What had started as a socio-economic crisis developed into a cultural, political and psychological phenomenon. By 1974 the urban historian of Paris Pierre Lavedan was prophetically noting the appearance of 'a change in the conception of life. We have seen emerge what is called the idea of the environment, and that of the quality of life.'[18] The May Events had given a foretaste of an ecological mentality and the presidential electoral campaign of 1974 saw environmentalism become a constituent part of a successful political programme. Giscard's electoral manifesto declared his intention to 'improve the quality of life in cities by reducing excessive density, preventing the proliferation of tower blocks and safeguarding all green space, public and private'.[19] Once in power, he took this agenda very seriously. He opposed the erection of tall tower blocks within the city: a giant building planned by the Place d'Italie was permanently shelved, for example, and new height regulations set the norm for the inner arrondissements at 25 metres. He also froze plans for an autoroute expressway on the Left as well as the Right Bank. His call for a conservationist approach to new projects was brilliantly illustrated by his decision to locate the museum of the nineteenth century in the long-disused Quai d'Orsay railway station (VIIe.): the Musée d'Orsay was to become one of the most visited sites in Paris. Many nineteenth-century monuments now received classified status for the first time, including many theatres and (surprisingly enough) the Eiffel tower. Giscard was lukewarm about the new-towns approach, and a decision was taken not to increase their number from five to eight, as had originally been planned. He also urged a cultural renaissance in the suburbs, situating *maisons de culture* in the *banlieue* and beginning the renovation of the rotting medieval basilica out at Saint-Denis.

If Giscard's approach to Paris was well attuned to a growing current of opinion within the capital, it also harmonized with a shift in the viewpoint of many architects and city planners. 'The age of giant cities and overlarge organizations is over,' he had declared. 'The time of concrete at any price has gone.'[20] These were sentiments increasingly shared by the professions which had been so infatuated with modernism and its attendant works over the previous two decades. The shift in professional opinion owed something to intergenerational rivalries, something to swings of fashion, and something also to corporate defensiveness. The media success of historian Louis Chevalier's *L'Assassinat de Paris* ('The Assassination of Paris': 1977) showed there was a public ready to believe that a conspiracy of short-sighted and corrupt politicians and money-grubbing and ignorant planners was hell-bent on destroying the historic texture of the city. The change of outlook by architects and planners also derived from their growing acceptance of the humanistic critiques of the *grands ensembles*. A return to tradition had been preached for some time by the influential think-tank *Atelier parisien de l'urbanisme* (APUR), and in 1977 it was enshrined in practice by the *Plan d'occupation des sols* built into a new *Schéma directeur* for Parisian urbanism. This new set of building regulations restored the street, the building line and the block as the framework for planning and also highlighted the need for greater sensitivity to context. The architect Christian de Portzamparc declared the aim of the new approach 'to architecturalize urban space rather than to assemble architectural objects'.[21] He exemplified his approach in his pioneering design for the Rue des Hautes-Formes (XIIIe.). Combining the spirit of the modern with a feel for Parisian traditions, the ensemble was elegant and complex, but also highly liveable.

This was also a moment at which the hard work put into the renovation of blue-chip conservation areas such as, most notably, the Marais, was starting to pay off. An insanitary district had been reclaimed as a model for modern living. The streets were restored to the *flâneur* and the casual shopper – to such an extent that, so intense was the pedestrian crush, the thoroughfare of the Rue des Francs-Bourgeois became almost impassable for vehicular traffic at weekends. The ersatz, it is true, was never far away. Façadism – the destruction of the entirety of a building except the facing wall – was a procedure sometimes too readily adopted. On the edge of the Marais the Quartier de l'Horloge (IIIe.) to the north of the Pompidou Centre, for example, is a medieval pastiche of *faux* passages, alleys and culs-de-sac, composed of concrete for the most part, behind the heavily restored wall facing onto the Rue Saint-Martin, one of the oldest streets in Paris. Façadism risked turning parts of these renovated areas into unreal stage-sets. But it was popular with planners since it meant that all the amenities of modern living could be provided easily behind this decorative external shell. The spectacular rise in property values in the district highlighted the social promotion which these architectural procedures entailed.

The way in which the renovation of the Marais conformed with developments in new building from the 1970s onwards showed that, to some extent, what was happening was a return to models and norms which had a long lineage in Parisian history, but which had got lost from view in the excitement and clamour of the late 1950s and 1960s. Symptomatically, the studies by historian François Loyer of Haussmann's Paris helped to nurture a growing respect in architectural circles for the great planner's visual sense and his sensitivity to the Parisian site.[22] Yet there was a dimension of democratic accountability and social justice which was quite un-Haussmannian, and quite new. The Le Corbusier-inspired modernizing projects of the 1960s had been top-down operations. Directed by businessmen and technocrats, who simply assumed that they were acting in the best interests of Parisians, they had been implemented with a breathtaking lack of public consultation. A concern for the views of the public was now coming back on the political as well as the architectural agenda. A government-commissioned report by Pierre Nora and Bertrand Éveno in 1975 highlighted the poor quality of the nation's housing stock, especially for the socially vulnerable such as the old. The government responded with a change of policy. A new body, the *Fonds d'aménagement urbain* (FAU) was created to oversee all urbanist projects, and it was instructed to include social equity as a factor in decision-making. Legislation in 1977 introduced *Opérations programmées d'amélioration de l'habitat* (OPAHs), which ran like small-scale conservation areas. Like the companies which ran the latter, OPAHs had wide-ranging powers of expropriation and responsibility for economic regeneration of a neighbourhood. But they gave local inhabitants a bigger say in affairs, and also had a clearer notion of end-use in renovation schemes. They put less emphasis on historical re-creation (or indeed creation) in the style of the Marais and more on getting buildings usable and used again. Historical precision mattered less than utility and liveability. They thus tended to build around the existing patterns of use and also to incorporate existing quality buildings into the development plans. The ambitious renovation of Bercy in the Twelfth arrondissement, for example, made a deliberate feature of the defunct wine warehouses, which were turned into trendy bars and restaurants.

The more humane and user-oriented strain of urbanism preached and practised by Giscard received unlikely reinforcement from a development which caused him a good deal of political damage – the appointment of a mayor of Paris. For nearly two centuries the city had been adjudged too important to the government to be allowed to have such a post. Giscard's decision, announced in 1975, to reject the message of history was partly motivated by his conviction that he could plant one of his minions in the Hôtel de Ville and undermine the Gaullist majority on the city council. As it turned out, Giscard was utterly outmanoeuvred by the maverick Gaullist Jacques Chirac, who convincingly won the popular vote in 1977, and went on to dig in the Gaullist movement from top to bottom of the municipal administration. Chirac had a more *dirigiste* conception of what a mayor should be than Giscard, and the city council became a rubber stamp for his energetic actions. Even a move in the early 1980s to decrease the mayor's powers by setting up arrondissement-level elected assemblies failed to blunt the mayoral juggernaut.

In addition Chirac proved a past master at stealing the clothes of his political combatant. On coming to power, Giscard had blocked plans for a world trade centre in the Les Halles development, and urged the provision of a greater amount of green space, overriding Pompidou's fears that if one placed a large park here 'it would soon be full of 60,000 young hippies'.[23] Chirac now imperiously declared himself 'architect in chief' of the project, and oversaw its final stages. This included the laying out of the ground-level park, the below-ground provision for offices and shops and the integration of business into the project. Significantly, however, he permitted an unofficial competition of 'counter-projects' criticizing what had been proposed.

Even though in planning terms the impact of the 'counter-projects' was meagre, and counted more as public relations, the episode underlined an increasing awareness of the desirability of consulting public opinion.

Paris was in a powerful position to benefit from having a president of the Republic and its own mayor using the enhancement of the city as part of their respective political programmes. This was even more the case after 1981, when Giscard was ousted as president by François Mitterrand. The latter was if anything even more captivated by the possibility of using Paris as a showcase for his policies. With one eye firmly fixed on posterity, he launched a set of eye-catching major initiatives. These became known as the *Grands Projets* ('big projects'), and though associated closely with Mitterrand in fact echoed similar ventures by his predecessors. De Gaulle had had the original idea for the development of Les Halles, for example, and Pompidou for the Centre Beaubourg. For his part, Giscard had brought both these initiatives to fruition, and made his own contributions, notably in establishing the Musée d'Orsay (which opened in 1986), in initiating plans which would lead to the creation of the Institut du Monde arabe, and in deciding to use the defunct abattoir out at La Villette as the basis of a new science museum and park. Mitterrand, as we shall see,[24] embarked on a whole raft of measures. The *Grands Projets* would be one of the defining features of the city at the dawn of the third millennium.[25]

Yet the mayor of Paris had not allowed the president of the Republic – into whose shoes he would step following the presidential elections of 1995 – to steal all the thunder. A number of major initiatives, often boasting the design hallmark of internationally acclaimed architects, came out of the Hôtel de Ville. The Palais-Omnisports de Bercy (XIIe.) was one such, and was an important component in the complete renovation of an area which had formerly been full of wine warehouses. The Catalonian architect Ricardo Bofil was responsible for the kind of nostalgico-baroque housing and office development around the Place de la Catalogne behind the Montparnasse station (XIVe.). The part of the Canal Saint-Martin where it joins the Seine was turned into a yachting centre.

A particularly striking development for which the Hôtel de Ville

can claim credit was the extension of green space within the city. Giscard had declared one of his aims to be 'to bring ecology into everyday life',[26] but it was to be Chirac who delivered on the promise. There had been absolutely no addition to Parisian green space since 1945, but Chirac changed this dramatically. Over the period of his mayoral office, from 1977 to 1995, no fewer than 134 gardens were created. This represented an increase of well over one-third above previous levels. The parks added 118 hectares of green space to the city aggregate – out of a total for Paris as a whole (excluding the Bois de Boulogne and Vincennes) of 484 hectares. The policy aim of ensuring that every Parisian was less than 500 metres away from an area of recreation highlighted the post-Giscard attention to environmental issues and leisure demands. Some of the parks were created as a result of removing defective and overcrowded housing plots – as with the Belleville park (XXe.). Others were located on the sites of former industrial plant and the like. In the XVe., for example, the Parc Georges-Brassens was sited over the old Vaugirard abattoir and the Parc André-Citroën was on the former premises of the famous car factory. A good deal of thought and imagination went into the design of these parks and gardens. The same qualities were evident in the opening of a planted walkway – the *coulée verte* – running over an old railway line between the Opéra-Bastille and the Bois de Vincennes (XIIe.).

The imaginative creation of green space marked a concern for the Parisian (or tourist) pedestrian which was a welcome post-Giscard development, although the pedestrianized walkways which were separated off from the buzz of traffic in the *grands ensembles* were not adjudged a success. More effort was put into developing the street as a site of sociability and exchange – a process of Parisian reinvention which linked with the city's past. Even the pavements on the *grands boulevards* were widened and made more welcoming as if to encourage a revival of *flânerie*. The pedestrianization of certain historic areas proved a disappointing failure, driving property prices up and small traders out, but the shift to a system of *quartiers tranquilles* where traffic speed was kept low and through traffic excluded was more successful. Another concession to the pedestrian was the opening of underground car parks – the first were at the Place Vendôme (Ie.:1972) and on the Rue Lagrange by Notre-Dame (Ve.: 1973). Even areas which seemed on the fast track to decay and which had little of architectural distinction about them – the Butte-aux-Cailles (XIIIe.), for example, the Rue Mouffetard (Ve.), the Rue Montorgeuil (Ie.–IIe.) and the Faubourg Saint-Antoine (XIe.–XIIe.) – were given a new lease of life. These changes chimed with the trend from the mid-1970s onwards to present Paris as a city with a human face. They made the areas more liveable – but also more expensive – and attracted tourists, who found within them the cleaned-up appearance of a backdrop to a photograph by Robert Doisneau or a film by Marcel Carné. In a somewhat round-about way, they also suggested that the 'outmoded aesthetic' denounced by Pompidou, in his call for Paris to adapt to the motor car[27] (rather than vice versa) still had some legs on it.

Conclusion
Big Projects in a Bigger City
Paris in the Twenty-first Century

Paris celebrated the advent of the new millennium on 31 December 1999 with one of the northern hemisphere's better firework displays. The year 2000 found this historic city in good form. Its economy had been through a series of crises since the 1970s, but it was doing well compared with international rivals. The city's cultural prestige helped make it the world's number-one tourist city and – in so far as such league tables have any value – it could also claim to be a world leader in fashion, luxury goods and gastronomy as well as being a major international centre for financial services and communications. The quality of life in the city ranks well against international comparators too. Paris also has good supply systems, is only moderately polluted, and is very well served by public transport. Property prices are high – but not compared with London and Manhattan. There is a problem of inner-city violence and insecurity. Yet these are problems in big cities the world over – and they are usually worse elsewhere than in Paris. With the partial and contested exception of 'French theory' (Lévi-Strauss, Foucault, Derrida, etc.), recent and current intellectual output is not highly rated internationally. Yet the range of cultural and leisure activities available to Parisians is particularly high and of outstanding quality. In addition the longevity of Parisians shades national averages, and residents' health is generally better too. The heavy concentration of world-class hospitals and other health services in the capital is a contributory factor in this.

Paris was, and is, a wonderful place in which to live – in the right circumstances. It contains the vast majority of the wealthiest individuals in the country, but also a solid phalanx of the homeless (SDFs, or *sans domicile fixe*), who spend their lives on the streets.

Overall the city's labour market is more robust than elsewhere in France, and unemployment rates middling when set against French averages. The housing problems which bedevilled Parisian politics until the 1950s have eased, though there are small enclaves of appalling housing conditions in which immigrant labour is forced to live. The active population is shrinking as a proportion of the overall population, which is clearly ageing. Individuals aged over sixty-five formed 10 per cent of the population in 1954; by the end of the century it was around 15 per cent and growing. Given the differences in longevity between the sexes, this is partly explained by the fact that Paris contains more women than men.

The second half of the twentieth century thus witnessed a remarkable renaissance of a city which after the Great War had seemed ground down by tensions and conflicts and oppressed by a feeling of faded grandeur. The revival of the French economy after 1945 – and particularly from the mid-1950s through to 1974 – was vital in this. Parisians secured for themselves the lion's share of economic prosperity. The material culture of the city's inhabitants – from consumer durables through to provision of transport, availability of housing and general living standards – registered a seismic shock. Against this glowing background, the downturn of the economy from the mid-1970s proved hard. In some senses the apogee of Parisian industrialism had been in the late 1950s and early 1960s, so the move towards deindustrialization was extremely painful. Over a very short period of time the city was effectively drained of the industry which had been such an important part of its nineteenth- and earlier twentieth-century identity. By the year 2000 only around five or six individuals in every hundred inhabitants were working-class – and half of these were foreigners. The city had become a 'tertiary city', as Haussmann had dreamed, where only the services counted. But it had recovered much of its erstwhile prosperity too.

The remodelling of the local economy had been helped by the position of influence that, from 1977, the mayor of Paris had carved out for himself. In 1995 Mayor Jacques Chirac was elected president of the Republic, and abandoned his office in the Hôtel de Ville for national preoccupations. The eighteen years which Chirac served as mayor were a tribute to his own stamina as well as a comment on the

impact of his performance on Parisian voters – for he was re-elected in 1983 and 1989. This bucked national political trends, but confirmed Paris's rather right-wing complexion. Chirac used his eighteen years in power within the city to build a ramp for his own ambitions, with a style which attracted accusations of serious corruption. Yet he had seized the opportunity offered by being appointed the first mayor of Paris since the French Revolution in order to bring a new and urgent focus on Parisian problems, and in particular to attract more funds towards the city. The decentralizing thrust of many of President Valéry Giscard d'Estaing's reforms was thwarted. By the 1990s President François Mitterrand was emulating the mayor in seeking to register his own renown in posterity by implementing a series of major presidential plans – the *Grands Projets*. Chirac was politically antagonistic to Mitterrand, but he supported the projects because he realized they raised Paris's international profile and had tourist appeal.

Chirac's successors as mayor were not without problems. His associate Jean Tibéri was investigated for corrupt dealings while still in office, and in 2001 was ousted by the Socialist Bertrand Delanoë, who almost fell foul of an assassin in October 2002. Yet the system which Chirac had established stayed in place, allowing his successors latitude to continue a range of high-profile policies. The mayor of Paris had become a key figure in the national political landscape. He commanded a budget and a staff larger than most ministries, while the location of the key sectors of the media within the capital also helped give Parisian problems a national dimension.

Many of the policies developed during the Chirac years have continued – the greening of the city, for example, the emphasis on sound environmental policies, attention to leisure pursuits, and cooperation with central government over major capital projects. Like Chirac, the next two mayors accepted the Haussmannian template which they inherited. Although there was an enormous amount of building from the late 1950s onwards, with some exceptions (such as the Fronts de Seine and the Bercy development) this was achieved while respecting the street plan which Haussmann and his early Third Republic successors had set in place. Similarly, although a lot was demolished, much of this was in the outer arrondissements and was of poor quality anyway. The stress on standard building heights which Haussmann had endorsed was frequently infringed in the outer arrondissements. Yet, again, with very few and usually glaring exceptions – such as the hideous seventeen-storey annex to the Hôtel de Ville opened in 1965 on the Boulevard Morland (IVe.) – the old regulations were observed in the historic central arrondissements. At an absolutely vital moment, Giscard's environmentalism beat off the love of tall buildings which President Pompidou had placed at the heart of his plans for the city. In this sense the urban transformation of the late twentieth century, though dramatic in its way, reinforced rather than undermined the sense of Paris as a Haussmannian city.

It remains less certain how long Paris can continue in this mould. Many of the major building projects of the last decades of the century were on sites made available as a result of industrial relocation. By 2000 these were fewer in number, at least within the twenty arrondissements. This kind of interstitial development is becoming more problematic. Attention has increasingly been given to creating new sites, for example by building platforms over railway lines – as with the Jardin de l'Atlantique over the Gare Montparnasse. Subterranean locations (a procedure which *le grand trou* of Les Halles may be said to have trialled) have also been mooted. Another possibility is simply overriding height limits, a process which would bring the city into line with its international comparators, albeit at the risk of losing some of its charm. The need for high-rise office blocks forming a business district has been hived off to La Défense, outside city walls, and if this prospers, the pressure on Paris for more office space may ease. But in all events hard choices seem to lie ahead, which will impinge on Paris's sense of its own identity.

Paris remains a highly international city. This fact has helped it to maintain its central place in the life of the nation, despite several campaigns of decentralization since the late 1940s. Sometimes those campaigns have looked to be swimming against the tide, such have been the continuing powers of attraction of Paris and its region. The establishment of a superb national communications system – particularly through the service of the TGVs (*Trains à grande vitesse*, the high-speed services initiated in the 1970s) – has actually favoured centralization rather than its opposite. The fact that Paris is, for example, only three hours by TGV from the Mediterranean coast and just over two hours from London, means that Palavas-les-Flots and Elephant and Castle become potential commuting suburbs of Greater Paris. The progressive Europeanization of the TGV services is also acting in Paris's favour.

By 2000 the conservation movement in favour of *le Vieux Paris* had become a significant force in planning developments. Conservationists were also by now able to point out how poorly some of the modernist building of the 1950s and 1960s had worn. The *grands ensembles* both inside and outside Paris were looking extremely shabby, especially with the added problem of juvenile vandalism. The Pompidou Centre closed for extensive repairs in 1998 too, after only two decades of use. Even so, the conservationists felt beleaguered. They had won many battles but seemed in danger of losing the war. The modernizers seemed always able to circumvent the obstacles they put up. The trend of façadism – anathema to the conservationists – was becoming widespread. In addition there was growing awareness of the dangers of so-called 'museumization' in parts of Paris which had kept the planners at bay. The Marais was the example always cited here – the conservationists had driven out the workers, it was said, and turned the neighbourhood into something between a museum exhibit and a film set. Paris, the city of nineteenth-century modernity, was in danger of being set in aspic, with modernity transformed into nostalgia. (But then quite a few Parisophiles were confirmed nostalgics . . .)

The conservationists were also placed on the back foot by the growing taste of both the municipality and the central government for 'big projects'. A revival of interest among architects and historians in Haussmann in the 1980s testified to the way in which thinking about these projects was influenced by the experience of the Second Empire. The *Grands Projets* are monuments; while most are not free-standing, they are planned in relation to their immediate environs. French architects had found it difficult to imagine what a public monument might look like, following the unfortunate liaison with pompous Fascist architecture in the 1930s. Glass seemed to provide the answer. It has been argued that the extensive use of glass in most of the *Grands Projets* not merely signified the new technical feats which could be achieved in this medium but also acted as a political metaphor for the values of transparency and accountability alleged to be dear to the heart of Socialist President François Mitterrand. Certainly the idea of the projects had come on the scene just as public consultation in planning issues was being discussed.

Mitterrand did not originate the idea of the *Grand Projet*, but he did make it his own. Pompidou had commissioned the Pompidou Centre at Beaubourg (1977), while Giscard d'Estaing had started work on the Cité des Sciences out at La Villette (1983–90), the Musée d'Orsay (1986), the renovation of the Louvre (1981–93) and architect Jean Nouvel's Institut du Monde arabe (1987). Many of these were brought to fruition by Mitterrand, who added projects of his own. The most important psychologically and politically was I. M. Pei's glass pyramid, created as the new entrance to the renovated Louvre (1993). The project excited an incredibly hostile reaction, especially from conservationists, who regarded it as little less than sacrilege. The manifest popularity of the pyramid as soon as it was unveiled, however, meant that, as one critic put it, 'the war is over'.[1] The way was open for new and even more daring projects.

Initially the *Grands Projets* looked as though they were merely embellishing the traditional east/west axis of power in the capital. Thus there were new monuments at La Défense, where the Grande Arche was aligned with the Arc de Triomphe and the Arc du Carrousel in 1989, through the Louvre pyramid and past the Pompidou Centre out to the Canadian Carlos Ott's Opéra Bastille, also inaugurated in 1989. Yet what became more apparent as time went on was that the *Grands Projets* were also realigning Paris's monumental space in two quite novel ways. First, far more was being situated on the working-class eastern side of the city than had been the case with prestige building in the past – a point which pleased the Left. Second, the projects were having the effect of reworking and re-emphasizing the river Seine.[2] Much of the new building between the 1920s and 1960 had been located in the space made available by the removal of the city fortifications. Between around 1970 and the year 2000 the river banks became the focus of major development. The removal of industrial plant from many sites along the Seine opened up space for major projects, of which the Hôtel de Ville as well as presidents of the Republic took advantage. Just in from the *boulevard périphérique* on the west side of Paris, the old Citroën car factory was turned into the Parc André-Citroën, characterized by huge glasshouses (1993), alongside the Front de Seine development. Between this site and the Musée d'Orsay (1986), Mitterrand's successor Jacques Chirac is currently planning the Musée du Quai Branly, which will house the contents of the museum of Oceanic Art and the Musée de l'Homme. The Grand Louvre, the Opéra Bastille and the Institut du Monde arabe are all riverside locations too. Downstream there was extensive modernization on the old wine warehouse site at Bercy, at one end of which was the futuristic Ministry of Finance building of Paul Chemetov (1989). Across the river the disinherited area of Tolbiac-Masséna has received huge investment, and the virtual creation of a new neighbourhood was oriented around the TGB – the Très Grande Bibliothèque, or the Bibliothèque de France François Mitterrand – which the president commissioned from Dominique Perrault and which opened in 1996.

The manifest grandiloquence of many of these projects is more than a little overpowering. Although their use of glass is supposed to highlight transparency and public accessibility, in fact the scale of a number of monuments and the reflectiveness of the glass make some of them rather sinister and forbidding buildings. Mitterrand was accused of having 'pharoah-like' ambitions. Though some monuments have an attractive human scale, others show little sign of public consultation. It seems highly unlikely that the TGB would have been built as it is (with books stored in glass towers which needs special air-conditioning and shading to prevent damage, for example), had care been taken to consult potential readers systematically.

One way or another the *Grands Projets* are marking the physiognomy of Paris in a very striking and durable way. Perhaps the greatest challenge to the city as it entered the twenty-first century, however, was its relationship with its suburbs. Distrust of the *banlieue* has been an abiding feature of Parisian history, even as the nature of the relationship between the two has changed. Once, the suburbs were the light frill around the walls of the most important city in Christendom. Those days are long past. The number of inhabitants of the *banlieue* overtook the size of Paris in the early twentieth century. By the turn of the twenty-first century the 2.1 million inside the *boulevard périphérique* contrasted with the ten and more million in the surrounding area, newly reorganized after 1976 as the region of the Île-de-France. Parisians make up around a thirtieth of France's population – but one French person in five or six is an inhabitant of the Paris region as a whole (the city included).

Relations between city and *banlieue* have become ever more complex. The population of the city swells each day by a million people. With the exception of tourists and long-distance travellers, these are nearly all inhabitants of the *banlieue* travelling in to work (and also to play) by RER, Métro, bus or private vehicle. There is a related movement regarding Parisians' family lifecycle. The majority of Parisian households are one-person affairs (the figure was one-third in 1962), and this has had an impact on housing demand. When an individual marries and has children, one of the first decisions will be whether to relocate in the *banlieue* where there are cheaper and more numerous larger apartments and houses. At retirement too, some Parisians choose to transfer to what they hope is a more rural environment in the *banlieue*.

Despite the growing interdependence of city and suburb, the long-established cultural lag is still in place. Regional infrastructure cries out for improvement. The RER and Métro extensions show a willingness to come to grips with the problem. Yet the everyday experience of *banlieusards* either travelling into Paris or else going to work in different parts of the suburban belt is often pretty grim. The fourteen years of Socialist Mitterrand's tenure as president produced less than one might imagine for the individuals who provided the labour on which Paris's prosperity is based.

Paris has always grown outwards from a central core, with boundaries radiating outwards like ripples in a pond. 'A city like Paris is in perpetual flood,' noted Victor Hugo in *Notre-Dame de Paris* in 1829.

> Within it is made a continual vegetation of wood and stone . . . Every year, every day, every hour by a kind of slow and irresistible infiltration, the city expands into the faubourgs and the faubourgs become the city and the fields become the faubourgs.[3]

Thus Philip Augustus's boundaries became those of Charles V: 'the houses finally jumped over Philip Augustus's Wall and scattered joyfully in the plain and chaotically like breakaways.'[4] The city boundaries of Louis XIV, and then of Louis XVI's Farmers-General, worked in much the same way. In 1859–60 Paris was extended out to the Thiers fortifications and the existing twenty arrondissements formed. Very few observers at that time would have imagined that a city so evidently in a dynamic phase of expansion would be confined within the same boundaries nearly a century and a half later. Napoleon I had imagined the city extending out to Saint-Germain-en-Laye in the west, while sundry science fiction writers and, eventually, Le Corbusier imagined it reaching to the English Channel. Expansion has been put back on the agenda, but only while keeping the major caesura of the *boulevard périphérique* in place. There has been talk of paving over these roadways into an underground tunnel, so that freer expansion becomes possible. We shall have to see.

At all events, Paris was not without its problems as it entered the twenty-first century. But it was in a good position to face up to them. In the Middle Ages the city's water-merchants adopted as Paris's motto the Latin tag, '*Fluctuat nec mergitur*' – 'It floats, nor does it sink.' How reassuringly apt.

544

Paris at a Glance

Date	Population	Surface area (in hectares)
250	6,000	c. 50
800	20,000	60
1100	3,000	30
1220	50,000	272
1328	200,000	300+
1500	150,000	439
1600	300,000	483
1700	500,000	1,100
1789	650,000	3,370
1815	700,000	3,370
1861	1.7 million	7,802
1914	2.9 million	7,802
1939	2.8 million	8,622
1946	2.8 million	10,516
1958	2.8 million	10,516
1982	2.2 million	10,516
1999	2.1 million	10,516

Characteristic Buildings

(plus arrondissement; architect; and dates of construction)
No terminal date given = major subsequent work
* = other architects involved

AD 250 Arènes de Lutèce (Ve.; 1st–2nd centuries); Thermes de Cluny (Ve.; late 2nd century).

1100 *Public buildings*: Louvre palace (Ie.; 1190); Philip Augustus Wall (1190–1213). *Religious buildings*: Priory of Saint-Martin-des-Champs (IIIe.; 1060–); Notre-Dame cathedral (IVe.; 1163–); churches of Saint-Pierre-de-Montmartre (XVIIIe.; 1147–) and Saint-Julien-le-Pauvre (Ve.; 1165–1220).

1220 *Public building*: Conciergerie (Ie.; late 13th century–). *Religious buildings*: Sainte-Chapelle (Ie.; 1242–8); churches of Saint-Germain-l'Auxerrois (Ie.), Saint-Nicolas-des-Champs (IIIe.) and Saint-Séverin (Ve.; all late 13th century–)

1328 *Public buildings*: Charles V Wall (1364–80); fortress of Vincennes (14th century). *Private buildings*: tower of John the Fearless (IIe.; 1409–11); Hôtels de Cluny (Ve.; 1485–1510) and de Sens (IVe.; 1498–). *Religious buildings*: Cloister of Les Billettes (IVe.; 1427–); churches of Saint-Étienne-du-Mont and Saint-Médard (both Ve. and late 14th century–).

1500 *Public buildings*: Hôtel-de-Ville (IVe.; Le Boccador; 1533; rebuilt in replica, 1873–); Louvre (Ie.; Pierre Lescot, Jean Goujon; 1546–); Fontaine des Innocents (Ie.; Jean Goujon; 1549). *Private building*: Hôtel Scipion (Ve.; 1532–). *Religious buildings*: abbot's palace, Saint-Germain-des-Prés (VIe.; Guillaume Marchant; 1586–90); churches of Saint-Jacques-de-la-Boucherie (IVe.; 1509– ; all but tower demolished 1797) and Saint-Eustache (Ie.; Jean Delamarre, Pierre Lemercier; 1532–).

1600 *Public buildings*: Luxembourg palace and gardens (VIe.; *S. de

Brosse; 1615–); Palais-Royal (Ie.; 1629–); Pont-Neuf (Ie.; J. B. Androuet de Cerceau; 1578–1607); Louvre colonnade (Ie.; C. Perrault; 1668); Invalides (VIIe.; L. Bruant; 1671–8; and church, J. Hardouin-Mansart; 1679–1708); Portes Saint-Denis (Xe.; J. F. Blondel; 1672) and Saint-Martin (Xe.; P. Bullet; 1674); Place des Vosges (IVe.; probably L. Métezeau; 1605–39), Dauphine (Ie.; L. Métezeau; 1607–), des Victoires (Ie.; J. Hardouin-Mansart; 1685–6) and Vendôme (Ie.; J. Hardouin-Mansart; 1699–1720); Jardin des Plantes (Ve.; 1640–); Institut de France (VIe.; *L. Le Vau; 1663–88); Observatoire (XIVe.; C. Perrault; 1667–72); hospitals of Saint-Louis (Xe.; C. Vellefaux and C. Chastillon; 1607–11) and La Salpêtrière (XIIIe.; L. Le Vau, 1657–). *Private buildings*: Hôtels de Sully (IVe.; J. B. Androuet de Cerceau; 1624–30), de Guénegaud (IIIe.; F. Mansart; 1652–5) and Salé (IIIe.; J. Boullier de Bourges; 1656–9); Musée Carnavalet (IIIe.; F. Mansart; 1660–). *Religious buildings*: Sorbonne chapel (Ve.; J. Lemercier; 1635–); Val-de-Grâce convent (Ve.; F. Mansart; 1645–); churches of Saint-Gervais (IVe.; 1616–), the Oratoire du Louvre (Ie.; C. Métezeau, J. Lemercier; 1621–30), Saint-Paul-et-Saint-Louis (IVe.; 1627–41), Notre-Dame-des-Victoires (IIe.; P. Le Muet; 1629–), Saint-Sulpice (VIe.; 1646–) and Saint-Louis-en-l'Île (IVe.; *L. Le Vau, 1670–).

1700 *Public buildings*: Farmers-General Wall (toll-houses by C. Ledoux; 1784–6); Palais-Royal (Ie.; rebuilding, 1781–4); Palais Bourbon (Assemblée Nationale) (VIIe.; 1722–); École militaire (VIIe.; *J. A. Gabriel; 1752–88); Place de la Concorde (VIIIe.; J. A. Gabriel; 1755–72); Bourse de Commerce (Ie.; 1765–); Hôtel des Monnaies (VIe.; J. Antoine; 1771–5); Odéon theatre (VIe.; M. J. de Peyre, C. de Wailly; 1779–82); Palais de l'Élysée (VIIIe.; C. A. Mollet; 1718–). *Private buildings*: Hôtels de Soubise (IIIe.; P. A. Delamair; 1705–9), and Matignon (VIIe.; J. B. Courtonne; 1722–3). *Religious buildings*: churches of Sainte-Geneviève (Panthéon) (Ve.; *J. G. Soufflot; 1757–90) and Saint-Philippe-du-Roule (VIIe.; J. F. Chalgrin; 1774–84).

1789 *Public buildings*: Pont des Arts (Ie.; 1803); Vendôme column (Ie.; 1810); Arc de Triomphe du Carrousel (Ie.; P. Fontaine, C. Percier; 1806–8); Arc de Triomphe (VIIIe.; *J. F. Chalgrin; 1806–36); Père-Lachaise cemetery (XXe.; A. Brongniart; 1804–); Bassin de La Villette (XIXe.; 1805–8). *Commercial buildings*: Passage des Panoramas (IIe.; 1800); Catacombs (XIVe.; 1808); Bourse (Ie.; A. T. Brongniart; 1809–26). *Religious building*: church of the Madeleine (Ie.; P. Vigon; 1807–42).

1815 *Public buildings*: Canal Saint-Martin (IIIe.–IVe.; 1822–5); obelisk, Place de la Concorde (VIIIe.; 1836); Gare de l'Est (Xe.; F. E. Duquesney; 1847–50); Fontaine Saint-Michel (VIe.; G. Davioud; 1858). *Commercial buildings*: Passages Vivienne (IIe.; F. J. Delannoy; 1823), Colbert (IIe.; J. Billaud; 1826) and Choiseul (IIe.; F. Mazois, A. Tavernier; 1826–7). *Religious buildings*: Chapelle expiatoire (VIIIe.; P. Fontaine; 1818–26) churches of Saint-Pierre-du-Gros-Caillou (VIIe.; E. H. Godde; 1822–3), Notre-Dame-de-la-Bonne-Nouvelle (IIe.; E. H. Godde; 1823–30), Notre-Dame-de-Lorette (IXe.; H. Lebas; 1823), Sainte-Marie-des-Batignolles (XVIIe.; A. Molinos; 1826–9), Saint-Denys-du-Saint-Sacrement (IIIe.; E. H. Godde; 1826–35) and Sainte-Clotilde (VIIe.; *T. Ballu; 1846–57).

1861 *Public buildings*: Théâtres du Châtelet (Ie.) and de la Ville (IVe.) (both G. Davioud; 1860–65); Tribunal de Commerce (IVe.; A. N. Bailly; 1860–65); Gares du Nord (Xe.; J. I. Hittorff; 1861–4), de Lyon (XIIe.; M. Toudoire; 1895–1902) and d'Orsay (VIIe.; *V. Laloux; 1900); Opéra (IIe.; C. Garnier; 1862–75); reading room, Bibliothèque Nationale (IIe.; H. Labrouste; 1869); Eiffel tower (VIIe.; G. Eiffel; 1889); Grand Palais and Petit Palais (VIIIe.; *C. Girault; 1897–1900); Pont Alexandre-III (VIIIe.; 1900). *Commercial buildings*: Hôtel Lutétia (VIe.; L. Boileau, H. Tauzin; 1907); Le Bon Marché (VIIe.; 1869–); Au Printemps (IXe.; *P. Sédille; 1881–); Galeries Lafayette (IXe.; 1895–). *Religious buildings*: Basilica of Sacré-Coeur (XVIIIe.; P. Abadie; 1876–1914); churches of Saint-Augustin (VIIIe.; V. Baltard; 1860–71), Trinité (IXe.; T. Ballu; 1861–5) and Saint-Ambroise (XIe.; T. Ballu; 1865).

1914 *Public buildings*: Musée National des Arts d'Afrique et d'Océanie (XIIe.; *L. Jaussely; 1931); Palais de Chaillot et de Tokyo (both XVIe; both· 1937); Cité universitaire (XIVe.; 1923–). *Commercial building*: La Samaritaine store (Ie.; F. Jourdain, H. Sauvage; 1926–8). *Religious building*: Mosque (Ve.; 1926).

1945 *Public buildings*: Maison de Radio-France (XVIe.; H. Bernard; 1955–62); UNESCO headquarters (VIIe.; 1958); Centre Georges-Pompidou (Beaubourg) (IVe.; R. Piano, R. Rogers; 1971); Forum des Halles (Ie.; 1979–88). *Commercial buildings*: La Défense (1958–); Maine-Montparnasse tower (XVe.; 1961–73). *Private building*: Front de Seine development (1960–); Rue des Hautes-Formes (XIIIe.; *C. de Portzamparc; 1979).

1982 *Public buildings*: Palais Omnisports de Paris-Bercy (XIIe.; 1984);

Parcs Georges-Brassens (XVe.; 1985), André-Citroën (XVe.; 1992) and de Bercy (XVIIIe.; 1993–5); Musée d'Orsay (VIIe.; formerly Gare d'Orsay, 1900; 1986); Institut du Monde Arabe (Ve.; *J. Nouvel; 1987); Louvre Pyramid (Ie.; I. M. Pei; 1988); Arche de la Défense (X.; *O. van Spreckelsen; 1989); Bastille Opera (XIIe.; C. Ott; 1989); Finance ministry (XIIe.; *P. Chemetov; 1989); Fondation Cartier (XIVe.; *J. Nouvel; 1994); Bibliothèque Nationale de France (XIIIe.; D. Perrault; 1997). *Private building*: Place de la Catalogne (XIVe.; R. Bofil; 1985).

Maps

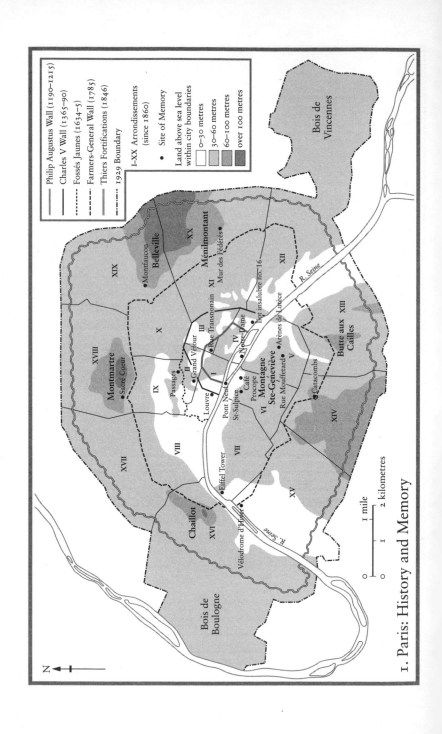

Legend:

— Philip Augustus Wall (1190–1215)
— Charles V Wall (1365–90)
---- Fossés Jaunes (1634–5)
-·-· Farmers-General Wall (1785)
—— Thiers Fortifications (1846)
-··- 1929 Boundary

I–XX Arrondissements (since 1860)
• Site of Memory

Land above sea level within city boundaries
0–30 metres
30–60 metres
60–100 metres
over 100 metres

N

1 mile
0   1   2 kilometres

Bois de Vincennes

Bois de Boulogne

Chaillot
XVI
• Vélodrome d'Hiver
• Eiffel Tower
XVII
VIII
Montmartre
XVIII
• Sacré Cœur
Passages
IX
X
XIX
• Montfaucon
Belleville
XX
Ménilmontant
• Mur des Fédérés
XI
Rue Transnonain
III
II
• Grand Véfour
I
Louvre
Pont Neuf
Café Procope
Café
St-Sulpice
VII
VI
Montagne Ste-Geneviève
Rue Mouffetard
V
• Arènes de Lutèce
IV
• Notre-Dame
• Îlot insalubre no. 16
XII
R. Seine
XIII
Butte aux Cailles
• Catacombs
XIV
XV
R. Seine

1. Paris: History and Memory

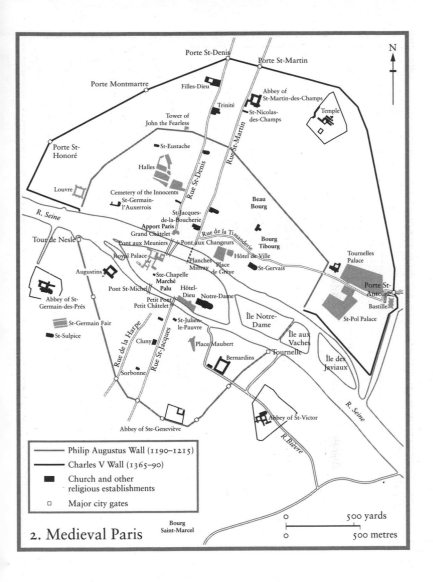

N

Porte St-Denis
Porte St-Martin
Porte Montmartre
Filles-Dieu
Abbey of
St-Martin-des-Champs
Trinité
St-Nicolas-
des-Champs
Temple
Tower of
John the Fearless
St-Eustache
Porte St-
Honoré
Halles
Rue St-Denis
Rue St-Martin
Cemetery of the Innocents
Beau
Bourg
St-Germain-
l'Auxerrois
Louvre
St-Jacques-
de-la-Boucherie
Apport Paris
Rue de la Tissanderie
Grand Châtelet
Tour de Nesle
Pont aux Meuniers
Pont aux Changeurs
Bourg
Tibourg
Royal Palace
Planches
Mibray
Hôtel de Ville
Place
de Grève
St-Gervais
Tournelles
Palace
Augustins
Ste-Chapelle
Marché
Pont St-Michel
Palu
Hôtel-
Dieu
Notre-Dame
Porte St-
Antoine
Abbey of St-
Germain-des-Prés
Petit Pont
Petit Châtelet
Bastille
St-Pol Palace
St-Germain Fair
St-Julien-
le-Pauvre
Île Notre-
Dame
St-Sulpice
Cluny
Rue de la Harpe
Rue St-Jacques
Place Maubert
Île aux
Vaches
Tournelle
Bernardins
Île des
Javiaux
Sorbonne
R. Seine
Abbey of Ste-Geneviève
Abbey of St-Victor
R. Bièvre

R. Seine

Philip Augustus Wall (1190–1215)
Charles V Wall (1365–90)
Church and other
religious establishments
Major city gates

2. Medieval Paris

Bourg
Saint-Marcel

500 yards

500 metres

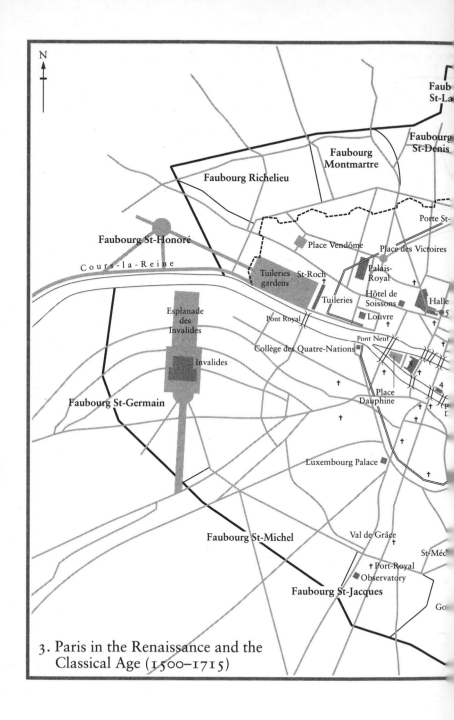

N

Faub
St-La

Faubourg
St-Denis

Faubourg
Montmartre

Faubourg Richelieu

Porte St-

Faubourg St-Honoré

Place Vendôme

Place des Victoires

Cours-la-Reine

Tuileries
gardens

St-Roch †

Palais-
Royal

†

Tuileries

Hôtel de
Soissons ■

Halle

Esplanade
des
Invalides

Pont Royal

■ Louvre
†

5

Collège des Quatre-Nations ■

Pont Neuf

†

Invalides

†

3

†

4

Faubourg St-Germain

†

Place
Dauphine

P
L

†

†

†

Luxembourg Palace ■

†

†

Faubourg St-Michel

Val de Grâce
†

St-Méd

† Port-Royal
■ Observatory

Faubourg St-Jacques

Go

3. Paris in the Renaissance and the
Classical Age (1500–1715)

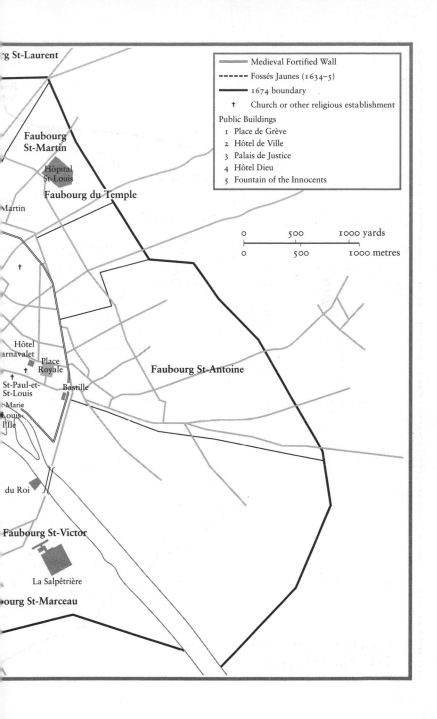

g St-Laurent

Faubourg
St-Martin

Hôpital
St-Louis

Faubourg du Temple

Martin

Medieval Fortified Wall
Fossés Jaunes (1634–5)
1674 boundary
† Church or other religious establishment
Public Buildings
1 Place de Grève
2 Hôtel de Ville
3 Palais de Justice
4 Hôtel Dieu
5 Fountain of the Innocents

0   500   1000 yards

0   500   1000 metres

†

Hôtel
arnavalet   Place
     Royale

Faubourg St-Antoine

†
St-Paul-et-
St-Louis

Bastille

Marie
Louis-
l'Ille

du Roi

Faubourg St-Victor

La Salpêtrière

ourg St-Marceau

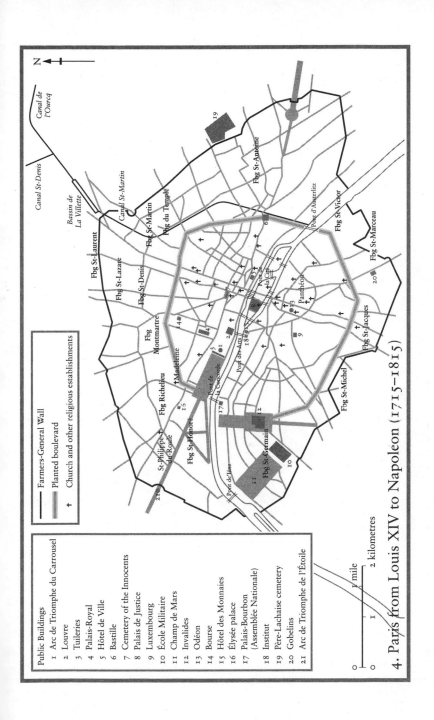

Public Buildings
1 Arc de Triomphe du Carrousel
2 Louvre
3 Tuileries
4 Palais-Royal
5 Hôtel de Ville
6 Bastille
7 Cemetery of the Innocents
8 Palais de Justice
9 Luxembourg
10 École Militaire
11 Champ de Mars
12 Invalides
13 Odéon
14 Bourse
15 Hôtel des Monnaies
16 Élysée palace
17 Palais-Bourbon
   (Assemblée Nationale)
18 Institut
19 Père-Lachaise cemetery
20 Gobelins
21 Arc de Triomphe de l'Étoile

——— Farmers-General Wall
▬▬▬ Planted boulevard
† Church and other religious establishments

4. Paris from Louis XIV to Napoleon (1715–1815)

0   ½   1 mile
0   1   2 kilometres

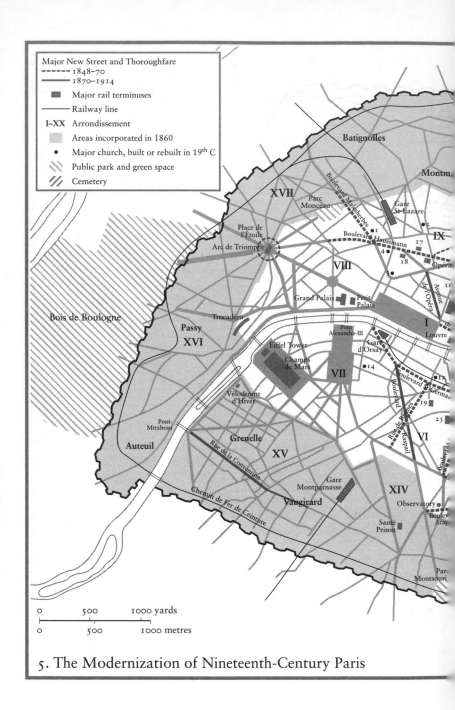

Major New Street and Thoroughfare
- - - - - 1848–70
———— 1870–1914
■ Major rail terminuses
—— Railway line
I–XX Arrondissement
Areas incorporated in 1860
• Major church, built or rebuilt in 19ᵗʰ C
Public park and green space
Cemetery

Batignolles

Montm...

XVII

Parc
Monceau

Boulevard Malesherbes

Gare
St-Lazare

Place de
l'Étoile

Boulevard Haussmann

IX

Arc de Triomphe

17

18

Opéra

VIII

I

Grand Palais

Petit
Palais

Louvre

Bois de Boulogne

Trocadéro

Pont
Alexandre-III

Gare
d'Orsay

Passy
XVI

Eiffel Tower

Champs
de Mars

VII

14

Boulevard St-Germain

12

19

Vélodrome
d'Hiver

Boulevard Raspail

23

Pont-
Mirabeau

Grenelle

VI

Auteuil

XV

Rue de la Convention

Gare
Montparnasse

XIV

Vaugirard

Observatory

Santé
Prison

Chemin de Fer de Ceinture

Parc
Montsouri

| 0 | 500 | 1000 yards |
| 0 | 500 | 1000 metres |

5. The Modernization of Nineteenth-Century Paris

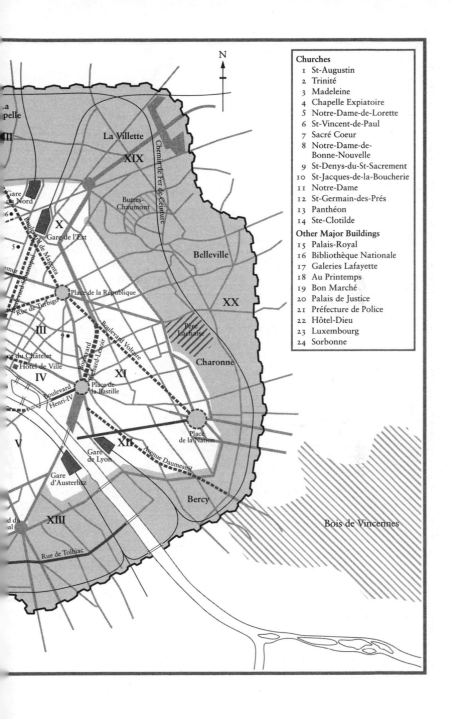

N

Churches
1 St-Augustin
2 Trinité
3 Madeleine
4 Chapelle Expiatoire
5 Notre-Dame-de-Lorette
6 St-Vincent-de-Paul
7 Sacré Coeur
8 Notre-Dame-de-
  Bonne-Nouvelle
9 St-Denys-du-St-Sacrement
10 St-Jacques-de-la-Boucherie
11 Notre-Dame
12 St-Germain-des-Prés
13 Panthéon
14 Ste-Clotilde

Other Major Buildings
15 Palais-Royal
16 Bibliothèque Nationale
17 Galeries Lafayette
18 Au Printemps
19 Bon Marché
20 Palais de Justice
21 Préfecture de Police
22 Hôtel-Dieu
23 Luxembourg
24 Sorbonne

La Villette

XIX

Chemin de Fer de Ceinture

Buttes-
Chaumont

Belleville

XX

Gare
du Nord

X

Gare de l'Est

5

Boulevard de Magenta

Rue de Turbigo

Place de la République

III

9

Père
Lachaise

Charonne

Boulevard Voltaire

Boulevard Richard-Lenoir

e du Châtelet
Hôtel de Ville

IV

Boulevard
Henri-IV

XI

Place de
la Bastille

Place
de la Nation

V

Gare
de Lyon

XII

Avenue Daumesnil

Gare
d'Austerlitz

Bercy

d du
al

XIII

Bois de Vincennes

Rue de Tolbiac

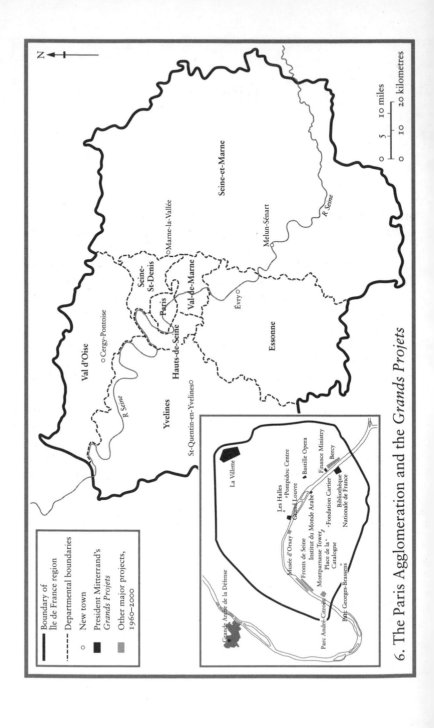

Boundary of
Île de France region

Departmental boundaries

○ New town

President Mitterrand's
Grands Projets

Other major projects,
1960–2000

N

0   5   10 miles
0   10   20 kilometres

Val d'Oise

○ Cergy-Pontoise

R. Seine

Yvelines

St-Quentin-en-Yvelines ○

Seine-
St-Denis

Paris

Hauts-de-Seine

○ Marne-la-Vallée

Val-de-Marne

Évry ○

Essonne

Seine-et-Marne

Melun-Sénart ○

R. Seine

Grande Arche de la Défense

La Villette

Les Halles
Pompidou Centre
Grand Louvre

Musée d'Orsay
Fronts de Seine
Institut du Monde Arabe
Montparnasse Tower
Place de la
Catalogne

Parc André-Citroën

Parc Georges-Brassens

Bastille Opera
Finance Ministry
Bercy

Fondation Cartier

Bibliothèque
Nationale de France

6. The Paris Agglomeration and the *Grands Projets*

Glossary

arrondissement   Name for the different jurisdictional areas into which Paris has been divided since the French Revolution. Legislation in 1795 established twelve arrondissements, which were also municipalities in their own right. When Paris was extended in 1859–60, the number of arrondissements was increased to twenty, and these still exist. It is helpful to think of the numbering system as taking the form of a snail's shell: starting with the first and second arrondissement, to the west of the historic heart of the city, then spiralling round in a clockwise direction. The inner spiral (IIIe. to XIe.) reaches around to the Bastille, where the outer spiral (XIIe. to XXe.) begins. (See Map 1.)

banlieue   Name for the suburbs, especially the workers' suburbs which developed outside the Thiers fortifications after 1841.

district   Electoral divisions of Paris, sixty in number, in which elections to the Estates General were organized in 1789; replaced by forty-eight sections from 1790.

faubourg   Originally, the term meant suburbs, but most faubourgs were gradually incorporated into the city over the seventeenth and eighteenth centuries and lie in the outer arrondissements.

grands boulevards   Name given from the middle of the nineteenth century to the line of boulevards (broad, tree-planted avenues) on the Right Bank running in a semi-circle from the Place de la Bastille to the Place de la Concorde. The line roughly follows the trace of the fortifications which Louis XIV converted into boulevards from c. 1670.

grands magasins   Major department stores developed in the late nineteenth and early twentieth centuries. Many are located on the *grands boulevards*.

Hôtel de Ville   Both a) the building on the Place de l'Hôtel-de-Ville (formerly Place de Grève) in which the city government has been located since the late Middle Ages; and b) by extension, the city government itself.

Île de la Cité   The largest and most important island on the river Seine on which Paris has been based, probably from pre-Roman times.

journée   'Day' of revolutionary action in the Revolution, 1789–99, and in other insurrectionary periods throughout the nineteenth century.

Latin Quarter   Name given in the nineteenth century to the university and student area around the Sorbonne in the Fifth and Sixth arrondissements, in which Latin was a common language from the Middle Ages.

Left Bank   The area of Paris to the left of the observer facing downstream. Otherwise, the area of Paris south of the Seine.

Marais   'Marsh'. a) Name given to the originally boggy areas outside the line of the *grands boulevards* on the Right Bank, which were developed for market gardening from the late twelfth century; b) name still given to the area roughly equivalent to the present-day Third and Fourth arrondissements, which was developed for elegant housing from the late fifteenth century onwards.

quartier   a) Historic name given to subdivisions of Paris, dating back to the Middle Ages; b) one of the four administrative areas into which the twelve arrondissements were subdivided in 1795, and into which the twenty arrondissements were subdivided in 1860; c) general name for 'neighbourhood'.

Right Bank   The area of Paris to the right of the observer facing downstream. Otherwise, the area of Paris north of the Seine.

section   One of the forty-eight units of local government into which Paris was divided between 1790 and 1795.

Abbreviations

ADH	*Annales de démographie historique*
AESC	*Annales. Économies. Sociétés. Civilisations*
BPIF	*Bulletin de la Société de l'histoire de Paris et de l'Île-de-France*
FHS	*French Historical Studies*
Lieux de mémoire	P. Nora (ed.), *Lieux de mémoire*, 3 vols. (pbk, 1997)
MPIF	*Mémoires de la Société de l'histoire de Paris et de l'Île-de-France* (from 1952, *Paris et l'Île-de-France. Mémoires*)
NHP	*Nouvelle Histoire de Paris*
pr.	present-day
RH	*Revue historique*
RHMC	Revue d'histoire moderne et contemporaine

Notes

(All works published in Paris unless otherwise stated.)

Introduction: An Impossible History of Paris?

1. The work does not seem to have been translated.
2. Ibid., pp. 24–5, 60.
3. In compiling this list, I have drawn on *Quid 2003* and *Paris en chiffres* (Mairie de Paris, 1994). Because of the time-lag leading up to the completion of this book, I am brave enough to admit that some figures may not be correct to the last digit.
4. Piganiol de La Force, *Description historique de la ville de Paris* (1765 edn), Introduction, p. xxiii.
5. *Memoirs of Charles-Lewis, Baron de Pöllnitz* (2 vols., London, 1739), ii, p. 189.
6. Edmondo De Amicis, *Ricordi di Parigi* (Milan, 1900), p. 22.
7. Balzac, *Ferragus* (1834).
8. Cited in G. Durieux, *Le Roman de Paris à travers les siècles et la littérature* (2000), p. 41.
9. On this theme, see esp. P. Higonnet, *Paris, Capital of the World* (London, 2002); but above all Walter Benjamin, *The Arcades Project* (English translation, Cambridge, MA, 1999).
10. Pierre Nora (ed.), *Les Lieux de mémoire*, 3 vols., paperback edition (1997). For translations of much of this massive work, see *Realms of Memory. Rethinking the French Past* (3 vols., New York, 1998) and *Rethinking France* (Chicago, 2001).
11. Raymond Queneau, *Zazie dans le métro* (1959). Queneau's Parisians seem divided too on what gender to ascribe the Eiffel tower.
12. Clébert, *Paris insolite* (1952), p. 14.
13. Cf. Chapter 1. Julius Caesar quite probably did not actually come to Paris.

14. P. Pinon, *Paris, biographie d'une capitale* (1999), p. 58.

15. Any of a numerous collection of literary anthologies provides a lengthy compilation of quotations which the lone scholar cannot hope to match. I have drawn on several of these. The best is I. Littlewood, *A Literary Companion to Paris* (London, 1987). But see too J. Barozzi, *Littératures parisiennes* (1997); S. Barclay, *A Place in the World Called Paris* (San Francisco, CA, 1994); and Durieux, *Le Roman de Paris*. Walter Benjamin's magnum opus, *The Arcades of Paris* (Cambridge, MA, 1997), is among other things a quite incredible anthology of quotations about especially nineteenth-century Paris, and repays much happy dipping.

16. Baudelaire, 'Le Cygne', *Les Fleurs du mal* (1857).

17. For medieval descriptions, see the recent compilation of R. W. Berger, *In Old Paris: An Anthology of Source Descriptions, 1323–1790* (New York, 2002).

18. J. C. Scott, *Weapons of the Weak: Everyday Forms of Peasant Resistance* (London, 1985).

19. L. S. Mercier, *Le Tableau de Paris* (12 vols., Amsterdam, 1780–88); Baudelaire, esp. *Les Fleurs du mal*. See below, Chapter 8.

20. W. Benjamin, *The Arcades Project*; H. Lefebvre, *Everyday Life in the Modern World* (London, 1968); G. Debord, *The Society of the Spectacle* (Detroit, 1983); M. de Certeau, *The Practice of Everyday Life* (Berkeley, CA, 1984).

21. G. Perec, *Perec/rinations* (1997); M. Augé, *Un Ethnologue dans le métro* (1986). For Simenon, cf. M. Carly, *Maigret: traversées de Paris. Les 120 lieux parisiens du commissaire* (2001). Many of Richard Cobb's writings on Paris are brought together in his *Paris and Elsewhere* (London, 1998).

22. Cf. Fernand Braudel, *Écrits sur l'histoire* (1969).

1: *Paris-Lutetia*

Feature Boxes: Main Sources

1.1: The *Arènes de Lutèce*

   D. Busson, *Carte archéologique de la Gaule. Paris* (1998)

   P. M. Duval, *Paris: De Lutèce oppidum à Paris capitale de la France* (NHP: 1993)

   Formigé, *Les Arènes de Lutèce* (1918)

   C. Jones, 'The archaeology of modernity in nineteenth-century Paris' (unpublished paper)

   P. Velay, *From Lutetia to Paris. The Island and the Two Banks* (1992)

1.2: A Parisian Child

L. Chevalier, *Classes laborieuses et classes dangereuses à Paris pendant la première moitié du XIXe siècle* (1958)

C. Delasalle, 'Les enfants trouvés à Paris au XVIIIe siècle', *AESC*, 30 (1975)

G. Dupont-Ferrier, 'Les enfants martyrs à la fin du moyen âge', *BPIF*, 64 (1937)

A. Farge & J. Revel, *The Vanishing Children of Paris: Rumor and Politics before the French Revolution* (Cambridge, MA, 1991)

Victor Hugo, *Les Misérables* (1862)

E. Toulouze, 'Mes fouilles', *Bulletin de la Montagne Sainte-Geneviève*, ii, (1897–8), pp. 215–16

1.3: Saint Geneviève

R. Amiet, *Le Culte liturgique de Sainte-Geneviève* (1984)

P. Chaunu, *La Mort à Paris (XVIe, XVIIe, XVIIIe siècles)* (1978)

J. Dubois & L. Beaumont-Maillet, *Sainte-Geneviève de Paris* (new edn 1982)

S. Kaplan, 'Religion, subsistence and social control: the uses of Saint Genevieve', *Eighteenth-Century Studies*, 13 (1979)

M. Sluhovsky, *Patroness of Paris. Rituals of Devotion in Early Modern France* (Leiden, 1998)

1. Julian, 'Misopogon', in id., *Works*, ed. W. C. Wright (3 vols., Cambridge, MA, 1913–23), ii, pp. 428–31.
2. Julius Caesar, *The Conquest of Gaul*, Book 7, ch. 57.
3. Antoine de Mont-Royal, *Les Glorieuses Antiquitez de Paris*, ed. V. Dufour ([1678]: Paris, 1879), p. 2; François Rabelais, *Gargantua*, Book 1, ch. 17.
4. Caesar stated that the capital of the Parisii was on an island in the Seine, but he did not necessarily thereby designate the Île de la Cité as the island in question. Recently, some archaeologists have wondered whether another island altogether might be indicated, especially in view of the quasi-absence of pre-Roman remains on the Cité. The jury is still out on this question.
5. Ammianus Marcellinus, *Histoire: Livres XX–XXII*, ed. J. Fontaine et al. (1996), Book xx, pp. 12–13, 25.
6. Julian, 'Misopogon', pp. 450–51, 480–81.
7. Gregory of Tours, *The History of the Franks*, Book 2, ch. 38.
8. Cited in M. Fleury, *La Naissance de Paris* (1997), p. 110.
9. Cited in E. James, *The Origins of France. From Clovis to the Capetians, 500–1000* (London, 1982), p. 29.

10. See below, p. 366.
11. Einhard, *Life of Charlemagne*, Book 1.
12. Abbon, *Le Siège de Paris par les Normands. Poème du IXe siècle*, ed. H. Waquet (Paris, 1942), p. 15.
13. Ibid., p. 81.
14. Ibid., p. 99.
15. Ibid., p. 13.
16. Ibid., p. 113.

2: 'Queen of Cities'

Feature Boxes: Main Sources
2.1: Saint-Denis
   C. Beaune, 'Les sanctuaires royaux' in *Lieux de mémoire*, i
   C. Beaune, *Naissance de la France* (1985)
   J. P. Brunet, *Saint-Denis, la ville rouge, 1890–1939* (1980)
   R. Mulryne & E. Golding (eds.), *Court Festivals of the European Renaissance. Art, Politics and Performance* (Aldershot, 2002)

2.2: The Philip Augustus Wall
   B. Fortier (ed.), *La Métropole imaginaire: Un atlas de Paris* (1989)
   B. Rouleau, *Le Tracé des rues de Paris* (1988)

2.3: Robert de Sorbon
   V. W. Egbert, *On the Bridges of Medieval Paris. A Record of Early Fourteenth-Century Life* (Princeton, NJ, 1974)
   A. L. Gabriel, *The Paris Studium. Robert of Sorbon and his Legacy* (Notre Dame, IN, 1992)
   J. Le Goff, *Les Intellectuels au moyen âge*, 2nd edn (1985)
   P. Kibre, *The Nations in the Medieval Universities* (Cambridge, MA, 1948)
   J. Verger, *L'Essor des universités au XIIIe siècle* (1997)

1. Guy de Bazoches, 'Description de Paris vers 1175', *BPIF*, 4 (1877), 38–40.
2. See Chapter 1 note 12.
3. Cf. pr. Place de Saint-André-des-Arts; and, for Saint-Côme, pr. Rue de l'École-de-Médecine (both VIe.).
4. The 'Beau-Bourg' (cf. Rue Beaubourg, IIIe./IVe.) had a number of locations itemized by Saint Louis as permitted for prostitution, including Rue Chapon. The Bourg Thibourg (cf. Rue Bourg-Tibourg, IVe.) may have been

named after Thiboult Riche, who was probably one of the bourgeois to whom Philip Augustus entrusted royal administration in 1190.

5. The traces of the encampment walls are retained in the streets around Rue Bertin-Poirée (Ie.).

6. Étienne Boileau, cited in G. Duby (ed.), *Histoire de la France urbaine. ii: La ville médiévale* (1981), p. 380.

7. *Letters of John of Salisbury*, W. J. Miller, H. E. Butler & C. N. L. Brooke (eds.) (2 vols., Oxford, 1979–86), i, p. 7.

8. Close to the Rue du Fouarre, for example, were to be found the pr. Rue de la Parcheminerie ('Parchment-maker Street'), the Rue de la Huchette (named after the tavern 'À la Huchette d'Or': 'At the Golden Breadbin') and the Rue des Enlumineurs ('Illuminators Street': pr. Rue Boute-Brie).

9. Suger, *Oeuvres*, ed. F. Gasparri (1966), p. 61.

10. *Oeuvres de Rigord et de Guillaume le Breton, historiens de Philippe-Auguste*, ed. F. Delaborde (2 vols., 1882–5), i, p. 297ff.

11. First use in *Oeuvres de Rigord*, i, p. 11.

12. *Civitas Parisius est patria communis velut Roma.*

13. Rabelais, *Pantagruel* (1542), ch. xv.

14. *Oeuvres de Rigord*, i, pp. 53–4.

15. These are, though heavily restored, observable from the Tour de l'Horloge to the Tour Bon-Bec on the Quai de l'Horloge (Ie.).

16. The Pré ran along the river as far as the present-day Palais Bourbon.

17. The Marché Palu (IVe.) adjoined the Petit Pont on the Île de la Cité; the Apport Paris (Ie.) was on the north-west corner of pr. Place du Châtelet; the Place Baudoyer (IVe.) is still existent – most notably as an underground car park.

18. The Fontaine des Innocents, built in 1549 and slightly relocated in 1865, bears present witness to this site. For the relocation of the cemetery, see below, pp. 240, 291–2.

19. Cited in Duby, *Histoire de la France urbaine*, p. 309.

20. For the most part it followed the course of the pr. *grands boulevards*. See above, p. 4.

21. The Ville-l'Évêque, which was at the heart of the *Culture l'Évêque*, was approximately at the site of the pr. Madeleine church (VIIIe.).

22. Cf. the Rue des Coutures-Saint-Gervais (IIIe.), and the Place Sainte-Catherine (IVe.).

23. To cite F. Lehoux, *Le Bourg Saint-Germain-des-Prés depuis ses origines jusqu'à la fin de la Guerre de Cent Ans* (1951).

24. No trace survives of the abbey, which was situated around pr. Place Jussieu (Ve.).

25. The locations are as follows: Saint-Martin, Rue de la Collégiale (Ve.); Saint-Hilaire, Rue des Carmes (Ve.); Saint-Hippolyte, Rue des Marmousets (XIIIe.).

26. Cited in Le Roux de Lincy & M. T. Tisserand, *Paris et ses historiens aux XIVe. et XVe. siècles* (1867), p. 56.

27. See above, p. 14.

28. R. de Lespinasse & F. Bonnardot, *Les Métiers et corporations de la ville de Paris. XIIe siècle. Le Livre des métiers d'Étienne Boileau* (1879), p. xcvi.

29. Rue des Lavandières is pr. Rue des Lavandières-Sainte-Opportune (Ie.); the Rue des Jongleurs linked the Rue Saint-Denis and the Rue Saint-Martin (Ie.); the Rue Coupe-Gueule was in the Ve. The present-day Rue du Petit-Musc is in the IVe.

30. Cited in J. Le Goff, *Les Intellectuels au moyen âge* (1985), p. 25.

31. Jacques de Vitry, *Histoire occidentale/Historia occidentalis (Tableau de l'Occident au XIIIe siècle)*, ed. J. Longère (1997), pp. 85–6.

32. The term *universitas* originally was applied to any corporative grouping, its purely academic meaning only gradually being established.

33. H. Denifle (ed.), *Chartularium universitatis Parisiensis* (4 vols., 1889–97), i, pp. 136ff.

3: *The City Adrift*

Feature Boxes: Main Sources

3.1: Montfaucon

    G. Le Halle, *De Montfaucon à la Place Colonel Fabien* (1973)

    D. Reid, *Paris Sewers and Sewermen. Realities and Representations* (Cambridge, MA, 1991)

    L. Tanon, *Histoire des justices des anciennes églises et communautés monastiques de Paris* (1883)

3.2: The Parvis of Notre-Dame

    F. Colletet, *Abrégé des antiquités de la ville de Paris* (1664)

    J. Depauw, *Spiritualité et pauvreté à Paris au XVIIe siècle* (1999)

    A. L'Esprit, 'Le Jeûneur de Notre-Dame', *La Cité*, 10–11 (1911–12)

    F. Rabelais, *Gargantua* (1534)

    L. Sieber (ed.), 'Description de Paris par Thomas Platter le jeune de Bâle (1599)', *MPIF*, 23 (1896)

3.3: François Villon

    J. Dérens et al., *Villon hier et aujourd'hui* (1993)

D. A. Fein, *François Villon and his Reader* (Detroit, 1989)

J. Le Goff, *Les Intellectuels au moyen âge*, 2nd edn (1985)

1. 'Éloge de la cité de Paris' (1323). Reprinted in Le Roux de Lincy & L. M. Tisserand, *Paris et ses historiens aux XIVe. et XVe. siècles* (1867), p. 25.

2. Eustache Deschamps, *Ballade* (1394).

3. The Rue des Poulies was subsequently incorporated into the Rue des Francs-Bourgeois (IIIe.–IVe.), which follows the line of the Philip Augustus Wall for some of its length. Towers of the Hôtel de Clisson are still visible on the corner of the Hôtel de Soubise (Archives Nationales) in the pr. Rue des Archives.

4. See above, p. 62.

5. *Chronique parisienne anonyme de 1316 à 1399, précédé d'additions à la chronique française dite de Guillaume de Nangis (1206–1316)*, ed. A. Hellot, *MPIF*, 11 (1884), 28.

6. *Journal de Nicolas de Baye, Greffier du Parlement de Paris, 1400–17*, ed. A. Tuetey (2 vols., 1885–7), i, p. 212.

7. *Journal d'un bourgeois de Paris*, ed. C. Beaune (1990), pp. 171–2, 393.

8. The Haudriettes were located on the pr. Rue des Haudriettes (IIIe.); the Quinze-Vingts was close to the Rue Saint-Honoré, though it moved to the Rue de Charenton (XIIIe.) just before the 1789 Revolution.

9. 'Éloge de la cité de Paris'.

10. Cited in M. Mollat, *Histoire de l'Île-de-France et de Paris* (Toulouse, 1971), p. 150.

11. Deschamps, *Virelai*. Cf. e.e. cummings, 'little ladies move', *Portraits XII* (1925).

12. *Journal de Nicolas de Baye*, i, p. 208.

13. *Journal d'un bourgeois de Paris*, pp. 67–8. A convenient list is provided in J. Delumeau & Y. Lequin (eds.), *Les Malheurs du temps. Histoire des fléaux et des calamités en France* (1987), p. 214.

14. The Tower of John the Fearless is visible and visitable on the Rue Étienne-Marcel (IIe.). The Tour de Nesle, 25 metres high, was on the Quai Conti (VIIe.), opposite the Louvre and on the site of the pr. Institut.

15. *Journal d'un bourgeois de Paris*, p. 112.

16. *Journal de Clément de Fauquembergue (1417–55)*, ed. A. Tuetey (3 vols., 1903), i, p. 136.

17. Charles had become Dauphin on the death of his two elder brothers Louis, who died in 1415, and John, who died in 1417.

18. *Journal d'un bourgeois de Paris*, pp. 153–4.

19. Ibid., p. 217.

20. Ibid., pp. 309–11.
21. *Chronique d'Arthur de Richemont, connétable de la France, duc de Bretagne (1393–1458)* (1890), p. 138.
22. G. Fagniez, 'Journal parisien de Jean Maupoint, prieur de Sainte-Catherine-de-la-Couture (1437–69)', *MPIF*, 4 (1877), p. 54.
23. Cited in G. Fourquin, *Les Campagnes de la région parisienne à la fin du Moyen Âge* (1963), p. 398.
24. *Chronique parisienne*, pp. 135–8. Cf. ibid., pp. 17–18, 34–5, 50.
25. J. Favier, *Les contribuables parisiens à la fin de la Guerre de Cent Ans. Les rôles d'impôt de 1421, 1423 et 1438* (Geneva, 1970), pp. 25–9.
26. The Musée Cluny (Rue du Sommnerard, Ve.) today incorporates the Museum of the Middle Ages as well as the Roman Baths.
27. *Journal d'un bourgeois de Paris*, p. 381. Cf. ibid., p. 441 (1445).
28. B. de Mandrot (ed.), *Journal de Jean de Roye connu sous le nom de Chronique scandaleuse (1460–85)* (2 vols., 1894), i, pp. 180–81.
29. Rue des Lions (IVe.). The nearby Rue de la Ceriseraie highlighted cherry-orchards which had been another striking feature of the site.
30. Hôtel d'Armagnac was located in the Rue des Bons-Enfants (Ie.); the Hôtel du Porc-Épic, on the pr. Passage Charlemagne (IVe.) and the Hôtel de Clisson on the pr. Rue des Archives.
31. Y. H. Le Maresquier-Kesteloot (ed.), *Les Officiers municipaux de la ville de Paris au XVe siècle* (1997), p. 135.
32. J. Le Goff, *Un autre moyen âge* (1977), p. 194.
33. B. Geremek, *Les Marginaux parisiens aux XIVe et XVe siècles* (1976), p. 178.
34. 'Vous ne valez point que je me mêle de vous': cited in J. Favier, *Paris au XVIe. siècle, 1380–1500* (NHP: 1974), p. 235.

4: Paris Reborn, Paris Reformed

Feature Boxes: Main Sources
4.1: The Louvre
  J. P. Babelon, 'Le Louvre' in P. Nora (ed.), *Lieux de mémoire*, ii
  R. W. Berger (ed.), *In Old Paris: An Anthology of Source Descriptions, 1323–1790* (New York, 2002)
  A. Fierro, 'A quoi le Louvre doit-il son nom?' in id., *Mystères de l'histoire de Paris* (2000)
  H. Sauval, *Histoire et recherches des antiquités de la ville de Paris* (1724)

4.2: The River Bièvre

J. K. Huysmans, *Croquis parisiens* (1880)

R. Pevear, 'Letter from Paris', *Hudson Review*, 54 (2001)

J. J. Rousseau, *Rêveries* (1776)

Senancour, *Oberman* (1804)

4.3: Henry III

K. C. Cameron, *Henri III, a Maligned or a Malignant King?* (Exeter, 1978)

P. Chevallier, *Henri III* (1994)

R. Dallington, *The View of France (1604)*, reprint edn, ed. W. P. Barrett (Oxford, 1936)

N. Le Roux, *La Faveur du Roi: mignons et courtisans au temps des derniers Valois* (2000)

1. A. Tuetey (ed.), *Registres des délibérations du Bureau de la Ville de Paris*, vol. ii (1886), p. 17.
2. Although the interest was based on royal wealth, the management of the scheme was entirely in the hands of the Paris municipality.
3. G. Corrozet, *La Fleur des antiquitez, singularités et excellences de . . . Paris* (1532).
4. *Registres des délibérations*, ii, p. 175.
5. Ibid., iii, p. 170.
6. Cited in R. Héron de Villefosse, *Solennités, fêtes et réjouissances parisiennes* (NHP: 1980), p. 61.
7. P. Lavedan, *Histoire de l'urbanisme à Paris* (NHP: 2nd edn, 1993), p. 146.
8. The Rue des Francs-Bourgeois marks the boundary between the pr. IIIe. and IVe. arrondissements. The Hôtel de Sévigné is on the Rue de Sévigné, the Hôtel Donon on the Rue Elzévir (along with other residences from this period), and the Hôtel Lamoignon on the Rue Pavée. The Rue Barbette marks one boundary of the Barbette estate.
9. The Hôtel de Flandre included the pr. Rue Coq-Héron (Ie.); the Hôtel de Bourgogne is on the pr. Rue Étienne-Marcel.
10. The church's pr. address is 286 Rue Saint-Honoré.
11. Pr. Rue de la Lune (IIe.), close to Bonne-Nouvelle Métro stop.
12. G. Raynaud, 'Paris en 1596 vu par un italien (Récit de F. G. d'Ierni)', *BPIF*, 12 (1885), 166.
13. Ibid.
14. Other churches manifesting the same tendencies include Saint-Jacques-de-la-Boucherie, Saint-Merri (both IVe.) and Saint-Séverin (Ve.).
15. J. P. Babelon, *Paris au XVIe siècle* (NHP: 1986), p. 286.

16. *Registres des délibérations*, iii, p. 221 (1550).

17. Cited in Lavedan, *Histoire de l'urbanisme*, p. 173.

18. A. Vidier, 'Description de Paris par Arnold van Buchel d'Utrecht (1585–6)', *MPIF*, 26 (1899), p. 155.

19. H. Omond (ed.), 'Une lettre de Paris au temps de la Réforme', *BPIF*, 8 (1881), p. 88.

20. Babelon, *Paris au XVIe siècle* (citing Crespin), p. 414.

21. The term may have been a derivation of the German '*Eidgenossen*', meaning confederates, highlighting that Calvinist communities were in league with Geneva where Calvin was based.

22. E. de Barthélemy, *Journal d'un curé ligueur de Paris sous les trois derniers Valois* (1865), p. 149.

23. G. Fagniez (ed.), 'Mémorial juridique et historique du Maître Guillaume Aubert, avocat au Parlement de Paris (deuxième moitié du XVIe siècle)', *MPIF*, 36 (1909), pp. 67–8.

24. M. Greengrass, *France in the Age of Henri IV: The Struggle for Stability* (London, 1995), p. 7.

25. *Mémoires de Luc Geitzkofler, tyrolien (1550–1620)* (Geneva, 1892), p. 64.

26. D. Crouzet, *La Nuit de la Saint-Barthélemy. Un rêve perdu de la Renaissance* (1994), p. 33.

27. *Mémoires de Luc Geitzkofler*, p. 74.

28. E. Barnavi & R. Descimon, *La Sainte Ligue. Le juge et la potence. L'assassinat du président Brisson (15 novembre 1591)* (1985), p. 45.

29. 'Balafré' (scarred) because his face had been disfigured by a wound incurred on the field of battle in 1575.

30. Barthélemy, *Journal d'un curé ligueur*, p. 133.

31. P. de l'Estoile, *Mémoires-journaux*, ii: *1585–6*, ed. G. Brunet et al. (1885), pp. 134–5.

32. Montaigne, *Essais*, Book 3, ch. 9.

33. Cited in M. Yardeni, 'Le Mythe de Paris comme élément de propagande à l'époque de la Ligue', *MPIF*, 2nd series, 20 (1969), p. 56.

34. Greengrass, *France in the age of Henri IV*, p. 13.

35. Babelon, *Paris au XVIe siècle*, p. 383.

36. Greengrass, *France in the age of Henri IV*, p. 58.

37. E. Saulnier (ed.), *Journal de François, bourgeois de Paris (23 décembre 1588–30 novembre 1589)* (1913), p. 15.

38. L'Estoile, *Mémoires-journaux*, iii (1886), p. 158.

39. A. Dufour (ed.), 'Relations du siège de Paris par Henri IV, traduit de l'italien de Filippo Pigafetta', *MPIF*, 2 (1876), p. 77.

40. Cited in J. P. Babelon, *Henri IV* (1982), p. 588.

5: *Grand Siècle, Great Eclipse*

Feature Boxes: Main Sources
5.1: The Pont Neuf
  V. R. Belot, *Le Pont Neuf. Histoires et Petites Histoires* (1978)
  F. de Dartein, *Le Pont-Neuf sur la Seine à Paris, 1578–1609* (1911)
  E. Fournier, *Histoire du Pont Neuf* (1862)
  R. M. Isherwood, *Farce and Fantasy: Popular Entertainment in Eighteenth-Century Paris* (New York, 1986)
  C. Jones, 'Pulling Teeth in Eighteenth-Century Paris', *Past and Present*, 166 (2000)
  B. Latour & E. Hermani, *Paris, ville invisible* (1998)
  [Jean-Paul Marana], *Lettre d'un Sicilien à un de ses amis* (Paris 1700 [but probably c. 1692])
  Raymond Queneau, 'Cris de Paris', *Courir les rues* (1967)
  M. Sélimonte, *Le Pont-Neuf et ses Charlatans* (1980)

5.2: Madame de Sévigné
  J. Queneau & J. Y. Patte, *L'Art de vivre au temps de Madame de Sévigné* (1996)
  Madame de Sévigné, *Correspondance*
  Madame de Sévigné (1996)
  Madame de Sévigné, Molière et les médecins de son temps (Marseille, 1973)
  J. Wilhelm, *La Vie quotidienne au Marais au XVIIe siècle* (1966)

5.3: The *Cour des Miracles*
  L. Bernard, *The Emerging City: Paris in the Age of Louis XIV* (Durham, NC, 1970)
  M. Chassaigne, *La Lieutenance-Générale de police de Paris* (1906)
  G. Dethan, *Paris au temps de Louis XIV, 1660–1715* (NHP: 1990)
  O. Ranum, *Paris in the Age of Absolutism* (new edn; Philadelphia, 2002)

1. Sieur Coulon, *L'Ulysée françois* (1643), p. 270.
2. Cited in R. Mousnier, *Paris capitale au temps de Richelieu et de Mazarin* (1978), p. 295.
3. A. M Boislisle (ed.), *Mémoires des Intendants sur l'état des généralités dressé pour l'instruction du duc de Bourgogne. Tome 1. Mémoire de la généralité de Paris* (1881), p. 1.
4. J. P. Babelon, *Henri IV* (1982), p. 830.

5. *Mercure françois*, cited in J. P. Babelon, *Demeures parisiennes sous Henri IV et Louis XIII* (1991), p. 21.

6. In addition the development included the present-day Rue Debelleyme (which incorporated the old Rues de Périgord and de Limoges) and the northern half of Rue de Turenne.

7. P. Pinon, *Paris, biographie d'une capitale* (1999), p. 63.

8. The Place Dauphine was named after the dauphin, Henry's son and successor Louis XIII. The new streets around the Place Dauphine reflected the same theme: Rue Christine and the Rue d'Anjou (pr. Rue de Nesle) were named after the king's younger children.

9. R. Dallington, *The View of France (1604)*, reprint edn, ed. W. P. Barrett (Oxford, 1936) (no pagination).

10. John Evelyn, *The Diary of John Evelyn*, ed. E. S. de Beer (6 vols., Oxford, 1955), ii, pp. 128ff.

11. R. Pillorget, *Paris sous les premiers Bourbons (1594–1661)* (NHP: 1998), p. 327.

12. Dallington, *View of France*.

13. See below for further discussion of the institutions.

14. O. Ranum, *Paris in the Age of Absolutism. An Essay* (New York, 1968), p. 110.

15. P. Lavedan, *Histoire de l'urbanisme à Paris* (NHP: 1975), p. 156.

16. See above, pp. 104ff.

17. Cardinal de Retz, *Oeuvres* (10 vols., 1870–96), ii, pp. 44–5.

18. Cited in A. Feillet, *La Misère au temps de la Fronde et Saint Vincent de Paul* (1865), p. 406.

19. Ranum, *Paris in the Age of Absolutism*, p. 292.

20. M. Pernot, *La Fronde* (1994), p. 303.

21. Pillorget, *Paris sous les premiers Bourbons*, p. 226.

22. G. Dethan, *Paris au temps de Louis XIV, 1660–1715* (NHP: 1990), pp. 19, 25.

23. The four nations in question were the provinces of Alsace, Artois, Piedmont and Roussillon. There were bursaries for students from each of these areas which had recently passed under French domination.

24. A. Vautier (ed.), *Voyage de France. Moeurs et coutumes français (1664–5): Relation de Sébastien Locatelli* (1905), p. 193.

25. Lavedan, *Histoire de l'urbanisme*, p. 189.

26. Ibid.

27. B. Causse, *Les Fiacres de Paris aux XVIIe et XVIIIe siècles* (1972), p. 13.

28. L. Bernard, *The Emerging City. Paris in the Age of Louis XIV* (Durham, NC, 1970), p. 10.

29. E. Brackenhoffer, *Voyage de Paris en Italie, 1644–6* (1927), pp. 70–72.

30. Louis XIV, *Mémoires*, ed. J. Longnon (1978).

31. La Bruyère *Les Caractères* (1696): VII: De la Ville.

32. M. Lister, *A Journey to Paris in the Year 1698* (London, 1699), p. 7.

33. R. Challes, cited in Dethan, *Paris*, p. 168.

34. Flaubert, *Dictionnaire des idées reçues* (1863).

6: The Kingless Capital of Enlightenment

Feature Boxes: Main Sources

6.1: The Café Procope

S. Barrows, 'Nineteenth-century cafés: arenas of everyday life', in B. Stern Shapiro (ed.), *Pleasures of Paris: Daumier to Picasso* (Boston, 1991)

J. C. Bologne, *Histoire des cafés et des cafetiers* (1990)

W. Scott Haine, *The World of the Paris Café: Sociability among the French Working Class, 1789–1914* (Baltimore, MD, 1999)

[Nemeitz], *Séjour de Paris, c'est-à-dire Instructions fidèles pour les voyageurs de condition* (2 vols., Leiden, 1725)

M. Oberthur, *Cafés and Concerts of Montmartre* (Salt Lake City, 1984)

6.2: Rose Bertin

E. Langlade, *La Marchande de modes de Marie-Antoinette: Rose Bertin* (1925)

E. Lever, *Marie-Antoinette* (1991)

P. de Nouvion & E. Liez, *Un Ministre des modes sous Louis XVI. Rose Bertin* (1911)

A. Ribeiro, *The Art of Dress. Fashion in England and France, 1750 to 1820* (London, 1995)

A. Ribeiro, *Dress in Eighteenth-Century Europe* (London, 1984)

D. Roche, *The Culture of Clothing. Dress and Fashion in the Ancien Régime* (Cambridge, 1994)

V. Steele, *Paris Fashion: A Cultural History* (Oxford, 1988)

N. Waugh, *The Cut of Women's Clothes, 1600–1930* (London, 1968)

6.3: Rue Mouffetard

H. Bresler, *Mouffetard . . . au faubourg au coeur de la ville* (1992)

G. Duhamel, *Biographie de mes fantômes* (1901–06); *Vie et aventures de Salavin* (1920)

J. Ferniot, *La Mouffe'* (1995)

E. Hemingway, *A Moveable Feast* (1964)

L. S. Mercier, *Le Tableau de Paris* (12 vols.; Amsterdam, 1782–8)

1. See below, p. 254.

2. On this episode, and the king's views on it, see A. Farge & J. Revel, *The Vanishing Children of Paris: Rumor and Politics before the French Revolution* (Cambridge, MA, 1991).

3. N. de La Mare, *Traité de la police*, tome 4, 39. Cited in J. N. Harouel, *L'Embellissement des Villes. L'Urbanisme français au XVIIIe siècle* (1993); see also above, p. 192.

4. Besides this quotation attributed to Marivaux, see too [Caraccioli], *Paris le modèle des nations étrangères, ou l'Europe française* (Venice & Paris, 1777), esp. p. 325.

5. See above, p. 196.

6. Mercier, *Le Tableau de Paris* (12 vols.; Amsterdam, 1782–8), iv, p. 258.

7. Peyssonel, *Les Numéros* (1782), p. 9.

8. The first edition was published in 1684; the ninth – which was published in facsimile edition in 1971 – in 1752.

9. Notably the Sainte-Geneviève church project. See below, p. 208–9.

10. [Mrs Cradock], *Voyage en France (1783–6)*, O. Delphin, ed. (1896), p. 21.

11. Quai Conti (VIe.)

12. Only the former Queen Regent's astronomical tower was retained – and still exists.

13. R. L. Cleary, *The Place Royale and Urban Design in the Ancien Régime* (Cambridge, 1999), p. 81.

14. N. Coquéry, *L'Hôtel aristocratique: le marché du luxe à Paris au XVIIIe siècle* (1998), pp. 188–9.

15. See above, pp. 160–61.

16. See above, p. 208.

17. The Rues d'Artois and de Ponthieu (VIIIe.) were at the heart of this development. The church of Saint-Philippe-du-Roule was inaugurated here in 1784.

18. The Opéra-Comique is still located here, Place Boïeldieu (formerly Place de la Comédie).

19. See above, p. 184.

20. J. Lough, 'Letters from France, 1788–9', *Durham University Journal* (1961), p. 2.

21. The artistic Salon is not to be confused with the salons run for the arts and sciences by well-connected ladies.

22. T. Crow, *Painters and Public Life in Eighteenth-Century Paris* (New Haven, CT, 1985), p. 6. From mid-century, the Luxembourg palace provided a permanent exhibition from the royal collections which was also highly popular.

23. Estimated total consumption in pre-Revolutionary Paris by A. Lavoisier, *Résultats extraits d'un ouvrage intitulé: De la Richesse territoriale de la France* (Paris, 1791).

24. See T. E. Brennan, *Public Drinking and Popular Culture in Eighteenth-Century Paris* (Princeton, NJ, 1988). Note that Brennan underestimates the role of bars in cross-class sociability. For tennis, see J. L. Ménetra, *Journal of my Life*, ed. D. Roche (New York, 1986), pp. 192–4.

25. V. Jamaray-Duval, *Mémoires. Enfance et éducation d'un paysan au XVIIIe siècle*, ed. J. M. Goulemot (1981), p. 313.

26. See quotation above, p. 205.

27. Cited in R. M. Isherwood, *Farce and Fantasy. Popular Entertainment in Eighteenth-Century Paris* (New York, 1986), pp. 154–5.

28. Goldoni, *Mémoires*, L. Jouvet, ed. (1946), p. 210.

29. Marquis de Bombelles, *Journal*, eds C. Grassion & F. Durif (2 vols., 1978–1993), ii, p. 206.

30. *Les Moeurs de Paris* (1748); cited in J. Chagniot, *Paris au XVIIIe siècle* (NHP: 1988), p. 46.

31. Peyssonel, *Les Numéros*, p. 34.

32. According to the student who is the subject in C. d'Arjuzon, 'Un étudiant à Paris au XVIIIe siècle. Lettres inédites', *Revue des Deux-Mondes*, 10 (July 1902), p. 426.

33. D. Roche, *The Culture of Clothing: Dress and Fashion in the Ancien Régime* (Cambridge, 1994), p. 178.

34. East of the present-day Père-Lachaise cemetery, for example, the family of financier and Revolutionary politician Lepeletier de Saint-Fargeau constructed an enormous estate in the early part of the century.

35. Coquéry, *L'Hôtel aristocratique*, p. 87.

36. The Six Corps were constituted by the drapers, grocer-apothecaries, furriers, silk merchants, goldsmiths and mercers.

37. J. Savary, *Le Parfait Négociant* (1675), p. 45.

38. Cited in M. Le Moel, *L'Urbanisme parisien au siècle des Lumières* (no date), p. 39.

39. Mercier, cited in Coquéry, *L'Hôtel aristocratique*, p. 52.

40. J. J. Rousseau, *Confessions*, Book IV.

41. J. J. Rousseau, *Émile*, in *Oeuvres* (5 vols., 1964–95), i, p. 277.

42. Fougeret, *La Capitale des Gaules, ou la Nouvelle Babilonne* (La Haye, 1759), p. 4.

43. P. J. B. Nougaret, *Les Astuces et les tromperies de Paris, ou Histoire d'un débarqué, écrite par lui-même* (Year VII), p. 2.
44. Menuret de Chambaud, *Essai sur l'histoire médico-topographique de Paris* (1786), p. 29.
45. P. Higonnet, *Paris, Capital of the World* (Cambridge, MA, 2002), p. 41.
46. Voltaire, 'Les embellissements de Paris'.
47. A. Furetière, *Dictionnaire universel*.
48. The phrase 'machines à guérir' is from Jacques Tenon, the surgeon and hospital reformer. See M. Foucault et al., *Les Machines à guérir: aux origines de l'hôpital moderne* (1976).
49. See below, pp. 291–4.
50. See above, pp. 199ff.
51. Mercier, *Tableau de Paris* is eloquent on this kind of behaviour.
52. See above, pp. 192–3.
53. M. Guillaute, *Mémoire sur la réformation de la police de France, soumis au Roi en 1749*, J. Seznec, ed. (1974), p. 96.
54. D. Garrioch, *The Making of Revolutionary Paris* (Berkeley, CA, 2002), p. 231.
55. J. L. Gay, 'L'Administration de la capitale entre 1700 et 1789. La tutelle de la royauté et ses limites', *MPIF*, 8 (1956), 9 (1957), 10 (1959, p. 205), 11 (1966).
56. T. Blaikie, *Diary of a Scottish Gardener at the French Court at the End of the Eighteenth Century*, F. Birrell, ed. (London, 1931), p. 212.
57. Mercier, *Tableau de Paris*, viii, p. 671.
58. For the Diamond Necklace Affair, see the overview of its importance in C. Jones, *The Great Nation: France from Louis XV to Napoleon (1715–99)* (London, 2002), pp. 336ff.
59. See above, p. 207.
60. E. Frémy, 'L'Enceinte de Paris, construite par les fermiers généraux et la perception des droits d'octroi de la ville, 1784–91', *BPIF*, 39 (1912), p. 119.
61. J. Godechot, *The Taking of the Bastille, July 14th 1789* (1965), p. 54.
62. The best of the several remaining Ledoux constructions is at La Villette.
63. Mercier, *Tableau de Paris*, vi, p. 26.

7: Revolution and Empire

Feature Boxes: Main Sources
7.1: Philippe-Égalité, duc d'Orléans
   R. T. Barnhart, 'Gambling in Revolutionary Paris: The Palais-Royal 1789–1838' (typed paper, Bibliothèque Nationale de France)

V. Champier & R. Sandoz, *Le Palais-Royal* (new edn, 1991)

E. Lever, *Philippe-Égalité* (1996)

Le Palais-Royal (Musée Carnavalet: 1988)

7.2: The Grand Véfour

J. P. Aron, *Le Mangeur du XIXe siècle* (1973)

Balzac, *Les Illusions perdues* (1837)

Baudelaire, *Les Fleurs du mal*: 'Tableaux parisiens, LXXXVIII'

J. C. Bologne, *Histoire des cafés et des cafetiers* (1990)

R. L. Spang, *The Invention of the Restaurant: Paris and Modern Gastronomic Culture* (Cambridge, MA, 2001)

7.3: The Catacombs

A. Clément & G. Thomas, *Atlas du Paris souterrain. La doublure sombre de la Ville lumière* (2001)

T. Laqueur, 'The Places of the Dead in Modernity', in C. Jones and D. Wahrman (eds.), *The Age of Cultural Revolutions: Britain and France, 1750–1820* (Berkeley, CA, 2002)

S. Rice, *Parisian Views* (Cambridge, MA, 1997)

R. Suttel, *Catacombes et carrières de Paris. Promenade sous la capitale* (1986)

1. G. Oliva, 'Voyageurs italiens face au Paris révolutionnaire, 1789–92', *Paris et la Révolution*, M. Vovelle, ed. (1989), p. 288.

2. Mallet du Pan, cited in J. Tulard, *La Révolution* (NHP: 1989), p. 32.

3. Alfieri, cited in Oliva, 'Voyageurs italiens', p. 358.

4. L. S. Mercier, *Le Nouveau Paris* (Year VII (1799)), 'Avant-propos'.

5. M. Dorigny, 'Les Girondins avant le "fédéralisme". Paris 'chef-lieu' de la Révolution', *Paris et la Révolution*, pp. 287–8.

6. Tulard, *La Révolution*, p. 227.

7. Ibid., p. 224.

8. *Archives parlementaires*, lxv, p. 320.

9. J. Tulard, *Le Consulat et l'Empire* (NHP: 1970), p. 158.

10. A. Fierro, *Histoire et dictionnaire de Paris* (1996), p. 145.

11. J. Favier, *Histoire de Paris*, (1997), p. 299.

12. Fierro, *Histoire et dictionnaire*, p. 145.

13. Cited in D. G. Levy et al. (eds.), *Women in Revolutionary Paris, 1789–95* (Urbana, IL, 1979), p. 216.

14. K. Alder, *Engineering the Revolution: Arms and the Enlightenment in France, 1763–1815* (Princeton, NJ, 1997), p. 262.

15. Tulard, *Le Consulat et l'Empire*, p. 317.

16. Ibid., p. 418.

17. P. Pinon, *Paris, biographie d'une capitale* (1999), p. 142.

18. Tulard, *Le Consulat et l'Empire*, p. 224.

19. Pinon, *Paris*, p. 145.

20. Tulard, *Le Consulat et l'Empire*, p. 243.

8: Between Napoleons

Feature Boxes: Main Sources

8.1: Rue Transnonain

J. Harsin, *Barricades: The War of the Streets in Revolutionary Paris, 1830–48* (London, 2002)

E. Hazan, *L'Invention de Paris. Il n'y a pas de pas perdus* (2002)

P. Mansel, *Paris between Empires, 1814–52* (London, 2001)

M. Traugott (ed.), *The French Worker: Autobiographies from the Early Industrial Era* (Berkeley, CA, 1993)

8.2: Victor Hugo

A. Ben-Amos, 'Les Funérailles de Victor Hugo: apothéose de l'événement spectacle', in *Lieux de mémoire*, i.

F. Choay, *The Invention of the Historic Monument* (Cambridge, 2001)

V. Hugo, *Choses vues. Souvenirs, journaux, cahiers, 1830–84*, ed. H. Juin (2002)

M. Ozouf, 'Le Panthéon', in *Lieux de mémoire*, i.

8.3: The Arcades

Aragon, *Le Paysan de Paris* (1926)

W. Benjamin, *The Arcades Project* (Cambridge, MA, 1999)

P. Chemetov & B. Marrcy, *Architectures. Paris 1848–1914* (1980).

J. C. Delorme et al., *Passages couverts parisiens* (1996)

P. de Moncan & C. Mahout, *Les Passages de Paris* (1990)

1. See below, Chapter 9.

2. D. Sultana, *From Abbotsford to Paris and Back: Sir Walter Scott's Journey of 1815* (Stroud, 1992), p. 96.

3. Chateaubriand, *Mémoires d'outre-tombe* (1849), Book 5, ch. 8.

4. The expiatory chapel is on the Rue d'Anjou (VIIIe.), and the Picpus cemetery on the Boulevard de Picpus (XIIe.). They and the Conciergerie monument may all be visited.

5. Notre-Dame-de-Bonne-Nouvelle is situated on the Rue de la Lune, just off the Boulevard de Bonne-Nouvelle; Notre-Dame-de-Lorette on the Rue

de Châteaudun; and Saint-Denys-du-Saint-Sacrement on the Rue de Turenne.

6. G. Bertier de Sauvigny, *La Restauration, 1815–30* (NHP: 1977), p. 456.

7. V. Hugo, *Choses vues. Souvenirs, journaux, cahiers, 1830–85*, H. Juin ed. (2002), p. 98.

8. As noted by J. Tulard, in 'Le Retour des cendres', *Lieux de Mémoire*, ii, p. 1747.

9. This was also helped by the fact that Lutetia – the Latin name for Paris – is a feminine noun.

10. This is clearly shown in Pierre Citron's wonderful *La Poésie de Paris dans la littérature française de Rousseau à Baudelaire* (2 vols., 1961).

11. A. Bazin, *L'Époque sans nom. Esquisses de Paris, 1830–3* (2 vols., 1833), i, pp. 59–60.

12. Cited in P. Mansel, *Paris between Empires, 1814–52* (London, 2001), p. 318.

13. Thomas Raikes, cited in Mansel, *Paris between Empires*, p. 308.

14. L. S. Kramer, *Threshold of a New World. Intellectuals and the Exile Experience in Paris, 1830–48* (Ithaca, NY, 1988), p. 17.

15. Ibid., p. 31.

16. Bazin, *L'Époque sans nom*, ii, pp. 298, 141.

17. Mrs Trollope, cited in Kramer, *Threshold of a New World*, p. 17. 'Gay' is taken in its nineteenth-century sense, of course.

18. Balzac, *Physiologie du mariage* (1829).

19. Cited in K. Stierle, *La Capitale des signes. Paris et son discours* (2001), p. 186. Despite its title, *Lutèce* was not concerned with the Roman city.

20. Bertier de Sauvigny, *La Restauration*, p. 169; Bazin, *L'Époque sans nom*, i, p. 35.

21. Here I am adopting the terminology of Louis Chevalier's classic *Classes laborieuses et classes dangereuses à Paris pendant la première moitié du XIXe siècle* (1958). In recent years Chevalier's thesis, which has equated crime and labour, has been contested by a number of historians, who have seen the question of the social danger of the workers as more of a cultural construction than a social reality. I follow this line of criticism here.

22. P. Vigier, *Paris pendant la monarchie de Juillet (1830–48)* (NHP: 1991), p. 178.

23. Rambuteau cited in J. Des Cars & P. Pinon, *Paris-Haussmann. 'Le Pari de Haussmann'* (1991), p. 22; and for Chabrol, see Bertier de Sauvigny, *La Restauration*, p. 18.

24. C. Lachaise, *Topographie médicale de Paris* (1822), p. 176.

25. G. Bertier de Sauvigny, *La France et les Français vus par les voyageurs américains, 1814–48* (2 vols., 1982), i, p. 74.

26. Mansel, *Paris between Empires*, p. 366.

27. See above, pp. 307, 311.

28. Vigier, *Paris pendant la monarchie de Juillet*, p. 499. Nouvelle Athènes was roughly bounded by the Rues Saint-Lazare and La Rochefoucauld.

29. The last-named street was re-named Rue Balzac in 1850.

30. See below, pp. 359–62.

31. Victor Hugo, *Les Misérables* (1862).

32. Chevalier, *Classes laborieuses et classes dangereuses*, p. xviii.

33. Vigier, *Paris pendant la monarchie de Juillet*, p. 87. Cholera statistics are from Chevalier.

34. Kramer, *Threshold of a New World*, p. 33.

35. See above, n. 21.

36. Balzac, *Traité de la vie élégante* (1830).

37. The most important works in question are Parent-Duchâtelet, *Essai sur les cloaques ou égouts de la ville de Paris* (1824) and his *La Prostitution dans la ville de Paris* (1828); Villermé, *Tableau de l'état physique et moral des ouvriers* (1840); Frégier, *Des Classes dangereuses dans la population des grandes villes* (1840); de Gérando, *De la Bienfaisance publique* (1839); and Buret, *De la Misère et des classes laborieuses en Angleterre et en France* (1840).

38. *La Peau de chagrin* (1831), cited in Stierle, *La Capitale des signes*, p. 239.

39. Balzac, *Fille aux yeux d'or* (1834).

40. Id., *Facino Cane* (1836).

41. Mansel, *Paris between Empires*, p. 397.

42. Ibid., p. 404.

43. E. Hazan, *L'Invention de Paris: Il n'y a pas de pas perdus* (2002), p. 333.

9: *Haussmannism and the City of Modernity*

Feature Boxes: Main Sources

9.2: The Mur des Fédérés

A. Horne, *The Fall of Paris: The Siege and the Commune, 1870–1* (London, 1965)

M. Rébérioux, 'Le Mur des Fédérés: rouge sang craché', in *Lieux de mémoire*, i

R. Tombs, *The Paris Commune, 1871* (1999)

NOTES

9.3: The Eiffel Tower

G. Apollinaire, *Alcools* (1913); *Caligrammes* (1919)

R. Barthes, 'La Tour Eiffel' (1963: repr. in id., *Oeuvres complètes, t. 2 (1962–7)*, ed. E. Marty (1994))

M. R. Levin, *When the Eiffel Tower was New: French Visions of Progress at the Centennial of the Revolution* (South Hadley, MA, 1989)

B. Marrey, *La Vie et l'oeuvre extraordinaire de Monsieur Gustave Eiffel, ingénieur . . .* (1984)

J. Milner, *The Studios of Paris. The Capital of Art in the Late Nineteenth Century* (London, 1988)

E. Tonnet-Lacroix, 'Le Thème de la tour Eiffel dans l'art et la littérature depuis 1909 jusques vers 1930', in J. Guichardet (ed.), *Errances et parcours parisiens de Ruteboeuf à Crevel* (1986)

1. Louis Bonaparte became dynastic pretender on the death of Napoleon's childless son and heir 'Napoleon II' in 1832. Louis was Napoleon I's eldest nephew, the son of Louis Bonaparte and Hortense de Beauharnais.

2. This theme is endlessly recurrent in Haussmann's *Mémoires*. See the excellent edition by F. Choay (2000).

3. See below, pp. 383–5.

4. See above, pp. 204–5.

5. G. Poisson, *Histoire de l'architecture à Paris* (NHP: 1997), p. 463.

6. M. Carmona, *Le Grand Paris: l'évolution de l'idée d'aménagement de la région parisienne* (2 vols., 1979), i, p. 36.

7. N. Chaudun, *Haussmann au crible* (2000), p. 76.

8. M. du Camp, *Paris, ses organes, ses fonctions et sa vie dans la seconde moitié du XIXe siècle* (6 vols., 1869–75), vi, pp. 333–4.

9. See the important article of P. Cassell, 'Les Travaux de la Commission des Embellissements de Paris en 1853: pouvait-on transformer la capitale sans Haussmann?', *Bibliothèque de l'École des Chartes*, 155 (1997). Cf. Choay, 'Introduction' to Haussmann, *Mémoires*, pp. 28–9.

10. Carmona, *Le Grand Paris*, i, p. 27.

11. L. Réau, *Histoire du vandalisme. Les monuments détruits de l'art français* (2nd edn, 1994), p. 746.

12. P. Pinon, *Paris, biographie d'une capitale* (1999), p. 218.

13. Carmona, *Le Grand Paris*, i, p. 33.

14. The Rue Étienne-Marcel is in the Ie.–IIe.; the Rue Réaumur in the IIe.–IIIe.; while the Rue de Turbigo extends from the Ie. through the IIe. to the IIIe.

15. N. Green, *The Spectacle of Nature: Landscape and Bourgeois Culture in Nineteenth-Century France* (Manchester, 1990), p. 43.

16. This explains why street numbering on the Rue de Rennes (VIIe.) starts at no. 41! Planners only really gave up on the idea of the extension in the 1940s, by which time it had dawned that Saint-Germain-des-Prés might be worth saving.

17. Completely incorporated into Paris were Passy, Auteuil, Monceau-Batignolles, Montmartre, La Chapelle, La Villette, Belleville, Charonne, Bercy, Vaugirard and Grenelle. Partly incorporated were Neuilly, Clichy, Saint-Ouen, Aubervilliers, Pantin, Saint-Mandé, Bagnolet, Ivry, Gentilly, Montrouge, Vanves, Issy and the Pré Saint-Gervais.

18. Pinon, *Paris*, p. 180.

19. Sainte-Clotilde is on the Rue Las-Cases (VIIe.); Saint-Ambroise just off the Boulevard Voltaire (XIe.); Saint-Pierre-de-Montrouge on the Rue Victor-Basch (XIVe.); the church of Auteuil on the Place d'Auteuil (XVIe.); and the Alexandre-Nevski cathedral on the Rue Daru (VIIIe.).

20. Carmona, *Le Grand Paris*, i, p. 33.

21. Haussmann, *Mémoires*, iii, p. 946.

22. D. Reid, *Paris Sewers and Sewermen: Realities and Representations* (Cambridge, MA, 1991), p. 27.

23. Ibid., p. 47.

24. Ibid., p. 41.

25. J. Merriman, *Aux Marges de la ville: faubourgs et banlieues en France, 1815–70* (1994), p. 294.

26. Chaudun, *Haussmann au crible*, p. 144.

27. Cited in A. Fierro, *Histoire et dictionnaire de Paris* (1996), p. 530.

28. V. Fournel, *Paris nouveau et Paris futur* (1865), pp. 29, 265.

29. As cited in an 1868 pamphlet, according to W. Benjamin, *The Arcades Project* (Cambridge, MA, 1997), p. 130.

30. Fournel, *Paris nouveau*, p. 16.

31. Haussmann, *Mémoires*, iii, p. 825.

32. Haussmann's favoured street surface was slippery in wet weather, a point which made cavalry manoeuvres difficult. For Engels on the obsolescence of the barricade, see Benjamin, *The Arcades Project*, p. 145.

33. See above, p. 29.

34. Fournel, *Paris nouveau*, p. 166.

35. See above, p. 181.

36. W. Benjamin, *The Arcades Project*.

37. Ibid.

38. Amédée de Cesena (1864), cited in D. J. Olsen, *The City as a Work of Art: London, Paris, Vienna* (New Haven, CT, 1986), p. 52.

39. The title of Ferry's *Les Comptes fantastiques* was a pun. *Compte* signified financial account, but *conte* (pronounced in the same way) was a tale or yarn. Hoffmann's *Contes fantastiques* were fairytales and the subject of Offenbach's opera, *Tales of Hoffmann*.

40. E. de Goncourt, *Journal*, ed. R. Ricatte (4 vols., 1956), iii, p. 274.

41. G. J. Becker (ed.), *Paris under Siege, 1870–1. From the Goncourt 'Journal'* (Ithaca, NY, 1969), pp. 185, 197.

42. Ibid., p. 309.

43. Rougerie, cited in Merriman, *Aux Marges de la ville*.

44. S. Rials, *Paris de Trochu à Thiers, 1870–73* (NHP: 1985), p. 522.

45. B. Belhoste et al., *Le Paris des Polytechniciens. Des ingénieurs dans la ville* (1994).

46. See above, p. 348–9.

47. See below, pp. 415.

48. Poisson, *Histoire de l'architecture*, p. 515.

49. Pinon, *Paris*, p. 223.

50. See above, p. 286.

51. Doncourt, cited in Benjamin, *The Arcades Project*, pp. 188–9.

52. J. Kinsman (ed.), *Paris in the Late Nineteenth Century* (Canberra, 1997), p. 58. The reference is to Jules Verne's *Around the World in Eighty Days* (1872).

53. B. S. Shapiro, *Pleasures of Paris: Daumier to Picasso* (Boston, MA, 1991), p. 12.

54. *Paris Guide* (1867), Introduction, p. vi.

55. Edmondo De Amicis, *Ricordi di Parigi* (Milan, 1900), p. 6.

56. Benjamin, *The Arcades Project*, p. 197.

57. Cited in V. Schwartz, *Spectacular Realities. Early Mass Culture in Fin-de-Siècle Paris* (Berkeley, CA, 1998), p. 75.

58. Benjamin, *The Arcades Project*, p. 524.

59. De Amicis, *Ricordi di Parigi*, p. 22.

60. 'The Painter of Modern Life'.

61. Cited in T. Reff, *Manet and Modern Art* (Washington, DC, 1982), p. 24.

62. R. L. Herbert, *Impressionism: Art, Leisure and Parisian Society* (London, 1988), p. 2.

63. Baudelaire, 'Salon de 1846'.

64. 'Le vieux Paris n'est plus (la forme d'une ville change plus vite, hélas! que le coeur d'un mortel).' Baudelaire, 'Le Cygne', *Les Fleurs du mal* (1857).

65. Du Camp, *Paris*, i, p. 6.

10: The Anxious Spectacle

Feature Boxes: Main Sources

10.1: Alphand

A. Alphand, *Les Promenades de Paris* (1867–73: reprint edn, 2002)

Discours prononcés à l'occasion des funérailles de J. C. A. Alphand (1892)

G. Surand, 'Haussmann, Alphand: des promenades pour Paris', in J. Des Cars & P. Pinon (eds.), *Paris-Haussmann: 'Le Pari d'Haussmann'* (1991)

S. Texier, *Les Parcs et jardins dans l'urbanisme parisien (XIXe.–XXe. siècles)* (2001)

10.2: *Îlot insalubre numéro 16*

A. Gady, 'L'îlot insalubre no. 16: un exemple d'urbanisme archéologique', *MPIF*, 44 (1993)

E. Paul, *The Last Time I Saw Paris* (1942)

P. Pinon, *Paris, biographie d'une capitale* (1999).

10.3: Sacré-Coeur of Montmartre

L. Chevalier, *Montmartre du plaisir au crime* (1980).

R. Jonas, 'Monument as ex-voto, monument as historiosophy: the basilica of Sacré-Coeur', *French Historical Studies*, 18 (1993)

R. Jonas, *France and the Cult of the Sacred Heart. An Epic Tale for Modern Times* (Berkeley, CA, 2000)

G. P. Weisburg, *Montmartre and the Making of Mass Culture* (New Brunswick, NJ, 2001)

1. Heartbroken, he committed suicide on his mistress's tomb in Ixelles in Belgium.

2. D. Silverman, *Art Nouveau in Fin-de-Siècle France. Politics, Psychology and Style* (Berkeley, CA, 1989), p. 5.

3. With the honourable exception of the Eiffel tower, of course. The *Galeries des Machines* lasted until 1910.

4. See below, p. 526.

5. It is for this reason that I am using the term.

6. D. Halévy, *Pays parisiens* (1932), p. 161.

7. J. Guichardet (ed.), *Errances et parcours parisiens de Ruteboeuf à Crevel* (1986), p. 147.

8. P. Pinon, *Paris, biographie d'une capitale* (1999), p. 341, n. 110.

9. A. Sutcliffe, *The Autumn of Central Paris. The Defeat of Town Planning, 1850–1970* (London, 1970), p. 191.

10. Pinon, *Paris*, pp. 228–9.

11. Cited in J. P. Rioux, *Chronique d'une fin de siècle. France 1889–1900* (1991), p. 47.

12. R. Magraw, 'Paris 1917–20: Labour Protest and Popular Politics', in C. Wrigley (ed.), *Central and Western Europe, 1917–20* (London, 1993), p. 127.

13. G. Jacquemet, *Belleville au XIXe siècle: du faubourg à la ville* (1984), p. 344.

14. See above, pp. 388–9.

15. R. L. Herbert, *Impressionism: Art, Leisure and Parisian Society* (London, 1988), p. 15; and P. Nord, *Impressionists and Politics: Art and Democracy in the 19th Century* (London, 2000), p. 82.

16. *Post-Impressionism. Cross Currents in European Painting* (London, 1979), p. 134.

17. Rioux, *Chronique*, p. 55.

18. S. Gilson Miller (ed.), *Disorienting Encounters. Travels of a Moroccan Scholar in France in 1845–1846. The Voyage of Muhammad As-Saffar* (Berkeley, CA, 1992), p. 135.

19. D'Avenel, 1902, cited in T. Gronberg, *Designs on Modernity. Exhibiting the City in 1920s Paris* (Manchester, 1998), p. 74.

20. P. D. Cate (ed.), *The Graphic Arts and French Society, 1871–1914* (New Brunswick, NJ, 1988), p. 28.

11: *Faded Dreams, Lost Illusions*

Feature Boxes: Main Sources

11.1: Josephine Baker

P. Higonnet, *Paris, Capital of the World* (Cambridge, MA, 2002)

D. & M. Johnson, *The Age of Illusion. Art and Politics in France 1918–40* (London, 1987)

C. Rearick, *The French in Love and War. Popular Culture in the Era of the World Wars* (London, 1997)

T. Stovall, *Paris Noir, African-Americans in the City of Light* (Boston, 1996)

E. White, *The Flâneur* (London, 2001)

11.2: The *Vespasiennes*

W. Benjamin, *The Arcades Project* (Cambridge, MA, 1999)

P. Borhan, *Charles Marville. Vespasiennes* (1991)

L. Chevalier, *The Assassination of Paris* (London, 1994)

R. Cobb, 'The Pissotière', in id., *Tour de France* (London, 1976)

A. Fierro, 'Toilettes publiques', in id., *Histoire et dictionnaire de Paris* (1996)

C. Maillard, *Les Précieux Ridicules. Les vespasiennes de Paris* (1967)

Henry Miller, *Letters to Emil* (1930)

B. S. Shapiro, *Pleasures of Paris. Daumier to Picasso* (Boston, MA, 1991)

M. de Thézy, *Paris, la rue. Le mobilier parisien du Second Empire à nos jours* (1976)

11.3: The Vel' d'Hiv

R. Anchel, 'Les juifs à Paris au XVIIIe. siècle', *BPIF*, 59 (1932)

J. J. Becker & A. Wievorka (eds.), *Les Juifs de France de la Révolution française à nos jours* (1998)

E. Benbassa, *Histoire de juifs de France* (1997)

P. Hildenfinger, *Documents sur les juifs à Paris au XVIIIe. siècle* (1913)

A. Kaspi & A. Marès, *Le Paris des étrangers depuis un siècle* (1989)

H. Michel, *Paris allemand* (1981)

D. Pryce-Jones, *Paris in the Third Reich. A History of the German Occupation, 1940–4* (London, 1981)

1. Several versions of the text are available in W. Benjamin, *The Arcades Project* (Cambridge, MA, 1999). To be fair, Gertrude Stein felt that Paris was capital of the twentieth century.

2. V. Bougault, *Paris Montparnasse. À l'heure de l'art moderne, 1910–40* (1997), p. 159.

3. T. G. Kennedy, *Imagining Paris: Exile, Writing and American Identity* (London, 1993), p. 12. Born to a half-Cuban, half-Danish mother and a Spanish father, Nin spent her childhood in the USA.

4. R. Schor, *L'Opinion française et les étrangers en France 1919–39* (1985), p. 100.

5. Alfred Perles, *My Friend Henry Miller* (London, 1955), p. 19.

6. T. Gronberg, *Designs on Modernity: Exhibiting the City in 1920s Paris* (Manchester, 1998), pp. 37–8.

7. A. Fourcaud (ed.), *Banlieue rouge, 1920–60* (1992), p. 222; B. Cendrars, *La Banlieue de Paris. Photographies de Robert Doisneau* (1983), pp. 41–2.

8. Some of the brick is yellow, but red predominates.

9. See above, p. 415.

10. P. Pinon, *Paris, biographie d'une capitale* (1999), p. 263.

11. Cited in S. Texier, *Les Parcs et jardins dans l'urbanisme parisien (XIXe.–XXe. siècles)* (2001).

12. R. Cobb, *Promenades* (London, 1980), p. 131.

13. See above, pp. 388–9, 422–3.

14. M. Nesbit, *Atget's Seven Albums* (London, 1992), p. 71.

15. Ibid.

16. See above, p. 450.

17. Cited in V. Cronin, *Paris, City of Light, 1919–30* (London, 1994), p. 123. (I have adjusted the translation.)

18. Cobb, *Promenades*, p. 150.

19. B. Belhoste et al., *Le Paris des Polytechniciens. Des ingénieurs dans la ville* (1994), p. 225.

20. See above, p. 453.

21. B. Basdevant, *L'Architecture française des origines à nos jours* (1971), p. 306.

22. J. L. Cohen in A. Fourcaud (ed.), *Banlieue rouge, 1920–60* (1992), p. 198.

23. P. Nivet & Y. Combeau, *Histoire politique de Paris au XXe. siècle* (2000), p. 90.

24. J. Jackson, *The Popular Front in France: Defending Democracy, 1934–8* (Cambridge, 1988), pp. 96–7. (I have slightly altered the translation.)

25. Cobb, *Promenades*, p. 24.

26. A. Monnier, *The Very Rich Hours of Adrienne Monnier* (London, 1976), p. 397.

27. J. H. Lartigue, *Diary of a Century* (London, 1970: no page nos.).

28. Colette, *Paris de ma fenêtre* (1944: 1948 edn), p. 25.

29. C. Rearick, *The French in Love and War. Popular Culture in the Era of the World Wars* (New Haven, CT, 1997), p. 248.

30. S. Barber, *Weapons of Liberation* (London, 1996), p. 41.

31. N. Evenson, *Paris. A Century of Change, 1878–1978* (New Haven, CT, 1979), p. 279.

32. Lartigue, *Diary of a Century*, n.p.

12: *The Remaking of Paris*

Feature Boxes: Main Sources

12.1: The Métro in Zazie

M. Augé, *Un ethnologue dans le métro* (1986)

R. Barthes, ' "Zazie" et la littérature', in id., *Oeuvres complètes, ii. 1962–7* (2002)

W. Benjamin, *The Arcades Project* (Cambridge, MA, 1999)

M. & S. Bigot, *'Zazie dans le métro' de Raymond Queneau* (1994)

R. Cobb, 'Queneau's itineraries', in id., *Promenades* (Oxford, 1980)

F. Kafka, *The Diaries of Franz Kafka 1910–23* (1992)

R. Queneau, *Zazie dans le métro* (1959)

12.2: The 'Algerian Bridge'

J. L. Einaudi, *La Bataille de Paris. Le 17 october 2001* (1991; rev. edn 2001)

J. House, 'Antiracist memories: The case of 17 October 1961 in historical perspective', *Modern and Contemporary France*, 9 (2001)

Y. Lemire & Y. Potin, ' "Ici on noie les algériens": Fabriques documentaires, avatars politiques et mémoires partagées d'une icône militante (1961–2001)', *Genèses*, 49 (2002)

12.3: The Marais

A. Gady, 'L'Îlot insalubre numéro 16: un exemple d'urbanisme archéologique', *MPIF*, 44 (1993)

E. Hazan, *L'Invention de Paris. Il n'y a pas de pas perdus* (2002)

R. Kain, 'Conserving the cultural heritage of historic buildings and towns in France since 1945', in M. Cook, *French Culture since 1945* (1993)

E. White, *The Flâneur* (2001)

1. See Chapter 11, p. 489.

2. A. Kaplan, *The Collaborator: the Trial and Execution of Robert Brasillach* (London, 2000), p. 143.

3. A. Beevor & A. Cooper, *Paris after the Liberation, 1944–9* (London, 1994), pp. 219–20.

4. Ibid., p. 261.

5. Though see below, p. 513.

6. F. Morris (ed.), *Paris Post-War, Art and Existentialism, 1945–55* (London, 1993), p. 25.

7. Beevor & Cooper, *Paris after the Liberation*, p. 422.

8. Morris (ed.), *Paris Post-War*, p. 35.

9. H. Lottman, *The Left Bank* (London, 1982), p. 233.

10. See above, p. 454.

11. See above, pp. 460–62.

12. I. Calvino, 'Préface', in G. Macchia, *Paris en ruines* (1988), p. 5.

13. N. Evenson, *A Century of Change, 1878–1978* (London, 1979), p. 59.

14. ZUPs are 'zones to be urbanized in priority'; ZACs, 'zones of concerted development'.

15. See above, p. 419.

16. Cf. the influential Guy Debord, *La Société du spectacle* (1971).

17. A. Sutcliffe, *Paris. An Architectural History* (London, 1993), p. 176.
18. P. Pinon, *Paris, biographie d'une capitale* (1999), p. 269.
19. M. Carmona, *Le Grand Paris. L'évolution de l'idée d'aménagement de la région parisienne* (2 vols., 1979), i, p. 154.
20. Ibid., p. 167.
21. Pinon, *Paris*, p. 276.
22. F. Loyer, *Paris XIXe. siècle. L'immeuble et la rue* (1987).
23. B. Marchand, *Paris, histoire d'une ville (XIXe.–XXe. siècles)* (1993), p. 299.
24. See below, Conclusion.
25. See Conclusion, esp. pp. 540–42.
26. Carmona, *Le Grand Paris*, i, p. 167.
27. See above, p. 508.

Conclusion: Big Projects in a Bigger City

1. F. Chaslin, cited in A. Fierro, *The Glass State. The Technology of the Spectacle, 1981–98* (Cambridge, MA, 1983), p. 179.
2. The exception here is the Parc de la Villette science museum and park in the XIXe.
3. Victor Hugo, *Notre-Dame de Paris* (1831).
4. Ibid.

Bibliographical Guide

The following Guide is an introductory survey. It merely skims the surface of works written on the history of Paris, and highlights those consulted in the writing of the present volume. See also the list of sources attached to each of the Feature Boxes and in the endnotes for each chapter. For a fuller listing of sources, see my website, http//:www.warwick.ac.uk/staff/Colin.Jones.

In the works cited below, unless otherwise indicated, works in French were published in Paris and those in English in London.

Although an enormous number of books has been written on Paris, there is currently no up-to-date, full-length treatment of **the history of Paris from earliest times to the present.** Alistair Horne's *Seven Ages of Paris, Portrait of Paris* (Basingstoke, 2002) is a colourful, episodic and anecdotal account, which starts in 1180 and stops around 1970. John Russell, *Paris* (1960) shows its age but is a high-quality historical essay, with photographs by Brassaï. Robert Cole, *A Traveller's History of Paris* (reprint edn, Moreton-in-Marsh, 1997) offers a brief general account. Alfred Fierro's *History and Dictionary of Paris* (Lanham, MD, 1998) is a very useful work of reference – though less full than the same author's strongly recommended *Histoire et dictionnaire de Paris* (1996). A. Sutcliffe, *Paris. An Architectural History* (1993) is an authoritative account of the environment in which Parisians lived. The best of the many works dedicated to exploring the image of Paris in literature is I. Littlewood, *Paris. A Literary Companion to Paris* (1987).

The reader in French is better served. Jean Favier's forbiddingly monumental *Histoire de Paris* (1997) adopts a thematic emphasis and is stuffed with excellent things. No serious historian of Paris or dyed-in-the-wool Parisophile in general can afford to neglect J. Hillairet's superb and erudite (though just occasionally plain wrong) *Dictionnaire historique des rues de Paris* (2 vols., 1957–61). P. Pinon, *Paris, biographie d'une capitale* (1999) and B. Rouleau, *Paris, histoire d'un espace* (1988) offer good up-to-date accounts centred on the built environment. Also valuable in this respect are J. R. Pitte, *Paris, histoire d'une ville* (1993); B. Rouleau, *Le Tracé des rues de Paris* (1988); and A. Friedmann, *Paris, ses rues, ses paroisses* (1952). An outstanding visual work of reference is D. Chadych and D. Leborgne, *Atlas de Paris. Évolution d'un paysage* (1999), which largely replaces P. Couperie, *Paris through the Ages* (1971). It can be read alongside A. Clément & G. Thomas (eds.), *Atlas du Paris souterrain: La doublure sombre de la Ville lumière* (2001); B. Fortier (ed.), *La Métropole imaginaire. Un atlas de Paris* (1989); and A. Picon & J. P. Robert, *Le dessus des cartes. Un Atlas parisien* (1999). Finally, there is an enormous amount on Paris to be gleaned from P. Nora (ed.), *Les Lieux de mémoire* (3 vols., paperback edn, 1997), parts of which have been translated as Nora (ed.), *Realms of Memory* (3 vols., New York, 1996). The enjoyably chatty yet erudite approach of E. Hazan, *L'Invention de Paris. Il n'y a pas de pas perdus* (2002) makes it the best introduction to the history of Parisian social and cultural life for the French reader. English readers have E. White, *The Flâneur* (2001), written in the same vein.

The most compendious introduction to the history of Paris in recent years is the 23-volume *Nouvelle Histoire de Paris* (NHP), nearly all of which is now in print. Regrettably, none of the volumes has been translated into English. They are listed in chronological order in the different sections below. There are also three thematic volumes: J. Beaujeu-Garnier, *Paris, hasard ou prédestination? Une géographie de Paris* (1993); R. Héron de Villefosse, *Solennités, fêtes et réjouissances parisiennes* (1980); and P. Lavedan, *Histoire de l'urbanisme à Paris* (2nd edn, 1993). A useful collection of the essays of Michel Fleury, redoubtable defender of *le Vieux Paris* and specialist on the archaeology and early history of the city, has been published as '*Si le roi m'avait donné Paris, sa grande ville . . .*' (1994). For the pre-modern myth of Paris, see M. Barroux, *Les Origines légendaires de Paris* (1955), and C. Beaune, *The Birth of an Ideology: Myths and Symbols in Late-Medieval France* (Oxford, 1991). A helpful short primer of sources is R. W. Berger, *In Old Paris: An Anthology of Source Descriptions, 1323–1790* (New York, 2002). See too A. Le Roux & L. M. Tisserand (eds.), *Paris et ses historiens aux XIVe. et XVe. siècles* (1867). Still useful are the products of early modern antiquarianism. See most notably Henri Sauval, *Histoire et recherches des antiquités de la ville de Paris* (2 vols., 1724), Nicolas de La Mare, *Traité de la police* (4 vols., 1705–38) and Germain Brice, *Description de la ville de Paris* (1685).

A large number of general works on the history of Paris focus on recent rather than ancient times. The best of these is now P. Higonnet, *Paris, Capital of the World* (2000), which is a kind of extended conversation with the spectre of the influential Marxist critic Walter Benjamin: see the latter's *The Arcades Project* (Cambridge, MA, 1999). The classic works of A. Sutcliffe, *The Autumn of Central Paris. The Defeat of Town Planning, 1850–1970* (1970) and N. Evenson, *Paris: A Century of Change, 1878–1978* (1979) offer wide-ranging interpretations of modern Paris. See too B. Marchand, *Paris, histoire d'une ville (XIXe.–XXe. siècles)* (1993); D. Harvey, *Consciousness and the Urban Experience* (Oxford, 1985) and id., *Paris, Capital of Modernity* (2003). On the myth of Paris as city of modernity, see also the colourful P. Citron, *La Poésie de Paris dans la littérature française de Rousseau à Baudelaire* (2 vols., 1961) plus the excellent recent analysis of K. H. Stierle, *La Capitale des signes. Paris et son discours* (2001). Also of value are C. Charle & D. Roche (eds.), *Capitales culturelles, capitales symboliques. Paris et ses expériences européennes, XVIIIe.–XXe. siècles* (2002) and R. Burton, *Blood in the City. Violence and Revolutions in Paris, 1789–1945* (Ithaca, NY, 2001).

For the period **from the very earliest times through to Roman Lutetia**, P. Velay, *From Lutetia to Paris. The Island and the Two Banks* (1992) is one of only very few specialized works to exist in English. The NHP volume is excellent: P. M. Duval, *De Lutèce oppidum à Paris capitale de la France* (1993). Also archaeologically well informed are D. Busson, *Carte archéologique de la Gaule, Paris* (1998); id., *Paris ville antique* (2001); and M. Fleury, *Naissance de Paris* (1997). Primary sources include Julius Caesar, *Gallic Wars* and Julian the Apostate, *Works*.

For **the Merovingian and Carolingian periods through to the death of Philippe-Augustus in 1225**, see J. Boussard, *Paris de la fin du siège de 885–886 à la mort de Philippe-Auguste* (NHP: 1976). Among primary sources, I drew esp. on Gregory of Tours, *History of the Franks* (numerous edns); Abbon, *Le Siège de Paris par les Normands. Poème du IXe. siècle*, ed. H. Waquet (1942); *Letters of John of Salisbury*, eds. W. J. Miller et al. (2 vols., Oxford, 1979–86); *Oeuvres de Rigord et de Guillaume Le Breton, historiens de Philippe-Auguste*, ed. F. Delaborde (2 vols., 1882–5); and Suger, *Oeuvres*, ed. F. Gasparri (1996). A useful synthetic overview is provided by R. H. Bautier, 'Quand et comment Paris devint capitale', *BPIF*, 105 (1978). A. Lombard-Jourdan, *Paris, genèse de la ville. La rive droite de la Seine des origines à 1223* (new edn, 1985) is nicely complemented by F. Lehoux, *Le Bourg Saint-Germain-des-Prés depuis ses origines jusqu'à la fin de la Guerre de Cent Ans* (1951). W. H. Newman, *Le Domaine royal sous les premiers Capétiens (987–1180)* (1937) is still useful, while J. W. Baldwin, *The*

Government of Philip Augustus (Berkeley, CA, 1986) offers an account of a highly Parisian monarch. V. Egbert, *On the Bridges of Mediaeval Paris* (Princeton, NJ, 1974) uses visual sources to good effect. Important aspects of the economic history of the period are covered in R. de Lespinasse & F. Bonnardot, *Les Métiers et corporations de la ville de Paris. XIIe. siècle. Le Livre des métiers d'Étienne Boileau* (1879) and T. Kleinsdienst, 'La Topographie et l'exploitation des "marais" de Paris du XIIe. au XVIIIe. siècle', *MPIF*, 14 (1963). Writing on Parisian intellectual and cultural life is extensive. In English, see J. W. Baldwin, *Masters, Princes and Merchants. The Social Views of Peter the Chanter and his Circle* (2 vols., Princeton, NJ, 1970); S. C. Ferruolo, *The Origins of the University. The Schools of Paris and their Critics, 1100–1215* (Stanford, CA, 1985); P. Kibre, *The Nations in the Medieval Universities* (Cambridge, MA, 1948); M. & R. Rouse, *Manuscripts and their Makers. Books and Book-Producers in Paris, 1200–1500* (London, 2000); and in French esp. J. Le Goff, *Les Intellectuels au moyen âge* (1985); J. Verger, *Les Universités françaises au moyen âge* (Leiden, 1985); and id. (ed.), *Histoire des universités en France* (Toulouse, 1986).

For the **period from the early thirteenth century to around 1500**, one may start with the NHP volumes: Boussard (cited above), plus R. Cazelles, *Paris de la fin du règne de Philippe-Auguste à la mort de Charles V, 1223–1380* (2nd edn, 1994) and J. Favier, *Paris au XVe. siècle, 1380–1500* (2nd edn, 1996). Primary sources start to become more numerous in this period. Besides the memoirs cited in endnotes, I have also drawn on Jacques de Vitry, *Histoire occidentale. Historia occidentalis* (*Tableau de l'Occident au XIIIe siècle*), ed. J. Longère (1997) for the early part of the period and, for later, the superb *Journal d'un Bourgeois de Paris de 1405 à 1449*, ed. C. Beaune (1990). See too the 'Chronique parisienne anonyme de 1316 à 1399', *MPIF*, 11 (1884). J. R. Strayer, *The Reign of Philip the Fair* (Princeton, NJ, 1980) is a classic, and may be complemented by J. Favier, *Philippe le Bel* (1978) and by R. Cazelles, *La Société politique et la crise de la royauté sous Philippe de Valois* (1958). On the Hundred Years War, R. Cazelles, *Étienne Marcel* (1984) is a useful biography. High politics is the focus in R. C. Famiglietti, *Royal Intrigue: Crisis at the Court of Charles VI (1392–1420)* (New York, 1986), but a broader social perspective is evident in B. Guénée, *Un Meurtre, une société: l'assassinat du duc d'Orléans, 23 novembre 1407* (1992) and the excellent G. L. Thompson, *The Anglo-Burgundian Regime in Paris, 1420–36* (1984) and id., *Paris and its People under English Rule: The Anglo-Burgundian Regime (1420–36)* (Oxford, 1991). For ritual and ceremonial, see B. Guénée & F. Lehoux, *Les Entrées* *royales françaises de 1328 à 1515* (1968), as well as C. Couderc, 'L'entrée solennelle de Louis XI à Paris (31 août 1461)', *MPIF*, 23 (1896). On the university, see S. Lusignan, '*Vérité garde le Roy . . .*' *La construction d'une identité universitaire en France (XIIIe.–XVe. siècles)* (1999) and G. Leff, *Paris and Oxford Universities in the Thirteenth and Fourteenth Centuries* (New York, 1968). Guy Fourquin's work is the best introduction to the economic history of the period. In English, see his *The Anatomy of Popular Rebellion in the Middle Ages* (New York, 1978), and in French 'La Population de la région parisienne', *Moyen Âge*, 52 (1956); 'Paris, capitale économique à la fin du moyen âge', *BPIF* (1960–61); and *Les Campagnes de la région parisienne à la fin du Moyen Âge* (1964). For the world of poverty, B. Geremek, *The Margins of Society in Late Medieval Paris* (1987) may now be read alongside S. Farmer, *Surviving Poverty in Medieval Paris: Gender, Ideology and the Daily Lives of the Poor* (Ithaca, NY, 2002).

For the sixteenth century, J. P. Babelon, *Paris au XVIe. siècle* (NHP: 1986) is a masterly work of synthesis. A key primary source is A. Tuetey (ed.), *Registres des délibérations du Bureau de la Ville de Paris* (numerous volumes, 1886–). Primary works consulted besides those cited in endnotes included F. Bournon (ed.), 'Chronique parisienne de Pierre Driart, chambrier de Saint-Victor (1522–55)', *MPIF*, 22 (1895); G. Fagniez (ed.), 'Livre de raison de Me. Nicolas Versoris, avocat au Parlement de Paris (1519–30)', *MPIF*, 12 (1886); E. Knobelsdorf, *Lutetiae descriptio (1543)*, ed. O. Sauvage (1978); and L. Lalanne (ed.), *Journal d'un bourgeois de Paris sous le règne de François I (1515–36)* (1854). For the Wars of Religion, see too A. Dufour (ed.), 'Relation du siège de Paris par Henri IV', *MPIF*, 2 (1876); G. Fagniez (ed.), 'Mémorial juridique et historique du Maître. Guillaume Aubert, avocat au Parlement de Paris (deuxième moitié du XVIe siècle)' (1560–89)', *MPIF*, 36 (1909); A. Franklin (ed.), *Journal du siège de Paris en 1590 rédigé par un des assiégés* (1876); *Mémoires de Luc Geitzkofler tyrolien (1550–1620)* (Geneva, 1892) and A. Vidier, 'Description de Paris par Arnold van Buchel d'Utrecht (1585–6)', *MPIF*, 26 (1899).

Secondary works of central importance in English include D. Thomson, *Renaissance Paris, Architecture and Growth, 1475–1600* (London, 1984) and B. B. Diefendorf, *Paris City Councillors in the Sixteenth Century* (Princeton, NJ, 1983). Excellent work has been done on royal ceremonial, notably R. E. Giesey, *The Royal Funeral Ceremony in Renaissance France* (Geneva, 1960); L. Bryant, *The King and the City in the Parisian Royal Entry Ceremony: Politics, Ritual and Art in the Renaissance* (Geneva, 1986); *Les Entrées. Gloire et déclin d'un cérémonial* (Pau, 1996); *Les Fêtes de la Renaissance* (3 vols., 1956–75); and V. E. Graham & W. McAllister Johnson

The Paris Entrées of Charles IX and Elizabeth of Austria (Toronto, 1974). There are several royal biographies of note: J. Jacquart, *François I* (1981); R. Knecht, *Renaissance Warrior and Patron: The Reign of Francis I* (Cambridge, 1994); and P. Chevallier, *Henri III* (1994). On the history of print and its relation to the history of (particularly religious) ideas, see L. Febvre & H. J. Martin, *L'Apparition du livre* (1958) and D. Crouzet, *La Genèse de la Réforme française, 1520–60* (1996). Key works on the religious wars include E. Barnavi, *Le Parti de Dieu. Étude sociale et politique des chefs de la Ligue parisienne* (Paris–Louvain, 1980); id. & R. Descimon, *La Sainte Ligue, le juge et la potence* (1985); D. Crouzet, *La Nuit de la Saint-Barthélemy. Un rêve perdu de la Renaissance* (1994); R. Descimon, 'Qui étaient les Seize? Étude sociale de 225 cadres laïcs de la Ligue radicale parisienne (1585–94)', *MPIF*, 34 (1983); M. Yardeni, 'Le mythe de Paris comme élément de propagande à l'époque de la Ligue', *MPIF*, 20 (1969); and F. A. Yates, 'Dramatic religious processions in Paris in the late sixteenth century', *Annales musicologues*, 2 (1954). On aspects of the social and economic history of the period, see too Cherrière, 'L'eau à Paris au XVIe siècle', *La Cité*, 11 (1912); E. Coyèque, 'L'assistance publique à Paris au XVIe siècle', *BPIF*, 15 (1888); and J. Jacquart, 'Le poids démographique de Paris et de l'Île de France au XVIe siècle', *ADH*, 1960.

For the 'long seventeenth century', from the reign of Henry IV to the death of Louis XIV, the two NHP volumes – R. Pillorget, *Paris sous les premiers Bourbons, 1594–1661* (1988) and G. Dethan, *Paris au temps de Louis XIV* (1990) – may be supplemented by O. Ranum, *Paris in the Age of Absolutism* (new edn, Philadelphia, 2002); L. Bernard, *The Emerging City. Paris in the Age of Louis XIV* (Durham, NC, 1970); A. Trout, *City on the Seine: Paris in the Time of Richelieu and Louis XIV* (new edn, 1996); and R. Mousnier, *Paris capitale au temps de Richelieu et de Mazarin* (1978). Key primary sources include the correspondence of Madame de Sévigné and Colbert and the memoirs of Tallemant des Réaux, the Cardinal de Retz, Madame de Motteville, Saint-Simon and many others. See too A. M. de Boislisle (ed.), *Mémoires des Intendants sur l'état des généralités dressé pour l'instruction du duc de Bourgogne. Tome 1. Mémoire sur la généralité de Paris* (1881); Marquis d'Argenson, *Notes intéressantes sur l'histoire des mœurs et la police de Paris à la fin du règne de Louis XIV* (1891); and Vauban, *De l'importance dont Paris est à la France* (reprint, 1821). Among antiquarian writings, besides Sauval, see esp. P. Bonfons, *Les Antiquitez et choses les plus remarquables de Paris* (1608); F. Colletet, *Abrégé des antiquitez de la ville de Paris* (1664); and J. Du Breul, *Le Théâtre des antiquitez de Paris* (1612). I have drawn heavily on travel writings. Besides the works cited in the endnotes, see also T. Coryate, *Voyage à Paris (1608)*, ed. R. Lasteyrie (1880); P. Fréart de Chantelou (ed.), *Journal de voyage du cavalier Bernin en France* (Aix-en-Provence, 1981); P. Lacombe, 'Antoine de Rombise: voyage à Paris, 1634–5', *MPIF*, 13 (1886); and G. Raynaud (ed.), 'Paris en 1596 vu par un italien (Récit de F. G. d'Ierni)', *BPIF*, 12 (1885). John Lough has edited *Locke's Travels in France, 1675–9* (Cambridge, 1953) and compiled a very useful anthology, *France Observed in the Seventeenth Century by British Travellers* (Stocksfield, Northumberland, 1985).

There are several highly usable biographical treatments of rulers: notably, J. P. Babelon, *Henri IV* (1982); M. Greengrass, *France in the Age of Henri IV* (1984); and F. Bluche, *Louis XIV* (1990). See also M. Wolfe, *The Conversion of Henry IV. Politics, Power and Religious Belief in Early Modern France* (Cambridge, MA, 1993); R. Mousnier, *L'Assassinat d'Henri IV* (1964); id., ed., *Un Nouveau Colbert* (1985); and M. Laurain-Portemer, *Études mazarines* (2 vols., 1981). For the administration and policing of the city, see A. Miron, *François Miron et l'administration municipale de Paris sous Henri IV de 1604 à 1606* (1885); A. Lebigre, *Les Dangers de Paris au XVIIe. siècle. L'assassinat de Jacques Tardieu, lieutenant criminel au Châtelet et de sa femme* (1991); and M. Chassagne, *La Lieutenance générale de police à Paris* (1906). Aspects of the Fronde and its aftermath are examined in J. L. Bourgeon, 'L'Île de la Cité pendant la Fronde: structure sociale', *MPIF*, 13 (1962); R. M. Golden, *The Godly Rebellion: Parisian Curés and the Religious Fronde, 1652–62* (1981); and A. Hamscher, *The Parlement of Paris after the Fronde* (1976). There is excellent material on the urbanization of the city, beginning with H. Ballon, *The Paris of Henri IV: Architecture and Urbanism* (1991). P. Francastel, *L'Urbanisme de Paris et de l'Europe, 1600–80* (1969) provides the wider perspective and can be supplemented by J. P. Babelon, *Demeures parisiennes sous Henri IV et Louis XIII* (1991); F. de Catheu, 'Le développement du faubourg Saint-Germain du XVIe. au XVIIIe. siècle', *BPIF*, 85 (1958); and R. Pillorget & J. de Viguerie, 'Les quartiers de Paris aux XVIIe. et XVIIIe. siècles', *RHMC* (1970). P. Breillat, *Versailles nouvelle, capitale moderne* (1986) provides a useful comparative context. More focused on the social history of the period are B. Causse, *Les Fiacres de Paris aux XVIIe. et XVIIIe. siècles* (1972); J. Jacquart, *La Crise rurale en Île-de-France, 1550–1670* (1974); J. P. Labatut, 'Situation sociale du quartier du Marais pendant la Fronde', *XVIIe. siècle*, 58 (1958); R. Mousnier, 'Recherches sur les structures sociales parisiennes en 1634, 1635, 1636', *RH* (1973); and id., *Recherches sur la stratification à Paris aux XVIIe. et XVIIIe. siècles* (1976). P. Chaunu, *La Mort à Paris,*

XVIe.–XVIIe.–XVIIIe. siècles (1978) provides a good introduction to the religious history of the period, and may be supplemented by J. Depauw, *Spiritualité et pauvreté à Paris au XVIIe. siècle* (1999) and J. Ferté, *La Vie religieuse dans les campagnes parisiennes (1622–95)* (1962). M. Ultee, *The Abbey of Saint-Germain-des-Prés in the Seventeenth Century* (New Haven, CT, 1981) and O. Krakovitch, 'Le Couvent des Minimes de la Place Royale', *MPIF*, 30 (1979) are good case studies. See too C. Jourdain, *Histoire de l'Université de Paris aux XVIIe. et XVIIIe. siècles* (1888).

For the eighteenth century, D. Garrioch, *The Making of Revolutionary Paris* (2002) is a splendid foil to the NHP volume, J. Chagniot, *Paris au XVIIIe. siècle* (1988). P. Gaxotte, *Paris au XVIIIe. siècle* (1982) is largely derivative. I have been particularly influenced by two superb primary sources: J. L. Ménétra, *Journal of My Life*, ed. D. Roche (New York, 1986); and L. S. Mercier, whose 12-volumed *Tableau de Paris* (Amsterdam, 1782–8) has been skeletally anthologized by J. Popkin as *The Panorama of Paris* (Philadelphia, 1999). Less well-known sources used include R. C. Alexander (ed.), *The Diary of David Garrick, being a record of his memorable trip to Paris in 1751* (New York, rev. edn, 1971) and J. Lelage (ed.), *Mémoires du chevalier de Mannlich (1740–1812)* (1949). Of almanac and guide-book sources, the pick are [Nemeitz], *Séjour de Paris, c'est à dire Instructions fidèles pour les Voyageurs de condition* (2 vols., Leiden, 1725); Peyssonel, *Les Numéros* (1782); Piganiol de La Force, *Description historique de la ville de Paris et de ses environs* (1765 edn); and Watin fils, *Le provincial à Paris ou État actuel de Paris* (4 vols., 1787).

On the urban environment, see esp. M. Le Moel (ed.), *L'Urbanisme parisien au siècle des lumières* (no date) and J. L. Harouel, *L'Embellissement des villes: l'urbanisme français au XVIIIe. siècle* (1993). Also useful are A. Chastel, 'L'Îlot de la rue du Roule et ses abords', *MPIF*, 16–17 (1965–6); B. Fortier, *La Politique de l'espace parisien à la fin de l'Ancien Régime* (1975); J. Pronteau, 'Le Lotissement de la "couture" extérieure du Temple à Paris et la formation de la nouvelle ville d'Angoulême', *BPIF*, 108 (1981); D. Rabreau, *Les Dessins d'architecture au XVIIIe. siècle* (2001); and O. Zunz, 'Étude d'un processus d'urbanisation: le quartier Gros-Caillou à Paris', *AESC*, 25 (1970). On the administration and policing of the city, to A. Williams, *The Police of Paris, 1718–89* (1979) may be added J. Chagniot, *Paris et l'Armée au XVIIIe. siècle, étude sociale et politique* (1985); R. Descimon & J. Nagle, 'Les Quartiers de Paris du Moyen Âge au XVIIIe siècle: évolution d'un espace plurifonctionnel', *AESC*, (1979); J. L. Gay, 'L'Administration de la capitale entre 1770 et 1789: la tutelle de la royauté et ses limites', *MPIF*, 8–11 (1956–60); *Les Institutions parisiennes à la fin de l'Ancien Régime et sous la Révolution française* (no date) as well as much of the work of S. Kaplan: see most notably his *Provisioning Paris: Merchants and Millers in the Grain and Flour Trade during the Eighteenth Century* (Ithaca, NY, 1984); *The Bakers of Paris and the Bread Question, 1700–75* (Durham, NC, 1996); and *La Fin des corporations* (2001).

The work of Daniel Roche has reshaped our understanding of eighteenth-century Paris. See his *France in the Enlightenment* (Cambridge, MA, 1998); his edition of Ménétra's memoirs, cited above; the path-breaking *The People of Paris: An Essay in Popular Culture in the Eighteenth Century* (Leamington Spa, 1987); *The Culture of Clothing: Dress and Fashion in the 'Ancien Régime'* (Cambridge, 1994); and *A History of Everyday Things: The Birth of Consumption in France, 1600–1800* (Cambridge, 2000). In addition, see his edited volume, *La Ville promise. Mobilité et accueil à Paris (fin XVIIe. siècle–début XIXe. siècle)* (2000). Contrasting images of the city are evident in S. Davies, *Paris and the Provinces in Eighteenth-Century Prose Fiction* (Oxford, 1982) and V. Milliot, *Paris en bleu. Images de la ville dans la littérature de colportage (XVIe.–XVIIIe. siècles)* (1996). For the world of ideas at all levels, D. Goodman, *The Republic of Letters: A Cultural History of the French Enlightenment* (Ithaca, NY, 1994) may be read alongside A. Farge, *Subversive Words: Public Opinion in Eighteenth-Century France* (Cambridge, 1994); R. Isherwood, *Farce and Fantasy: Popular Entertainment in Eighteenth-Century Paris* (New York, 1986); C. Jones, 'Pulling Teeth in Eighteenth-Century Paris', *Past & Present*, 166 (2000); and R. A. Etlin, *The Architecture of Death: The Transformation of the Cemetery in Eighteenth-Century Paris* (Cambridge, MA, 1984). On the legal and political elites, R. M. Andrews, *Law, Magistracy and Crime in Old Régime Paris, 1735–89* (Cambridge, 1994) may be read alongside D. Bell, *Lawyers and Citizens. The Making of a Political Elite in Old Régime France* (Oxford, 1994).

For social structure, see A. Daumard & F. Furet, *Structures et relations sociales à Paris au milieu du XVIIIe. siècle* (1961). On the urban elite, see F. Bluche, *Les Magistrats du parlement de Paris au XVIIIe. siècle* (1960); Y. Durand, *Les Fermiers Généraux au XVIIIe. siècle* (1971); and M. Marraud, *La Noblesse de Paris au XVIIIe. siècle* (2000). Their leisured lifestyle may be glimpsed in N. Coquéry, *L'Hôtel aristocratique. Le marché du luxe à Paris au XVIIIe. siècle* (1998); M. Gallet, *Les Demeures parisiennes: l'époque de Louis XV* (1964); *La Maison parisienne au Siècle des Lumières* (1985); A. Pardailhé-Galabrun, *The Birth of Intimacy: Privacy and Domestic Life in Early Modern Paris* (Cambridge, 1991); R. Fox & A. Turner (eds.), *Luxury Trades and Consumerism in Ancien Régime Paris* (Aldershot,

1998); and K. Scott, *The Rococo Interior* (1995). On the poorer part of the population, J. Kaplow, *The Names of Kings*. *The Parisian Laboring Poor in the Eighteenth Century* (New York, 1971) is still useful, as is D. Garrioch, *Neighbourhood and Community in Eighteenth-Century Paris* (Cambridge, 1986). See too C. Crowston, *Fabricating Women: The Seamstresses of Old Régime France, 1675–1791* (Durham, NC, 2001); A. Farge, *Fragile Lives: Violence, Power and Solidarity in Eighteenth-Century Paris* (1993); and R. Darnton, *The Great Cat Massacre and Other Episodes in French Cultural History* (New York, 1984). Issues of popular crime and public order are discussed in S. Barles, *La Ville délétère: médecins et ingénieurs dans l'espace urbain (XVIIIe.–XIXe. siècles)* (1999); E. M. Bénabou, *La Prostitution et la police des moeurs au XVIIIe. siècle* (1987); P. Petrovitch, 'Recherches sur la criminalité à Paris dans la seconde moitié du XVIIIe. siècle', in *Crimes et criminalité en France, XVIIe.–XVIIIe. siècles* (1971); P. Piasenza, 'Juges, Lieutenants de police et bourgeois à Paris aux XVIIe. et XVIIIe. siècles', *AESC*, 45 (1990); and T. Brennan, *Public Drinking and Popular Culture in Eighteenth-Century Paris* (Princeton, NJ, 1988). Also useful are E. Frémy, 'L'Enceinte de Paris construite par les fermiers généraux et la perception des droits d'octroi de la ville (1784–91)', *BPIF*, 39 (1912) and J. M. Peysson, 'Le Mur d'enceinte des fermiers-généraux et la fraude à la fin de l'Ancien Régime', *BPIF*, 109 (1982).

For the Revolutionary decade (1789–99), works specifically dedicated to Paris as a city (rather than as a venue for political action) are less ubiquitous than one might imagine, and they become quite rare for the Consulate and Empire. The original NHP volume on the Revolution, M. Reinhard, *La Révolution* (1971; and still usable) has been updated by J. Tulard, *La Révolution* (1989). Also highly useful is E. Ducoudray et al., *Atlas de la Révolution française. 11. Paris* (2000). The primary materials are voluminous. Among memoirs and correspondence, I have a particular liking for L. S. Mercier, *Le Nouveau Paris* (1799) and N. Ruault, *Gazette d'un Parisien sous la Révolution* (1975). Documentary collections include Buchez & Roux, *Histoire parlementaire de la Révolution française* (40 vols., 1834–8); A. Aulard, *La Société des Jacobins. Recueil de documents* (6 vols., 1889–97); P. Caron et al. (eds.), *Paris pendant la Terreur. Rapports des agents secrets du ministère de l'Intérieur*, 6 vols. (1910–64); C. L. Chassin, *Les Élections et les cahiers de Paris en 1789*, 4 vols. (1888–9); B. Gille, *Documents sur l'état de l'industrie et du commerce de Paris (1778–1810)* (1963); W. Markov & A. Soboul, *Die Sansculotten von Paris. Dokumente zur Geschichte der Volksbewegung* (1957); and W. A. Schmidt, *Paris pendant la Révolution d'après les rapports de la police secrète, 1789–1800* (4 vols., 1880–94).

Paris et la Révolution (1989) comprises a valuable, wide-ranging collection of essays covering all aspects of Paris's Revolutionary experience. On the origins, see esp. R. Chartier, *Cultural Origins of the French Revolution* (Durham, NC, 1991); T. Crow, *Painters and Public Life in Eighteenth-Century Paris* (1985); R. Darnton, *Mesmerism and the End of the Enlightenment in France* (Cambridge, MA, 1968); and S. Maza, *Private Lives and Public Affairs. The Causes Célèbres of Pre-Revolutionary France* (Berkeley, CA, 1993). On key events in the Revolutionary decades, see J. Godechot, *The Taking of the Bastille, 14 July 1789* (1970); T. Tackett, *The King Takes Flight* (2003); M. Reinhard, *Le 10 août: la chute de la monarchie* (1969); R. Bienvenu (ed.), *The Ninth of Thermidor: The Fall of Robespierre* (Oxford, 1968). Useful on the emergence and flourishing of the Parisian popular movement are R. B. Rose, *The Making of the Sans-Culottes* (Manchester, 1983); G. Rudé, *The Crowd in the French Revolution* (Oxford, 1959); A. Soboul, *Les Sans-culottes parisiens en l'an II* (1958); R. Cobb, *The Police and the People: French Popular Protest, 1789–1820* (Oxford, 1970); id., *Paris and its Provinces, 1792–1802* (1975); H. Burstin, *Le Faubourg Saint-Marcel à l'époque révolutionnaire* (1983); and R. Monnier, *Le Faubourg Saint-Antoine, 1789–1815* (1981). The female dimension is covered in D. Godineau, *The Women of Paris and their Revolution* (Berkeley, CA, 1998) and O. Hufton, *Women and the Limits of Citizenship in the French Revolution* (Toronto, 1982). On the Thermidorian and Directorial period, see esp. F. Gendron, *La Jeunesse dorée sous Thermidor* (1983) and I. Woloch, *The Jacobin Legacy. The Democratic Movement under the Directory* (1970).

Most of the most illuminating analyses of Revolutionary Paris have set the 1790s in a broader chronological framework. See, for example, C. Backouche, *La Trace du fleuve: la Seine et Paris, 1750–1850* (2000); A. de Baecque, *The Body Politic: Corporeal Metaphor in Revolutionary France, 1770–1800* (Stanford, CA, 1997); A. Corbin, *The Foul and the Fragrant. Odor and the French Social Imagination* (Cambridge, MA, 1986); M. Fitzsimmons, *The Parisian Order of Barristers and the French Revolution* (Cambridge, MA, 1987); D. Garrioch, *The Formation of the Parisian Bourgeoisie, 1690–1830* (Cambridge, MA, 1996); C. Hesse, *Publishing and Cultural Politics in Revolutionary Paris, 1789–1810* (Berkeley, CA, 1991); J. Johnson, *Listening in Paris. A Cultural History* (Berkeley, CA, 1995); P. Metzner, *Crescendo of the Virtuoso: Spectacle, Skill and Self-Promotion in Paris during the Age of Revolution* (Berkeley, CA, 1998); W. Scott Haine, *The World of the Paris Café. Sociability among the French Working Class, 1789–1914* (1996); and R. Spang, *The Invention of the Restaurant: Paris and Gastronomic Culture* (2001).

The pickings specific to the **Napoleonic period** are slim. J. Tulard's NHP volume *Le Consulat et l'Empire* (2nd edn, 1983) stands out by the quality of its analyses. Tulard is also the author of *Paris et son administration, 1800–30* (1976). Primary sources include – besides a mountain of memorialists – A. Aulard, *Paris sous le Consulat. Recueil de documents* (4 vols., 1903–9) and id., *Paris sous le Premier Empire. Recueil de documents* (3 vols., 1912–23). See also G. Poisson, *Napoléon et Paris* (1964); M. D. Sibalis, *The Workers of Napoleonic Paris, 1800–15* (1979); and J. Bertaut, *La Vie à Paris sous le Premier Empire* (1943).

For the period **from the Bourbon Restoration through to the Second Republic,** as for later periods, the general works devoted to modern Paris cited on p. 595 start to become relevant. The NHP volumes for the period are G. de Bertier de Sauvigny, *La Restauration* (1977); P. Vigier, *La Monarchie de Juillet* (1991); and L. Girard, *La Deuxième République et le Second Empire* (1981). Balzac, Hugo and Sue provide lightly disguised fictional accounts full of authentic Parisian detail. Of other contemporary accounts, I found especially useful A. Bazin, *L'Époque sans nom: esquisses de Paris, 1830–33* (1833); G. Claudin, *Mes Souvenirs: les boulevards de 1840 à 1870* (1884); C. Lachaise, *Topographie médicale de Paris* (1822); H. Meynadier, *Paris sous le point de vue pittoresque et monumental* (1843); L. Montigny, *Le Provincial à Paris: Esquisse des moeurs parisiennes* (1825); and A. Parent-Duchâtelet, *De la Prostitution dans la ville de Paris* (1836). Of visitors' accounts, especially useful is F. Trollope, *Paris and the Parisians in 1835* (1985). Secondary literature surveying the genre includes G. Bertier de Sauvigny, *La France et les Français vus par les voyageurs américains, 1814–48* (2 vols., 1982) and L. S. Kramer, *Threshold of a New World. Intellectuals and the French Exile Experience (1830–48)* (Ithaca, NY, 1988).

Louis Chevalier drew heavily on fictional accounts in his *Laboring Classes and Dangerous Classes in Paris during the First Half of the Nineteenth Century* (1973) – probably the most influential single work on the period in recent decades. Chevalier has, however, been criticized for over-egging the pudding: see esp. the remarks of B. M. Ratcliffe, '*Classes laborieuses et classes dangereuses à Paris pendant la première moitié du XIXe. siècle?* The Chevalier Thesis Reexamined', *FHS*, 17 (1991). Accounts drawing heavily on fiction and poetry, but more aware of the work of mythologization, include the works by P. Citron and K. Stierle cited above. Also excellent in this respect are C. Prendergast, *Paris and the Nineteenth Century* (Oxford, 1992) and P. Parkhurst Ferguson, *Paris as Revolution: Writing the Nineteenth-Century City* (Berkeley, CA, 1994).

BIBLIOGRAPHICAL GUIDE

There is now a good politically oriented account of the period in English:
P. Mansel, *Paris between Empires, 1814–52* (London, 2001), and this may
be read alongside the invaluable collection of essays, K. Bowie (ed.), *La
Modernité avant Haussmann: formes de l'espace urbain à Paris, 1801–56*
(2001), which is esp. strong on pre-Haussmann urban change. On this see
too J. C. Delorme & A. M. Dubois, *Passages couverts parisiens* (1997); S.
Marcus, *Apartment Stories. City and Home in Nineteenth-Century Paris
and London* (Berkeley, CA, 1999); P. de Moncan & C. Mahout, *Les
Passages de Paris* (1990); D. Morel, *La Nouvelle Athènes* (1984); and J.
Pronteau, *Construction et aménagement des nouveaux quartiers de Paris
(1820–8)* (1958). A. Daumard, *La Bourgeoisie parisienne de 1815 à 1848*
(1963) provides a statistical account of the most powerful social grouping.
See too A. M. Fugier, *La Vie élégante ou la Formation du Tout-Paris, 1815–
48* (1991). The world of bohemians is the focus of J. Seigel, *Bohemian Paris.
Culture, Politics, and the Boundaries of Bourgeois Life, 1830–1930* (1999)
and J. Richardson, *The Bohemians, 1830–1914* (1969). Other social groups
to receive attention include B. H. Moss, *The Origins of the French Labor
Movement: The Socialism of Skilled Workers, 1830–1914* (1976); M.
Caron, *Générations romantiques: Les Étudiants de Paris et le Quartier latin
(1814–51)* (1991); N. Papayanis, *The Coachmen of Nineteenth-Century
Paris* (1993); and D. Reid, *Paris Sewers and Sewermen: Realities and Representations* (1991). On Paris's role in the 1848 Revolution, see P. Amann,
Revolution and Mass Democracy: The Paris Club Movement in 1848
(Princeton, NJ, 1975) and M. Traugott, *Armies of the Poor. Determinants
of Working-Class Participation in the Parisian Insurrection of June 1848*
(Princeton, NJ, 1985). See too J. Harsin, *Barricades: The War of the Streets
in Revolutionary Paris, 1830–48* (2001). On urban pathology, see F. Dela-
porte, *Le Savoir de la maladie: essai sur le choléra de 1832 à Paris* (1990); R.
Fuchs, *Poor and Pregnant in Paris. Strategies for Survival in the Nineteenth
Century* (New Brunswick, NJ, 1992); and C. Kudlick, *Cholera in Post-
Revolutionary Paris: A Cultural History* (Berkeley, CA, 1996).

The period **from the Second Empire through to circa 1890**, includes the
work of Haussmann and his collaborators and continuators. G. Haussmann,
Mémoires, rev. edn F. Choay (2000) provides an excellent starting-point
here, and should be read alongside A. Alphand, *Les Promenades de Paris*
(2 vols., 1867–73) and E. Belgrand, *La Seine* (3 vols., 1869–83). See too
the important study of P. Cassell, 'Les Travaux de la Commission des
Embellissements de Paris en 1853: pouvait-on transformer la capitale
sans Haussmann?', *Bibliothèque de l'École des Chartes*, 155 (1997). Of
Haussmann's contemporaries with a view about his work, see esp. M. Du

Camp, *Paris. Ses organes, ses fonctions et sa vie dans la seconde moitié du XIXe. siècle* (6 vols., 1869–75); V. Fournel, *Ce qu'on voit dans les rues de Paris* (1858); id., *Paris nouveau et Paris futur* (1868); J. K. Huysmans, *Croquis parisiens* (1880); L. Lazare, *Les Quartiers de l'est de Paris et les communes suburbaines* (1870); and id., *Les Quartiers pauvres de Paris: le XXe. arrondissement* (1870). The Rougon-Macquart cycle of novels by Emile Zola make compelling reading. Besides the NHP volume by L. Girard noted above, the best general accounts are those which highlight the architectural and planning changes: see esp. J. Des Cars & P. Pinon, *Paris-Haussmann* (1991); N. Chaudun, *Haussmann au crible* (2000); F. Loyer, *Paris Nineteenth Century: Architecture and Urbanism* (1988); J. Gaillard, *Paris, la ville, 1852–70: l'urbanisme parisien à l'heure de Haussmann* (1976); P. Chemetov & B. Marrey, *Architectures: Paris 1848–1914* (1983); and D. Van Zanten, *Building Paris. Architectural Institutions and the Transformation of the French Capital* (Cambridge, 1994). For the history of street furniture, see the quirky and scholarly M. de Thézy, *Paris, la rue. Le mobilier parisien du Second Empire à nos jours* (1976); and for one example, C. Maillard, *Les Précieux ridicules. Les vespasiennes de Paris* (1967). D. Jordan, *Transforming Paris: The Life and Labors of Baron Haussmann* (1995) and D. H. Pinkney, *Napoleon III and the Rebuilding of Paris* (1958) are very solid accounts of the main protagonists of change. D. J. Olsen, *The City as a Work of Art: London, Paris, Vienna* (1986) offers a valuable broader geographical perspective. A wider chronological frame is provided by the classic works of A. Sutcliffe (*The Autumn of Central Paris*) and N. Evenson (*Paris: A Century of Change*) cited above.

The artistic and cultural impact of the new Paris is underlined in T. J. Clark, *The Painting of Modern Life. Paris in the Art of Manet and His Followers* (revised edn, Princeton, NJ, 1999); R.L. Herbert, *Impressionism: Art, Leisure and Parisian Society* (1988); A. Boime, *Art and the French Commune: Imagining Paris after War and Revolution* (Princeton, NJ, 1995); P. Mainardi, *Art and Politics of the Second Empire: The Universal Expositions of 1855 and 1867* (1989); id., *The End of the Salon. Art and the State in the Early Third Republic* (Cambridge, 1993); P. Nord, *Impressionists and Politics. Art and Democracy in the Nineteenth Century* (2000); id., *The Republican Moment. Struggles for Democracy in Nineteenth-Century France* (Cambridge, MA, 1995); and T. J. Walsh, *Second Empire Opera: The Théâtre Lyrique: Paris 1851–1870* (1981). For photography, S. Rice, *Parisian Views* (1997) is very stimulating. See too C. Condemi, *Les Cafés-Concerts: Histoire d'un divertissement (1848–1914)* (1992).

On social tensions and class conflict, see the excellent L. Berlanstcin, *The Working People of Paris, 1871–1914* (1984), plus L. M. Greenberg, *Sisters of Liberty: Marseille, Lyon, Paris and the Reaction to a Centralized State, 1868–1871* (1971) and A. L. Schapiro, *Housing the Poor of Paris, 1850–1902* (Madison, WI, 1985). Specifically on the Commune, besides the works cited in endnotes, see the NHP volume, S. Rials, *De Trochu à Thiers, 1870–3* (1985); R. Christiansen, *Paris Babylon: The Story of the Paris Commune* (1996); R. V. Gould, *Insurgent Identities: Class, Community and Protest in Paris from 1848 to the Commune* (Chicago, 1995); and G. L. Gullickson, *Unruly Women of Paris: Images of the Commune* (1996). E. de Goncourt, *Paris under Siege, 1870–1871: from the Goncourt Journal* (1969) is a colourful account from a dyspeptic opponent of the Commune, who authored the most compelling of diaries in the period. See too J. Milner, *Art, War and Revolution in France 1870–1, Myth, Reportage and Reality* (2000). On the emergence of the suburbs, J. Bastié, *La Croissance de la banlieue parisienne* (1964) may be read alongside N. Green, *The Spectacle of Nature. Landscape and Bourgeois Culture in Nineteenth-Century France* (Manchester, 1990).

For the **fin de siècle** and until **1914**, much of the bibliography in the previous paragraphs is relevant. The characteristic mixture of hedonism and anxiety of the period is brought out vividly in E. Weber, *France Fin de Siècle* (Cambridge, MA, 1986); C. Charle, *Paris fin-de-siècle* (1998); C. Prochasson, *Paris 1900: essai d'histoire culturelle* (1999); and C. Rearick, *Pleasures of the Belle Époque. Entertainment and Festivity in Turn-of-the-Century France* (1985). R. Shattuck, *The Banquet Years* (1968) is still a good read – and nothing excels Proust for giving a feel for the period. D. Silverman, *Art Nouveau in Fin-de-Siècle France. Politics, Psychology and Style* (1989) is good on the Expositions, on which see also J. P. Rioux, *Chronique d'une fin de siècle; France 1889–1900* (1991) and P. Ory, *Les Expositions universelles de Paris* (1982). The artistic perspective is further explored in B. S. Shapiro, *Pleasures of Paris. Daumier to Picasso* (Boston, MA, 1991); J. Kinsman, *Paris in the Late Nineteenth Century* (Canberra, Australia, 1997); *Post-Impressionism. Cross-currents in European Painting* (1979); P. D. Cate (ed.), *The Graphic Arts and French Society, 1871–1914* (New Brunswick, NJ, 1988); J. Milner, *The Studios of Paris. The Capital of Art in the Late Nineteenth Century* (1988); and R. R. Brettell & J. Pissarro, *The Impressionist and the City. Pissarro's Series Paintings* (1993). For the longer term see too J. Dethier & A. Guiheux (eds.), *La Ville, art et architecture en Europe, 1870–1933* (1994). For the rise of consumerism, the classic works by M. Miller, *The Bon Marché: Bourgeois Culture and* *the Department Store, 1869–1920* (Princeton, NJ, 1981) and R. Williams, *Dream Worlds: Mass Consumption in Late Nineteenth-Century France* (Berkeley, CA, 1982) are now joined by V. Schwartz, *Spectacular Realities. Early Mass Culture in Fin de Siècle Paris* (Berkeley, CA, 1998). The working-class experience is explored in J. P. Brunet, *Saint-Denis, la ville rouge, 1890–1939* (1980); G. Jacquemet, *Belleville au XIXe. siècle: du faubourg à la ville* (1984); A. Fourcaut (ed.), *Un Siècle de banlieue parisienne (1859–1964)* (1988); and A. Faure et al., *Les Premiers Banlieusards: aux origines de la banlieue de Paris, 1860–1940* (1991); while the gender perspective is examined in A. Martin-Fugier, *La place des bonnes. La domesticité feminine à Paris en 1900* (1979) and M. L. Roberts, *Disruptive Acts. The New Woman in Fin-de-Siècle France* (2002).

For the **Great War (1914–18)**, see J. J. Becker, *The Great War and the French People* (Leamington Spa, 1985); J. L. Robert, *Les Ouvriers, la patrie et la Révolution: Paris, 1914–19* (1985); and the comparative perspectives in J. Winter & J. L. Robert (eds.), *Capital Cities at War: Paris, London, Berlin, 1914–19* (Cambridge, 1997), as well as the excellent early chapters of the NHP volume, J. Bastié & R. Pillorget, *Paris de 1914 à 1940* (1997).

The **Inter-War period (1918–39)** is covered by the NHP volume, J. Bastié & R. Pillorget, *Paris de 1914 à 1940* (1997). It is also the object of a popular study, V. Cronin, *Paris, City of Light (1919–39)* (1994). D. & M. Johnson, *The Age of Illusion. Art and Politics in France, 1918–40* (1987), E. Cohen, *Paris dans l'imaginaire national de l'entre-deux-guerres* (1999) and C. Rearick, *The French in Love and War: Popular Culture in the Era of the World Wars* (1997) provide vivid accounts of cultural life. For the latter part of the period, see too E. Weber, *The Hollow Years. France in the 1930s* (1995). Cultural life is the focus of T. Gronberg, *Designs on Modernity: Exhibiting the City in 1920s Paris* (Manchester, 1998); V. Bougault, *Paris Montparnasse. À l'heure de l'art moderne, 1910–40* (1997); *L'École de Paris, 1904–29. La Part de l'autre* (2001); *L'Esprit nouveau: le Purisme à Paris, 1918–25* (Grenoble, 2001); and M. Sheringham (ed.), *Parisian Fields (19th Century to c. 1920)* (1996). For photography, see M. Nesbit, *Atget's Seven Albums* (1992), and for the cinema, *Paris, grand-écran. Splendeur des salles obscures, 1895–1945* (1994). The expatriate contribution is explored in J. G. Kennedy, *Imagining Paris: Exile, Writing and American Identity* (1993); S. Benstock, *Women of the Left Bank: Paris, 1900–40* (1987); and T. Stovall, *Paris Noir. African-Americans in the City of Light* (Boston, MA, 1996). The work of the authors and artists who are the subject of these works comprises an important documentary contribution to the period.

The growth of and problems within the *banlieue* have attracted some major studies. See esp. T. Stovall, *The Rise of the Paris Red Belt* (Berkeley, CA, 1990); M. Carmona, *Le Grand Paris*. *L'évolution de l'idée d'aménagement de la région parisienne* (1979); A. Fourcaud (ed.), *Banlieue rouge, 1920–60* (1992); J. L. Cohen & A. Lortie, *Des Fortifs au périf* (1991); and P. Fridenson, *Histoire des usines Renault: la naissance de la grande entreprise, 1898–1939* (1972). For urbanism and city planning, see K. Burlen (ed.), *La banlieue oasis: Henri Sellier et les cités-jardins 1900–40* (Saint-Denis, 1987); P. Chemetov et al., *Paris-banlieue, 1919–39. Architectures domestiques* (1982); D. Calabi, *Marcel Poëte et le Paris des années vingt: aux origines de l'histoire des villes* (1997); and P. W. Wolf, *E. Hénard and the Beginnings of Urbanism in Paris, 1900–14* (1968). For the social, cultural and political crises of the late 1930s, see J. Jackson, *The Popular Front in France. Defending Democracy, 1934–8* (Cambridge, 1988); H. Lebovics, *True France. The Wars over Cultural Identity 1900–41* (Ithaca, NY, 1992); and R. Schor, *L'Opinion française et les étrangers en France (1919–39)* (1985).

For the Second World War, including German occupation, D. Pryce-Jones, *Paris in the Third Reich. A History of the German Occupation, 1940–4* (1981) is a well-illustrated guide. See too H. Michel, *Paris allemand, Paris résistant* (2 vols., 1982) and G. Perrault and P. Azéma, *Paris under the Occupation* (New York, 1989). For the Jewish experience, see J. Adler, *The Jews of Paris and the Final Solution (1940–4)* (Oxford, 1997) and the works cited in endnotes. A. Horne, *To Lose a Battle: 1940* (1969) is a gripping account of *l'année terrible* and Marc Bloch's *Strange Defeat* (1968, but penned in 1940) an important contemporary analysis. There is a huge primary literature on Paris under Vichy (de Beauvoir, Brasillach, Cocteau, Colette, Galtier-Boissière, Morand, etc.). Excellent on the Liberation and its dilemmas is A. Beevor & A. Cooper, *Paris after the Liberation: 1944–9* (1994) and A. Kaplan, *The Collaborator: The Trial and Execution of Robert Brasillach* (2000).

For post-Second World War and for contemporary Paris, the NHP volume is J. Bastié, *Paris de 1945 à 2000* (2003). For the post-Liberation mood, Beevor and Cooper, cited above, offer a racy start, as do the writings of de Beauvoir, Sartre and the other existentialists. See too S. Barber, *Weapons of Liberation* (1961); T. Judt, *Past Imperfect: French Intellectuals, 1944–56* (Oxford, 1992); H. Lottman, *The Left Bank: Writers, Artists and Politics from the Popular Front to the Cold War* (Boston, MA, 1982); F. Morris (ed.), *Paris Post-War. Art and Existentialism, 1945–55* (1993); and J. P. Bernard, *Paris rouge (1944–64)* (1991). Two vivid cultural accounts of the longer term are R. F. Kuisel, *Seducing the French: The Dilemma of Americanisation* (Berkeley, CA, 1993) and K. Ross, *Fast Cars, Clean Bodies. Decolonization and the Reordering of French Culture* (Cambridge, MA, 1995). P. Nivert & Y. Combeau, *Histoire politique de Paris au XXe. siècle* (2000) is especially useful for this period. L. Chevalier, *The Assassination of Paris* (Chicago, 1994) is a stirring, populist account of the rapid urbanization of the city since 1950. See too C. Eveno et al., *Paris perdu: 40 ans de bouleversements* (1992); J. F. Gravier, *Paris et le désert français en 1972* (1972); L. Réau, *Histoire du vandalisme* (new edn, 1994); and, for what they thought they were up against, *Les Plans Le Corbusier de Paris, 1956–62* (1956). The writings of Richard Cobb combine Chevalier's analysis with a plangent nostalgia all his own: see esp. *A Second Identity* (1969), *Tour de France* (1976), *The Streets of Paris* (1980); *Promenades* (1980), and *People and Places* (Oxford, 1985). J. Bastié & J. Beaujeu-Garnier, *Atlas de Paris et la région parisienne* (1967) is by now a historical document as much as an analysis. F. Boudon et al., *Système de l'architecture urbaine. Le quartier des Halles* (1977) is an important account. On the *Grands Projets* and their context, see the excellent A. Fierro, *The Glass State. The Technology of the Spectacle, 1981–98* (Cambridge, MA, 1983), plus B. Marrey & J. Ferrier, *Paris sous verre: La ville et ses reflets* (1997). See too J. L. Cohen & B. Fortier (eds.), *La Ville et ses projets. A City in the Making* (1988). F. Chaslin, *Les Paris de François Mitterrand* (1986); and E. Biasini, *Grands Travaux* (1995). F. Maspéro, *Roissy Express: A Journey through the Paris Suburbs* (1994) is a memorable account of the *banlieue*. See too J. Lucan (ed.), *Paris des faubourgs. Formation. Transformation* (1996). For the recent 'greening' of Paris, see S. Texier, *Les Parcs et jardins dans l'urbanisme parisien (XIXe.–XXe. siècles)* (2001). F. Loyer (ed.), *Ville d'hier, ville d'aujourd'hui en Europe* (2001) is a historically well-grounded exercise in futurology.

List of Illustrations

26 (pp. 278–9). Arrival of Napoleon Bonaparte at Notre-Dame cathedral, 18 August 1802 (photo copyright © The Art Archive/Musée Carnavalet/ Dagli Orti)

27 (p. 295). The catacombs photographed by Nadar, c. 1890 (photo copyright © Hulton-Deutsch Collection/Corbis)

28 (pp. 300–301). Russian soldiers bivouacking on the Champs-Élysées, 31 March 1814 (Photo copyright © The Art Archive/Musée Carnavalet/ Dagli Orti)

29 (pp. 304–5). Transporting the body of Napoleon to the Invalides, 15 December 1840 (photo copyright © AKG images)

30 (pp. 308–9). Funeral carriage used to transport the bodies of the Heroes of the 1830 Revolution to the Place de la Bastille, 28 July 1840 [Estampes, coll. Hennin 14721 71 C 47220] (photo copyright © Bibliothèque Nationale de France)

31 (p. 314). Giuseppe Fieschi attempts the assassination of king Louis-Philippe, 28 July 1835 (photo copyright © AKG images)

32 (p. 333). Passage de l'Opéra. Photograph by Charles Marville, c. 1860–70 (photo copyright © Roger-Viollet/Rex Features)

33 (pp. 346–7). A Café, Place du Théâtre Français, by Édouard Manet (photo copyright © Burrel Collection/Glasgow Museums)

34 (pp. 350–51). Map of Haussmann's Paris (photo copyright © The Art Archive/Marc Charmet)

35 (pp. 360–61). Place de l'Opéra in 1889 (photo copyright © AKG images)

36 (pp. 374–5). Burning houses in the Rue de Rivoli during the Commune, 24 May 1871 (photo copyright © The Art Archive/Musée Carnavalet/ Dagli Orti)

37 (p. 377). Barricade during the Commune [Arch.K.e.41 Page 1] (photo copyright © Bodleian library)

38 (pp. 398–9). Punch and Judy show in the Luxembourg gardens. Photograph by Eugène Atget, 1898 (photo copyright © Bibliothèque Historique de la Ville de Paris/J.-C. Doerr)

39 (pp. 402–3). Paper model of the Eiffel tower. Construction game from the Imagerie d'Épinal, made for the 1889 Universal Exhibition (photo copyright © RMN – Jean Schormans)

40 (pp. 424–5). Henri de Toulouse-Lautrec, At the Salon of the Rue des Moulins, 1894 (photo copyright © The Art Archive/Toulouse-Lautrec Museum Albi/Dagli Orti)

41 (pp. 436–7). French soldiers at the time of mobilization, August 1914 (photo copyright © TAL/Rue des Archives)

LIST OF ILLUSTRATIONS

Acknowledgements

In his great *Tableau de Paris*, written on the eve of the French Revolution, Louis-Sébastien Mercier claimed not only to have written his book but to have walked it too. I think I now understand what he meant. The pleasure of writing the present book on Paris has been compounded by regularly visiting the city from the late 1960s onwards, and getting to know it. I have especially good memories from spending two years living there – in 1969–70, as an undergraduate student, and in 2001–2. Besides combing the city, I have worked a great deal in French libraries and archives and I gratefully acknowledge the help of numerous archivists and librarians over the years – particularly in the Bibliothèque Nationale (in its old and new manifestations) and the Bibliothèque Historique de la Ville de Paris. There cannot be a better spot than the latter in all the world for any historian of Paris to work in.

In writing this book, I have drawn particular inspiration from the writings and my memories of two great and utterly inimitable historians: my former supervisor, Richard Cobb, lover of all things Parisian, and Roy Porter, whose vivid history of London gave me something to bounce off. I am sorry they are not around to read my efforts. Of scholars who have worked on the history of Paris, I have gained most insight into the city from Daniel Roche. Some of my ideas on late eighteenth-century Paris were tried out in lectures at the Collège de France which he kindly invited me to give in 2003.

In 2001–2 I was fortunate to be Visiting Fellow at Columbia University's Institute for Scholars at Reid Hall in Paris. My thanks are due to the Institute's Director Danielle Haase-Dubosc and to her colleagues Mihaela Bacou and Maneesha Lal for their support. They, and fellow scholars at the Institute, especially Phyllis Birnbaum, Greg Brown, Sandra Burman, Gene Lebovics, Cathy Schneider and Steve Ungar, were a most convivial group to work alongside. I also thank most sincerely those friends and colleagues who have read the manuscript, or parts of it: Nigel Aston, Gerd-Rainer

Horn, Peter Jones, Neil McWilliam, Roger Magraw, Patrick Major, Penny Roberts and Chris Wickham. They should not feel responsible for any of the book's shortcomings; these would have been more glaring without their kind help. There simply is not space enough to list all the individuals on whom I have tried out ideas or consulted for help and guidance. Those involved will know who they are, and I salute them. My parents Lawrence and Joyce Jones helped by amassing newspaper cuttings from the early 2000s. My agent Felicity Bryan, has provided constant encouragement. The enthusiasm for the project and the editorial skills of Penguin's Simon Winder through the entire process have been vitally important. I also thank Isabelle de Cat at Penguin and Matthew Beaumont for their help with the pictures; Matt Milner for research assistance; Kevin Gould for technical help; Tim Reinke-Williams for time spent on the index; and Molly Rogers for her photographic skills.

Finally, the book has been thought, lived, worried over, written – and walked – in the company of my wife Josephine McDonagh, who also read the manuscript and provided many invaluable insights. The book is dedicated to her with all my love, thanks and affection.

Colin Jones
August 2004

Index

autoroutes 468, 508, 526
avant-garde 400, 426, 430, 464, 498

Bailly, Antoine-Nicolas (architect) 358
Bailly, Jean-Sylvain (mayor) 260, 277,
Baker, Josephine 447–50
Ballu, Théodore 363
Baltard, Victor 358
Balzac, Henri de xvi, xxii, 217, 234,
  284, 293, 318, 320, 321, 325, 333,
  340, 341, 387, 520
banks 353, 413, 435, 473
banlieue (general) xxiii, 48, 411, 412,
  413, 414, 419, 420, 421, 422, 423,
  427, 438, 453, 454, 455, 466, 467,
  469, 471, 479, 488, 490, 503,
  504–6, 508, 514, 515, 517, 522,
  526, 542–3
banlieue (individual localities)
Argenteuil 227, 389
Arpajon 227
Asnières 227, 389, 411, 423
Aubervilliers 419, 469, 566
Bagnolet 227, 566
Bellevue 214, 228
Bicêtre 188, 233, 264
Bobigny 14, 420, 422, 471
Bougival 389
Boulogne(-Billancourt) 58, 411, 413,
  438, 469
Charenton 168, 195, 414
Château-Landon 432
Chatou 389
Clamart 227, 420
Clichy 14, 566
Drancy 462, 486, 513
Fontainebleau 51, 111, 125, 194,
  313, 362, 406, 422
Gennevilliers 420
Gentilly 14, 99, 337, 566
Issy 566
Ivry 14, 99, 227, 411, 420, 471,
  566
Meudon 228
Meulan 884
Montreuil 471
Montrouge 99, 566
Nanterre 227

Neuilly 209, 566
Pantin 420, 566
Poissy 228
Pré-St-Gervais 566
Rueil 84
Rungis 10, 523
St-Cloud 84, 86, 94, 227, 228, 275,
  290, 468
St-Germain-en-Laye xix, 111, 194,
  544
St-Mandé 566
St-Maur-des-Fossés 7, 227
St-Ouen 419, 566
St-Quentin 130
Sarcelles 516–17
Sceaux 228
Sèvres 227, 228, 389, 500
Suresnes 420, 462
Vanves 227, 337, 566
Villejuif 227, 462, 470
Vincennes 58, 88, 96, 227, 228, 362,
  373, 406, 428, 451, 532
  see also St-Denis, Versailles
Barbie, Klaus 513
Barbier, Le 185
Barillet-Deschamps 405
barricades xxiii, xxiv, 18, 70, 147, 178,
  310, 315, 316, 324, 342, 366, 369,
  459, 488, 523
bars, wineshops and inns 217, 218,
  221, 234–5, 283, 423, 433, 447
Barthes, Roland 393, 517, 522
Basin, Thomas 99
Bastille xx, 58, 77, 88, 96, 98,
  200–201, 205, 209, 245, 252, 253,
  256, 258, 289, 296, 297, 358
bateaux-mouches 385, 421
bath-houses xxi, 10, 14, 36, 44, 101,
  132, 355
'Battle of Paris' (1961) 502, 509–14
battles
Agincourt 95
Alésia 8
Arcques 149
Bouvines 51
Brémoule 4
Corbie 17
Crécy 8

bridges – *contd.*
　Neuf (Ie.–VIe. and IVe.–Ve) 144,
　　153–4, 156–9, 162, 176, 185,
　　195, 250, 307, 386, 389
　Notre-Dame (IVe.) 78, 120, 185
　Petit Pont (IVe.–Ve.) 33, 37, 43, 44,
　　53, 60, 78, 234, 239
　'Planches Mibrai' (IVe.) 78
　Royal (Ie.–VIIe.) 185
　Saint-Michel (Ie.–VIIe.) 78, 509, 512
　Sully (de: IV.–Ve.) 358
　Tournelle (de la: IV.–Ve.) 23, 161
　Tripes (aux: Ve.) 125
brothels 64, 131, 132, 257, 319, 340,
　423, 430, 465
Bruant, Aristide 430
Bruant, Libéral 167, 188
building regulations 122, 161, 240,
　241, 328
　(eighteenth century) 212, 298, 382,
　　414
　(nineteenth century) 414, 415, 390,
　　391, 401, 406
　(twentieth century) 401, 409, 415,
　　515, 526
built environment 40, 54, 55, 122, 123,
　124, 130, 133, 152, 156, 160, 161,
　162, 163, 164, 168, 185, 186, 197,
　204, 205, 209, 211, 212, 213, 247,
　286, 287, 288, 296, 297, 298, 328,
　329, 333, 337, 338, 353, 354, 355,
　356, 357, 358, 359, 382, 383, 408,
　414, 415, 452, 454, 455, 456, 462,
　466, 467, 478, 479, 490, 505–6,
　514, 517–19, 520–21, 526–8
burial places 10, 14, 15, 26, 29, 36, 40,
　234, 240, 292, 293, 294, 306, 484
　Cemetery of the Innocents 16, 57,
　　122, 146, 238, 240, 291, 292
　Père-Lachaise xvi, 291, 321, 323,
　　337, 378, 379, 404

Caesar, Julius xix, xxi, 1, 5, 6, 7, 8
cafés and coffee-houses xi, xv, xxvii,
　166, 168, 216, 217, 219, 221, 222,
　236, 254, 256, 257, 274, 283, 284,
　319, 330, 331, 339, 389, 410, 423,
　426, 430, 433, 434, 439, 485, 497

Anglais (des) 218, 330
Beaubourg 219
Chartres (de) 284
Deux-Magots 496, 497
Flore 496
Hauteurs (des) 219
'Maison Dorée' 330
Marly (de) 219
'Nouvelle Athènes' 430
Paris (de) 330
Procope xxvii, 216–20
Régence (de la) 218
Riche 218
Tortoni 218, 330
cafés-concerts 218, 423, 429, 430
Cain, Georges 463
Calvin, Jean 138, 168
Camp, Maxime du 349, 390
Camus, Albert 496–7
can-can 430
canals 336
　d'Ourcq 125, 294, 298, 327
　St-Denis 48, 125, 294, 326, 410
　St-Martin 125, 294, 326, 364, 367,
　　466
Canard enchaîné (Le) 440, 450
Carco, Francis 430
Carné, Marcel 466, 507, 533
carnival 107, 158, 319
carriages 192, 193, 241, 281, 421
Cartier-Bresson, Henri 464
catacombs 240, 291–4, 295, 341, 463
cathedral chapter 41, 43, 57, 68, 131,
　161, 189
ceinture 454, 506
ceinture de fer 186, 299
ceinture rouge 48, 422, 453, 455, 471,
　472
Céline 332, 482
Cendrars, Blaise 394, 453
censorship 173, 174, 192, 216, 263,
　381, 440
ceremonial and rituals 90, 92, 98, 118,
　119, 121, 144, 146, 150, 158, 173,
　197, 205, 206, 210, 241, 242, 268,
　289, 298, 307, 311, 321, 322, 380;
　see also royal *entrées*
Cézanne, Paul 389, 426

INDEX